# The Rebel Scribe

# The Rebel Scribe

*Carleton Beals and the Progressive Challenge to U.S. Policy in Latin America*

Christopher Neal

**Hamilton Books**

Lanham • Boulder • New York • Toronto • London

Published by Hamilton Books
An imprint of The Rowman & Littlefield Publishing Group, Inc.
4501 Forbes Boulevard, Suite 200, Lanham, Maryland 20706
Hamilton Books Acquisitions Department (301) 459-3366

86-90 Paul Street, London EC2A 4NE, United Kingdom

Copyright © 2022 by The Rowman & Littlefield Publishing Group, Inc.

*All rights reserved.* No part of this book may be produced in any form or by any electronic means, including information storage and retrieval systems,without written permission from the publisher, except by a reviewer who may quote passages in a review.

British Library Cataloguing in Publication Information Available

**Library of Congress Cataloging-in-Publication Data Available**

Names: Neal, Christopher, 1954– author.
Title: The rebel scribe : Carleton Beals and the progressive challenge to U.S. policy in Latin America / Christopher Neal.
Description: Lanham : Hamilton Books, 2022. | Includes bibliographical references and index. | Summary: "American journalist Carleton Beals's combative reporting of U.S. intervention in Latin America from Mexico to Cuba in the 20th century won him millions of readers. The Rebel Scribe tells his story in a way that sheds new light on Western Hemisphere history while also showing how probing journalism drives change"—Provided by publisher.
Identifiers: LCCN 2021050323 (print) | LCCN 2021050324 (ebook) | ISBN 9780761873105 (paperback) | ISBN 9780761873112 (epub)
Subjects: LCSH: Beals, Carleton, 1893–1979. | Foreign correspondents—United States—Biography. | Foreign correspondents—Latin America—Biography. | Latin America—Politics and government—20th century.
Classification: LCC PN4874.B35 N43 2022 (print) | LCC PN4874.B35 (ebook) | DDC 070.4/332092 [B]—dc23/eng/20211115
LC record available at https://lccn.loc.gov/2021050323
LC ebook record available at https://lccn.loc.gov/2021050324

For Mayra Zeledon Neal
cuyo amor me enseñó a cruzar fronteras para entender mejor

# Contents

| | |
|---|---|
| List of Figures | ix |
| Acknowledgments | xi |
| Abbreviations | xiii |
| Introduction | 1 |
| 1  Conscientious Objector Heads South | 9 |
| 2  Rags to Respect in Mexico City | 25 |
| 3  Witness to Rising Benito Mussolini | 41 |
| 4  Return to Mexico | 49 |
| 5  Revolutionary and Literary Adventures from Manhattan to Mexico | 67 |
| 6  Sandino's Mythmaker | 91 |
| 7  Mexican Maze | 131 |
| 8  The Crime of Cuba | 159 |
| 9  Fire and Love on the Andes | 183 |
| 10  Crossing Swords with Trotsky and the American Left | 207 |
| 11  Wartime Visions of America North and South | 233 |
| 12  Hitting a Wall | 259 |
| 13  Second Act in Cuba | 281 |
| 14  Radical in Winter | 311 |
| 15  A Stranded Ghost's Journalistic Legacy | 325 |
| Bibliography | 341 |

| | |
|---|---|
| Additional Sources | 353 |
| Index | 359 |
| About the Author | 375 |

# List of Figures

| | | |
|---|---|---|
| Fig. 4.1 | Carleton Beals (front row, center, with mustache) is pictured here in 1924 with fellow teachers at the Miguel Lerdo de Tejada High School in Mexico City's northern industrial neighborhood of Vallejo, where he taught English. | 50 |
| Fig. 6.1 | Carleton Beals on his way to Sandino's camp, 1928. At one point, he was thrown from his horse, suffering a back injury that left recurring pain to remind him of the trip for the rest of his life. | 106 |
| Fig. 6.2 | Carleton Beals (right with knotted kerchief around his neck) in Sandino's camp on El Remango, near San Rafael del Norte, Nicaragua, February 1928. | 112 |
| Fig. 6.3 | Augusto César Sandino, photography by Carleton Beals taken on February 2, 1928, the day of his interview near San Rafael del Norte. At the time, US officials sought a photo of Sandino to help the US Marines find him. Beals did not share this one. | 113 |
| Fig. 8.1 | Walker Evans's photograph, Havana Street (1933), was featured on the cover of Beals's *The Crime of Cuba*. | 165 |
| Fig. 11.1 | Carleton Beals in a photo from the jacket flap of *Pan America*, one of three books Beals | |

|  |  |  |
|---|---|---|
|  | published in 1940. His expression reflects the satisfaction of an author at the pinnacle of his career. | 247 |
| Fig. 12.1 | Blanca Rosa (Leyva y Arguedas) Beals was for almost twenty years happily married to Beals, whose work she supported and with whom she traveled and enjoyed an active social life. Their marriage collapsed after a furious row at their home in Sachem's Head, Connecticut that coincided with Beals's professional crisis in 1953, not long after this photo was taken. | 261 |
| Fig. 13.1 | Carolyn Kennedy Beals in the living room of the home she shared with Beals from 1958 until his death in 1979, in Killingworth, Connecticut, c. 1960. | 282 |
| Fig. 13.2 | Carleton Beals and Jorge Ricardo Masetti, head of Cuba's *Prensa Latina* news agency, 1960, are all smiles as they sign a contract for Beals to be a "correspondent-at-large." It would not end happily. | 295 |
| Fig. 14.1 | Carleton Beals, aged eighty-two, at a dinner held in his honor before delivering a lecture at the University of Massachusetts (Dartmouth), near New Bedford, in March 1975. | 321 |
|  |  | 375 |

# Acknowledgments

Researching and writing this biography has been a labor of love that began in 2001 and continued whenever I could find time squeezed between full-time jobs and family responsibilities. Over several years, I spent weeks reading through the material in over two hundred boxes containing Beals's Papers at the Howard Gotlieb Center for Archival Research at Boston University. Its founder, the late Dr. Gotlieb, received me and graciously offered initial guidance. The Center's Assistant Director Sean Noel, and its team of archivists were unfailingly helpful, knowledgeable, and courteous. I would like to mention, in particular, Charles Niles, whose thorough knowledge of the Beals collection was invaluable, as well as Sarah Pratt, Perry Barton, Diane Gallagher, and Alex Rankin.

Melvin B. Yoken, who befriended Beals in the 1970s, steered me to his correspondence with Beals entrusted to the John Hay Library at Brown University, while also offering his own memories. Beals's nephews, Alan R. Beals and Ralph Carleton Beals, respectively in California and Ontario, generously provided insights and memories, photographs and a memoir by their father, Ralph Leon Beals. Lenny Cavallaro, a relative of Bertha Klausner, shared memories of Beals's longtime literary agent.

I am grateful too, to the staff at the US National Archives and Records Administration in College Park, Maryland, the US Library of Congress, Milton Eisenhower Library at Johns Hopkins University in Baltimore, Howard University Library, George Washington University Library, Georgetown University Library, George Mason University Library, Katherine Anne Porter Room at the University of Maryland in College Park, and the New York Public Library.

Enrique Krauze, distinguished Mexican historian, author and editor gave me an early boost by publishing an excerpt from my work in *Letras Libres*, along with encouraging advice, for which I thank him. Michael Shifter, President of the Inter-American Dialogue in Washington, DC, the late Nicaraguan politician and economist Arturo J. Cruz, as well as journalists Tim Johnson, Lucy Conger, David Wimhurst, Bryan Demchinsky and Mark Abley read drafts of the manuscript and gave me useful criticisms and guidance. Historian Malcolm Deas, Senior Fellow at St. Antony's College and former director of Oxford University's Latin American Centre, and Marc Raboy, professor emeritus at McGill University, read the final manuscript, making corrections and offering insightful suggestions.

Historian James Herschberg, professor of US foreign policy history at George Washington University (GWU), provided helpful feedback on the Sandino and Crime of Cuba chapters. I am also grateful for guidance from Henry Nau, professor emeritus of political science at GWU, and historian Peter Klarén, also at GWU, for his valuable insights on Latin American populism. Journalist Peter Katel's advice on the Trotsky chapter was pointed and helpful, even if he disagreed with some of my conclusions. Robert Nedelkoff kindly invited me to join the Washington Biographers' Club, where I benefited from the solidarity and support of like-minded writers.

The late Susannah Joel Glusker, author of a biography on her mother, Anita Brenner, who was a friend of Beals, received me at her Mexico City home, where she allowed me to read her mother's diaries. An earlier Beals biographer, John A. Britton, was collegial in sharing thoughts on the phone and by email, as was Gregg Andrews of Texas State University.

I would like to thank Maureen Kelleher, who introduced me to Beals's widow, the late Carolyn Kennedy Beals, and acknowledge the late Lewis Scranton and Janet Scranton, who gave me access to Beals's Killingworth home and schoolhouse study. In the final stages, I benefited from Sam Brawand's meticulous editing and the management skill of Brooke Bures, associate editor at Hamilton Books, who shepherded the manuscript's transformation into a published book.

Finally, I would like to thank my spouse, Mayra Zeledon Neal. She not only read the first drafts of chapters as I produced them, making valuable observations and corrections, but never tired of discussing and supporting the work. Without her, this book would not have come to fruition.

# Abbreviations

| | |
|---|---|
| ABC | Cuban political organization, with membership based on lettering |
| ACLU | American Civil Liberties Union |
| AFP | American and Foreign Power Corporation |
| AP | Associated Press |
| APL | American Protective League |
| APRA | Alianza Popular Revolucionaria Americana |
| CBC | Carleton Beals Collection, Howard Gotlieb Archival Research Center, Boston University |
| CNC | Christopher Neal, Private Collection, Westmount, Quebec. |
| CO | Conscientious Objector |
| COM | Casa del Obrero Mundial |
| CP | Communist Party |
| CROM | Confederación Regional Obrera Mexicana |
| DEU | Directorio Estudiantil Universitario |
| FDR | Franklin Delano Roosevelt |
| FMLN | Farabundo Martí National Liberation Front |
| FPCC | Fair Play for Cuba Committee |
| FSLN | Frente Sandinista de Liberación Nacional (Sandinista National Liberation Front) |

| | |
|---|---|
| FWP | Francis White Papers, Milton Eisenhower Library, Johns Hopkins University, Baltimore |
| HUAC | House Committee on Un-American Activities |
| IMF | International Monetary Fund |
| ISI | Import-Substitutiing Industrialization Theory |
| JFK | John F. Kennedy |
| IWW | Industrial Workers of the World |
| LBJ | Lyndon B. Johnson |
| MBYC | Melvyn B. Yoken Collection, Brown University Library, Providence, Rhode Island. |
| MIT | Massachusetts Institute of Technology |
| NAACP | National Association for the Advancement of Colored People |
| NARA | US National Archives and Records Administration |
| NBC | National Broadcasting Company (early radio chain) |
| NCDPP | National Committee for the Defense of Political Prisoners |
| NSA | US National Security Agency |
| NSC | US National Security Council |
| OAS | Organization of American States |
| PAYCO | Pasos, Arellano y Companía |
| PLI | Independent Liberal Party |
| PNR | Partido Nacional Revolucionario |
| POUM | Partido Obrero de Unificacion Marxista |
| PRI | Partido Revolucionario Institucional |
| PST | Prebisch–Singer (or Singer–Prebisch) thesis |
| RA | Resettlement Administration (federal) |
| SIP | Sociedad Interamericana de Prensa (Bogotá, Columbia) |
| UFCO | United Fruit Company |
| UN | United Nations |
| UPI | United Press International |
| USSR | Union of Soviet Socialist Republics (or Soviet Union) |

# Introduction

In the early 1980s, while working as a freelance journalist in what was then revolutionary Nicaragua, I was struck by the mythic status of Augusto César Sandino (1895–1934), the long-dead leader of a nationalist army fighting a US Marine occupation in the 1920s. In this land of devout, often mystical Roman Catholics, Sandino's image had been fashioned by the leftist government as a kind of secular, revolutionary saint. A giant poster of him was erected on the façade of Managua's earthquake-shattered cathedral, with a white nimbus about his head and signature wide-brimmed sombrero.

Salman Rushdie, in his account of a Nicaraguan journey, *The Jaguar Smile*, observed that images of the sombrero alone were talismans for Sandino's message of anti-imperialist defiance, that "his hat, and not his face . . . had become the most potent icon in Nicaragua."[1]

The image was visual shorthand for the Sandino story that the Nicaraguan Marxist Carlos Fonseca Amador (1936–1976) had retrieved and mythologized in the early 1960s, instrumentalizing it as a rallying narrative for the eponymous Frente Sandinista de Liberación Nacional (FSLN) (Sandinista National Liberation Front), which he founded. The FSLN was vindicated in 1979, when it led the movement that toppled the country's Somoza dictatorship.[2]

Even if the corrupt, repressive remnant of the FSLN, led by Daniel Ortega that rules Nicaragua today, is widely reviled even by most former supporters; Sandino's mystical hold endures. As a journalist myself, I was fascinated to learn that Sandino's mystique derived, at least partly, from the account left by the only American journalist to interview him: Carleton Beals (1893–1979).

Beals was once described in *Time* magazine as "the best informed and the most awkward living writer on Latin America."[3] His career as a freelance journalist, spanning the 1920s in Mexico and Central America to the 1960s in Cuba, coincided with America's rise to become a military and economic power of global reach. A World War I draft resister and left-libertarian, Beals became, for the generation between the wars, the most influential US journalist who was writing about Latin America at that time. He was an acerbic, unsparing critic of America's stance in the region, whether manifest in the dispatch of gunships or US Marines, or in looking askance as tyrants ruled, so long as they were in America's pocket. His radicalism, more Jeffersonian than Marxist or ideological, made him something of a fringe figure, but he did achieve prominence as a writer, and sustained it for two decades, ending in the mid-1940s. He also made an unusual comeback as a pro-revolution journalist in Cuba, from 1959 to the early 1960s.

His articles were published in the *Nation,* the *New Republic,* the *New York Times,* and *Current History,* among others, and his many books were reviewed by the *Times,* the *Washington Post,* and all the literary magazines. Some made the bestseller lists. Most important, his signature critique of US foreign policy and military intervention presaged that of later dissenting journalists and pundits, also in the radical tradition, since his time inside America and abroad. He identified Third World revolution as a twentieth-century theme at its very beginnings in Mexico and Nicaragua in the 1920s. This equipped him to argue, by the 1950s, that these struggles and others like them predated and were unrelated to the Cold War, although often distorted by it. Beals was among the first to identify these movements in Latin America as the result of desperately poor majorities, disenfranchised and exploited by privileged elites, in which the latter's dominant position was sustained by an alliance with US oil, mining, and fruit companies, and investors and bankers who were often shored up by military force. Later, he cautiously welcomed President Franklin D. Roosevelt's (FDR) Good Neighbor Policy in the region. Still later, he bitterly criticized Washington's Cold War approach to Latin America, and to the world, in which dictators were given succor, as a betrayal of America's commitment to democratic freedom.

Through most of his long career, Beals focused on Latin America. From his wild trip across the Sonora desert to Mexico City in 1918, he chose a quixotic path that took him to remote rebel camps and presidential palaces. The world he chose to inhabit and observe was an amalgam of Mexico, Central America, Cuba, Peru, literary New York City, fascist Italy, and, of course, America, especially as seen by its excluded and disenfranchised.

There are appearances in his life by prominent figures Mexico's revolutionary era: Presidents Venustiano Carranza, Álvaro Obregón, and Plutarco Elías Calles, as well as muralist Diego Rivera and painter Frida Kahlo. Also in Mexico, Beals crossed paths with photographers Edward Weston and Tina Modotti and a decade later, crossed swords (polemically) with Leon Trotsky and philosopher John Dewey. Elsewhere in Latin America, he befriended

Peruvian populist leader Victor Raúl Haya de la Torre and Marxist writer José Carlos Mariátegui, while also interviewing Cuban dictator Fulgencio Batista and the *fidelistas* (Fidelists) who toppled him in 1959. He associated with writers Bertram Wolfe and Katherine Anne Porter, and magazine editors Herbert Croly, Lewis Gannett and Oswald Garrison Villard. His life was storied and full, peopled by journalists, political activists, cartoonists, spies, diplomats, leatherneck generals, roués, bandits, poets, friends, lovers—and four wives.

Beals's fame as a journalist was secured in 1928, when he rode a horse through Nicaragua's forested mountains to find and interview for the *Nation*, Augusto César Sandino, who led a guerrilla war of resistance against nearly three thousand US Marines sent there by President Calvin Coolidge (1872–1933) to smoke him out.[4]

Fifty-one years later, on July 19, 1979, just three weeks after Beals died, Sandinista guerrillas rode triumphantly into Managua, Nicaragua's capital. The celebration that greeted them, and the decade-long revolution that followed, marked the culmination of an anti-imperialist struggle started by Sandino, whose example inspired these revolutionaries two generations later. Although that revolution has since atrophied into a kleptocracy run by the Ortega family, Sandino's example and its lasting hold on public imagination gives enduring relevance to Beals's writings in Nicaragua. He was the only American journalist ever to have interviewed Sandino, and his account helped shape the myth surrounding the man.

By the 1980s, President Ronald Reagan's administration, convinced that the latter-day Sandinistas were a Soviet proxy in America's backyard, financed *Contra* rebels seeking to overthrow them. In this war and intrigue, and the forces behind it, a continuing arc from beginning to end of the century can be discerned. US policy in Latin America, as Beals covered it, included the US Marines' war on Sandino; the Mexican Revolution (1910–1920) and US resistance to it; Cuban dictator Gerardo Machado, whom the United States supported, and the 1933 student-led revolution to topple him, which the United States opposed; the CIA-engineered 1954 coup in Guatemala, in which America replaced an elected President with a military man; and, finally, the Bay of Pigs fiasco. That was followed by a Cold War–US freeze on relations with Cuba which, by the twenty-first century, had become a museum piece recalling another era, shelved by President Barack Obama in 2015, only to be re-introduced by Donald Trump.

While the Nicaraguan story put Beals's journalism before a nation-wide audience, Mexico is the country he knew best, and about which he wrote the most. Aside from the *Nation* series, "With Sandino in Nicaragua," Beals's freelance work and several of his books described Mexico's long journey of revolutionary accommodation. Read in sequence, they offer a colorful and nuanced description of Mexico's leaders and the bitter struggles through the

1920s and 1930s. His work reached diverse readers, from foreign policy wonks and diplomats thumbing *Current History*, to reformists in the *Progressive* and pacifists in *World Outlook*. He is probably the only journalist who wrote, simultaneously, for the Soviet news agency TASS and the *New York Times*. He also published forty books. They include chronicles blending political analysis with travel writing, such as *Mexico: An Interpretation* (1923) ("the best book on Mexico written by any American," wrote the late Senator Ernest Gruening), *Banana Gold* (1932), about Central America, *Mexican Maze* (1931), *The Crime of Cuba* (1933), *Fire on the Andes* (1934), and *America South* (1937). Beals also published four novels, one of which, *Dawn Over the Amazon* (1943), an imagined German-Japanese Axis invasion of South America, sold about 200,000 copies the year it was released. He wrote biographies on Huey Long and Mexican dictator Porfirio Díaz (1830–1915), among others, along with histories of Latin America and overlooked corners of America's past. Contemporary endorsements and reviews describe Beals as, "one of the ablest journalists in this country . . . like Richard Harding Davis, he is the true American journalist—historian—novelist—adventurer . . . his work is based upon study and investigation and not upon the half-baked impressions of a round-trip ticket . . . an idol of the youth movement in Cuba . . . the dean of correspondents in Latin America."[5]

Beals's fame proved ephemeral, and today he is a stranded ghost in the history of American journalism. He was a young romantic, a member of the "lost generation" of the 1920s, part of a loosely-linked group of left-leaning writers, editors, and activists such as John Dos Passos, Mike Gold, Kyle Crichton, Lewis Gannett, Oswald Garrison Villard, Victor Calverton, Ernest Gruening, and Anita Brenner. Absenting himself from America during its World War I xenophobia, followed by a post-war Red Scare, Prohibition, and Teapot Dome corruption, the younger Beals viewed his homeland from revolutionary Mexico, in the company of similarly disaffected writers and artists. Mexico City was then a hothouse of "isms," of artistic license, and of sexual freedom, a Latin version of 1920s Paris, but cheaper and closer to home. These young dissidents led the culture war of their time against the American establishment. For them, Mexico was refuge and an example. For Beals, it was a point of departure.

Throughout the career that followed, in his reporting, stories, and chronicles, Beals had important things to say about America's role in the hemisphere, and in the world. His messages are still relevant, predating and anticipating discourses that we hear today. "We Latin Americans owe much to Carleton Beals," Mexican writer Carlos Fuentes once commented, attesting to the resonance that Beals's perceptions still held in some quarters.[6] By contrast, conservative historian Mark Falcoff has written that Beals left a "doleful legacy" of excessive negativism that prevailed among US journalists covering America's role in the hemisphere in the late twentieth century.[7]

British scholar Malcolm Deas calls Beals "the prototype of a certain sort of Anglo-Saxon journalist in Latin America, one prone to vent domestic frustration in foreign radicalism, [and] to overstate the culpability of imperialism."[8]

Beals has his defenders too, among whom he was acknowledged in his time as the dean of US correspondents in Latin America. "Carleton is one of the most valuable gadflies in existence . . . he should be subsidized and encouraged," wrote liberal historian Hubert Herring, also director of the Committee on Cultural Relations with Latin America, in 1933.[9] Political scientist Martin Needler described Beals as "an unusually clear-eyed leftist . . . taken in by the sectarian maneuvers of the Communists no more than he was by the hypocrisy of the State Department."[10]

Beals's story is a cautionary tale that sheds light on enduring aspects of foreign policy discourse and journalism in America. His Sandino interview earned him lifelong enmity in US government and military circles and was a kind of harbinger of ostracisms to be visited on later contrarian journalists such as I. F. Stone, Seymour Hersh, Raymond Bonner, and Glenn Greenwald, among others. As was the case with Beals, their combination of investigative and polemical journalism had or has a subterranean flavor, building a following through liberal publications such as the *New Yorker,* and the *New York Review of Books*, or edgier media such as the *Nation* and *Mother Jones,* and more recently, online outlets such as the *Intercept.* In addition to his critical stance from the Left, Beals was also a gonzo journalist *avant la lettre*, freely hurling earthy epithets, but nonetheless sure of their targets. It is reminiscent not only of Hunter S. Thompson, but also of the late Christopher Hitchens. For example, Beals launched withering attacks on FDR's foreign policy strategist Sumner Welles, and earlier on Henry Lane Wilson, for their duplicitous roles behind violent removals of Cuban and Mexican presidents whose regimes Washington wanted to change. It was much in the same vein as Hitchens' campaign to have President Richard Nixon's foreign policy supremo Henry Kissinger tried for alleged war crimes in Vietnam and Chile.

Beals was dismissed by some Americans for "siding with our enemies." But others considered him an agent of change, whose work challenged acceptance and approval of America's emerging hegemon status as a necessary hedge to defend freedom. Instead, Beals's analytical framework questioned the neo-imperialist character of the still-nascent US foreign policy stance, along with its costs and consequences. His story illustrates concepts later developed by critical theory philosophers such as Louis Althusser, Michel Foucault, Edward Said, Herbert Marcuse, and the Frankfurt School; it shows how *awkward* is a journalist who systematically challenges a society's hegemonic discourse. Controversial at home, Beals was widely respected in Latin America, where his analysis was more closely aligned with mainstream opinion.

By the 1940s, and the red-baiting early 1950s, Beals found it difficult to get his work published, and his career began to crumble. It was briefly revived in the late 1950s, when the *Nation* sent him to Cuba, where he covered—sympathetically—Fidel Castro's revolution and, famously, warned that a US invasion was being planned. Later, while serving as co-chair of the Fair Play for Cuba Committee, he wrote for the Cuban news agency Prensa Latina, and was tailed by US diplomatic staff, until he resigned over Communist-Party-driven censorship of his copy.

Beals challenged the widespread assumption that America intervenes abroad mostly to defend freedom. He saw this everywhere as cynical posturing. His reporting illustrated that, often, this impulse to solidarity, to uphold the right to life, liberty, and the pursuit of happiness, is stilled and undermined by someone with an interest at stake. Usually, that interest involves investment, a valuable resource, a market, or an alliance that pays in some way. Beals made a plea for genuineness over hypocrisy in America's diplomatic discourse. In 1957, he decried a double standard in which the US welcomed Hungarian refugees escaping Soviet repression while ignoring "thousands of refugees from Latin American dictatorships (about whom) our press is silent."[11]

In his journalistic forays inside America, he chose subjects—the 1936 Scottsboro trial in which nine black farm boys were framed for rape, the lot of Alabama sharecroppers and migrant fruit-pickers in California—that allowed him to interpret social realities through the lens of the victims of injustice, the downtrodden, and the excluded.

This practice made him enemies, combined as it was with take-no-prisoners denunciations of the powerful, such as US diplomats, as "stuffed shirts" and "apologists" of businessmen, as "kissers of the feet of aristocrats" and so on.[12] The very oddness of Beals' story and work commands our attention. His crackling critique was hard to dismiss because it was combined with a sure grasp of his subject. It was a cocktail strong enough to prompt the FBI and US State Department to keep files on him. In the *zeitgeist* of the late 1940s and early 1950s, poisoned by McCarthyism, editors of mainstream papers and journals, too, found his voice too strident, too awkwardly contrarian, and turned away from it.

With every new overseas military entanglement undertaken by a US president, there is fresh evidence of media subservience to power, of controlled access to information, of *faux*-patriotic groupthink, even of outright censorship or, at least, of censured journalists. These repeated, almost cyclical instances remind us that peddlers of "fake news" have been with us for a long time. Sometimes, however, during these episodes, a voice cries out to denounce what is happening. Such dissident voices are rare, enduring despite the high cost often imposed on them, and even when actively suppressed, as happens from time to time. In his time, Carleton Beals was one of these voices: dismissed as awkward in his time, but in truth, awkwardly prophetic.

"The only axe I have ever had to grind," Beals wrote shortly before his death, "is to write the truth as I have seen it. That, in this world of snoop and smear, is a hazardous business."[13] One of its hazards is to be forgotten. This biography seeks to rescue the stranded ghost that Carleton Beals has become and restore his place in our collective memory.

## NOTES

1. Salman Rushdie, *The Jaguar Smile: A Nicaraguan Journey* (London: Pan Books, 1987), 22.

2. The Somoza dictatorship began in 1934, after General Anastasio Somoza García, head of Nicaragua's US-trained National Guard, murdered the nationalist rebel Augusto César Sandino. He ruled directly as president from 1937–1947 and from 1950 until he was assassinated in 1956. He was succeeded by his eldest son Luís and, subsequently, by his second son Anastasio Somoza Debayle, both of whom ruled both directly and through presidents subservient to them. The regime was toppled by the Sandinista revolutionary movement on July 19, 1979.

3. Book Review: "Stone-Thrower," of *Glass Houses*, by Carleton Beals, *Time* 31, no. 18 (April 25, 1938).

4. Carleton Beals, "With Sandino in Nicaragua," *Nation*, February 22 & 29, 1928; March 7, 15, 21 & 28, 1928.

5. Carleton Beals, *Glass Houses—Ten Years of Free-Lancing* (jacket back cover), (Philadelphia: J. B. Lippincott & Company, 1938).

6. Letter to Beals's widow, Carolyn Kennedy Beals, 1990, Christopher Neal, Private collection, Westmount, Quebec (hereafter cited as CNC).

7. Mark Falcoff, "The Doleful Legacy of Carlton [sic] Beals," in *A Culture of its Own: Taking Latin America Seriously*, by Falcoff (New York: Routledge, 1998), 131–42.

8. Malcolm Deas, "John A. Britton, Carleton Beals. A Radical Journalist in Latin America," *Journal of Latin American Studies* 21, nos. 1–2 (1989): 187–88, https://doi.org/10.1017/S0022216X00014723.

9. Hubert Herring to Lewis Gannett (Editor, *New York Herald Tribune*), April 10, 1933, CBC.

10. Martin C. Needler, Book Review of "Britton, *Carleton Beals: A Radical Journalist in Latin America* (Albuquerque: University of New Mexico Press, 1987)," *Hispanic American Historical Review* 68, no. 2 (1988): 374–75, https://doi.org/10.1215/00182168-68.2.374.

11. Carleton Beals, "Where Does Charity Begin?" *Christian Century*, January 30, 1957, 136–37.

12. Carleton Beals, Letter, *Saturday Review of Literature*, February 7, 1935; Beals, *Under the Fifth Sun* (Unpublished autobiography), CBC, Box 45.

13. Carleton Beals, "Snoop and Smear—The Golden Calf of Democracy" (undated, but after 1975), 9. CBC.

*Chapter One*

# Conscientious Objector Heads South

During the 1970s, the last decade of his life, Carleton Beals's neighbors on Fire Tower Road in Killingworth, Connecticut, just north of Long Island Sound, hardly knew him. Most were retired couples whose tidy homes were separated by hillocks forested with beech and maple from the hobby farm that Beals shared with his wife Carolyn. A few were vaguely aware that he was—or had been—an author of some kind, but even they were at a loss to name a book he had written. He was seen as an eccentric, a recluse.

He reinforced this perception. Even if he did not deliberately avoid contact with what he called "Killingworthies," he did not seek it either. Sometimes he accompanied Carolyn when she drove into the village by the Sound to buy groceries or to go to the post office. He sat on the passenger side of their Chevy station wagon, as Carolyn, seventeen years his junior, insisted on driving. From there, he would gaze quietly out the window, stroking his long, tangled blond-white beard. The curls hanging over his lips were tinted with the mustard color of nicotine, giving him the outward appearance of a vagrant. "He looked like one rough old man," a neighbor recalled.

He stayed up late into the nights, tapping on a manual typewriter in the remodeled Revolutionary-era schoolhouse he used as his study. There, amid thousands of books and stacks of files, manuscripts, and clutter, he had written seventeen books and hundreds of articles. Most of the books were popular histories and biographies, such as his 1957 *John Eliot: The Man Who Loved the Indians* and his 1963 *Eagles of the Andes* (about South American struggles for independence), produced to order for high-school library markets.[1] His freelance career had left him without a pension, so this work earned Beals just enough money to sustain his modest country life with Carolyn, his fourth and last wife, the daughter of a wealthy New York banker whose inheritance, by the 1970s, had been depleted.

His financial straits kept him busy writing at an age by which most reporters would have retired. Earlier, in the 1960s, he had sustained the combative journalism that had been his trademark when his career was in high gear. For just over a year around 1960, he wrote articles for the Cuban news agency Prensa Latina, as well as for the *Nation*, the liberal weekly with which he had had an association since the 1920s.

But by the mid-1970s, he was into his eighties, and had withdrawn into an elegiac solitude, to reflect and to take stock of his life. It was unfamiliar ground for him. A lifelong witness, Beals was a perceptive observer of all things, save himself. And though he published over forty books during his life, he never finished the autobiography to which he devoted these final years in his Killingworth schoolhouse. It served mostly as a vehicle for his own nostalgic return to his childhood and youth, in Kansas and California around the turn of the century, and to his years as a student in New York City, which is where our story begins.

\*\*\*

In mid-summer of 1917, a notice ordering Carleton Beals to report for his US Army physical exam was delivered to the attic apartment he shared with two friends at 43 Washington Square in New York City's Greenwich Village. It languished there unacknowledged. In May, Beals, then twenty-three years old, had completed his studies at Columbia University, obtaining at once a master's degree in political science and a teachers' certificate. Immediately upon graduation, he had left for his family's home in Berkeley, California.

For young Beals, blond, blue-eyed, and callow when he had first arrived in Manhattan, university had been an intellectual awakening. Literature, history, and anthropology—this last taught by the legendary Franz Boas—engaged him most, prompting him to read voraciously. This bookish bent was combined with an evolution in his personality. His earnest manner was now lightened by an emerging sardonic disposition. He had grown irreverent, a non-conformist who sought the company of bohemians who dreamed of becoming artists. His roommates were Harold Speakman, an artist and then-aspiring novelist, and Clark Wing, an acutely sensitive pianist and an aesthete who was a decade older than Beals and who introduced him to the city's art, architecture, and its more obscure little restaurants.[2] This sojourn had offered Beals an escape from Berkeley and from his domineering mother Elvina, a stern disciplinarian who had raised him and his younger brother Ralph by her hybrid code of puritan temperance and prairie socialism.

He retained an attachment to living-by-principle and to the sententious instincts he had inherited from his mother, but his years in New York had enabled him to cultivate a new raffish charm, while the big-city electric nights had given him a veneer of sophistication. But now, he was out of money, and so had little choice but to return to Berkeley, where he could live rent-free with his parents while getting established as a schoolteacher. Or so he thought.

He had been dreading the draft notice. Once President Woodrow Wilson (1856–1924) obtained Congressional approval to declare war on Germany on April 6, 1917, Beals knew he faced the danger of conscription. He wanted no part of it. Like his parents, Beals was a member of the American Socialist Party, for whose followers the war was a disingenuous sham in which Europe's rival countries' elites sought to settle accounts, and for which mostly working-class soldiers were being drafted and slaughtered. He was bitter that America had entered the war. It was a betrayal of Wilson's 1916 re-election campaign promise to stay out of it.

This politically-inspired opposition to the war joined his personal reasons for resistance. The war would ruin his plan to teach public school in Berkeley, and he had decided that he was a pacifist. "For three years," he wrote, "we had been learning about the horrors of war, the folly of war, the stupid greed of all the nations involved, the ruin to civilization, and here we had drifted in."[3]

Now, though, Beals faced the practical problem of how to resist the draft. He was young and vigorous, though small in stature at just over five feet. He could find no medical grounds for a waiver.

While pondering what to do, Beals was reunited with Lillian Rhein, the lighthearted Texas girl with whom he had fallen in love before he had left for New York, while both were undergraduates at the Berkeley campus of the University of California. She was warm and loyal and, like him, she wanted to be a schoolteacher. But Beals's conscription predicament would complicate their plans.

He had proposed marriage and she had accepted. Their engagement was a tender respite that temporarily allayed his anxiety about military service. The couple shared magic weeks that summer, savored after the long winter separation while Beals had been at Columbia. They traveled from California to Niagara Falls and back south again to the Grand Canyon, finally returning to Berkeley in early August, where they took long walks, hand in hand, watching the sun drop over the yellow hills surrounding the city.[4]

As Beals prepared to meet the draft board, opposition to US entry into the war mounted. It reached Congress, where fifty-six Representatives and Senators voted against the war declaration, conscious of the views of their constituents.

But despite significant and tenacious opposition, much of it based on a traditional isolationist reflex, Americans were increasingly lining up to support US participation in the war. This shift to mounting public outrage was triggered by a German U-boat's 1915 torpedoing of the British passenger liner *Lusitania*, in which 1,198 perished, including 124 Americans. It deepened with the continuing threat that the Germans posed to US merchant ships. A final straw came with disclosure of the Zimmerman Telegram, in which Germany's foreign minister Arthur Zimmerman sought to enlist the Mexican government in a plan to destabilize the United States. Having made the decision to declare war, the Wilson administration launched a propaganda effort to bolster popular support for it, while its repressive tactics cowed many opponents.

Opinion remained more evenly divided among young American men who were being asked to fight and die. The military draft was unpopular: in addition to the draft evaders, or "slackers" as they came to be known, some 60 percent of those who registered for the draft requested exemptions.[5]

Beals was one of these. After having registered in New York, "putting down a list of claims for exemption as long as my arm," he reported on August 10 to a US Army recruiting center at Berkeley City Hall. An officer and military clerks, smartly dressed in pressed uniforms, were seated at the registration table set up in the lobby. Beals's pulse quickened as he approached them. The officer had a breezy manner, an easy cheer that failed to stem Beals's agitated state. His banter evaporated altogether when Beals nervously announced his refusal to take the pre-induction physical exam.

"I am opposed to war in general," he said, "and seek conscientious objector status."

His request had "a religious basis," he wrote later in a bid for release from military prison, where he was held as a draft resister. His conscientious objector (CO) stance, he claimed, was based on "the tenets of Positivism, at once a science, polity, and a religion." He typed on his application a windy summary of "this dominant synthesis . . . conceived by August Compte [*sic*] and Frederick Harrison [which] expresses itself in the worship of Humanity as the Supreme Being, irrespective of race, creed, or national lines." War, he said, was a "profanation" of his idea of the Supreme Being, and military service, a deprivation of his right to life, liberty and the pursuit of happiness."[6]

Beals's opposition to the war was influenced less by his putative positivism, which was largely contrived, than by the antiwar stand taken by the American Socialist Party, whose leader and five-time presidential candidate, Eugene V. Debs, was the Beals family's hero. Beals's parents, Leon and Elvina Blickensderfer Beals who, like Debs, traced their origins to the Midwest, embraced the cause of the downtrodden western farmer during the 1890s, first as activists in the Populist Movement and later, in the American Socialist Party.

Debs was a stirring orator who had started his political career as a Democratic representative in the State of Indiana Assembly, and went on to lead the American Railway Union. When workers at the Pullman Palace Car Company went on strike in 1894 to roll back layoffs and wage cuts caused by a nationwide depression, Debs called out the railway workers in a sympathy strike. The protests ended in repression by federal troops, who were sent to Chicago by President Grover Cleveland. Seven strikers were killed, and Debs was sentenced to six months in jail, where his reading and reflection led him to declare himself a socialist.

Influenced by Marxist ideology and the Industrial Workers of the World, an international anarchist labor alliance also known as the Wobblies, Debs became leader of the Socialist Party when it was founded in 1901. Lean and ascetic-looking, but with an ebullient enthusiasm, "Gene" appealed to large audiences of workers, telling them that capitalist exploitation was un-American, a violation of the nation's founding constitutional principles. Urging workers to think for themselves, he denounced "this capitalist war," saying that, "we have no enemies among the workers of other countries, and no friends among the capitalists of any country."[7]

In 1918, Debs would be charged with sedition and sentenced to ten years in prison for delivering an antiwar speech in Canton, Ohio. In that speech, Debs said wars are always declared by "the master class" while, "the subject class has always fought the battles. The master class has had all to gain and nothing to lose, while the subject class has had nothing to gain and all to lose—especially their lives."[8]

Beals's parents had moved the family from his birthplace in Medicine Lodge, Kansas, to Oxnard, California, while he was still a child. In Kansas, his father, Leon Elverson Beals, had been editor of the local Farmers' Alliance newspaper, the *Barber County Index*, and was later elected county attorney.[9] In 1896, the family moved to Oxnard, California, where Leon borrowed enough money to buy a racket (general) store, serving the families of workers in the American Beet Sugar Company mill owned by the town's eponymous Henry T. Oxnard.[10]

That venture did not work out, so the family moved inland to Pasadena, where Leon found a job as a postal clerk. In 1911, they moved again, to Berkeley where Beals's mother Elvina was the Socialist Party's candidate for the US Senate in 1920, and the US House of Representatives in 1922.[11]

While a student at Columbia, Beals organized rallies for Debs, including one paid-attendance meeting that drew a crowd of two thousand. When he returned to Berkeley, he organized a local branch of an anti-war umbrella organization headed by another socialist, the political economist Scott Nearing, known as the People's Council of America for Peace and Democracy.[12]

Beals viewed Wilson's decision to enter the war as a betrayal of the President's own professed principles. The war was only being sold as a patriotic duty, Beals believed, while Wilson's darker purpose was to secure a seat at the table, at Versailles in 1919 as it turned out, where "imperialist pacts" would be concluded to divide the spoils of victory. The DuPont munitions interests and the House of Morgan had pressed Wilson to enter because war was good for business, according to Beals, whatever the cost in American lives.[13]

But opposition to the war on political grounds did not excuse a young man from the military draft. Only religious faith could accomplish that, so Beals was forced to invent his adherence to the *religion* of Positivism.

When Beals refused to take the Army physical, he was promptly sent to Berkeley's municipal jail, and spent the next six months in and out of municipal and federal prisons, including a cell at Alcatraz. Four months into this ordeal, a bureaucratic snafu stemming from his failure to respond to his original draft notice in New York, led to his being charged as a deserter. He was incarcerated in the San Francisco Presidio, where he was beaten up, kicked, and did time in solitary.[14] Eventually, he was assigned to crews of convicts cleaning streets and collecting trash around San Francisco.

Beals's mother, Elvina, was campaigning as a Socialist candidate for a seat on Berkeley city council that fall, but she made time to lobby for her son's release. She contacted Roger Baldwin, Secretary-General of the National Civil Liberties Bureau (later the American Civil Liberties Union), who had himself been jailed earlier for refusing to register for the draft.[15] Baldwin took up Beals's case, advising him to offer to perform non-combatant service. This he did, in a letter to the Commanding General of the Presidio in San Francisco, in which he petitioned for release from prison, or the "disagreeable compromise" of non-combatant service. "I have a rough knowledge of typewritting [*sic*]—this letter is a sample," he wrote. "Whether this constitutes sufficient ability to warrant my being placed at some other employment than my present one of shoveling coal is, of course, for you to decide."[16]

Elvina also fired off protest letters to US Representative J. A. Elston, of California's Sixth Congressional District, and California Republican Senator Hiram Johnson, whose secretary replied: "The Senator has asked me to say that it would be futile to protest against the enforcement of the provisions of the draft law, adopted by both Houses."[17]

Given Elvina Beals's status as a local politician—in addition to running for city council, she had earlier been elected as a member of the Berkeley school board—Beals's campaign to be excused from military service was covered in the local press. He augmented this with opinion articles published in the local paper that outlined his views on the war, and defending his right, as a citizen of a democratic country, to oppose it. "The roots of the present world conflict . . . take hold on the sordid schemes for commercial and imperialistic control which have featured the policy of the great powers of Europe during the past half century," Beals wrote in the *Oakland World*.[18] While jailed on the desertion charge, Beals managed to scribble a letter in which he complained of being held in a dark, cold cell without blankets or even a bench, and fed only bread and water, "thrust in on the dirty spit-covered floor." His mother got the account published in the *Oakland Tribune* under the headline: "Carl Beals Tortured."[19]

One of the military officers handling his case privately appealed to Elvina Beals for her help in persuading her son to take the physical examination because, if he failed, it would provide a face-saving way out for everyone. "He would make a very bad soldier," the officer told her. "I wouldn't want him in any unit I command."[20]

This advice was followed, and Beals finally obtained his military discharge on March 9, 1918, based on a War Department assessment that he had a weak heart that rendered him "totally unfit for military service."[21]

While Beals had been embroiled in securing his release, the climate for anti-war dissidents had grown forbidding. Pacifism was construed as cowardice or treason. The War Department authorized local army officers to repress "acts committed with seditious intent," often with the collaboration of local chapters of the American Protective League (APL). This quasi-vigilante, volunteer security force gave itself the mission of supporting the war effort at home by enforcing conscription, checking on dissidents, and launching "slacker raids" to arrest draft resisters.[22]

This officially-sanctioned repression targeted the Socialist Party, among other dissident groups, deepening Beals's discomfort. In September 1917, the party's national headquarters in Chicago was raided and searched by federal agents for three days. Following Socialist gains in the November 1918 elections, the Red Scare shifted to high gear, with many Socialist Party leaders indicted and sentenced to twenty years for sedition. Their imprisonment ended only with a US Supreme Court ruling in their favor in 1921.[23]

Beals's objection to and discharge from military service, even if based on his purported pacifist predisposition against all wars, gave him a convenient excuse for the exile he wanted anyway. While not entirely spurious—as he would have been a hopelessly insubordinate soldier—his refusal to serve seemed as much driven by a thirst for freedom as it was by pacifism, or by philosophical, "positivist" objections to war. "I ached to do remarkable and unusual things [and] hoped for fame, but above all for freedom, personal freedom, always freedom," he recalled years later.[24]

The edgy jingoism and xenophobia that swept America once war had been declared, combined with Beals's own youthful rebellion, pushed him south in the summer of 1918. "What sent a man to Mexico was the goddamn war, the great patriotic and noble expedition that saved the world for democracy," he recalled.[25] "Just a few months before, I had looked with pride on those huge campaign posters [in 1916] that covered whole billboards with American workmen, full dinner-pail, happy smile, going to the humming factory, with a beatific portrait of Woodrow Wilson, and the exclamation, 'He kept us out of war!'"[26]

Added to this was Beals's daily mind-numbing grind and dismal prospects. The schoolteacher position he had lined up at a Berkeley high school while studying for his Teachers' Certificate in New York City had vanished while he had been behind bars. After his release in March, the only job he could find was cataloguing oil drums at the Standard Oil Company.

Beals soon improvised an escape plan that had infinitely greater appeal: a one-way trip to Mexico. The idea also captivated his seventeen-year-old brother Ralph, himself still eligible for the draft, although he had not been called up. So in early July, the Beals brothers, callow and thirsty for adventure, set off for "new worlds." They had no passports, a minor consideration, they surmised, compared to being recalled for military service in Carleton's case, or to being called for the first time, in Ralph's.

"We were sick of a life of suspicion, of losing friends, of intolerant war spirit, and it appeared such a glorious adventure," Ralph Beals later recalled.[27]

With two hundred dollars between them, they packed camping gear and climbed aboard a dilapidated Ford they had nicknamed "Fannie" and headed south. The vehicle was actually the property of the Socialist Party of America, on loan to Elvina for political organizing trips. As she could not drive, Ralph had been her chauffeur. But now, concern for her sons weighed more heavily than party loyalty, and she dispatched Ralph to drive Carleton, a notoriously inept driver, to what would become his self-imposed exile.[28]

The brothers were bound for the northwestern Mexican desert state of Sonora. It was an unlikely destination, chosen partly because any journey requires an object, but also because it had been suggested to Beals months before, by one Mike O'Shaughnessy. O'Shaughnessy was an adventurer whom Beals had met in a bar on the San Francisco waterfront. The young Beals was fascinated by his boozy tales of travels from Dublin to Tahiti, to the Klondike, and to the streets of Buenos Aires.

Although only forty years old, O'Shaughnessy sensed his approaching death: "I've a queer hunch that somethin's goin' to happen to little Mike. Fate's an upper-cuttin' sonnabitch," he told Beals. Over many whiskeys in the smoky bar, he entrusted to Beals a creased, yellowed map of the Rio Yaqui in Sonora, with detailed directions to a cache of hidden gold, penciled on the back.[29]

The gold-seeking gave the young Beals brothers' journey a purpose, a plausible pretext for the flight from America that they wanted, not only to escape the war frenzy, but in Carleton's case, to pursue his vague notion of becoming a writer. Mexico, torn by revolutionary chaos, seemed a more congenial venue for this than the United States.

By mid-1918, then, Beals was like a bluebottle fly banging against a windowpane, bored and despondent, his anti-war dissidence silenced, and "sick of wartime hysteria which had outlawed Beethoven, Mozart [and] Wagner, and smashed restaurant dishes 'Made in Germany.'"[30]

The Beals brothers rode through the San Joaquin Valley to Bakersfield, over the Tehachapi Pass, and across the Mohave Desert to Barstow and Needles, California. They crossed the Colorado River and followed a barely marked track southeast through a parched wasteland, unpopulated but for a few mining camps, until they reached the blistered, ramshackle town of Wenden, Arizona.

About twenty miles before making it to Wenden, one of Fannie's tires blew. They drove on, finally reaching Wenden, but destroying the wheel in the process. There, they abandoned the jalopy in the care of a rapacious garage owner who told them it was un-repairable and kept repeating that Wenden was "the asshole of creation."[31] Bereft of vehicle, the Beals brothers were swindled into paying $10 each for a couple of "town donkeys" that lived off trash heaps, useless charges they expected would serve as pack animals for their journey south. No matter. They plodded south through "Burnt-in-the-Middle country" for what was to be an arduous, and seemingly pointless, desert trek.[32]

Ralph described the journey in a self-deprecating memoir fourteen years later, in which he recalled that soon after leaving Wenden, "we were virtually lost in a welter of haphazard arroyos, twisting, turning, with only narrow ridges between . . . the burros became stubborn, balking or else running away to the infinite confusion of our badly-made packs. A paper bag full of beans broke (Imagine greenhorns packing in paper bags)."[33]

Carleton described the same trip in a breezy travelogue, *Brimstone and Chili*, published by Knopf in 1927. The two accounts match in many instances, with Carleton's leaning more to hyperbole.

All the same, it is faithful enough to the facts to be, as claimed, more a diary of "personal experiences in the Southwest and Mexico" than fiction, and as such, it documents Beals's introduction to Mexico. At turns cantankerous and comical, the first-person narrative follows the brothers as they stumble awkwardly through the hot, inhospitable barrens of northern Sonora, and then, after having lost their donkeys, as they hitch freight trains south to Culiacán and Mexico City.

They chase their errant donkeys up and down ravines, on one occasion while bathing and completely naked, and bicker and curse at one another, frequently mad with thirst and fatigue.

At one point, they are held prisoner in an alfresco desert *jail* in a village called Querobabi, where the local *constable* demanded a bribe for their release. They finally induced the extortionate policeman to release them by convincing him, through loud conversations in pidgin-German, that they were not Americans, but Swiss, and that their last $80 had been stolen. In fact, they had stashed the money in a nearby tree-trunk, from which they retrieved it as they fled Querobabi.

Soon after, having disposed of the useless *burros* and now traveling on foot with a lone nag named Prince, Beals suffered a poisonous bite from an unidentified animal, probably a tarantula. The ensuing leg wound swelled ominously, prompting him to slit it open to release the poison. Fortuitously, they met an Indian who applied a medicinal salve of crushed leaves to the wound. The swelling receded. Leg recovered, the brothers approached the city of Hermosillo, in Sonora, getting chilling warnings of warlike Yaqui Indians along the way.

From Hermosillo, they boarded a third-class coach—"a mélange of scarlet sarapes, yellow and red shawls, bright, embroidered blouses, dusky faces, music, noise, and promiscuity"—on a train south to the Pacific coastal cities of Guaymas and Empalme. Once there, by now penniless and discouraged, they hitched a ride on another train, this one a freight to Esperanza, on the long-sought Río Yaquí (Yaqui River). But being broke, their first order of business was getting work and food, not hunting gold.

In Cajemé, a town just south of Esperanza on the Pacific coastal highway, they were recruited by the Swedish foreman on an outlying rice farm owned by an expatriate American named Boyd. When they got there, Boyd, "a lean, Mexicanized, wry-mouthed, vicious-looking, ex-Texas ranger, dessicated [*sic*], penurious, a completely brutalized miser, hated by everyone," put the brothers to work clearing weeds from irrigation ditches.[34] This lasted a few days, ending when Carleton was reassigned to replace the Chinese cook, who had been fired after farmhands in the mess hall complained that his meals were revolting, all either burnt or undercooked.

In this new job, Beals faced a trial of a different sort. Boyd's plump Mexican companion, Margarita, approached him in the kitchen one day, a sensual smile on her face. Clad only in a dressing-gown, she threw her arm around his neck.

"Kiss me," she commanded.

Beals, fearful of the consequences of such a dalliance, and not quite taken by Margarita's charms, rebuffed her advance. She was insulted.

"You'll pay for this," she said. "Wait 'til I tell Boyd." She laughed with an air of mischievous triumph as she climbed the stairs.

The next day, Carleton and Ralph were ordered to clear out, and cheated out of the two weeks' pay owed them. They were in a helpless blind rage, penniless, and outcast just as the region was hit by a rainstorm lasting days. They waded, almost waist-deep, across flooded cornfields back to Cajemé, without food for thirty hours.

While the Beals brothers surmounted these sometimes hair-raising, sometimes banal misadventures, Mexico was bitterly divided, mired in a bloody revolutionary civil war that was draining the country's resources, and provoking widespread hunger. At the same time, the global influenza epidemic was raging across the country, unstalled by any preventive measure.

The two California vagrants managed to escape illness, but they encountered violence near Cajemé, where Carleton witnessed the beating death of two traveling companions by Yaqui fighters, then battling federal government troops.

The Yaqui Indians of Sonora were fierce warriors who had resisted outsiders' incursions since the Spanish conquest. They now chafed under the rule of President Venustiano Carranza (1859–1920), a conservative former Senator in dictator Porfirio Díaz's time, and later Governor of the northern state of Coahuila, who had emerged from Mexico's revolutionary turmoil to become a compromise leader—an unelected, so-called First Chief of the Revolution.

Most Yaqui soldiers owed little or no allegiance to Carranza, but answered instead to two other leaders, Francisco "Pancho" Villa and General Álvaro Obregón. Both of these military chiefs had broken with Carranza, whose regime was rife with corruption, by the time the Beals brothers arrived in Yaqui country.

The Yaquis were also at war with the state government of Sonora, then led by Governor Plutarco Elías Calles (a future Mexican President, whom Beals would come to know), who had sought to pacify Yaqui rebels in 1916 with promises of land.[35] By 1918, this agreement was in tatters, and the Yaquis accused the state government of reneging on its commitments.

A Yaqui band attacked the town of Esperanza in December 1917, and again in the late summer of 1918, when the Beals brothers were in nearby Cajemé. Carleton recalled that in the later attack, they "drove out the garrison, seized the military supplies and captured the Commandant and his aide, [whom they] tied to their horses' tails and galloped with them heads down, up one street and down another until they were dead."[36]

Still, the Beals brothers felt relatively safe in Cajemé, just ten kilometers south of Esperanza, because the town's commandant, an uncharacteristically passive Yaqui, was unlikely to be molested by his brethren. But they abandoned their plan to find O'Shaughnessy's cache of gold, as it would have involved extensive traveling in the back country, where Yaquis were on the warpath. Carleton and Ralph remained in Cajemé a few weeks as the cool autumn descended, building a hut for a German immigrant farmer named Schneider, in return for a pittance and space to sleep in a haystack.

When that job was finished, they hired on as farmhands at an isolated cornfield near Esperanza. But this employment did not last either, as their enthusiasm for the job suddenly vanished when an unidentified sniper took potshots at them from his perch in the surrounding forest.

Joe, Schneider's clerk, then announced a plan to sink his savings into a melon farm on thirty acres of rented land south of Cajemé. He offered Carleton and Ralph jobs as laborers. Joe would pay the Beals brothers one peso a day plus a share of the melon sale proceeds. They accepted.

But the fearsome Yaquis made sure it was not to be. Carleton, Joe, and another farmhand set off for Esperanza to buy farm tools and seeds they would need to plant the melons. Along the way, they came upon a group of Yaquis burning a railroad bridge, hooting as they watched the flames engulf it.

"I'm not going on," Beals told his companions. "You can do what you like. But you'll not risk it if you aren't suicide-seeking fools." The other two ignored him.

Beals turned and headed back the way they had come. But after proceeding about a hundred feet, he felt he "couldn't leave them to their fate," so he veered back toward the bridge, through the bush this time, out of sight and undetected. He was horrified as he watched the Yaquis cluster around the two men and force them to strip off their clothes. They tied their hands behind their backs, hurled them to the ground, and began beating them with clubs.

The shaken Beals retreated and crawled through the brush, then ran to the Commandant's quarters in Esperanza, demanding that he gather his men to try to rescue his two unlucky companions. The Commandant demurred. "Better that we go tomorrow morning. We can't fight the Yaquis in the dark," he replied.

"But those boys may still be alive," Beals insisted.

"Alive! Not if the Yaquis got hold of them." The next day, Beals and the Commandant found the bodies.

At this point, the Beals brothers decided to try to make it to Mexico City alone. They managed to feed themselves, barely, by unloading boxcars, telling fortunes to credulous Indians, and by selling postcards of the Virgin of Guadalupe, this in partnership with a blind street minstrel.

In early November, they reached Culiacán. Along the way, they met another draft evader, "a red-headed, self-educated, Jewish communist" from New York, also on his way to Mexico City.[37] Here, the trio stayed with Ernesto Weisner, a boozy German-American expatriate who befriended them. "Don Ernesto" enjoyed the young Americans' company so much that he tried to dissuade them from heading south, saying the trip through the mountains as winter set in was dangerous enough, even if they managed to evade the bandits who preyed on travelers just like them. When he failed to shake the group's purpose, he proposed that Ralph stay behind and work at the electric light plant at which Weisner was the engineer. To Ralph's indignation and dismay, Carleton and the New Yorker "turned on [him]," saying this was a good idea, as two travelers would find it easier to find food than a threesome.[38]

One morning before they left, Weisner's vivacious *mestiza* (woman of mixed race) partner, Panchita, seized a moment while her husband was away at the plant, to pour out a tale of woe to Carleton. Weisner, she said, though he seemed kind and generous, was "a brute." She pounded the breakfast table. "I hate him, hate him," she cried, and begged Beals to send for her once he got to Mexico City. She showed him an ugly scar on her bosom, saying, "He did that. He gets drunk and brings in other women and carouses with them and even makes me stay in the same room." She broke into sobs and threw her arms around Beals, "the fire of her round young body running through me," he wrote.[39]

Beals promised to ask Ralph to bring her with him to Mexico City once he was established there. It never happened. Ralph would stay in Culiacán with the unhappy Weisner couple for several months before returning to California.[40]

Carleton and Ralph would remain in contact over the years, with the peripatetic Carleton making sporadic visits to his more settled brother, who became a celebrated professor of anthropology at the University of California in Los Angeles, specialized in indigenous cultures of Mexico. Ralph also acquired a wife, Dorothy Manchester, with whom he had two sons and two daughters. Carleton, to his nieces and nephews, was "a little like the character Uncle Ben [who makes cameo appearances] in *Death of a Salesman*," one of them recalled.[41]

For now, Beals and his companion continued to Mexico City on foot. This was complicated by his shoes having given out, to be replaced by *huaraches*, or Indian sandals of cured leather, that he fashioned himself, out of old tire rubber and wire. As he forded back and forth across the Tamazula River, sand stuck to the sandal thongs, which then fretted sores into his feet. This became chronic, even threatening gangrene, until Beals finally received medical attention from a kindly nurse who took pity on him.

On this trip, Beals discovered and practiced what became a lifelong passion for sharing the daily lives of the poor. His own pain and poverty never blocked his capacity to empathize with the poor, and to endow their miserable lives with a kind of noble dignity. As a journalist, Beals, when addressing the poor, would try "to lift them up a few notches," and when dealing with the wealthy and powerful, "to knock them down a few."[42] This bias, or vocation, originated with the reforming socialist passions he inherited from his mother Elvina. But it was during his quixotic overland journey of some 1,500 miles to Mexico City in 1918, and especially its last leg, through Mexico's more heavily-populated highlands, where he traveled among Mexico's great masses of rural poor, that his deeply-felt—if ingenuous and idealized—devotion to the downtrodden was reinforced.

After leaving Ralph, for some days, Beals and his companion traveled and camped out with a mule-train carrying salt and other supplies over the western Sierra Madre from Culiacán, which the muleteers sold to housewives who rushed out from their thatched huts in mountain hamlets along the trail. Once, when suffering from fever and chills, Beals was nursed to health by a venerable old medicine woman, who pasted green leaves on his temples, provided hot, pungent herbal tea, and dispatched him to perspire in a temascal, a low, conical, stone bath-house, like a sauna.

In Topia, in Durango, Beals lodged with a peasant family as the mountain village was hit by the worldwide pandemic, known as the Spanish flu. "In many houses, the whole family was ill, and people died as in some Oriental pest-hole, the dead bodies being pushed out of the door into the street by the person most capable of movement," Beals later wrote.[43] He found himself nursing his hosts as they succumbed, and helped dig the grave of the youngest, a sixteen-year-old girl.

From Durango, Beals rode a freight train again. Suffering from flu himself now, Beals was attended by a fifteen-year-old Indian girl, Evangelina Huitrón, from Jalisco. Evangelina described herself as an *agrarista*, part of a federal military corps whose mission was to break up large landholdings for redistribution to peasant farmers. She told Beals that her objective in Mexico City was to see Carranza and demand that his government deliver on its promise to redistribute land to the peasants, and to stop its repression.[44]

She said her father, who had fought in the revolution, had lost patience waiting for Carranza's administration to return lands to the peasants. The restitution of lands that the previous dictatorial Porfirio Díaz regime had stolen from smallholders and ejido communities was, to Mexico's rural poor, the revolution's very purpose. Evangelina's father, joined by six of his neighbors, tore down the fences of unused land near his village, and settled on it. Soon, soldiers came and marched them off to prison. Later, Evangelina learned that her father had been killed.[45]

"I went through the village telling everybody they should take the lands, they should fight the government if necessary," Evangelina told Beals as they sat in the shadows of the cold, empty boxcar as it rattled south towards Mexico City. "One day I even got up and made a speech. I made many speeches."[46]

Finally, Evangelina said, she was shot in the hand by federal soldiers who came to break up a farmers' protest rally at which she had given a speech denouncing the government. "Now I have run away from the village," she said. "I will go to President Carranza and tell him what the soldiers are doing in our village and that the people must have their lands. And that is why I am here."[47]

In the final stretch before Mexico City, Beals and Evangelina had to scramble aboard a car of pigs, to avoid being seen and ejected by train inspectors. They stood with their backs pressed against the door, kicking the pigs away from them when they crowded too close. Beals looked through the slats of the car to behold below, the gleaming lake of Texcoco, and later, the great towers of the cathedral poking above the plain. The freight skirted on through the tree-clustered suburbs, past quaint lanes and adobe houses to the terminal.

Evangelina bade him farewell through tears. "To part will be easier for both of us," she said, holding his hands. "You are of another people. You will find your own friends to help you and give you clothes, all you need. And I too must go among my own people. Goodbye."[48]

## NOTES

1. Carleton Beals, *John Eliot: The Man Who Loved the Indians* (New York: Messner, 1957); and Beals, *Eagles of the Andes: South American Struggles for Independence* (Philadelphia: Chilton Books, 1963).
2. Carleton Beals, "Under the Fifth Sun" (unpublished autobiography, c. 1972–1978), Carleton Beals Collection (CBC), Howard Gotlieb Archival Research Center, Boston University, box 45 (hereafter cited CBC); this is one title among several Beals gave his unfinished and unpublished autobiography.
3. Beals, "Under the Fifth Sun" (unpublished autobiography), CBC.
4. Beals, "Under the Fifth Sun" (unpublished autobiography), CBC.
5. Robert Justin Goldstein, *Political Repression in Modern America: From 1870 to 1976* (Chicago: University of Illinois Press, 2001), 107.
6. Carleton Beals to Commanding General, The Presidio, San Francisco, California, December 29, 1917, CBC, box 165.
7. See Harold W. Currie, *Eugene V. Debs* (Boston: Twayne, 1976), 88.
8. Currie, *Eugene V. Debs*, 89.
9. Carleton Beals, *Cyclone Carry: The Story of Carry Nation* (Philadelphia: Chilton Books, 1962), 107–8.
10. Beals, "Under the Fifth Sun" (unpublished autobiography), CBC.
11. Beals, "Under the Fifth Sun" (unpublished autobiography), CBC; see also Ralph L. Beals, "Memories of My Brother, Carleton Beals," (1982), prepared for Melvin B. Yoken, Melvin B. Yoken Collection (MBYC), John Hay Library, Brown University, Providence, Rhode Island (hereafter cited MBYC).
12. Beals, "Under the Fifth Sun" (unpublished autobiography), CBC.
13. Beals, "Under the Fifth Sun" (unpublished autobiography), CBC.
14. Beals, "Under the Fifth Sun" (unpublished autobiography), CBC.
15. Beals, "Under the Fifth Sun" (unpublished autobiography), CBC.
16. Carleton Beals to Commanding General, The Presidio, San Francisco, California, December 29, 1917, CBC, box 165.
17. Hiram Johnson to Elvina Beals, August 1917, CBC, box 165.
18. Carleton Beals, "Eastern Trade As a Factor in the World War," *Oakland World*, September 14, 1917, in Christopher Neal, Private collection, Westmount, Quebec (hereafter cited CNC).
19. Carleton Beals, "Carl Beals Tortured," *Oakland Tribune*, December 1917, in CNC.
20. Ralph L. Beals to Melvin Yoken, MBYC.
21. US War Department, Letter of Military Discharge to Carleton Beals, quoted in "Army Frees Beals," *San Francisco Chronicle*, March 10, 1918, CNC.
22. Goldstein, *Political Repression*, 110–11.
23. Goldstein, *Political Repression*, 119.
24. Beals, "Under the Fifth Sun" (unpublished autobiography), CBC.
25. Beals, "Under the Fifth Sun" (unpublished autobiography), CBC.
26. Beals, "Under the Fifth Sun" (unpublished autobiography), CBC.

27. Ralph L. Beals, "Prospective Diary of Trip to Mexico in 1918–1919" (unpublished manuscript, c. 1932), 1, courtesy of Alan R. Beals, now in CNC.

28. Beals, "Prospective Diary of Trip to Mexico in 1918–1919" (unpublished manuscript, c. 1932), now in CNC.

29. Carleton Beals, *Brimstone and Chili: A Book of Personal Experiences in the Southwest and in Mexico* (New York: Knopf, 1927), 1–3.

30. Beals, "Under the Fifth Sun" (unpublished autobiography), CBC.

31. Letter Ralph Beals to Yoken; Carleton Beals, *Brimstone and Chili: A Book of Personal Experiences in the Southwest and in Mexico* (New York: Knopf, 1927), 128, and in Ralph L. Beals, "Prospective Diary" (unpublished manuscript), 12–13, in CNC.

32. Beals, *Brimstone and Chili*, 67.

33. Ralph L. Beals, "Prospective Diary" (unpublished manuscript), 3, in CNC.

34. Beals, *Brimstone and Chili*, 128, in Ralph L. Beals's "Prospective Diary" (unpublished), in CNC, Boyd is referred to as "Bruce."

35. Mark T. Gilderhus, *Diplomacy and Revolution: US-Mexican Relations under Wilson and Carranza* (Tucson: University of Arizona Press, 1977), 75.

36. Carleton Beals, *Mexican Maze* (Philadelphia: J. B. Lippincott, 1931), 179.

37. Ralph L. Beals, "Prospective Diary" (unpublished manuscript), 15, in CNC.

38. The Beals brothers' accounts differ as to the names of the family with whom Ralph L. remained in Culiacán. In *Brimstone and Chili*, Carleton refers to them as James Langdon and his Mexican wife Josefina, while Ralph calls them Ernesto Weisner and Panchita. Ralph's L. account seems the more reliable, as he actually lived with the family for several months. Also, Carleton may have wanted to disguise the names in a published book to avoid repercussions, and to guard the secrecy of the unhappy Mexican wife's longing for escape.

39. Beals, *Brimstone and Chili*, 199.

40. Ralph L. Beals, "Prospective Diary" (unpublished manuscript), in CNC.

41. Alan R. Beals, telephone interview by Christopher Neal, January 7, 2002.

42. Carolyn Kennedy Beals, interview by Christopher Neal, September 15, 2001, Madison, CT.

43. Beals, *Brimstone and Chili*, 227.

44. Beals, *Brimstone and Chili*, 267.

45. Beals, *Brimstone and Chili*, 266.

46. Beals, *Brimstone and Chili*, 266.

47. Beals, *Brimstone and Chili*, 266–67.

48. Beals, *Brimstone and Chili*, 266.

*Chapter Two*

# Rags to Respect in Mexico City

Years later, Carleton Beals looked back, self-satisfied and nostalgic, on his phoenix-like rise from utter destitution after his arrival in Mexico City. He had been delivered there on a freight car loaded with pigs, and broke, speaking only the rudiments of Spanish. At just a few inches over five feet tall, he was a kind of man-child whose wispy blond beard now gave him a seedy aspect. His shirt and trousers were greasy and threadbare and his feet, a mess of festering sores. Even the regulars in the *cantinas* of the city's historic center, where he first lodged, wanted nothing to do with him, as he wandered the streets in his makeshift *huaraches* (Mexican sandals).

But less than a year later, in 1919, he had acquired status—in the American expatriate community, at any rate. He was principal of the American School. In his spare time, he served as a gracious volunteer lecturer, offering weekly talks on Shakespeare over tea and cakes in genteel parlors of the wives of American oilmen, executives, and diplomats posted to the Aztec capital. And later in the year, he was invited by the nation's *Primer Jefe* (First Chief), Venustiano Carranza himself, to teach English to Mexico's senior military staff.

It was a dizzying climb from the crisp early December day in 1918 when Beals had first arrived in Mexico City. Just twenty-six years old, he was captivated immediately, even in his penury. On the broad Paseo de la Reforma, gentlemen on horseback and horse-drawn coaches competed for space with open-air automobiles and gas-powered trolleys. The boulevard was a grand affair, bordered by green islands of palms and eucalyptus trees, granite urns, and statues of minor military heroes. In the crowds filing past the gaily-painted storefronts and *pulque* (agave liquor) shops, mahogany-skinned peasants clad in cotton pajamas, handwoven red *serapes* (shawls) slung over their shoulders, were mixed with businessmen in three-piece suits cut in Paris.

The golden Angel of Independence, like Mercury set atop a towering monument, centerpiece of the Paseo's principal traffic circle, had been unveiled nine years earlier by Porfirio Díaz to mark the centenary of Mexican independence. It gave the city a decorative crowning touch and counterpoint to the mushrooming slums around it.

But Mexico City's stately downtown hardly concealed the fact that it, too, was mired in the conflict and suffering that racked the whole country. By 1920, almost two million Mexicans—about one-eighth of the population—had died over the previous decade from starvation, epidemics of disease, and straight-out violence, all rooted in the revolutionary turmoil.

War still raged as Beals struggled to find his way in the city. "From Mexico City itself," he wrote:

> I could see the watch fires of the agrarian rebel Emiliano Zapata blazing brightly in lofty Milpa Verde. The picturesque Desierto de Los Leones, only an hour or so out from the capital, was still Zapata country. I went out there once with a special detachment of federal soldiers. Elongated wind-dried human cadavers, hung from trees or telegraph poles, turned slowly in the breeze . . .
>
> Mexico City itself was wild, with a murderous night-life. Prostitutes—unfortunate women washed up by the disorder—swarmed everywhere. I counted 47 streetwalkers in one block right by the main post office, a street not particularly devoted to this activity. There were four vast red-light districts—not to mention the scores of houses of every category scattered over the city, or the wild dance-hall saloons all the way from the center out through the Peravillo and Guerrero districts. Sometimes women came to bachelor doors and for small sums offered their 12 or 13-year-old daughters "to work" for a week or so. As wreckage drifted in from the European war, more sophisticated talent of the Old World capitals competed with the charms of native women. Wide-open gambling flourished. Generals, drunk with sudden power, splattered their ill-gotten wealth around recklessly, shot up cafés, even looted homes.[1]

Lacking the capacity he would later acquire to understand the subtleties of Mexico's revolutionary convulsion, Beals's first impressions of Mexico City were gilded ones, reflecting his relief after the months of privation and hard travel across the deserts and mountain ranges between the capital and the US border. After a night spent in a rooftop room at the downtown Hotel Juárez, he strolled through the central Alameda Park:

> Something in this Mexican scene calmed my nerves, banishing all fear of the future. I no longer felt the pariah, the outcast. I had enough money for a night's lodging, perhaps for two nights. The sun shone luxuriously upon me.
>
> The mass of semi-tropical vegetation and the soft green lawns, the delightful bronzes, the paths laid out in French style, the splashing fountains, all was

lyric, soothing. I gave myself sensuously to the lover-like caress of the balmy air and the beauty of the deep shadows over rich green grass. I drowsed among the calls of the bootblacks, the vendors of oranges, candy, and ices, and the chirrupings of the canaries. . . . Fringing the park rose buildings, the stately unfinished National Theatre, churches, arcades, tiled palaces, bell towers. On the wings of the soft air came the constant boom of mellow bells; beautiful women passed by; carriages and autos rolled down the avenue.

I began to dream dreams, extravagant dreams. I would stay here in this city of the Aztecs and the Conquistadores and live and achieve success. I would make money. I would enjoy life and win women, the beautiful women who passed me by.[2]

First, however, there was the more urgent matter of finding something to eat and more secure lodging. Beals, friendly and articulate, turned serendipitous encounters to his advantage, helping him on the way to realizing his dreams. The Alameda Park was a magnet for some of the estimated 30,000 American war resisters, known as "slackers" in Mexico. Another of these, Linn A. E. Gale and his wife Magdalena, had just arrived in Mexico City from upstate New York by way of Louisiana, where they had lived in a socialist commune.[3] Like Beals, they were homeless, and so the trio agreed to share a rented second-floor room at a boarding house at the corner of Nuevo Mexico and Dolores Streets, overlooking a block of Chinese restaurants and grocery shops.

Days later, Beals stopped a dapper Mexican ambling on a city street to ask directions. Juan de Dios Avellaneda, a member of Mexico's Chamber of Deputies, had lived in the United States, and responded affably in fluent English, inviting Beals to dine with his family at his home, just blocks away. He also gave the disheveled young drifter access to his shower, shaving gear, and outfitted him with a new pair of trousers, jacket, and tie, so that he looked the part of the English teacher he hoped to be. "What American Congressman—indeed, what American—would do the same for a homeless foreigner?" Beals asked himself.

At the boarding house, meanwhile, Beals had so endeared himself to the concierge that she allowed him to remain for three months as a lodger, for which he "paid" by giving English lessons to her children. Gale and his wife, however, had run out of money, and so were evicted. He blamed Beals for having abandoned him, cutting a separate deal with the concierge, who had taken a shine to Beals. Months later, Gale founded and edited *Gale's International Monthly*, one of several socialist and communist publications that surfaced in Mexico in the late 1910s and early 1920s.[4] His "radical magazine" irritated the Álvaro Obregón (1880–1928) government enough to deport him from Mexico in 1921. Upon arrival in the United States, Gale was arrested on a charge of desertion, later convicted by a military court-martial, and sentenced to seven years in prison.[5]

These early positive experiences stirred in Beals what would be a lifelong affection for Mexicans. He did not love them blindly, for he catalogued some faults, but in his writings about Mexico, there is a distinctly respectful, even admiring tone. "Half-poet, half-musician, and who feels in terms of beauty and an all-pervading mysticism, [the Mexican] is usually kindly in his human relations," he wrote in 1923. "Above all he is sympathetic, courteous, generous, boundless in his hospitality. His great Latin *dignidad* [dignity] promptly melts if he finds that a person is *simpático* [friendly]; and the foreigner is more kindly treated in Mexico than anywhere else in the world."[6]

Beals soon became established in Mexico City, after a fashion. Life at the boarding house on Dolores Street settled into a pattern, and he befriended some of his fellow residents there, "subterranean crew" that they were. Next door was a dashing and amorous freelance journalist, living at a breakneck pace, and down the corridor, an engineering student and his sister, for whom he pimped. There was a thin but pretty vaudeville actress, doing a song-and-dance act in the cheaper movie houses. A "threadbare socialist lawyer" named Santibañez entertained the boarders with his pamphleteer rants at the dinner table. And a retired sea captain, quite mad, dressed in full uniform and gesticulated with a pulpy stump, shorn of all fingers, save the thumb. With great solemnity, he invited Beals to an interview in his room one day and tried to entice him to help sell some fantasy military technology to American capitalists.[7]

Beals's roster of students grew, as businessmen and bored wives of aristocrats, and other idle rich, responded to his ads for English lessons in the daily newspaper, *El Universal*. In mid-1919, he was approached by George Poltiol, another English teacher and British expatriate in his mid-twenties, who suggested they go into business together. The pair had soon rented two large rooms at the corner of Independencia and Lopez Streets, installed lights, desks, and blackboards, and opened what they called "The English Institute." Within six months of his arrival as a ragged beggar, Beals proudly recorded that he was earning twice his salary at the Standard Oil Company back in Richmond, California, a year before.

He felt vindicated, and also exhilarated by the heady freedom he sensed in Mexico. Here he found a "new and richer existence . . . more satisfying than any I had ever known."[8] Touching bottom, living by his wits in absolute poverty, and then rising from it in a city at once alien and inviting, inspired him to write. He recorded his impressions, wrote poems, and started to write feature news stories, which he tried to sell to American magazines. These early efforts met with a string of rejection slips, but Beals was undeterred, and reveled in having discovered his calling as a writer.

He had taken a decisive and irrevocable step away from his earlier life in the United States, which he now saw as a forlorn existence driven by what he called "the American herd gospel: success, college friends, a conventional engagement, [where] everything led me to a job in a shipping-office instead of to a garret of books and cobwebs and poetry."[9] In Mexico, he felt as if delivered from the fears that had plagued him earlier, fear of poverty, of censorious opinion, of love, of emotion, of the future, of life itself.

He churned out poems with an intensity he would later apply to books of reportage, travelogues, political analyses, novels, history, and biography. In his fantasy, he imagined himself a new Percy Bysshe Shelley, composing ballads of lusty freedom, a curious beginning for someone who would later focus his work on polemics and personalities. By early 1920, he had finished enough poems for a collection, which he called *Aztec Arrows*, and tried to sell to Harcourt, Brace & Howe, Poet Lore, the Bookman, and Harper and Brothers, all of whom sent it back.[10]

Beals also translated forty poems by Amado Nervo, a hugely popular Mexican laureate of the Modernist school who had died at the age of forty-nine years, in 1919. Again, he tried to interest American publishers in the poems and again, was rebuffed. Given his own ambition to make it as a poet, Beals was fascinated by Nervo's limpid, emotive verse, and even more so by the outpouring of public grieving at his death. Over fifty thousand people turned out to receive Nervo's remains when they arrived at Mexico City's train station from Montevideo, Uruguay, where he had died. The following day, two hundred thousand people filed past his bier at the Foreign Ministry, and his funeral service was attended by cabinet ministers and Mexican Supreme Court justices.[11]

After the funeral, Beals wrote a laudatory obituary on Nervo, which he sent to *Harpers* and the *Atlantic Monthly*. Both rejected it, although eleven years later, the same piece was published in the *Saturday Review of Literature*.[12]

Through most of 1919, Beals found few outlets willing to publish his literary efforts. It was not for want of trying, as Beals approached the *New York Times*, *St. Louis Globe-Democrat*, *Chicago Tribune*, *Baltimore American*, the *Dial*, *Everybody's Magazine*, *Southern Woman's Magazine*, the *New Republic*, and the *Nation*, among others.[13] The steady stream of rejections for his poetry finally convinced him that he was not quite Shelley, and so he shifted his focus to journalistic pieces which, later in the year, drew glimmers of interest.

*Collier's*, one of the more popular magazines of the time, rejected a story on *pulque*, Mexico's national home-brew liquor made with fermented juice of the maguey cactus, but its editor urged Beals to write articles on Mexico, "as it affects the US and not internal Mexican problems."[14] Herbert Croly, editor of the *New Republic*, commented on an article about the political situation, saying it "made a great many assertions which I am sure you fully believe to be true, but which we have no way of verifying."[15] Ernest Gruening, editor of the *Nation*, sent him an encouraging rejection note, asking for more on "important happenings in Mexico City."[16]

Soon after launching the English Institute with Poltiol, Beals was able to move from the rooming house where he had shared space with Gale into an apartment on his own. He began to make friends in the bohemian expatriate community, with young writers and artists at the leftist newspaper, the *Masses*, as well as with well-heeled Americans, diplomats, and business people. His association with the latter group arose when one of the trustees of the American High School in Mexico City suggested to Beals that he apply for a teaching position there. To his astonishment, he was not only appointed at once, but also, within a few months, named principal.

Now outwardly established as a prominent member of the expatriate community, Beals found himself in demand. Some of the country club women of the American colony asked him to give them informal lectures on English literature once a week, each time in a different lady's parlor. This became the Shakespeare Club, for which Beals served as an unlikely scholar. Though well-read for his age, the Bard of Avon was not his forte, and usually, he had to scramble to read the plays just hours before he would pontificate on them for the ladies.

His work and associations multiplied, as many of these same women enjoined him to tutor their children, as they prepared themselves to attend universities in the United States. Beals showed the prodigious industry that later would make him so prolific, as he juggled private tutoring with his responsibilities as principal of the American School, and with the courses he continued to teach with Poltiol at the English Institute. Meantime, he had started work on a book, an extended political essay that would become *Mexico: An Interpretation*, published in 1923 by the independent New York house owned by liberal Ben Huebsch.

Though Beals was part of this expatriate American community, he soon learned that he was not of a mind to embrace it. He most enjoyed the company of bohemians with whom he identified, but he was able to move easily among vastly different social circles throughout his life, and this practice became evident during his first extended sojourn in Mexico City.

Although his writings are strident and uncompromising, Beals was mild-mannered in social intercourse. His humor was dry, and he would usually fall silent or make only a subtle dig, when he disapproved of something, rather than make a scene. Always serious-minded, he was happiest with talk of books and literature. This he enjoyed at the Shakespeare Club.

But now, he was drawn also to the underground life of Mexico City. "The gossip of the teacups had the good effect of driving me to drink," he wrote. "Association with the good women of the Shakespeare Club was quite too prophylactic, and my fondness for good, honest, low-brow association would violently reassert itself."[17] Often, he repaired to Fat Sing's, a dingy Chinese café on his now-beloved Dolores Street, to drink beer and tequila late into the night.

There he met an unlikely assortment of political activists and intellectuals, mixed with expatriate roués and would-be artists. Mexico's disorderly and still largely undefined revolution offered a climate in which political intrigue flourished. Fat Sing's was the hangout for the underground foreign chattering classes, a kind of leftist clubhouse. Once again, Gale was there, as well as Mike Gold, later the editor of the New York-based Communist newspaper *New Masses*, along with Manabendra N. Roy, a Hindu nationalist refugee seeking home rule for British India.[18]

Roy introduced Beals to a Soviet agent named Mikhail Borodin, who had come to Mexico in September 1919, via New York and Chicago, entrusted by Lenin and Trotsky with the task of establishing a Communist Party there. Borodin used his real name, Michael Gruzenberg, while assuming a fake identity as a hardware merchant. At thirty-five years old, Borodin was already an experienced Bolshevik operative, whose objective was to cement diplomatic ties to Mexico's government, while also establishing a Moscow-linked Communist Party to promote Mexican participation in the Soviet strategy to foment world revolution.[19] To these ends, Lenin had appointed Borodin as Soviet Consul to the Mexican government in April.

Borodin had met Roy soon after the Russian's arrival in Mexico City, quickly developing a friendship with him. Unlike Borodin, Roy spoke Spanish. He had also managed to finagle money from the German government early in World War I to build overseas support for the Indian nationalist movement, thus fulfilling a German goal of undermining the British.[20] Borodin was short of funds, having lost a cache of stolen Tsarist jewels that was to have financed his mission. His association with Roy had reciprocal payoffs: Borodin obtained a well-financed Spanish-speaking go-between connected to Mexico's mostly expatriate leftists, while Roy gained a vital contact to win over Soviet support for his goal of an independent India.

Roy and his wife, a Stanford graduate named Evelyn Trent, had become Beals's friends, close enough that they allowed Beals to live in their apartment when they left Mexico in 1920. Beals took an immediate dislike to Borodin, however, but kept his opinion to himself. This was a show of deference to his friend Roy, who had agreed to help Borodin set up a Mexican Communist Party in return for which Borodin had promised to help Roy not only secure Soviet backing for the Indian nationalist movement, but also place Roy as Indian representative in the Comintern.[21]

Roy, Borodin, and American expatriates Mike Gold and Charles Phillips joined a handful of others to seize control of Mexico's Socialist Party, itself a tiny klatch dominated by American "slackers," then nominally led by Linn Gale. They succeeded in removing Gale, whom they considered a "pseudo-socialist" who would block their project of transforming the party, such as it was, into a Moscow-aligned entity.[22] Roy, under Borodin's influence, had converted, at least outwardly, to Marxism, and was named Mexico's delegate to the Second Congress of the Communist International in Moscow in July and August 1920. Upon arrival there, however, he ceded this role to fellow delegate Charles Phillips, and represented India instead.[23]

Despite his outward charm, mystery, and even charisma, Borodin was a hard, dogmatic man, Beals believed, whose purpose, under Trotsky's direction, "seemed to me brutal and dastardly . . . the same sort of *realpolitik*, dressed up in a red flag, which I disliked so heartily in old feudal and capitalist Europe [and] which had already led to universal tragedy."[24] Borodin left Mexico in December 1919 for Russia by way of Barcelona and Amsterdam, setting up a Comintern presence in the first, and attending an abortive Comintern congress in the second. He would later be dispatched by Lenin to Canton, where he became an influential advisor and conduit for Soviet weapons to Chinese nationalist leaders Sun Yat-Sen and, tepidly, to Chiang Kai-shek, before the latter purged Communists from the ranks of the Kuomintang.[25]

Along with his exposure to this shadowy world, Beals experienced his sexual awakening during this period, and began a decade of joyful promiscuity. He remained engaged to Lillian, and their plan was for her to join him as soon as he had gotten on his feet financially. But Beals's long absence in Mexico had reinforced skepticism about him in the minds of Lillian's parents. They feared that their daughter would rue this choice of a draft-evading, seemingly aimless drifter now living, without much in the way of what they considered real prospects, in tumultuous Mexico City. They implored her to break the engagement.

Beals was lonely, of course, and after having been reared to an almost fanatical and idealistic canon of sexual purity and chastity, he was now thrust into a world in which attractive young women, even strangers, arrested him with what he called "the frank, open gaze of the Latin which makes no attempt to hide its interest."[26] Imbued with the atheistic, free-love theories of his hero, the poet Shelley, Beals now found himself presented with an opportunity to a celebrate them. He was fair and blond, of small stature but trim, vigorous, and handsome. His Spanish had grown fluent enough that he could make women laugh with his stories. And at twenty-six years old, he was still a virgin.

But not for long. At the boarding house, the concierge, Doña Concha, had offered herself to him, but he had turned her away, a bit shocked by the frank advance. Shortly thereafter, he slept with two *mestiza* girls in rapid succession, and then with Virginia, a young woman who attended his weekly Shakespeare lectures. She lived with her parents in a handsome low-roofed, green dwelling on a sprawling estate not far from the San Angel Inn, then as now, a precinct of privilege in the federal district. One hot day, when her father was out of town on business, she sent the servants home for the day and invited Beals to tea.

Turned out in a fluffy dress, Virginia welcomed him warmly, ushering him to a divan in a splendidly decorated sitting room, everything bearing the stamp of wealth and good taste.

"We're all alone," she said portentously, as she seated herself beside him on the divan.

"You know, I brought you here under false pretenses. I want to read some of my poetry to you and get your opinion about it."

She brought out a thick stack of lavender-colored pages with scalloped edges and began to recite. The verses were pedestrian, sprinkled with abundant references to flowers, stars, and love, but she read in a lilting, full-bodied voice that had a soporific effect on Beals, who soon dozed off.

Some time later, he awoke with a start. She had been gazing at him as he slept.

"I am sorry . . ."

"Poor boy, you were tired . . . please rest." She had drawn the shades and removed his shoes.

"I am very much ashamed."

"Oh, not at all. Lie back and take it easy."

She stroked his forehead. He enjoyed the gentleness of her cool hand. He embraced her, and found she had nothing on under her dress.

"I'm crazy about you, darling," she announced suddenly, taking his cheeks in her hands. Soon she had wriggled out of the fluffy dress, and Beals was "drowned in a hammering sea of delight."

This episode, while a welcome release for Beals, pricked his conscience, as he thought of Lillian, his fiancée. Only a few days later, he received a wire from her, saying she would arrive by train three days hence.[27]

Her train pulled into the pre-dawn gloom of Mexico City's Colonia Station at about 4 a.m., six hours late. Beals had fallen asleep on a bench and was awakened only moments before her arrival by a vagrant trying to steal his shoes.

It was a strangely joyless reunion, an anti-climax. Both had, for a time, almost lost hope that their marriage would actually take place. Now their dream was restored. But time, indecision, and Beals's infidelities had dulled some of its luster.

She smiled nervously, fussing as Beals struggled with her huge trunk of linen, clothes, and American luxuries. She had not seen him for over a year, and now it seemed as though a gulf had opened between them. He seemed changed somehow, grown distant, and had acquired a new fugitive light in his eyes that made her uncomfortable.

It was a difficult adjustment for her, to be plunged suddenly into daily life with this strange version of the Carleton Beals she once knew, no longer the college man he had been. Before, his politics had been unconventional, but it had seemed part affectation. Now he struck her as being adrift. She had not imagined him having gone so native. His apartment was almost bare, furnished mostly with terra cotta bowls, urns, and glazed gourds, a lone bed, and a kind of brazier stove, on which she would try gamely to cook American meals. His friends dismayed her; they seemed as refugees, reedy, chain-smoking artists and radicals, drifting in and out at all hours.

They were married on November 6, 1919, a week after her arrival, by a judge in a courthouse near the *Volador*, or Thieves' Market. The witnesses were Henry Glintenkamp, an artist, and Art Young, a cartoonist, both of whom Beals knew from the Communist magazine, *The Masses*, as well as Indian refugee, Hernamba Gupta.[28] Lillian was dazed by the casual arbitrariness of what she had imagined would be, should be, a more solemn ceremony, a grander and more festive wedding.

To match the earnestness with which she had preserved her virginity for him, Beals forced himself to adhere to the lie that he had done the same, concealing his recent embrace of *free love* as a lifestyle. So began their marriage.

Although she suffered, sometimes crying softly in the night during the first weeks, she adapted, finding friends of her own among the American community. She learned to rekindle her taste for Beals's sometimes wild abandon. Once, for example, they made love on top of the large Pyramid of the Sun at Teotihuacán, under a cloudless sky, heat waves shimmering over the great fertile valley and villages all around.

\*\*\*

In late 1919, Beals shared cocktails in a café with a member of President Carranza's personal staff who suggested that he and his fellow officers would benefit from instruction in military English.[29] Beals promptly agreed to the proposal, and was soon giving lessons to about twenty young officers—"a jolly barrack-room crowd"—in the offices of the Mexican Secretary of War, located above the north entrance of Mexico City's National Palace.[30] This new function gave Beals a ringside seat to the Carranza regime, by then rotting from within as corrupt generals appropriated the spoils of power for their personal use. His classroom was next to the offices of Generals Barragán and Urquizo, who shared the role of Secretary of War. Beals depicted Barragán as Mexico's military ruler, unrestrained by the remote and ineffectual Carranza, as "a military upstart of less than thirty years—a dude and a braggart, who swaggered around the capital with a gold-headed cane and women of ill-repute, who came to own a string of mansions on the fashionable Paseo de la Reforma, who brazenly defied the traffic regulations by dashing through the streets with his feet cocked on the windshield of his auto."[31]

He met Carranza too, several times, including at least a few private interviews in the President's office, during which he was always received so that Carranza's face remained in the shadow. He found the white-haired patriarch to be, "chilly and inscrutable behind his flowing whiskers and blue spectacles," his office adorned with statues of Napoleon and Porfirio Díaz, the latter under whom Carranza had served as a Senator. This choice of political heroes gave Beals "a subtle clue to understanding [Carranza's] inflexible obstinacy." By the spring of 1920, Carranza's erstwhile ally turned bitter rival, General Obregón of Sonora, challenged him openly from the outside, at the head of what became the "revindicating revolution."[32]

The split had emerged when Obregón announced his candidacy for the presidency on June 1, 1919, setting himself up in opposition to Carranza's handpicked successor, Ignacio Bonillas, whom Carranza had appointed as Mexico's ambassador to Washington. Bonillas, an engineer trained at Massachusetts Institute of Technology (MIT), was widely ridiculed as "Meester" Bonillas, because his long residence in the United States showed in his gringo-sounding Spanish.

More to the point was Carranza's failure to deliver on promises to redistribute land to peasant farmers, or to pass legislation to raise workers' wages and recognize their rights. The free-running corruption in his administration, with "loot-spirit infecting every department," as Beals put it, had destroyed his credibility. Also, most of the high command of the army wanted Obregón, a military man, to be president.[33]

As government officials sold foreign exchange at big discounts to cronies, and pocketed bribes in return for oil, timber, and mining concessions, plans to build schools were shelved, and teachers went unpaid. The labor movement, led by the Casa del Obrero Mundial (COM) (House of the World's Worker), was suppressed, with federal troops sent to break strikes, and labor leaders jailed.

Meanwhile, Obregón's candidacy for president ignited a rebellion led by his partisans in his home state of Sonora. Carranza further provoked them, and the state government by declaring federal jurisdiction over the vital Sonora River. He also rejected Sonoran Governor Álvaro de la Huerta's peace agreement with the state's Yaqui Indians.[34] In March 1920, Carranza sent federal troops into Sonora, prompting opposition forces, including business leaders and military officers backing a third candidate, Pablo González, to unite behind Obregón, with De La Huerta heading the newly-minted anti-Carranza Constitutionalist Liberation Army.[35]

Carranza, always a reluctant revolutionary and more civic politician than military leader, was neither able to manage the pressures for radical change to which the revolution had given birth, nor rein in the thieving generals who were waging—and now losing—the war. Beals watched as, one by one, his officer students mysteriously disappeared from the classroom. By April

1920, when Obregón's troops were closing in on the capital, only three remained, all the others having fled or defected to Obregón's ranks.

Beals's ability to insinuate himself into situations affording a close-up view of Mexico's revolutionary leadership gave him an understanding of the real forces at work in the political upheaval that was unrivaled among the few American journalists there at the time. He was able to draw on direct observation of the crude and crafty maneuvers driven by greed and power-lust, concocted by bosses and generals, and their respective hangers-on. Through the 1920s, Beals would describe, in dispatches to the *Nation*, the *New Republic*, and *Current History*, and in his first three books on Mexico, how these forces interacted with the broader social convulsion and uprising of Mexico's poor masses to send the revolutionary train lurching through a long night of chaos and bloodshed. By decade's end, a modicum of stability was achieved, clouded, however, by an increasingly repressive state and party apparatus. Although Beals was not yet established as a journalist in 1920, his observations of Carranza and his coterie gave him the context and background that endowed *Mexico: An Interpretation,* published three years later, with the bracing ring of truth that prompted Ernest Gruening, then editor of the *Nation*, to call it, "without question, the best volume on Mexico written by any American."[36]

As Obregón's forces neared the capital, Beals found "everything in wildest confusion" in the Secretary of War's offices. In *Brimstone and Chili*, he left an account of the panicky, doomed escape:

> The government was attempting to pack up its effects and skip out to Vera Cruz, still held by General Candido Aguilar, the loyal son-in-law of the President. Men were tearing in and out of the offices with telegrams, orders, news. Bearded, travel-stained officers, in from the front, strode nervously to and fro.
>
> The War offices were being stripped; soldiers and officers were bawling about like so many calves; everything was being hauled out: old bugles and broken drums, hoary with dust; pins, furniture, type-writers, files. This saturnalia of mad last-minute packing was going on in every public building. The government had completely lost its head.
>
> Down in the train-yards fourteen trains were waiting to transport the departing Government and its effects. There, too, everything was in the wildest disorder. Great ragged heaps of records, files, furniture, stood along the tracks waiting to be loaded—even the treasury of the nation: great open coffers full of gold coins had been flung down haphazardly, spilling their valuable contents over the runway under the very heels of the frantic train-hands and pacing officials.[37]

Finally on May 7, 1920, Carranza left Mexico City bound for Veracruz with a convoy of railroad cars, carrying his loyal staff and soldiers, weapons, and the paraphernalia of office, including cars stuffed with gold bars from the National Treasury. His object was a tactical retreat to Veracruz, where he hoped to repeat the ultimately successful campaign strategy he had used against the counter-revolutionary Victoriano Huerta, launched in 1913 from the same Gulf coast colonial city. But it was not to be.

Carranza's train was attacked repeatedly until May 14 when, informed that that the railway to Veracruz was blocked, the Primer Jefe mounted a horse and rode north with a handful of his generals. On May 20, Carranza was murdered as he slept in peasant's hut where he had taken shelter.

As Obregón's army approached the capital on May 7, Beals rushed to cover the fleeing Carranza caravan, witnessing the aftermath of a horrific train crash. A rebel colonel, among the first of Obregón's men to reach the city, finding that the enemy had fled, dashed to the railway station near the Basilica of Guadalupe. Accompanied by about twelve men, the crazed colonel leapt aboard the cab of an engine and hurtled down the track in pursuit of the last Carranza train, which was full of cavalry men. After pulling the throttle all the way, the colonel and his men jumped into the ditches on either side, sending the engine smashing into the rear of the cavalry train, causing it to derail.

Beals arrived to find "mangled bodies being laid out in an irrigation ditch to be taken off by the Red Cross." Two cars were half-telescoped into two others, and a fifth was smashed to bits, while others lay on their sides, jack-knifed off the track. As a reward for his mad exploit, Beals recorded, the colonel was later made a general.[38]

Beals then hurried back to Mexico City's historic center to watch as one of Obregón's generals, Jacinto Treviño, declared from the balcony of the National Palace that his troops had seized control of the city on behalf of Obregón and the "revindicating revolution." Obregón, meanwhile, had holed up in a hotel in the suburb of Tacubaya. He wanted to enter the city at the head of a triumphant procession that would send a powerful message: the Revolution has won and I am in charge. He sent word to his troops, some fifty thousand in all, to gather in Tacubaya the following Sunday. All week long, they arrived on horseback and by the trainload. It was a sweltering day when Obregón made his entrance, ruddy and jovial in a blue shirt and red suspenders, mounted on a cayuse, riding into the city, the conquering hero. The four-mile parade that followed him included fierce Yaqui Indian battalions, Zapatista agrarians in gray felt sombreros riding behind black Jolly Roger flags, and goose-stepping cadets in red and black uniforms. The Paseo de la Reform was jammed from end to end, the crowds shouting, "Viva Obregón! Viva la Revolución Reivindicadora!"[39]

This whirlwind of Carranza's fall and Obregón's takeover was, to Beals, a godsend. It made Mexico a big story in America, leading the magazines he had cultivated with only spotty success, to actually press him for stories. His accounts of Obregón's dramatic seizure of power became his first published articles, in the *North American Review* and the *Nation*.

Even if it made news, Carranza's demise also ended Beals's English classes for the senior military staff. This coincided with problems for him at the American School. The parents' association there, annoyed by what they perceived as excessive taxes on American oil and mining properties imposed by the Mexican government, passed a resolution denouncing Mexico's posture toward the United States. This was fully consistent with the position taken by US petroleum companies, who had found a champion in Republican US Senator Albert Fall of New Mexico. Fall chaired a Senate subcommittee which gave these oilmen a platform for their anti-Carranza views, even depicting him as a "Bolshevik."[40]

Beals immediately dissociated himself from the resolution, saying that if Mexicans were to say such things in the United States, they would be deported. The parents' association, unconvinced by his arguments, demanded and got his dismissal.[41]

Beals, having lost both of his jobs in rapid succession, and without obvious prospects, was suddenly broke again. The American School trustees, in addition to firing him, had refused to offer any severance pay, or to compensate him for unused vacation time. He and Lillian, no longer able to pay their rent, were rescued by a wealthy couple Beals had befriended, Albert Blair and Antonieta Rivas, the latter having been a regular attendee at his Shakespeare talks. They invited the Beals couple to stay at their renovated colonial mansion behind a high iron fence on Calle de los Héroes. Blair was a British expatriate who had married into one of Mexico's most prominent families; his wife, Antonieta, sensitive and willowy, was the daughter of Antonio Rivas, the architect who designed the famous Ángel de la Independencia monument on the Paseo de la Reforma, still Mexico City's signature landmark. Blair, who had been known as "Capitán Adelante" when he fought with Madero's revolutionary forces, was now in business with his father-in-law, building a residential subdivision in Chapultepec Heights.

Years later, the couple would separate and divorce, and Antonieta, deeply disturbed, would jump to her death from the tower of Notre Dame Cathedral in Paris.

Beals had reached an impasse in Mexico and decided that it was time to leave. His confidence bolstered by having successfully placed his first four articles in national US magazines, and by having almost completed the manuscript of *Mexico: An Interpretation*, he felt sure he could make it as a freelance writer. He convinced Lillian that they should travel to Spain and Italy, from which he would file stories to support them. She was skeptical, suggesting they should return instead to the United States, but had little choice after Carleton was rebuffed by the US consul when he tried to obtain a passport. The consul, hitherto unknown to Beals, but aware of his dustup with the American School trustees, offered only to send his papers to Washington, adding, "I am not inclined to help you at all. I don't like the company you keep."[42]

"The company I keep is none of your damn business," Beals retorted. "You can go to hell." He arranged instead, through a Mexican lawyer, to obtain a Mexican passport. In August 1920, he and Lillian, fourth-class steerage tickets in hand, boarded the ocean liner *Lafayette* for a twenty-one-day passage to Coruña, Spain.

## NOTES

1. Carleton Beals, *Glass Houses: Ten Years of Free-Lancing* (Philadelphia: J. B. Lippincott, 1938), 19–20.
2. Carleton Beals, *Brimstone and Chili: A Book of Personal Experiences in the Southwest and in Mexico* (New York: Knopf, 1927), 289–90.
3. Dan La Botz, "American 'Slackers' in the Mexican Revolution: International Proletarian Politics in the Midst of a National Revolution," *Americas* 62, no. 4 (2006): 574. https://www.jstor.org/stable/4491137.
4. Beals, *Glass Houses*, 50; and John A. Britton, *Carleton Beals: A Radical Journalist in Latin America* (Albuquerque: University of New Mexico Press, 1987), 19–20.
5. "LINN A. E. GALE SENT HERE TO BE TRIED," *New York Times*, June 29, 1921, 8, https://www.nytimes.com/1921/06/29/archives/linn-ae-gale-sent-here-to-be-tried-alleged-draft-deserter-expelled.html (accessed May 15, 2021).
6. Carleton Beals, *Mexico: An Interpretation* (New York: B. W. Huebsch, 1923), 211.
7. Beals, *Brimstone and Chili*, 311–12.
8. Beals, *Brimstone and Chili*, 317.
9. Beals, *Brimstone and Chili*, 317.
10. Carleton Beals Collection (CBC), Howard Gotlieb Archival Research Center, Boston University, Correspondence, box 165 (hereafter cited CBC).
11. Beals, *Mexico: An Interpretation*, 206.
12. Carleton Beals, "Poet of Mexico," *Saturday Review of Literature*, August 16, 1930, 57.
13. CBC, boxes 45 and 165.
14. *Collier's* magazine to Carleton Beals, October 19, 1919, CBC, box 165.
15. Herbert Croly of the *New Republic* to Carleton Beals, July 24, 1919, CBC, box 165.
16. Ernest Gruening of the *Nation* to Carleton Beals, May 20, 1920, CBC, box 165.
17. Beals, *Brimstone and Chili*, 327; Carleton Beals, Beals, "Under the Fifth Sun" (unpublished autobiography), CBC; see also Ralph L. Beals, "Memories of My Brother, Carleton Beals," (1982), prepared for Melvin B. Yoken, Melvin B. Yoken Collection (MBYC), John Hay Library, Brown University, Providence, Rhode Island. (hereafter cited MBYC).
18. Beals, *Glass Houses*, 43–53.
19. Dan N. Jacobs, *Borodin: Stalin's Man in China* (Cambridge, MA: Harvard University Press, 1981), 59; Beals, *Glass Houses*, 45.
20. Jacobs, *Borodin*, 67–68.
21. See Daniela Spenser, *Stumbling Its Way Through Mexico: The Early Years of the Communist International* (Tuscaloosa: University of Alabama Press, 2011).
22. Spenser, *Stumbling Its Way Through Mexico*, 59, 67.
23. Dan La Botz, "The Mexican Communist Party," *El Machete (Medium)*, December 18, 2019, https://medium.com/@danlabotz/the-mexican-communist-party-83a3f5ffbca1 (accessed May 15, 2021).
24. Beals, *Glass Houses*, 48. Eighteen years later, in 1937, when Beals's renown as an author of progressive opinions would lead American Trotskyists to name him to a panel to hear Trotsky respond to charges laid against him by Stalin, this obscure encounter with Borodin would resurface. Beals would cite Borodin in a provocative question to Trotsky, publicly

suggesting that the Bolshevik leader—by 1937 an exile and guest of the Mexican government—had earlier sought to destabilize Mexico's revolution. See chap. 10.

25. See Jacobs, *Borodin*, for a thorough, analytical account of Borodin's influence on Sun Yat-Sen and the 1920s Chinese revolutionary nationalist movement, including its 1927 "Northern Expedition" against regional warlords led by Chiang Kai-Shek. Jacobs's account reveals Borodin's outsized—if, ultimately, failed—role in mobilizing political and military support for this early phase of China's revolution. Borodin later directed the *Moscow Daily News*, the Kremlin-directed English-language newspaper. He was arrested there in 1949 and exiled to a Siberian prison for having approved publication of a pro-Mao Zedong article by *Daily News* contributor Anna-Louise Strong, this when Stalin's xenophobic paranoia over Mao's "heretical brand of Communism" was at its height.

26. Ralph L. Beals, "Prospective Diary of Trip to Mexico in 1918–1919" (unpublished manuscript, c. 1932), 1, courtesy of Alan R. Beals, now in Christopher Neal, Private collection, Westmount, Quebec (hereafter cited CNC); and Beals, *Brimstone and Chili*, 295–96.

27. "Under the Fifth Sun" (unpublished autobiography), CBC.

28. "Under the Fifth Sun" (unpublished autobiography), CBC.

29. Beals, *Brimstone and Chili*, 325.

30. Beals, *Brimstone and Chili*, 325.

31. Beals, *Mexico: An Interpretation*, 58.

32. Beals, *Brimstone and Chili*, 326.

33. Beals, *Mexico: An Interpretation*, 59 and 69–70.

34. Berta Ulloa, "La lucha armada (1911–1920)" (The Armed Struggle), in *Historia General de México*, 4th ed., ed. Daniel Cosío Villegas (México City: El Colegio de México, 1998), vol. 2, 1173.

35. Ulloa, "La lucha armada," 1173.

36. Ernest Gruening to Carleton Beals, January 22, 1924, CBC, box 165.

37. Beals, *Brimstone and Chili*, 331.

38. Beals, *Glass Houses*, 62–63.

39. Beals, *Brimstone and Chili*, 332; *Mexican Maze*, 177; *Under the Fifth Sun* (Unpublished autobiography), CBC.

40. Mark T. Gilderhus, *Diplomacy and Revolution: US-Mexican Relations under Wilson and Carranza* (Tucson: University of Arizona Press, 1977), 97–99.

41. Beals, *Glass Houses*, 72.

42. Beals, *Glass Houses*, 75.

*Chapter Three*

# Witness to Rising Benito Mussolini

Carleton Beals and his wife, Lillian, enjoyed unusual quiet and privacy during their Atlantic crossing, as all but five of the four hundred bunks in the ship's hold were empty. Reaching Coruña at daybreak, they leaned on the railing and watched as a team of Spanish immigration officers sculled in unison toward the ship. The ancient port city shimmered in its own reflection in the still water of the harbor. They disembarked and gazed at the early morning streets from behind the flowered curtains of a horse-drawn hackney carriage that took them to their hotel. Not so different from say, Veracruz, Beals thought, but then every detail bore the mark of time, of an un-American patience. The townspeople were shod in wooden clogs. Market women cried out to one another in a Spanish argot that sounded quaint, somehow more subdued, to Beals's ears, more attuned to the Mexico City sing-song.

From Coruña, the couple spent several weeks touring Spain, stopping in Santiago de Compostela, Madrid, Avila, Toledo, Sevilla, and Merida. Although strapped for funds, they took their time to wander through museums, while lodging in cheap pensiones and eating simple meals of bread, cheese, and Valdepeñas wine.

From Barcelona, they boarded a ferry for a stormy crossing to Genoa, Italy, from which they immediately headed north to Milan. Here, Beals and Lillian set themselves up in a low-end hostel run by a buxom Neapolitan named Maria Guazzarini. Broke again and suffering from a recurrence of the rheumatism that had begun to afflict him while he was imprisoned in California and living rough in Mexico, Beals was nevertheless determined to make a go of it as a writer in Italy.

In his 1938 memoir *Glass Houses*, Beals describes this period with a series of breezy vignettes in the style of "strange characters I have met," but in letters to his parents, the relentless penury of his daily life is laid bare. Beals's two years in Italy were the hardest, most miserable of his life, but also deeply formative from multiple perspectives.

In Italy, he found a nation left limping by the war, mired in a deepening crisis of joblessness, poverty, and disillusionment, its economy ruined, and its Liberal Party political leaders aged and spent. This was fertile ground for the birth and seizure of power of the world's first-ever fascist movement, led by Benito Mussolini (1883–1945).

As a witness to this pivotal event of the twentieth century, Beals came into his own as a journalist and political analyst. He watched street battles between Mussolini's *fasci di combattimento* (fighting bands) and communist youths. He followed and interviewed the Blackshirts, men and women of his own generation, as they gathered for Mussolini's contrived, rain-soaked "March on Rome," in late October 1922. At the same time, he undertook a study of Mussolini, absorbing his manner and use of language in public, and reading everything he had written, focusing on his doctrine of violence.

His observations were published in a series of dispatches documenting Mussolini's rise to power published in the *Nation*, and later expanded into his first book, *Rome or Death: The Story of Fascism*, published by the Century Company in 1923.

From the beginning, Beals saw the dangerous artifice and mendacity in the *fasci*'s empty slogans and martial songs. He watched the Italian *Duce* (leader) transform an established democracy into a dictatorship in just weeks. That it was done mostly through clever manipulation of democratic institutions themselves, combined with deft use of legal organization and propaganda, made it all the more disturbing. In this unfledged Italian fascism, Beals grasped its horrific portents, and developed a worldview dominated by a withering dread of demagogic political leaders.

As Beals and Lillian immersed themselves in Milan daily life in the fall of 1920, reading and speaking to one another only in Italian so as to more quickly gain the language, the country was restive on many fronts. Italy had lost nearly half a million men in the war, only to see its Prime Minister Vittorio Orlando (1860–1952) storm angrily out of the 1919 Paris Peace Conference and return home empty-handed.[1]

A few months later, as if to restore the nation's trampled dignity, Gabriele d'Annunzio, a flamboyant poet, playwright, and aviator twice wounded during the war, led a band of nationalist war veterans across the border into Croatian Dalmatia to seize the city of Fiume (now Rijeka, Croatia) and to hold it for just over a year. A wild and ultimately embarrassing incident for Italy, d'Annunzio's illegal occupation and attempt to establish a martial state in Fiume was an example that inspired Mussolini, whose Fascists were still perceived as marginal and vaguely comic at this point.

D'Annunzio's exploit also highlighted a widespread popular perception of the Italian government, now led by seventy-seven-year-old Liberal Party Prime Minister Giovanni Giolitti, as inept in defending the nation's interest. The "irredentist" demand for the "restoration" to Italy of Fiume—about half its population being Italian-speaking—had been among Italy's postwar demands that were brushed aside at Versailles.

The Fiume Occupation, although forcibly ended after fourteen months by Italian troops dispatched by Giolitti, was celebrated by many Italians as an unapologetic display of decisive action in a nation that was stumbling at the brink. Veterans had returned home to find their compatriots embittered by Italy's political and military leadership, whose incompetent stewardship on the battlefields of World War I had proved so costly. By 1920, emboldened by Socialist Party gains in the November 1919 parliamentary elections, urban labor unions and rural Socialist land leagues launched a wave of factory and land seizures.

A coordinated wave of nearly three hundred union-led factory takeovers in northern Italy in September 1920 shocked the country and was later used by Mussolini to stoke fears that Italy was at risk of sliding into Communist barbarism.

Beals, in Milan shortly after the seizures had started, assessed the Socialist- and union-led movement as doomed to failure from the outset. Giolitti sought compromise to resolve the labor conflict, proposing a law that would create a form of industrial democracy in factories. It failed to pass, and its debate caused a delay in which the Socialists lost momentum. Their project soon foundered as economic conditions deteriorated.

Just two months later, in January 1921, Giolitti's parliamentary base was crippled, as his Socialist Party allies, meeting for their annual congress in Livorno, split into three factions. Amadeo Bordigas and Antonio Gramsci bolted to form Italy's Communist Party as they judged—incorrectly—that the factory seizures had the earmarks of a prelude to an incipient proletarian revolution. The remaining Socialists split into so-called Maximalists, or radicals, led by Giacinto Serrati, and moderates led by Filippo Turati.

This urban strife was exceeded by that on the countryside, where the fascist movement wedged itself between landowners locked in a struggle with the Socialist land leagues, as landless peasants sought access to small plots, or jobs working on larger estates.

As Beals found during a spring 1921 walking tour through the Po Valley, around Bologna and Ferrara, it was Socialist-led land seizures that had provoked landowners to counterattack. The landowners, many of whom had invested heavily before the war to turn swamps into viable farms, now saw their assets being taken from them, just as the economy slid into decline. Many aligned themselves with the urban-based Blackshirts to counter the powerful socialist land leagues. Once the *fascisti* had broken the socialist land league leadership, they set about attracting peasants to their camp by offering them land for rent, under contract with the landowners.

As Beals observed, this was disingenuously described as "land to the one that works it," a slogan used by Socialists twenty years before, "now having an entirely different significance."[2]

Those who were not drawn to the *fascisti* in this way, were intimidated or even beaten up. By 1922, Beals reported, agrarian fascism was peasant-led. These *ras*, as they were known, were loosely aligned with Mussolini and the *fascisti* movement, but also kept both the *Duce* and the landowners on edge, as both recognized that the *ras* were not always easy to control.[3]

"It was easy to see that Italy—and the world as well—was coiling itself into a new knot of war and strife . . . but there was going to be no proletarian revolution," Beals later wrote of this period.[4]

Here, Beals came to question the received truths of his family's Debsian socialism, as he witnessed the Italian Socialists collapse before the fascist rise in Italy. "Look at the photographs of genial, bearded [Italian 1920s socialist leaders] Turati and Serrati," he wrote, "schooled in parliamentary debate, benign and fatherly, alongside one of the ferocious and relentless Mussolini, and one can understand in part why the radical movement in Italy was doomed, even though the Socialist Party at the moment held the largest bloc [of seats] in the Chamber [of Deputies]."[5]

In Milan, Beals witnessed the street fights provoked by Mussolini's Blackshirts. He watched them march on the cobblestoned streets, chanting their quick-step anthem, "Giovinezza, Giovinezza [Youth, Youth]," and falling down with fists, knives, and revolvers on Communist groups, or trashing leftist newspapers and party headquarters.

The deepening political crisis in Italy was combined, for Beals and Lillian, with a daily struggle to survive. They were in constant poverty, living from bank drafts wired by their parents, a flow that was sometimes interrupted when banks and telegraph offices were closed due to strikes and civil disobedience. The political analyses he started filing to the *Nation* in 1921 brought him some income, but far from enough to live on.

He also remained determined to try his hand at literary efforts, writing and seeking publishers for poems and short stories, which were rejected one after another. In a letter to his "dear, dear Mumsey," he reports, "our income in May [1921] was $5.50 for a poem in the *London Graphic*."[6] This precarious income was the result of Beals's vacillation between journalism and literature. Even if his timely analyses of Italy's turmoil proved to be the only writings for which he had found a market, he still devoted more than half his time to producing poems, short stories, and plays, almost none of which would ever be published.

His early journalism, though, had a depth and insight that reflected his emerging method. In Italy, Beals developed an approach that would become his signature. He undertook what seemed like leisurely walking tours of rural areas—in Italy, he fortuitously chose the Po Valley, the cradle of fascism—but which allowed him to take the pulse of popular feeling. This kind of impromptu man- or woman-in-the-field [or street] survey would always be his starting point, and it is the method behind his remarkable and enduring prescience about political events. In this case, his walk around Bologna and Ferrara informed a descriptive analysis of the rise of agrarian fascism that stands up remarkably well against historians' accounts of the forces behind Mussolini's rise.

In *Rome or Death*, Beals delivered firsthand reporting of events he had witnessed, including strikes, political rallies—of both Fascists and Socialists—and finally, the March on Rome. His account attests to the strange staging that attended this last event, which Mussolini would later seek to mythologize. Beals describes Rome, sodden through days of driving rain, suspended between confusion and curiosity. Crowds gathered in its *piazzas* (public square) while black-shirted marchers seized control of traffic, telephone lines, and post offices, and were armed with canes, table-legs, and tree roots. The government had already resigned after the king, Vittorio Emanuele III (1869–1947; r. 1900–1946), had refused its request to impose martial law to stop the *Fascisti*.

"Certainly," Beals reported, "there has been no show in Rome of blocking the Fascisti, merely a half-hearted attempt to preserve order."[7] He describes government machine-gun lorries sitting idle, and cavalry on horses hanging their heads, "waiting in the rain . . . waiting for the Fascisti . . . waiting for orders from a resigned cabinet minister . . . waiting for the decision of the king."[8]

Beals also painted a nuanced portrait of the relatively young Mussolini. It is in contrast to the caricature the *Duce* now evokes, revealing the shrewd calculation that brought him to power, but also the impulsiveness and vanity that ultimately brought him to ruin. Beals first saw him in Bologna in 1921, when Mussolini addressed about five thousand *fascisti* at the Teatro Communale.

> He does not flatter his audience but treats it aggressively, at times even abusively. . . . He has absorbed a few philosophic tags from Sorel, Proudhon, Spinoza, and the Italian idealists, which he has the knack of expressing in the form of dilute, disconnected, and sweeping generalizations—frequently with a rather poetic originality . . . his favourite posture is that of raising his left shoulder slightly and leaning forward with hand tense and close to the body. This accentuates his large semi-bald cranium and causes the whites of his eyes to gleam in an almost "darky" fashion . . . there is a veiled quality to his eyes, not a dreaming expression but the indefinable smouldering haziness that one may observe in the eyes of a person who has enjoyed some new and delicious

emotional experience and is still slightly intoxicated, as though he were always a bit drunk with life.[9]

In the same book, Beals includes an exploration of the Fascist doctrine of violence, which arose from Mussolini's idea that Italy's parliamentary leaders, by their ineffectual deadlock and empty bickering, had betrayed the nation. Salvation, he concluded, had to come from without, led by patriotic revolutionaries whose violence was made legal by its high purpose of rescuing the nation from its inept custodians. He quoted Georges Sorel's (philosophical father of anarcho-syndicalism) and Pierre-Joseph Proudhon's concepts of violence, as "the force that creates right." Fascist violence was "moral" because it sought to "destroy in order to create."[10]

What is striking about *Rome or Death* is the extent to which Beals correctly assessed the larger significance of the fascists' takeover before it was fully manifest, even in Italy. Writing just after the March on Rome had ended, on October 30, 1922, he noted that, "political democracy means as little as it did under the sway of Cromwell. It makes no difference that the herd has bent the neck willingly to the new yoke. The significant thing: a new era has begun in Italy—as it began in Rome with the dictatorship of Sulla. The events of these last few days are a part of a European tendency that began with the Great War, embraced the Russian Revolution, [and] that may not end in our generation."[11]

Political violence, and the fascist justification for it, was deeply troubling to Beals. It would influence his choice and treatment of journalistic subjects throughout his life. From the 1920s to World War II, almost every nation in the world hosted a movement that was either wholly fascist or bearing its tinge. Beals's observation in Italy of fascism's founding father at work would lead him to scrutinize what he saw as related, quasi-fascist political movements, in Mexico, Cuba, and the United States, in the light of this first experience. His observation of fascism at its wellspring, and his immediate understanding that it was a fraudulent pseudo-ideology, a utilitarian grab-bag of nationalist propaganda, and tactics of intimidation whose real purpose was to catapult demagogues into power, would henceforth inform all his political analysis.

To the extent that he has been remembered, Beals is usually identified as a "radical journalist" associated with Latin America. But this overlooks the major problem Beals sought to address in his work, that is, authoritarian rule and related aspects such as dictatorship, populism, militarism, corporatism, and imperialism. In the twentieth century, all these phenomena defined Latin America's, and indeed much of the world's political history. In all cases, fascism was present too, as an influence, an inspiration, or at least as the source of some tactics.

For most of the developed world, fascism ended with the defeat of the Axis powers in World War II. But in Latin America, a fascist echo, arguably even an indigenous variant of fascism, lingered for a generation thereafter. By having witnessed the world's first fascist movement at its beginnings, Beals was singularly qualified to grasp its offshoots in Latin America.

Like early twentieth-century Italy, Latin America presented fertile ground for fascist-type regimes: poverty and inequality, and intense social strains caused by a relatively late and rapid emergence of an industrial economy. This led to the rise of militant labor movements and a credible leftist challenge in many countries, in turn alarming traditional elites who presided over semi-feudal agricultural estates, or *latifundias*, worked by landless peasants. With the growth of democracy, however fledgling and erratic, there emerged a pronounced proclivity among the laboring classes to embrace charismatic *caudillos* skilled in the art of mass manipulation. Often, these populist leaders exhibited marked fascist characteristics.[12]

\*\*\*

By early 1923, Beals's relationship with Lillian had crumbled. Lillian had grown fed up with Beals's footloose lifestyle, his unwillingness to compromise his independence as a writer, and to give up freelancing for a secure, salaried job as a journalist. Their unending poverty, and the real hunger that attended the forever anxious anticipation of the next miserable check for a published article or poem, had depleted Lillian's enthusiasm for this life of freedom. Adventure, in such strapped circumstances, was, to her, a humiliating bore. With her family's resources and her own training as a schoolteacher, it was unnecessary too. She was wasting her time, her life. But Beals, absorbed in his projects, himself sinking into depression, no longer had the psychological strength, nor the will to ease her anxieties. She had become a burden to him.

One day in late spring, Beals found, in the mail he picked up at the American Express office, a letter from the liberal New York publisher Benjamin Huebsch. Without Beals's knowledge, Huebsch had received a copy of the manuscript of *Mexico: An Interpretation* from Beals's father Leon. He had read it, liked it, and wanted to publish it. While obviously elated at the news, Beals was also puzzled, because he had received rejections from four or five publishers to whom his mother had sent the manuscript and had told her to stop trying to flog it, as it was no longer timely. His father, unaware of this instruction, had sent a barely legible, incomplete carbon copy to Huebsch.

As more than two years had elapsed since it was written, Huebsch wanted Beals to return to Mexico to revise the book—within two months. Beals, thrown into a state of almost euphoric happiness, scrambled to prepare. He had been thrown a lifejacket, rescued from his torpor of entanglement with depression. The collapse of his marriage, his failure to publish, and his poverty, had triggered what he called a "nervous breakdown." He had lost his bearings, and "plunged into despair."[13] Huebsch's letter, coming when it did, was his big break, an affirmation that blew away the gloom that had invaded his spirit. He hastened with anticipation, leaving Rome by train, crossing France and the Atlantic to Veracruz, and finally arriving in his beloved Mexico City.

## NOTES

1. See Margaret MacMillan, *Paris 1919: Six Months That Changed the World* (New York: Random House, 2001), 279–305.
2. Carleton Beals, *Rome or Death: The Story of Fascism* (New York: Century, 1923), 134.
3. Beals, *Rome or Death*, 142.
4. Carleton Beals, *Glass Houses: Ten Years of Free-Lancing* (Philadelphia: J. B. Lippincott, 1938), 113.
5. Beals, *Glass Houses*, 113.
6. This would be about $550 in today's dollars. Carleton Beals to Elvina Beals, August 1921, CBC.
7. Beals, *Rome or Death*, 295.
8. Beals, *Rome or Death*, 293.
9. Beals, *Rome or Death*, 244–46.
10. Beals, *Rome or Death*, 208.
11. Beals, *Rome or Death*, 298.
12. See Robert O. Paxton, *The Anatomy of Fascism* (New York: Andrew A. Knopf, 2004), 78–80, for a discussion of how fascist movements in Europe, between the wars, took hold more easily in societies that were relative *latecomers* to industrialization. In such societies, Paxton argues, the crisis of the liberal state was deeper and more stressful, due to the power and radicalism of labor unions, at a moment when the Left threatened elites by seeking to enlist support for class struggle. As democracy now compelled these elites to compete for popular support, many of them saw an alliance with Fascists—who had showed their ability to mobilize mass audiences with nationalist symbols—as a way of preserving privileges threatened by the radical Left. Paxton also cites the work of Jurgen Kocka, who argued that the persistence of powerful pre-industrial elites was the most important precondition for the growth of fascism, as it created a polarized social order in which largely rural landowners, artisans, and rentiers were pitted against a new industrial managerial and working class. This latter situation certainly applied to many Latin American societies in the early twentieth century, including Mexico, Cuba, Peru, and Central America, among others. All faced social disruptions with the arrival of US capital investment and Taylorist production models, which challenged rural latifundistas who had hitherto maintained a paternalistic dominance, both economic and political, through their ownership of land in agrarian societies. See also Thomas F. O'Brien, *The Revolutionary Mission: American Enterprise in Latin America, 1900–1945* (Cambridge: Cambridge University Press, 1996).
13. Beals, *Glass Houses*, 172.

## Chapter Four

# Return to Mexico

After spending his first night in Mexico City, April 3, 1923, at the run-down Grand Hotel, Carleton Beals, nearly broke, strode into the office of his well-connected friend Robert Haberman, director of the languages department for the city's public schools. The son of Romanian Jewish immigrants to California, Haberman was a socialist lawyer who had come to Mexico in 1917 to work in the state of Yucatán, where a utopian socialist experiment was under way. There, he had administered the cooperative stores of the state's "Resistance League" led by the idealistic Mayan leader and later martyred governor, Felipe Carrillo Puerto (1874–1924).

In 1919, when Carrillo Puerto and other governing Yucatán Socialist Party leaders broke with the *Primer Jefe* Carranza to side with his rival Álvaro Obregón (1880–1928), Haberman, probably because of anxiety about keeping his Mexican visa, had found it prudent to leave for Mexico City.

Haberman, dark of complexion, lean and muscular, had a mischievous sense of humor that beguiled Beals when they first met in 1920. Not least, Beals was impressed that Haberman's easy charm also had the happy result that he always found himself in the company of an attractive young woman, and often several at a time.

Haberman was grateful to Beals for having left the English Institute, which Beals and George Poltiol had founded in 1919, under Haberman's direction when both left Mexico in 1920. Now it was Haberman's turn to respond. He welcomed his long-lost friend and quickly found work for him. Beals was to teach English at the Miguel Lerdo de Tejada High School in the poor, north-end neighborhood of Colonia Vallejo, and at a secretarial college for girls.

Haberman also introduced Beals to Soledad "Cholita" Gonzalez, personal secretary—and lifelong mistress—to Plutarco Elías Calles (1877–1945), the

**Figure 4.1.** Carleton Beals (front row, center, with mustache) is pictured here in 1924 with fellow teachers at the Miguel Lerdo de Tejada High School in Mexico City's northern industrial neighborhood of Vallejo, where he taught English. *Photo courtesy of the Carleton Beals Collection, Howard Gotlieb Archival Research Center at Boston University, and Ralph Carleton Beals.*

ex-Governor of Sonora who was now Secretary of Government (roughly equivalent to Secretary of the Interior) in President Obregón's cabinet.[1] Cholita wanted to learn English too, so it was not long before Beals was rising before dawn three mornings a week, to make it to her office at 6 a.m. to deliver a two-hour private lesson. These quite relaxed and friendly sessions were conducted over breakfast, served in a salon of the Gobernación building on Bucareli Street, a baronial building with rooftop parapets and a grand balcony.

Cholita was tough and savvy, and Calles relied on her to warn him of enemies and conspiracies, so that he could undo them before they posed a threat. A plump, attractive *mestiza* who liked to dress like a New York flapper, she was already on her way to becoming a wealthy entrepreneur and investor.[2] She was also a vital conduit for Beals, providing him with privileged access to Calles, who would soon become one of the century's most important, though not much beloved, Mexican presidents.

Beals found Mexico dramatically changed after his three-year absence. Obregón had been President almost all of that time. A wealthy garbanzo bean farmer from the state of Sonora, General Obregón had a wisecracking shrewdness that won him the loyalty of the army's high command, combined with a steely readiness to return to battle at a moment's notice. His right arm had been blown off in 1915 by an exploding shell on the battle lines against Pancho Villa; he used the incident as a prop, telling one visiting journalist that he got elected because, with only one arm, "the people know I can only dip one hand into the Treasury."[3] But beneath this affability was a sang-froid that sent many of his enemies to the firing squad. These qualities had stemmed, for now, the murderous rivalries that had plagued the country over the previous decade.

It was no surprise, then, that Beals found Mexico City, "was tamer, but more of a city; order, law, stability were more apparent . . . it had grown prodigiously, [and] the better residential districts had more than doubled in size."[4] This new stability had allowed the revolution's cultural dimension to flourish, and attracted a new kind of *émigré* community to the capital. It was made up of political activists, artists, and dilettantes, mostly American, but also European and Russian. They were quite a change from the Texas oil and mining company types, along with other fortune-seekers, who had dominated the expatriate scene just a few years earlier.

This was in equal measure the result of revolution in Mexico, and the flight of young American freethinkers after World War I. Many had grown disillusioned with a state apparatus in the United States, which they saw as having been captured by the country's most conservative, conventional, and regressive elements: bankers, big business, and Christian fundamentalists. Reform-minded intellectuals had looked to the government to deliver women's emancipation, end child labor, and break up monopolistic capitalism during the Progressive Era and the early years of the Woodrow Wilson presidency. To their chagrin, it had failed to deliver on these promises, had entered the war in Europe over the objections of many of them, and had been party to an unjust division of the spoils at the Paris Peace Conference of 1919. At home, meanwhile, federal agents rounded up dissidents in "Palmer Raids," so named for US Attorney General A. Mitchell Palmer who directed a fierce national campaign against anarchists and other radicals, the first so-called Red Scare. And, of course, the country was so in thrall to puritanical tendencies that even drinking alcohol was outlawed.

This was too much for a young, educated generation that had burst upon the scene, radicalized by its exposure to war, and embracing freedoms offered by the automobile, the vote for women, and a new frankness about sex. They found these fledgling freedoms were too often stymied by narrow attitudes and rigid laws. America's *culture war* began to emerge, as young people derided the cant and hypocrisy of old-time religion and fusty attitudes.

But while many younger urbanites sought to be moderns, their more numerous compatriots still plumped for status-quo politicians, such as Warren Harding and Calvin Coolidge, who refused to come out fighting against Ku Klux Klan marches in downtown Washington, or state laws banning the teaching of Charles Darwin's Theory of Evolution in public schools.

Although he had been out of the United States since 1918, Beals was at home with this community of disillusioned American intellectuals of the 1920s. Indeed, he was ahead of the curve, having chosen exile years earlier, for just these kinds of reasons. Among his influences were H. L. Mencken, editor of the *American Mercury*, who denounced America as a vast collection of peasants, boobs, and hillbillies, forever chained to an "imbecilic patriotism" and an "absurd" Christian morality.[5] Another was Sinclair Lewis, whose 1920 best-seller *Main Street*, with its withering satire of arid, midwestern small-town life in fictional Gopher Prairie, deeply impressed Beals, born in his own Gopher Prairie, namely Medicine Lodge, Kansas.[6]

For some among this *lost generation*, people who simply did not like the society in which they lived, Mexico offered a freer cultural air that could be breathed in the company of like-minded expatriates. With its revolutionary effervescence, its social ferment, its profusion of contending "isms," and its native art renaissance, Mexico City was a kind of Paris closer to home, attracting, by 1923, artists and activists of the avant-garde for whom life in the United States had become a straitjacket.

Beals's new neighbors in Mexico City were drawn from this movement of "political pilgrims."[7] Haberman suggested he seek lodging in a building on Bucareli Street, just a few blocks from the Gobernación building, toward the Paseo de la Reforma, facing the offices of the daily newspaper *Excelsior*. It had been converted from an old girls' convent, with the small apartments abutting a shared, sunlit courtyard. His fellow residents there included Bertram "Bert" Wolfe and his petite, chatty wife, Ella Goldberg Wolfe, New York radicals whose Communist Party activities had made them targets during the Red Scare, forcing them to go underground. During a visit to New York City, Haberman had recruited them, like Beals, to be English teachers assigned to the Tejada high school.[8] The Wolfes also studied literature at the National University and dedicated themselves to activist work in the Mexican Communist Party, which was dominated by expatriates. Bert became a member of the Party's central committee and led seminars in "proletarian tactics" for Mexican Communist labor union activists, while Ella organized the Mexico City branch of International Red Aid. She also helped launch a newspaper, *El Libertador*, "the organ of the Pan-American Anti-Imperialist League," a Communist organization.[9] Fluent in Russian as well as Spanish, Ella also worked, undercover, as a decoding clerk at the Soviet embassy.[10]

The couple's social circle included Mexican artists, communist activists, labor leaders, writers, and Soviet diplomats, to whom they also taught English.

Their years in Mexico, as for many in their circle, became a defining experience. Bert would later write what is widely considered the definitive biography of Diego Rivera, and Ella became a confidante of Frida Kahlo. By the 1950s, however, both had become fierce anti-Communist Republicans.

Another couple living in the same building was Frances Toor, later to be editor of the cultural magazine, *Mexican Folkways*, and her husband, J. L. Weinberger, a dentist who headed up Mexico City's B'nai B'rith office in his spare time.[11] Frances, or "Paca" as she was nicknamed, and Ella became close friends of Beals. Toor exuded energy with a firm handshake and a sweeping stride. Canny, curious, and sure of herself, she found in Mexico a cultural complexity that she would spend her life seeking to disentangle and understand. As with Beals, Mexico itself was her grand obsession, which she sought to share with American readers and visitors in meticulously catalogued books and travel guides, updated every year.

Ella Wolfe's diminutive stature, liquid black eyes, and sensuous lips gave her a sweetness that was in contrast to her hard, uncompromising militant's opinions. Born in Ukraine's Black Sea port city of Kherson, she had moved, with her coal-and-lumber merchant father, to Brooklyn at the age of ten years. There she had met Bert, lean and lanky, on a tennis court in Prospect Park, and with him, had campaigned for Morris Hillquit, the Socialist candidate who won 20 percent of the vote in New York City's 1917 mayoral race.[12] Now in Mexico, she and her husband had tied their destinies to that of the Communist Party.

Paca Toor and Ella Wolfe shared a jaunty energy, poured out in a whirl of projects and causes, and both found in Beals a kind of indulgent, surrogate brother, for whose attention and approval they almost competed. Wolfe pressed him to write articles for the Soviet news agency TASS, and to file intelligence reports for pay to "his nibs [Ambassador Stanislav Pestkovsky] at the Soviet legation."[13] Toor soon sought his advice, moral support, and stories for *Mexican Folkways*, her cultural magazine funded by the Mexican Department of Education. Each of these women appealed to one of Beals's coexisting passions: Wolfe to his commitment to revolutionary social change, and Toor, to his idealization of native, pre-industrial culture and art.

From these, Beals's social contacts expanded to include Edward Weston, already a distinguished photographer but unlike the Wolfes, utterly apolitical. This "picturesque figure with his big stick, rough corduroy clothes and scarlet-lined Spanish peasant cape" arrived in Mexico in August 1923 on the cruise ship *S.S. Colima* from California.[14] He was accompanied by his sometime lover and assistant, Tina Modotti, a twenty-seven-year-old artist and actress of breathtaking beauty who had left a promising Hollywood movie career, and later became a photographer and Stalinist agent. Weston, besotted with Tina, had run off with her, leaving his wife Flora and four sons behind in California.

Beals also began what would be a lifelong friendship with Howard Phillips, a British expatriate and former newspaperman with a patrician manner and a taste for immersing himself in Mexico that matched his own. A stocky man of dark complexion, Phillips had immigrated to Chicago, where he had become a naturalized American, and worked as a newspaper reporter, while moonlighting as a vaudeville actor.[15] He then moved to south central Texas, where he had run a daily paper during the oil boom. Tiring of the cultural limitations there, he moved to Mexico City, where he bought a moribund magazine and transformed it to *Mexican Life*, an English-language monthly he would edit for more than fifty years, and in whose pages Beals's articles frequently appeared.

The iconoclastic Phillips was a model of sartorial elegance in the British style, clad in smart tweed jackets, often punctuated with a pearl gray Stetson cocked over one ear. He would twirl a Malacca cane like a boulevardier as he sauntered along Calle Madero, and his good-natured conversation was sprinkled with obscure words and references that sent his friends scurrying for an encyclopedia.[16]

Phillips and Beals liked to explore the valley of Mexico City on horseback on weekends, in English saddle, wearing white breeches and boots. Both fluent in Spanish, the two men also shared a penchant for the coquetry of certain Mexican women and took their dates together to dinner at the Café Tacuba, and dancing at the many clubs around the Zócalo. Phillips later married—and much later, divorced—Dolores Olmedo, who would become a famous Mexican real estate developer, art collector and patron of the muralists, notably Diego Rivera.

Beals's growing circle included Mexicans as well as expatriates, including Rivera himself, then painting socialist motifs on the interior panels of the Department of Public Education building, in the Juárez neighborhood of Mexico City, as well as José Clemente Orozco, and David Alfaro Siqueiros, all now legends of Mexico's artistic renaissance.

This explosion of art and ideas was stage-managed by José Vasconcelos (1882–1959), a writer and rector of the National University whom President Obregón had named Secretary of Education. In a grand vision to be copied later by revolutionary leaders in Cuba and Nicaragua, Vasconcelos dispatched corps of secular missionary teachers to the countryside where they taught peasants, 85 percent of whom were illiterate, to read and write.[17] To take art from the parlors of wealthy homes and deliver it to the common people and ennoble them, Vasconcelos urged Mexican painters living abroad to return home. He then commissioned them—Rivera, Orozco, Siqueiros, Jean Charlot, Roberto Montenegro, Francisco Goitia, and others—to pour their creative energies into transforming the drab interiors of Mexico City's public buildings. In the space of just a few years, poster-art frescoes, bold and haunting, covered the walls at the National Palace, the National Preparatory School, the Education Department, the agricultural college at Chapingo, and many others. They depicted the struggle of the Mexico's Indian farmers, sugarcane workers, henequén (fiber extracted from an agave plant) pickers, factory hands, and miners, accompanied by revolutionary vanguards from Vladimir Lenin (1870–1924) and Karl Marx (1818–1883) to Frida Kahlo (1907–1954), as they marched through history, ultimately victorious, cutting down their adversaries—here a helmeted Spanish conquistador, there a Royalist guard, here a bloated Mexican bourgeois *criolla* (Spanish-descended) family at a sumptuous feast, there a leather-faced likeness of John D. Rockefeller amid fat-cat bankers.

Vasconcelos facilitated this artistic flowering in Mexico as a way of making manifest his concept of the new "cosmic race" in Latin America, a cultural awakening which coincided and interacted with an idealistic political vision that included militant nationalism, anti-imperialism, embracing both workers and peasant farmers, and celebrating the continent's hitherto denigrated indigenous heritage. This movement deeply influenced Beals, now thirty years old and excited by the possibilities offered by this original interaction between politics and art. He was excited by the explosive emergence of artistic genius, from the murals, to street theater, to an "estridentista" (noisemaker) movement in poetry and prose, in which writers experimented with new genres that broke convention, "shouting out" both new revolutionary ideals, and ancient mestizo and Indian realities, long obscured behind the sterile European masquerade of the Porfirio Díaz years.[18]

Beals also finally met Ernest Gruening, who had helped him when he was still an untried journalist, by publishing several of Beals's early articles in the *Nation*, filed from Mexico in 1920, and from Italy in 1921 and 1922. A physician turned journalist from a well-to-do New York family, Gruening came to Mexico in December 1922 with his wife and two young sons, to spend six months preparing in-depth articles for *Collier's*, as well as for the *Nation*. His status as managing editor of the *Nation*, his wealth, and his polished presence gave him easy access to President Obregón, with whom he struck up a friendship, and to others in the country's elite circles. He rented a well-appointed home in the Roma neighborhood, where he hosted dinner parties for Mexican government officials, intellectuals, diplomats, and expatriates.

Through Paca Toor and Weinberger, Beals met eighteen-year-old Anita Brenner, to whom he soon became a literary mentor. The daughter of Latvian Jews who had emigrated to Aguascalientes by way of Chicago, Brenner had spent her early years on her parents' farm. The revolutionary turmoil sent the family packing to San Antonio, Texas, where she spent her adolescence. This was followed by a semester at the University of Texas at Austin, where she studied writing under the tutelage of J. Frank Dobie, famous for his books on Texas folklore.

Brenner was captivated by the bohemian circle of writers, artists, and activists she found upon her arrival in Mexico City. Beals, already close to Paca Toor, welcomed Brenner to this enchanted world with a courtly attentiveness, taking her to dance at the Salón México, and for leisurely breakfasts at Sanborn's House of Tiles. "You lounge through your meal, and interesting people whom you know—or ought to know, drop along, and talk—oh, books and politics and the threatre and gossip—over the cigarettes and the coffee," was how Brenner described it.[19]

She and Beals grew close, though never romantically attached. He introduced her to Gruening, who hired her to write for the *Nation*, and later to help him research his book on Mexico. Beals became her confidant, offering critiques of her writing, and dropping by to talk into the early hours of the morning. Though friends, they sometimes bickered and belittled one another. "She is something of a poseur," Beals wrote of Brenner, while she disparaged his "individualistic chip-on-the-shoulder short man's character."[20]

Brenner would later become an important promoter of Mexican artists in the United States, and an accomplished journalist. In 1943, she would publish *The Wind That Swept Mexico*, a minor classic for its lyrical portrait of the Mexican Revolution, accompanied by over a hundred rare photos of critical events and protagonists.

Beals plunged into this whirl of Mexican politics and art with a kind of rapture. While his finances remained precarious, dependent on the erratic delivery of checks for published articles, he now found himself part of a congenial and supportive social network.

Single and free to indulge his vigorous sexual appetite once again, he began a string of casual affairs with young Mexican women, mostly from the lower middle classes. These relationships were separate from his intellectual friendships with journalists, writers, artists, and political activists. After the collapse of his marriage to Lillian, Carleton's attitude toward women grew cavalier. Perhaps this was due to unresolved conflicts between his prudish upbringing by his headstrong mother Elvina, to whom he remained unusually close, and his embrace of a free love philosophy espoused by his literary hero, Shelley. To this was added a highly active libido which, until he reached Mexico, had been frustrated.

Beals enjoyed trying out a new persona as a lady's man, able to roll out solicitous courtesies like a red carpet when a pretty girl caught his eye. His disarming manner and gentle, teasing conversation captured the attention of many women, followed by intensely physical but fleeting liaisons. For many of his paramours, flattered by the attentions of an American of some prominence, social ambition probably played a role in their interest. But Beals, a disastrous marriage behind him, now sought sexual partners rather than another wife. His romantic attachments, usually with unschooled women who could share his interests only superficially, lacked the depth of his friendships.

"How strange it is to me that you have not written in so long," demanded pert twenty-year-old Guadalupe in a reproachful letter. "What is the reason? You have forgotten that I love you, with all my soul. If you no longer love me, if you already love another, why not tell me."[21]

"Lupe" would be followed by Constancia, Carlota, Rina, Maria-Isabel, Chela, and others, with whom the pattern was repeated. "I'm desperate," pleaded Carlota, "Two weeks have passed and I've only received two short notes from you." Later, Chela writes, "I love you so much. But do you still love me? Or are you fooling around?"[22]

Katherine Anne Porter, the Texas-born short story writer, felt a certain kinship with Beals's wife Lillian and feigned friendship with Beals in the early 1920s while privately contemptuous of him. She was so disgusted by his womanizing that she sought revenge of a sort by sketching a portrait of him as a pretender of modest talent in her short story, "That Tree," published in 1934. Porter's use of Beals as the model for the story's journalist-hero, a "cheerful bum lying under a tree in a good climate, writing poetry," with his failed marriage as its defining focus, can be discerned in her own comment on the story:

> That Tree has for its hero something like ten thousand wistful American boys who have been brought up in dull ways and dull surroundings, and are infected with the notion that romance and glory lie in other places, and in a different occupation. To be a poet is the most romantic thing he can imagine. So he decides to be one, in a strange, fascinating country where he can forget his provincial beginnings. . . . He is defeated, of course, because he has a grudge, he blames it on all sorts of things, but mostly he blames it on his wife, who is the same kind of person he is, socially and economically, but who has stuck by her own training and her own beliefs. She is his Nemesis, the instrument of his defeat, but the defeat was in him from the beginning. I laid the scene in Mexico because I felt at home there, and because so many persons of this sort were there then.[23]

While nursing this opinion of Beals, Porter nonetheless wrote him on at least one occasion, to ask for a job. "You don't need an assistant on TASS?" she asked him.[24]

Despite his busy social life, so much in contrast to his isolation with Lillian in Italy, he worked long hours through April, May, and June 1923. Bent over a table in his small apartment, and rushing about the city, he interviewed contacts, gathered updated statistics, and reworked the manuscript of *Mexico: An Interpretation*. Influenced by his closeness to Haberman and, through him, to Luis Morones, Beals added a detailed update on Mexico's labor union politics, and Obregón's presidential record, the uneven progress of land reform, education drive, renegotiation of the national debt, and Obregón's battle with the panoply of US oil companies, which Beals described as, "a Soviet capable of exercising a more powerful pressure upon the Governments of the United States and Mexico than many a foreign power."[25]

The book was finally published in September 1923. In its preface, Beals acknowledged Haberman's help, and that of Morones, "who has looked over the chapters on Labor and Reconstruction," along with the support of other Mexican officials. He also notes that he is, "above all . . . indebted to the patient assistance, criticism, and sympathy of my wife, Lillian," even though they were, by then, irreconcilable.

As journalism, *Mexico: An Interpretation* was arresting, laced with often sententious opinions, in sharp contrast to the more measured tones of other Mexico analysts, both contemporary and in subsequent years, such as Frank Tannenbaum and Gruening. Beals staked out his position as an uncompromising critic of US imperialism in Mexico, a stance from which he would never deviate.

In the two concluding chapters of *Mexico: An Interpretation*, "American Capital" and "The United States Government," Beals describes a campaign by US oil companies in Mexico to goad the Wilson administration into a military intervention aimed at rolling back Article 27 of the Mexico's revolutionary-era 1917 "Querétaro" Constitution.

In fact, Article 27 merely reaffirmed that Mexico owned the sub-soil minerals—including oil—on its territory, a principle dating back to Spanish colonial times, and upheld in the country's 1857 constitution. It was controversial, however, as it enabled the government to levy taxes on foreign companies pumping oil in Mexico. This stirred the virulent opposition of Edward L. Doheny, Mexico's pre-eminent American oil tycoon, who had made his first investments under the Porfiriato, when they were granted an initial ten-year tax holiday. Francisco Madero (1873–1913), Mexico's first revolutionary president (and 37th President of Mexico) from 1911 to 1913, had imposed a tax of fifty cents per ton of oil produced; this was raised to seventy-five cents by the counter-revolutionary President, General Victoriano Huerta, then lowered to sixty cents by Carranza. In 1920, the tax was amended to be a sliding 10 percent of the assessed value of the oil.[26]

The oil companies, organized under the aegis of the New York-based Association of Oil Producers in Mexico (what Beals had termed a "Soviet"), enlisted copper, silver, and gold-mining interests to form an Association for the Protection of American Rights in Mexico, tellingly located in the same Fifth Avenue office as the oil producers' organization.[27] Together, they refused to pay their taxes to the Mexican government. President Warren G.

Harding's US Secretary of State, Charles Evans Hughes, backed them up, saying the United States "could not accept the constitutional principle of government ownership of the subsoil, whether enforced by decrees or by law."[28]

Beals noted that this same principle had been upheld by the US Supreme Court in at least two cases involving the states of Pennsylvania and Indiana, in which the justices ruled that "petroleum is a public thing, subject to the absolute control of the state."[29]

The oil issue chilled relations between Wilson and Carranza. After elections in both countries in 1920, US-Mexican relations lapsed into a deep freeze. The newly-elected Harding suspended diplomatic recognition of Mexico under Obregón, also just elected. This was due, in large part, to the efforts of Republican US Senator Albert B. Fall of New Mexico, who took up the cause of the oil companies and others clamoring for intervention.

In August 1919, Fall obtained the chairmanship of a three-man subcommittee of the US Senate Foreign Relations Committee, formed to investigate Mexican affairs. The subcommittee's hearings were farcically one-sided, as the other two members, Senators Frank Brandegee of Connecticut, a Republican, and Marcus Smith of Arizona, a Democrat, were usually absent, as they leaned toward intervention themselves and trusted Fall to defend the position.[30] The most contentious witness to appear before the subcommittee was missionary and scholar Samuel Guy Inman, executive secretary of the Protestant churches' Committee on Cooperation in Latin America, who had just published a book, *Intervention in Mexico*, strongly opposing US intervention.[31]

Fall treated Inman with derision, questioning him for two days, seeking to demolish the anti-interventionist arguments in his book, by picking holes in some of its allegations that could not be substantiated with hard evidence. The day after Inman's appearance, Edward Doheny took the witness stand, enjoying a fawning deference. "The parties in power in Mexico," he told the subcommittee, "had determined to make an enemy of me on account of my success; and I want that to go on the record."[32]

Not surprisingly, the subcommittee's report recommended that the US government insist that Americans be exempt from the Mexican Constitution's Article 27. If this were not forthcoming, the report advised, and if "disorder" continued, the United States should intervene in Mexico. By the time the report was published, however, Carranza had been assassinated, and the interim Adolfo de la Huerta administration was preparing elections that would put Obregón in power. The situation had stabilized. Also, Fall's imperious manner with Inman and other anti-interventionists had backfired, as American public opinion turned against intervention. Inman's book, meanwhile, mysteriously vanished from bookstore shelves; it was rumored that Doheny had personally ordered his staff to buy every copy.[33]

Fall's appointment as Harding's US Secretary of the Interior ensured that, even if intervention was not in the cards, non-recognition of Mexico would be the government's policy—pending Mexican acceptance of the Fall subcommittee's conditions, namely that Mexico promise, in writing, not to apply the terms of its constitution to American citizens and companies. The *Nation*'s Gruening wrote that, with few exceptions, the US news media also upheld Fall's biases against Mexico. "News stories about Mexico were both inaccurate and inflammatory; the Hearst papers in particular proclaimed regularly that Mexico was overrun by "reds" and bandits," he reported.[34]

This position held until 1923, when it was ended by the Bucareli Treaty, a protocol signed by the two governments to mediate claims held by nationals, including oil companies, of each country against the other, and so pave the way for restored diplomatic relations on August 31. In his book, Beals attributed the thaw which led to the Bucareli Treaty to "expediency alone" on the part of the large petroleum companies with investments in Mexico. Smaller, independent US companies and "wild-catters" unaffiliated with the Association of Oil Producers in Mexico, as well as the British Cowdray oil interests, had entered the field, and agreed to obey all Mexican laws based on Article 27. This alarmed the US petroleum companies, led by Doheny and Harry F. Sinclair, Beals wrote. Suddenly, chastened and fearful of losing everything, they reversed course, started paying their taxes to the Mexican government, following the new rules, and abandoned their campaign to overthrow Obregón.[35]

This thaw in Mexican-American relations roughly coincided with the Teapot Dome scandal, in which Secretary of the Interior Fall's links to the oil companies were exposed by a US Senate investigation. Fall had issued leases to oilman Sinclair to exploit the Teapot Dome oil reserves on federal land in Wyoming, in exchange for a "loan" of $308,000 and a herd of cattle. The scandal also concerned a $100,000 bribe Fall received from none other than Edward Doheny. In return, Fall had authorized access to the Elk Hills federal oil reserve in New Mexico by Doheny's Pan-American Petroleum and Transport Company. When the deals were revealed, Fall was forced to resign, after which he immediately took a position with Sinclair's oil company. Much later, in 1929, Fall was convicted and sentenced to a year in New Mexico state prison.

Fall's troubles were fortuitous for Beals, as publisher Ben Huebsch read the manuscript for *Mexico: An Interpretation* against the background of the Teapot Dome scandal, the investigation of which had highlighted the Mexican antecedents of the scandal's villains. Given Doheny's effort to suppress Inman's earlier book on oil and intervention in Mexico, there was no strongly-argued critique available that explained the forces at work behind the official antipathy between the Harding administration and Mexico under Obregón. Beals's book had landed on the right desk at the right time.

*Mexico: An Interpretation* covered more than the oil issue, of course. Organized into four parts, it includes a historical account of the chaotic and contradictory events of the Mexican Revolution, along with its background of Indian heritage, Spanish colonization, and the independence struggle. A central section deals with the agrarian problem, sketching a detailed portrait of life among the country's poor, while the final part is the most damning; it covers the "foreign invasion," namely that by Mexico's neighbor to the north.

Beals's *Interpretation* identified problems that would plague Mexico through the century and that still defy easy solution: land redistribution, education, credit for small-scale farmers, deforestation, and the need for better transport. Drawing on his earlier penniless trek across the countryside, he colored his analysis with firsthand descriptions of poverty. The poor Mexican's home was "one small, cold, dark, un-floored, windowless room, reeking with moisture and sewer gas." Average earnings were insufficient to cover the cost of corn, beans, beef, rice, sugar, and lard, all of which he documented meticulously.[36]

On "the most important problem" of agrarian reform, to which Beals devoted the book's second-longest chapter after that on US policy toward Mexico, he explains that Obregón's administration chose not to push land redistribution everywhere, but rather respond to popular demand. Policy makers believed it unwise to launch a radical program in the absence of a well-organized agrarian reform movement. This meant redistribution was "conservative" in most states, Beals reported, except in Morelos, Yucatán, and Vera Cruz. In Morelos, home of Emiliano Zapata, there were persuasive reasons to proceed quickly: before the Revolution, all of the state's landholdings were owned by just thirty-three individuals. After 1911, the Zapatistas had remained in a state of defiant rebellion for a decade. Anything less than thorough land distribution there, Beals wrote, "would precipitate armed revolt in one of the most strategically defensible districts of the Republic, [located] on the highway to all the southwestern areas."[37]

While Beals recognized the inherent risks of land reform, many of which he would cite, years later, as having contributed to its eventual failure, he also underlined its political urgency: "Its immediate importance was to make a contented Indian through putting him on the land regardless of his capacity for conducting his farming operations according to scientific methods."[38]

Beals's exposure to farming while growing up in California equipped him to ask the right questions in formulating an assessment of the emerging Mexican land policy's prospects. The measure of its success would depend not so much on momentarily contented Indians, he observed, but on increased productivity, bolstered by state-sponsored investments in agricultural training, irrigation, roads and railways, schemes to provide credit to smallholders, and reforestation to increase rainfall and reduce surface wastage. In an insight that resonated even in 2003 when Mexican small-holding corn farmers rose in protest over the removal under the North American Free Trade Agreement of protective tariffs against US corn imports, Beals predicted that, "the modern world will not tolerate inefficient cultivation of corn."[39]

Seven years later, Beals would describe Mexico's agrarian reform as a "colossal failure." Speaking in July 1930 at an annual seminar of Mexico analysts, he lamented that seven million peasants had been thrust off the haciendas without having been provided the proper means of earning a decent livelihood.

> The communal system of landholding which has been resuscitated in Mexico is a failure . . . because it represents a primitive village system based upon the production of maize and beans for local self-support and therefore runs counter to the national needs and to modern industrial tendencies.
> The true agricultural wealth of Mexico, [he added] resides in tropical products such as sugar cane, tobacco, coffee, banana, rubber, henequén and hardwoods. But these can be produced efficiently only on large plantations with capital and technical equipment and knowledge. The henequén industry is in ruins. The peasants are burning off vast areas of precious hardwoods to plant maize and beans. The Mexican Revolution has never frankly faced those problems.[40]

Most striking about *Mexico: An Interpretation* is its crusading tone, as it denounces US policy toward Mexico throughout the revolutionary period, and stoutly defends Obregón's regime. This engaged advocacy would become a Beals trademark, to be cited by some critics as undermining the credibility of his analysis. The same applied to the bare-knuckled descriptions he offered in this early book, of the Mexican aristocracy, the middle-class, the Church, the military class, and the foreigner in Mexico; they are so bombastically grotesque—and for that, entertaining—as to stretch credulity. On the Mexican aristocracy, for example, Beals writes: "The son of the Mexican aristocrat is brought up a snob and a tyrant . . . [while the daughter] is prepared for connubial and concubinal slavery of a jewel-and-silk order by being taught to dance, play the piano, speak French, read sensuous poetry and French pornographic novels, embroider, talk sex, flirt, and win a husband."[41] He goes on to detail examples of widespread drunkenness, morphine use, incest, philandering, and syphilis among the upper classes, while he ridicules the middle class for trying to imitate the behavior of their so-called betters. Is this an exaggeration, or an accurate depiction of the kind of excess and abuse that sparked a revolution? It is hard to say, but it is the kind of tirade to which Beals would return, again and again.

*Mexico: An Interpretation*, as an apologia written when the bloom was still on the rose of the Mexican Revolution, endeared Beals not only to

Obregón but also to his successor, Calles. A Calles presidential campaign pamphlet in 1924 quoted and praised Beals's book as "the only authentic study in English of present-day Mexico."[42]

But if Mexico's political leaders liked it, US business people, especially oilmen and State Department diplomats, dismissed it as an ideological rant. Soon after Coolidge was inaugurated as US President in March 1924, he named career diplomat James R. Sheffield as Ambassador to Mexico. Sheffield was a hardliner who considered Calles and Morones "Bolsheviks." He regarded Beals, whose book was one of just three non-fiction works on Mexico published in the United States in 1923, as belonging to a group of Americans living in Mexico City who were "communistic in ideals and anti-American in practice . . . who were able to get their views published in many magazines and newspapers in the United States and to some extent influence public opinion."[43] Sheffield ordered his staff to open a file on Beals.

The book enjoyed a warmer reception among literary critics. "It is the best current book on Mexico," wrote Tannenbaum in the *Survey Graphic*, while also praising Beals for a "genuine sympathy with the people of Mexico, a sense of color, broad historical perspective and economic insight."[44] Tannenbaum, then a young intellectual also studying Mexico and a friend of Beals, would later join the faculty at Columbia University and publish two books on Mexico. Gruening, perhaps predictably, also offered a friendly review in the *Nation*. While gently taking issue with Beals' "slightly overcolored" portraits of "the worst and to some extent departed elements" of the American expatriate community in Mexico, he judged it, "on the whole . . . an extraordinary achievement in artistic photography, shrewd analysis, and masterly condensation. It has lifted the steadily rising level of contemporary literature about Mexico several notches."[45]

In November 1923, the relative stability established by Obregón's regime was suddenly broken by a bloody rebellion. De la Huerta, who had been interim President before Obregón's election in 1920, and later Treasury Secretary in his cabinet, had assumed that he, not Calles, would be anointed as Obregón's successor. Obregón stalled, then declared his support for Calles. De la Huerta declared that the fix was in, and launched a military revolt, led by anti-Calles generals and backed by segments of the middle class and the business community. He also had the support of some labor unions who resented the strong-arm tactics of Luis Morones' Confederación Regional Obrera Mexicana (CROM) (Regional Confederation of Mexican Workers), and some Catholic politicians who mistrusted Calles' anticlericalism.[46] In states dominated by rich landowners, such as Yucatán, the De la Huerta uprising sparked renewed civil war. Felipe Carrillo Puerto (1874–1924), the storied Mayan Governor of Yucatán who wanted to redistribute the henequén planters' land (Beals called him "the Mexican Gandhi") was stood against a wall and shot, along with members of his family.[47]

Carrillo Puerto's final year had included a storybook romance with Alma Reed, an arts writer and suffragette from San Francisco sent to Yucatán by Lester Markel, editor of the *New York Times Magazine*, to report on the Carnegie Institution's excavations at the Mayan site of Chichén Itzá. Reed, lithe, blond, and blue-eyed, interviewed Carrillo Puerto as part of her assignment there in early 1923. The Yucatán governor, a feminist who had appointed women to key posts in his state government and established the first birth control clinics in the Americas, was enchanted by Reed on their first meeting. Her modest beauty, aesthetic sensibility, and commitment to social reform so stirred the fifty-one-year-old Mayan politician that he abandoned his wife. Carrillo Puerto courted Reed, sending orchids, introducing her to his mother and, before she left for California, proposed to her. Their affair continued during another visit in the fall of 1923, and they were to be married in January 1924.

Reed was at her parents' home in San Francisco, preparing to return to the Yucatán capital of Mérida for the nuptials when she received the tragic news on January 3 that Carrillo Puerto had been murdered. In Yucatán, that day is now a holiday bearing his name, and his serenade to Alma Reed, "La Peregrina," (The Pilgrim), summons the memory of one of the state's enduring romantic legends.[48] For Beals and many in his circle, who knew both Carrillo Puerto and Reed, the day was a tragic watershed. It was a reminder that the threat of violence lay just beneath the surface of the country's revolutionary optimism. It was not enough for Mexico's leaders to be strong and popular; they needed to be ruthless to survive, and to ensure that the revolution survived.

The De la Huerta revolt was crushed within a few months, but only after seven thousand people had been killed. Obregón's victory was due to his having won US support (a stunning reversal after years of antipathy), and the prevailing opinion among the high command of Mexico's army that favored a military man, Calles, over the civilian De la Huerta. Calles stood for election in July 1924 and won with a huge majority.

## NOTES

1. Álvaro Obregón, a general during the Mexican Revolution, was the 46th President of Mexico, in office from December 1, 1920–November 30, 1924. He would be succeeded by Plutarco Elías Calles, the 47th President of Mexico, in office from December 1, 1924–November 30, 1928.
2. Carleton Beals, *Glass Houses: Ten Years of Free-Lancing* (Philadelphia: J. B. Lippincott, 1938), 177.
3. Ernest Gruening, *Many Battles: The Autobiography of Ernest Gruening* (New York: Liveright, 1973), 109.
4. Beals, *Glass Houses*, 177.

5. See H. L. Mencken, *Prejudices: First Series* (New York: Alfred A. Knopf, 1919); *Prejudices: Second Series* (London: Jonathan Cape, 1921); and *Prejudices: Third Series* (New York: Alfred A. Knopf, 1922).

6. Sinclair Lewis, *Main Street* (New York: Harcourt, Brace and Howe, 1920). Sinclair Lewis was awarded the Nobel Prize for Literature in 1930.

7. Helen Delpar traces this term to sociologist Paul Hollander, who used it to characterize intellectuals who visited the Soviet Union and other revolutionary societies in the twentieth century.

8. Helen Delpar, *The Enormous Vogue of Things Mexican: Cultural Relations between the United States and Mexico, 1920–1935* (Tuscaloosa: University of Alabama Press, 1992), 32.

9. Ella Wolfe to Carleton Beals, March 25, 1925, Carleton Beals Collection (CBC), Howard Gotlieb Archival Research Center, Boston University, Correspondence, box 165 (hereafter cited CBC).

10. Margaret Hooks, *Tina Modotti: Radical Photographer* (New York: Da Capo Press, 1993), 111.

11. Susannah Joel Glusker, *Anita Brenner: A Mind of Her Own* (Austin: University of Texas Press, 1998), 33.

12. Sam Tanenhaus (The Lives They Lived) "Ella Goldberg Wolfe, b. 1896: A Tale of Three Centuries," *New York Times Magazine*, January 7, 2001, 28, https://www.nytimes.com/2001/01/07/magazine/lives-they-lived-01-07-01-ella-goldberg-wolfe-b-1896-tale-three-centuries.html

13. Ella Wolfe to Carleton Beals, July 10, 1925, CBC, box 166.

14. Beals, *Glass Houses*, 242–43.

15. Carleton Beals, "Under the Fifth Sun" (unpublished autobiography, c. 1972–1978), CBC.

16. Pepe Romero, "Howard Phillips" (obituary), *News* (Mexico City), June 20, 1972.

17. Carleton Beals, *Mexican Maze* (Philadelphia: J. B. Lippincott, 1931), 199–200.

18. CBC, box 47, folder 7, 49; and Beals, *Mexican Maze*, 246.

19. Glusker, *Anita Brenner*, 33.

20. Beals, "Under the Fifth Sun" (unpublished autobiography), CBC; and Glusker, *Anita Brenner*, 156.

21. Lupe to Carleton Beals, December 16, 1924, CBC, box 165.

22. Carlota to Carleton Beals, June 9 and August 4, 1926, CBC, box 166; Chela to Carleton Beals, December 1, 2, and 3, 1926, CBC, box 166.

23. Katherine Anne Porter's short story, "That Tree," quoted in Thomas F. Walsh, *Katherine Anne Porter and Mexico: The Illusion of Eden* (Austin: University of Texas Press, 1992), 169.

24. Katherine Anne Porter to Carleton Beals, January 16, 1926, CBC.

25. Carleton Beals, *Mexico: An Interpretation* (New York: B. W. Huebsch, 1923), 244.

26. Beals, *Mexico: An Interpretation*, 239–40.

27. Beals, *Mexico: An Interpretation*, 244.

28. Beals, *Mexican Maze*, 345.

29. Beals, *Mexico: An Interpretation*, 238.

30. Kenneth F. Woods, "Samuel Guy Inman and Intervention in Mexico," *Southern California Quarterly* 46, no. 4 (1964): 357, https://doi.org/10.2307/41171358.

31. Samuel Guy Inman, *Intervention in Mexico* (New York: Association Press, 1919).

32. US Congress, Senate, Subcommittee of the Committee on Foreign Relations, Hearings, Investigation of Mexican Affairs, 66th Congress, 1st Session (1919), I, 272. See also Mark T. Gilderhus, *Diplomacy and Revolution: US-Mexican Relations under Wilson and Carranza* (Tucson: University of Arizona Press, 1977), 96–99.

33. Woods, "Samuel Guy Inman and Intervention in Mexico," *Southern California Quarterly*, 46, no. 4 (1964): 363.

34. Gruening, *Many Battles*, 108.

35. Beals, *Mexico: An Interpretation*, 246.

36. Beals, *Mexico: An Interpretation*, 128.

37. Beals, *Mexico: An Interpretation*, 102.

38. Beals, *Mexico: An Interpretation*, 109.
39. Beals, *Mexico: An Interpretation*, 92.
40. Carleton Beals, "CALLS AGRARIAN MOVE IN MEXICO FAILURE; Carleton Beals Says 7,000,000 Peasants Lack Proper Means of Earning Livelihood," *New York Times*, July 25, 1930, 4, https://www.nytimes.com/1930/07/25/archives/calls-agrarian-move-in-mexico-failure-carleton-beals-says-7000000.html.
41. Beals, *Mexico: An Interpretation*, 151–53.
42. Carleton Beals to Ben Huebsch, December 7, 1923, CBC, box 165.
43. Sheffield, "Mexico" (unpublished memoir, Sheffield Papers), quoted in John A. Britton, *Carleton Beals: A Radical Journalist in Latin America* (Albuquerque: University of New Mexico Press, 1987), 57.
44. Frank Tannenbaum, Foreign and International Affairs, "The Texture of Mexican Social and Radical Life . . .," *Survey Graphic*, 52, May 15, 1924, 251. https://archive.org/details/surveycharityorg52survrich.
45. Ernest Gruening, "A Real Interpretation," Review of *Mexico: An Interpretation*, by Carleton Beals, *Nation*, 117, no. 3048, December 5, 1923, 660. https://books.google.com/books?id=1D5HpEUpprMC&pg=PA660.
46. Anita Brenner and George R. Leighton, *The Wind That Swept Mexico: The History of the Mexican Revolution of 1910–1942*, new ed. (Austin: University of Texas Press, 1971; first published in 1943), 77.
47. Brenner and Leighton, *Wind*, 77.
48. Erna Ferguson, *Mexico Revisited* (New York: Alfred A. Knopf, 1955), 115; "La Peregrina" was written by poet Luis Rosado de la Vega and composer Ricardo Palmerín, in 1923, commissioned by Felipe Carrillo Puerto, then the governor of Yucatán.

*Chapter Five*

# Revolutionary and Literary Adventures from Manhattan to Mexico

In early 1924, Beals was struggling again with the threat of nervous depression. "I cannot bring myself to write anything extensive," he wrote his mother in May. "Everything seems to go in a blind circle."[1] He was without money, two months behind on his rent, and there was a lull in demand for articles about Mexico.

Even if the previous year had delivered him a double breakthrough, with his first two published books favorably received by critics in the smart liberal magazines, Beals's mood plunged. The separation from Lillian still troubled him, and beneath the cover of his outwardly enthusiastic attentions to various women, he felt overcome by loneliness. He sent a copy of *Mexico: An Interpretation* to Irene McKinnon, an American woman with whom he had a brief relationship shortly after breaking up with Lillian, in mid-1923, and included an intimate dedication that sought to revive their affair. She replied frostily that the inscription, "was somewhat tardy and stupid, inasmuch as I selected my future novio [fiancé] some six months previous."[2]

Having been out of the United States for almost six years now, Beals was also suffering from homesickness. He felt he was losing touch and wanted to build literary contacts in New York City. He also thought, vaguely, that he would like to find and fall in love with an American woman. He decided to try using his status as the author of a book on Mexico to market himself as a speaker on the lecture circuit in the United States. He wrote to several speakers' booking agencies but elicited only a string of rejections.

Dejected, Beals booked passage on a ship to New York City, arriving at a Brooklyn dock on a foggy August morning. Within a few days, he had rented an apartment in The Munroe, a new fourteen-story building at 415 West 115th Street, between Columbia University, where he had taken his degree eight years earlier, and Morningside Park. It was a congenial location, removed from the bustle of downtown Manhattan and agreeably familiar.

New York bubbled in 1924, with floods of European immigrants filling tenements with children and the chatter of strange tongues. Radio was the latest thing, and Standard Oil Company filling stations sprouted like mushrooms to service the Ford motor cars that clogged the streets. Babe Ruth was building his legend as the greatest hitter of all time, while young people danced through electric nights to jazz in forbidden speakeasies. Girls tried to impress as *flappers* in cloche hats and silk stockings, suggestively discussing Freud with their college-boy dates. Miss America contests had taken off, alongside their sultry cousin, the Ziegfield Follies, where pink lights celebrated bare skin, velvet, and buckets of champagne. Along with vaudeville night life and Broadway shows, New York was the pulsating heart of America's celebration of brash, swaggering capitalism, driving an expanding web of chain stores across the land. Families with money learned quickly to shop at Safeway and Sears-Roebuck, stocking up on new appliances such as refrigerators and electric stoves and washing machines. While most workers struggled to keep their families afloat, some social progress was being made. Most city homes had electricity, gas, and plumbing by now, and many had telephones. Despite the trust-busting of Teddy Roosevelt, though, a huge share of America's wealth was amassed in the fortunes of a few families: Rockefeller, Morgan, Carnegie, and Mellon.

Journalistic and literary New York was effervescent too. The *New York World*, started by Joseph Pulitzer (1847–1911), had sustained its legacy as a people's champion under the stewardship of Frank I. Cobb, whom Pulitzer had handpicked for the editor's job. Cobb died of cancer in 1923, and the *World* was now struggling to compete for readers with William Randolph Hearst's two papers, the *Journal* and *American*, as well as the *Herald-Tribune*, the *New York Post*, and, of course, the venerable *New York Times*. All were hawked on the streets by newsboys shouting the headlines, while passers-by browsed at newsstands stocked with *Collier's, McClure's, Survey Graphic, Ladies Home Journal* and *Vanity Fair*. It was the era, too, of the glib wits who met for lunch at the Round Table of the Algonquin Hotel on West 44th Street: Dorothy Parker, Robert Benchley, and Robert Sherwood of *Vanity Fair*, Harold Ross, the founding editor of the *New Yorker*, and Heywood Broun, the columnist and founder of the Newspaper Guild.

While many writers in New York remained focused on the manners and repartee of smart-set urban moderns, another group, more somber, perhaps, but also clever, unapologetic, and crackling with ideas, articulated the aspirations of a subterranean movement for social reform. They included Broun, as well as liberals Herbert Croly, editor of the *New Republic*, and Oswald Garrison Villard, editor of the *Nation*. Further to the Left were writer-activists such as Upton Sinclair, Norman Thomas, Waldo Frank, John Dos Passos,

Mike Gold, and Theodore Dreiser, whose work appeared in a succession of socialist and communist journals, including the *New York Call*, the *Masses*, the *Liberator*, and, from 1926, *New Masses*. More enduring literary marks were made by Sinclair Lewis, who had won the Nobel Prize for Literature in 1930 for his novels of social satire,[3] and Eugene O'Neill, whose bitter and mordant vision of American family life was the toast of serious theater. Uptown, the Harlem Renaissance was underway, with bold, fresh black American voices such as poet Langston Hughes, and baritone-activist Paul Robeson.

But in his torpor of depression and culture shock, Beals seemed unable, at first, to embrace this abundance of literary fertility. He felt stifled, out of place, and disconnected from his surroundings. He had been away from New York for too long, and now he found that he no longer wanted to be there. The ever-solicitous and suave Ernest Gruening, working as publicity director for Wisconsin Senator Robert La Follette's Presidential bid under the Progressive Party banner in 1924, asked Beals to join the campaign staff. He declined, his mind still immersed in Mexico. He did succeed in getting several articles published; tellingly, almost all of them were on Mexican subjects. There was a profile of Mexican President-elect Plutarco Elías Calles for the *Survey*, a piece for *Current History* on the Mexican situation, an article for the *Yale Review* on Tlaxcala, an irreverent portrait of Mexicans for H. L. Mencken's *Laughing Horse* magazine, and more serious analyses for the *American Mercury*, and the *World Tomorrow*, a progressive pacifist journal published by the Quakers' Fellowship of Reconciliation.[4]

Throughout this period, Beals maintained a regular correspondence with Ella Wolfe and Paca Toor, both still in Mexico. He poured out his disgust with life in New York, with what he saw as the petty rivalries among writers and intellectuals. The road to quick literary success in the city, he concluded, was to "pick out your clique, stick to it, [and] do a lot of back-scratching of your fellow-members." Much like today's media pundits, Beals found New York's *literati* could be classified by the fad or dogma to which they and their respective circles subscribed. Many years later, he reflected on the phenomenon:

> Mr. X conforms to the party line; you will know therefore whether he writes on Proust, the TVA, Charlie Chaplin or hog-calling, what his interpretation will add up to. Mr. Y has become a Trotskyite, so that you know he will be more radical than the radicals, but against the Soviet Union and with a degree of respectability. Mr. Z is a member of this particular Liberal group, and therefore you know that whether he writes on the Ku Klux Klan, the Spanish revolution, or hay fever, just what he is going to say on peace, civil liberties, and the Mooney case. Mr. A belongs to the smart aleck set; you know that he will be witty, cynical and shallow. Mr. B belongs to the sacred family complex; you know, before he starts to write, that he will parade his piety, mention

his children, damn labor and speak awesomely of all powerful persons. Most intellectuals are merely walking placards.[5]

Despite his dismissive tone, Beals's goal was to make a niche for himself in this literary marketplace, and he worked hard to make contacts with other writers, editors, and publishers. But he felt frustrated much of the time, and most of his pursuits in the city involved Mexican connections and issues. Ella's gossipy letters from Mexico City kept him up to date on political developments there, as President Calles consolidated his hold on the country.

In late October 1924, the newly-elected Calles came to New York City as part of a world tour prior to his inauguration, to take place in early 1925. The President-elect was accompanied by Manuel C. Téllez, Mexico's Ambassador to the United States, and a friend of Beals's. As Beals was assigned by the *Nation* to cover Calles' visit to the United States, he looked up Téllez at the Waldorf Astoria Hotel, where the Mexican delegation was staying. Téllez embraced him and congratulated him on his book.

"Carleton," he said, "you've got to help me work on the President's speech for the business people. It has to be in English, and I am at a loss."

Beals liked Téllez, admired his intellect, and was flattered to be asked. He agreed immediately, apparently feeling no discomfort that such closeness might compromise his journalistic objectivity. The two men worked late into the night on the speech, in which Calles, whom Beals found "more forceful and polished" than before, was to tell the business audience that his government's policy would not be radical, but rather friendly to American capital, which he invited to invest in Mexico.[6]

Two nights later, on October 30, Beals actually accompanied Calles on the stage at the Stuyvesant High School auditorium, where the Mexican President-elect spoke to an audience very different from the businessmen in the Waldorf Astoria dining room the day before. Here, he faced an enthusiastic crowd of labor unionists and students. Calles was joined on the stage by American Socialist Party leaders Norman Thomas and Morris Hillquit who, along with Beals, made brief remarks expressing solidarity with Mexico's Revolution.

Calles then rose, his expression stern and portentous. "I am a socialist and a man of the people," he declared, forefinger raised affectedly as he scanned the faces of the audience. "Before I will betray the proletariat, I will wrap myself in the red flag and hurl myself into the abyss."[7] Years later, Beals would write: "Since then, of course, he has betrayed his dear proletariat over and over again, and incidentally even before then had made himself a multimillionaire by his advocacy of revolutionary principles."[8]

As autumn gave way to the chilly days of December, Beals secured engagements as a lecturer for small stipends. Luncheons and cultural evenings, at which chamber music was combined with one or two lecturers, and tea, were a popular diversion for thoughtful New Yorkers. They also offered intellectuals an opportunity to exchange ideas and socialize. Beals addressed the Society for Ethical Culture about Mexico a few days before Christmas, and in January 1925, shared a stage with Gruening at the Civic Club, where he outlined "Who's who and what's what in Mexico."[9]

In these lectures, and in his journalism during this period, Beals's descriptions of Mexico were much in the same vein as in *Mexico: An Interpretation*.[10] They usually included a defense of Mexican government positions, and frank criticism of US big-footing of Mexico's revolutionary projects. He maintained his defense of outgoing President Obregón, whom he called "a social patriot" and for the incoming Calles, about whom many in the newly-elected Coolidge administration remained skeptical.

Over the decade, Beals would emerge as the pre-eminent American journalist writing about Mexico, publishing over thirty magazine articles and three books on the country, including its politics, social and economic issues, art, and literature. Given Mexico's *vogue* during this period, other American writers immersed themselves in the subject too. There was Frank Tannenbaum, a voluble labor activist with the Industrial Workers of the World who first went to Mexico in 1922, and published articles in the *Survey*, *Century*, and the *New Republic*. In these pieces, and his subsequent academic studies on Mexico, Tannenbaum's balanced tone belied his radical background. His rosy assessments of the Revolution's achievements on land reform and labor legislation, even by 1933, when Calles had turned the Revolution into a ghost of its earlier promise, led Beals to view Tannenbaum as naïve and given to single-track theses.[11] Unlike Beals, Tannenbaum thought Mexico—and Latin America—were unlikely to industrialize, as he assumed the region would be unable to generate the necessary capital or gain sustained access to US markets, whose huge growth he did not anticipate.[12] Gruening, a moderate Liberal in counterpoint to Beals's and Tannenbaum's more radical ideological stances, nonetheless more closely shared Beals' disillusionment with the Calles regime by the early 1930s.[13]

Neither Gruening nor Tannenbaum, however, combined Beals's industry, depth, and range. Neither of them, and no other US correspondent in Mexico, matched his unusual voice or outright ballsy attitude. Perhaps this was because they did not share his proclivity for traveling on horseback in the back country, or in third-class trains with the peasants, or for lodging in the homes of the rural poor, while also developing close friendships with artists and poets, as well as love affairs with young showgirls and secretaries.

During these years, Calles was the dominant figure in Mexican politics and so Beals, though quite distant in his personal relations with him, became the tough Mexican *caudillo*'s (strongman) principal interpreter to American opinion leaders. Beals's perceptions of Calles shifted over time, from enthusiastic support at first, to grudging respect and, by the early 1930s, to outright disgust. This reflected Calles' complexity and evolution, amid bitter struggles, including a religious civil war, to maintain control of the country, the army, the state, and the Revolution. It also traced the unfolding, over time, of his ruthlessness, corruption, and sensual enjoyment of the trappings of power, including an opulent mansion in Cuernavaca, not far from the aptly-nicknamed Ali Baba Street.

Calles was a despot, a hard-fisted political boss who would set up Mexico's Party machine called, in his day, the Partido Nacional Revolucionario (PNR) (National Revolutionary Party), sardonically nicknamed "Plutarco Needs to Rob" by some Mexicans. Later, it would become the Partido Revolucionario Institucional (PRI) (Institutional Revolutionary Party), and remain in power, uninterrupted, until 2000. Calles aligned himself with the equally shrewd and tenacious Luís Morones, the portly labor leader known for his affinity for fat jewel-bedecked rings and cufflinks, along with sleek black limousines. By the mid-1920s, Morones had stared down challenges, hired thugs, and rigged elections to make himself the uncontested leader of Mexico's labor movement. Morones' organization, the Confederación Regional de Obreros Mexicanos, or CROM, became an obedient tool and weapon of the so-called revolutionary state, at once docile in following its orders, but fierce in crushing its opponents. This co-opting of organized labor was underscored when Calles named Morones as Minister of Industry.

While Beals was in New York in early 1925, Communist activist Ella Wolfe wrote him in outrage from Mexico of Calles' "steady move to the right," as the Mexican leader took steps to distance himself from the Soviets, while Morones and the CROM were busting unions of Mexico City trolley, bakery, and railroad workers, to wipe out all Communist influence, all with backup support from Calles government troops.[14]

The Wolfes faced expulsion from Mexico, Ella told him, as their erstwhile mutual friend Robert Haberman, now working as Morones' liaison with Samuel Gompers' American Federation of Labor, was "rabid" to put an end to their Communist labor union activism by having their Mexican visas revoked. Bertram Wolfe was expelled in July, and journeyed to Moscow, with Ella joining him there some months later.

Beals's life would, at various turns, be deeply affected by this emerging global Communist movement, which had gained purchase on the minds of many young intellectuals in Mexico and across Latin America, as in New York City and Europe. Before she left Mexico in 1925, Ella Wolfe referred Beals to Kenneth Durant, then correspondent in New York City for Rosta, later renamed TASS, the Soviet news agency. Beals, in need of work, met Durant soon thereafter, and began a relationship with TASS that would last for several years.[15]

Durant, a doctrinaire Marxist from a wealthy Philadelphia family, received Beals in the shabby TASS office, its walls covered with agit-prop

Russian posters, furnished only with capacious yellow desks. Durant had come to this role by an unlikely route. After graduating from Harvard in 1912 and working as a reporter with the *Philadelphia Bulletin* and as a publicist in the federal War Agency, he was hired as an aide to Colonel Edward M. House, advisor to President Woodrow Wilson.[16] This role resulted in his joining the US delegation at the Versailles Peace Conference in 1919. During this period, he was drawn to the Russian Revolution, possibly influenced by his friendship with John Reed whose pro-Bolshevik book, *Ten Days that Shook the World*, was published the same year.[17] When he returned to the United States, Durant signed on as press secretary to the then-unrecognized Soviet envoy, and in 1923 opened the Rosta/TASS office. He proposed, and Beals agreed, that Beals would be the agency's Mexico correspondent, filing analytical pieces on Mexican-US relations immediately.

Prone to ill humor, Durant remained aloof as Beals developed a close friendship with his wife at the time, Ernestine Evans. Moody and restless herself, Ernestine would shift from being eager and full of ideas, to phlegmatic and standoffish. She lived with Durant in a New York apartment full of antique furniture and pine boughs stuffed into large vases. Their domestic life was stormy as Durant's saturnine temperament was punctuated by icy rudeness toward Ernestine, often displayed in public. The couple separated by the early 1930s.[18]

For many years, Evans worked off and on as Beals's literary agent, placing his articles in New York magazines, and most importantly, introducing him to Jefferson Jones, managing editor at J. B. Lippincott and Company, who would publish twelve Beals titles over the next decade. Evans also obtained for Beals a Guggenheim fellowship to write a biography of Porfirio Díaz, the Mexican dictator whose forty-year rule was brought to an end in 1911 by the Revolution. She also became one of his most loyal friends, corresponding with him until her death in 1967.[19]

By joining the TASS network, Beals established a personal connection to the Soviet Communist system. This gave him privileged insights, but also complicated perceptions about his objectivity. An early example of this came in 1925, a year in which Beals became an active public speaker at New York events held to denounce persecution of dissidents around the world. Beals's role at these rallies, usually organized by the International Committee for Political Prisoners, was to lend his credibility as a journalist to demand the release of journalists and activists in Spain under dictator Primo de Rivera, and Italy under Benito Mussolini's fascist Blackshirts. The Prisoners' Committee was headed by Roger Baldwin who, in 1917 as head of the American Civil Liberties Union (ACLU), had helped Beals obtain his discharge from military service as a conscientious objector during World War I.

But when the Committee published a report on political prisoners in Russia, Beals's TASS connection placed him in a dilemma. He immediately wrote Baldwin asking him to remove his name from the list of supporters on the Committee's stationary—a group that included the [John Thomas] "Scopes Monkey Trial" defense attorney Clarence Darrow, black activist and intellectual W. E. B. Dubois, social reformer Jane Addams, and Oswald Garrison Villard, editor of the *Nation*. The report, Beals wrote, "is a grave tactical error . . . whatever the truth of the contents, it is being used entirely by those who have no love for political freedom in Russia or anywhere else, and who will be the first to clap Roger Baldwin, Carleton Beals or Eugene Debs in jail here in the US if they had half a chance."[20] It was an argument that would become a familiar refrain in many leftist circles, especially Soviet-leaning, for decades.

In his reply, Baldwin suggested that Beals's action was prompted by Durant's and Beals's work with TASS, adding, "I cannot understand your having acted on a partisan presentation of objections to the Committee's book or attitudes, because I know you to be a believer in the principle to which this Committee is devoted, and wherever it applies."[21]

The extent and depth of Beals's Soviet and Communist Party connections are something of an enigma. He never actually joined the Communist Party, contrary to the charge leveled at him in State Department and FBI files and given currency by some US diplomats at cocktail parties. In 1929, he would report his dismay at conditions he witnessed during a brief trip to Russia. But he did write for TASS, and he enjoyed cordial relations with senior Soviet diplomats in New York and Mexico, accepting their frequent invitations to receptions and dinners, through the 1920s and 1930s.

He also filed reports on his observations, while traveling around Latin America, to the Soviet ambassador in Mexico. It appears that the incentive for this was money, rather than ideological fealty. Living as a freelancer was dodgy from a financial standpoint, so Beals was strapped for funds throughout 1925. He needed a source of income as he struggled to finish the manuscript of *Brimstone and Chili*, the account of his 1918 trip to Mexico with his brother Ralph. The Soviets were willing to pay him for his reports, and they did not impose any conditions on him.[22]

In July, he moved out of the city to stay for a month with his friends from Mexico days, artist Maurice Becker and his wife Dorothy Baldwin, at their home in Tioga, in northern Pennsylvania. Becker was busy organizing the revival of the defunct socialist magazine the *Masses*, which had been shut down in 1918 for a supposed violation of the *Espionage Act of 1917*.[23] In April 1926, the inaugural edition of *New Masses* was published; Beals's name was included on the masthead, along with Becker, editor Michael Gold, a Communist, and novelist John Dos Passos, among many other left-leaning writers and intellectuals.[24]

In Tioga, Beals savored long country walks, a daily swim in the creek near Maurice and Dorothy's home, and quiet days during which he was able to finish *Brimstone and Chili*. This absorption in the Mexican subject, along with his failure to find satisfaction or intellectual pursuits on the New York literary scene, reinforced his decision to return to what he now realized had become his muse: Mexico. Once he finished the manuscript, Beals spent a few weeks hitchhiking around New Brunswick and Prince Edward Island, Canada, then returned to New York City to pack his things.

In late September 1925, Beals boarded a train at Pennsylvania Station, bound for Laredo, Texas, and on to Mexico City. As he sat smoking cigarettes, gently rocking, and gazing at the cornfields whizzing by, a mood of nostalgia descended upon him. He felt as though he was returning home rather than going abroad. Nearing the border, he reflected on how far he had come since his last entry into Mexico, eight years before, as a vagrant dragging a useless donkey.

\*\*\*

Once back in Mexico City, Beals stayed at a *pensión* (boarding house) at 104 Bucareli Street, facing the Secretaría de Gobernación, where he had given Cholita Gonzalez early-morning English lessons in 1923, and just a few blocks from his friends Howard Phillips and Frances Toor. Phillips and Toor were living in a red-brick high-rise on Abraham Gonzalez Street, both of them having launched their magazines, respectively *Mexican Life* and *Mexican Folkways*. Beals was delighted to be reunited with them, and with Anita Brenner, to whom he had become a literary mentor and who now was at work on her first book, *Idols Behind Altars*, with the help of French muralist Jean Charlot.[25]

In early October 1925, just days after his return to Mexico City, Tina Modotti invited Beals to a spaghetti and wine dinner party that she and Edward Weston were hosting and at which the guest of honor was Tina's older sister Mercedes, visiting from San Francisco. During Beals's thirteen-month absence from Mexico, Tina's talent as a photographer had bloomed in a flurry of still-life studies of calla lilies, telegraph wires, sugar cane, and architectural interiors, as well as portraits of friends, including folksinger Concha Michel, actress Dolores del Rio, and Soviet Ambassador Stanislav Pestkovsky.

Included among her portraits was a compelling study of Beals, taken in July 1924, after Tina had sent him a slip of paper, on which she had written: "This 'coupon' entitles you to have your 'mug' immortalized by the supreme 'artiste,' undersigned Tina Modotti."[26] In the portrait, Beals is captured gazing intently into the camera, lips pursed, his expression earnest, even stern. His neck is wrapped in a black fabric that Tina had discreetly provided as a prop to conceal his weak chin, and he looks younger than his thirty-one years of age. It is the image of a man in his prime, suggesting not only youthful vigor, but also intellect and depth.

Weston had left Tina in December 1924, to spend several months in California, where he had rejoined his four sons, and finalized his divorce from Flora, the estranged wife he had left behind. Tina had remained in Mexico, refining her photographic technique and posing as a model for Diego Rivera, then at work on studies and sketches as he prepared to undertake the painting of murals in the chapel of the agricultural college at Chapingo, twenty-five miles outside Mexico City. This involvement with Rivera, as well as her friendship with another artist, Xavier Guerrero, drew Tina—fatefully—into the Communist Party that absorbed both men at this time.

Weston returned to Mexico in late August 1925, accompanied by his second eldest son Brett. The pair joined Tina in Guadalajara, where she had arranged an exhibition of photographs by both of them at the Jalisco state museum. While elated to see her again, Weston found Tina much changed from the callow acolyte and assistant she had been two years earlier. She had become a Marxist and, though still interested in photographic art, increasingly believed it had little value unless it served the Communist revolutionary cause. A telling detail: when they bought tickets at Guadalajara station for the train to Mexico City, Tina insisted on traveling second-class, on wooden benches with the peasants, chickens, goats—and smells—instead of joining Edward and Brett in the comfort and relative luxury of their Pullman coach.

Beals's reunion with the couple a few weeks later in Mexico City, marked the resumption of what was, for him, a more congenial social life than that in New York City. Tina and Edward's parties were lively events at which artists and activists mingled. A guitar would often be pulled out, and piñatas hung and pelted open to celebrate birthdays. There were costumes and cross-dressing, dancing, poetry recitals, and intense political discussions, fueled by rounds of tequila. Tina was a charismatic presence whose charm was irresistible. Although he was never romantically involved with Tina, Beals's roving eye enjoyed her striking beauty and "exquisite artistic sensitivity," while Edward was among his preferred friends.[27] On this occasion, however, Beals's attention was focused on Tina's vivacious sister Mercedes. His interest was returned with matching enthusiasm. They were inseparable from the moment they met; Mercedes jokingly nicknamed Beals *cognato*, or brother-in-law.

A few days after this first encounter, Beals procured a government car, and drove Mercedes, Tina, Weston, and his son Brett to Chapingo, where Diego Rivera was at work on frescoes that would cover the walls and ceilings of the agricultural college chapel. Tina posed in the nude while Rivera rendered her, in two panels, as an allegorical figure depicting various stages in the natural cycle of life. The result remains immortalized there in the Chapingo chapel, in a masterpiece of muralist art. It depicts a secular Mexican Eden, in which idealized naked figures are building a new world where natural evolution and fertility are fused with the utopian promise of social revolution and land reform.

As Rivera painted and Tina Modotti posed, arms raised above her head for the section to be called *Canto a la tierra* (Song to the Earth), Beals and Mercedes spent the afternoon in the shade of a tree, gazing rapturously into one another's eyes, leaving Weston and his son to explore the college buildings and grounds on their own.

Like many Americans in Mexico in the 1920s, Beals was fascinated by Rivera, drawn by his artistic genius and personal charisma. "Don Diego is a huge man with a Pilsner paunch," he wrote, "[who] involves every utterance in gargantuan fantasy; he is a legend-maker and Munchausen liar; yet at the heart of his fables, in the pitch of their meaning, lurks absolute truth."[28] Chapingo was his finest effort, in Beals's assessment. It was, he believed, "the Sistine Chapel of the Americas . . . [Rivera's] most organic synthesis; there, passion, intellect and technique have formed a holy trinity."[29]

Beals was first introduced to Rivera about two years before, by Fred Leighton, an American wire reporter, while the painter was starting work on the inside walls of the Secretariat of Education building in Mexico City's historic center. They struck up an amiable relationship, based on easy banter and a shared disdain for capitalist imperialism and social pretension. Rivera was helpful to Beals too, introducing him to key Mexican politicians and intellectuals, and in 1930, agreed to provide pen-and-ink illustrations on revolutionary themes for Beals's fifth book, *Mexican Maze*.

Mercedes extended her visit to Mexico by a month, largely to continue enjoying her infatuation with Beals. They spent several days together with Tina and Edward at the elegantly-landscaped home in Cuernavaca of art and antiques dealer Fred Davis, the place he later sold to Dwight W. Morrow, a J. P. Morgan executive whom Coolidge would name US Ambassador to Mexico in 1927. Carleton and Mercedes both remembered it fondly as the setting for their affair at its most passionate apogee.

"An enchanting spot," Beals reminisced, "with its tall mirador, wide gardens and gigantic white palm trunks, of which Weston made some beautiful moonlit studies."[30] Mercedes wrote Beals later, sharing the memory of "our faces under the palm on that unforgettable night, in a moment of great love, great abandonment, and infinite sweetness."[31] On November 21, the couple visited Brenner, in hospital recovering from injuries she had suffered in a car accident. Brenner recorded acidly in her diary that, "Carleton is perpetually 'feeling a Latin' and thereby losing his dignity."[32]

On December 1, Tina and Edward hosted a farewell party for Mercedes on the rooftop of their home at Veracruz 42, in Mexico City's convivial Condesa neighborhood, overlooking tree-lined avenues and outdoor cafés. Beals, of course, was the one for whom Mercedes' departure, made necessary by her mother's illness, caused most distress. The party was a grand affair, attended by Rivera and his then-wife Lupe, Toor, and Brenner, carried up the stairs and solicitously attended by the French artist Charlot, along with the bronzed and handsome Guanajuato Senator Manuel Hernández Galván.[33]

Beals and Mercedes would stay in touch through 1926, exchanging passionate letters, even while Beals enjoyed relationships with several other women. There was substance to their relationship and chagrin on both sides that sustaining it proved elusive.

In the end, though, their romance would be ephemeral, and soon Beals's untroubled attentions drifted to others. Lupe, with whom he had had an affair in 1923, wanted to reunite now that he was back in Mexico. Constanza, who worked with the eccentric artist Gerardo Murillo, better known as Dr. Atl, sought to rekindle another affair. Carlota professed that her heart was his, and that she was desperate to see him again. No wonder that when Brenner—with whom he had an enduring platonic friendship, not an affair—saw him in mid-April, he seemed "slightly burned out."[34]

That same week, Beals received the good news from his friend Harry Block, an editor at Alfred Knopf Publishers, that they would publish *Brimstone and Chili*, the account of his 1918 journey to Mexico with his brother Ralph.[35] That success, achieved after flogging the manuscript for more than two years, prompted Beals to think of undertaking a trip to Central America, to produce another travelogue of the same genre. In late May, he set off for a month-long visit to Guatemala and Honduras, during which he researched articles for the *Nation* and *Current History*, and for the book *Banana Gold*, which would be published in 1932.[36]

\*\*\*

While Diego Rivera and other muralists of Beals's acquaintance enjoyed the sponsorship of Mexico's revolutionary state in return for idealizing its goals in their art, rumblings of fierce opposition to the Calles administration were gathering strength among the hierarchies of the country's twin pillars of traditional power: the Roman Catholic Church and the army. The clerics' ire had its roots in Calles' odd status as an unabashed atheist leading a nation of devout Catholics. Calles almost bristled when he talked about church leaders, seeing them as thinly-disguised counter-revolutionaries, propagandizing against his regime from the sacrosanct safety of their pulpits. He was determined to stop them.

In February 1925, Calles had approved the initiative of a dissident, pro-revolution priest to set up a breakaway Orthodox Catholic Apostolic Mexican Church. The bishops were furious, while thousands of Catholics rioted in cities and towns. Together, they denounced the anticlerical provisions of the 1917 Constitution, such as limits on the number of clergy and the secularization of education.

Calles only stiffened his resolve. He ordered Catholic schools shuttered, and deported foreign-born priests. The Church reacted by calling a nationwide strike, closing the churches to worshippers, and suspending not only masses, but also baptisms, marriages, and funerals. The Cristero War (*La Cristiada*), with its battle cry of "Viva Cristo Rey!" (Long Live Christ the King!) had begun.

While initial skirmishes were easily put down by the army, the Cristeros shifted to guerrilla warfare tactics, targeting agrarian reform workers and state-appointed schoolteachers for assassination. The army reacted by killing civilians and looting church property. By mid-1927, more than twenty thousand armed Cristeros were fighting the federal army in five states.[37]

Beals's bias in favor of Mexico's revolutionary state in its war against what he perceived as a reactionary Church was pronounced at first but grew more nuanced as both sides accumulated their share of brutality. In mid-1926, he filed a report to the *Nation*, in which he laid all blame for the conflict on the Church. "It has opposed every necessary reform of the past fifteen years, and its priests have alienated the rural population by excommunicating peasants accepting ex-church lands, and by hobnobbing with large landowners."[38]

The Mexican government welcomed this kind of reporting and made use of it for propaganda purposes. Later in 1926, the Mexican embassy in Washington produced a pamphlet which included a reprint of the chapter including a vitriolic attack on the Church from Beals's first book, *Mexico: An Interpretation*. The pamphlet was part of a Mexican government campaign, supported by the socialist paper *New York Call*, to counter the offensive by the US Catholic Church to discredit the revolutionary government for allegedly persecuting Catholics. There is no evidence that Beals objected to this use of his work by Mexican authorities, even though it exposed him to charges of propagandizing for the Calles regime.[39] His generally laudatory writings about Calles during this period, combined with his almost-visceral antipathy to the Church, suggest that he was quite willing to be counted as a supporter.

"The Roman-Aztec Church has been jealous of its right to rule, its wealth, and its luxuries," Beals writes in the selected excerpt. "For this right to rule, it has returned majestic temples that tower above the plains throughout the length and breadth of the land, but it has returned very little toward the material, mental or moral elevation of the people."[40]

The US Catholic Episcopate reacted swiftly, printing over a million copies of a booklet-length pastoral letter in December 1926, in which it dismissed the charges laid against the Mexican Church, defended its record in social uplift, and warned of a "new paganism" that threatened to "eliminate the divine," resulting in slavery of the individual in Mexico.[41]

Beals further endeared himself to the Mexican government, while infuriating US officialdom, in December 1926, with provocative remarks he made at a conference in Washington on the Cause and Cure of War. He was invited to speak on the Monroe Doctrine and US policy towards Mexico at the conference, which was organized by a coalition of women's groups headed by former suffragette leader Carrie Chapman Catt. His presentation followed that by anti-imperialist campaigner Parker Moon; in it he outlined what he saw as the State Department's duplicitous role in Mexico since the very beginnings of the revolution.

At some point in his peroration, Beals referred to the role played by Henry Lane Wilson, the US Ambassador to Mexico appointed by President Taft. In 1913, Beals said, Ambassador Wilson had signaled tacit approval as Mexican army chief of staff Victoriano Huerta prepared to overthrow Mexican President Francisco Madero. Madero had won Mexico's presidency in 1911 in the country's first democratic election after the revolution that toppled dictator Porfirio Díaz.[42] He was a gentle revolutionary, inspired, oddly, by the Bhagavad Gita and of a dreamy rather than calculating nature. He seemed aloof as his unstable cabinet tried to govern, torn between a Senate still stacked with pro-Díaz legislators, and rebellions led by rivals Emiliano Zapata, Bernardo Reyes, Pascual Orozco, and Félix Díaz.

Egged on by incendiary reports from Ambassador Henry Lane Wilson and responding to the anxieties of oil tycoon Edward L. Doheny, the US State Department grew skeptical of the wobbly Madero's ability to restrain the radicals within the revolutionary tent. Lane Wilson, both architect and executor of that policy, had told Huerta that the United States would not stand in the way of his coup against Madero, which ended with Madero's murder. Because of this, Beals told the conference, Wilson had "a direct moral responsibility" for Madero's assassination, as well as that of his Vice-President, Pino Suárez.[43]

Mrs. Rufus Dawes, sister-in-law of Coolidge's Vice-President Charles G. Dawes, rose from the audience during the question period and angrily rebuked Beals for making the allegation against Lane Wilson. Her voice shaking with emotion, she accused him of injecting "arsenic" in the discussion and of attacking the character of an honorable man who was not present to defend himself. Beals brushed her off, saying Dawes' agitated state made her comments too incoherent to follow, and suggested that if he had injected arsenic into the discussion, "evidently the dose had not been strong enough."[44]

Beals's remarks were reported in the *Washington Post*, *New York Times*, and *Herald-Tribune*, stirring the outrage of the target of his barbs, Lane Wilson, now retired and living in Indianapolis. Concerned that a textual version of Beals's comments would be printed in a book of the conference proceedings to be published by the Carnegie Endowment for International Peace, Wilson sent letters of protest to Beals and to Carrie Chapman Catt. Beals, he said, was "a paid propagandist of the Mexican government" and the charge that he had participated in a conspiracy to topple and kill Madero was libelous. He demanded that it be withdrawn in the published version of the conference proceedings.[45]

Beals responded to all the parties, agreeing to Catt's polite entreaty to modify the wording of his original statement so as to avoid a libel suit that would perforce involve the Carnegie Endowment. But he dug in his heels in his direct response to Wilson. Also, in a letter responding to Wilson's in the *Herald-Tribune*, Beals repeated his charges that Wilson had, "abused his latitude, and that he had a powerful influence in shaping the Taft Mexican policy and bringing about acts which . . . tended toward the undermining of the Madero Government and toward friendship with the usurper Huerta."[46]

These responses were hardly the retraction Wilson had sought. They actually lent greater publicity and credibility to the allegations against him, contributing to the now-widespread acceptance among historians that Henry Lane Wilson's acquiescence was a key factor—probably the determining one—in Madero's overthrow and murder.

\*\*\*

In January 1927, Beals received a visit in Mexico City from Herbert Croly, the founding editor of the *New Republic*. Croly, then fifty-eight years old, was in the city to participate in the third annual Mexico Seminar organized by Hubert Herring, head of the Committee on Cultural Relations with Latin America. These seminars, held from 1925 to the mid-1930s, were organized by Herring with Beals's assistance and usually attracted about one hundred Mexican and American academics, politicians, and journalists. They reflected Herring's personal mission to promote deeper understanding between the two countries, and more sympathetic US policies toward Mexico.

Croly was an exceedingly private and inscrutable man, an introvert caught in an extravert's profession. He came to found the *New Republic* in 1914 at the invitation of its owners, Willard and Dorothy Straight, who had been influenced by Croly's *The Promise of American Life*, published in 1909. That book came to be regarded as the seminal philosophical work underpinning American Progressivism, as it purportedly had influenced the political thinking of Theodore Roosevelt and Woodrow Wilson, and the later development of modern American liberalism.

Croly's thesis in favor of a planned economy and increased public spending to foster social progress, grew from his conviction that a middle way had to be found between socialism and capitalism. He was alarmed at the huge wealth amassed by the turn-of-the-century titans of big business, banking, and oil, and by the corresponding radicalism of the labor unions. To Croly, America's widening gulf of economic inequality originated, paradoxically, with the "equal rights" upon which the Founding Fathers had insisted. A so-called level playing field of legal equality between rich and poor, he observed, would always favor the already-rich. Those who believed in the notion of an equal start but an unequal finish, he wrote, "are wholly blind to the fact that under a legal system which holds private property sacred, there may be equal rights, but there cannot possibly be any equal opportunities for exercising such rights."[47]

Croly struggled to define the terms of a balance he believed the state needed to strike between protecting individual liberties on one hand and promoting the "national interest" in genuine political or economic reform which, he recognized, would sometimes entail depriving some (privileged) individuals in order to improve the opportunities of others.

While Croly's views earned him suspicion among the well-heeled, he was also dismissed by those on the far left. The staff under Croly's direction at the *New Republic*, sniffed Max Eastman, writing in the Communist organ the *Masses* in 1915, "still live in a world in which fundamental democratic progress comes by telling, and persuading, and showing how, and propagating reasonable opinions, and better social feeling. The real world is a world in which privilege can only be uprooted by power."[48]

Beals found Croly to be a taciturn but thoughtful companion, whose views on the role of journalism in promoting social change coincided with his own. Croly had been impressed by *Mexico: An Interpretation*, especially its analysis of how the US oil industry lobby shaped a destructive US foreign policy toward Mexico. The recent notoriety Beals had gained through the Henry Lane Wilson furor also drew the journalist to Croly's attention, as did a speech Beals had given in New York City, which was reported in the *New York Times*. Addressing the League for Industrial Democracy—organized by Upton Sinclair—at the Civic Club in downtown Manhattan, Beals had urged the United States to use its great power, "generously, nobly and high-mindedly" to help Mexico establish its new constitution. Even if the country's needed social adjustment would cause difficulties for a few individuals, he said, the Mexican government "cannot do much if it leaves 99 percent of its people without property, nor can it build up a nation unless it controls the resources of the country."[49]

Croly became convinced that Beals was a journalist with an aroused individual conscience, able to make the connections between business exploitation and political corruption that the gruff editor saw as the *New Republic*'s role. He wanted Beals to be the magazine's Mexico City correspondent. But there was a problem in that Beals's long affiliation with the *Nation*, based on his friendship with its former managing editor Gruening, precluded him from writing for the *New Republic*, its direct competitor in the liberal magazine market. Croly solved it by offering to double Beals's rate at the *Nation*, which enticed him to shift his allegiance. A happy collaboration followed, between a journalist at the height of his powers, a supportive editor on the same political wave-length, and a compelling subject that entranced them both, namely Mexico's internal turmoil and its entanglement with US interests. The combination delivered some of the best journalism of Beals's career.

He uncovered the holdings of US oil companies in Mexico and outlined how US Secretary of State Frank B. Kellogg insisted on protecting the "rights" of a minority of twenty-one US-owned petroleum companies that had refused to submit to Mexican law and register their properties in order to receive drilling permits. The most important of these companies, Beals found, were owned by Edward L. Doheny, of Teapot Dome fame.

Beals's digging led him to the conviction that Secretary Kellogg, whose trembling hands gave him the moniker "Nervous Nellie," had become Doheny's tool. His research, which included secret oil company documents passed to him by an industry insider, suggested that Doheny sought US annexation of Mexico's oil-rich northern desert if necessary, that is, if Calles "overstepped" in his effort to impose government regulation and taxation on Doheny's oil holdings and production.

In this, Doheny found a staunch ally in US Ambassador to Mexico James R. Sheffield. A former corporate lawyer, Sheffield was a hardliner whose reports to Kellogg warned that Calles and his cabinet were "Bolshevists" leading Mexico down a Soviet-inspired path. In Beals's assessment, Sheffield was "a choleric soul . . . [who] lacked the slightest inkling of what the Mexican revolution really meant."[50]

Cautious to avert libel charges, Beals took pains to avoid directly mentioning Doheny's name in his *New Republic* reports, alluding to "a trail of corruption and bloodshed, falsification of records, fraud, bribery, and even murder" in the acquisition of oil titles by Mexican companies set up as fronts for Doheny's holdings.[51] But the implication was clear enough, and the danger of an explosion in Mexico, in Beals's view, was greater than at any time since the Huerta-Carranza War of 1914.

On April 20, 1927, Mexico's stability was shaken on another front as the Cristero Rebellion exploded with news of an atrocity in the state of Jalisco. Fifty-four civilians—including women and children—were among some 150 people massacred in an attack on a passenger train between Guadalajara and Mexico City. Four hundred men shouting "Long Live Christ the King!" had attacked the train, setting fire to rail cars and bayoneting passengers in their seats.

Beals traveled to the state of Jalisco to investigate. He started by interviewing the state's Governor José Guadalupe Zuno, a flamboyant artist-politician and Communist, who had lashed out at the Catholic clergy in fiery speeches, calling them "effeminate products of shameful colleges."[52] Beals gained access to him through a letter penned by Diego Rivera, introducing "my esteemed friend, Carleton Beals, the journalist and the writer . . . whom I have no doubt you will receive as a friend and intelligent revolutionary."[53]

Beals's tour of Jalisco, however, made him reassess his earlier assumptions about the Cristero Rebellion, and its impact. Testimony from peasants and townspeople revealed their mistrust of the government; the mayor of a small town told him, "We have the saying in Jalisco now, 'Whoever visits the barracks headquarters comes away fleeced—if he comes away!'"54 In reconstructing the train massacre from the accounts of seven survivors, Beals developed a more balanced picture of the forces behind the conflict. He now found that the rebellion, while fueled by the big landowners and conservative clergy, also fed "on the disorder and injustices falsely created by unprincipled army commanders."55

Mexican army officials had reacted to the train attack, Beals reported, by declaring a large swath of Jalisco a 'neutral zone' and ordering residents to concentrate in just twelve towns or be considered rebels. The government, meanwhile, censored the press and news cables, to prevent news of the repression from getting out.56

By the late summer of 1927, Beals remained a supporter of Mexico's revolutionary process, while also acknowledging, ruefully, that it had sacrificed its earlier idealism for a "dangerous retrogression" into *caudillismo* (system of political power, based on strongman rule), and one-man rule. Obregón, the one-armed Sonora general and former President, was preparing to run for re-election in 1928, when Calles' term would end. One strongman was to follow another. But Beals stopped short of condemning the revolution's current leaders, as he weighed the challenges they faced.

Calles and Obregón were also suddenly challenged by a revolt from within the military, as two rival generals, Francisco "Panchito" Serrano and Arnulfo Gómez, mobilized to derail Obregón's comeback. They organized a coup attempt, backed by more than half the army, as well as the radical Catholics and landowners. It failed, as did another plot to assassinate Obregón by hurling a bomb at his passing car in Chapultepec Park. Calles ordered that the conspirators, and their accomplices, be shot by firing squads without trial, and within forty-eight hours of their arrest.

Beals judged Calles' increasingly repressive rule, while unfortunate, as understandable, even necessary. The summary execution of the conspirators was, he wrote, a "moral blot on an administration which has, on the whole, been energetic, far-sighted, and constructive."57 Such "blots" were the consequence of turmoil that was itself a legacy of the brutality of Mexico's colonial era. The revolution's gains were under threat as dissident generals in cahoots with the Church, foreign capital, and the reactionary *hacendados* (landowners), wanted to turn back the clock. For his part, Obregón was obliged to violate the "no re-election" principle, a defining tenet of the revolution, Beals wrote, "to preserve the main drive . . . toward agrarian reform, regulation of foreign capital, conservation of resources, anti-clericalism, and labor emancipation."58

Calles, whose indifference to brutal measures was matched by his shrewd calculation, also came to realize, by mid-1927, that it was time to negotiate an end to the Cristero Rebellion hostilities. The Rebellion had spread to thirteen states, the number of dead was nearing 70,000, and refugees were flooding across the border to the United States in an exodus that would soon total half-a-million.[59]

The Mexican President's opportunity came in early October 1927, when Coolidge announced the appointment of Dwight W. Morrow as US Ambassador to Mexico, a move that was interpreted in both countries as a conciliatory gesture. A trusted former Amherst College classmate of Coolidge's, Morrow had become a highly-regarded executive with J. P. Morgan. Unlike Doheny's companies in Mexico, the House of Morgan had rejected confrontation in favor of negotiating its differences with the Mexican government. Combined with Morrow's personal qualities, which included passable Spanish (a first for a US Ambassador to Mexico) and an absent-minded, bookish charm, this augured well for a new era in US-Mexican relations.

Morrow's mandate was to broker a settlement to the oil claims issue, to press for an end to the Cristero Rebellion that was causing economic ruin and undermining income from US investments, and to resolve Mexico's outstanding debt issues. All were spectacularly thorny problems that had festered for years under the inept intransigence of previous ambassadors.

Within mere weeks, Morrow had engineered a sea change in relations, surprising even skeptics like Beals, who met Morrow soon after his appointment. Working from the premise that Calles was a moderate pragmatist with whom the US could do business, Morrow cultivated him. He invited Calles to ham-and-eggs breakfasts at his home, where he promised sensitive accommodation to the domestic political pressures the President faced. He also hosted Calles, accompanied by his entire cabinet, at full-dress embassy dinners. He made a show of convivial friendliness, accompanying the President at public ceremonies and visits around the country.

In return, Calles prevailed upon the pliable Mexican Supreme Court justices to rule in a landmark oil claims case so that the American companies' contention would be at least partly recognized. Morrow reciprocated by pressing Doheny and the other US oil investors to shave down their demands to the bone and agree to observe Mexican laws.

This was an extension of the strategy employed by the Morgan interests of giving ground on the oil issue—so important to the Mexicans—in order to lay the foundation for new loans, and to secure other concessions of equal or greater long-term value. With the same goals in mind, Morrow led talks to reschedule Mexico's debt service payments to US banks, primarily J. P. Morgan, in the conviction that leaving money to circulate in-country would stimulate the economy, thereby improving later repayment prospects.

Beals, writing for the *Nation* again, welcomed Morrow's "victory over the dying political elements revolving around Teapot Dome, and over the traditional short-sighted, heavy-footed, hairy-breasted cudgel diplomacy of the past."[60]

Morrow enjoyed similar, if short-lived, success in brokering an end to the Cristero Rebellion. As it became clear that Washington favored accommodation with the Calles regime, even Vatican opposition could not stop a peace pact hammered out by Calles and Mexican Church leaders at a secret meeting on the island of San Juan de Ulúa, off Veracruz. Once again, the man at the center of the parley was Morrow.[61]

The event that stands out from Morrow's time in Mexico, his "cleverest, most dramatic" achievement in Beals's view, has become the remembered story to which Morrow himself has become a footnote. It was Charles Lindbergh's solo flight to Mexico.

In December 1927, Morrow decided that a fly-in visit by Lindbergh, whose trans-Atlantic flight earlier that year had made him the world's most famous aviator, would be just the thing to celebrate the new, friendly Mexico-US ties. Lindbergh swept all Mexico off its feet, along with Morrow's daughter, Anne, whom he met during this trip and later wed.

Beals was asked by Clarence "Pete" Dubose, the Associated Press (AP) correspondent, to file reports from the Valbuena Airfield where Lindy, as Lindbergh was called, was to land December 13, 1927. As the appointed hour of Lindbergh's arrival came and went with no sign of him, the swelling crowd grew restless as the day grew hotter. As noon passed, and then Mexican *comida* (meal) time, the expectant mood shifted to one of foreboding. Had Lindbergh's plane crashed?

Finally his plane appeared, bursting out of a cloud. He made three broad sweeps around the valley before landing in a long perfect glide, his gas tank almost empty. Later at a US embassy reception after his triumphant ride through Mexico City in an open car showered with bouquets, Lindbergh told Beals and other reporters, that he was late because he had gotten lost.

"Mexican railway stations don't have their names painted on the roofs, as in America," he said. "Besides, I got my maps from the War Department in Washington, and they aren't any good."[62]

Beals left this thumbnail portrait of Lindbergh:

> One simply had to be proud of Lindy. One has to be proud of the best of anything. One could be proud that the United States had turned out one of the best flyers in the whole world. A mechanical genius, a sort of super-chauffeur, quick with hands and body, excellent reflexes, sensatory alertness, a typical American product, he was precisely the sort of hero that adolescent America, with all its mechanical gadgets, can fully appreciate and honor. But now all Mexico idolized Lindy, precisely because he was so American, and that indeed was an achievement.[63]

But Beals, and other correspondents in Mexico, saw Lindbergh's testy side too, when they followed him to Cuernavaca, where he was a guest at Morrow's majestic home, the place previously owned by art dealer Fred Davis. Lindbergh turned on the media, angrily demanding that they leave him alone. The reporters were already miffed that Lindbergh had cut a commercial deal to give interviews exclusively to the *New York Times* and resented having to scramble for scraps. "Don't imagine that we enjoy this any more than you do, Mr. Lindbergh," one of the journalists reminded him.[64]

While his Mexican landing was welcomed, Lindbergh's flight to Nicaragua a month later was another story. His arrival in Managua, which coincided with that of humorist Will Rogers, who was to entertain some of the nearly three thousand US Marines occupying Nicaragua, prompted charges in the Latin American press that Lindbergh had come, "to help whitewash American aggression." Carleton Beals's visit to Nicaragua a few weeks later, would have rather the opposite effect.

## NOTES

1. Carleton Beals to Elvina Beals, May 1924, Carleton Beals Collection (CBC), Howard Gotlieb Archival Research Center, Boston University (hereafter cited CBC).
2. Irene M. McKinnon to Carleton Beals, April 25, 1924, CBC, box 165.
3. Sinclair Lewis, *Main Street* (New York: Harcourt, Brace and Howe, 1920).
4. CBC, box 165.
5. Carleton Beals, *Glass Houses: Ten Years of Free-Lancing* (Philadelphia: J. B. Lippincott, 1938), 226–27.
6. Beals, *Glass Houses*, 228–29.
7. Beals, *Glass Houses*, 229.
8. Beals, *Glass Houses*, 229.
9. Lecture at the Civic Club, January 1925, CBC.
10. Carleton Beals, *Mexico: An Interpretation* (New York: B. W. Huebsch, 1923).
11. CBC; and Carleton Beals' review of Frank Tannenbaum's book, *Peace by Revolution: Mexico after 1910* (New York: Columbia University Press, 1933), in *Nation*, January 10, 1934, 50–51.
12. See Frank Tannenbaum, *Whither Latin America? An Introduction to Its Economic and Social Problems* (New York: Thomas Y. Cowell, 1934); and Jefferson R. Cowie, *The Emergence of Alternative Views of Latin America: The Thought of Three US Intellectuals, 1920–1935*, Working Paper 3 (Durham, NC: Duke-University of North Carolina Program in Latin American Studies, September 1992).
13. See John A. Britton, *Revolution and Ideology: Images of the Mexican Revolution in the United States* (Lexington: University Press of Kentucky, 1995), 70–71. Britton's ideological typology categorizes the American journalists and academics who studied Mexico in the 1920s to explain their variegated depictions of the Revolution's progress over the decade.
14. Ella Wolfe to Carleton Beals, June 10, 1925, CBC.
15. Ella Wolfe to Carleton Beals, May 8, 1925, CBC.
16. Alan M. Wald, *Exiles from a Future Time: The Forging of the Mid-Twentieth-Century Literary Left* (Chapel Hill: University of North Carolina Press, 2002), 232.
17. John Reed, *Ten Days that Shook the World* (New York: Boni & Liveright, 1919).
18. Ione Robinson, *A Wall to Paint On* (New York: E. P. Dutton, 1946), 124.
19. Carleton Beals, "Under the Fifth Sun" (unpublished autobiography, c. 1972–1978), CBC.

20. Carleton Beals to Roger Baldwin, December 10, 1925, CBC.
21. Roger Baldwin to Carleton Beals, December 16, 1925, CBC.
22. Carleton Beals, *Brimstone and Chili: A Book of Personal Experiences in the Southwest and in Mexico* (New York: Knopf, 1927).
23. US Congress, *Espionage Act of 1917*, Pub L. 65–24, 40 Stat. 217, 65th Cong., 1st sess., June 15, 1917.
24. Other contributing editors of *New Masses* included Sherwood Anderson, Stuart Chase, Max Eastman, Edmund Wilson, Lewis Mumford, Waldo Frank, Eugene O'Neill, and cartoonist Miguel Covarrubias, while the Executive Board was composed of Freda Kirchwey, Rex Stout, Art Young, Helen Black, and Joseph Freeman. Beals later asked that his name be struck from the list of contributing editors, as the magazine became, under Michael Gold's editorial direction, what Beals described as an "official organ" of the Communist Party, whose "ramrods" were using the more literary group of writers for their own ends.
25. Anita Brenner, *Idols Behind Altars* (New York: Payson & Clarke, 1929).
26. Tina Modotti to Carleton Beals, June 29, 1924, CBC
27. Beals, *Glass Houses*, 243.
28. Carleton Beals, *Mexican Maze* (Philadelphia: J. B. Lippincott, 1931), 278.
29. Beals, *Glass Houses*, 181.
30. Beals, *Glass Houses*, 243.
31. Mercedes Modotti to Carleton Beals, CBC.
32. Anita Brenner (unpublished journal, November 21, 1925), courtesy of Susannah Joel Glusker, Mexico City.
33. Anita Brenner (unpublished journal, December 2, 1925), courtesy of Susannah Joel Glusker, Mexico City.
34. Brenner (unpublished journal, November 21, 1925).
35. Harry Block to Carleton Beals, April 12, 1926, CBC.
36. Carleton Beals, *Banana Gold* (Philadelphia: J. B. Lippincott, 1932).
37. W. Dirk Raat, *Mexico and the United States: Ambivalent Vistas.* (Athens: University of Georgia Press, 1992), 136–37.
38. Carleton Beals, "The Mexican Church Goes on Strike," *Nation*, August 18, 1926, 146.
39. Carleton Beals and Edward Alsworth Ross, *The Church Problem in Mexico* (New York: Academy Press, 1926).
40. Beals and Ross, *Church Problem in Mexico*, 28–29.
41. Catholic Church, National Conference of Catholic Bishops, *Pastoral Letter of the Catholic Episcopate of the United States on the Religious Situation in Mexico*, Committee of the American Episcopate (New Haven, CT: Committee of the American Episcopate, 1926).
42. Beals, Glass Houses, 251.
43. Beals, *Glass Houses*, 251.
44. Beals, *Glass Houses*, 251.
45. H. L. Wilson to Catt, January 14, 1927, CBC.
46. Carleton Beals to *New York Herald-Tribune*, February 14, 1927, CBC.
47. See Herbert Croly, *The Promise of American Life* (Princeton, NJ: Princeton University Press, 2014).
48. Max Eastman, "Writing About the *New Republic*," *Masses*, May 29, 1915.
49. Carleton Beals, "For Generosity to Mexico - Carleton Be ls [*sic*] Speaks at Civic Club on Land Laws There," *New York Times*, December 11, 1926, 8.
50. Beals, *Glass Houses*, 260.
51. See Carleton Beals, "Whose Property is Kellogg Protecting?" and "Who Wants War with Mexico?" *New Republic*, February 23, and April 27, 1927.
52. Brenner (unpublished journal, November 21, 1925).
53. Diego Rivera to José G. Zuno, May 2, 1927, CBC.
54. Carleton Beals, "Civil War in Mexico—How It Strikes an Observer," *New Republic*, July 6, 1927.
55. Beals, "Civil War in Mexico."
56. Beals, "Civil War in Mexico."
57. Carleton Beals, "Whither Mexico?" *New Republic*, December 21, 1927, 133.

58. Carleton Beals, "Mexico's Coming Election," *New Republic*, August 17, 1927.
59. Enrique Krauze, *Mexico: Biography of Power: A History of Modern Mexico, 1810–1996*, trans. Hank Heifetz (New York: HarperCollins, 1998), 423.
60. Carleton Beals, "Dwight Morrow Agrees with Mexico," *Nation*, January 25, 1928.
61. Beals, *Glass Houses*, 275.
62. Beals, *Glass Houses*, 333.
63. Beals, *Glass Houses*, 334.
64. Beals, *Glass Houses*, 336.

*Chapter Six*

# Sandino's Mythmaker

Late in the afternoon of January 5, 1928, Carleton Beals ambled into the cable office on San Juan de Letrán Street in Mexico City, as he did most days, to pick up his messages. The wicket attendant passed him an urgent telegram that had arrived that morning from Oswald Garrison Villard, editor of the *Nation*. While his closest contact at the *Nation* had been the magazine's now-departed, previous managing editor, Ernest Gruening, Beals had met Villard several times during his last extended stay in New York City in 1924.

Villard was "the product of an interesting experiment," columnist Heywood Broun once wrote. "His mother's father was an abolitionist and his father a railroad magnate." Villard was the grandson, on his mother's side, of the anti-slavery crusader William Lloyd Garrison (1805–1879), and the son of Henry Villard (1835–1900) who, in 1881, had used some of his railway fortune to buy the *New York Evening Post*.[1] The elder Villard had started his career as a journalist, and always sustained a passion for newspapers.

A driven, hardy, and intense man, the younger Villard was a champion of liberal, pacifist, and anti-imperialist intellectual activism in the city. He had carried the legacy of his grandfather's abolitionist cause forward by helping to found the National Association for the Advancement of Colored People (NAACP) in 1905, and he served as an officer of the Anti-Imperialist League.

From his perch at the *Nation*, a weekly journal he had detached in 1918 from its companion daily, the *New York Evening Post*, which he had inherited from his father and later sold, Villard led what he called a "family" of dedicated journalists, all liberal idealists like him. The articles they wrote and commissioned for the *Nation* on "politics, literature, science and art" combined intellectual curiosity with a progressive outlook, and pressed for social justice, equality, and an end to racism.[2] Among their more cherished causes was opposition to the Monroe Doctrine (1823) and, more specifically, the way it was used to justify US military intervention in Latin America.

In recent months, the fifty-six-year-old Villard had enthusiastically embraced a solidarity effort on behalf of Augusto César Sandino, a Nicaraguan nationalist rebel fighting US Marines dispatched by President Calvin Coolidge a year earlier to that Central American republic. The troops were there to prop up the regime of the pro-US Conservative President Adolfo Díaz, and to supervise elections to be held in November 1928.

Today, Sandino is an iconic figure in Nicaragua, his role as inspiration of the eponymous Sandinista Front (by the early twenty-first century, divided and tarnished by its corrupt leader and Nicaraguan President Daniel Ortega) reflected in the ubiquity of his image around the country. Often it is just a silhouette, a Stetson riding the back of his head, a Smith and Wesson revolver hanging from his hip, and riding breeches above leather puttees laced to the knee.

In January 1928, however, he remained a shadowy figure, both in Nicaragua and in the US. "The bandit Sandino" was the label given him by US Secretary of State Frank B. Kellogg, with the *New York Times* and the Hearst papers repeating the epithet. He was said to have somewhere near one thousand peasant volunteers in his army, whose battle cry was, "a free country—or death!" No American, not even one among the over 2,500 US Marines trying to smoke him out of Nicaragua's northern Segovia mountains, had actually met him, face to face. Indeed, the US legation staff in Managua had been frustrated in their efforts to obtain a photo of Sandino, so they would know their quarry when they found him.[3] Certainly, few Americans had any real understanding of what seemed a quixotic rebellion.

Villard supported Sandino's cause, which he saw as an example of a subject people rising in arms to throw off an imperialist enemy and its puppet regime. Together with other liberals and Progressives, as well as the American Civil Liberties Union (ACLU), Villard had been busy that cold first week of 1928 organizing a mass rally in Manhattan of the All-American Anti-Imperialist League, to be held January 15 to raise funds for medical supplies for Sandino's army.[4]

A "Hands-Off Nicaragua" committee had been struck, with chapters in several US cities, and Mexico as well. Its volunteers sold facsimile Sandino postage stamps, which supporters pasted on their letters. Villard was also preparing for publication in the *Nation*, a paean to Sandino by the exiled Nicaraguan poet Salomon de la Selva. "Sandino is of the breed of Bolivar and Sucre and San Martín and Martí," de la Selva wrote. "In the Hall of National Heroes at the Pan-American Union in Washington, Nicaragua's pedestal is empty. She now has a candidate."[5]

Villard was determined to counter what he saw as malicious propaganda spread by the US State Department, as well as by US companies and banks with interests in Nicaragua's banana trade, rail and riverboat concessions, and outstanding unpaid debt owed them by the Nicaraguan government. Their campaign to discredit Sandino as a bloodthirsty outlaw had shown some success in influencing media coverage to support the US Marines' war, which nonetheless remained unpopular among the public. Clifford Ham, the US-appointed collector general of customs in Managua, supplemented his salary with reports he filed to United Press, all uniformly friendly to US policy.[6] Harold Norman Denny, the *New York Times'* Caribbean correspondent, described Sandino as "motivated by . . . a wild patriotism . . . touched with megalomania . . . a *poseur*."[7]

Finally, Henry L. Stimson, who had as Coolidge's special envoy, negotiated an agreement with Liberal General José María Moncada (1870–1945) to end a civil war between Nicaraguan Conservatives and Liberals in May 1927, had published a three-part series in the *Saturday Evening Post* in October 1927, in which Sandino was (erroneously) described as having "served under Pancho Villa" in Mexico. "I was told," Stimson wrote, that Sandino "only came back to Nicaragua at the outbreak of the revolution in order to enjoy the opportunities for violence and pillage which it offered."[8]

To confront these images, and boost Sandino's reputation as a patriotic anti-imperialist—so as to bolster a campaign against US intervention by Progressives in Congress—Villard came up with the idea of sending a journalist to find Sandino and tell his story in his own words. Such a feat would reach beyond the twenty-five thousand readers of the *Nation*, he surmised. It would raise the magazine's profile, while also delivering a satisfying poke in the eye to Coolidge for his imperialist policy.

But who could handle such an assignment? Villard thought immediately of Carleton Beals. His articles on Mexico's fight with US oil king Edward L. Doheny over petroleum leases, and its Church-state civil war, published in the *Nation*, as well as Herbert Croly's rival liberal weekly the *New Republic*, had won Villard's admiration. His telegram to Beals contained his proposal.

Beals tore open the envelope, and felt his excitement rise as his eyes raced across the block letters pasted on the page:

CAN YOU PROCEED IMMEDIATELY NICARAGUA FOR NATION SENDING EXCLUSIVE STORIES AMERICAN POLICY MARINE RULE POPULAR FEELING ET CETERA REACHING SANDINO IF POSSIBLE. TRIP PROBABLY OCCUPY MONTH. CAN OFFER HUNDRED A WEEK + EXPENSES. WIRE COLLECT WHETHER POSSIBLE URGENTLY HOPE YOU CAN GO.[9]

Beals recalled Villard's peculiar emphatic manner of speaking, inherited from his Bavarian immigrant father. He could see his hard-boiled newsman's glare behind the thick lenses of his glasses, a gruff façade that never quite concealed his gentle soul.[10]

He was thrown, agitated. He paced as he contemplated the challenge, and the adventure it promised. He had gained a basic familiarity with Central America during his trip there a year earlier, but this was a prospect of another order, a clandestine journey through a war zone. He sat down at one of the cable office desks, trying to focus.

"Would Sandino receive me? Or shoot me?" he wondered. "Would the Marines let me land? Could I get my stories out?" He stuffed the message in his pocket and walked around the block, his mind on fire.

Half an hour later, he was back in the cable office, composing his game reply:

> WILL GLADLY GO LEAVING HERE SATURDAY VIA GUATEMALA. GATES TO SANDINO OPEN BUT UNADVISABLE TO ANNOUNCE THIS PARTICULAR FACT BEFOREHAND FOR IT WOULD INCREASE RISK SPOIL CHANCES. EYE ESTIMATE FIVE WEEKS NECESSARY. ADVISABLE WIRE ME FIVE HUNDRED TOMORROW. BEALS.[11]

That evening, Beals had dinner with his friend Howard Phillips and Dr. Carlos León, head of the Union of Central and South America and the Antilles, an anti-imperialist organization. León was an exile from Venezuela, having escaped after nine years at hard labor in a Caracas prison. A former diplomat and teacher, León had incurred the wrath of Venezuelan strongman Juan Vicente Gómez, known as "The Sorcerer" and the "Tyrant of the Andes," when he refused to serve his regime as education minister. At sixty years old, his ordeal hardly showed. Freckled, with spiky, close-cropped hair, he retained a youthful appearance and disposition, and now took vicarious delight in contemplating Beals's plan to reach Sandino.[12]

León was a critical contact for Beals, as he was part of the Manos fuera de Nicaragua (Hands Off Nicaragua) committee, the Mexican chapter of Sandino's underground network opposing US intervention in the country, which had also reached Villard in New York. The three men talked late into the night, charting plans for Beals's itinerary. León also wrote letters of introduction for Beals to Froylán Turcios, Sandino's representative in Tegucigalpa, Honduras, and to Sandino himself.

At León's suggestion, Beals called on Sandino's "ambassador" to Mexico, Dr. Pedro José Zepeda, the following day. Zepeda, burly and corpulent in a dapper suit and tan fedora, was a personable and effective diplomat. He had built a Sandino solidarity movement in Mexico City, securing money, arms, and ammunition for the Sandinista uprising, all on a shoestring.

Before his role as Sandino's man in Mexico, he had been the nexus between Nicaragua's "provisional" Liberal government, led by Juan Bautista

Sacasa, and Mexican President Plutarco Elías Calles. From early 1926 until Sacasa's forced exile in May 1927, Zepeda had worked assiduously to build a channel of sympathy between Sacasa, with whom Sandino had been briefly aligned, and Calles. It had paid off, as Calles, eager to challenge the United States for commanding influence in Central America, had been the first leader to recognize Sacasa's government, and had supplied it with weapons.

Zepeda, stimulated by the possibilities offered by coverage of Sandino's cause by a sympathetic American journalist, welcomed Beals and motioned for him to join him in his office. He then brought him up to date on the situation in Nicaragua.

\*\*\*

Beals was already well-acquainted with Nicaragua's polarized, corrupt political culture and its entanglement with the interests of US mining, fruit, and riverboat companies, and banks. These companies repeatedly called on US politicians and State Department officials to protect their interests, in several cases, by sending the US Marines. Beals had visited the country during a Central American tour in late 1926 and had written from Managua about the grubby machinations that determined power there.

In November 1926, during Beals's last visit, Conservative Adolfo Díaz had just been installed as Nicaragua's President at the insistence of the United States, in a bid to end the "Constitutionalist War." That war was another episode in an entrenched, bitter rivalry that had split Nicaragua's ruling elite for generations. On one side were Conservative landowners, near-feudal in economic practice and deeply Catholic, around the city of Granada, on Lake Nicaragua. Against them were the more modernizing, nationalistic Liberals, with some anti-clerical tendencies, based in León, on the country's hot Pacific coastal plain.

The roots of the war went back to 1924 when the Liberals, hungry for power after a decade of Conservative rule, mostly under the control of the "strongman of Nicaragua," Emiliano Chamorro (1871–1966), had aligned themselves in an electoral coalition with those Conservatives who had fallen out with Chamorro. This coalition, they hoped, would capitalize on growing Liberal popularity among the people to end the *caudillo* Chamorro's rule. Chamorro had been President from 1916 to 1920, and thereafter ruled by proxy, with his aged uncle, Diego Chamorro, in the President's chair; the formula had collapsed in October 1923, when Diego died.

The Liberal-Conservative coalition's 1924 presidential ticket against Chamorro combined Carlos José Solórzano (1860–1936), a genial, pliable Conservative businessman, with the Liberal Juan Bautista Sacasa (1874–1946) as nominee for Vice President. The pair won by 48,000 to 28,000 votes in the 1924 election, supervised by US soldiers.[13]

But the Conservative chieftain Chamorro had no intention of exiting from the political stage. Almost immediately, he launched an intrigue to topple Solórzano's government. He waited until the US government—now reasonably confident that stability had been restored and satisfied with a settlement in which the Nicaraguan government was buying back stock from US bankers Brown and J. & W. Seligman in the country's Pacific railway and national bank—decided to send the last US Marines home in mid-1925.[14]

On August 28, 1925, Chamorro began to roll out his plot. A band of armed Conservative brigands was dispatched to storm a dinner party attended by Liberal cabinet ministers and generals at Managua's International Club. Fortified with rum, a Conservative ringleader, Alfredo Rivas, dressed in breeches, boots, and spurs, fired his pistol in the air. Panic ensued, and the more prominent guests were quickly taken as captives. They included the chief Liberal General, José María Moncada, who was dragged out with a gun pressed to his head, cursing his captors. All the hostages were conveyed to La Loma, a citadel garrison on a hill with a commanding view of the sleepy capital city.[15]

President Solórzano, who had fortuitously left the dinner party early, dithered in the face of this challenge to his authority, appealing to the US legation for "protection." The US Marines having left Nicaragua, American Minister Charles Eberhardt urged the Nicaraguan President to order his own troops to retake the Loma from the conspirators. But Solórzano demurred. The plot degenerated into farce. Its leader, Rivas, was the President's own brother-in-law. He proved willing to call the whole thing off when Solórzano offered the right amount.

In fact, Rivas' plot was just a trial balloon sent by the wily Chamorro. Once reassured by the Americans' supine response to this coup "rehearsal" that they would not send the US Marines back to Nicaragua, Chamorro ordered his own followers to seize La Loma once and for all, allowing him to retake the presidency in a coup aptly called the "Lomazo." Chamorro then manipulated the National Assembly—dominated by Conservative deputies who remained loyal to him—to force Solórzano to resign the presidency and quit the country.

Sacasa, as Solórzano's Vice President, immediately invoked his constitutional right to accede to the presidency in Solórzano's place. But Chamorro maneuvered the Assembly once again, this time to vote on January 13, 1926, to impeach Sacasa and banish him from Nicaragua for two years.[16]

Sacasa traveled to the United States and Mexico to lobby for support for his claim as the constitutional President of Nicaragua. Rebuffed by the United States, he secured Mexican support, and established a "provisional" government in Puerto Cabezas, a steamy Caribbean port on Nicaragua's Mosquito Coast, separated from Managua by 320 miles of impregnable rainforest. From this unlikely staging area, Sacasa, a respected physician, his hair silver at the temples, led an armed challenge to Chamorro and Nicaragua's old Conservative party establishment. His troops in the field were led by one of those who had been taken prisoner at the Managua International Club dinner party, General Moncada.

After months of intensifying war, in which Mexican support for the Liberals was evident in captured weapons, cartridge shells, and even captured Mexican volunteer soldiers on the Liberal side, the United States was in a quandary. It could not openly support its longtime staunch ally, Chamorro, without violating a commitment by Charles Evans Hughes, President Harding's Secretary of State. Hughes had backed the signatories at the 1922 Central American conference in Washington, who agreed to withhold recognition from governments coming to power through unconstitutional means.[17] America could not now come to the aid of a dictator who had seized power in a coup, without making a mockery of its stance in favor of democracy.

The US State Department decided to launch a peace initiative. Acting on orders from Secretary of State Kellogg, the American chargé d'affaires in Managua, a bold thirty-two-year-old Lawrence Dennis, pressured Chamorro to resign. Dennis got him and his cronies to agree that an interim administration led by another Conservative, Adolfo Díaz, be installed until new elections could be held in 1928.[18] Above all, the United States was alarmed by what it perceived as a radicalized and nationalist Sacasa who, during his recent visit to Mexico, had been received warmly by Calles as a comrade-in-arms against US imperialism.

Sacasa's potential seizure of power had to be prevented, US officials came to believe. Their view was shaped by suspicion of Mexican designs on Central America, evident in Mexico's gifts of high-power radio transmitters to the isthmian countries, trade missions, new steamship, and cable links, and cultural overtures, as well as arms shipments.[19] Adolfo Díaz egged on US diplomats in this vein, warning them that Sacasa was a stalking horse, armed by Mexico's President Calles, who would overthrow Nicaragua's Conservatives unless the United States brought back the Marines to shore up the Díaz regime. Such a turn of events, he argued, would jeopardize US access to Nicaragua for a potential alternative canal route through the Río San Juan and Lake Nicaragua, which had been secured under the 1914 Bryan-Chamorro Treaty in return for US agreement to pay Nicaragua's $3 million debt.[20]

In an article he filed from Guatemala for *Current History* during his first visit to Central America in 1926, Beals wrote that he was "convinced that Mexico assisted materially in the installation of the Liberal government [in Nicaragua] and that it is now assisting in the movement to overthrow Chamorro."[21] President Coolidge, in a statement to Congress January 10, 1927, said he would not allow Calles, full of socialist rhetoric, and already locking horns with US oil companies over royalties, and mineral and land rights in Mexico, to spread his revolutionary cancer to Central America.[22]

Dennis, who left the diplomatic service soon after his tour of duty in Nicaragua, wrote archly in *Foreign Affairs* five years later: "Continued Mexican support (for Sacasa) against a government we had recognized . . . was an assault on our national prestige amounting to a piece of international *lèse-majesté* [offense against US sovereignty]. Thereafter, affronted dignity dictated largely our course of action and determined events."[23]

In November 1926, having finally prevailed upon Chamorro to resign, Dennis had brokered a deal under which the assembly elected Conservative Adolfo Díaz to serve as President until general elections set for November 1928.

Díaz had been President once before, from 1912 through 1916, when he was thrust into power with the support of US Marines sent to Nicaragua in 1909 by President William Howard Taft (1857–1930), to back a Conservative rebellion first against Liberal President José Santos Zelaya (1853–1919), and then his successor, José Madriz Rodríguez (1867–1911). The Conservatives had seized an opportunity created when independent creole banana planters along the Río Escondido rose against Zelaya. They had felt betrayed when Zelaya authorized a monopoly riverboat concession for the United Fruit Company, which promptly dropped prices paid to the planters for their bananas. Zelaya reacted by breaking the agreement, thereby antagonizing United Fruit, which turned to the US State Department for support.[24]

Before that, Díaz had been a clerk for the US-owned La Luz and Los Angeles Mining Company, with gold mining operations in Nicaragua, for which Philander Knox, US Secretary of State under Theodore Roosevelt and Taft, had once served as legal counsel.[25] It had been under Knox's watch at the State Department that this first US intervention in Nicaragua had been launched. Díaz emerged at that time, Beals would later write, "with $600,000 to back a revolution against Zelaya and became, thereafter, the fair-haired office-boy for the State Department . . . a dapper, glib, neatly-tailored little man uttering incredible falsehoods."[26] Now, once again, in this new war against the Liberals, Díaz was backed by a growing force of returning US Marines, who had begun regularly disembarking on both of Nicaragua's coasts starting in September 1926.

This was the status quo when Beals had first visited Nicaragua. In an article he filed to the *Nation* in December 1926, he had described "traditional Nicaraguan governing practices" as of a piece with Central American governments in general which, he wrote, "[are] patterned after the old Spanish vice-regal regimes; they are still, in spirit, colonial fiefs, ruled by a number of bitterly contentious, semi-creole families, whose heads are alternately in power or in exile, fighting to grab the lion's share of the spoils. In the last century one faction has gained its support by catering to American imperial interests, the other by catering to the growing nationalist, racial, and anti-clerical sentiment."[27]

The situation as Beals prepared to go to Nicaragua in January 1928, was similar in that Díaz's puppet regime was still in power thanks to US Marine protection, without which it likely would have fallen. But in the interim, a mission to Nicaragua undertaken in April 1927 by President Coolidge's envoy, Henry L. Stimson, had completely changed the configuration of the war.

Stimson, already sixty years old in 1927, was an experienced soldier and commanding officer, as well as the US Secretary of War in the Taft administration. Coolidge was frustrated with Nicaragua's civil war, uncomfortable with the growing US military commitment there and the opprobrium it was earning him in Latin America. He dispatched Stimson to broker a peace deal. He was to get the Liberals and Conservatives to lay down their arms and abide by the results of an election to be organized and supervised by the United States.

On the face of it, Stimson seemed to have succeeded. He had secured Díaz's agreement to the plan and then sought a meeting with Sacasa. Sacasa, however, refused to abandon his "capital" of Puerto Cabezas, and sent three representatives instead. They arrived at the appointed meeting with Stimson in the Pacific port of Corinto, after a hurried passage via the Panama Canal aboard the battleship *USS Preston*. Initially skeptical, they were impressed by Stimson's courtly manner and dignified military mien. His peculiarly American way of pronouncing "Nicaraguew-a" reassured them. As he had obviously never visited their country before, they concluded that he was incapable of playing favorites. They considered his proposal and asked to consult with their own Secretary of War, José María Moncada.

Stimson saw in this an opportunity and quickly invited Moncada to meet with him directly, offering him safe conduct under US Marine escort. A forty-eight-hour truce was hastily arranged, and the two men met on May 4, 1927, in the shade of a blackthorn tree at Tipitapa, a dusty village on the shore of Lake Managua. There, they concluded the "Espino Negro Accord," or the Peace of Tipitapa, in which Moncada accepted Stimson's proposal that he suspend Liberal hostilities against the government.

Moncada fancied himself a political philosopher and had even written a book outlining his large ambitions for Nicaragua. He was also a smart military tactician whose campaign had outmaneuvered Díaz's government forces, so much so that the Liberals easily would have taken the National Palace long before Stimson arrived in Managua, but for the presence of the US Marines.

In addition to his battlefield wits, Moncada had an opportunistic streak that quickly asserted itself when he recognized in Stimson's offer a chance to make himself Liberal candidate for President in 1928, possibly with US sponsorship. "In less than thirty minutes," Stimson wrote, "we had understood each other and had settled the matter."[28] Immediately after meeting

Moncada, Stimson wired US Secretary of State Frank Kellogg: "The civil war in Nicaragua is now definitely ended."

Moncada called on his generals to surrender their weapons, and rally to his leadership. Most of them promptly acquiesced. Sacasa, of course, was furious at this betrayal. But without an army, he had no choice but to give up the struggle, and flee, to Costa Rica. He later rallied to Moncada. One Liberal general, however, refused to surrender: Augusto César Sandino.

Sandino, just thirty-two years old, was the son of Gregorio Sandino, a coffee farmer from Niquinohomo, in the department of Masaya, and Margarita Calderón, one of his family's servants. He had been raised alone by his teenaged mother until he was eleven, when his father, having reached the age to take responsibility for the farm, took him into his house. After primary school, and some technical training in Granada, the younger Sandino worked as the accountant for his father's farming operation. But in 1915, after a heated argument, Sandino shot and wounded a man in the plaza of Niquinohomo and fled the country to avoid arrest.[29] He crossed into Honduras and got a job in the Caribbean banana port of La Ceiba, as a warehouseman and mechanic in the Montecristo sugar mill, owned by the Vaccaro Brothers and Company, later to be reorganized as the Standard Fruit Company. After some years there, he moved on to Quiriguá, another Caribbean port town in neighboring Guatemala, where he worked as a mechanic for the United Fruit Company.

In 1923, Sandino arrived in Tampico, an oil-boom city and bustling port on the Gulf of Mexico. Coincidentally, Carleton Beals also visited Tampico around this time; he described it as, "a wide-open town, with one of the largest red-light districts in the world . . . money did not flow but gushed like oil."[30] Sandino stayed there for three years, working first with the South Pennsylvania Oil Company, and then as a gasoline salesman with the Huasteca Petroleum Company, owned by Doheny. He lived in the night watchman's house along a pipeline on Cerro Azul, just outside the city, with a young woman with whom he had a child in 1925.

It was during this period that Sandino's revolutionary ideology was formed. While employed by a US company, he was exposed in Tampico to a hothouse of labor activism, with anarchist Industrial Workers of the World (IWW) unions vying for workers' loyalties with Morones' government-affiliated CROM and conservative labor organizations tied to the American Federation of Labor. At the same time, he studied theosophical books, was drawn to the Seventh Day Adventist Church, and became inspired by a biography of Simón Bolívar, whose selfless devotion and determination in the face of impossible odds deeply impressed him.

In May 1926, Sandino received a letter from his father asking him to return home, to which he immediately acquiesced. It is not clear whether he planned at the outset to throw himself into Sacasa's war against Chamorro's coup, but once back in Nicaragua, it wasn't long before he did so.

After a short stay in Niquinohomo, Sandino found himself a job as assistant paymaster at an American-owned gold mine called San Albino, in the department of Nueva Segovia. Laborers at the San Albino mine, like most people living in the Segovia mountains, were drawn from poor Indian and *mestizo* peasants and tenant farmers. By the 1920s, their lives had been transformed by the penetration of US capital investment and expansion of the coffee economy. Many had been pushed off their subsistence farms, or *milpas*, as coffee growers obtained legal title to the best land to set up plantations. These peasants then became laborers bonded by debt to coffee plantation owners, or they found jobs at gold mines such as San Albino.

Violent gang warfare arose in this environment, as coffee planters and mine owners, all paying only bare subsistence wages, used coercion to keep their workers in line. This rural elite was tied to Nicaragua's central governing power through its patronage of the Conservative and Liberal parties. To maintain control, local party bosses paid gang leaders to "protect" landowners of the same party allegiance. In the Segovias in 1926, the Conservatives held the government positions and garrisons, giving Conservative-sponsored gangs the spoils of office. These gangs protected—or rather, abused—their privileges by unleashing terror among the opposition Liberal-inclined local populace. Beatings, rapes, and murders became commonplace. Many of the farm workers and landowners, who wound up the losers in this system, sought protection in their turn by joining or sponsoring Liberal armies and bands that had surfaced since Chamorro's coup. These Liberal gangs, led by local chieftains, matched the Conservative gangs' mayhem with terror of their own, often targeting government garrisons and patrols.[31]

The casual attitude toward violence of these rural gangs is evident in the names they gave their atrocities: the *corte de cumbo* or "skull cut," in which the top of the head was cut off and the brain exposed, and the *corte de blumers*, in which the legs were severed at the knees, and the hands cut off. It was this climate of brutish lawlessness in northwestern Nicaragua that led to the easy categorization of Sandino as a "bandit."[32]

In October 1926, an armed band of Conservatives killed two men, raped two girls, and burned a home in Murra, a village near San Albino. A survivor ran to San Albino with news of the atrocity, inflaming the mining community.[33] Sandino was outraged. For weeks, he had grown increasingly frustrated with his role as a US mine employee, and this incident provoked him to shift from vague efforts to stir mine workers' demands for better working conditions, to direct action. While working in the paymaster's office, Sandino had incited the workers to demand payment in dollars rather than company scrip.[34] He used such gambits as a way of passing on to the mine workers some of the revolutionary ideas he had acquired in Tampico, and in so doing, he quickly found that he had an ability to capture their imagination. As he grew comfortable in this new role, he denounced the Chamorro dictatorship, a message that resonated among the laborers.

Now, with his companions' wrath ignited by the Conservative attack, Sandino gathered twenty-nine men, armed them with rifles he had bought with his own Tampico savings from Honduran gun-runners and led an attack on a government garrison at Jícaro, near the mine, on November 2. The attack failed, but Sandino's men managed to kill a few soldiers.[35]

Some of his men were discouraged and left the group, but a few then followed Sandino to Puerto Cabezas, where he sought out Sacasa and Moncada, offering to mount and lead a column of fighters for their cause in Nueva Segovia, and asking for arms and ammunition to do so. Neither was much interested. Moncada, upon hearing Sandino's comments about the need for workers to struggle against the rich, dismissed him as a communist.

Sandino was disgusted with this reception, but not dissuaded. On December 23, 1926, when US Marines seized control of Puerto Cabezas and ordered Sacasa to move his weapons and soldiers out of the town, Sandino's followers took advantage of the confusion to seize about thirty rifles and ammunition left behind by Sacasa's men. He then marched to Prinzapolka, further down the coast, where he met Moncada once again. Moncada ordered him to turn his rifles over to Liberal forces, which Sandino refused to do. Finally, after prodding from other Liberal military officers, Moncada relented and named Sandino a general in the Liberal "Constitutionalist" army, in command of its forces in Nueva Segovia.[36]

Just four months later, Moncada agreed to peace terms with Stimson, ending the civil war and calling on Liberals and Conservatives to disarm as the country prepared for "free and fair" elections. To Sandino, this amounted to treason. In the Segovias, meanwhile, he faced Conservative-sponsored gangs who, pointedly, were not disarming. Instead, they were now determined to disrupt the elections which they knew would deliver power to the Liberals, given widespread disenchantment with long years of Conservative rule, repression, and exploitation. Moncada, in Sandino's view, was no better than the Conservatives Díaz and Chamorro: a Yankee sellout and a corrupt opportunist.

By now, too, Sandino had begun to believe in his own messianic mission, a sense of "calling" which would become more pronounced as his rebellion developed. He gathered his troops in Jinotega, a town in the semi-tropical, heavily-wooded Segovia mountains, and vowed "to fight, understanding that I was the one called to protest the betrayal of the Fatherland."[37]

From the start, Sandino's rebellion had a David-and-Goliath quality. The US plan Stimson had brokered called for determined US backing of the interim Díaz regime, and sponsorship of elections in which Moncada would be the Liberal candidate, heavily favored to win. This scenario was thrown into jeopardy by Sandino's determination to keep fighting, with his prime enemy having now shifted from the Conservatives to the US Marines who, once again, were deployed in growing numbers to "uphold the peace" agreed at Tipitapa.

At this point, Sandino's army was made up of only a few hundred mostly illiterate peasant farmers and laboring poor armed with Krag and Enfield rifles. His project of leading them to confront the US Marine Corps, equipped with state-of-the-art weaponry, including Vought Corsair and Curtiss Falcon aircraft able to carry bombs, seemed laughable.[38]

Despite the mismatch, Sandino would fight US troops for seven years, holding them to a stalemate and creating a legend of resistance that would endure for generations across Latin America. Carleton Beals brought that legend to Americans.

\*\*\*

With letters to contacts along the way and credentials provided by Dr. Zepeda in hand, along with $500 wired him by the *Nation*'s foreign editor Freda Kirchwey, Beals set off for Nicaragua on January 7, 1928.

It was a nerve-racking, arduous journey, which Beals first described in his famous six dispatches published as exclusives in the *Nation* in February and March of 1928, and later, in more detailed form, in his 1932 book, *Banana Gold*.

After trains to the Guatemalan border, and travel by road from there, Beals reached San Salvador, capital of El Salvador. He located his contact, a young, high-strung physician, Dr. José de Jesús Zamora, who was also president of the Nicaraguan Independence Association. Zamora received him in his cluttered clinic, between appointments with patients. He advised Beals to invent a scheme to hide his letters of credentials to Sandino, as he would certainly be searched on his way. Beals came up with the ruse of sealing them in an envelope which he addressed to the US Minister to Honduras, in the capital of Tegucigalpa, George Thomas Summerlin.

Zamora also dispatched a Nicaraguan messenger named Rivas to accompany Beals on a launch across the Gulf of Fonseca to San Lorenzo, Honduras, from which he would go to Tegucigalpa by road. Rivas turned out to be a liability. "A tough customer, with a heavy blunt nose and flat face," was how Beals described him. "At first glance, I felt he was a man without principles of any sort. A brutal irresponsibility ruled him."[39]

Rivas turned out to be excessively fond of drink, malarial, chronically late and dangerously indiscreet, bragging of their plan to meet Sandino to strangers who crossed their path. He also encumbered the little party by picking up a buxom, stringy-haired *mestiza* girl named Margarita, who, Beals wrote, "clucked around generally, attracting much unnecessary attention."[40]

Upon boarding the launch to Honduras, the three were subjected to a body search (Margarita stripped completely) by Salvadoran police, who confiscated all of Beals's letters, save the ones he had presciently enclosed in an envelope addressed to the American Minister.

"*This*, we will respect," the Salvadoran police chief said, handing it back to Beals with a deference hitherto absent. On the Honduran shore, however, Rivas was arrested and deported to Nicaragua. Beals felt unburdened rather than troubled.

Rivas, meanwhile, was turned over to the US Marines in Nicaragua, who questioned him (under torture, Beals later alleged), and to whom he testified that Beals was carrying 238 letters to Sandino on behalf of Zamora.[41] He added that Beals had cabled the *Nation* from San Salvador that "all collections and all medical supplies and cotton gathered were to be remitted to Dr. J. J. Zamora, President of the Anti-Imperialist League in San Salvador."[42]

In Tegucigalpa, Beals found Turcios, Sandino's clandestine envoy in the Honduran capital. At the time, the Honduran government was aligned with Coolidge's policy against the Sandinistas, and most of the country's army was deployed along the Nicaraguan border to prevent supplies from reaching Sandino.

Honduran press reports of Sandino uniformly described him as a bandit. This was not accidental, as anti-imperialist media interpretations of his uprising were suppressed at the behest of the US legation. "It is only in virtue of this [strict] censorship that we are not deluged with the publication of violently anti-American articles coming out of the Sandino activities in Nicaragua," Jefferson Caffery, US Minister in San Salvador, reported to Kellogg.[43] "As long as Sandino is permitted to terrorize portions of Nicaraguan territory, rumors about him serve only to keep alive an unpleasant agitation against the US."[44]

It was Caffery who first alerted the US legation in Managua that Beals was on his way to Sandino. "The [Salvadoran] Chief of Police tells me an alleged American citizen Carlton [*sic*] Beals acting as Sandino's courier in Central America now in Tegucigalpa," he cabled Eberhardt.[45]

Turcios, a poet and former Honduran Secretary of State, was publisher of a pro-Sandino journal titled *Ariel*, after the 1900 essay by Uruguayan poet José Enrique Rodó, which borrowed the protagonists of Shakespeare's *The Tempest* as metaphors, with *Ariel* representing the creative spiritualism of Latin America against the base, subterranean materialism of Caliban, who personifies North America. The journal had been banned shortly before Beals's arrival, on US Minister Summerlin's orders. US officials had denounced what they called Sandino's "flamboyant propaganda among the natives" in such journals, in which he related "imaginary decisive victories over the "Yankees" and sought to rally recruits to the cause of throwing the marines out of Nicaragua."[46]

Turcios prepared Beals's "passport" to Sandino which stated frankly, that "though an American, he is worthy of every confidence." A photo of Beals was affixed to the margin.[47] He also introduced his guide, "General" Santos Siqueiros. A dusky man of ectomorphic build and a manner at once haughty and nervous, he had been a soldier in Luís Mena's Liberal revolt in Nicaragua in 1911 and later the same year, in Manuel Bonilla's successful armed bid to take over the Honduran government. He was now eager to return to his native Nicaragua and join Sandino's ranks.

After two days' delay, Siqueiros procured horses and a Honduran guide, a native ranch hand named Simón, dressed in a red sash and conical sombrero. They set out on what would be a grueling two-week journey across a harsh landscape, dodging Marine patrols amid rainstorms and baking heat, without enough food or sleep. At one point, Beals was upended and thrown off his horse, leaving him with a back injury that sent him painful reminders of the trip for the rest of his life.

By late January, they had crossed into Nicaraguan territory, arriving in Limones, from which the little party was guided by seven Sandinista soldiers with red and black ribbons in their hats.

Near Jícaro, renamed "Ciudad Sandino" to commemorate the rebel leader's first attack, the party's trail passed a solidly-built log cabin with a Union Jack flying on a pole in its front yard, as if to warn off Marine bombing.

"Which cloud did you drop from!" a man cried out in British-accented English. George Williams was a homesteader who had married a Nicaraguan woman, with whom he was raising several daughters. "You've got your nerve," he told Beals. "Any one of these fellows is likely to take a whang at an American."[48]

Over a meal served by Williams's wife, Beals's first decent food since Tegucigalpa, Williams reported that the US Marines had been past his cabin the day before. They had tried to enlist Williams as a guide to Sandino's main camp on the nearby mountain popularly known as "El Chipote." He had refused, he said, and hinted to Beals that he had sent one of his daughters to tip off the Sandinistas on the Marine movements.

"I doubt if Sandino will receive you," he repeated to Beals, while puffing on corncob pipe. "An American! I'll be damned! I don't see how you got this far without trouble . . . any of these ignorant fellows is likely to pull a gun on you."[49]

Indeed, the journey now grew more perilous, but the danger facing Beals originated not with his guides, but from the air, as the area had been subjected for weeks to heavy shelling by US planes, the first-ever such bombardment in the Western hemisphere. The US Marines had launched a fierce offensive seeking to capture or kill Sandino, and thereby deliver a trophy for the US delegation to show off at the Pan-American Conference, a six-week hemispheric jamboree of Latin American Presidents just getting under way in

Figure 6.1. Carleton Beals on his way to Sandino's camp, 1928. At one point, he was thrown from his horse, suffering a back injury that left recurring pain to remind him of the trip for the rest of his life. *Photo courtesy of the Carleton Beals Collection, Howard Gotlieb Archival Research Center at Boston University, and Ralph Carleton Beals.*

Havana, and at which President Coolidge was to deliver the only overseas speech of his presidency. The Marines' campaign focused, as Williams had explained, on El Chipote, a mountain near the San Albino mine where Sandino's main camp had been located, and which Beals now approached.

But Beals found the region suddenly deserted. Frightened refugees hurried along the trail, confiding that "the Machos (Americans) have taken El Chipote." His plan to find and interview Sandino had suddenly fallen into a jumble. The refugees' stories were accurate: the US Marines had taken El Chipote, on January 26. But they had found it abandoned, Sandino having given them the slip.[50]

Beals's party had also lost track of the route Sandino had followed to evade the Marines, and the whole mission seemed doomed. As Beals struggled to convince his guides to continue the effort, an Indian courier arrived with a letter signed by Sandino himself, instructing the party to conduct Beals to El Remango, where the general's most trusted aide, Captain Pedro Altamirano, would bring them "to the place where I [Sandino] am to be found." Much as US diplomats had identified Beals's presence as a potentially disruptive factor, Sandino had clearly identified him as an ally in the propaganda war for US and Nicaraguan public opinion.

His plan back on track, Beals described the scene at the Sandinista camp where he waited to be summoned by Sandino:

> Though the wind howled over El Remango, we spent the night convivially in the long barracks room. The soldiers were as free and easy as though the enemy were a thousand miles away instead of actually on the next ridge. The barracks room was made of driven poles and high thatched roof. At one end stood the kitchen tables, heavy tree trunks split in half, or slabs of stone on wooden posts. By their side were the grinding *metates* (stones) for making tortillas, the braziers, and the adobe ovens, the fronts of them indented with features of human faces by some humorous artist. The barracks was lined with bunks, rawhide stretched over poles and the flaps pegged up against the walls as protection from the wind.
>
> In a free wall space, the camp Juanas had set up a little shrine presided over by St. Anthony, decorated with colored tissue paper, before which burned a carbide lamp. From the smoky rafters dangled great loops of fresh and dried meat. Hung down, too, gourds with corn-cob plugs, terra-cotta jars, pieces of harness, home-made fiber ropes, and long strips of rawhide. A baby squealed from a sisal hammock with multicolored tassels.
>
> The soldiers, each with his rifle ready by his side, clustered in groups. Some were talking, telling stories—the attack on Ocotal, the surprise assault on the Machos in Las Cruces, the burning of Hacienda El Hule and the violation of the women by the hated Gringos—and I, here in their midst, a Macho, a Yankee, a Gringo, yet treated with super-deference. Other soldiers, seated on sawed-off stumps, were reading by the light of the *jocote* (spondias purpurea) torches—novels, the latest number of *Ariel*, stray newspapers. One fellow was making love to a Juana who wore a high red comb with sparkling glass di-

amonds. Another in white "pajamas" grimy from use, roasted meat, using his ramrod as a spit. A guitarist thrummed a Sandino song, with simple Whitmanesque flavor and love of proper names, to the tune of the Mexican *La Casita* (cottage):

> Yo soy de los defensores
> Que con sangre y no con flores
> Lucho por conquistar
> Mi segunda independencia
> Que traidores sin conciencia
> Han querido profanar.
> Es mi patria la sultana,
> Linda Centroamericana
> De los lagos y el pinar.
> No quiero ser esclavista
> Del nórdico expansionista
> Que nos viene a asesinar.[51]
>
> [I am of the defenders
> Who with blood and not with flowers
> Struggled to win
> My second independence that
> Shameless traitors have smeared.
> This is my beautiful
> Central American nation
> Of lakes and pines.
> I don't want to be a slave dealer
> For the imperialists of the North
> Who come to kill us.][52]

"To the sound of such music and words, we began to dance, and danced most of the night away—a crowded confusion of babble and smoke, song, smell, flame and color."[53]

From El Remango, Beals's party proceeded under the command of "Pedrón" Altamirano, a stocky and ruthless outlaw whom Sandino had converted to a revolutionary captain (and would later promote to general). Their destination was San Rafael del Norte, a small town of adobe huts and red-tiled roofs on the borderline between the departments of Nueva Segovia and Jinotega, recently seized by the Sandinistas in their flight from El Chipote. The little group included Beals, Siqueiros—who spent the time showing off, berating soldiers they met on the way, and giving unsolicited advice on troop discipline to Pedrón—another Sandinista named Juan Colindres, and a woman named Blanca. Their horses were the worst of the lot, left behind by the Sandinista army in their hurried flight from El Chipote. Beals's mount was a white horse with asthma, "clumsier than a cow and completely indifferent to spur or quirt," prompting him to clamber down and continue on foot. They had to take a circuitous route to avoid the town of Quilalí, which was under

Marine attack. For several days, they followed a trail for miles over sunburnt bare hills studded with cactus and prickly acacias, and which then plunged into humid river valleys, shaded by great ceiba trees, entangled with matted vines. The party finally reached San Rafael del Norte late at night, where they were welcomed by a skirl of bugles and an entire company of soldiers, who snapped their rifles from ground to shoulder.

Colonel Francisco Estrada, of Sandino's general staff, told them Sandino would receive Beals the following morning. Beals described the scene in what became the signature story of his career:

> At a grim hour, the strident *diana* of the bugler shrilled me through the door and brought me out of bed fumbling for matches and shoes. Two hours of rest. I was red-eyed and shaky. In less than half an hour, General Sandino received me in his office in the rear of the main barracks. By the light of a lantern, we were served coffee and sweetbread by his wife, Blanca [at that time telegraph operator for the town], who spread out the cups on a red plaid cloth. As we talked the yellow tongue of the lantern flame grew feebler and finally faded into the light of common day.
>
> Sandino is short, probably not more than five feet. On the morning of our interview he was dressed in a new uniform of almost black khaki, and wore puttees, immaculately polished. A silk red and black handkerchief was knotted about his throat. His broad-brimmed Stetson, low over his forehead, was pinched into a shovel-like shape. Occasionally, as we conversed, he shoved his sombrero far back on his head and hitched his chair forward. The gesture revealed his straight black hair and full forehead. His face is straight-lined from temple to sharp-angled jawbone, which slants to an even, firm jaw.
>
> His regular curved eyebrows are high above liquid black eyes without visible pupils, eyes of remarkable mobility and refraction to light—quick intense eyes. He is a man utterly without vices, with an unequivocal sense of justice, a keen eye for the welfare of the humblest soldier.
>
> "Many battles have made our hearts hard, but our souls strong," is one of his pet sayings.
>
> I am not sure of the first part of the epigram, for in all the soldiers and all the officers to whom I talked, he has stimulated a fierce affection and a blind loyalty and has instilled his own burning hatred of the invader.
>
> "Death is but one little moment of discomfort; it is not to be taken too seriously," he repeated over and over again to his soldiers.
>
> And another, "Death most quickly singles out him who is afraid of death."
>
> There is a religious note in his thinking. Frequently he mentions God. "God is the ultimate arbiter of our battles." "If God wills it, we shall go on to victory." "God and our mountains fight for us."
>
> His sayings, pithy and wise, run from tongue to tongue in his little army—ideas which are the wonder of simpler minds.
>
> His most frequent gesture was the shaking of his forefinger, a full-armed motion behind it. Invariably, he leaned forward as he spoke, and once or twice took to his feet, emphasizing a point with his whole body.

>His utterance was remarkably fluid, precise, evenly modulated, his enunciation absolutely clear; his voice rarely changed pitch, even when he was visibly intent upon the subject matter. Not once during the four and a half hours during which we talked, almost continually without prompting from me, did he fumble for the form of expression or indicate any hesitancy regarding the themes he intended to discuss. His ideas are precisely, epigrammatically ordered. There was not a major problem in the whole Nicaraguan question that he dodged or that I even needed to raise. In military matters, however, he was quite too flamboyant and boastful, and exaggerated his successes. [54]

Beals scribbled notes furiously as Sandino spoke. As the early morning gave way to the heat of the day, he posed more direct questions, repeating some of the charges of atrocities widely leveled against him.

"The American officers are very bitter," Beals said, "because when they recover a body, the penis had been cut off and stuffed in the man's mouth."

Sandino was unmoved. "It is an old Indian custom in the Segovias. Four centuries ago, the Spaniards also complained of it. It is a ritualistic act. If the gringos would get out, they wouldn't have their penises cut off." Sandino then looked at his watch. "It's five minutes to ten. The planes will come over at ten."

Sandino rose and led Beals out the front door of the house. The street was deserted. The horses had all been tethered under cover, in patios or in thickets of trees. Sandino told the sharpshooters posted in doorways not to fire unless the planes fired first. One of them begged impatiently to be allowed "just one shot."

"You shoot one shot," Sandino said, "and I will have your penis cut off."[55]

The American planes roared overhead, as predicted, at ten. Sandino's men held their fire so as not to give the US Marines an excuse to bomb the town. Six months before, in July 1927, the Marines had bombed Ocotal, killing up to 300 civilians. The slaughter had provoked a public outcry in the United States and abroad, which resulted in the order that US planes were to fire only if fired upon. Sandino stood in the middle of the cobblestoned street, his thumbs in his belt, and sneered as the planes flew low over the town, and then vanished.

The following day, Beals, elated at having accomplished his goal and anxious to write up the story and file it to New York, prepared to leave for Managua. As he packed his things, Siqueiros rushed to him, agitated, suddenly terrified that Sandino planned to kill him. How had Siqueiros come by this idea? Beals wondered. He tried to reassure him, pointing out that Siqueiros was equipped with proper credentials, and that Sandino had shown him every courtesy and consideration.

"You don't know our people," Siqueiros replied. "Give me an *abrazo* [hug], for this is the last time you will see me alive."

Beals reflected that the diminutive Sandino had "an uncanny power of domination over his men" in which "the lift of his finger was law with men knowing only lawlessness."[56] During the interview, which Siqueiros had attended, Sandino had somehow completely terrorized this arrogant and battle-worn soldier, "through some intricate Oriental mannerism too recondite for me to comprehend."[57] Six months later, Beals would learn that Sandino had indeed sent Siqueiros to a firing squad for having allegedly plotted to betray the Sandinistas in a scheme concocted with US officials, including US Army General Frank R. McCoy, sent to Nicaragua to organize the 1928 elections.

Beals, outfitted with a horse, left Siqueiros and rode to the Sandinista barracks in the town. The troops were outside, waiting to bid him farewell. Sandino emerged from his quarters, and gave Beals two handwritten letters, both of which would be published in the *Nation*, along with Beals's reports. In the first, to the Pan-American Congress (then meeting in Havana), Sandino denounced the "illegal delegates of the so-called President Adolfo Díaz . . . and the hypocrisy of Coolidge, who speaks of good will and sends an army to murder Nicaraguans." He also protested "against the indifference and servility of the Latin American delegates in the face of the encroachments of the United States," and called on them to "insist on the immediate withdrawal of North Americans who are violating the autonomy of my country."[58]

The second letter was a response to a leaflet air-dropped by the US Marines calling on Sandino to surrender. Addressed to Rear Admiral David F. Sellers, "Representative of Imperialism in Nicaragua," Sandino's letter took issue with Sellers' contention that the war had its origin in the political struggle between Liberals and Conservatives. "Today," he wrote, "it is the entire Nicaraguan people who fight to drive out the foreign invasion from my country. . . . The only way this struggle can be ended is by the immediate withdrawal of the invading forces from our territory; the substitution of the present President by some Nicaraguan not a candidate for the Presidency; and the supervision of the coming elections by Latin-American representatives instead of American marines."[59]

The day before, during the interview, Sandino had left his chair and paced to and fro to emphasize these conditions. The rebel leader denied that he sought public office for himself, claiming to want only to return to his trade as a mechanic. He told Beals he would not fight in a domestic war, only against "foreign invasion."

> We have taken up arms from the love of our country because all other leaders have betrayed it and have sold themselves out to the foreigner, or have bent the neck in cowardice. We, in our own house, are fighting for our inalienable rights. What right have foreign troops to call us outlaws and bandits and to say

Figure 6.2. Carleton Beals (right with knotted kerchief around his neck) in Sandino's camp on El Remango, near San Rafael del Norte, Nicaragua, February 1928. *Photo courtesy of the Carleton Beals Collection, Howard Gotlieb Archival Research Center at Boston University, and Ralph Carleton Beals.*

>that we are the aggressors? I repeat that we are in our own house. We declare that we will never live in cowardly peace under a government installed by a foreign Power. Is this patriotism or is it not? And when the invader is vanquished, as some day he must be, my men will be content with their plots of ground, their tools, their mules, and their families.[60]

Beals took the letters and extended his hand. He told Sandino that he would interpret what he had seen and heard according to his own criteria, but offered to withhold information about Sandino's location, or other aspects, that might provide a military advantage to his enemy.

"If you wish," Sandino replied, "tell the first marine commander you meet everything you have seen and heard." And he added, with a little smile, "In fact, that would fit my plans admirably."[61]

As Beals made his way back to Managua, he was struck by Sandino's hold on the popular imagination. "The simple folk with whom we talked were all agog over Sandino," he wrote. "He had been seen here; he had been seen there. In every town, Sandino had his Homer. He was of the constella-

**Figure 6.3.** Augusto César Sandino, photography by Carleton Beals taken on February 2, 1928, the day of his interview near San Rafael del Norte. At the time, US officials sought a photo of Sandino to help the US Marines find him. Beals did not share this one. *Photo courtesy of the Carleton Beals Collection, Howard Gotlieb Archival Research Center at Boston University, and Ralph Carleton Beals.*

tion of Abdel-Krim, Robin Hood, Villa, the untamed outlaws who knew only daring and great deeds, imbued ever with the tireless persistence to overcome insurmountable odds and confront successfully overwhelming power. His epos will grow—in Nicaragua, in Latin America, the wide world over. For heroes grow ever more heroic with time."[62]

In Managua, Beals checked into a cheap hotel, shaved, and cleaned off the dust of his three weeks in the mountains, jettisoning his disheveled straw hat and oilcloth bag. The following day, he bought himself a Palm Beach suit and a new suitcase, and ordered a taxi to the Hotel Lupone, the capital's finest. There he worked day and night, pounding out on a rented Royal typewriter the articles which became the *Nation*'s series, "With Sandino in Nicaragua."

After finishing and cabling them to New York, he sought interviews with President Díaz, Moncada and Chamorro for further stories explaining the country's turmoil. In one hour's talk, Beals later recalled, Chamorro told him "more outright lies than all the other politicians" he had ever interviewed.

The day after Beals had checked into the Lupone, the US legation's intelligence officer, a Lieutenant Larsen, paid him a visit.

Beals had some fun at the earnest lieutenant's expense. Larsen had seen intelligence reports based on Beals's letters, which had been confiscated during his journey from Mexico by Salvadoran and Honduran border police, and turned over to US diplomats. He suspected that Beals was trying to get to Sandino, and launched into a stern interrogation.

"How did you get into Nicaragua?"

Beals pretended to be at a loss to remember the names of towns through which he had come, blaming it on his bad Spanish ("all these names confuse me, they all sound so odd"). He kept asking Larsen to repeat his own name. Larsen finally revealed the purpose of his visit: "I just come to tell you—we know you intend to try to see Sandino and we can't give no guarantees."

Beals replied that he had the idea of doing just that, but feigned to be convinced by Larsen's warning that he ought to give it up, as Sandino "hates Americans" and "he'd just kill you, that's all."

"All you say makes me believe I had better abandon the project," Beals told him. Larsen then pressed Beals to come to the US legation in Managua and see Minister Charles Eberhardt. The journalist demurred, saying he was too busy, much to Larsen's irritation.

Two days later, however, Beals did call at the legation, and met the lanky and affable American Minister. Eberhardt received him immediately; indeed, he had keenly anticipated his visit. Three days earlier, Eberhardt had cabled the State Department that he had received "a letter from Mexico addressed to Carleton Beals, a radical American newspaper writer . . . [who] was in Tegucigalpa recently and expressed the intention of attempting to join Sandino to obtain information for his projected articles."[63]

"I would be glad if we could be of service to you while you're here," Eberhardt told Beals. "But I understand you are pretty much against our policy here."

Again, Beals used the encounter to play coy with the diplomat. "I have come with an open mind to be shown the true facts," he replied. "You are the first person in Managua upon whom I have called."

Eberhardt was visibly relieved and offered to help Beals obtain interviews with President Díaz, as well as Moncada and Chamorro. Beals thanked him and asked if he could arrange an interview for him with Sandino.

> "Don't you think he is one of the important men on the scene?"
>
> Eberhardt was taken in. "Undoubtedly," he replied, "but the marines have been trying to interview Sandino for almost a year. I imagine it would be a trifle dangerous."
>
> Beals decided to end the playful charade. "Mr. Eberhardt," he said, "you are the first person on whom I have called in Managua, but you are not the first

person I have called on in Nicaragua. I have already interviewed General Sandino."

"Impossible! How did you do that?"

"Very simple. I hired a horse in Tegucigalpa, and rode overland for two weeks."

"And where did this interview take place?"

"In San Rafael del Norte, on February 2nd, five days ago."[64]

Eberhardt quickly called in his assistant, the chargé d'affaires Dana Gardner Munro, a scholar who had already written the first of several books on Central America, as well as General McCoy, who was in charge of organizing the November 1928 US-supervised election.

They began questioning Beals on the details of his trip, on Sandino, and conditions on the countryside. While Beals was guarded, he enjoyed the flattery of being interviewed by, rather than interviewing diplomats, an experience with which road-tested journalists are familiar.

"What does Sandino want?" demanded General McCoy. Beals reflected that it was an odd question, given that Marines fighting him for more than a year should know his purpose.

Beals's encounter with the embassy staff, and with General McCoy in particular, provided him with material for a withering critique of the election plans, also published in the *Nation*. Considered in the light of later US-sponsored elections in Latin America, such as those in El Salvador in 1982, where America was arming and training government forces as it supervised the voting, Beals's assessment of the Nicaraguan experience in 1928 is remarkably prescient.

"How can there be free elections [in Nicaragua]," he wrote, "when four important departments out of seventeen are in an uproar? What chance for free elections in the localities where the marines have driven the people out like cattle and burned their homes?"[65]

Beals singled out McCoy as an American imperial prototype, combining innocence, unshakeable self-confidence and a sense of mission. McCoy, he wrote, was "one of these iron-willed, super-logical, single-track types whose stern jaw carries not an ounce of compromise." He was determined to implement his election program for Nicaragua, whatever the conditions, and "nothing that he might discover on the Nicaraguan scene would cause him to alter by one iota the program he had mapped out."[66]

As for Munro, then deeply involved in guiding McCoy's electoral law through Nicaragua's assembly, Beals acknowledged in a later memoir that he had earlier written "a sincere book" book on Central America but had now "acquired the air of an apologist."[67]

"American officials nimbly assure me that we will hold a fair election and get out. We are likely to get in deeper and deeper," Beals concluded.[68] Indeed, the election rules, governance and enforcement machinery was completely controlled by McCoy. As Coolidge's special envoy, he had a free hand to over-rule a rival draft of the electoral law proposed by the Chamorro-dominated assembly, and impose his own version, which came to be known as *la ley McCoy*. He also disallowed applications by two smaller parties seeking to field presidential candidates, as these could split the Liberal vote and thereby, under Nicaragua's constitution, force the assembly—again, likely to be dominated by deputies loyal to Chamorro—to decide the winner. Finally, he had himself named chairman of the national electoral board, and US Marine officers as chairman of all the country's departmental electoral boards.[69]

By its "made in the USA" character, the election also actually prolonged the US military presence in Nicaragua. In the first instance, both Díaz and Moncada agreed that this was necessary until the polling took place. Upon winning the election, Moncada, undeceived by the momentary calm that ensued, insisted that the Marines stay to back up his regime. McCoy shared this view.[70]

Beals's dispatches relating his adventure in Nicaragua, published in the *New York Herald-Tribune* as well as the *Nation*, created a sensation that catapulted him to journalistic fame, making him something of a hero among Latin Americans and left-leaning Americans. Excerpts from the Sandino interview stories were also picked up by newspapers across the United States and around the world, including *El Sol* of Madrid, several Mexican dailies, and *La Nación* in Buenos Aires. While officially on assignment for the *Nation*, Beals also filed accounts of his Sandino interview to the Soviet news agency, TASS. They were picked up by newspapers across the United States and recounted across the new radio medium by the National Broadcasting Company (NBC) chain.[71]

Beals himself soon grasped the impact of his story. His exploit had been reported in the Nicaraguan papers too, with screaming headlines and photos of Beals on horseback and with Sandino's men.[72] When he reached San José, the genteel little capital of Costa Rica, having taken ferryboats from Managua, he found the press "aflame with my visit to Sandino," and his arrival treated as front-page news, much to the dismay of resident US diplomats. "*The Nation* is the most talked-of periodical in Latin America," he reported breathlessly to foreign editor Kirchwey.[73]

In the United States, Beals's version of Sandino's war, promoted as a mega-scoop, gave it wide currency among a domestic audience and Peace Progressive Congressmen who were already mounting a campaign to end US intervention in Nicaragua. In an advance news dispatch published on the front page of the *Washington Post* on February 11, Beals reported that "Sandino [said] . . . that he is able to sustain himself indefinitely and that he would continue fighting as long as American marines remained in Nicaragua."[74]

The report provoked a rapid counter-spin effort by US Rear Admiral Sellers. "Sandino's ammunition is practically gone," Sellers wrote in a cable the day before to the US Navy Department. The cable seemed aimed more at the press than naval intelligence officers, as it was immediately distributed to reporters. Sandino, concluded Sellers, "is finished and is simply trying to escape."[75]

US Secretary of the Navy Curtis D. Wilbur repeated Sellers' assessment in his opening remarks February 11, 1928, at the first of two US Senate Foreign Relations Committee hearings on the use of the US Navy in Nicaragua. "We received a very important telegram this morning," Wilbur testified, "to the general effect that Sandino had escaped into Honduras."[76]

"That is very different from what the morning paper says," interjected committee member Frederick H. Gillett, Republican US Senator of Massachusetts and a former US Speaker of the House, citing Beals's report.[77]

The hearings of the US Foreign Relations Committee, chaired by Idaho Republican US Senator William E. Borah, leader of the "Outlawry of War" movement and the so-called Peace Progressives in the US Congress, took place as the intervention in Nicaragua was the focus of intense controversy in Washington. They came after two months during which the US military presence in Nicaragua had doubled in size, with an additional 1,233 troops having been sent there, raising the total deployed to over 2,570. The air war was boosted too, with the dispatch of three Fokker transport planes, six Vought Corsairs and six Curtiss Falcons.[78]

The escalation was in reaction to the rising intensity of Sandino's campaign, reported in October 1927 as having grown "from banditry to a state of insurrection" with most of the territory of three departments under the rebels' control.[79] In the first three months of 1928, there were 269 stories about Nicaragua in the *New York Times*, many of them reports of ambushes and marine casualties that raised alarm. After five US Marines were killed and twenty-three wounded in a battle with Sandino's forces at Quilalí January 1, 1928, two US Senators, James Heflin and Gerald Nye, both Democrats, proposed resolutions calling for withdrawal, while in the US House, several Representatives sharply criticized the US Marine intervention in Nicaragua.[80] Parents of some of the slain US Marines also denounced what they called "murder...in a disgraceful war against this little nation."[81] A frustrated Kellogg cabled McCoy in Managua: "People cannot understand why the job cannot be done, and frankly I do not understand myself."[82] The military escalation continued, stirring renewed opposition from anti-imperialists in Congress.

In April 1928, Wisconsin US Senator John J. Blaine introduced an amendment to a naval appropriations bill for Nicaragua stating that the United States should, "in no event have recourse to arms or resort to force in any manner" to protect the commercial interests and investments of US citizens in foreign countries.[83] As former US Secretary of State Charles Evans Hughes led the US delegation at the Sixth Pan-American Conference that opened in mid-January in Havana, Blaine rose in the Senate to denounce Coolidge for having wrongfully applied the Monroe Doctrine in a way that "exalted greed" and transformed Americans into "monsters of imperialism" who could no longer credibly oppose the expansionist actions of European powers and Japan.[84]

In April, Blaine introduced an amendment to the Naval Appropriations Bill, calling for a cutoff of funds for the Marines' occupation of Nicaragua after February 1929. It was defeated, but received twenty-two votes (seven Republican, fifteen Democrat), and was followed by three successive amendments seeking the same cutoff, proposed by US Senators James Thomas Heflin and Clarence Cleveland "C. C." Dill, of Washington. Dill's amendment was actually passed a year later, in February 1929, but narrowly reversed the following day after heavy lobbying by Coolidge's White House.[85]

These US Senate initiatives were bolstered by Beals's depiction of Sandino as a patriotic nationalist, as the Coolidge administration had justified the intervention on the portrait of Sandino as "a bandit" propagated by Stimson in his October 1927 *Saturday Evening Post* articles, drafted with the assistance of Francis White, Assistant Secretary of State.[86] "These men are regarded as ordinary bandits, not only by the Government of Nicaragua, but by both political parties in that country," asserted a US State Department communiqué in early January.[87] Senior military officers testifying along with Secretary Wilbur repeated this characterization. Brigadier General Rufus Lane said the Nicaraguan people, "look upon [Sandino] as a bandit" and depicted his support as being limited to a band of followers in the province of Nueva Segovia, and whose arms came from Honduras.[88]

But Beals's dispatches, published in the *Nation* in six installments from late February until late March, "left the bandit story pretty flat," the *Nation*'s Kirchwey cabled Beals.[89]

On March 20, for example, Senator Heflin quoted Sandino's response to Beals on the Senate floor: "I shall never recognize a government imposed by a foreign power." This, Heflin thundered, was "good American doctrine . . . that we have inculcated in our children from Revolutionary days to this good time, and now we are in Nicaragua pursuing a patriot who is fighting for the same principle."[90]

Meantime, the State Department launched a damage control effort in the wake of publication of Beals's account. At Eberhardt's request, Kellogg ordered American diplomats in Mexico, and in Central and South America to press host governments to crack down on individuals and groups raising funds for Sandino, and to intercept any shipments of supplies bound for the Nicaraguan rebels.[91] In Honduras, police acting on US orders held another journalist, Charles Yale Harrison of the *New York Graphic*, for three days of questioning aboard the steamship from which sought to disembark. They sent him back to the United States after he acknowledged that he too was trying to reach Sandino to match Beals's scoop.[92]

In addition to evoking—or constructing—Sandino as a charismatic personality with his prose, Beals also delivered on his promise to serve as a messenger for the rebel leader. Along with his stories, he sent Lewis Gannett, deputy editor of the *Nation,* a copy of the leaflet dropped into Sandinista-held territory in Nicaragua, in which US Rear Admiral Sellers had demanded that Sandino respect the "so-called Stimson agreements" and lay down his arms. "Your refusal and that of your companions to accept and consent to the provisions of the Stimson agreements, reinforced by the illegal operations of your men, have caused considerable harm, spilling much unnecessary blood, and creating an intolerable situation" Sellers wrote.

The *Nation* published Sellers' ultimatum, along with Sandino's reply, in which he outlined his three conditions for ending hostilities. These were the same he had related to Beals in the interview: immediate withdrawal of the Marines, substitution of Díaz as President by a Nicaraguan citizen not previously a President, and new elections observed only by Latin American governments.

These demands were never entertained by the United States and as a result dismissed by the Nicaraguan parties, before and after the election. Instead, American diplomats and military officers remained focused on hunting down Sandino, and on denouncing him as a bandit.

On both counts, they failed. Sandino ended his rebellion when US Marines left the country in 1933 and, despite his murder in 1934 and suppression of his story there throughout the Somoza years, his image in Nicaragua—and the world—became that of an almost mythical icon symbolizing tenacious, patriotic resistance to [US] imperialism.

That the US State Department's official description of Sandino as a bandit was similarly disingenuous is borne out by a frank assessment offered by Munro, at the time chargé d'affaires in Managua, in a private letter to his superior, US Assistant Secretary of State Francis White: "It cannot be denied that Sandino's is distinctively a liberal and not a bandit movement. If he did not have political aims he would not remain in the field after all opportunities for loot had been shut off by garrisoning the towns."[93] Munro added that Moncada, "despite his apparent reasonableness and friendliness, is mean man to deal with and a contemptible character personally."[94]

Beals would much later find evidence for vindication from an unlikely source. During a US book tour in 1933, he met General Logan Feland, former commander of the US Marines in Nicaragua, by then retired in Columbus, Ohio. Recalling his Nicaragua experience, Feland told Beals: "I was doing my duty as an officer, but I really had no stomach for it. You were right all the time. We were in the wrong. I couldn't show my feelings to you then, but I was with *you.*"⁹⁵

The enduring relevance of Beals's role in covering Sandino in Nicaragua lies in the fact that it illustrates at once the importance of discourse in US politics and foreign policy, and the effect of a "propaganda model" affecting US media.⁹⁶

The US State Department's effort to label Sandino as a bandit was aimed at removing him as a serious political actor. US diplomats sought to destroy his appeal among Nicaraguans, as well as political elites and publics in other Latin American countries. This, they believed, would help justify to the American public an increasingly costly military intervention that was distinctly unpopular.

This pattern of behavior among US government leaders was repeated in 1979 through 1990 with respect to the leaders of Nicaragua's Sandinista Revolution, who were dismissed as Communists. As Michael J. Schroeder has observed, in both cases, "these imposed names and narratives have a weight and power of their own, comprising crucial components in the efforts of dominant groups to retain their superior power."⁹⁷

Beals's Sandino series was an outlier on the US media landscape of his time. It challenged a 1920s version of what Noam Chomsky and Edward S. Herman later termed the propaganda model, in which US media are seen to operate within restricted assumptions, to depend heavily and uncritically on elite information sources—such as the White House, US State Department, and the military—and to participate in propaganda campaigns helpful to elite interests.⁹⁸

Ultimately, Beals's Sandino scoop was a blip in a minor US war; it was a historical footnote. It did not change the outcome. But his stories did confront the US State Department discourse about Sandino with sufficient force and credibility to shift popular perceptions and influence US Congressional action. Without a non-mainstream medium such as the *Nation* and its crusading editor Villard, they never would have existed, and the framing of Sandino as a bandit might never have been discredited.

As it was, Beals's account also exposed the sham that was the US-sponsored 1928 Nicaraguan election, touted as the introduction of democracy to the country. Its result was Moncada's election as Nicaragua's president, and continued US military presence for another five years, which had the perverse consequence of giving even greater currency to Sandino's rebellion. This sowed the seeds for the dictatorship led by Anastasio Somoza (1896–1956), a Nicaraguan military officer whose fluent English and attentive manner won him the confidence of Henry Stimson and key US Marine commanders.⁹⁹

In 1934, Somoza—then head of Nicaragua's National Guard—would lead a conspiracy to murder Sandino after the rebel leader's peace talks over dinner with Sacasa, who had been elected president in 1932. In 1936, Somoza, having stripped Sacasa of most of his powers, seized power for himself after a rigged election.[100] He was Nicaragua's president for all but short interludes in which he ruled through proxies, until he was shot by an assassin in 1956.

Sandino thus became a martyr and, later, the rallying symbol that provided the inspiration for the Frente Sandinista de Liberación Nacional (FSLN) (Sandinista National Liberation Front), founded in the early 1960s by Carlos Fonseca, a law student from Matagalpa influenced by Marxism and the Cuban Revolution. The latter-day Sandinistas finally overthrew the last of the Somozas in 1979, their defining position, like that of their progenitor, being their rejection of US imperialism.

\*\*\*

Beals's return to Mexico from Nicaragua via a circuitous route, by skiff down the San Juan River and to Puerto Limón in Costa Rica, was not so low-profile as his clandestine entry just a month earlier. His exploit had been reported in the Nicaraguan and Costa Rican papers, with photos of Beals on horseback and with Sandino's men.[101] At the wharf in Greytown, a damp, overgrown town on the Caribbean coast, at the mouth of the San Juan River, he was welcomed by an elderly American grinning under a straw hat.

"You are Mistah Beals," the man said. "My niggah boy [in fact, a white-haired man with a stoop] will take you' baggage ovah to the hotel. Ah heah you intention gawin' Costa Rica. Now while my boy takes you' baggage to the hotel, suppose we go ovah yondah and have a few drinks?"[102]

Beals was stunned that a perfect stranger would so recognize him and know his plans. The man, a Mr. Bland, was what Beals termed a "canal hopper," a member of that "stranded specimen long settled in Greytown, waiting for the canal."[103] From the 1849 California gold rush to the present, "canal hoppers" have bought land in southern Nicaragua, invested in hotels, and sought concessions on the clammy malarial riverfront, speculating on the possibility that some financier would, one day, offer them cool millions for the would-be canal-zone properties they had so presciently acquired.

Bland and Beals were later joined by a couple of other quirky specimens washed up here on the fringes of empire, Stacomb and Wolff, both agents of the United Fruit Company who were trying to undermine a concession obtained by the company's rival for the banana trade, Cuyamel Fruit. Not so informed as Bland, they suspected Beals of being a Cuyamel spy. Stacomb tried to trap Beals into confessing by getting him drunk and setting him up with a local prostitute. It did not work, so he befriended him instead.

From Greytown, Beals took a coastal banana boat north to the lagoon of Bluefields, which he found to be "another grass-grown town of wooden houses, sheet-iron roofs and board walks . . . with a winding muddy street

[that] curved up from the launch landing, past the extensive buildings of the Moravian mission to the main stores, the radio station and the Tropical Club."[104] Bluefields was under what Beals described as a "reign of terror," occupied by US Marines whose captain had reportedly beaten and even killed several townspeople.

As Beals stood in line there to embark on another boat, this one loaded with coconuts, headed south to Puerto Limón in Costa Rica, he witnessed US Marine officers searching luggage and "confiscating" a camera case from a young Nicaraguan couple, after one had said to the other, "If you run across a good Kodak, Jim, you know I want one."

Beals reached into his suitcase, pulled out his own camera, and put it on his suitcase.

"Suppose you take this one."

"You're one of those fresh guys, aren't you?" the second marine said.

Beals then demanded to know why he was keeping the couple's camera case.

"What'n hell are you butting in for? This ain't none of your damn business."

"I'm making it my business. Why are you taking that case?"

"Regulations."

"Regulations, my eye. Let's see your regulations. Go call the officer in charge."

"I thought it was a Kodak," the marine retorted. "We have orders to confiscate all kodaks."

He gave the case back to the Nicaraguan couple, saying, "It's not a Kodak, it's just some case."

"If that is the regulation," Beals persisted, "I demand that you confiscate my Kodak."

"If you know what's good for you, you'll go on board and shut up."

Beals, not wishing to be delayed, decided to let the issue drop.

By the time he reached San Jose, Costa Rica, he found evidence that his movements were being monitored. A letter awaited him at the check-in desk at San Jose's Europa Hotel, from a Mr. Venditti, the owner of the Hotel Roma in Tegucigalpa, Honduras, where he had stayed more than a month before. Venditti told him that two policemen had come to the hotel asking for him the day after he had left for Nicaragua. They had learned of Beals's plan to reach Sandino, probably from Rivas, his first guide who had been arrested upon their arrival in Honduras.

Beals, quick to poke ridicule at police and military authorities whenever he had the chance, replied to the Tegucigalpa police chief by collect radio message—at eleven cents a word—that he would be willing to return to Tegucigalpa to meet with him. The police chief paid for the message but did not respond.

After granting an interview to *La Nueva Prensa*, in which he repeated his testimony that Sandino could anticipate Marine attacks, and march well in advance to avoid them, Beals left for Puntarenas, on Costa Rica's Pacific coast. There, he was to board the coastal freighter *Corinto*, which was to take him to Guatemala, where he planned to disembark and return overland to Mexico City.

Before he embarked, though, the innkeeper at the Puntarenas hotel at which he was lodging took him aside.

"First of all," he told Beals, "I want to tell you how proud I am to meet you; second, to warn you, two secret service men are following you."

One of the two men, whom he had seen in the hotel dining room, was an agent of Nicaragua's President Díaz, while the other, he claimed, was a US embassy official. He warned Beals not to disembark from the *Corinto* when it stopped in the Nicaraguan port of the same name. "You'll get into trouble if you do," he said. "Merely an ordinary dogfight just before the boat leaves, and you are detained as a witness."

Beals gave little credence to the warning, and when the ship docked in Corinto, he sauntered down the gangplank, and ambled around the town. When he returned aboard, the ship's steward told him a Captain Bleasdale had come aboard earlier, asking for him.

Victor Bleasdale, a US Marine veteran decorated for heroism in France during World War I, was commander of the Nicaraguan National Guard corps assigned to Corinto. The steward led Beals to the deck and pointed below to a lean officer on the wharf, directing the handling of supplies being unloaded. "That's him," he said.

Beals could not resist engaging the captain. He walked down the gangplank again and approached Bleasdale, amiably posing general questions, one American to another, about Nicaragua, then recounted how he had heard of Bleasdale's derring-do against the Sandinistas.

"Who the devil are you anyway?" Bleasdale asked.

To which Beals responded by offering his calling card.

The following morning, Bleasdale returned, accompanied by an aide. He found Beals concentrated on a chess game with the ship's doctor. "I'd like to talk to you about Sandino," Bleasdale said.

"I'll be glad to talk to you," Beals replied, "just as soon as I finish this game."

The game dragged on, and Bleasdale grew impatient. "I'm rather busy," he said. "Why don't you come to the barracks for supper?" Bleasdale replied. We eat at six and the boat doesn't leave until ten. You'll have plenty of time to make it."

Now Beals remembered the Puntarenas innkeeper's warning. Was this a trick to make me miss my boat? he wondered.

"I'm sorry," he said, "but I have invited friends to eat with me on board. Why don't you join us?"

Bleasdale agreed. He made no attempt to arrest Beals, but used the occasion to present a passionate argument to justify the US Marines' presence in Nicaragua.

"This is a nasty job we have here," he said. "We're going to get it in the neck from the American public whether we succeed or fail. We're only trying to help out the Nicaraguans."

"It seems to me," Beals said, "that the only ones you're helping out are a bunch of lickspittle politicians."[105]

That night, the *Corinto* sailed for San Jose, a small port town on Guatemala's Pacific coast. Here again, Beals's arrival was expected. The military commandant who boarded the ship told Beals he could not land, by order of Guatemalan President Lázaro Chacón González (1873–1931).

The reasons for the order were never made clear, but Beals's Sandino stories, also published in the Guatemalan papers, along with plans afoot for a pro-Sandino demonstration in Guatemala City that week, were probably the key factors.

Another influence might have been Beals's description, in an article in *Current History* in 1926, of the previous Guatemalan President José Maria Orellana (1872–1826) as "of mixed Indian and Negro blood—a zambo."[106] At the time, Beals's Mexican diplomat friend posted in Guatemala City, Luís Quintanilla, told him that race-conscious Guatemalan officialdom was "scandalized" by the reference.[107] Beals himself had been oblivious and, in fact, had come away from his interview quite favorably impressed by Orellana.

Now, however, Beals fumed as he was held in limbo aboard the ship for three days. The *Corinto* remained anchored some distance from shore, separated by a sandbar, which slowed down unloading, as freight had to be ferried across the shallow harbor to the San Jose dock in light boats. He fired off radio messages to the American Minister in Guatemala, as well as dispatches describing his situation to all the papers he could think of in Central America, to pressure the Guatemalans into relenting and letting him disembark. Finally, thanks to an entreaty by the US Minister to Guatemala, Arthur H. Geissler, President Chacón conceded and authorized that Beals be allowed to disembark, but ordering him to leave Guatemala within forty-eight hours.

Finally, on March 28, 1928, he reached Mexico City. Here again, his return qualified as news for the local press. Both major dailies, *El Universal* and *Excelsior*, sent reporters to interview him. Beals savored his scoop. This newfound fame allowed him to poke ridicule at usually impassive US diplomatic and military authorities, many of whom had caused him grief in the past. Suddenly, he commanded their respect on his own terms.

He told the Mexican reporters that, "if Sandino had the arms and the ammunition, he'd have 10,000 men with him and he would march into Managua and be received as a hero."

"The Marines say Sandino's men don't know why they are fighting," he sniffed. "But the truth is that the Sandinistas know better why they are fighting than the Marines . . . I suppose the Marines are fighting for the Monroe Doctrine."[108]

Just days after his return, the exiled Cuban student leader and Communist Party activist Julio Antonio Mella invited Beals to speak at a rally organized by the Manos Fuera de Nicaragua (Hands Off Nicaragua) committee, to raise money to treat wounded Sandinistas. The April 1 meeting drew a standing-room only crowd of more than five thousand, packed into the Fabregas theatre hall. When Beals, dressed in a formal dark suit, white hankie in pocket, was introduced, the crowd rose to its feet in thunderous applause. It was the largest audience he had ever addressed.

A bit awkwardly, Beals—always uneasy as a public speaker—allowed that the ovation unnerved him even more than the US airplanes on bombing raids over Nicaragua. Finding his stride, he paid tribute to the crowd's expression of solidarity.

"The fact that I could go and interview Sandino without a hair on my Nordic head being touched shows that people can understand one another, over the top of the capitalist interests that seek to pit one against the other," he said. "The American people are healthy and even idealistic, but corrupted by a group of governors and businessmen who represent there what the group of Díaz, Moncada and (Venezuelan dictator Juan Vicente) Gómez represent here."

He concluded by repeating a phrase which he said Sandino had asked him to transmit: "I want you to know that not all Nicaraguans are bandits, and not all the bandits are Nicaraguans!" The crowd leapt to its feet once again.[109]

Beals's Nicaraguan adventure and his sympathetic portrait of Sandino boosted opponents of Coolidge's Nicaragua policy, whose April 14, 1928, picketing of the White House was broken up by police who arrested 107 demonstrators.[110] It won him kudos in the journalistic community too, turning him into a prominent writer literally overnight. While Lester Markel, the *New York Times*' Sunday editor, now regularly sought Beals's contributions to the newspaper, his notoriety also sealed his reputation in the US State Department as an unfriendly critic who warranted close monitoring.

Alexander Weddell, American Consul General in Mexico, dispatched a note to the US Secretary of State, accompanied by a copy of *El Libertador*, the newsletter of the Hands-Off Nicaragua Committee, in which Beals's address at the Fabregas theater was reported. This address, Weddell wrote, was "of the type generally to be heard at gatherings of this character, being marked by abuse of the United States, Wall Street and its prominent representatives, etc."[111]

With his freelance status, unusual depth of knowledge of Latin America, and his journalistic talent, Beals would prove himself able, over more than a decade, to build his reputation while thumbing his nose at US officials, whom he often dismissed as "stuffed shirts." But eventually, the tide shifted, and the effects of officialdom's disapproval grew insidiously destructive.

## NOTES

1. Victor Navasky, "Oswald Garrison Villard," *School of Cooperative Individualism* (1990), https://www.cooperative-individualism.org/navasky-victor_oswald-garrison-villard-1990.htm (accessed May 20, 2021).

2. Sara Alpern, *Freda Kirchwey: A Woman of "The Nation"* (Cambridge, MA: Harvard University Press, 1987), 33.

3. U. S. National Archives and Records Administration (NARA), US Diplomatic Records for Nicaragua, Record Group 84, Volumes 82–88, College Park, Maryland, Managua, 1928, vol. 083 (hereafter cited NARA).

4. Dana Gardner Munro, *The United States and the Caribbean Republics, 1921–1933* (Princeton, NJ: Princeton University Press, 1974), 246–47.

5. Salomon de la Selva, "Sandino," *Nation*, January 18, 1928, 63.

6. Carleton Beals, *Great Guerrilla Warriors* (Englewood Cliffs, NJ: Prentice-Hall, 1970), 94. Karl Bickel, president of United Press, told Beals in an interview that the State Department required such collaboration in return for its protection. "It was either play ball or not provide *any* service," Beals quoted him as saying.

7. Harold Norman Denny, *Dollars for Bullets: The Story of American Rule in Nicaragua* (New York: L. MacVeagh, Dial Press, 1929; reprint Westport, CT: Greenwood Press, 1980), 332.

8. Henry L. Stimson, *American Policy in Nicaragua: The Lasting Legacy* (New York: Markus Weiner, 1991; original publication, 1927), 35.

9. Carleton Beals Collection (CBC), Howard Gotlieb Archival Research Center, Boston University, box 143 (hereafter cited CBC).

10. See Carleton Beals, "Under the Fifth Sun" (unpublished autobiography, c. 1972–1978), CBC.

11. CBC, box 143.

12. This narrative of Beals's journey to Sandino's camp draws from various sources within the Carleton Beals Collection (CBC) at the Gotlieb Archival Research Center at Boston University, including drafts of Beals's "Under the Fifth Sun" (unpublished autobiography); Beals's correspondence with *Nation* editor Freda Kirchwey and with Beals's parents during his trip; and in Beals, *Great Guerrilla Warriors*, 74–98.

13. Munro, *United States and the Caribbean Republics*, 178.

14. Munro, *United States and the Caribbean Republics*, 174.

15. See Lester D. Langley, *The Banana Wars: United States Intervention in the Caribbean, 1898–1934* (Wilmington, DE: Scholarly Resources, 2002), 177–79.

16. Munro, *United States and the Caribbean Republics*, 192.

17. Betty Glad, *Charles Evans Hughes and the Illusions of Innocence: A Study in American Diplomacy* (Urbana: University of Illinois Press, 1966), 244.

18. Lawrence Dennis, "Revolution, Recognition and Intervention," *Foreign Affairs* 9, no. 2 (1931): 213–14, https://doi.org/10.2307/20030344 213-14.

19. See Litton Wells, "Mexico's Bid for Supremacy in Central America," *New Republic*, May 18, 1927, 348–50.

20. Emily S. Rosenberg, *Financial Missionaries to the World: The Politics and Culture of Dollar Diplomacy, 1900–1930* (Cambridge MA: Harvard University Press, 1999), 85; Denny, *Dollars for Bullets*, 242–47.
21. Carleton Beals, "Mexico Seeking Central American Leadership," *Current History* 24, September 6, 1926, 840.
22. Denny, *Dollars for Bullets*, 252–53.
23. Dennis, "Revolution, Recognition and Intervention," 214.
24. Thomas F. O'Brien, *The Revolutionary Mission: American Enterprise in Latin America, 1900–1945* (Cambridge: Cambridge University Press, 1996), 65–66.
25. George Black, *The Good Neighbor: How the United States Wrote the History of Central America and the Caribbean* (New York: Pantheon, 1988), 25.
26. Beals, *Great Guerrilla Warriors*, 81. See also Denny, *Dollars for Bullets*, 78–79, who claimed, based on his journalistic investigation, that the $600,00 furnished by Adolfo Díaz on behalf of the US government to back the Mena revolt against Madriz, though a "Liberal assertion," was nonetheless credible as, he wrote, "there is little doubt that foreigners contributed to the revolution whose early success they greeted so rapturously."
27. Carleton Beals, "The Nicaraguan Farce," *Nation*, December 15, 1926, 631–32.
28. Stimson, *American Policy in Nicaragua*, 32.
29. Stimson, *American Policy in Nicaragua*, 50; and Instituto de Estudio del Sandinismo, *General Augusto C. Sandino* (Managua: Instituto de Estudio del Sandinismo/Editorial Nueva Nicaragua, 1986), 14.
30. Carleton Beals, *Mexican Maze* (Philadelphia: J. B. Lippincott, 1931), 337.
31. Michael J. Schroeder, "Horse Thieves to Rebels to Dogs: Political Gang Violence and the State in the Western Segovias, Nicaragua, in the Time of Sandino, 1926–1934," *Journal of Latin American Studies* 28, no. 2 (1996): 399, https://doi.org/10.1017/S0022216X00013055. For an analysis of the impact of the coffee economy on rural life in northern Nicaragua in the early twentieth century, see also Jeffrey L. Gould, "Vana Ilusión!": The Highlands Indians and the Myth of Nicaraguan Mestiza, 1880–1925," in *Identity and Struggle at the Margins of the Nation-State*, ed. Aviva Chomsky and Aldo Lauria-Santiago (Durham, NC: Duke University Press, 1998), 52–93; and Julie A. Charlip, "At Their Own Risk: Coffee Farmers and Debt in Nicaragua, 1870–1930," in *Identity and Struggle at the Margins of the Nation-State*, ed. Aviva Chomsky and Aldo Lauria-Santiago (Durham, NC: Duke University Press, 1998), 94–121.
32. Schroeder, "Horse Thieves to Rebels to Dogs," 427.
33. Schroeder, "Horse Thieves to Rebels to Dogs," 416.
34. Neill Macaulay, *The Sandino Affair* (Chicago: Quadrangle Books, 1971), 54.
35. Macaulay, *Sandino Affair*, 54.
36. Macaulay, *Sandino Affair*, 56.
37. Macaulay, *Sandino Affair*, 61.
38. Macaulay, *Sandino Affair*, 103, 247.
39. Carleton Beals, *Banana Gold* (Philadelphia and London: J. B. Lippincott, 1932), 180.
40. Beals, *Banana Gold*, 185.
41. Logan Feland to Charles Eberhardt, American Minister in Managua, July 9, 1928, NARA, US Diplomatic Records for Nicaragua, RG84/82-88.
42. Logan Feland to Charles Eberhardt, July 9, 1928, NARA.
43. Caffery to Kellogg, January 17, 1928, NARA, US Diplomatic Records for Nicaragua, RG84/82-88.
44. Caffery to Kellogg, January 17, 1928, NARA.
45. Caffery to American Legation, Managua, January 30, 1928, NARA, US Diplomatic Records for Nicaragua, RG84/82-88.
46. Harold N. Denny, "Marines Again in Battle, Lose 1 Killed, 5 Wounded; Nicaraguans Well-Armed," *New York Times*, January 3, 1928, 2.
47. Beals, *Banana Gold*, 191.
48. Beals, *Banana Gold*, 233; and Macaulay, *Sandino Affair*, 88.
49. Beals, *Banana Gold*, 233.
50. Instituto de Estudio del Sandinismo, *Ahora sé que Sandino Manda* (Managua, Nicaragua: Editorial Nueva Nicaragua, 1986), 317.

51. Adapted lyrics to the song, *La Casita*, by Manuel José Othón (1858–1906), music by Felipe Llera (1877–1942), recorded in 1923 by vocalist Alcides Briceño (1886–1963). https://www.loc.gov/item/jukebox-67326/ (Library of Congress (LOC) audio-recording, accessed May 31, 2021).

52. Author's translation.

53. Beals, *Banana Gold*, 253–54.

54. Beals, *Banana Gold*, 265–66. This and the previous passage are slightly adapted, by Beals, from his original dispatches to the *Nation*, "With Sandino in Nicaragua," (IV. "Sandino Himself), *Nation*, March 14, 1928, 288–89, and (V. "Send the Bill to Mr. Coolidge") *Nation*, March 21, 1928, 314; these formed a series printed in the *Nation*, February 22 & 29, 1928; March 7, 15, 21 & 28, 1928.

55. Beals, *Great Guerrilla Warriors*, 88–89.

56. Beals, *Banana Gold*, 272.

57. Beals, *Banana Gold*, 273.

58. Beals, "With Sandino in Nicaragua, V. Send the Bill to Mr. Coolidge," *Nation*, March 21, 1928, 317.

59. Beals, "With Sandino in Nicaragua, V. Send the Bill to Mr. Coolidge," *Nation*, March 21, 1928, 316.

60. Beals, "With Sandino in Nicaragua IV, Sandino Himself," *Nation*, March 14, 1928, 289.

61. Beals, *Banana Gold*, 274.

62. Beals, *Banana Gold*, 276–77.

63. Eberhardt to Secretary of State, February 2, 1928. NARA, US Diplomatic Records for Nicaragua, RG84/82-88.

64. Beals, *Banana Gold*, 291–92.

65. Carleton Beals, "The McCoy Election Law," *Nation*, April 4, 1928.

66. Beals, *Banana Gold*, 291–94.

67. Beals, *Banana Gold*, 292.

68. Beals, "McCoy Election Law."

69. See Andrew J. Bacevich, *Diplomat in Khaki: Major General Frank Ross McCoy and American Foreign Policy, 1898–1949* (Lawrence: University Press of Kansas, 1989), 114–37.

70. Bacevich, *Diplomat in Khaki*, 135.

71. Elvina Beals to Villard, March 12, 1928, CBC.

72. *La Noticia* and *La Prensa* (Managua), February 11 and 12, 1928, CBC.

73. Carleton Beals to Freda Kirchwey (on board the *Corinto*), March 1928, CBC.

74. Carleton Beals, "Fighting in Managua Soon, Sandino Predicts," *Washington Post*, February 11, 1928.

75. US Rear Admiral Sellers, quoted in "Mexico and Central America," *Current History*, April 1928, 122–23.

76. US Senate. Hearings before the Committee on Foreign Relations. *Use of the United States Navy in Nicaragua*. 70th Congress, 1st Session, Pursuant to S. Res. 137, Use of the United States Navy in Nicaragua. February 11 and 18, 1928, on February 11, 1928, 1.

77. US Senate. Hearings before the Committee on Foreign Relations. *Use of the United States Navy in Nicaragua* (1928), 9; and "New Fights Predicted by Sandino," Associated Press file quoting Carleton Beals, *Los Angeles Times* (among others), February 11, 1928, 3.

78. US Senate. Hearings before the Committee on Foreign Relations. *Use of the United States Navy in Nicaragua* (1928), 9.

79. "Rebellion Spreads in North Nicaragua," Associated Press file in *New York Times*, October 22, 1927, 3.

80. "Nicaragua Fighting Rouses Congress to Attacks Policy," *New York Times*, January 5, 1928, 1–2.

81. "Marines' Fathers Bitter," *New York Times*, January 5, 1928, 2.

82. Bacevich, *Diplomat in Khaki*, 127.

83. Robert David Johnson, *The Peace Progressives and American Foreign Relations* (Cambridge, MA: Harvard University Press, 1995), 133. See also United States Congressional Record, US Senate, April 24, 1928, 7042.

84. Johnson, *Peace Progressives*, 135.

85. Rosenberg, *Financial Missionaries*, 237.
86. Stimson to White, September 2, 1927, in Francis White Papers (FWP), Milton Eisenhower Library, Johns Hopkins University, Baltimore (hereafter cited FWP).
87. "1,000 Additional Marines are Ordered to Nicaragua to Quell Sandino Revolt,"*New York Times*, January 4, 1928, 3.
88. US Senate. Hearings before the Committee on Foreign Relations. *Use of the United States Navy in Nicaragua*. 70th Congress, 1st Session, Pursuant to S. Res. 137, Use of the United States Navy in Nicaragua. February 11 and 18, 1928, on February 11, 1928, 27.
89. Freda Kirchwey to Carleton Beals, March 30, 1928, CBC.
90. US Congress, *Congressional Record*, 70th cong., 2nd sess., vol. 70, pt. 6 (December 3, 1928 to March 4, 1929), 9–236, https://www.govinfo.gov/app/details/GPO-CRECB-1929-pt6-v70/GPO-CRECB-1929-pt6-v70-1 (accessed May 13, 2021), see entry for March 20, 1928.
91. Eberhardt to Kellogg, March 6, 1928; Kellogg to Eberhardt, March 7, 1928, NARA, US Diplomatic Recrods for Nicaragua, RG84/82-88.
92. "Newspaperman is Held," *New York Times,* February 10, 1928, 4.
93. Munro to White, November 4, 1927, FWP.
94. Munro to White, November 4, 1927, FWP.
95. Carleton Beals, *Glass Houses: Ten Years of Free-Lancing* (Philadelphia: J. B. Lippincott, 1938), 298.
96. See Edward S. Herman and Noam Chomsky, *Manufacturing Consent: The Political Economy of the Mass Media* (New York: Pantheon, 1988).
97. Michael J. Schroeder, "Bandits and Blanket Thieves, Communists and Terrorists: The Politics of Naming Sandinistas in Nicaragua, 1927–36 and 1979–90," *Third World Quarterly* 26, no. 1 (2005): 83, https://www.jstor.org/stable/3993764.
98. Edward S. Herman, "The Propaganda Model Revisited," *Monthly Review* (July 1996).
99. Godfrey Hodgson, *The Colonel: The Life and Wars of Henry Stimson, 1867–1950* (New York: Knopf, 1990), 84.
100. Lars Schoultz, *Beneath the United States: A History of US Policy Toward Latin America* (Cambridge, MA: Harvard University Press, 1998), 271.
101. See *La Noticia* and *La Prensa* (Managua), February 11 and 12, 1928, CBC.
102. Beals, *Banana Gold*, 324.
103. Beals, *Banana Gold*, 325.
104. Beals, *Banana Gold*, 338.
105. Beals, *Banana Gold*, 344–46.
106. Beals, "Mexico Seeking Central American Leadership," *Current History*, September 6, 1926.
107. Luis Quintanilla to Carleton Beals, September 6, 1926, CBC.
108. *Excelsior*, March 30, 1928, CBC.
109. *El Machete*, April 7, 1928, CBC.
110. "Arrest 107 Pickets at the White House," *New York Times*, April 15, 1928, 21.
111. American Consulate General, Mexico City, June 6, 1928, no. 1579, Subject: Citizenship of the United States; Beals Carleton, Anti-American Activities of, copy in CBC.

*Chapter Seven*

# Mexican Maze

Just three-and-half months after Beals's return to Mexico City, the country was thrown into sudden turmoil by the assassination on July 17, 1928, of General—and President-elect—Álvaro Obregón. The veteran military chief and former president had been drawn back into politics after a short retirement on his chickpea farm in Sonora. An improvised constitutional reform had enabled his re-election as president for a second time, just seventeen days before.

In the absence of political parties in Mexico, Obregón had gained power through a kind of triangulation strategy that earned him the support of disparate, even opposed groups: the Mexican Army, radical peasantry, and conservative foreign investors.

During his first presidential term in the early 1920s, Obregón had mended his differences with the United States by shrewdly playing off British oil companies with holdings in Mexico against American ones. This won him grudging respect in Washington. The President Warren G. Harding's administration found it expedient to recognize his government as a result, and settle outstanding claims, mostly so that the California oil tycoon Edward L. Doheny's wells in the Mexican desert would be saved from expropriation.

This time, Obregón's support from the landless poor made Washington uneasy, as the president-elect would surely have to respond to their "radical" demands. This was counterbalanced, however, by his closeness to President Plutarco Elías Calles and friendliness to foreign capital, which offered some reassurance that the cordial relations US Ambassador Dwight Morrow had cultivated with Calles could be sustained.

At home, Obregón remained the object of visceral disgust among Catholics. Together with Calles, Obregón had pressed for the anti-clerical laws that triggered the *Cristero* War. First, the two Sonora political bosses had brought the Church under the thumb of the state, as they sought to neutralize the Vatican's counter-revolutionary influence. Then, they manipulated the Chamber of Deputies and Senate into amending the Constitution to allow Obregón to run a second time, succeeding Calles. The organizing purpose of Mexico's revolution—"No to Re-election!"—was stood on its head.

Their maneuvers had already triggered one attempt on Obregón's life. In November 1927, a conspirator had thrown a fire bomb at Obregón's passing limousine. Within two days, the would-be assassin and Padre Humberto Pro, a Catholic priest allegedly involved in the plot, were shot by a firing squad, without trial.

This was the context in which José de León Toral, a quiet and slight man of twenty-eight years old, nudged his way to the head table at which Obregón sat during a luncheon celebrating his recent election victory. A member of a shadowy cult of Catholic extremists, Toral—who called himself Escapulario (scapular, a Christian garment worn on the shoulders)—was on what he considered a divine mission to rid Mexico of its heretic leader. He had gained entry to La Bombilla, a fashionable restaurant of airy rooms in San Angel where the banquet was being held, by posing as a caricaturist from a local magazine, sketching personalities attending the event. The festive ambiance provided cover for Toral's approach. No suspicions were raised as the young man quickly penciled a profile of the president and showed it to him.

The ever-affable Obregón was pleased and agreed to Toral's request to remain close to him to perfect his sketch. Toral then drew a pistol from his coat and pumped five bullets into Obregón's back. As the president slumped forward, dying, Toral announced, "It was I who did it."[1]

Beals learned about the murder from a newsboy's cries of, "The President is shot! The President is dead!" later that afternoon, as he was leaving his apartment on Minerva Street. He was suddenly stirred from a relaxing week during which he had been showing his parents around Mexico City. Elvina and Leon Beals, full of pride at their son's newfound status as a journalist of some stature, had come down from Berkeley for their first-ever visit to Mexico.

Beals now covered the investigation and Toral's subsequent trial for the *New York Times*. One result of his Augusto César Sandino scoop was that Lester Markel, the *New York Times*' Sunday editor, had taken notice of Beals. The week before, Markel had commissioned him to produce a profile of Obregón upon the Mexican leader's election as president. Oddly, the piece, headlined, "Obregón: Bold Master of Mexico," was published five days after the assassination, as the magazine had been printed beforehand and could not be recalled. In it, Beals predicted "a greater test" for Morrow in establishing friendly relations between the United States and Mexico under Obregón than with Calles, as the president-elect's status as champion of the peasantry clamoring for land, placed his political interests in opposition to those in the United States who sought a more moderate regime.[2]

Now, of course, Beals's cables to the *New York Times*—and to the *Nation*, whose editor Freda Kirchwey also asked him for a piece—focused instead on the ascetic-looking assassin and on the political jockeying that followed the murder. Toral, it turned out, belonged to a group of young men devoted to one "Madre Conchita," a large-framed self-styled "nun" whose imposing stature and charisma impressed Beals. "She . . . was not overly physically attractive, yet in few women have I ever sensed greater, more potent sex appeal. There was something diabolic in her physical magnetism, something monstrously primitive, yet supremely sophisticated."[3]

Madre Conchita and Toral faced trial together in a crowded second-floor courtroom of San Angel's *Palacio de Justicia*. Again, Beals, like many Mexicans and almost in spite of himself, could not help but be impressed by the co-defendants. The "pale, neurasthenic" Toral, Beals wrote, was "completely calm, his sunken eyes glowing with a strange fire. He was sure of himself, of his role, his righteousness."

In a strange way, the defendants' self-possession seduced the spectators at the trial. The bitter images of the government's underhanded waging of the war against Catholics, including the killing of Father Pro without trial just months before, were reawakened in many minds, Beals reported. Toral and Conchita, meanwhile, "bested the State's prosecution at every turn of phrase, every bit of repartee."[4]

The government's frustration was evident. It reversed itself on a promise to broadcast the courtroom drama on radio, and cleared most of the onlookers from the building, claiming that its creaking structure could not hold them. Then, toward the close of the trial, about fifty members of the Chamber of Deputies burst into the courtroom. Outraged at the growing public sympathy the defendants had elicited, they shouted angrily at the defense attorney and the jury, waving pistols and threatening them with death, while yelling obscenities at Madre Conchita.

Toral was convicted and executed in February 1929, while Madre Conchita was sent to Islas Marías prison for twenty years. Toral's funeral was attended by thousands and marked by clashes between mourners—passively approved by the Church—and the police.

These events were the high-water mark of a shift in the Mexican Revolution, and in Beals's perception and journalistic rendition of it. The Cristero War, in which lay the roots of Obregón's assassination, opened a yawning wound in the Mexican Revolution that was never really resolved. Calles manipulated events following Obregón's murder, to seize control of the government and hold it for another six years, pulling the strings behind a succession of three presidents who did his bidding. It was called the "Maximato," and it at once institutionalized the revolution while destroying its momentum.

This new approach began with Calles delivering a "political testament" to Congress on September 1, in which he declared an end to the era of *caudillos*; it was a statement rich in irony, coming from a general whose nickname was "El Jefe Máximo" (Supreme Chief).

The *Maximato* began with the 1928 appointment as interim president of Emilio Portes Gíl (1890–1978), nominally an Obregón loyalist and Governor of the state of Tamaulipas.

With Obregón having been murdered by a Catholic, the government suspended its talks with Church leaders aimed at ending hostilities and stepped-up repression against the *Cristero* movement. By 1929, the *Cristeros* had twenty thousand fighters, concentrated in Jalisco—which Beals had visited in 1927—Guanajuato, Colima, and Michoacán. Even if their offensives never really threatened the government's survival, putting down the rebellion was slow, and atrocities committed by the army complicated the situation. [5]

Meantime, Calles's determination to end the domination of Mexican politics by military cabals was immediately challenged by two generals, José Gonzalez Escobar and Francisco Manzo, who launched a military revolt in the northern states.

In an analysis of the military uprising in *Current History* magazine—then owned by the *New York Times*—Beals classified it as a reaction against the progress of the Revolution. "They hate Calles, not because he has violated the law of the land, but because he has curbed [the generals'] power to plunder," Beals wrote. Comparing this latest revolt to two previous failed military plots, in 1923 and 1927 respectively, he noted that the old-time supremacy of the militarists was "seriously menaced" by the social improvements brought by Obregón, Calles, and Portes Gíl. However imperfect, land reform, rural schools and farm credits, irrigation investments, as well as the freedom to organize for self-betterment, were all material changes that had gained support on the countryside. [6]

These disruptions coincided with US Ambassador Morrow's continuing effort to cultivate a sounder relationship with Mexico, aimed at protecting the Mexican holdings of US oil and mining companies, and the banks that financed them. With Obregón out of the way, Morrow's ham-and-eggs breakfasts with Calles found a restored influence. For their part, Calles and Portes Gíl, and the ruling elite over which they presided, had grown wealthy in power, and now sought US capital investment, along with military aid to put down both the *Cristeros* and rebellious generals.

As he had done in 1927, Morrow once again persuaded the Mexican president to reopen negotiations with Church leaders. The Church, with Vatican approval, had suspended celebrations of Mass, baptisms, and marriages, to protest Mexico's anti-clerical edicts, which included the closing of religious schools and deportation of 200 foreign priests. With Morrow's sponsorship, however, the two sides soon came to terms, and the churches reopened for Mass again in June 1929.[7]

Calles' determined consolidation of power and drift to the right was also reflected in mounting repression directed at the Communist Party. Although it was small and vastly outweighed nationally by labor and peasant organizations whose leaders were members of—or had been co-opted by—ruling elites, either in the capital or the states, many intellectuals, artists, and expatriates, such as Diego Rivera and David Siqueiros, were Communist Party members.

Communist Party influence in Mexico had achieved a fleeting zenith in mid-1928, as Obregon's election had been supported by the Mexican Communist Party, along with its allied railway workers' union and National Peasants' League, which claimed to have 300,000 members. The much-bigger and more influential Confederación Regional Obrera Mexicana (CROM), meanwhile, was about to lose its inner-circle status as Calles prepared to relinquish power to Obregón. Even with Obregón dead, this shift was set in motion.

In an effort to calm the waters and maintain a hold on power after the shooting and Toral-Madre Conchita trial, Calles, Congress and the army had settled on the choice of Portes Gíl as interim president, in large part, *because* of his ties to Obregón. Portes Gíl, no fan of Luís Morones, pushed the once-powerful CROM to the margin.

Calles, meanwhile, devoted himself to backroom politics and to creating a new revolutionary party machine, the first step in building the one-party corporatist state model that would control Mexican politics for the rest of the century. In this enterprise, Beals reported in the *Nation*, Calles was no longer interested in supporting Morones and the CROM; indeed, to do so would contradict and undermine Portes Gíl, whom Calles himself had named to the Presidency.[8]

But the Communist Party, which Portes Gíl hitherto had tolerated, now stepped over the line in trying to seize control of the labor movement. Its activists organized workers' and peasants' marches against a new labor code Portes Gíl had introduced, provoking violent clashes and repression in the states of Durango, Veracruz, Coahuila, and Jalisco. Communist Party activists reacted to the military repression that ensued by denouncing the most Left members of Portes Gíl's cabinet, and calling on soldiers to refuse orders to fire on demonstrators.

This stretched state tolerance to the breaking point. Portes Gíl, already facing a military rebellion, and seeking an end to the Cristero War, banned the Communist Party outright in March 1929.

\*\*\*

The hard edge of anti-Communist repression had already sent shock waves through the lives of Beals's circle of friends. On January 10, 1929, Julio Antonio Mella, the Cuban student revolutionary leader, was gunned down as he walked home on a Mexico City street.

Mella was fine-featured, his aquiline nose and classic profile calling to mind an Athenian statue. These natural endowments were joined with an eloquence and aplomb beyond his twenty-five years of age. He combed his longish, wavy black hair straight back over his head in a way that drew attention to a prominent brow. His skin was richly toned, his lips sensuous, cheekbones high, and he held his listeners with an intense gaze, inspiring many to join in the political struggles to which he was devoting his life.

In 1923, he had unveiled his gift for leadership by directing a students' strike at the University of Havana, demanding and getting the dismissal of teachers whom the students considered anachronistic, inefficient, or corrupt. He also articulated the students' call for free education, among other demands.[9]

Just over a year later, however, the tide turned when Gerardo Machado (1869–1939), a gregarious general, was elected president of Cuba. Machado's path to office was eased by a campaign financed by the US-owned Electric Bond and Share Company, which owned most Cuban utilities, and of which Machado himself was vice-president.[10] It also involved intrigue, deal-making with the army and intimidation at the polls.

Mella quickly declared his opposition to Machado and was soon expelled from the university and jailed on charges of terrorism. He launched a hunger strike, which sparked a popular campaign for his release. When Machado ordered Mella freed in December 1925, the young activist left for exile in Mexico City.

In Mexico, Mella joined an international network of Cuban expatriates seeking Machado's removal and, more broadly, an end to Cuba's dependency and subservience to the United States. His links to the Communist Party, which had been tenuous in Cuba, deepened in Mexico. By the summer of 1927, he was organizing, with other exiles, the Mexican effort in the international campaign to exonerate Sacco and Vanzetti, Italian anarchists on trial in New York—and eventually executed—on a widely-contested charge of murder. A year later, inspired by Sandino's example and foreshadowing Fidel Castro's thirty years later, Mella organized a guerrilla expedition that was to set out for Cuba by boat from Veracruz. It was aborted when an informer alerted Machado, thereby prompting the Cuban dictator to target Mella for assassination.

It was during this period that Mella met Tina Modotti. By early 1928, they were working closely together on the Communist newspaper *El Machete* and had fallen in love. They had even informed the Party's Central Committee of their relationship, as the rigid party discipline required. Julio

Antonio asked Tina to move into his apartment on Abraham Gonzalez Street, where they lived as a couple, committed to one another, and to the international Communist struggle. Beals was their neighbor and friend.

Mella and Modotti were walking home together, arm in arm, from an evening Party meeting on January 10, when at least one gunman, perhaps two, stepped from the shadows behind a billboard. Two shots were fired. Mella collapsed, fracturing his elbow as he hit the cobblestoned street. "Machado has done this!" he cried.

An ambulance arrived. Its attendants collected Mella, bleeding from abdominal wounds, and rushed him to the hospital where, incredibly, medical treatment was delayed as police questioned him about the incident.

Neighbors who had witnessed the shooting quickly informed Mella's friends, including Frances Toor, who scribbled a message to Beals and slipped it under the door of his apartment, urging him to go to the General Hospital.

Mella was still alive when Beals got there. Three surgeons struggled to save his life, but it was slipping away. "It was agonizing to see the blood gradually drain from his face and body," Beals recalled. "He was one of the finest, most brilliant men I have ever known."[11] The memory of Mella's final hours was henceforth etched in Beals's memory and would prompt him to travel to Cuba three years later, to research and write a book denouncing Machado's crimes, and what he saw as US complicity in them.[12]

The Mexican police response to Mella's murder further disgusted Beals and his circle. Mexico City police chief Valente Quintana, the man who had tracked down Obregón assassin Toral's links to Madre Conchita, disingenuously concluded that Mella was likely murdered by Tina Modotti. Already succumbing to a grief that stamped dark sockets around her eyes, Modotti found herself in a struggle to clear her name, now linked to the murder in the screaming headlines of Mexico City's dailies.

Beals remained in Mexico City as he and Modotti's friends, including Diego Rivera, made a point of showing up to be photographed as the police staged a re-creation of the crime, to publicly pressure the authorities to drop all charges against her.

*\*\*\**

Just weeks later Beals, depressed and dismayed by these events, returned to the United States for a lecture tour organized by his publisher. He had spent four consecutive years in Mexico by this point—save for the two trips to Central America—and was keen to spend some time in the United States, and tour Europe, including the Soviet Union. The lecture fees would help cover the cost of the travel.

Beals disliked the lecture circuit routine; he got bookings through his publishers easily enough, but his strident views did not always play well with audiences. When discussing issues about which his opinions were fiercely held, his denunciations were sometimes so caustic as to alienate those accustomed to more decorum in public discourse. More than one of his publishers received a complaint from the host about his podium performance.

After this tour of five cities including New York, Beals undertook a whirlwind five-month trip to Europe traveling through Spain, Morocco, Algeria, Tunisia, by boat from Tunis to Palermo, and then from Italy to Turkey, across the Black Sea to Odessa, and then by train to Kiev, Baku, Moscow, Leningrad (St. Petersburg), and returning by boat through the West Pomeranian port of Stettin (now Szczecin), and then Berlin.

In Spain, Beals looked up his friend, Mexican author Martin Luis Guzmán (1887–1976), who introduced him to a *tertulia*, or regular gathering of literary figures, held at Madrid's Café Regina. Here, he met intellectuals who would soon emerge as key leaders in the Republican government which would take power just two years later, starting the chain of events which culminated with the Spanish Civil War (1936–1939).

The *tertulia*'s leading lights included the playwright Ramón del Valle Inclán, the writer and future Second Republic President Manuel Azaña, and Julio Álvarez del Vayo, a socialist journalist who later, as Foreign Minister of the Republican government, would lead the diplomatic effort to secure Joseph Stalin's (1878–1953) support for the Republican side in the civil war.[13]

With Guzmán as his guide—a man so trusted by Azaña that the latter placed him in charge of the pro-government daily *El Sol* during the Second Republic—Beals gained access to a network of privileged experts, upon whom he drew heavily for a four-part series on Spain published in the *Nation* in the summer of 1929.[14]

In these dispatches, Beals depicted the dictatorship led by Falange Party founder Miguel Primo de Rivera as a corrupt prop for the weak King Alfonso XIII (1886–1941; r. 1886[1902]–1931). The regime relied for its survival, he wrote, on generals returned from the outposts of a collapsed empire, notably in Morocco, where Spanish troops had been routed in the early 1920s by nationalist Berber rebels led by Abd el-Krim. This Spanish military cadre, having lost its colonial vocation, now turned its attention to ruling Spain.

As Beals told it, the generals colluded with an over-privileged Roman Catholic hierarchy to shore up Primo de Rivera's rule, backing his press censorship and suspension of rights of assembly, in their shared goal of stopping the mounting challenge to it, led by socialists and communists.

While sympathetic to the latter two parties, Beals was pessimistic about the ultimate prospects for success of this embryo of what would later become the Popular Front that led the Second Republic. Primo de Rivera's dictatorship was an "opera-bouffe enterprise" in Beals's assessment, but it still held sway, in large part due to its alliance with the country's clerical elite and the

100,000-odd priests, nuns and monks who controlled the educational system. Outwardly at least, this group supported the regime, whose cabinet was composed almost entirely of generals.

The left-wing Republicans' program aimed at ending repressions of church and militarist state seemed an enticing prospect, as Beals heard it—and reported in the *Nation*—from its leaders Azaña, Indalecio Prieto, and Alvaro de Albornoz, just out of jail.[15] It included overthrow of the monarchy, the breakup of the large estates in the south, an enlightened labor code, the separation of church and state, an end to ecclesiastical privileges, and the creation of an independent judiciary.

But these same Republicans were also "woefully split," Beals reported.[16] And the separatists in Catalunya, whose support might have decided the outcome, were themselves ably manipulated by Primo de Rivera, and not in a position to offer a national solution. These observations were prescient in foreshadowing some of the factors in the collapse, a decade later, of Spain's Second Republic after three years of civil war.

From Spain, Beals crossed the Strait of Gibraltar to Ceuta, and spent several days touring the Moroccan cities of Chechaouen, Tangier, Fez, and Casablanca, before taking trains to Algeria, with stops in Oran and Algiers, and finally, Tunis. From Tunis, he took a berth on the overnight ferry to Sicily. It was a short, nostalgic return to Italy, which he had first visited in a penniless state almost a decade earlier with his now long-estranged first wife, Lillian.

By August, Beals entered the Soviet Union, alighting at Odessa after crossing the Black Sea from Istanbul aboard the *Tchitcherin*, an antiquated passenger vessel painted bright red, and named for a Soviet foreign minister.

Russia was a rude awakening for Beals. Given his work as TASS correspondent in Mexico and the close relations he had entertained with Soviet diplomats there as a result, he might have expected a warmer reception. As it was, he was greeted at Odessa by soldiers armed with bayoneted rifles, herding him along with the other passengers, from one luggage search to another in a process that lasted most of the day.

"This *is* dictatorship," Beals wrote in a chronicle of his trip. "Mussolini is just a child at this sort of thing."[17]

Over the course of his tour, Beals found in Stalin's regime a "lust for intrigue [grown] into a monstrosity," with its "shadow of authority always peering over your shoulder," prompting Muscovites to talk in whispers. Twelve years after the Bolshevik takeover, he concluded, Russia had progressed a great deal in material terms, but at the cost of smothering the lives of a whole generation in dark terror.[18]

"He got a jolt in Russia," Anita Brenner wrote shortly after a reunion with Beals upon his return to Mexico a few months later. "It wasn't as pretty as he romantically had imagined the carrying out of his ideas might be. In fact, he found it distinctly ugly and irksome to his individualistic, chip-on-the-shoulder, short man's character."[19]

Beals did not publish any journalistic accounts of his two-week Soviet tour, as he did not consider himself qualified to write about Russian matters. His purpose was to satisfy his curiosity while trying "to maintain an open mind," thereby developing an understanding of the Stalinist system that would inform his analyses of international affairs. He did, however, devote about a third of his 1940 memoir, *The Great Circle: Further Adventures in Free-Lancing*, to a "personal chronicle" of his stops in Odessa, Kiev, Baku, Moscow, and Leningrad.

It is a compelling account, told from the distance of an intervening decade during which Stalin's purges and show trials became widely known, along with evidence of the 1932–1933 forced famine in Ukraine. Beals ventured into Soviet Russia alone, without official guides or minders. He was consequently not allowed, despite his repeated requests to officialdom, to see cooperative farms, schools, factories, or hospitals. At the same time, he experienced a Russia unsweetened by any diplomatic charm offensive.

His story is peppered with incidents in which Russian officials, waiters, hotel concierges, train conductors, and taxi drivers treat him with discourtesy and disdain. While feeling unwelcome throughout his visit, he was at once conflicted as his illusions were shattered one by one.

He seems, for example, strangely forgiving in relating a tale involving agents of the GPU, the secret police.[20] An American engineer he met on the train from Odessa to Baku, one Henry Blake, told him that he had been arrested by the GPU for having illegally imported the drug salvarsan to distribute to workers suffering from syphilis at the Baku oil refinery at which Blake was employed.

After holding Blake for questioning in Moscow for several days, the GPU finally released him, with warm congratulations. "The GPU boys are pretty tough babies," Beals quoted Blake as saying. "But the men I saw impressed me as trying hard to do what they thought to be right." While Beals acknowledged abundant evidence that the GPU fabricated false political plots to justify the murder of Stalin's enemies, he also placed the GPU in a larger context, comparing it to all police forces that serve dictators elsewhere.

"Nearly every Russian and Mexican revolutionist I have ever met has had this greedy ego, this lust for dictatorial authority, coupled with harsh intolerance," he wrote. "Certainly Stalin is the type of dictator, schooled in long violence and intrigue, now raised to the status of God by his adulators, who is unable to tolerate the slightest whiff of personal criticism."[21]

While in Moscow, Beals was invited for dinner at the home—a made-over carriage house—of United Press correspondent Eugene Lyons and his wife. In 1935, Lyons caused a sensation with a *mea culpa* article in *Harper's* magazine, later expanded into a book, *Assignment in Utopia*.[22] In both, he recanted his previously laudatory reports on life in the Soviet Union filed during his six-year posting, especially his earlier denunciation of the British journalist Gareth Jones's account of the Ukraine famine as a fabrication. *Assignment in Utopia* also influenced George Orwell; its chapter, "Two Plus Two Equals Five," referring to Stalin's push to achieve the goals of the Five-Year Plan in four years, resurfaced in altered context as a theme in *Nineteen Eighty-Four*, Orwell's imaginary totalitarian dystopia.[23]

Beals found the "intense, self-contained" Lyons to be "already considerably soured" with the Soviets as early as 1929, when he had been there only a year. "He parried my questions, but several times remarked in an ironical tone that some of my own statements smacked of heresies," Beals recalled.[24] The delayed memoir of Beals's visit is informed not only by the subsequent tumultuous history of the 1930s in Russia and worldwide, but also by Beals's own maturing through his participation in the fractious debates within the international political left during those years.

Although Beals neither joined the Communist Party, nor adhered to its doctrine, his leftist inclinations and anti-imperialist views are reflected in his journalistic accounts that often seem at pains to present Soviet and American systems—and their respective imperialist designs—as two sides of a coin. He balanced criticism of the Soviet system's police apparatus, in a typical example, with a jab at racial inequality in the United States.

As for the US version of foreign intervention, his analytical framework anticipated critiques of US foreign policy by C. Wright Mills, Cold War revisionist historian William Appleman Williams and the libertarian anarchist academic Noam Chomsky. In all his political writings, Beals held to the contention that US foreign policy was directed by and for an elite that dominates America's banks, corporations, government, military—and media. This serving of *elite* interests was aimed, ultimately, at maintaining an Open Door to enable US corporations to invest, extract resources, and market their products overseas with little or no regard for local implications and consequences. Beals argued that the single-minded pursuit of these elite interests had resulted in US foreign interventions and policies that were often wrongheaded, costly, and damaging to the *public* interest, both in America and abroad. Still, he was not a Communist. He was an anti-ideologue, deeply suspicious of all political leaders, parties, and dogma.

A real Communist sensed this immediately. One such was Joseph Freeman, who took over Beals's contract as correspondent for TASS in Mexico City, after Beals—his trip to Russia having aroused his disgust at Stalinism—abruptly decided in 1929 to stop working for the Soviet news agency and asked that his name be removed from the masthead of *New Masses*, the pro-Communist magazine. Freeman, a Communist Party member since 1921, had been working in the New York City TASS—or Rosta, as it was then known—office with Kenneth Durant. He had spent several months in Mexico in 1929, where he stood in for Beals during the latter's European tour.

While there, Freeman met and fell in love with Ione Robinson, a lithe, sensitive, and strikingly attractive twenty-year-old artist working as an assistant to Diego Rivera on a Guggenheim fellowship. At the time, Rivera had started work on his frescoes in Mexico's National Palace.[25]

Back in New York, the newlywed Freeman couple hosted Beals at their apartment upon his return—by way of Mexico—from Europe.

"I don't understand how Joe could invite [Beals] after criticizing him so," Ione wrote in her diary. "Joe complained all last summer that [Beals] never really covered the news well in Mexico because of his bourgeois background."[26]

\*\*\*

Before leaving for Europe, Beals had submitted the manuscript for his first novel, *Destroying Victor*, to Macauley publishers.[27] He returned to find it had been published. It is a strange concoction, in which Beals unwittingly reveals some of the demons that plagued his inner world, undermining his peace of mind and often giving a hard edge to his perceptions of the forces driving events and people.

Angie Rosser, an aspiring poet from Texas with whom Beals had had a brief love affair in the early 1920s, put her finger on it in a review of the novel, published in the *Dallas News*: "With savage intensity, the author reveals an appalling meanness, an illuminating vice, or some inane vacuity in each of his puppets. Knowing Mr. Beals to be the kindest and most humane of gentlemen, I find this fact curious. Somewhere in *Brimstone and Chili* [his memoir of his discovery of Mexico, published in 1927] he describes the Mexican cantinas as, "an unending, entrancing spectacle of human depravity." I think perhaps this is the way Mr. Beals has chosen to view life."[28]

Beals would have four novels published during his lifetime. All of them must qualify as attempts rather than successes, as they were flawed, some spectacularly so. This is certainly true of *Destroying Victor*. The plot is so utterly improbable as to be laughable: it revolves around Henry Proctor Scroggin, a priggish classics professor at a small-town west coast university who is also a member of the local censorship board. Scroggin grows so besotted with Yvonne Dadant, a French actress he has invited to star in a campus staging of *Medea*, that he leaves his wife, Minnie, for her. This enrages a former suitor of Yvonne's, Elbert Maples, who just happens to have recently married Charlotte, one of Scroggin's two daughters. But Maples is still in love with Yvonne, and visits her at her hotel. In a fit of jealousy, he stabs Yvonne to death. Her body is discovered by Scroggin, who is falsely charged and convicted of the murder. The hapless Scroggin, his marriage and career in tatters, is jailed. A trial eventually exonerates him, and he is released from prison.

After his release, his fortunes slide. He becomes a skid-row vagrant. Almost overnight, though, he is redeemed as a Socialist Party newspaper editor, a politician, and finally, as an advertising executive. In the end, he remarries his wife Minnie and is thereby restored to domestic tranquility and self-respect.

Beals's *Destroying Victor* is a shambles of a story, fantastic in incident, with characters like paper maché stereotypes or discordant composites that give the reader no grounds for recognition in real life. Such a haphazard pastiche would hardly earn him a pass in a fiction-writing seminar. It is hard to fathom how it got published. In the event, it was dismissed by most reviewers who, nonetheless, seemed to restrain themselves even when faced with such a palpably bad book. Perhaps they were influenced by Beals's reputation based on his recently-celebrated journalism and three earlier nonfiction works, all of which had won reviewers' respect. "The style is sometimes adolescent," said one, while another allowed that the novel's theme "has been outmoded time and again" and lamented that Beals "is not yet at ease in this [novel] form."[29]

In considering Beals's overall legacy, it is probably judicious—and charitable—to overlook most of his fiction. His brother Ralph implicitly offered this counsel to a would-be biographer, warning that while Carleton was "a first class reporter or journalist . . . I'm afraid he was an inept novelist."[30]

Katherine Anne Porter, in reviewing Beals's 1936 novel of Mexico, *The Stones Awake*, described his fictional method as, "kidnapping his characters whole and sound out of real life" instead of imagining them. This, she said, made it impossible for him to "follow his characters into the locked doors of their hearts and minds because he did not create them."[31]

The same criticism applies to *Destroying Victor*, many of whose characters were closely drawn from people Beals had known, namely his father Leon, his first wife Lillian, and of course, himself. Even so, amid the pottage of ill-conceived invention, one finds some sharply observed reportorial gems. This sketch, for example, of 1920s California Socialist Party activists in their newspaper office, is wrought from close-up intimacy:

> A small railed-in reading-room was hung with perpetual tobacco-smoke, carpeted with expectoration, and fragrant with the odor of unwashed bodies. The loungers who frequented these dingy rooms were like the building itself, run down at the heels—shabby earnest people with soft, pleading eyes, misfits, on the whole, men with strange visions but no capacity for wrenching from society a decent existence. To the regular meetings, however, came a group somewhat higher on the social scale; men with trades, and their wives, small shopkeepers, the lower fringe of the middle-class, and clerks—"white-collar slaves," they facetiously called themselves . . . All were sincere, honest people

with considerable moral courage that comes from true conviction, people whom the world, for some strange reason feared; but, if the world only knew it, harmless people, with few exceptions quite satisfied to have their candidates on the ballot, to listen to wild speeches instead of paying for tickets to melodrama, and to scatter leaflets in defiance of city ordinances.[32]

\*\*\*

In November 1929, Beals returned to a "clear zestful fall" in Mexico City. After his eight-month absence in Europe, he was flattered to be asked to sit for a feature interview by the daily *Excelsior*. The story, "El periodista Carleton Beals ha regresado a nuestra capital" (Journalist Carleton Beals has returned to our capital)" reflected a growing notoriety; it was also published in the major Central American dailies.[33] In it, he tells the reporter that his firsthand experience of Stalinism taught him that Mexico, despite its devastating civil wars, had "recovered much more rapidly than Russia." Even if subject to "unruly ambitions" and its share of brutality, Mexico remained a society trying to improve itself without being "hammered half-lifeless" by dogmatism. "Mexico might have had a revolution—one was not always sure of it—but the deep-rooted culture was a spreading tree that had not been stripped."[34]

Beals's upbeat assessment soured quickly. His return coincided with the November 17 election as Mexican president of Pascual Ortiz Rubio (1877–1963), the first-ever candidate for the Partido Nacional Revolucionario (PNR). Ortiz Rubio, fully backed by Calles' military and political machine, easily defeated José Vasconcelos, the former Mexican Secretary of Education, despite the latter's vigorous campaign. Vasconcelos, who in the early 1920s brought education to the Indians and dreamed of the Latin-American *mestizos* (people of mixed race) as a new *raza cosmica* (cosmic people/race), had since moved to a pro-Catholic position, leading a self-styled campaign under the banner of the opposition "Anti-Re-election Party."

Vasconcelos, "round head and stubby short hair constantly betokening a frenzied seriousness," Beals wrote, "was an impetuous man, of an experimental and imaginative turn of mind, full of eager ideas, but in no sense an able executive."[35] He got five percent of the vote according to the official count and denounced the election as a fraud. Three weeks later, Vasconcelos issued a Guaymas Plan in which he called on his supporters to take up arms against Ortiz Rubio, while he himself went into exile in the United States.

As the political right—represented by Vasconcelos—found itself fighting for survival, so too did the extreme left. Mexico's Communist Party, now clandestine, still enjoyed Stalin's support and was egged on into aggressive anti-government tactics by Communist International organizers dispatched from Moscow. The Mexican Communists were now in declared opposition to the government, calling for a peasant uprising.³⁶ Portes Gíl, in his last weeks as interim president, reacted by ordering raids in December on the offices of communist youth, peasants, and workers organizations. At the same time, the Mexican foreign minister, Genaro Estrada, announced that Mexico was rupturing diplomatic relations with the Soviet Union.

This was a dramatic reversal. Mexico had had a revolution, it was true, but it was not a Bolshevik one. Its characteristic *ideology*—to the extent that it had one—had always been more nationalistic, more rooted in the Mexican liberal reformist tradition of Benito Juárez, than it was inspired by Marx and Lenin. Still, Mexico was the first *New World* country to establish diplomatic ties with the Soviets. Even if those relations blew hot and cold through the mid-1920s, the Soviet legation enjoyed a prominent status in Mexico City. As Mexico correspondent for the Soviet news agency TASS during this time, Beals witnessed the shifting tides of this relationship up close.

He got to know—and gain the trust of—three successive Soviet ambassadors. First, there was the booming-voiced Stanislav Pestkovsky, brusque and tactless, but also jovial and friendly. Pestkovsky mixed with the artistic circle around Diego Rivera, openly cultivated the Communist unions, while disparaging Morones and the CROM. He also lavished funds on the Communist *El Machete* newspaper.³⁷

Pestkovsky was followed by Alexandra Kollontai, an elegant fifty-year-old Ukrainian aristocrat who had written a marriage manual in Russia. Fluent in English and fond of the company of younger men, she often asked Beals to guide her on horseback rides around the Valley of Mexico. The last Soviet envoy was Alexandr Makar, a plump sybarite and former physician who had become a career diplomat under the Soviet regime.

When the Mexican foreign ministry issued a communiqué announcing Makar's expulsion, Beals rushed to the Soviet embassy on Eliseo Street. In happier times, he had been a frequent guest there at Makar's dinners, where abundant food was oddly served on frayed and ragged table linen.

Beals found himself in the odd role of informing Makar of what had transpired; he "hadn't the slightest inkling that this was brewing." Indeed, he reflected, it was ironic that this particular ambassador should be held responsible for Mexican Communist Party agitation. Makar's choice of company was in keeping with his preferred attire of morning coats, tails and silk hats. He "scarcely allowed [Communist Party activists] to step inside the Legation, or, if he did so, very secretly," Beals wrote. Instead, he "cultivated . . . the best society he could wedge into."³⁸

Several days later, however, Makar found himself headed for Veracruz to board a steamer bound for Russia. Before leaving, Mexican police arrested him long enough to confiscate most of his trunks as supposed evidence of Soviet espionage and intrigue.

Two months later, another wave of repression was unleashed when Ortiz Rubio—just inaugurated—was shot in the jaw as he sat in the back seat of his car leaving the National Palace. His wife and a niece were also injured in the February 1930 attack.

Ortiz Rubio survived the assassination attempt but was traumatized by it and reacted by demanding a roundup of critics and opponents of his government, especially Communists, whose hand he suspected in the plot on his life.

Bruce Bliven, who had taken over from the dying Herbert Croly as editor of the *New Republic*, asked Beals for an article that would assess the veracity of the Vasconcelist charges of electoral fraud, as well as describe the government's conservative tilt and break with the Soviets.

"The new government has abused its power . . . and is moving to the right in every sense of the word and in a most brutal fashion," Beals replied in a letter. "This, naturally, will provide fuel for the Vasconcelistas. The government is using the attempted assassination of Ortiz Rubio to persecute all of its political enemies . . . but this does not necessarily justify Vasconcelos."[39]

Indeed, Beals took a dim view of the "erratic, egoistic" Vasconcelos and the constituency he sought to represent.[40] It was a middle- and upper-class movement in a rough-and-tumble revolutionary society, which sought, somewhat idealistically, to gain power through an appeal for a moral recovery in Mexico, rather than by cutting deals among army officers, labor and peasant leaders, the Church, and foreign capital. Later, many historians would adjudge Vasconcelos' ill-fated candidacy to be a defining moment in which Mexico missed its opportunity to transform its revolution to a functioning democracy.

But Beals, still convinced that Calles, warts and all, was best equipped to steer Mexico through this new round of turmoil, disparaged the Vasconcelos candidacy for playing to "reactionary student elements, some fanatic religious old ladies, and the fairy-like sons of the aristocrats." As for Vasconcelos' program, he found it to be, "a marvel of mystical obfuscation and brilliant verbal pyrotechnics meaning nothing."[41]

Along with his letter to Bliven, Beals cabled an article detailing the anti-Communist repression. It would get him into trouble.

Soon after the cable was sent, Beals was seized in his apartment by two men who took him to the Valley of Mexico's military headquarters, where he was interrogated by General Eulogio Ortiz [no relation to Ortiz Rubio], the local Commandant.

Eulogio Ortiz had ordered the arrest, Beals surmised, after reading a reference to himself in Beals's cable to Bliven, which the military censor had intercepted. In the cable—which was published in the *New Republic* a week later—Beals cited allegations against Ortiz of embezzling funds, making arbitrary arrests, and even torturing a detained labor leader. He also recounted a tale told by Ernest Gruening in his recently-published *Mexico and Its Heritage*, in which General Ortiz was said to have seized several bulls from a rancher to turn them over to his personal friend, a bullfighter who wanted them to organize a highly profitable corrida.[42]

While the offending article likely played some role in it, Beals's arrest was more directly caused by his well-known association with Communists and their sympathizers. Already, close to twenty foreign Communists had been deported, and some 150 people associated with the political left, including two of Sandino's representatives in Mexico, had been jailed.[43]

Determined to inform the US embassy of his arrest, Beals insisted on typing out a letter to the US chargé d'affaires before leaving his rooftop apartment with the plainclothes military officials sent to pick him up.

But the officials' patience quickly wore thin. They snatched the letter from him and hauled him out of his apartment by force. But as they bundled him into their car, Beals's shouts drew the attention of his neighbor, an expatriate American writer named Susan Smith. She quickly informed the embassy.

"Hijo de la verga," (son-of-a-bitch) Eulogio Ortiz shouted as Beals stood before him at the headquarters. He waved a carbon copy of the offending cable Beals had sent Bliven two days earlier. "Can you prove the things you say in these letters?"[44]

An agitated Beals replied that his own "illegal" arrest was proof, in part, of Ortiz's abuses. "Take him and lock him up incommunicado," Ortiz ordered his aides.

"We'll deport you," he growled at Beals, who was then taken to a basement room, joining about a dozen political prisoners from across the spectrum, mostly students, Vasconcelistas, Communists, a labor leader, and a few Catholics.

Meantime, Susan Smith had contacted the US military attaché, a Colonel Gordon Johnston, who presently showed up at the Commandant's headquarters.

Ortiz remonstrated with Johnston, showing him Beals's offending cables, but relented and released Beals to his custody.

\*\*\*

As the summer of 1930 approached, Beals decided he needed a change of scenery after his encounter with General Ortiz. Upon learning that Harry Block, the editor who had handled the *Brimstone and Chili* manuscript for the Knopf publishing house, was to visit Mexico, Beals proposed that the two of them set off on a five-week ramble on horseback through the mountains of the southern state of Oaxaca.

Block's interest in Mexico had been sparked not only by editing Beals's book, but also as a result of sharing his New York City apartment with the

Mexican cartoonist Miguel Covarrubias. On this summer tour, Block would meet Marilú Cabrera, daughter of Carranza's finance minister Luis Cabrera, whom he would marry a year later.

Tapping his contacts in the government, Beals obtained an introductory letter to the Oaxaca's state superintendent of federal schools, Rafael Ramírez. Block and Beals spent several days in Oaxaca City, enjoying nighttime drinks in its storied *zocalo* with Ramírez and other state officials, before embarking on their journey. Ramírez was proud to show off his effort to establish schools in the state's most remote villages, so he assigned the pair a Mixtec Indian teacher as a guide, and loaned them four mules.

The two roughed it at a leisurely pace, enjoying ceremonious welcomes with brass bands and processions in Indian villages such as San Sebastián Etla, San Augustín Etla, Cuicatlán, and Valeria Trujano. In the latter, they were serenaded upon waking with a traditional *mañanita*, a "haunting melody [that] invades one's consciousness like a slow caress," as Beals described it.[45]

This tour reminded him that despite the slide of many revolutionary leaders into abuses of power and corrupt self-enrichment, Mexico's Indians had still made gains. "They had been serfs on the hacienda until a few years before," he wrote. But now, they had their communal lands, and despite their poverty, they had their schools.[46]

Beals underlined these observations in *Mexican Maze*, on which he was working through 1930. It was published the following year by J. B. Lippincott, an established Philadelphia-based house boasting a list of top-drawer authors. Arguably among his best books, it combined redrafted articles that had appeared earlier in Howard Phillips' *Mexican Life* magazine, with new material.

Its twenty chapters provide a broad survey of Mexico's revolutionary society. One chapter describes pastoral village life in Tepoztlán, near Mexico City. Another relates the day-to-day interactions between a local chieftain who has embraced the revolutionary state, and the bitter priests whose earlier mantle of leadership he now holds. The book also explores the oil boom, the growing machine age, street theatre, and crisp observations of the emerging painters and writers whose work both defined—and was defined by—the Revolution.

In several chapters, including an introductory "The Maze," Beals foreshadows aspects of Octavio Paz's *El laberinto de la soledad* (*The Labyrinth of Solitude*) (1950). His portrait of Mexico's collective psychology is remarkably similar to that developed a generation later by Mexico's Nobel laureate:

> Underneath the involved functioning of the Mexican Mind is the stolid, fantastic, brooding temperament of the native races, a disturbing interplay of hidden

purposes, too subtle for ready analysis, complicated by centuries of oppression. This lends a gargoyle externality to Mexican thinking and art. This grotesqueness of conduct and aesthetics results from the unruly surge of forces beneath the crust of political disorder—a baffling labyrinth, a jungle of cross-purposes . . . a series of blistered layers of so-called civilizations holding down the seething native life, which . . . bursts to the surface and flows over government and institutions, leaving long black scars.[47]

At one level, a passage like this has a purplish tinge, but at another, it offers insight into the complexity and contradictions in the Mexican national character, a theme Paz made his signature. In both Beals's *Maze*, and Paz's *Labyrinth*, we find parallel observations: the Mexican's outward formality and reticence, combined with a love of ceremony and fiesta, the *masks*, the simultaneous coexistence—often in the same person—of exaggerated courtesy and grotesqueness, an obsession with death and the afterlife, and the ever-present, lurking threat of violence in both art and life, a simmering tension always ready to explode.

Elsewhere in the same book, which confirmed Beals's status as one of America's foremost interpreters of Mexico, he delivers a knowing assessment of the Mexican Revolution's singularity: it "had no prophet and no body of positive theory; it was obliged to formulate its own ideology and own program as it went along, a halting, fumbling, misdirected series of experiments that have brought the masses little but a sense of freedom—a freedom not too easily demonstrable."[48]

Its depth and variety complemented by seventy-five evocative pen-and-ink illustrations by Diego Rivera, *Mexican Maze* enjoyed a generally warm reception from reviewers. Another Latin-Americanist and novelist, Waldo Frank, writing in the *New Republic*, paid tribute to Beals for having "a grasp of the country's myriad phases which few Mexicans can equal." He added, however, that Beals had failed to bring order to his observations, so that readers are left, "as if we had visited a maze . . . [where we have] dimly sensed a principle of life—an order and direction; and we know that this principle would be an inestimable treasure, if it were made so clear that we could assimilate and use it."[49]

Other reviewers such as Arthur Ruhl, who had covered the Spanish-American War when Beals was still a child, made a similar critique, lamenting that the "solid value of his firsthand observations . . . is marred pretty generally by his fierce determination to make the reader sit up and take notice of him as a writer, cost what it may."[50] On balance, however, these were quibbles. *Mexican Maze* was selected as one of the year's fifty notable books by the American Association of Libraries.

As the summer of 1930 waned, Beals decided "on a whim" to join his riding companion Harry Block, as well as their mutual friends Warren Vinton and Helen Augur, on a passenger ship to New York City. He was still feeling at loose ends in Mexico after the episode with General Ortiz and thought some time in Manhattan would rekindle his spirit.[51]

It was not long before he was back in Mexico. It was his signature subject, he quickly realized, giving him a more secure source of income than anything on offer in Manhattan. This was all the more evident, as the freelance journalism market narrowed with the Great Depression that had descended on America in the wake of the 1929 Wall Street crash.

\*\*\*

Having decided—for now—to settle in Mexico for a longer time, Beals moved to a house at 11 Avenida Ave Maria, in Coyoacán, just outside Mexico City. Coyoacán, an uncommonly pastoral setting so close to the huge metropolis, offered a more upscale domesticity than Beals had ever experienced. His house on the cobblestoned street lined by adobe walls garlanded with bougainvillea and hibiscus, exuded a relaxed elegance. And, flush with the success of *Mexican Maze*, Beals could now afford hired help in the form of Petra, a Mexican housekeeper.

This move from an apartment to a house was prompted mostly by his sudden romantic involvement with a twenty-six-year-old schoolteacher from San Antonio, Texas, Elizabeth "Betty" Daniel. Beals left few clues as to where or how he met Betty, an attractive redhead, but their marriage seemed to their friends to be a bolt out of the blue. The wedding ceremony at Cortes Palace in Coyoacán was held on August 17, 1931, with Beals's journalist friends Howard Phillips, John Lloyd, and Charlie and Eleanor Nutter in attendance.[52]

His new marriage seemed to crown success on all fronts. Beals was now at the pinnacle of his career. As America's deepening economic crisis triggered a similar one in Mexico, Beals was riding high. *Mexican Maze* had been chosen for distribution by the Book League of America and was winning accolades everywhere. The *New York Times* regularly commissioned him to write Sunday magazine pieces. And now, the Guggenheim Foundation had granted him its annual Mexico fellowship to research a biography of Porfirio Díaz, Mexico's president who served as president seven times from 1876 to 1911.

Soon after the wedding, Beals prepared for another horseback trip in the states of Guerrero and Oaxaca, accompanied this time by Eyler Simpson, manager of the Guggenheim Foundation's Mexico City office and himself a writer. His purpose was to trace the marches of his biographical subject, Porfirio Díaz, whose road to power had begun with military campaigns, first in the war against the dictator Santa Anna, and then in Benito Juárez's army, in which he rose quickly to the rank of general during the resistance against French troops who had invaded Mexico in 1862. The army was sent by

Napoleon III (1808–1873), whose imperial ambition drove him to try to seize Mexico by force on the pretext that it had defaulted on its debt to France.

While Beals and Simpson rode off into the back country, Betty, whose romance with Beals had flourished during what was, for her, an extended visit to Mexico, found herself married, but nonetheless left alone in Coyoacán, and without a purpose.

Although her union with Beals had begun under nearly idyllic conditions, its joys were soon mixed with frustration and growing bitterness as they found their temperaments and life plans to be wholly incompatible. Beals's footloose way of living and his hardboiled rejection of mainstream American values soon grated with Betty. She was, by her own admission, high-strung and nervous. "A truly appalling upper-middle-class female with all the false values of a genteel Texas background," was how Carleton's brother Ralph, whom the couple once visited in California, remembered her.[53]

As inconceivable as it was for her to rough it in Mexico's highlands, so it was just as unlikely that Beals would ever accommodate her idea of settling in San Antonio where she would teach school and live close to her parents. Only weeks after their hastily-arranged marriage, she left for San Antonio, naively thinking, perhaps, that Beals would eventually join her there.

Beals and Simpson, meanwhile, spent five weeks following Díaz's march during the 1860s campaign against the French imperial army. In Oaxaca, not only the site of numerous battles and skirmishes through Díaz's life as a soldier and officer, but also his birthplace, Beals explored La Toronja (the grapefruit), the house in which the future *caudillo* had spent his boyhood. Díaz's father had cured animal hides in its courtyard there, while his mother and sisters spun cotton yarn, with which they wove *rebozos* (shawls). Beals also visited the school Díaz had attended as a boy, the convent at which he had studied briefly for the priesthood, and La Noria (water wheel), the ranch bestowed upon Díaz years later by a grateful nation to reward him for having trounced the French.

Beals's research on Díaz was thorough in the style of an investigative journalist. He tracked Díaz as if his subject had only recently departed, seeking out local archives and even surviving contemporaries who might shed light, however fleeting, on an episode in the great man's life.

In addition to the horseback ride with Simpson, Beals made separate trips to Puebla, site of Díaz's most famous battle and where he was also twice imprisoned. He toured the old fortresses to reconstruct the events of May 5, 1862, in which then-Colonel Díaz had led a victorious cavalry charge against the French army. The Battle of Puebla, after which Díaz was promoted to general, is now immortalized in the *Cinco de Mayo* (May 5th) celebrations marked by Mexicans everywhere.

Returning to his Coyoacán house after this and other research trips to Veracruz, Querétaro and the Valley of Mexico, Beals threw himself into drafting a manuscript of 1,200 pages in just six weeks, "in forced sittings, not even taking off Sundays."[54]

By the eighth draft, he had trimmed it down to six hundred pages. Published in 1932 by J. B. Lippincott as *Porfirio Díaz: Dictator of Mexico*, it was generally well-received by American reviewers. Its exhaustive research was applauded for having broken new ground in detailing Díaz's thuggish methods, including assassination, throttling the press, and violating civil rights.

The biography's coverage of the Porfiriato's ignominious aspects challenged most existing accounts that had emphasized Mexico's economic expansion and industrial development during the years of the Porfiriato. It also counterbalanced those observers who focused on the dictator's selection of the so-called *científicos* (scientists) for his cabinet in the latter part of his rule, as if this absolved Díaz from responsibility for his repressive regime.

While the *New York Times*' reviewer found it "a superb picture of a remarkable personality," some others regretted his "occasional descent to vulgar invective against Díaz" and "melodramatic" style.[55]

Two years after its appearance in English, the book stirred an academic controversy when the Mexican weekly, *El Universal Ilustrado* (The Illustrated Universal), translated and published it in a serialized version. As Beals's account of the Porfiriato was among the first of its kind to be published in post-revolutionary Mexico, popular interest in the pirated *El Universal Ilustrado* series reportedly boosted the magazine's circulation.[56]

It also sparked indignation among some survivors of the *científicos* circle. Salvador Quevedo y Zubieta, an author, historian, and former diplomat under Díaz, was outraged that Beals's account had singled him out for having been "subsidized to write a eulogistic biography of Díaz," and also for having served the dictator as a "pamphleteer."[57]

In addition to having produced histories and novels, Quevedo y Zubieta was also a prestigious physician. Seventy-five years old in 1934, he was embarrassed that his earlier role as an apologist for the Díaz regime was suddenly dredged up in a post-revolutionary society that would disapprove of it. Even more galling to him was that this public opprobrium was triggered by an American!

In a blistering attack published in *Excelsior*, Quevedo y Zubieta took particular aim at Beals's account of the administration led by General Manuel González (1833–1893), president of Mexico from 1880 to 1884. Quevedo y Zubieta, author of widely-respected biographies of both Díaz and González—respectful and protective of the former, harshly critical of the latter—took issue with Beals's reversal of this interpretation.

Four years after seizing power, Porfirio Díaz had nominated González, his *compadre* and loyal fellow officer, for president. Díaz, despite having himself been Finance (*Fomento*) Minister throughout much of González's term, sharply criticized the González administration's handling of a monetary crisis provoked by the Mexican government's decision to honor a debt owed to Britain. By 1884, Díaz was already distancing himself from earlier decisions in which he had played a role as Minister, leaving González to take public responsibility for the economic crisis that ensued.

Beals gave an unusually positive review of the González administration in his book, claiming that it "certainly . . . instituted more industrial progress than all previous administrations put together, and more than any single administration after him."[58] But despite Manuel González's unswerving loyalty to Díaz, the latter had sought to discredit him as his term neared its end in 1884. He wanted to make sure González would not seek to remain in power for another term, and the best way to do that was to smear him. Or so Beals presented the case.

But Quevedo y Zubieta, in his account, *General González and His Government*, depicted the González administration as being rife with corruption. Díaz, he wrote, far from seeking to escape blame for the crisis, had intervened to rescue the country from González's misrule, marked by alleged misuse of public funds to support the lavish lifestyles of mistresses he had imported for his pleasure from Russia and Europe.

This Quevedo y Zubieta version, seen as the definitive one in Mexico, was described by Beals in *Dictator of Mexico* as "a violent, pitiless, though undocumented exposé . . . a brilliant but unreliable piece of pamphleteering [that] has been the chief source of information about the González administration."[59]

Quevedo y Zubieta reacted with furious pique. "This American gentleman," he retorted in *Excelsior*, "who came to Mexico to prepare a book on "the dictator Porfirio Díaz" is satisfied with listening to this or that friend or relative of former President Manuel González and repeats what these biased observers told him in response to his rapid tourist's questions . . . this mister Carleton Beals has not even checked his testimonials in our libraries."[60]

In fact, Beals had befriended González's grandson Enrique, who gave him access to the former president's archives, hidden on the family's ranch in the state of Tamaulipas. Beals was "able to read every letter he had ever written while president and many others, and also go through his own diary and personal account books."[61] He found it "incredible" that the impression of González that emerged from these documents was "the exact opposite to that which had been painted for half a century."[62]

It led Beals to conclude that, even if González's government was tainted by corruption, this was no different than any other Mexican administration before or since. González, he wrote, "was probably the most honest president Mexico ever had." He also judged it "a filthy business" that Díaz had stirred up opposition to González, to which Quevedo y Zubieta "had loaned himself and his talent—for a very rewarding amount."[63]

Beals responded publicly to Quevedo y Zubieta's critique three days later, also in the pages of *Excelsior*. He was on firm ground in denouncing Quevedo y Zubieta's earlier role as an apologist for the Díaz regime, but less so in defending his failure to respect academic conventions. His decision not to include footnotes to back up his findings and assertions made him an easy target for charges that he was not able to substantiate many of his allegations.[64]

The controversy over the series led the *Ilustrado*'s editors to suspend its further publication on January 3, 1935, after forty-eight installments.[65] For his part, author Beals noted that they did so just before the chapters cataloguing the duplicity of other former Porfirian *científicos*—some of whom were still living in 1935—were to be published.[66]

The weaknesses of *Dictator of Mexico* are balanced by its significant strengths. The nature and first-hand character of the research that Beals undertook—finding personal archives and interviewing dozens of witnesses and near-witnesses—was at once innovatively distinct from that of earlier Díaz scholars, and not replicable by those who followed. The flaws were seized upon by critics like Quevedo y Zubieta and, more recently, by Paul Garner, author of a revisionist biography of Díaz published in 2003, who dismissed Beals's account as "erratic, anecdotal, passionate and anti-Porfirian."[67]

Garner's comment suggests that the debate around Porfirian historiography has not been laid to rest. But, along with the polemics provoked by Quevedo y Zubieta, it does help us to locate Beals's account in that historiography as the first "anti-Porfirian" treatment, between the earlier "Porfirian" apologists' school, and the later "neo-Porfirian" school to which Garner belongs.

# NOTES

1. "Slayer Is Young Cartoonist," *New York Times*, July 18, 1928, 1, https://timesmachine.nytimes.com/timesmachine/1928/07/18/91695893.html?auth=login-email&pageNumber=1.

2. Carleton Beals, "Obregon: Bold Master of Mexico," *New York Times Magazine*, July 22, 1928, https://www.nytimes.com/1928/07/22/archives/obregon-bold-master-of-mexico-the-presidentelect-strides-into.html.

3. Carleton Beals, *The Great Circle: Further Adventures in Free-lancing* (Philadelphia: J. B. Lippincott, 1940), 207.

4. Beals, *Great Circle*, 207.

5. Lorenzo Meyer, "El primer tramo del camino" (The First Leg of the Journey), in *Historia General de México*, 4th ed., ed. Daniel Cosío Villegas (México City: El Colegio de México, 1994), vol. 2, 1191.

6. Carleton Beals, "Mexican Military Adventurers in Revolt," *Current History* 30, no. 2. (May 1929), 222.

7. Meyer, "El primer tramo del camino," 1190–91.

8. See Carleton Beals, "Mexico's Labor Crisis," *Nation*, March 13, 1929; and Beals, "Mexico and the Communists," *New Republic*, February 19, 1930.
9. Luis E. Aguilar, *Cuba 1933: Prologue to Revolution* (New York: W. W. Norton, 1974), 73.
10. Aguilar, *Cuba 1933*, 50; and Carleton Beals, *The Crime of Cuba* (Philadelphia: J. B. Lippincott, 1933), 242
11. See Carleton Beals, "Under the Fifth Sun" (unpublished autobiography, c. 1972–1978), in Carleton Beals Collection (CBC), Howard Gotlieb Archival Research Center, Boston University, 126–28 (hereafter cited CBC).
12. See chap. 8 in this book.
13. After the Civil War ended, Julio Álvarez del Vayo sought exile in the United States, where he became foreign editor of the *Nation*. He was at the center of a celebrated case in 1951, in which the *Nation*'s editor Freda Kirchwey sued rival weekly the *New Leader* for libel over published allegations by a former *Nation* art critic that Del Vayo was using his access to the *Nation*'s columns to spread unfiltered propaganda for Stalin and the Soviet Union.
14. See Carleton Beals, "Spain: The Wreck of an Empire (1)." *Nation*, June 26, 1929; "Spain: How Strong is the Dictatorship? (2)" *Nation*, July 3, 1929; "Modern Spain: Censorship (3)." *Nation*, July 10, 1929; and "Modern Spain: Official Corruption (4)." *Nation*, July 17, 1929.
15. Beals, "Spain," 13.
16. Beals, "Spain," 13.
17. Beals, *Great Circle*, 118.
18. Beals, *Great Circle*, 155–59.
19. Susannah Joel Glusker, *Anita Brenner: A Mind of Her Own* (Austin: University of Texas Press, 1998), 156.
20. Beals used the term GPU to refer to the Russian state security police, whose Russian acronym was, in fact, OGPU.
21. Beals, *Great Circle*, 155.
22. Eugene Lyons, *Assignment in Utopia* (New York: Harcourt, Brace, 1937).
23. George Orwell, *Nineteen Eighty-Four: A Novel* (London: Secker & Warburg, 1949).
24. Beals, *Great Circle*, 181.
25. A stormy affair that combined sexual rivalry and intra-Communist Party schisms erupted after Ione Robinson told Tina Modotti that Diego Rivera had seduced her in July 1929. Modotti told her new companion, Comintern agent Vittorio Vidali, about it and Vidali informed Joseph Freeman, arousing furious jealousy. At the Mexican Communist Party's annual meeting that same month, Freeman was named to "investigate" Rivera's position vis-à-vis the Party; his report led to Rivera's expulsion from the Communist Party in September 1929. See Margaret Hooks, *Tina Modotti: Radical Photographer* (Boston: Da Capo Press, 1993), 188; Bertram D. Wolfe, *The Fabulous Life of Diego Rivera* (New York: Stein and Day, 1963), 266–70; and Ione Robinson, *A Wall to Paint On* (New York: E. P. Dutton, 1946), 106–7.
26. Robinson, *Wall to Paint On*, 126–27.
27. Carleton Beals, *Destroying Victor* (New York: Macaulay, 1929).
28. Angie Rosser, Review of *Destroying Victor* (1929), by Carleton Beals, *Dallas News*, December 29, 1929, CBC.
29. .Carleton Beals, reviews: *New York Herald-Tribune*, October 27, 1929, 14; "A Professor Sees Life," *New York Times Book Review*, November 24, 1929, 7.
30. Ralph Beals to Mel Yoken, October 7, 1982, Melvin B. Yoken Collection (MBYC), John Hay Library, Brown University, Providence, Rhode Island (hereaftere cited MBYC).
31. Katherine Anne Porter, review of *The Stones Awake : A Novel of Mexico*, by Carleton Beals (Philadelphia: J. B. Lippincott, 1936), *New Republic*, November 18, 1936, 82.
32. Beals, *Destroying Victor*, 260–62.
33. *Excelsior*, December 2, 1929. See also Rafael Heliodoro Valle, *El Imparcial* (Guatemala), *El Norte* (San Pedro Sula, Honduras), *El Cronista* (Tegucigalpa, Honduras), *El Diario* (El Salvador), CBC.
34. Beals, *Great Circle*, 199–200.
35. Beals, *Great Circle*, 218.

36. Patrick Marnham, *Dreaming With His Eyes Open: A Life of Diego Rivera* (Berkeley: University of California Press, 2000), 213.
37. Carleton Beals, *Glass Houses: Ten Years of Free-Lancing* (Philadelphia: J. B. Lippincott, 1938), 340.
38. Beals, *Glass Houses*, 345, 355.
39. Carleton Beals to Bliven, February 10, 1930, CBC, box 170.
40. Beals, *Great Circle*, 218.
41. Beals, *Great Circle*, 218–19.
42. Beals, "Mexico and the Communists," 10–12. See also Ernest Gruening, *Mexico and Its Heritage* (New York: Century, 1928).
43. Beals, "Mexico and the Communists," 10–12; and *New York Herald-Tribune*, February 20, 1930.
44. Beals, *Great Circle*, 232–33.
45. Beals, *Great Circle*, 283.
46. Beals, *Great Circle*, 282.
47. Carleton Beals, *Mexican Maze* (Philadelphia: J. B. Lippincott, 1931), 34–35.
48. Beals, *Mexican Maze*, 45.
49. Waldo Frank, Review of *Mexican Maze*, by Carleton Beals (Philadelphia: J. B. Lippincott, 1931), *New Republic*, July 1, 1931, 183.
50. Arthur Ruhl, Review of *Mexican Maze*, by Carleton Beals (Philadelphia: J. B. Lippincott, 1931), *Saturday Review of Literature*, June 20, 1931, 907.
51. Beals, *Under the Fifth Sun* (unpublished autobiography), CBC, box 47.
52. Social News, "Carleton Beals Marries: Author and Lecturer Wed to Elizabeth Daniel in Mexico," *New York Times*, August 18, 1931, 18.
53. Ralph L. Beals, "Memories of My Brother, Carleton Beals." 1982. Prepared for Melvin B. Yoken. Melvin B. Yoken Collection (MBYC), John Hay Library, Brown University, Providence, Rhode Island, 17, undated, but likely August, 1982.
54. Beals, "Under the Fifth Sun" (unpublished autobiography), CBC, 109.
55. R. L. Duffus, "The Strong Man of Mexico – Carleton Beals Writes a Dramatic Biography of Porfirio Díaz," *New York Times Book Review*, November 27, 1932, 1; James C. Barden, "The Mexican Revolution," *Virginia Quarterly Review* (Vol. 10: 1), January 1934, 135–40; Robert Briffault, *Scribner's Magazine* (undated); and C. W. Ervin, *Baltimore Sun* (undated), CBC.
56. Beals, "Under the Fifth Sun," (unpublished autobiography), CBC, 112–13.
57. Carleton Beals, *Porfirio Díaz: Dictator of Mexico* (Philadelphia: J. B. Lippincott, 1932), 247.
58. Beals, *Porfirio Díaz*, 246.
59. Beals, *Porfirio Díaz*, 247.
60. Salvador Quevedo y Zubieta, "Los Generales Presidentes Porfirio Díaz y Manuel González, el Sr. Carleton Beals y Yo" (General-Presidents Porfirio Díaz and Manuel González, Mr. Carleton Beals and me), *Excelsior*, November 9, 1934, 5, CBC; translation of quotation by the author.
61. Beals, "Under the Fifth Sun" (unpublished autobiography), CBC, 117.
62. Beals, "Under the Fifth Sun" (unpublished autobiography), CBC, 117.
63. Beals, "Under the Fifth Sun" (unpublished autobiography), CBC, 117.
64. Beals, "Under the Fifth Sun" (unpublished autobiography, c. 1972–1978), CBC, 109: "I have little sympathy for prevailing academic writing which parades all the authorities and witnesses, with many ifs and ands and voluminous footnotes. It achieves no synthesis and is usually the work of an industrious dullard."
65. Alejandra López Torres, "La biografía 'histórica' de Carleton Beals a través de sus lectores" (The 'historical' biography of Carleton Beals through its readers), *Tzintzun: Revista de Estudios Históricos* 40 (2004): 115. http://www.tzintzun.umich.mx/index.php/TZN/article/view/316
66. Beals, "Under the Fifth Sun" (unpublished autobiography), CBC.
67. Paul Garner, *Porfirio Díaz del héroe al dictador: Una biografía política* (Porfirio Díaz, from Hero to Dictator: A Political Biography) (Mexico: Planeta, 2003), 255, quoted in López

Torres, "La biografia 'historica'"; Beals, "Under the Fifth Sun" (unpublished autobiography, c. 1972–1978), CBC.

*Chapter Eight*

# The Crime of Cuba

Once Carleton Beals had finished his Porfirio Díaz manuscript in December 1931, he and Betty moved out of the house on Avenida Ave Maria in Coyoacán where she had earlier rejoined him and left for New York City. They settled there in a small apartment that rented for $62 a month at 105 East 15th Street, half a block from Union Square.

Within weeks, Beals was planning his next book project, this one inspired by his earlier friendship with the late Cuban revolutionary Julio Antonio Mella (1903–1929), whose tragic final hours he had witnessed in a Mexico City hospital three years before. It was to be an investigation of the regime led by Cuba's President, General Gerardo Machado.

President Machado had been elected by popular vote in 1925 and again in 1928, after which he had manipulated the island nation's Congress to amend the constitution to extend his term from four to six years. In addition to Machado's brutal repression of protests stemming from the economic collapse in Cuba, Beals was convinced that the Cuban ruler had dispatched Mella's assassins to Mexico.[1] He had something of a score to settle.

By early 1932, Machado had contrived to extend his term by yet another year, to 1935, but now faced mounting unrest. The Great Depression in Cuba's largest export market, the United States, had driven down the price and demand for Cuba's sugar, its primary source of income. This was made worse by the US *Smoot-Hawley Tariff* (*Tariff Act of 1930*), which had raised the duty on Cuban sugar to two cents a pound.[2] Cuban sugar producers received less than half the price paid American producers, and the Cuban share of the US sugar market was to drop from half to a quarter in just four years by 1934.[3] From a high point in 1920, of nearly four million tons harvested, with a value of over $1 billion, the crop had dropped by 1933 to less than two million tons, worth only $54 million.[4]

Across the island, unemployment was provoking widespread misery. Even among those who had work, daily life had become a struggle for survival, as sugar mill owners cut output, along with working hours and wages, setting off a wave of strikes and violence. The daily wages of cane cutters and mill operators respectively had fallen from $1.60 and $2.00 in 1929 to $0.50 and $0.80 in 1933.[5]

As popular opposition to Machado grew, he reacted by suspending constitutional guarantees on freedom of assembly and of the press and used Cuba's police and armed forces to put down strikes by sugar workers and by students. Conspiracies against his rule took root, with radical university students and labor unions, along with a more right-leaning, middle-class, corporatist underground movement called the ABC, planting bombs and attacking police stations. These were met by revenge killings meted out by the *Porra*, Machado's secret police. In August 1931, an armed uprising led by the old-line opposition politicians was easily put down by Machado, and its leaders, Carlos Mendieta and Mario García Menocal, arrested.[6]

In addition to his personal motivations for investigating and denouncing the regime, Beals's news instinct told him that Cuba was a cauldron ready to boil over. In late September 1932, he took a train from New York to New Orleans and from there, booked passage to Havana on the *Tela*, a freighter owned by the United Fruit Company. He found its deck cluttered with light armored cars, and its hold loaded with ammunition, all bound for Machado's army to bolster his repression and protect his cabinet and cronies from assassins.

Upon disembarking at Havana in September 1932, Beals checked into the spanking new Ambos Mundos Hotel, in the city's old quarter. Amid Havana's elegant Spanish colonial buildings dominated by its commanding *Capitolio* (Capitol), completed just three years earlier, he was shocked to find, "whole families of starving people . . . piled up under every arcade for miles around the central plaza."[7] His hotel was largely vacant, as the tourism trade had dried up. Within a couple of days, he had relocated to a small apartment across town in Vedado, a tidy residential suburb, and hired a Chinese houseboy to cook his meals.

He had made only one short visit to Cuba before, a week-long stopover on his way to Spain with Lillian in 1920. But this time, Beals had a valuable guide who eased his introduction to the island. He was José Antonio Fernandez de Castro, an editor at the *Diario de la Marina* (Navy Daily Journal), Cuba's oldest newspaper and the only prominent daily that was not owned or controlled by Machado. Beals had first met Fernandez de Castro in Mexico City in 1925, when both lived in the same boarding house on Bucareli Street.

Through Fernandez de Castro, and the paper's owner, José "Pépin" Rivera, descended from the Spanish aristocrats who founded it a hundred years earlier, Beals was able to secure appointments with a wide range of contacts across the spectrum of Cuban political and economic life.

Among his first interviewees was Orestes Ferrara, then Cuba's Secretary of State, a flamboyant former Italian anarchist who had fled to Cuba as a young man in 1896 and been awarded honorary Cuban citizenship for having fought in the struggle for independence. A mustachioed bon vivant who loved a good table, Ferrara had returned to Italy long enough to get a law degree, after which he had returned to Havana.

By dint of a canny business sense, shrewd judge of character, and an ebullient personality, Ferrara had become a wealthy man and a key player in Cuba's political elite. Machado had earlier appointed him to be his envoy to Washington. While in the United States, Ferrara had cut a deal with Sosthenes Behn, founder of the International Telephone and Telegraph Company (now ITT Corporation), under which Behn and his brother Hernan had acquired the Cuban telephone monopoly, as well as control of the Havana Docks Corporation.[8]

Ferrara was also a prolific author. In addition to an admiring biography of Machiavelli, he had just published—when Beals met him—*Las enseñanzas de una revolución* (Lessons of a revolution), a compilation of articles from the pro-government newspaper he controlled, *El Heraldo*. "A clever defense of the Machado regime, while at the same time criticizing its methods," was how Beals described it.[9]

The wily Ferrara sought to play the role of honest broker, placing the best face possible on the Machado regime he served. With Beals, he maintained the polite fiction that he welcomed a crusading left-leaning journalist's interest in interviewing a wide range of political figures. When Beals told him, over a sumptuous lunch at the Hotel Nacional, that he wanted to interview "the student leaders, the revolutionaries and the terrorists," Ferrara momentarily blanched.

"The people [police] might not like that," he said, but relented and asked if Beals would tell him what they said. "Gladly, if they give me permission," he replied. For his part, Ferrara—*quid pro quo*—promised to resolve any difficulties Beals might encounter with the authorities.

He also arranged for Beals an interview that would place him in the middle of what became a deadly tit-for-tat series of political assassinations. It was to have been with Clemente Vásquez Bello, president of Cuba's Senate, and a close friend of Machado's.

But on the very day of his appointment with Beals, September 27, Vásquez Bello was shot to death while leaving his Havana yacht club, apparently by a cell of the ABC.[10] This was the first part of an ABC plot whose second part targeted Machado himself. The assassins had planned to detonate explosives hidden at Havana's cemetery during Vásquez Bello's funeral, which they expected Machado and his cabinet would attend. The plan failed, however, when Vásquez Bello's widow decided instead to have her husband's remains buried in Santa Clara, his hometown in Las Villas province. The buried explosives were later found by a gardener.[11]

The second interview Beals had scheduled for September 27 was with Gonzalo Freyre de Andrade, a prominent legal scholar, Conservative party legislator, and outspoken critic of Machado, as well as his brother Leopoldo, author of a recent book on Cuba's sugar economy. But, upon arriving at their home at 13 B Street in Havana, Beals found them and their elder brother, Guillermo, a planter, lying in their own blood.[12] They had been murdered, apparently by Machado's secret police, to avenge the killing of Vásquez Bello. Had he arrived only a short time earlier, Beals reflected, "I would have been included in the massacre."[13]

Later the same day, another opposition congressman, Miguel Angel Aguiar, was murdered on his doorstep in Vedado, while dozens of prominent dissidents sought refuge in the embassies of Spain, Mexico, Colombia, and Uruguay (but not the United States), to escape a similar fate.[14]

Shaken by these events, Beals threw himself into a whirlwind of long days of research, interviews, and writing. The depth of despair he witnessed everywhere, and his view that much of it was due to unrelieved US exploitation of Cuba's people and resources, stirred in him a fury more intense and passionate than any previous journalistic subject. He was predisposed to despise Machado for the dictator's role in ordering Mella's murder. Now, during six weeks in Cuba, Beals found much that not only confirmed his preconceived ideas, but that showed Machado's rule to be even worse than he anticipated.

In *The Crime of Cuba*, the book whose manuscript he produced in less than three months, Beals delivered an unforgiving indictment of what he saw as a criminal—hence the title—compact between American and Cuban elites to sustain Machado's tyranny. This compact had been concocted over time among US investors in Cuban sugar, utilities, and transport, the US bankers who financed their operations, and the US State Department and military who protected them, Beals charged.

The compact was enshrined in and sustained by the Platt Amendment, a neo-imperialist legalism that dated back to 1901.[15] This amendment to a 1901 US Army Appropriations Bill was forced on the Cubans as a condition for the withdrawal of US troops from Cuba after the Spanish-American War. Named for Orville H. Platt, the Republican US Senator from Connecticut who proposed it on behalf of its real author, Theodore Roosevelt's Secretary of War Elihu Root, the "amendment"—which was incorporated into the Cuban constitution—stipulated that the US could intervene militarily in Cuba at any time it judged necessary, "to preserve political order and protect private property." It was the price Cuba paid for independence from Spain but had the practical effect of substituting America for Spain as a twentieth-century neo-colonial master.

Deeply resented by the Cubans, the Platt Amendment defined the terms of Cuba's dependent relationship with the United States, and at once distorted its politics and economy. By applying the Platt Amendment, Beals wrote, "we merely recognized existing governments [such as Machado's] which had seized power in the fashion we supposedly opposed, thus helping to perpetuate non-elected governments, while denying the people the right to remove them."[16] Harry Frank Guggenheim, the US Ambassador in the early 1930s, made much the same point in a long letter to US Secretary of State Henry Stimson, calling the Platt Amendment's provision for US intervention, "obnoxious to the Cuban people and which, in effect, impedes their political growth."[17]

While focused on Machado, about half of *The Crime of Cuba* is devoted to a colorful account of Cuba's history from the arrival of the Spaniards, the almost complete disappearance of the aboriginal Siboney, Taíno, and Guaríbo peoples they found there, through the island's colonization by Spaniards and the African slaves they imported, the independence struggle and finally, the twentieth century under US tutelage. The role of sugar is highlighted throughout, "black Cuba and black sweat and black song and dance, crystallized into a snow cube, held in silver prongs."[18]

Beals then recites Machado's crimes in a long section that reads like a Human Rights Watch report, followed by a chapter, "American Penetration," in which he draws links between the dictator's ties to various US companies and their support for his regime. The line he traces starts with Henry Catlin, President of the US Electric Bond and Share Company, who had bought up Cuba's electric utilities in the early 1920s, and then financed Machado's 1924 election campaign to the tune of half a million dollars.[19] Citing Catlin's parallel role as legal advisor to the Chase National Bank for the arrangement of loans to Cuba, Beals then marks a path through a welter of people with overlapping directorships of US companies with Cuban interests. The trail, itself a remarkable effort of investigative journalism, ends with a convenient scapegoat in Guggenheim, the US Ambassador.

Guggenheim was an early patron of American aeronautics whom President Herbert Hoover (1874–1964) appointed US Ambassador to Cuba in 1929, partly as a reward for a $35,000 campaign donation.[20] After listing Guggenheim's connections to individuals and to companies with investments in Cuba—not surprising, given the ambassador's family lineage and corporate directorships—Beals charged that Guggenheim "propped up the hated Machado to prevent impending collapse from bankruptcy and the gale of popular wrath."[21] He also held Guggenheim to account for failing to denounce the murders of Cuban civilians, and for employing local Cuban police to guard the US embassy, thereby ensuring that anyone seeking US protection from the dictatorship would immediately be denounced to Machado's *Porra*.[22] He even criticized Guggenheim for socializing with Machado, a diplomatic practice which an ambassador could hardly be expected to forswear.

The credibility of his pursuit of this angle was compromised by the fact that Beals never interviewed Guggenheim, who was absent from Cuba during his six-week visit. Lack of access seemed only to increase the flow of Beals' invective. Indeed, the otherwise prodigious research evident in *The Crime of Cuba*'s pages is undermined by a bilious tone that pervades the book, giving it the character of a screed rather than a balanced account. This is unfortunate, as Beals makes what is a legitimate case against the conflicts of interest that arise when political appointees with corporate interests hold diplomatic posts in countries where their companies have a stake. But Beals makes it with a sledgehammer rather than a scalpel and, in his haste to publish, failed to document all of his allegations. It is an example of what Carey McWilliams, a former editor of the *Nation*, once called Beals' "slapdash" style.[23]

Even before the book came out in late July 1933, US public opinion had turned severely against Machado. Indeed, the foreign policy elite was likely influenced, in part, by advance excerpts from *The Crime of Cuba* published in *Common Sense* magazine, and in the April 1933 edition of *Readers' Digest*, the sale of which was banned in Cuba.[24]

In these articles, Beals cited evidence of the Machado regime's murderous practices, including dropping arrested students "through a medieval trapdoor in Morro Castle [a Havana waterfront landmark] to serve as food for the sharks—an ancient custom." This was demonstrated when initialed cufflinks and clothing belonging to Claudio Brouzon, a young Spaniard detained for putting up anti-imperialist posters around Havana, were found in a shark's belly.[25]

While such reports of Machado's atrocities were uncontested, Beals' attack on Guggenheim provoked a sharp reaction from the ambassador, who sought to forestall it before *The Crime of Cuba*'s publication. After an account of Beals' criticisms of the US Ambassador's role in Cuba appeared in October 1932, in *La Prensa*, a Spanish-language newspaper in New York City, Guggenheim enlisted intermediaries to urge Beals to temper his attack.[26] Guggenheim wrote his well-connected friend Jacob Billikopf, director of Jewish Charities of Philadelphia, who then contacted the liberal educator John Dewey and Ernest Gruening, asking them to persuade Beals to balance his account by at least interviewing Guggenheim before publishing further articles, or indeed, his book.[27]

Beals, alerted to Billikopf's missive, responded directly to him, saying that his attack on Guggenheim was not personal, but that the ambassador had "become involved in a very iniquitous situation . . . due to the peculiar

*The Crime of Cuba* 165

**Figure 8.1.** Walker Evans's photograph, Havana Street (1933), was featured on the cover of Beals's *The Crime of Cuba*. *Photo courtesy of Metropolitan Museum of Art, New York.*

position of the American embassy in Cuba."[28] He added that, "the situation in Cuba is so grievous that no decent man can stand by at this time without doing his utmost in behalf of that unfortunate people."[29]

As he had done earlier in Mexico and Nicaragua, Beals held a US diplomat—political appointee Guggenheim, in this case—to individual account for a US foreign policy stance. It was a novel approach for a journalist to take, violating the usual implicit decorum that attends public foreign policy discussion. Beals used it as a tactic to denounce what he saw as elite capture of US foreign policy, to expose what he called "blue-bloods" and political appointees whom he held responsible for "crimes" against the people in the countries to which they were posted. It was also analogous, in many ways, to later styles such as Hunter Thompson's "Fear and Loathing" gonzo journalism and Michael Moore's bare-knuckled documentary films and shares similar strengths and weaknesses. In this case, however, it was unsupported by persuasive evidence and contradicted by Guggenheim's own cables to Washington in which he denounced Machado's repression, and vainly sought clearance to take more forthright action to work with local political leaders to end it.[30]

Guggenheim, concerned that this attack on his record might expose him to public and Congressional criticism under the new President Franklin Delano Roosevelt (FDR) (1882–1945) administration in Washington, built a case in his own defense by leaking selected cables to *New York Times* reporter Russell Porter, with whom he was friendly.[31] He also worked feverishly on his own memoir of his time in Cuba, published in May 1934, whose purpose was, in large part, to refute Beals's account.[32] Frustrated that Beals refused to yield, Guggenheim circulated a memo about the affair to a small group of influential and interested parties inside and outside government. In the memo, leaked and published upon Guggenheim's April 1933 departure from Cuba in the *Havana American-News*, he complained that "an American writer named Carleton Beals" had published "abusive" and "unfair" articles that accused the ambassador of supporting Machado, and held him and US policy "directly responsible for the grim conditions" in Cuba.[33] Another recipient of the memo was Hubert Herring, then US Secretary of the Committee on Cultural Relations with Latin America, who chose to forward a copy of it to Beals.

Beals reacted with characteristic high dudgeon, firing off a letter of complaint to Cordell Hull, just installed as FDR's first US Secretary of State. He also forwarded his copy of Guggenheim's memo to Bruce Bliven, editor of the *New Republic*, asking him to publish it. Bliven refused, saying Herring had asked him not to, given that it was marked "confidential and not for publication."[34] Beals, undeterred, retold the story of Guggenheim's memo in *The Crime of Cuba*.

Gruening and Herring, both longtime friends of Beals, were dismayed by what they perceived as the misplaced target of his critique, as well as his lack of discretion in going public about Guggenheim's memo, which Herring had sent him in confidence. While they shared Beals' passionate interest in Latin America, both men espoused a liberal reformist, as opposed to radical anti-imperialist critique of US foreign policy, as well as an aversion to personal attacks in public discourse.[35]

"I know you are an impetuous rascal," Herring wrote Beals after having learned that he had sent the memo to Bliven, "but really you shouldn't pull a machete on your friends until you find out exactly what they have been doing . . . I sent the precious document to you and eight others because I thought that you would like to analyze it and tear it up."[36]

Six months later, Gruening sent Beals a blistering note: "I was deeply shocked on reading *The Crime of Cuba* to find you using the Guggenheim-Herring incident in a way which deliberately conveys an impression of improper conduct on the part of Herring. . . . As for your attitude toward Guggenheim . . . I disagree in toto. The worst that can be said about Guggenheim is that he was too light for the job—a job that would have taxed the greatest abilities. . . . Did you ever see Guggenheim? Did you ever present to him and get his answer to your charges? If you didn't, it seems to me you are extremely vulnerable as impartial historian."[37]

While it is true that Beals' rush to publish and passionate intensity undermine *The Crime of Cuba*'s value as a reliable historical account, the book did provide documentary evidence of Machado's abuses in a way that got noticed. In addition to the advance excerpts published in prominent magazines, Beals delivered several public lectures in New York City and elsewhere and at least three radio broadcasts, including one on CBS, about Cuba through the winter months of 1933. Arguably, this was among the influences on US public opinion that led to FDR's decision later that year to abolish the Platt Amendment.

Beals's influence can be gauged by the gratitude he received from the Cuban-American Friendship Council, a Washington-based anti-Machado organization. Its president, Fernando Ortiz, wrote Beals in January 1933, saying "we are certain that your campaign has been one of the starting points to this display of publicity and opposition to Machado that we are now witnessing."[38]

*The Crime of Cuba* is also both prescient and useful for its analysis of Cuba's sugar economy in the 1920s and 1930s. Its presentation of discriminatory US tariff policies against Cuban sugar exports depicts a textbook case of rich-country protectionism targeted at a developing country's most competitive income-earning export. It is a story that has been repeated many times and illustrates a pattern that has long bedeviled development efforts in low-income countries dependent on agricultural commodity exports to industrialized economies.

For many, however, the book's enduring value has more to do with its thirty-one aqua-tone photographs by Walker Evans, than with its Cuban history or polemics. Evans, recruited by Beals's agent at the time, Ernestine Evans [no relation], sailed to Cuba in early May 1933, just two months after J. B. Lippincott had accepted Beals's manuscript.

For Walker Evans, then a callow thirty-year-old just starting his photographic career, Cuba was his first major assignment. Armed with a list of Havana contacts Beals had given him, Evans produced images of families, street vendors, and newsboys, captured at random as they milled about Havana, as well as studies of empty streets and storefronts. There is in them a mood akin to that he would later refine in his documentary stills of Appalachia and Alabama during the Great Depression.

He also found Ernest Hemingway in Havana, with whom he struck up an awestruck acquaintance over hot nights and cold drinks. Evans apparently offered the writer a sounding board to ventilate over his growing estrangement from his second wife, Pauline Pfeiffer. Hemingway was also fuming over Max Eastman's review in the *New Republic* of his recent book, *Death in the Afternoon*. Eastman had claimed that that the book revealed more about Hemingway's sexual insecurity than it did about bullfighting.[39]

But Walker Evans and Beals never met during this period. By the time Evans returned to New York in late June 1933, Beals and his wife Betty were on a trip west through Wyoming to Berkeley, where they visited Carleton's parents and brother Ralph, and then south to San Antonio, to spend some time with Betty's family. Evans wrote Beals, though, telling him that Cuba was "a grand place" where Carleton's friends had been "invaluably helpful as well as immense entertainment." He also predicted that the photographs, "if they are reproduced precisely my way . . . will be something noticeable, and that could help the book."[40]

## THE REVOLUTION OF 1933

Even if his crusade against US Ambassador Guggenheim was intemperate, Beals's forceful denunciation of Machado and of US policy gave him an unrivalled authority on "the Cuba issue," just as both Cuba and America went through almost coinciding transitions. Between February 1933, when Beals completed *The Crime of Cuba* manuscript, and its publication in late July, Roosevelt had been inaugurated as President. Although absorbed by the first hundred days and its flurry of New Deal initiatives, FDR was concerned enough by the deteriorating situation in Cuba to dispatch his top foreign policy advisor, Sumner Welles, to the island. Welles' mission in Cuba, as outlined in Cordell Hull's instructions to him (in all likelihood, drafted by Welles himself), was to engineer Machado's peaceful exit, followed by elections, through "friendly mediation" with the opposition.[41]

Welles, though just forty years old in 1933, was a self-assured, and by many accounts a pompously self-important diplomat, fluent in Spanish, and skilled at political brinkmanship. He had already managed political crises in Haiti, the Dominican Republic, and Cuba, while serving as director of the US State Department's Latin America Bureau in the early 1920s. Born to a wealthy Long Island family, Welles had early childhood ties to the Roosevelts. His cousin, Helen Schermerhorn Astor, had married FDR's older half-brother James "Rosy" Roosevelt Jr., and Sumner had roomed at Groton—FDR's alma mater—with Eleanor Roosevelt's brother.[42] As Assistant Secretary of the US Navy in 1915, FDR had written Welles a letter of recommendation to support his application to the US State Department.[43] Years later, after having served in senior posts at State under Harding and Coolidge, Welles had shrewdly rekindled his closeness to FDR after Coolidge had barred him from the US State Department in 1925, reportedly because the puritanical Coolidge disapproved of Welles' divorce from his first wife, Esther.[44] As FDR, then Governor of New York, prepared for his presidential bid, Welles gave him foreign policy advice. Though Welles professed to seek an end to US intervention in Latin America and claimed authorship of what would become FDR's Good Neighbor Policy, his role in Cuba would contradict this.

Just weeks after his arrival in Havana in May 1933, Welles convened the opposition, namely the Union Nacionalista (nationalist union), the ABC, a more radical group called the Organización Celular Radical Revolucionaria (Radical Revolutionary Cellular Organization), as well as leaders of educators' and women's organizations. The governing coalition was represented by leaders of the Liberal, Conservative and Popular parties, as well as Machado's Secretary of War, General Alberto Herrera.[45] The Communist Party was excluded, however, while the Directorio Estudiantil Universitario (DEU) (University Students' Directory), a left-leaning nationalist students' movement, declined to participate, stating that the mediation "makes light of the Cuban people's right to self-determination and it tends to inculcate in the population, once again, the view that our internal difficulties can only be solved through foreign collaboration."[46]

The mediation effort produced a consensus that Machado should resign and turn over power to a Vice President acceptable to all until elections would be held in 1934. Machado was furious, but his protests—and the mediation process—were overtaken in early August by a nationwide general strike, which brought public transport to a standstill.

An underground radio station controlled by the ABC Radical movement—a breakaway faction from the ABC group which, unlike ABC, was excluded from the mediation effort—repeated a false rumor that Machado had resigned. A celebrating mob surged through the gates of the Presidential Palace. The police fired on the crowd, killing twenty protestors and wounding over a hundred. The situation was critical; "a race between mediation by the United States ambassador and open revolution," the *New York Times* reported.[47]

Within days, a faction of army officers—emboldened by the strike, public outrage over the massacre, the support of the ABC and, most importantly by Welles's discreet encouragement—launched a rebellion, forcing Machado to resign. He was quickly replaced by Carlos Manuel de Céspedes, a former diplomat and son of an ex-President, whose friendship with Welles prompted many witnesses and historians to suggest he was handpicked by the US envoy.[48] Indeed, Welles himself described an "intimate personal friendship" with Céspedes and "a very close relationship with all of the members of his Cabinet."[49]

Beals, almost obsessed with Machado's crimes and deeply cynical in his assessment of what he saw as imperialist foreign policies of Republican presidents Harding, Coolidge, and Hoover, seemed unable at first to appreciate the extent to which the ground was shifting under FDR's New Deal administration.

This blinded him, initially, to the fact that Welles's purpose was to seek a negotiated exit by Machado, not prop him up.[50] Indeed, even Guggenheim—as we have seen—had prodded Machado, albeit timidly, to negotiate with opposition leader Carlos Mendieta of the Union Nacionalista. He *had* also recommended to the US State Department as early as January 1932 that the US government publicly make known its lack of sympathy for Machado's policies of repression.[51] The key difference was that Welles was given much greater license; "Guggenheim would have been in paradise if he could have had as free a hand (as Welles)," observed Ed Reed, a US diplomat who served successively as deputy to both men at the Havana embassy.[52]

*The Crime of Cuba* was published just two weeks before Machado finally resigned and fled to Nassau, and then to Montreal. Even if Machado had been deposed, the revolutionary convulsion that followed in Cuba presented the new Roosevelt administration with its first foreign policy challenge. It was a coincidence that seemed, at first, to promise change in the established pattern of US domination of Cuba's politics.

Appearing just as these events unfolded and were reported on the front pages of America's dailies, *The Crime of Cuba* received a high-profile and generally respectful reception. The *New York Times Book Review* featured it on its front page, illustrated by a Walker Evans photo of a Havana shantytown. In the review, Harold Denny judged Beals' depiction of Cuba "essentially convincing," noting that Beals had suppressed his "tendency to see everything in black and white where American relations with Latin-

American countries are concerned."[53] In the *Survey Graphic*, Herring, despite having taken issue with Beals over the Guggenheim memo, nonetheless endorsed his attribution of "a share of guilty responsibility for Cuba's sufferings" to Wall Street, the State Department and, ultimately, the American people.[54] Russell B. Porter, a *New York Times* staff member who reported on Cuba in January 1933, praised *The Crime of Cuba* in the *Saturday Review of Literature* for offering, "the whole story, all the facts, fully documented, of the Cuban situation, including the links between economic imperialism here and political despotism there." But he challenged Beals' suggestion in *Crime*'s final chapter that Welles would "buttress up" Machado. "The trouble with this theory is simply that it ignores the fact that Roosevelt sent Welles to get Machado out, not to "buttress him in power."[55] The *New Yorker*'s book reviewer Clifton Fadiman called *Crime* "an intensely stirring and valuable job, for which the author deserves all possible praise. It must be read."[56]

Moving from the book to those rapidly changing events, Beals would soon find that the promised change in US policy towards Cuba—and Latin America as a whole—was more tactics than substance. For this, he blamed the adept scheming, interference and partiality of Sumner Welles. Here, in contrast to his jeremiad against Guggenheim, Beals had a convincing case.

While Welles played an important role in conceiving FDR's Good Neighbor Policy in Latin America and had purportedly sought to apply the new policy of "non-intervention" in seeking a *mediated* end to Machado's repressive rule in Cuba, Beals would find that Welles's later action utterly contradicted these promising first steps.

Carlos Manuel de Céspedes (1871–1939), installed as Cuba's new President while Beals's book on Machado was going through its promotional blitz, would not last long. Having neither a strong base of support nor leadership gravitas, he was unable to stem what had become an insurrection. Even with immediate US recognition, he was overthrown after just twenty-three days in office.

This second coup, on September 4, was mounted by mutinous army sergeants against the officer class that had backed de Céspedes. It was a barracks revolt led by Sergeant Fulgencio Batista and supported by the DEU, as well as other opposition factions. The resulting student-army revolutionary government, led by anatomy professor and physician Ramón Grau San Martín (1887–1969), who became President, was thus a mix of radicals, socialists, and reformists, uneasily grafted on to the rebellious sergeants. Grau, tall and reserved, struggled to gain control of this improbable coalition, riven by internal contradictions and intrigue, and beset by continuing economic ruin and labor unrest across the country. Most critically, however, it faced the immediate hostility of the US Ambassador, who was incensed and embarrassed that his carefully nurtured de Céspedes government had been so easily toppled.

Welles, after having wrongly celebrated de Céspedes' brief takeover, and having basked in US mainstream media praise of his diplomatic skill in bringing it about, now telephoned US Secretary of State Hull to recommend that the US land troops to restore de Céspedes.[57] When Hull refused, saying this "might provoke trouble rather than quiet trouble," the ambassador immediately began casting about for alternatives to the student-army government.[58] Meantime, he parried Hull, requesting—and getting—the dispatch of "at least two warships to Havana and one to Santiago."[59] Within four weeks, thirty-one US Navy vessels had been sent to circle Cuba, or to stand by at Key West.[60]

Welles nonetheless met on September 15 with about thirty DEU leaders and tried to insinuate himself into their confidence by saying that were he a Cuban, he would consider it an honor to be a DEU member.[61] The students correctly sensed that his conciliatory tone was an affectation to mask his hostility to Grau. Indeed, Welles was at the same time counseling the US State Department to withhold recognition of the provisional government, which he described as "an undisciplined group . . . representing the most irresponsible elements in the city of Havana with practically no support whatsoever outside the capital."[62] He also urgently pressed Hull to ignore his earlier cable calling for a hike in the US Cuban sugar import quota (under de Céspedes), as it would "at once be misconstrued here as a demonstration of friendship by the US towards the present regime."[63] Earlier, Welles had advised Hull that a US failure to adjust the sugar quota in Cuba's favor would be "disastrous for the Cuban people."[64] But Grau, Welles reported, was "utterly impractical" and "obsessed with the idea that the soldiers are so devoted to the ideals of the 'revolution,' as he terms the mutiny, that they will take it upon themselves without any orders to maintain order and guarantee life and property."[65]

With Batista however, whom Welles met on September 21, and whose "reasonableness, intelligence and apparent patriotism" impressed him, he began plotting against the revolutionary government. The US envoy signaled to Batista that Washington would recognize any government that met "accepted standards," and intimated that the Grau regime would not pass the test.[66] Batista quickly grasped his meaning.

By some accounts, the student-army government was a chaotic affair. On September 14, two days after Grau's cabinet was sworn in, the Presidential Palace was like "a lunatic asylum with all the inmates turned loose," according to Ruby Hart Phillips, a longtime Havana-based American reporter, then married to *New York Times* correspondent James Doyle Phillips. "Soldiers and *revolucionarios* [sat] on all the desks and typewriters shouting at each other," she reported, while in the cabinet room, Grau, surrounded by about two hundred members of the DEU, would respond to a journalist's question, "but no one around him pays the slightest attention or stops talking an instant."[67]

Amid the disorder, a progressive government agenda emerged: an eight-hour workday, minimum wages for cane-cutters, compulsory arbitration to settle strikes, a rule that at least 50 percent of companies' employees be Cuban citizens (as opposed to Spanish migrants), the vote for women, autonomy for the university, land reform, and significantly, deletion of the Platt Amendment from the Cuban constitution.[68]

By the middle of October, the divisions within the Provisional Government grew clear. A leftist group gathered around Antonio Guiteras, a member of the DEU from eastern Cuba who was Interior Minister. A centrist group aligned with Grau, and a right-wing group lined up behind Batista. But Batista, despite his misgivings about Grau, could not move against him until he was sure the army would follow suit. He also knew that he needed to forge an alliance with an alternative President who could win—through Welles—Washington's support.

While Grau gave Fernando Ortiz (he of the Cuban-American Friendship Council) the task of negotiating a plan to unite the revolutionary factions, Batista met secretly—at the invitation of Welles—with the opposition Union Nacionalista and the ABC, both of which had previously supported de Céspedes. They agreed to back the old-line opposition Union Nacionalista leader Carlos Mendieta for President.

Some of the students learned of Batista's betrayal and moved quickly to stop him. They convened a meeting on November 4 at the home of War and Communications Minister Sergio Carbó, who had promoted Batista to Colonel, at which Grau was to confront Batista.

In a dramatic faceoff, Grau charged Batista with treason. Batista, playing for time, made a show of recanting and begged Grau's forgiveness. In a move that stunned and dismayed the radicals and many of the students, Grau accepted his apology, and reaffirmed his support for Batista's leadership of the army.[69]

\*\*\*

Beals, absorbed by a promotional tour for *The Crime of Cuba*, was not able to get to Cuba to cover these events until early December 1933. It was a heady visit for him, in which the notoriety stirred by his book followed him to Havana, while his visit coincided with what was to be Grau's final month in power, and the climax of this revolutionary episode.

A gaggle of journalists huddled under a wet snowfall at the dock in New York City to bid Beals farewell as he boarded the ship to Cuba on December 9. Upon his arrival in Havana, Beals was welcomed once again by his friend

Antonio Fernando de Castro, who accompanied him to a dinner in his honor hosted by Grau at the Presidential Palace.

Before that, however, Beals attended a press conference at the US embassy, at which Welles—"tall, bald-headed, immaculately dressed, with a glacial stuffed-shirt manner," he wrote—announced that he would return to Washington the following day to be Assistant Secretary of State in FDR's administration. Just hours later over dinner, Grau complained to Beals about Welles's "secret machinations against my government."[70]

Grau, whom Beals described as "a tall, lean man, with long arms and long, expressive fingers," thanked him for his book and articles denouncing Machado.[71] Now, however, he sought the journalist's help in making public the intrigue in which Welles was engaged to destabilize the student-army government.

He accused Welles of having protected some four hundred former Machado Cuban army officers whom Grau held responsible for a failed coup plot in early October. The plotters had holed up in the Hotel Nacional—where Welles was also staying, as he prepared to return to the United States—after de Céspedes' overthrow. While this conspiracy was aborted when the army—then still loyal to Grau—attacked the hotel on October 2, Welles had not been dissuaded, Grau told Beals. The ambassador had given assurances of tacit US support to an expanded group of ABC militants and Carlos Mendieta's Nationalist partisans who then conspired with factions of the army and air force to launch a second coup attempt on November 8. Grau had successfully resisted this one too, thanks to the support of the rest of the army, led by Batista—who had pledged his support at Minister Carbó's house after receiving Grau's forgiveness. The rebels had retreated to Havana's Atarés fortress, where hundreds had been killed.

By crushing this rebellion, Grau's government had gained a momentary boost of confidence. But the turmoil quickly resumed, fueled by the strikes, the Communist challenge, the government's own confusion and inexperience, the deepening economic crisis, and Sumner Welles's backroom destabilization campaign.

Grau's frustration with Welles was palpable. "The United States has not recognized my government," he told Beals, "so Welles has no right to be here."[72] Grau sensed that his time was running out. He had told Welles privately that he would resign but insisted that it would be unseemly for him to do so while Welles remained in the country. Perhaps he hoped that Jefferson Caffery, who would soon replace Welles as US Ambassador, would be more amenable to a deal enabling the revolutionary government to survive.

Indeed, just days before, US Secretary of State Cordell Hull, aboard the *S.S. American Legion* on his way to the Pan-American Conference in Montevideo, told the Associated Press that he "and President Roosevelt would like to recognize the Cuban government."[73] This difference between Welles and Hull, who, in his address to the Montevideo Conference, would hint at US plans to abolish the Platt Amendment, was an early indication of the friction that developed into rivalry between the two men over the direction of foreign policy under FDR.

In this case, Welles had gotten the jump on Hull. He took advantage of Hull's absence from the United States to seek and obtain a meeting with Roosevelt at Warm Springs, Georgia on November 19, at which he pressed his view that US commercial and export interests in Cuba could not be revived under Grau's government. He secured the President's agreement with his recommendation against recognition, contradicting Hull's instructions.[74]

Beals's encounters with Grau and Welles quickly deflated the remarkably optimistic view he had developed of the student-army government's prospects for survival under the supposedly benevolent watch of FDR. In a *Scribner's* magazine piece published just before his December 1933 trip to Havana, Beals wrote that Cuba, now "definitely on the move to win economic and political independence" could count itself, "fortunate that we have a man in the White House who can view this movement with tolerance, for had we acted in the customary manner of past decades, on this occasion we should probably have had on our hands a Cuban Sandino to arouse not only the patriotism of the islanders but to inspire statues, verse and moral sympathy in the rest of Latin America."[75]

This optimism was sustained in a second piece in *Scribner's*, published in January 1934, in which Beals still held out hope that the newly-minted Good Neighbor Policy would be observed in Cuba.[76] Ironically, even as this issue was being snapped up in newsstands, its author's views had undergone a complete reversal. Over three weeks in Cuba, Beals had been impressed by an exuberant determination he found among the young Cuban leaders—this despite the country's descent into chaos, and the ominous sight of thirty US warships that circled the island.

Welcomed by them as *el gran periodista yanqui* (the great Yankee journalist) and a comrade-in-arms, Beals was escorted on a tour of the countryside, where he witnessed the revolutionary leaders greeted enthusiastically in spontaneous encounters with townsfolk. He was hosted at meals and given fawning interviews by pro-government Cuban journalists. The attention led Ruby [R.] Hart Phillips, wife of the *New York Times* correspondent in Havana and herself a stringer for the North American Newspaper Alliance, to dismiss Beals as being among "a group of pinkish writers" who "cause Uncle Sam more trouble in Latin America than do the Latin Americans."[77]

But by late December 1933, Beals learned that Batista had given up on his effort to convince other members of the student-army government to reach agreement with Welles. Batista was about to turn on them a second time; he openly told Beals as much in an interview at the army barracks at Camp Columbia.

"Grau has to go," Batista said as he walked with Beals around the drill grounds. "Even if he were an archangel, the United States will never recognize him . . . and no government can survive in Cuba that does not have United States government support."[78]

It was the "rankest betrayal," Beals wrote years later.[79] It also showed beyond doubt that the non-recognition policy adopted by FDR at Welles's recommendation was decisive in precipitating the collapse of the student-army government.

The final straw was a dispute over electricity rates. At his dinner with Grau upon arrival in Havana, Beals listened as the President complained about the US-owned American and Foreign Power Corporation (AFP) electric company's conspiracy with Welles. They sought to reverse Grau's December 6 decree reducing Cuba's electricity rates by 45 percent, a move that had outraged the AFP, and triggered a protest from Welles. The AFP was already unpopular for having cut its Cuban staff from 4,000 to 2,000 since 1929, and for having instituted a 25 percent pay cut for those making more than sixty dollars a month.[80] AFP workers merged their two unions and drew up a list of demands. Negotiations followed—held at the US embassy and involving AFP executives and Batista—but these broke down when the company rejected most of the union demands. The power utility workers went on strike January 14, and the Grau administration intervened, firing the AFP's management team and replacing it with union leaders. The same day, Batista—who had convened a civilian-military junta at his Camp Columbia barracks—demanded that Grau resign, which he did the following day.

Batista seized control of Cuba, installing Carlos Hevia (1900–1964), agriculture minister in the revolutionary government, as interim President. Two days later, Carlos Mendieta (1873–1960), the Union Nacionalista leader who had been jailed and exiled by Machado, was installed as provisional President, a post he held until December 1935. His government gained US recognition on January 23, prompting "wild celebration" in Havana.[81] Three days later, the US government announced $2 million in emergency aid to Cuba, followed by a pledge in early February to increase Cuba's annual quota for sugar exports to the US by 244,000 tons to nearly two million tons.[82] Although many Cubans welcomed the restoration of order, the chaos soon resumed with over a hundred strikes in the first three months of 1934, along with intra-elite turmoil that Batista manipulated to divide and rule for the rest of the decade and beyond.[83]

His *de facto* dictatorship lasted for twenty-five years, until Batista's own overthrow in 1959 by Fidel Castro (1926–2018). "The Cubans will not soon forgive Welles his meddling and his partisanship," Beals wrote in the *Nation*. "He has sowed and reaped a fresh crop of hatred for the United States."[84] In the same article, he compared Welles's role to that of US Ambassador Henry Lane Wilson in Mexico in 1913, "who contributed greatly to the downfall of [President Francisco] Madero and hence to his subsequent assassination."[85]

This Cuban episode, which had the effect of extinguishing democratic aspirations in Cuba and arguably setting the stage for a leftist revolution a generation later, was an ignominious beginning for the Good Neighbor Policy, made possible only because Roosevelt, fully occupied with implementing the New Deal, left Welles to manage the Cuban situation as he saw fit. Indeed, even if Welles had gained FDR's confidence in the 1920s and pushed the non-interventionist ideals of the Good Neighbor Policy, his apprenticeship suggested more traditional instincts; his mentor in his early years at the US State Department had been Charles Evans Hughes, Secretary of State in the Harding Administration, and GOP presidential candidate in 1916.

Welles's visceral and instant rejection of the Grau government drove what was a freelance effort carried out by a supremely confident operator with the skills and hubris to pull it off. His partiality and instrumental role in torpedoing the 1933 Cuban Revolution, widely recognized by historians ever since, was repeatedly cited and condemned by Beals whenever he reported on Cuba.

"Through the machinations of Sumner Welles," Beals wrote in his 1938 book, *America South*, "the popular aspirations were choked off, and Cuba, after considerable violence and disorder, has been saddled with an equally brutal and more ignorant Machado, in the person of the upstart army sergeant, Fulgencio Batista, who now enjoys the full blessings of the State Department."[86]

A more detached observer, historian Frederick Pike, assigns more responsibility to FDR for the dénouement of the 1933 Cuban Revolution, pointing to his "Talleyrand-like tricksterism" which showed "that non-intervention was a policy meaning fundamentally very much the same thing as intervention."[87] Indeed, over the rest of his Presidency, Roosevelt would sustain a jovial forbearance with a large party of Latin dictators, making him, in Beals's assessment, "undoubtedly the best-liked American President in the rest of the hemisphere in the history of the United States."[88] In Cuba, the Platt Amendment was erased from the constitution, and a reciprocity agreement signed with the US—the first of many to mark the Good Neighbor Policy era—allowing Batista to depict himself as a nationalist revolutionary who got results. In Cuba, as across the hemisphere, tyrants kept watch on US investments, obviating the need for Marine interventions and gunboat diplomacy. Carleton Beals would find much to criticize.

***

Beals's tumultuous professional life in 1933 was matched by turmoil in his marriage. While consumed by this Cuban maelstrom, Beals had largely ignored Betty, his still-recent bride. Except for a summer holiday together through Wyoming, California, and Texas in 1933, they had been separated much of the time. In early September 1933, Beals had left her with her parents in San Antonio, and had taken a train to New York, from which he launched his promotional tour for *The Crime of Cuba*. Betty was frustrated, and by the fall of 1933, was preparing to file for divorce.

In an apparent last-ditch effort to save their marriage, she half-heartedly suggested that she take time off from her teaching job with the San Antonio Board of Education to join Beals on his planned trip to Havana, and then on to Panama and Peru, the next stops on his planned itinerary. She was even reading books on Peru to prepare for the journey.[89] Beals had rejected this idea, probably because her proposed timing of early November did not suit his plans. A month later, she took a train to New York, after having sent Beals an advance telegram: "Arrive Pennsylvania station Sunday morning at six fifty. Please be there. I want to talk to you. Betty."[90]

It was not a happy visit, Betty's purpose being to tell Beals, face-to-face, that she wanted out of the marriage. Beals agreed not to contest her suit for divorce, and a week later, he received a letter from her lawyer.

In the divorce suit, Betty alluded to "a constant clash of wills between them, resulting in unhappiness and heartaches." She was, she admitted, "high-strung and extremely nervous," while Carleton had "what is known as an artistic temperament, with very fixed ideas on all subjects."[91] Beals's mother Elvina, a clinging presence who freely shared her views on all matters, sought to comfort him: "I grieved over that affair as I sensed its utter lack of the elements necessary to success and the happiness and accord such a hasty union required . . . the court complaint shows how the very beginning of your life together was marred by discord and unhappiness."[92] Given his lifestyle and personality, it is unlikely that Beals could have sustained a relationship with any but the most accommodating of women, ready to drop everything to travel with him or be left alone for weeks, without complaint. Fortunately, for him, he would soon find such a woman.

## NOTES

1. In *The Crime of Cuba* (Philadelphia: J. B. Lippincott, 1933), Beals relates Machado's efforts to curry favor with senior Mexican government and police officials in order to gain their collaboration in suppressing anti-Machado activities by Cuban exiles in Mexico. Mexican authorities, notably Valente Quintana, then chief of Mexico's secret police, responded positively. Quintana was behind an effort to cast suspicion for Mella's murder on Tina Modotti, thereby distracting attention from the possible Machado connection and a second suspect named Magriñat, who was released soon after the crime. Investigation of the case was later reopened, and testimony implicating Magriñat surfaced, but no convictions ever resulted. Beals recorded in his unpublished autobiography that several men allegedly involved in the assassination were identified by Mella's widow, in 1959, as officials serving in Cuba's then-new revolutionary government led by Fidel Castro. They were fired from their government posts and, Beals

claimed, later played a role in the CIA's "Mad Dog" operation against Cuba, a precursor to the Bay of Pigs fiasco. Carleton Beals, "Under the Fifth Sun" (unpublished autobiography, c. 1972–1978), in Carleton Beals Collection (CBC), Howard Gotlieb Archival Research Center, Boston University (hereafter cited CBC).

2. Robert Whitney, *State and Revolution in Cuba: Mass Mobilization and Political Change, 1920–1940* (Chapel Hill: University of North Carolina Press, 2001), 58–59; US Congress, *Tariff Act of 1930*, 19 USC. ch. 4, Pub. L. 71–361, 71st Cong., 2nd sess., March 13, 1930.

3. Whitney, *State and Revolution in Cuba*, 58–59.

4. Philip Dur and Christopher Gilcrease, "US Diplomacy and the Downfall of a Cuban Dictator: Machado in 1933," *Journal of Latin American Studies* 34, no. 2 (2002): 257.

5. Dur and Gilcrease, "US Diplomacy," 257.

6. Louis A. Pérez Jr., *Cuba Under the Platt Amendment, 1902–1934* (Pittsburgh, PA: University of Pittsburgh Press, 1986), 289. The ABC, founded in 1931 by a group around lawyer Juan Andrés Lliteras, comprised three levels of secret cells denominated by the letters A, B and C, in which each cell member knew only his own cell's leader, and the seven members of a cell of which each member was responsible for founding and leading. This structure prevented the collapse of the terrorist anti-Machado organization in the event of a police arrest of any or several of its members. See Luis E. Aguilar, *Cuba 1933—Prelude to Revolution*, New York: W.W. Norton and Company, 1972, 118–19.

7. Beals, "Under the Fifth Sun" (unpublished autobiography), CBC, 132, box 45.

8. Beals, *Crime of Cuba*, 378.

9. Beals, "Under the Fifth Sun" (unpublished autobiography), CBC, 141.

10. Beals, "Under the Fifth Sun" (unpublished autobiography), CBC, 141; and Edward Reed to Cordell Hull, September 27, 1932, NARA, 837.00/3353, DS/RG59.

11. Jaime Suchlicki, *Cuba: From Columbus to Castro and Beyond*, 5th ed. (Dulles, VA: Brassey's, 2002), 92.

12. Beals, *Crime of Cuba*, 259; and *Havana Post*, September 28, 1932, CBC.

13. Beals, "Under the Fifth Sun" (unpublished autobiography), CBC, 145; *The Crime of Cuba*, 259–60.

14. Edward Reed to Cordell Hull, October 7, 1932, NARA. 837.00/3368, DS/RG59.

15. US Congress, Platt Amendment, in 1901 US Army Appropriations Bill, 31 Stat. 895, Pub. L. 56–803. 56th Cong., 2nd sess., March 2, 1901, https://govtrackus.s3.amazonaws.com/legislink/pdf/stat/31/STATUTE-31-Pg895.pdf (accessed May 22, 2021).

16. Beals, *Crime of Cuba*, 182.

17. Harry Guggenheim to Secretary of State Henry Stimson, January 20, 1933, NARA 711–37/174, Records of US Department of State Relating to Latin American & Caribbean States 1930–1934. LM 157, Reel #67.

18. Beals, *Crime of Cuba*, 25.

19. Beals, *Crime of Cuba*, 242–43. This finding, although its source is not attributed by Beals, has been corroborated by sources consulted by historian Thomas F. O'Brien, including records of the American and Foreign Power Corporation (AFP)'s Cuban interest, in *The Revolutionary Mission: American Enterprise in Latin America 1900–1945* (Cambridge: Cambridge University Press 1996), 227.

20. Beals, "Under the Fifth Sun" (unpublished autobiography), CBC, 146.

21. Beals, *Crime of Cuba*, 329.

22. In an internal report on the allegations, a US State Department official reported that Guggenheim, while acknowledging that two Cuban policemen were stationed at the embassy, "doubted whether either one of them is of sufficient intelligence to be able to report important matters to Police Headquarters even should he desire to do so." Memorandum: Matthews to Edwin G. Wilson, October 20, 1932, NARA, 837.00/124.373 DS/RG59.

23. Carey McWilliams, "Second Thoughts," *Nation*, July 14–21, 1979, 38.

24. Carleton Beals, "Accused of Cuban Plot," *New York Times*, March 29, 1933, 6, https://timesmachine.nytimes.com/timesmachine/1933/03/29/99217449.html?pageNumber=6

25. Carleton Beals, "The Crime of Cuba," *Readers Digest*, April 1933, 3–6.

26. Carleton Beals, "No intervengan EE.UU en Cuba sino dejen arreglar a los cubanos sus problemas" (US should not intervene in Cuba, but allow Cubans to solve their problems), *La Prensa*, October 20, 1932, in NARA, 837.00/33398 DS/RG59.

27. See Harry Guggenheim to Jacob Billikopf, November 19, 1932; Jacob Billikopf to Ernest Gruening, November 28, 1932; John Dewey to Carleton Beals, March 19, 1933, CBC.

28. Carleton Beals to Jacob Billikopf, December 8, 1932, CBC.

29. Beals to Billikopf (1932), CBC.

30. Harry Guggenheim to Secretary of State Henry Stimson, December 17, 1930, NARA, 711.37/146, Records of US Department of State Relating to Latin American & Caribbean States 1930–1934. LM 157, Reel #67. Also Edward Reed to Francis White, June 13, 1933, Francis White Papers (FWP), Johns Hopkins University, Baltimore.

31. Edward Reed to Francis White, February 20, 1933, FWP.

32. See Harry Frank Guggenheim, *The United States and Cuba: A Study in International Relations* (New York: Macmillan, 1934), 179–91; and Henry A. Armstrong, "A First-Hand Study of Cuban-American Relations," *New York Times Book Review*, May 27, 1934, B3.

33. Harry Frank Guggenheim, "Memo," *Havana American-News*, April 2, 1933.

34. Bruce Bliven to Carleton Beals, March 30, 1933, CBC.

35. See John A. Britton, *Carleton Beals: A Radical Journalist in Latin America* (Albuquerque: University of New Mexico Press, 1987), 108–22.

36. Hurbert Herring to Carleton Beals, March 23, 1933, CBC.

37. Ernest Gruening to Carleton Beals, September 6, 1933, CBC.

38. Fernando Ortiz to Carleton Beals, January 24, 1933, CBC.

39. See Belinda Rathbone, *Walker Evans: A Biography* (New York: Houghton Mifflin, 1995), 80–81.

40. Walker Evans to Carleton Beals, June 25, 1933, CBC. Indeed, these photographs have retained their appeal, especially as Walker Evans's work grew more famous with his photographs of Depression-era white tenant farmers in Alabama for James Agee's 1941 book, *Let Us Now Praise Famous Men* (Boston: Houghton Mifflin). They have also surfaced in exhibitions of Evans's work, as well as in *Cuba: Art and History from 1868 to Today*, edited by Nathalie Bondil, produced by the Montreal Museum of Fine Arts and the Museo Nacional de Bellas Artes and the Fototeca de Cuba in Havana, 2008. Among all of Beals's now out-of-print books, *The Crime of Cuba* commands the highest price, due to Evans's illustrations.

41. US Secretary of State Cordell Hull to Sumner Welles, May 1, 1933. NARA, 711.37/177, Records of US Department of State Relating to Latin American & Caribbean States 1930–1934. LM 157, Reel #67.

42. Irwin F. Gellman, *Secret Affairs: Franklin Roosevelt, Cordell Hull, and Sumner Welles* (Baltimore: Johns Hopkins University Press, 1995), 59.

43. Gellman, *Secret Affairs*, 60.

44. Gellman, *Secret Affairs*, 63.

45. Louis A. Perez Jr., "In Defense of Hegemony: Sumner Welles and the Cuban Revolution of 1933," in *Ambassadors in Foreign Policy: The Influence of Individuals on US-Latin American Policy*, ed. C. Neale Ronning and Albert P. Vannucci (New York: Praeger, 1987), 36.

46. Whitney, *State and Revolution in Cuba*, 89.

47. Associated Press, "Open Revolution Held Possible," *New York Times*, August 7, 1933, 7.

48. See Aguilar, *Cuba 1933*, 150; and R. Hart Phillips, *Cuban Sideshow* (Havana: Cuban Press, 1935), 72.

49. Sumner Wells to Secretary of State Cordell Hull, August 19, 1933, NARA, LC 711.37/183, Records of US Department of State Relating to Latin American & Caribbean States 1930–1934. LM 157, Reel #67.

50. Beals, *Crime of Cuba*, 368.

51. Harry Guggenheim to Secretary of State, January 25, 1932, US Department of State, *Foreign Relations of the United States: Diplomatic Papers*, 1932, Vol. 5, Latin America (Washington, DC: United States Government Printing Office), 5:538.

52. Ed Reed to Francis White, June 13, 1933, FWP.

53. Harold N. Denny, "The Crucified Republic," *New York Times Book Review*, August 20, 1933.

54. Hubert Herring, *Survey Graphic*, November 1933.

55. Russell B. Porter, "Before Machado Fell," *Saturday Review of Literature*, August 26, 1933, 66.

56. Clifton Fadiman, "Books," review of Beals, *Crime of Cuba*, *New Yorker*, September 2, 1933, 51.

57. Benjamin Welles, *Sumner Welles: FDR's Global Strategist* (New York: St. Martin's Press, 1997), 171.

58. Memorandum of a Telephone Conversation between Secretary Hull at Washington and Ambassador Welles at Havana, 5:30 p.m., September 5, 1933, NARA, 837.00/3764, DS/RG59.

59. Sumner Welles to Secretary of State Cordell Hull, September 5, 1933, NARA, 837.00/3740, DS/RG59.

60. Op. 38-A-MW. Office of Naval Operations, Distribution of Vessels in Cuban Waters, October 4, 1933, NARA, 0930. 837.00, DS/RG59.

61. Benjamin Welles, *Sumner Welles*, 176.

62. Sumner Welles to Secretary of State Cordell Hull, September 6, 1933, NARA, 837.00/3767, DS/RG59.

63. Sumner Welles to Secretary of State Cordell Hull, September 12, 1933, NARA, Records of US DOS Relating to Political Relations between US and Latin American & Caribbean States, 1930–1944 (1930–44), 711.37/LM 157, Reel 67.

64. Sumner Welles to Secretary of State Cordell Hull, September 25, 1933, NARA, 837.00/4007, DS/RG59.

65. Sumner Welles to Secretary of State Cordell Hull, September 5, 1933, NARA, 837.00/3756, DS/RG59.

66. Benjamin Welles, *Sumner Welles*, 176.

67. Phillips, *Cuban Sideshow*, 131–33.

68. Whitney, *State and Revolution*, 103.

69. See Aguilar, *Cuba 1933*, 189–93.

70. Beals, "Under the Fifth Sun," (unpublished autobiography), CBC, box 45.

71. Beals, "Under the Fifth Sun," (unpublished autobiography), CBC, box 45,

72. Beals, "Under the Fifth Sun" (unpublished autobiography), CBC, box 45.

73. Aguilar, *Cuba 1933*, 209.

74. See Benjamin Welles, *Sumner Welles*, 178–79; Robert Dallek, *Franklin D. Roosevelt and American Foreign Policy, 1932–1945* (New York: Oxford University Press, 1979), 64; William Appleman Williams, *The Tragedy of American Diplomacy* (New York: W. W. Norton, 1959), 174–76; and Gellman, *Secret Affairs*, 81.

75. Carleton Beals, "Young Cuba Rises," *Scribner's Magazine*, November 1933, 270.

76. Carleton Beals, "A New Code for Latin America," *Scribner's Magazine*, January 1934, 27–34.

77. Phillips, *Cuban Sideshow*, 238.

78. Carleton Beals, *Latin America: World in Revolution* (New York: Abelard-Schuman, 1963), 133.

79. Beals, *Latin America*, 133.

80. O'Brien, *Revolutionary Mission*, 235.

81. New York Times (Special), "Roosevelt Grants Cuban Recognition," *New York Times*, January 24, 1934, 1, 6.

82. New York Times (Special), "$2,000,000 in Food to be Sent to Cuba," *New York Times*, January 27, 1934, 30; and New York Times (Special), "Workers Return to Jobs in Havana," *New York Times*, February 9, 1934, 12.

83. Whitney, *State and Revolution in Cuba*, 124.

84. Carleton Beals, "American Diplomacy in Cuba," *Nation*, January 17, 1934, 70.

85. Beals, "American Diplomacy in Cuba," 70.

86. Carleton Beals, *America South* (Philadelphia: J. P. Lippincott, 1937), 510. Sumner Welles would later go on to be FDR's principal foreign policy advisor, eclipsing Cordell Hull until 1943, when he was forced to resign after details came to light about Welles' 1940 attempt

to solicit sexual favors from Pullman car porters aboard a train. The resignation, reluctantly accepted by FDR, came as Welles was absorbed in the early stages of the US initiative to establish a United Nations Organization, once the war had ended.

87. Frederick B. Pike, *FDR's Good Neighbor Policy: Sixty Years of Generally Gentle Chaos* (Austin: University of Texas Press, 1995), 173.

88. Carleton Beals, *America South* (Philadelphia: J. B.Lippincott and Company, 1937), 510.

89. Betty Daniel to Carleton Beals, October 21, 1933, CBC.

90. Betty Daniel to Carleton Beals, November 15, 1933, CBC.

91. Honorable W. W. McCrory, Judge of District Court of Bexar County, no. 74390, February 17, 1934, CBC.

92. Elvina Beals to Carleton Beals, March 29, 1934, CBC.

*Chapter Nine*

# Fire and Love on the Andes

Carleton Beals sensed by late December 1933 that President Ramón Grau's regime in Cuba was about to collapse under the combined pressure of Sumner Welles' hostility and Fulgencio Batista's (1901–1973) ambition. Still, he left the scene as the story's climax approached. Just before New Year's, Beals launched his next project: a book on Peru.

His editor at J. B. Lippincott, Jefferson Jones, had proposed Peru as "our next best bet" and advanced him $1,200 in late November for this, as well as for the manuscript of the novel Beals had sent him, *Black River*.[1] The latter was an ambitious and fast-paced moral tale of oil, corruption and violent injustice set in the Mexican Gulf coast port of Tampico around 1915. At the time, Tampico was at the apex of an oil boom and hotly contested in the civil war between the forces of constitutionalist leader President Venustiano Carranza and his rivals Emiliano Zapata and Francisco "Pancho" Villa.

Also, Beals had earlier accepted an assignment from *American Traveler* to deliver a piece on native foods in Mexico in return for his passage—already booked—from New York to Cuba, and then on to Panama.[2] So instead of covering the final disintegration of the Cuban Revolution, he boarded a ship south, through the canal to Panama City, from which he sailed two days later aboard the Grace Line's *Santa Clara*, bound for Lima's port of Callao.

It was an exceptionally pleasant trip for him, made so by an unlikely shipboard flirtation with a blushing Peruvian teenager named Blanca Rosa Leyva y Arguedas. Petite, almost childlike in appearance, the nineteen-year-old had enough puckish vivacity to beguile Beals, all the while seemingly unaffected by the watchful eye of her father, Carlos Samuel Leyva, a colonel in the Peruvian military. By the time their ship moored at Callao four days later, Beals was smitten.

There was a playfulness in his interactions with Blanca Rosa, her black eyes brimming with fun and seductive charm, that he now realized had been absent in his two failed marriages. It was a tonic that erased the troubling echoes of his drawn-out estrangement from Betty, placing him, by his own admission, in a disorganized state, almost giddy.[3]

Through the six months Beals spent in Peru, he became a regular visitor at the Leyva y Arguedas' home in Lima, stopping there between his forays to Trujillo, Cuzco, Ayacucho, Huancayo, and other centers on the Peruvian *sierra* (Andean highlands), as well as the coast, and the Amazonian jungle. Although the forty-year-old Beals was twice Blanca Rosa's age, her parents did not disapprove of the blossoming romance, apparently impressed by Beals' status as a published author, famous enough to meet the country's leading personalities and be interviewed by local newspapers. Within weeks, it was already clear that they would wed.

But first, Beals had to carry out his purpose in Peru, which was to research and write what became *Fire on the Andes.* Upon his arrival in Callao, he was met by Carlos Manuel Cox, one of the founders of the Peruvian Aprista Party, so-called for its affiliation with the Alianza Popular Revolucionaria Americana (APRA) American Popular Revolutionary Alliance, led by Victor Raúl Haya de la Torre.[4]

Two nights later, Beals was reunited with Haya, accompanied by Cox and the writer Luis Alberto Sánchez, over dinner in a German pension facing the sea at La Punta, Callao. Beals had last seen Haya a decade earlier in Mexico City, where the latter had sought exile after being expelled from Peru by the dictator Augusto Leguía (1863–1932).[5]

Beals was impressed that Haya, though now Peru's most celebrated—and persecuted—politician, had lost none of the warmth and jovial informality of his youth. On the contrary, he exuded an uncanny air of almost joyful serenity, intensely focused now on Beals, "*mi viejo amigo*" (my old friend), embracing him affectionately, emphasizing his points here with a squeeze of his forearm, there a pat on the hand.

Haya, Cox, and Sánchez shared with Beals their perception that after two years of often-horrific bloodshed and repression, conditions had now coalesced in a way that favored the *Apristas*' (APRA members) prospects for seizing power. Peru's President Óscar R. Benavides (1876–1945), a military man who claimed to be holding the post on an interim basis until elections two years hence, had ordered Haya's release from prison five months earlier.[6]

Benavides had promised Haya upon his release that he would be free to organize political meetings, but his Prime Minister José de la Riva Agüero, a self-declared fascist sympathizer, was of another mind. He made sure that police harassment of APRA sharply intensified after Haya had delivered an inspirational call to action to a crowd of 40,000 gathered in Lima's *Plaza de Toros de Acho* (bullring) the previous November.[7]

A month later, Haya had flown to his support base of Trujillo, in Peru's northern Chicama Valley, to pay homage to the estimated 1,500 *Apristas* who had been massacred and buried in open graves at the nearby Chan Chan ruins in July 1932. Again, his visit had drawn a multitude of APRA militants whose revolutionary spirit he whipped up with another of his almost mystical oratorical flights:

> I don't have words! I don't have words! I have to extract them, one by one, from the painful depths of two years that seem like two centuries, two centuries of suffering, two centuries of intense work on the evolution of our spirit. Because that is the achievement of our two years of work: a work of the spirit. That is what our land was missing. It was bereft, without the wind of the cosmic, of the eternal, of the high, of the pure which, because it we did not have it, we had to ask the dead to provide it.[8]

Beals had arrived in Peru as the country was emerging from a tumultuous period of bloodletting between troops loyal to President and erstwhile Lieutenant Colonel Luís Sánchez Cerro (1889–1933)—assassinated the year before—and militants of Haya's APRA.

Sánchez Cerro, whom Beals dismissed as "a troglodyte," had overthrown President Augusto Leguía in August 1930, ending the dictator's *oncenio*, or eleven-year rule. Leguía's administration had been marked by a welcoming posture toward foreign—especially US—investment, and high prices for Peru's mineral, sugar, and cotton exports, and consequently, a decade of prosperity for the creole elite that also created jobs in mining and agriculture for many among the *mestizo* and Indian majority. The formula foundered, though, as export prices tumbled after the 1929 stock market crash. The ambitious Sánchez Cerro, whom Leguía had earlier appointed commander of the battalion in the southern city of Arequipa, Peru's second-largest urban center, launched a revolt. After taking power in the coup, Sánchez Cerro purged the high command of the army, air force, Guardia Civil, and the navy, including a US naval mission of several years' standing, replacing Leguía's appointees with his own loyalists.[9]

But Sánchez Cerro's honeymoon was short. His cozying up to the country's conservative business and landowning elite, including some of the old *Civilista* Party leaders ousted from power in 1919 by Leguía, alienated many civilian and military supporters who had initially rallied to his cause.[10] They grew dismayed as Sánchez Cerro, a dark-skinned *cholo* (*mestizo*) who, they thought, would respond to the demands of the poor, now seemed increasingly co-opted by the wealthy.

Opposition groups, including APRA, demanded elections in which only civilians would be allowed to run. On March 1, 1931, with the country drifting towards civil war after weeks of protests, Sánchez Cerro resigned his military post and as President, and left for a brief exile in France, vowing to return to join the electoral fray later that year as a civilian.[11]

It would be a battle royal, with his opponent the formidable Haya de la Torre, who had first come to prominence as leader of a students' strike in 1919, and as organizer of the so-called *universidades populares* (people's universities), in which students gave night classes in literacy and political economy to industrial and service workers. In 1923, Haya had also emerged as the leader of protests at Leguía's ultra-Catholic gesture of consecrating Peru to the Sacred Heart of Jesus. This latter episode, in which Haya's nascent political skills became apparent, had disturbed Leguía enough to dispatch Haya to his exile in Mexico.

While in Mexico, Haya founded the APRA, an ideological hybrid movement that called for a pan-American revolution across what he called "Indo-America," that was at once anti-imperialist, pro-indigenous, socialist, and nationalist. It unsettled elites, certainly, but it also eventually stirred opposition among Marxists such as the Cuban revolutionary Julio Antonio Mella, and later in Peru, José Carlos Mariátegui. Both of them dismissed Haya de la Torre's insistence on the need for a revolutionary alliance including workers, peasants, Indians, *and* the middle class, along with students. For their more doctrinaire bent, Haya's concept was a strategically unsound departure from Marxist theory which called for class struggle *against*, among others, the middle class.

Beals and Haya became friends in Mexico in 1924. Even if Beals—by 1934—found Haya's eclectic political program "fuzzy," as well as tarnished by "opportunistic vacillations" and even "a bureaucratic Fascist tinge," he also conceded that "[Haya's] eloquence made everything sound logical."[12] APRA was, he concluded in an excerpt from *Fire on the Andes* published in *Foreign Affairs*, "the first stirring of a long-oppressed people . . . the beginning of a new Peru."[13]

Haya had returned to Peru after seven years of exile in July 1931, to enthusiastic crowds adopting what became an APRA signature of waving white handkerchiefs, as the *jefe maximo* (Supreme Leader) held them spellbound with speeches appealing to what he called his fellow soldiers in "the civilian army" of APRA.[14]

Haya's support base was in Peru's north, where he won the backing of local sugar planters who had dominated the local economy until they had been forced to sell out to foreign-owned companies.[15] Haya was also supported by miners, manufacturing, and dockworkers in Lima and Callao, as well as a large swath among merchants and middle-class white-collar workers. "We must free the small land owner and miner who is forced to sell his property to 'la gran empresa,' [big business]" he exhorted his followers.[16]

But it was not enough to win the election. Sánchez Cerro also returned from his much-shorter exile, and proved an effective campaigner too, in addition to being better known than Haya and benefiting from the support of the sectors of the army and the business elite, including, significantly, the Miro-Quesada family that owned *El Comercio*, Lima's major daily. Sánchez Cerro was proclaimed the victor at the October polls with 152,062 votes to Haya's 106,007.[17] Haya and his APRA militants immediately denounced an electoral fraud—a charge Beals echoed in his book three years later—but this was not supported by convincing evidence, nor has it been sustained in most historical accounts.[18]

If Sánchez Cerro's mandate was fairly won, once in power, he quickly reverted to habits of violent repression of his APRA opposition. APRA activists, for their part, were actively seeking support within the army and Guardia Civil for an insurrection that would prevent Sánchez Cerro from being inaugurated in December.[19] In early 1932, Sánchez Cerro imposed martial law, and exiled all twenty-three *Aprista* congressmen who had been elected in the 1931 election. With Haya in hiding, an *Aprista* teenager—apparently acting alone—shot and wounded Sánchez Cerro on March 6, 1932.

Two months later, Haya was captured and jailed on suspicion of having masterminded the plot on Sánchez Cerro. The following day, the crews of two Peruvian navy cruisers mutinied in what was ostensibly part of an incipient APRA-inspired revolt to topple the regime. Sánchez Cerro reacted quickly and decisively. Eight alleged instigators of the mutiny were identified, court-martialed, and executed by a firing squad within three days.

With Haya now in prison, his brother Agustín led another revolt in Trujillo in July 1932, seizing the garrison and gaining control of the city. But the *Aprista* conspiracy fell apart due to a lack of coordination, and troops loyal to Sánchez Cerro retook control. Before the rebels fled, however, they executed thirty-five Guardia Civil officers they had held captive.[20]

Government troops exacted a pitiless revenge, killing somewhere around 1,500 Trujillo residents, many of them sugar workers suspected of participating in or sympathizing with the attempted insurrection.[21]

Two years later, Beals was taken by *Aprista* activists to the pre-Inca Chimú ruins of Chan Chan, outside Trujillo, where the massacre victims had been left buried in mass graves. He described the scene in *Fire on the Andes*:

> We penetrated on into the tangle of Chan Chan. There people, taken out on trucks, had been lined up alongside of ancient holes, ditches, and reservoirs and shot into their graves. Weeks passed before the townsfolk dared sneak out to cover over their bones, by then picked clean by vultures, rodents and town curs which had repaired here by hundreds to snarl over the unburied remains. For months Chan Chan was a carnal house. Its pestiferous stench rose to high heaven for miles about, even to Trujillo.[22]

Even as Sánchez Cerro needed the military to protect his regime from internal assault, his lack of control over it was evident when Peruvian troops invaded neighboring Colombia, taking Leticia, a contested territory Peru had ceded to Colombia in 1922.[23] This sparked yet another revolt, this one led by Colonel Gustavo Jiménez, the former commander of the Lima garrison. Jiménez was virulently opposed to Sánchez Cerro, and suspected the president was behind the Colombian invasion, which Jiménez saw as leading Peru into a humiliating military disaster.

Desperate to regain control, Sánchez Cerro recalled Óscar Benavides (1876–1945) from his post as Peru's Ambassador to Britain to take charge of the military.[24] Benavides was a highly-respected former military chief of staff who had been President briefly after overthrowing the populist leftist President Guillermo Billinghurst (1851–1915) in 1914.

It was a fortuitous move for Benavides, as Sánchez Cerro was assassinated while attending a military ceremony in April 1933; the killer, a seventeen-year-old *Aprista* named Abelardo Mendoza Leyva, was beaten to death on the spot by the outraged mob. Peru's assembly named Benavides to serve out the rest of the slain Sánchez Cerro's presidential term.

Beals' arrival in Peru came eight months after these events, as Benavides was establishing his power. Given the turmoil Benavides sought to quell, and the military intrigue that had fueled it, the new President launched a transformation of the military. It was to become a self-directed institution that would serve as guarantor of political stability rather than a tool in the hands of one or another faction, or itself a staging area for revolts and counter-revolts.

Though deeply skeptical of Benavides as a military autocrat, Beals saw grounds for hope in this, as the army offered an opportunity for advancement and political influence to Peru's Indian majority, elsewhere excluded and denigrated. "Peru's army . . . has often been an escape for oppressed native groups," Beals wrote. "Ultimately, as in Mexico, the army may, however blunderingly, whatever the ensuing evils, contribute to social justice."[25]

Beals' analysis of Peru's prospects in 1934 was influenced not only by his closeness to Haya de la Torre and sympathetic study of *Aprismo*, the political philosophy and policies advocated by *Apristas*. It was also informed by his experience of Mexico, and seminal works by Peruvian thinkers Luís Eduardo Valcárcel, an archeologist, and especially José Carlos Mariátegui, probably Latin America's most famous Marxist theorist.

In a gesture that showed the esteem Beals enjoyed in Latin America's leftist circles, Mariátegui had mailed him a copy of his *Seven Interpretive Essays on Peruvian Reality* in 1929.[26] Mariátegui and Beals never met though, as the Peruvian died a year later at thirty-six years old of complications related to a rare form of tuberculosis, as well as a bone disease that dogged him throughout his short life and which had resulted in the amputation of one of his legs.

Even so, his influence on Beals was such that one reviewer was led to accuse Beals of plagiarizing from Mariátegui's essays in *Fire on the Andes*.[27] Indeed, Beals was effusive in his praise of Mariátegui who, as editor of the literary and political journal *Amauta* (a Quechua term meaning "master" or "wise one" in the Inca empire era) in the 1920s, was the predominant voice of opposition during the final years of the Leguía dictatorship.

His seven essays, Beals wrote, "are a tour de force of social and economic analysis unequalled in any other South American country," and his work "has something of the inimitable strength of a majestic tree."[28]

The guiding principle uniting the work of Mariátegui, Valcárcel, and Haya de la Torre, and which Beals adopted as the defining theme of *Fire on the Andes*, is their denunciation of the systematic and deliberate exclusion of indigenous people from Peruvian society. These polemicists all condemned, with an uncompromising force that was new at the time, that a whole race had been exploited and brutalized into silent submission since the arrival of Pizarro's *conquistadores* in the sixteenth century.

The parallels between Beals's book and Valcárcel's *Tempest in the Andes*, published in 1927, are as striking as the titles are similar. Valcárcel warned that four million indigenous people—80 percent of the Peru's population—were in a state of incipient mass rebellion. Their plea of "Let us live!" would soon explode.[29]

Beals titled a chapter of *Fire on the Andes* after Valcárcel's "Tempest in the Andes" to present the case, calling Valcárcel's book "a challenge and a gospel . . . a message to all Indo-America."[30] He also repeated the formula Valcárcel defined as a solution, reinforced by Mariátegui in his preface to Valcárcel's book, that Peru's ascent to true nationhood depended on breaking the semi-feudal *gamonal* (bossist) system that kept the country's indigenous people landless and enslaved.

"The Indians are both a cultural bloc, i.e., a nationality, and also an oppressed class," Beals wrote. "Revalidation of Indian culture strikes a blow at class exploitation. Economic liberation [through a restoration of Inca-era land tenure and the village *ayllu* governance systems] forges new weapons for invigorating native culture."[31]

As was the case with Augusto César Sandino in Nicaragua, Beals again cast himself in the role of interpreter of Haya de la Torre, as well as of Valcárcel and Mariátegui, to an American audience.

For example, Mariátegui had approvingly pointed out that Valcárcel resolved his *indigenist* philosophy politically, through socialism, and repeated his prophecy that "the indigenous proletariat awaits its Lenin."[32] Beals paraphrased this to "the indigenous dictatorship of Peru approaches; it is merely waiting its time and leader."[33]

Beals rationalized his flights of infatuation with some politicians—such as Álvaro Obregón and Plutarco Elías Calles in Mexico, Sandino, Grau in

Cuba, and now Haya in Peru—by his contention that political theory was only as good as those who shaped it into a program and inspired large numbers of people to support it.

Even if he had some premonitions of doubt about Haya and *Aprismo*, Beals's portrait of both was exceedingly favorable; it was publicized not just in his book aimed at American readers, but inside Peru as well.

When Beals visited Trujillo, for example, he was received by the editors of the *Aprista* newspapers *El Norte* and *Acción Aprista*, both of which reported his glowing praise for Haya and his philosophy: "Haya de la Torre is the most interesting, the most noble, the highest order of leader in Latin America," Beals is quoted as saying.[34] *Aprismo*, he added, is "a movement of formidable realism and authentically of the left in the semi-colonial countries. I admire its ideology, but I admire even more the nearly mystical fervor that it has awakened in the soul of the people. One way or another it has to win . . . my sense is that the problem it faces is surviving as a political organization. If it resists . . . despite the cruelty that the adversary puts into persecuting it, the battle will be won. And even if it is destroyed, which I don't think will happen, its ideology will prevail."[35]

He repeated similar observations in his piece on APRA in *Foreign Affairs*. There too, he cut quickly to the nub of why APRA so aroused the antipathy of communists, fascists, and capitalists at once: "For the communists this is obviously a new brand of fascism; for the feudal elements it is obviously little removed from outright communism." Based on an observation that capitalism and democracy could not be saved in Latin America because they had never existed there, Beals endorsed APRA as "the only type of movement that meets the actual issues and is likely to succeed."[36]

It is difficult to gauge what influence this had with the US foreign policy elite. Certainly, US companies such as Grace Brothers (later W. R. Grace and Company) and Cerro de Pasco Corporation, which had major investments in Peru's copper mines, sugar plantations, and refineries, were alarmed at the prospect of an APRA government. But with Franklin Delano Roosevelt's (FDR) hands-off, Good Neighbor approach in Latin America, and Haya's astute reassurances to US diplomats, Beals's positive review reinforced the idea that Haya was a democrat and, for all his radical oratory, a politician of moderate instincts.

One influential reader, Josephus Daniels, the onetime FDR mentor who was now US Ambassador to Mexico, wrote Beals that he had read both the article and *Fire on the Andes,* which he found "so interesting that I could not go to sleep until I had finished it."[37]

In *Fire on the Andes*, Beals rendered Peru in what had by now become a kind of Bealsian genre. Similar in format to *Mexico: An Interpretation*, *Mexican Maze*, and *The Crime of Cuba*, the book, published in November 1934, combined history with a travelogue full of sketches of characters he met and cities and regions he visited. Throughout, it is salted with opinions and digs at favorite targets such as Lima's phony elite for its "artificial aping" of European and American culture "with instincts of parvenu wealth, ostentation, snobbishness, and contempt for [their] native land."[38] He also skewers with equal relish Catholic priests, political bosses, faded aristocrats, and military brass, providing thumbnail sketches of these archetypes drawn from characters he met. The last two chapters—the best in the book—combine political analysis with cultural criticism that reflects an exhaustive review of Peruvian literature. This last illustrates his reading of Mariátegui's *Literature on Trial* essay, as well as, perhaps, his adoption of a methodology similar to that of his friend Victor F. Calverton, who had recently published *The Liberation of American Literature*.[39]

Despite his withering portraits of certain Peruvians, the narrative is more controlled than in the earlier books. Beals reins in his sentacious instinct to allow the injustices and atrocities he either witnessed or learned about to speak for themselves, instead of inflating his prose to underline his outrage.

In his customary nod to the need for some racy elements in his book, he included a bizarre sketch of a half-European, half-indigenous woman he met in the jungle near Juanjí in the Huallagua Valley, the remote northern region made infamous in the 1980s for its coca labs. The She-Devil of the Huallagua, as Beals called her, was rumored by his indigenous guides to have ensnared a German and another American traveler who had vanished. Beals waved off these fears ("such things happen in Chicago") and forged on.

He soon met her along their path, "about twenty-five, body supple, features uncommonly handsome . . . a mocking smile illuminating her tanned face." As his guides urged that they all flee, Beals insisted on tarrying, fascinated by this barefoot Amazon Lorelei who "carried herself like a Queen."[40] After at least a couple of days, during which Beals swims in a lagoon with the she-devil, who introduces herself as Matilda, enjoys a couple of meals prepared by her, and watches her dance by firelight, he relates that "she crept softly into my arms . . . lay still for a while, then her lips sought mine."[41]

Beals later offered that particular chapter to *Esquire* Magazine, where editor Arnold Gingrich called it "the best combination of sex and adventure that we had had to date," and thereupon lamented not being able to publish it because it had already appeared as part of the published book.[42] Fun to read, which was Beals' purpose, but it is the kind of anecdote that pervades his work and has been seen by some critics as a tall tale, purple, or puerile, or all three. In this case, its inclusion likely drew more readers to the subject, but also diminished Beals's credibility, especially in elite and academic circles, in his time, and ever since.

That he was able to produce this 448-page book in a matter of months, while traveling and doing other pieces besides, is evidence of a near-manic capacity for work that would endure throughout the 1930s. It was also made possible, in part, by his new agent, Maxim Lieber, whose eager marketing and promotion of Beals's work freed Carleton from this burden, enabling him to focus on writing.

During Beals's extended stay in New York City in 1932, Lieber had approached him much as he had other writers of dissident left inclination. Formerly editor-in-chief at the publishing arm of the bookstore chain Brentano's, Lieber had first dealt with Beals when he asked him, in 1929, to supply a preface for the English edition of *Los de Abajo* (*The Underdogs*), the classic novel of the Mexican Revolution by Mariano Azuela.

A garrulous and high-strung son of Polish *émigrés*, Lieber launched his own literary agency after Brentano's liquidated its publishing business in 1930. Short, with a toothbrush mustache, he was an energetic agent, well-connected, not only with book publishers, but also with editors of magazines such as *Harper's*, *Esquire*, *Current History*, and *Vanity Fair*, among others. He was also a Communist Party member, whose enthusiasm for the cause was such that he would sometimes encourage his clients to join as well.[43] In 1951, he would flee the country after Whittaker Chambers, testifying before the US House UnAmerican Activities Committee, identified Lieber as a Communist.

Although their business relationship had some growing pains, with Beals often prone to bypass Lieber and deal directly with his publishers, he soon came to rely heavily on his agent, who became a close friend.

With the Depression hurting all book sales, and *Fire on the Andes*' November 15 publication too late to get the full benefit of the holiday season, it failed to earn back Beals's advance from J. B. Lippincott.[44] By late March, it had sold only 3,172 copies.[45] Nonetheless, its critical reception was respectful. In the *New York Times*, Robert Luther Duffus qualified Beals's story as being of interest "not only to students of Latin American civilization, but to those who are looking for light on the nature of civilization itself."[46] Beals's manner, wrote Louise Bogan in the *New Yorker*, "as always, is fervent and even feverish, but it keeps you interested."[47]

Even the pro-Communist weekly *New Masses* liked it, with reviewer Maurice Halperin (writing under the pseudonym Frank L. Gordon, so as not to expose himself to dismissal from his post as a lecturer at the University of Oklahoma) somewhat condescendingly praising Beals for having overtaken his earlier work, "that of a first-class muckraker and a highly entertaining travel writer," by having now grasped the "social fascist nature of *Aprismo*, the essential opportunism of Haya de la Torre and the class basis of Peru's coming revolution."[48]

Ernest Gruening, in contrast to the Communist Halperin, adopted a critique in keeping with his more liberal reformist position. He thought Beals too harsh on Haya, whom Gruening described as "high-minded, courageous, steadfast, enlightened . . . intellectually and morally . . . far ahead of his contemporaries."[49]

***

In early March, while Beals was still in Peru, J. B. Lippincott published his novel *Black River*. The logic behind releasing it even as *The Crime of Cuba* was still selling briskly seemed questionable, and may have undermined the novel's sales, which turned out to be desultory. Most mainstream critics panned it as a clumsy attempt at anti-imperialist propaganda. A *New York Times* review described it as "a furiously written morality play" which, despite "a fine, Gothic strength," nonetheless, "as a novel, leaves much to be desired."[50]

*Black River*'s failure as a novel is especially unfortunate as Beals displays an informed and credible backing for his moral theme, namely a denunciation of the rapacious hunger for oil which corrupts or destroys everything and everyone in its path. As with his other novels, he drew many of his characters straight from real life, rendering them, for the most part, as grotesque caricatures. Simon J. Bartlett, the grasping oil tycoon from California, is an obvious takeoff on Edward Doheny, while the local Tampico commander, General Yarza, is a composite derived from the corrupt and lascivious officers to whom Beals gave English classes in Mexico City during the Carranza administration.

He paints a picture of a noble Mexican peasant family robbed of their land, meager possessions, and dignity by Bartlett and his ex-Marine enforcer, Tom Guard, both of whom are depicted as cartoonish criminals. The canvas is filled out by an entourage that includes Bartlett's vacuous wife, a spoiled daughter and son, the latter entangled with a manipulative fiancée who flirts with others, notably Guard, at every opportunity while sneering at, and eventually abandoning, her husband-to-be. Sleazy lawyers, raucous prostitutes, and a weak and dissipated young Mexican, Mico, manipulated by an extortionate mistress named *La Paloma* (The Dove) complete the tableau of degradation. Woven around this fictional circus is a summary thread of political history, with cameos by Carranza in his fight with US oil companies, the Pershing expedition, and the Mexican dimension of the Teapot Dome scandal.

Beals's haste in producing this work is evident in the choppy sentences, jolting transitions, and hackneyed dialogue. At its core, however, it is redeemed by its moral clarity and the depth of knowledge Beals displays of the interplay between Mexico's long revolutionary convulsion, US oil interests, and US policy towards Mexico. Indeed, Beals consciously sought in *Black River* to give impressionistic voice to material on the fraudulent awarding of oil drilling titles to Doheny that he had gathered in the 1920s while investigating the oil boom in Mexico. The resulting pieces, which he had then submitted, in turn, to the *New Republic* and the *Nation*, were never published, as editors of both magazines feared libel action from Doheny interests.[51]

In *Black River*, Beals reproduced not only characters from real life but plot as well. At one point in his narrative, as if recognizing that he is writing a kind of history rather than a novel, he includes a footnote to advise readers that he has compressed the time intervals between political events in Mexico to knit his story more tidily. The core of the plot is a scheme concocted by Bartlett to provoke US military intervention in Mexico to secure his company's oil wells, and thereby cast aside the Mexican government's insistence on legal title and royalty payments. Bartlett and the US Consul in Tampico, the "glandulous" Charles Sadler, conspire over what they baptize as the "Artichoke Plan."

> "The US may have to intervene in this cock-eyed country," [Bartlett said].
> Sadler shook his head mournfully. "If I had my way we'd march in tomorrow. Pershing should go on to Mexico City at once. But there's still too much opposition sentiment in our country for such a step."
> Bartlett raged. "We backed Carranza. Now look at his pronouncements, his anti-American attitude. By George, we'll take over the oil region—by force if necessary. If the American government can't get up backbone enough to do it, why, we'll do it ourselves."
> "Did you ever hear of Signor Cavour, Minister of the House of Savoy?" asked Mr. Sadler. "He's one of my heroes."
> "So!" Bartlett concealed his ignorance.
> "Do you remember his remarks as to how he was going to unify Italy: 'I'll eat it, leaf by leaf, like an artichoke.'"
> "Ha, Ha! Not bad."
> "Perhaps we can apply that nearer home. 'Leaf by leaf.'"
> "An artichoke plan!" Bartlett brought his fist down.
> "You're right. You've hit on the idea I've been working on for some time. The oil region must be split off from Mexico. Suppose the United States is engaged in world-struggle tomorrow. An unfriendly government here—and where are we at? Are we going to let some ragged General stand in our way? We can't permit the oil supply to be cut off under any circumstances. I'm a patriot, Sadler. Constantly I have my country's needs in mind. Won't it be better to settle the whole problem beforehand?"[52]

Though cast as fiction, this conspiracy bore almost photographic resemblance to real events between 1915 and the early 1920s. United States oil companies had lobbied President Woodrow Wilson and Congress in favor of a forceful US rejection of Mexico's 1917 Querétaro constitutional provisions, which claimed subsoil oil and mineral rights. They got a sympathetic hearing from the US State Department and powerful Republican US Senators Henry Cabot Lodge and Albert Fall, both of whom also appear, behind pseudonyms, in *Black River*.

But Wilson, even when confronted by Carranza's refusal to negotiate the constitutional provisions, preferred a conciliatory approach. Once re-elected in 1916, Wilson withdrew the Pershing Punitive Expeditionary troops that had remained in northern Mexico since March of the previous year. Because he shared Carranza's democratic constitutionalist posture and adhered in principle to the idea that every people has the right to determine its own form of government, Wilson resisted pressures for military intervention from the oil interests and his own State Department.[53]

In early 1927, two articles by Beals were published in the *New Republic*—one of which presented "the Great Artichoke Theory of International Relations" as applied to US-Mexico relations—and suggested that Frank B. Kellogg, President Coolidge's US Secretary of State, was risking war with Mexico to protect the oil companies, notably Doheny's, which held 1.3 million acres and 36 percent of Mexico's petroleum production capacity at the time.[54] Beals had been frustrated, however, as he had obtained copies of correspondence between Doheny and the US State Department that documented what his *New Republic* articles only implied. Had his articles that openly proved the existence of a conspiracy been published, they might have precipitated Kellogg's resignation.

Though its setting is Mexico and its theme anti-imperialism, *Black River* is a less doctrinaire variation on the *proletarian novel* genre popular among leftist American writers in the 1930s. Beals combines his indictment of lockstep US military and diplomatic support for a big-footing US oil tycoon in Mexico with an anti-materialist social critique of American culture. In this, *Black River* is in a similar category, though sloppier and less assured, as Sinclair Lewis's *Main Street*, or novels around the same period by John Dos Passos, Ring Lardner, James T. Farrell, and Josephine Herbst. In some ways, too, *Black River* can be seen as a novelistic treatment of upstart American neo-imperialism that is analogous to George Orwell's take on the British Empire version, then in decline, in *Burmese Days*.

Despite its weaknesses, *Black River*'s fast-paced plot and sharply-defined conflict sparked a ripple of interest from Hollywood. James M. Crofton, owner of the Agua Caliente Casino Hotel, a lavish Tijuana resort and racetrack with its own airstrip, announced at a press conference in November 1934 that he planned to finance a film based on *Black River*. Crofton's idea was invented with the boxer-turned-actor Max Baer, then visiting Mexico. Baer, Crofton claimed, would play the character Tom Guard, while Mexican movie star Dolores del Rio would play *La Paloma*. Meantime, a Fox Motion Pictures representative had already approached J. B. Lippincott for an exclusive option on the movie rights. The prospect fizzled, however, as the promoters' partnership broke up, probably as a result of Mexican President Lázaro Cárdenas' (1895–1970) decision to ban gambling in 1935, which dealt a blow to Crofton's casino revenues.[55]

Although the idea of a movie based on his novel excited both Beals and Lippincott, Lieber discouraged him from pursuing fiction. "I know that every writer's ambition is to succeed in fiction," Lieber wrote Beals just after *Fire on the Andes* was published in November, "but your gift truly lies in the field of first-class journalism. Now don't get sore at me."[56]

\*\*\*

Beals finished his intensive round of traveling and research in Peru and drafted his *Fire on the Andes* manuscript in marathon writing sessions through May and June 1934, during which he was also absorbed by his new love affair with Blanca Rosa. She was his fiancée now, and the urgency of their marriage was quickened by Carleton's impending departure.

Beals left first, aboard a ship to Mexico, where he made arrangements through the US Embassy, under the friendly stewardship of Josephus Daniels, to obtain immigration papers for Blanca Rosa, who joined him in Mexico City in August.

Beals and Blanca Rosa were wed in September and celebrated the event with a relatively intimate group that included Blanca Rosa's sister Seyna, and about twenty of Carleton's Mexico City friends. After the wedding, Blanca moved from the hotel to Beals's apartment on Insurgentes Boulevard. They lingered there for three months, sleeping late mornings, strolling around the city, sharing meals in restaurants and cafés, and touring the surrounding area. By the time they left for New York, Blanca Rosa was pregnant.

The couple arrived in New York just before Christmas, where they settled initially in Beals's apartment at 105 East 15th Street, near Union Square. It was a busy period, exciting and full of promise as Blanca Rosa, though callow and her English halting, charmed Carleton's friends with her Latin warmth and vivacity. Their idyll was blemished, however, when she suffered a miscarriage in late January, followed by a hysterectomy.[57] They would never have children.

They nonetheless enjoyed the big-city lifestyle, as Beals's success ensured a steady stream of requests to speak, as well as dinner invitations from Lieber, with whom he locked horns in friendly rivalry over long games of chess. Other friends included Maurice Becker, the artist, and his wife Dorothy Baldwin, now living in Manhattan, and left writers such as Kyle Crichton, a columnist (under the pseudonym of Robert Forsythe) for *New Masses*, but who supported his wife and three children by simultaneously serving as a senior editor with the mainstream *Scribner's* and later *Collier's* magazine.[58]

Another friend at this time was Victor F. Calverton (né George Goetz), the loquacious editor of the radical *Modern Monthly*, and his companion, actress and writer Nina Melville. Beals had agreed to be on the *Monthly*'s masthead as a contributing editor, sharing with Calverton the often-awkward independent radical space between the pro-Stalin Communist Party of the

USA, then at loggerheads with the Trotskyists and a smaller group of intellectuals who followed labor activist Jay Lovestone. He also enjoyed Calverton's prolix banter on sexual politics and American literature, occasionally enlivened by a shared marijuana reefer.

The Beals couple's Union Square neighborhood was a major New York staging area of leftist protest as America lurched into the depths of the Depression. Just a few minutes' walk from Beals' apartment, along Fourth Avenue, weekly left-wing parades often ended with clubbing of demonstrators by mounted police.[59]

\*\*\*

While in Peru working on *Fire on the Andes*, Beals developed the idea that he would try to apply his journalistic method to the United States.[60] Having acted as a kind of public witness to denounce dictators in Latin America, he fastened on what he saw as an analogous US target, a *made in America* demagogue, namely Louisiana's populist US Senator—and previously Governor—Huey P. Long. After some handwringing about the danger of a libel suit that a critical book on Long might provoke, Jefferson Jones at J. B. Lippincott relented and endorsed the project, advancing him $800 for it.[61]

To complement his imminent Louisiana tour, Beals pitched George Merritt Bond, editor of the *New York Post* and the North American Newspaper Alliance, on the idea of a series on Cuba. The island had slid into chaos once again, with a general strike under way, which Batista met with repression and the jailing of some four thousand protestors. Bond agreed and so, with Blanca Rosa on his arm, Beals boarded a Pullman coach from New York to Miami, from which they took the short-hop Pan-American flight to Havana on March 13, 1935.

Within a week of his arrival in Cuba, Beals's first stories had already aroused the ire of US Ambassador Jefferson Caffery. Caffery, a laconic career Foreign Service officer from Louisiana who had replaced Welles in Cuba in December 1933, had granted Beals an interview soon after his arrival in Havana. He was suspicious of Beals, of whom he knew from the Sandino stories which had been published when Caffery was the US minister in San Salvador.

Any hope Caffery may have had of influencing Beals's reporting was soon dashed. Beals's reports, published in member papers of the Newspaper Alliance as well as the *New York Times* and later in the *Nation*, quoted the envoy's enthusiastic approval of Batista's regime in juxtaposition to vivid descriptions of the regime's beating and jailing of union leaders during the wave of strikes that had paralyzed the island for months.[62]

The Cuban government, led by President Carlos Mendieta but whose real seat of power was in Batista's Camp Columbia barracks office, was roiled by labor unrest arising from the impact on its sugar exports of the Great Depression, a plunge which continued despite the Roosevelt administration's moves to restore credits and exempt Cuba from the US *Smoot-Hawley Tariff* (*Tariff Act of 1930*).[63] Antonio Guiteras, the most radical of the 1933 revolutionary junta leaders, now headed *Joven Cuba*, a political-military organization he had formed in May 1934. It was leading an armed struggle against the regime, calling for land reform, labor rights and decentralization of power.[64]

Beals's new round of reports on Cuba, reminiscent of his *Crime of Cuba* episode in their criticism of an American neo-colonial grip on the island, prompted new denunciations of US policy by Roger Baldwin's International Committee for Political Prisoners. It also led New York-based leftists, all members of the Communist Party-backed League of American Writers headed by Waldo Frank, to dispatch a fifteen-person "American Commission to Investigate Labor and Social Conditions in Cuba" in July, led by playwright Clifford Odets, known as the "Golden Boy" of left theater.[65] It also included Manning Johnson of the Food Workers Industrial Union and Dora Zucker of the Needle Trades Union, as well as student leaders and a Congregational Church pastor, Reverend Herman F. Reissig.[66]

A sendoff event was organized to mark the Commission's departure from New York harbor. Beals was among the speakers who denounced Batista and underlined the Commission's purpose of exposing US complicity, despite the abolition of the Platt Amendment,[67] with a dictatorship that oppressed the Cuban people, and denied them access to democratic means to replace it.

Upon their arrival in Havana, the Commission's members were arrested, marched through the city's streets at gunpoint by customs police, and detained overnight at Tiscornia detention center, Havana's version of New York's Ellis Island.[68] Hours earlier, a Cuban reception committee of writers, activists, and labor leaders had been clubbed by police, and many of their number jailed. The visitors were ordered deported the following day, and forced to return to New York, their mission unaccomplished.

By its refusal to accept such scrutiny, though, the Mendieta-Batista regime implicitly acknowledged its guilt and triggered a controversy that embarrassed it, along with Caffery. The commission members were met upon their return to New York's Pier 13 by several hundred supporters waving placards denouncing Cuba's tyranny and US complicity with it.[69] Odets recounted the story of the group's detention in the *New York Post*, as well as *New Masses*, and addressed several public meetings about it, accompanied by Roger Baldwin, poet Archibald MacLeish, and Beals.[70] He also teamed up with Beals to publish a thirty-one-page nickel pamphlet, *Rifle Rule in Cuba*, in which their complementary essays delivered a blistering critique of Caffery's role in making the US embassy a "propaganda bureau for the Cuban government."[71]

In his contribution, Beals counterpoised the Odets-led commission with Caffery's earlier initiative with Cuban business leaders to mount a petition signed by 300,000 Cubans and presented by the sponsors to FDR, expressing gratitude for US support during the island's travails. Beals claimed the signatures had been extracted for pittances paid to desperately poor Cubans and described the petition as a "blood book" and "a monstrous joke."[72]

"Caffery should receive a salary as press-agent for the Batista tyranny," Beals wrote, alleging that the ambassador frequently pressured US journalists in Cuba to suppress all news unfavorable to the Cuban regime. Odets, meanwhile, described a visit by the US vice-consul, a Mr. Edgar, to his commission members during their detention. "Apparently, the Cuban government doesn't want you," [Edgar] said. We asked: 'Why?' 'You know why,' was his answer."[73]

Even the *New York Post*, which had commissioned Odets beforehand to report on the group's mission, joined the chorus of protest. Its publisher, J. David Stern, wired US Secretary of State Hull, urging that Caffery be replaced for failing to protect an accredited US newspaper representative.[74] His was one of hundreds of telegrams and letters urging Caffery's recall. It was followed by the publication in major New York dailies of a petition calling for the same, signed by prominent editors and writers, including the *Nation*'s Oswald Garrison Villard, Bruce Bliven of the *New Republic*, Roger Baldwin and, once again, Carleton Beals.[75] The petition held Caffery and the US government "directly responsible . . . for the regime nominally headed by President Mendieta, but in fact controlled by the army under Colonel Batista."[76]

Caffery complained to Merritt Bond that Beals's allegations were unfounded. Beals was well-armed to respond, however, citing Caffery's threat to *New York Times*' Cuba correspondent J. D. Phillips, to have him deported if he continued to file stories that threatened American interests.[77] Beals's source for this was a letter he had received from Phillips' wife Ruby, in which she also suggested that Caffery's purpose was to shore up the Mendieta-Batista regime against more radical remnants of the abortive 1933 revolutionary junta, in return for which Mendieta would recognize Cuba's outstanding debt to the Chase Bank.[78] The urgency of the effort was heightened by the Roosevelt administration's concern that a Cuban explosion would undermine the still-new Good Neighbor policy, and jeopardize FDR's prospects for re-election in 1936.

By late summer 1935, after the killing in May by Batista's forces of *Joven Cuba* leader Guiteras, Beals described the Cuban dictator as a "hated tyrant" in an article in the *Nation* titled "The New Machado in Cuba." Read many decades later, in the light of the later rise of Castro and the collapse of US-Cuba relations, as well as nearly fifty years of US support for right-wing dictators across the hemisphere, its analytical lens is at once sharp and eerily prophetic:

Batista's type, that of the Latin American caudillo or military chieftain who leaps from the dregs to whip up a powerful personal and military following to conquer the state, has long commanded the curious attention of novelists and psychologists, but of few sociologists. The Batistas are a sociological phenomenon resulting from militarism, political corruption, race and cultural conflicts, feudal colonialism and imperialism. Depending for victory on desperate rebellion rather than prior mass organization, such ambitious types, however noble their expressed purposes, have invariably failed because the day after their success, not having the wit, ability, or patience to create a mass following, they have found their only sure support in machine-guns. The gulf between the literate and illiterate, between countryside and urban life, is so vast that popular leaders have usually soon been weaned away from dangerous alliances with the people they promised to help and promptly have become the petty tools of feudal aristocrats, foreign capitalists, and American pro-consuls, thus rapidly converting themselves into hated tyrants against whom new revolutions have inevitably been started.[79]

\*\*\*

From Havana, Carleton and Blanca sailed in early April 1935 to New Orleans, where they booked a room in a small hotel in the city's Garden District. There Beals met up with Abel Plenn, a cousin of Anita Brenner's whom he frequently hired to type manuscripts for him. Plenn, an aspiring writer, was about ten years younger than Beals. He was chronically broke, his ambition frustrated by a combination of modest talent and a freelance-writing market shrunk by the Depression. Beals had earlier decided to help Plenn—and himself—by inviting the younger man to collaborate on his planned biography of Huey P. Long.

Plenn had been at work for several weeks in Louisiana, compiling notes and outlining chapters, drawing on newspaper archives, statistics, and local interviews, notably with black and white farmers. Now Beals set to work on fleshing out and expanding the manuscript. He wrote and rewrote chapters, stamping them with his customary flourishes of strident reproof, adding portrait descriptions of key characters and most of all, giving the book a distinctive point-of-view.

Huey P. Long was, by the spring of 1935, the most talked-of man in America. Propelled by his oratory and promises to the poor, Long had roared from the relative obscurity of northern Louisiana. Elected at twenty-five years old to the state's railroad commission, he parlayed this victory into a successful 1928 run for Governor. A populist outwardly in the mold of William Jennings Bryan, Long inveighed against the Old Ring New Orleans bosses who had run the state for generations, channeling the anger of the little man.

"Every man a king, but nobody wears a crown," he demanded, taking Bryan's phrase for his own. In just two years as Governor, he had built hundreds of miles of roads, 111 bridges, distributed free textbooks to every one of the state's schoolchildren, and lavished public funds on Louisiana State University. All the while, he denounced the Standard Oil Company, and finally succeeded in imposing a five-cent tax for every barrel of oil refined in the state.

After fighting off an impeachment drive, Long had taken his ambition from the Louisiana state capital of Baton Rouge to Washington, winning a US Senate seat in 1930. Once on Capitol Hill, the newly-minted Louisiana Senator launched a nationwide "Share-Our-Wealth" movement, his self-styled plan to cap personal fortunes at $10 million, and redistribute the excess so as to ensure that each family owned a home, an automobile, and a radio. By early 1935, driven by his restless energy, power lust, and charisma, he boasted that his movement had attracted seven million adherents.

In fact, it was not just boasting. Long had hired as many as sixty stenographers to handle his fan mail, which had reached ten thousand letters a day. His filibusters of down-home riffs in the Senate, arms wheeling like a windmill, one fist pounding into the other palm, left his opponents flummoxed. Meantime, he retained a chokehold on Louisiana's state government, including its Governor O. K. Allen—Huey's handpicked successor—the legislature and every state regulatory body.

All this was making FDR's White House distinctly uncomfortable. The President's brain-trusters had stopped reassuring themselves that the Kingfish's buffoonish exterior, with his screeds of Bible-quoting and bar-room name-calling, would make him a laughing-stock. They now worried that Long, perhaps in league with the fire-breathing radio priest, Father Charles Coughlin of Detroit, was poised to launch a third-party bid for the Presidency in 1936.

In early March, public attention had been directed to the populist Louisiana US Senator when Brigadier General Hugh Johnson, formerly head of the National Industrial Recovery Administration, had delivered a blistering attack on Long in a nationally-broadcast speech delivered at New York's Waldorf-Astoria Hotel.

"You can snort at Huey Long," Hugh Johnson fulminated before his well-heeled and influential audience, "but this country was never under a greater menace."[80]

Johnson's speech was initially welcomed by mainstream pundits such as Walter Lippmann and Arthur Krock. But the media debate it stirred lasted several weeks and only raised Long's national profile, prompting many liberal critics to conclude that Johnson had done more to fuel his political prospects than douse them.[81]

All this seemed fortuitous timing for Beals, who had undertaken the Long project partly to build his profile by expanding his audience beyond the relatively small number of readers interested in Latin America.

Just weeks after Beals had completed the manuscript, Long was assassinated on September 8 in the lobby of the grandiose thirty-story Louisiana State Capitol Building he had erected. His publishers asked him to add an epilogue chapter and hastened to get the book out before public interest in Long subsided.

*The Story of Huey P. Long* was published in early December 1935. It was the first biography of the Kingfish to appear after his death, and thus became prologue to a vast literature that includes *All the King's Men*, the classic 1947 political novel by Robert Penn Warren. Beals's characterization of Long as a "dictator" was not original either in its time or since, but he did offer an apt comparison of Long's "undisciplined picturesque-ness" and "insurgent" appeal in Louisiana to what he saw as analogous populist movements in Cuba, Mexico and Peru.

Beals used his Latin American experience to place Long—and Louisiana's political culture—in context. When Long faced impeachment as Louisiana's Governor in 1929, Beals opined that he was, "no worse than most of the men attacking him" and acknowledged that, "whatever his ultimate purpose, however insincere, he had stood on the side of righteous if befuddled measures."[82]

His rule in Louisiana was an odd conglomeration of Hitlerism, hokum, and Tammany Ring methods, Beals wrote. And his Share-Our-Wealth campaign, in full throttle in 1935, was "either demagogic hypocrisy or else economic ignorance so abysmal as to inspire awe, a monstrous and tragic joke, which can only bring disillusion and defeat and stave off the real achievement of economic justice."[83]

In this last observation, closely parallel to his similar comments on Batista in Cuba, Beals touches the heart of populism. Huey's brand-built support for promised change by channeling the vague emotions, longing, frustrations and sympathies of "the ignorant unemployed, the poor, the wage-earner, the farmer, the precarious middle-class." But it was a shell game, Beals concluded, as Long's plan "could not be made effective, and the attempt to do so would have plunged [America] into chaos, he would have been forced by dictatorial methods . . . to push us more rapidly into feudal military capitalism, as has happened on a small scale in Louisiana."[84]

Compared to subsequent Long biographies, such as T. Harry Williams' *Huey Long*, awarded a Pulitzer Prize in 1969, Beals's effort has to be considered modest. He was not an expert on Louisiana, and his research was hasty and mostly confined to newspaper reports of the period. He did not interview Huey Long, and spoke only once to Gerald L. K. Smith, deputy leader of the Share-Our-Wealth movement. Still, his account is balanced, well-informed and clear-eyed. Like most people who observed Long, Beals "came away with a sense of mingled admiration and contempt," reviewer Francis Brown wrote in the *New York Times*.[85]

Beals's treatment of the Long story is probably most valuable for the analytical perspective he uses in describing the "feudal, semi-colonial" Louisiana political culture that produced Huey Long, and which he finds more closely akin to those of Latin America than Connecticut.

Such a comparison was not just the result of Beals's own personal experience of demagogues and gangster rule from Mussolini to Batista. It was appropriate to compare Louisiana with much of Latin America in the early 1930s; like the southern republics, Louisiana was dirt-poor, economically dependent, and divided socially and racially.

Its northern white farmers were, he wrote, "under the heel of the plantation creoles in the South, [and] later under the banks and corporations." Black disenfranchisement, and widespread white illiteracy and poverty had "prevented true democratic practices."[86]

This situation, combined with what Beals identified as a failure of poor-white farmers to join political forces with black farmers, allowed a new "feudal-industrialist alliance" to emerge. Long took advantage of this to seize power by promising reform to both black and white poor farmers, all the while adeptly skirting the race issue. At the same time, he co-opted sections of the creole elite, both rural and urban, by reassuring them that he was merely a power-seeker, not a revolutionary. It was a theme to which Beals would return.

## NOTES

1. Jefferson Jones to Carleton Beals, November 23, 1933, Carleton Beals Collection (CBC), Howard Gotlieb Archival Research Center, Boston University (hereafter cited CBC); see Carleton Beals, *Black River* (Philadelphia: J. B. Lippincott, 1934).
2. Andrew Freeman to Carleton Beals, November 7, 1933, CBC.
3. Maxim Lieber to Carleton Beals, June 27, 1934, CBC.
4. Carleton Beals, "Aprismo: The Rise of Haya de la Torre," *Foreign Affairs* 13, no. 2 (1935), 242.
5. Beals, "Aprismo," 242.
6. Luis Alberto Sánchez, *Haya de la Torre y el APRA* (Lima: Editorial Universo, Segunda Edición, 1980), 284.
7. Sánchez, *Haya de la Torre y el APRA*, 2nd ed. (Lima, Perú: Editorial Universo, 1980), 285.
8. Sánchez, *Haya de la Torre y el APRA*, 288.
9. Daniel M. Masterson, *Militarism and Politics in Latin America: Peru from Sánchez Cerro to Sendero Luminoso* (Westport, CT: Greenwood Press, 1991), 43.
10. Peter F. Klarén, *Modernization, Dislocation, and Aprismo: Origins of the Peruvian Aprista Party, 1870–1932* (Austin: University of Texas Press, 1973), 121.
11. Masterson, *Militarism and Politics*, 44.
12. Carleton Beals, *Fire on the Andes* (Philadelphia: J. B. Lippincott, 1934), 429; Carleton Beals, *Latin America: World in Revolution* (New York: Abelard-Schuman, 1963), 106.
13. Beals, *Fire on the Andes*, 429.
14. Jorge Basadre, *Historia de la República del Perú, 1822–1933* (translation), 6th ed. (Lima, Perú: Editorial Universitaria, 1963), vol. 14, 133–36.
15. Klarén, *Modernization*, 123.

16. Klarén, *Modernization*, 133.
17. Klarén, *Modernization*, 168.
18. See Basadre, *Historia*, 167. Jorge Basadre, Peru's foremost historian, and neither *Aprista* (pro-APRA), nor *Sanchezcerrista* (pro-Sanchez Cerro), described the 1931 election as having been conducted with "exemplary tranquility" and "respect by citizens for one another."
19. Masterson, *Militarism and Politics*, 48.
20. Masterson, *Militarism and Politics*, 50.
21. Klarén, *Modernization*, 141.
22. Beals, *Fire on the Andes*, 190.
23. Masterson, *Militarism and Politics*, 51.
24. Peter F. Klarén, *Peru: Society and Nationhood in the Andes* (New York: Oxford University Press, 2000), 276.
25. Beals, *Fire on the Andes*, 390.
26. Beals, *Latin America*, 105.
27. A. Torres-Rioseco and Carleton Beals, "Correspondence: On Peruvian Literature and an Article by Carleton Beals," *Books Abroad* 9, no. 2 (1935): 147–49, https://doi.org/10.2307/40076208
28. Beals, *Fire on the Andes*, 447.
29. See Luis E. Valcárcel, *Tempestad en los Andes* (1927) (*Tempest in the Andes*) (Lima, Perú: Populibros Peruanos, 1964).
30. Beals, *Fire on the Andes*, 316.
31. Beals, *Fire on the Andes*, 319–20.
32. Jose Carlos Mariátegui, *Seven Interpretative Essays on Peruvian Reality*, trans. Marjory Urquidi (Austin: University of Texas Press, 1971), 29 footnote.
33. Beals, *Fire on the Andes*, 324.
34. *Acción Aprista*, April 22, 1934, in CBC, box 144.
35. *Acción Aprista*, April 22, 1934, in CBC, box 144.
36. Beals, "Aprismo," 245.
37. Josephus Daniels to Carleton Beals, January 5, 1935, CBC.
38. Beals, *Fire on the Andes,* 182.
39. See Mariátegui, *Seven Interpretative Essays*; and Victor F. Calverton, *The Liberation of American Literature* (New York: Charles Scribner, 1932).
40. Beals, *Fire on the Andes*, 158.
41. Beals, *Fire on the Andes*, 165.
42. Arnold Gingrich to Maxim Lieber, December 31, 1934, CBC.
43. Albert Halper, *Good-Bye Union Square: A Writer's Memoir of the Thirties* (Chicago: Quadrangle Books, 1970).
44. Jefferson Jones to Carleton Beals, January 25, 1935, CBC.
45. Maxim Lieber to Carleton Beals, April 3, 1935, CBC.
46. R. L. Duffus, "Clashing Civilizations in Peru: *Fire on the Andes* Illuminates a Land of Fantastic Qualities," *New York Times*, November 25, 1934.
47. Louise Bogan, "Books," *New Yorker*, November 24, 1934, 108.
48. Maurice Halperin [pseud. Frank L. Gordon], on Beals, *New Masses*, January 8, 1935.
49. Ernest Gruening, "The Drama of Peru," *Nation* 140, no. 3627, January 9, 1935, 52.
50. New York Times, Review "A Novel of Mexico, BLACK RIVER," by Carleton Beals, *New York Times*, March 4, 1934, BR7.
51. Carleton Beals, "Under the Fifth Sun" (unpublished autobiography, c. 1972–1978), in Carleton Beals Collection (CBC), Howard Gotlieb Archival Research Center, Boston University: "I prepared four articles on the titles. Bruce Bliven, then editor of *The New Republic* accepted them at once and paid me on acceptance, not a usual procedure. Unfortunately, he soon got cold feet, telling me that the penalties for libel of property were terrific and could put them out of business. They resold the articles to the *Nation*, which was equally delighted. But they too got cold feet and sent them on to a Senator from Massachusetts (David I. Walsh), noted for his liberal views. He said that their publication would serve no good purpose. Later I found out he was in the pay of the Standard Oil Company, which had recently acquired the Doheny properties in Mexico. There were many millions of dollars in escrow pending the

establishment of proper proof of ownership. It was then I discovered that the whole Teapot Dome matter had been a battle between rival oil interests."

52. Beals, *Black River*, 239–40.

53. See Mark D. Gilderhus, *Diplomacy and Revolution: US-Mexican Relations under Wilson and Carranza* (Tucson: University of Arizona Press, 1977), 8–9.

54. Carleton Beals, "Whose Property is Kellogg Protecting?" *New Republic*, February 23, 1927; and Carleton Beals, "Who Wants War with Mexico? The Operation of the Great Artichoke Theory of International Relations," *New Republic*, April 27, 1927.

55. Jefferson Jones to Carleton Beals, November 22, 1934, CBC, and Beals, "Under the Fifth Sun" (unpublished autobiography), CBC, 91.

56. Maxim Lieber to Carleton Beals, November 22, 1934, CBC.

57. Frances ["Paca"] Toor to Carleton Beals, February 11, 1935, CBC.

58. Beals, "Under the Fifth Sun" (unpublished autobiography), CBC.

59. Halper, *Good-Bye Union Square*, 79.

60. Carleton Beals to Roy Temple House [editor of *Books Abroad*], December 9, 1934, CBC.

61. Jefferson Jones to Carleton Beals, January 25, 1935 & February 8, 1935, CBC.

62. Carleton Beals, "Big Gains in Cuba cited by Caffery," *New York Times*, March 19, 1935, 6; Carleton Beals, "Batista Sees Need of 'Good' Dictators," *New York Times*, March 22, 1935, 14; Carleton Beals, "Two Slain in Cuba by Secret Police," *New York Times*, March 28, 1935, 22. https://timesmachine.nytimes.com/timesmachine/1935/03/28/93465705.html?pageNumber=22.

63. US Congress, *Tariff Act of 1930*, 19 USC. ch. 4, Pub. L. 71–361, 71st Cong., 2nd sess., March 13, 1930.

64. Robert Whitney, *State and Revolution in Cuba: Mass Mobilization and Political Change 1920–1940* (Chapel Hill: University of North Carolina Press, 2001), 144.

65. Daniel Aaron, *Writers on the Left* (New York: Harcourt, Brace, and World, 1961), 303; John A. Gronbeck-Tedesco, *Cuba, the United States and Cultures of the Transnational Left, 1930–1975* (New York: Cambridge University Press, 2015), 43.

66. Carleton Beals and Clifford Odets. *Rifle Rule in Cuba.* American Commission to Investigate Labor and Social Conditions in Cuba (New York: Provisional Committee for Cuba, 1935).

67. US Congress, Platt Amendment, in 1901 US Army Appropriations Bill, 31 Stat. 895, Pub. L. 56–803. 56th Cong., 2nd sess., March 2, 1901, https://govtrackus.s3.amazonaws.com/legislink/pdf/stat/31/STATUTE-31-Pg895.pdf (accessed May 22, 2021).

68. Beals and Odets, *Rifle Rule in Cuba*, 26.

69. Margaret Gibson-Brenman, *Clifford Odets: American Playwright, The Years 1906–1940* (New York: Applause Theatre and Cinema Books, 2002), 365.

70. Odets, "What Happened to Us in Cuba" (1935); and Gibson-Brenman, *Clifford Odets*, 366.

71. Beals and Odets, *Rifle Rule in Cuba*, 1.

72. Beals and Odets, *Rifle Rule in Cuba*, 7.

73. Beals and Odets, *Rifle Rule in Cuba*, 19.

74. Gibson-Brenman, *Clifford Odets*, 365.

75. Carleton Beals, "American Envoy to Cuba Called Batista Friend," *New York World Telegram*, July 3, 1935.

76. Beals, "American Envoy" (1935).

77. Ruby Phillips to Carleton Beals, May 2, 1935, CBC.

78. Ruby Phillips to Carleton Beals (1935), CBC.

79. Carleton Beals, "The New Machado in Cuba," *Nation* 141, no. 3657, August 7, 1935, 153.

80. "Text of General (Hugh S.) Johnson's Denouncement of Father Coughlin and Huey Long," *New York Times*, March 5, 1935, 10. https://www.nytimes.com/1982/07/11/books/american-demagogues.html (accessed May 23, 2021).

81. Alan Brinkley, *Voices of Protest: Huey Long, Father Coughlin, and the Great Depression* (New York: Alfred A. Knopf, 1982), 4–7.

82. Beals, *The Story of Huey P. Long* (Philadelphia: J. B. Lippincott, 1935), 164.
83. Beals, *Story of Huey P. Long*, 312.
84. Beals, *Story of Huey P. Long*, 313.
85. Francis Brown, "The Political Meteor That Was Huey Long," *New York Times*, December 8, 1935, BR3.
86. Beals, *Story of Huey P. Long*, 15.

*Chapter Ten*

# Crossing Swords with Trotsky and the American Left

In the summer of 1935, Carleton and Blanca Rosa Beals rented a clapboard cottage on Brockett's Point, in Branford, Connecticut. It was built on a low promontory overlooking a then-isolated curve of beach, called Short Beach, on Long Island Sound. They enjoyed a swim there on days when the weather allowed it, and their home soon became a magnet for their city-bound friends.

They were happy in their new intimacy and this pastoral setting captivated them, offering Beals a tranquil workplace away from the distractions of Manhattan, where he nonetheless kept his small apartment near Union Square.

Between 1935 and 1938, a period during which Beals gradually moved his permanent residence to the Branford area, its quiet helped him concentrate and produce books at an unprecedented rate, even for him. In 1936, he would publish *The Stones Awake*, a novel set during the Mexican Revolution, followed in 1937 by *America South*, a retrospective survey of Latin America, in 1938 by *The Coming Struggle for Latin America*, and in 1939 by *American Earth*, an early plea for sustainable agriculture and environmentalism in the United States.[1]

Brockett's Point is just east of New Haven, a two-hour train ride from Manhattan's Pennsylvania Station. The distance changed the couple's social life. Beals's trips to the city became infrequent, each defined by a specific purpose—to have lunch with an editor, to deliver a lecture at the New School for Social Research, or to attend, with Blanca Rosa, a party or reception to which they had been invited. They deepened a few chosen friendships, though, with Beals's literary agent Max Lieber, his first wife Sally, and from 1937 forward, his second wife Minna, George Goetz (Victor F. Calverton) and his partner, actress Nina Melville, all of whom made weekend visits to the Beals cottage.

Now more settled in the United States and, despite the Depression, doing rather well, Beals wanted, somehow, to serve America's oppressed, its sharecropping farmers, black and white, its industrial workers, coal miners, and prisoners of conscience. Awakened to the injustice that plagued Latin America's masses of poor, urban and rural, mestizo, and Indian, now in the 1930s, he rediscovered the injustice of his native land, and he wanted to write about it.

In addition to his journalism during this period, he joined committees—but no political parties—and wrote letters of support for multiple causes. He was an executive committee member of the Popular Front-organized National Committee for the Defense of Political Prisoners (NCDPP), founded by Theodore Dreiser, and which also counted among its supporters Beals's sometime associates such as Michael Gold, Kyle Crichton, Malcolm Cowley, Aaron Copland, Langston Hughes, and Sherwood Anderson.[2] Beals once spoke at a meeting of the NCDPP in New York City on behalf of political prisoners in Latin America, and signed letters pleading for the release of many others, in America and abroad.

At home, the NCDPP sponsored a writers' tour to investigate conditions in the mines of Harlan County, Kentucky. It also financed attorneys for the defense in Alabama's infamous Scottsboro Boys case, in which nine innocent black teenage boys were jailed for years on charges of raping two white women, an accusation which one of the alleged victims recanted, and accused the other of lying.[3]

In January 1936, Beals lined up contracts from the *New York Post*, *Philadelphia Record*, and the *Nation* to cover the trial of Haywood Patterson, one of the nine Scottsboro boys, in Decatur, Alabama. The trial was one episode in a saga of gross injustice in which the teenagers were arrested in 1931, falsely convicted of rape and jailed, most of them for decades. Beals's vivid rendering of the trial, which ended with Patterson found guilty and sentenced to seventy-five years, contributed to securing for the Scottsboro case status as a defining nadir of racial injustice in the South. "No one who was not present," Beals reported, "can realize the inflections of the court and the subtly changed meanings that were put upon words."[4] He concluded:

> In charging the jury Judge Callahan said that if such and such things were true, in a tone implying they probably were, then the defendant was a "rapist" and should be convicted. As he said these words, he glared over at the defendant in fury, his lips drew back in a snarl, and he rolled out the word "r-r-rapist" in a horrendous tone. The record will never show such things; but continue them hour after hour and day after day in an already prejudiced courtroom, and the sum total weighs upon the minds of the jurors.[5]

Beals remained in Alabama for several weeks after the trial, interviewing poor black farmers on the state's red hillsides around Dadeville and Auburn. His driver and guide was Clyde Johnson (alias Tom Burke), a white Communist from Minnesota and an organizer of the Alabama Share Croppers Union.[6] The result was a two-part *Nation* series, "Red Clay in Alabama" which revealed the failure there of the federal Resettlement Administration (RA), part of the New Deal agency Federal Emergency Relief Administration, to improve the lot of landless tenant farmers, almost all of them black.

Beals found that landlords were gaming a system devised by the RA's creator, President Franklin Delano Roosevelt (FDR) brain-truster and economist Rexford Tugwell, to extract money from tenants as well as the government.[7] The tenant farmers used federal help to end the debt bondage that had kept them dependent on their landlords, but Beals found that this had been replaced in many cases by new charges the landlords assessed them for firewood, water, pasturage, and house rent. These were added to the interest payments sharecroppers now had to pay the RA. "Many 'rehabilitated' farmers have merely exchanged one bad master for two worse ones," Beals wrote.[8]

\*\*\*

Upon his return to Brockett's Point, and through the spring and summer of 1936, Beals bore down to finish what he hoped would be his great novel of the Mexican Revolution, *The Stones Awake*, which J. B. Lippincott published in October of that year.

Its title was inspired by an Aztec myth in which a goddess of the ninth heaven gives birth to a stone instead of a child. The other gods, frightened and disgusted, hurl it to earth where it shatters into thousands of fragments scattered across Milpa Alta (highland cornfield)—or as Beals renamed it for his novel, Milpa Verde (green cornfield)—in the southern reaches of Mexico City's valley. Luis, one of the novel's protagonists, relates that one day, these stones will awaken and become gods again. Beals weaves this and other mystical folk tales with labyrinthine plot twists and blends them with real events into a proto-version of magical realism.

His story, by turns gripping and meandering, focuses on a group of characters we first meet on the same hacienda in Mexico City's southern valley. It takes on a kind of *Les Misérables* flavor as we follow their often coincidental encounters and re-encounters through a decade-long revolutionary tumult that shapes their destinies.[9]

At the center of Beals's story is Esperanza Huitron, who is drawn from the real-life Luz Jimenez, an artists' model for Diego Rivera, among others, in Mexico City in the 1920s.[10] She is also an idealized version of the Indian teenage girl Evangelina Huitron, whom Beals wrote about having met on his 1918 train ride into Mexico City.[11] At the beginning of the novel, Esperanza, just seventeen years old, joins Luis, a hacienda foreman who bolts to sign up for Madero's revolutionary forces. They have a child, with whom she is left after Luis is killed in a firefight in Mexico City. Ever stoic and resilient amid the corruption, betrayals, and violence around her, Esperanza resurfaces later in the story with David Muñoz, a character who seems a composite of various revolutionary artists.

For Beals, Mexico's Revolution was a defining experience, and *The Stones Awake* was his effort to distil its embrace of the whole range of human experience: the syncretic conflation of indigenous cosmology and faith-healing with Catholicism, corruption among priests and generals, violence, class divisions, exploitation, great wealth, miserable poverty, prostitution, Indians, mestizos, and American intrusion. It is an expansive prose mural, combining fact and fiction, and reflects Beals's personal identification with the revolution's ideals of redistributing land to peasants, of exalting indigenous art and indigenous people themselves, of building village schools and spreading literacy, and of strengthening workers' rights. It also lays out his disdain for the fallen oligarchy, cruel and complacent landowners, and their majordomo guards, many of whom are rapidly converted into gendarmes for the most venal of the so-called revolutionary generals.

The novel has some familiar Bealsian flaws, such as rat-tat-tat dialogue like a 1930s Hollywood screenplay, as well as a tendency to over-describe and lapse into melodrama. There is a peculiar uneven quality to *The Stones Awake*, in which passages of studied insight sit uneasily with truncated subplots and tangents that go nowhere. But it nonetheless achieves an authenticity with more sharply-drawn, believable characters than those found elsewhere in Beals's fiction.

This was recognized by Katherine Anne Porter, who in a *New Republic* review praised his creation of the character Esperanza, as "worth knowing" even while dismissing Beals as someone who "would have made a good novelist if he'd taken the time to learn."[12]

For members of Beals's Mexico City circle of the 1920s, the book's description of a house party of artists and intellectuals was familiar; Diego Rivera, Frida Kahlo, Julio Antonio Mella, Tina Modotti, cartoonist Miguel Covarrubias, Dr. Atl and Nahui Olin, among many others, were all there, thinly-disguised behind pseudonyms.[13] This underscored another of Porter's observations, that Beals—ever the reporter—captured his characters whole from real life rather than creating them.

Toward the end, the plot grows overly tangled as Beals crams in every element he considers important to his general thesis of a deeply tarnished revolution that is nonetheless worth defending. It has value as an impressionistic treatment of the Mexican Revolution, at once entertaining while accurately sketching Mexican characters to convey a revolution whose legacy includes both transformation and continuity.

Porter's praise, though backhanded, found company with others whose reviews found both qualities and faults in *The Stones Awake*, but who, on balance, treated it as worthy of respect. Stanley Young of the *New York Times* recognized its "authentic flavor" as "a fresh and vivid panoramic understanding of Mexicans in the mass."[14] The *Saturday Review of Literature* described it as, "all of Beals's books on Mexico put into the story of an Indian woman, Esperanza," and *The Boston Transcript*'s S. A. Lavine approved its "epic style."[15]

\*\*\*

Beals was by now established as the pre-eminent journalistic interpreter of Latin America within the subculture of America's leftist intellectuals. But even if his social and professional circle was dominated by people from this group, his readership reached beyond it.

He had earned his radical bona fides in the 1920s by contributing articles to left magazines such as the *Liberator*, the *Masses*, and *New Masses*, but he was not a Communist Party member, a fellow traveler, or a Trotskyist. By the early 1930s, he had cut his links to *New Masses*, which had become a Stalinist organ, and preferred to be published in liberal magazines such as the *Nation*, *New Republic*, *Common Sense*, and *Scribner's,* as well as *The New York Times*. Not incidentally, these were better able to pay for his articles as well.

His combination of free-thinking and mainstream media credibility combined with an enduring left orientation drew the attention of at least some American sympathizers of Leon Trotsky (1879–1940) who had a specific purpose in mind. They considered Beals a natural candidate for a commission of inquiry they were setting up in Mexico, where the former Bolshevik leader and Soviet Minister of War was exiled. This "Preliminary Commission of Inquiry" would hold "hearings" in Mexico, offering Trotsky a platform from which to refute conspiracy charges laid against him in the Moscow trials set in motion by Soviet Marshal Joseph Stalin.

These Moscow trials were at the center of what became Stalin's Great Terror, which he launched in supposed response to the December 1934 assassination in Leningrad (St. Petersburg) of Sergei Kirov (1886–1934), a Bolshevik leader who was then head of the Leningrad branch of the Communist Party. Other Bolshevik leaders, including former Politburo members Lev Borisovich Kamenev, Grigory Zinoviev, Karl Radek, and Nikolai Bukharin were also soon arrested on Stalin's orders. They were forced to make confessions at show trials, after which they were first sentenced to prison terms, where they either died or were later shot. By March 1937, two public trials had been conducted. A third would follow in June.

Trotsky, forced into exile by Stalin in 1929, first sought refuge in Turkey, then in France, Norway, and finally Mexico. His name was invoked in all of the trials, in which he was accused of being the mastermind of a conspiracy with Hitler's Nazi Germany and Imperial Japan to overthrow the Stalinist regime.

In early March 1937, while Beals and Blanca were visiting his parents in Berkeley, he received a letter from George Novack, a young lawyer and secretary of the American Committee for the Defense of Leon Trotsky, formally inviting him to join the Commission. Novack related that the Commission would include American Socialist Party leader Norman Thomas, or his deputy Devere Allen, and indicated that historian Charles A. Beard, Oswald Garrison Villard, and Amalgamated Association of Iron and Steel Workers lawyer Frank P. Walsh were also being approached.[16]

Putting the Commission together was a challenge for Novack and its other sponsors on the Trotsky defense committee. They wanted members of unquestioned integrity with reputations for fair-mindedness. They would have to be sufficiently progressive that the peculiar (to most American ears) Marxist dialectic that was Trotsky's everyday vernacular would not confuse or disturb them. At the same time, they could not be formally or publicly associated as sympathizers with either the Stalinist or Trotskyist camps.

The committee had accomplished a coup by convincing John Dewey to be chairman of the Commission. Dewey, seventy-eight years old at the time, was widely esteemed as a wise elder, a much-published philosopher of the pragmatist school, a progressive humanist, as well as a theorist and practitioner in the field of education. That he would lend his prestige to this enterprise gave the Commission an imprimatur of rigor, impartiality and justice that stood in stark contrast to Stalin's Moscow show-trials.

Getting Dewey on board had been the second signal achievement of the Committee, following its successful brokering of Trotsky's asylum in Mexico. That had been accomplished in large measure by Anita Brenner, Beals's friend from his Mexico days, now an editor at the *Menorah Journal*, a New York-based leftist Jewish journal sympathetic to Trotsky. Brenner had connected Trotsky with her friends Diego Rivera and Frida Kahlo, who appealed on the Old Man's behalf to the populist Mexican President Lázaro Cárdenas, with whom they had close personal ties.[17]

Novack's letter to Beals coincided with another from Benjamin Stolberg, who sought to persuade him on a more personal level, appealing to Beals's instinctive sense of outrage, noting that Stalinists had tried to shut down the Commission's work by "an incredible campaign of slander and pressure: calling people up at 2 a.m. to tell them that Dewey and others had resigned."[18]

Beals knew Stolberg from New York literary circles and as a fellow contributor to the *Nation*. Diminutive, plump and just two years older than Beals, Stolberg was a Marxist labor historian who had emigrated to the United States from Germany in his teens. Author of a book on the history of the Ladies Garment Workers Union, he was independent-minded, even iconoclastic by nature, but nonetheless sympathetic to Trotsky's plight. He was also an accomplished raconteur whose hilarious mimicry of literary and political celebrities could reduce his audience to tears of laughter. Beals liked his company, and so when Stolberg approached him with an insistent request that Beals join the Commission, it was hard to say no.

Stolberg added that the Commission was becoming "quite fashionable" with its prominent members having publicly denounced the Stalinist calumnies and pressure tactics. He also noted that two other friends of Beals, writer Louis Adamic and literary critic John Rensselaer Chamberlain had also joined.[19]

In fact, the eleventh-hour arm-twisting of Beals, as well as that directed to others had become necessary as many previous invitees had declined to join. Beard who, with his wife Mary, was America's most famous progressive historian, begged off claiming that one could not prove a negative—in this case, the nonexistence of a conspiracy—as the emerging Commission proposed to undertake to do.[20]

In other cases, intellectuals aligned with or at least sympathetic to the Stalinist Popular Front, were actively hostile to the whole enterprise. Eighty-eight of them—including Beals's associates Malcolm Cowley, *Nation* editor Carey McWilliams, Anna Louise Strong, and Tess Slesinger—signed an "Open Letter to American Liberals" in which they urged Commission members to reconsider their position.[21] "The demand for an investigation of trials carried on under the legally constituted judicial system of the Soviet government," they argued, "can only be interpreted as political intervention in the internal affairs of the Soviet Union with hostile intent."[22]

A somewhat different case was that of James T. Farrell, author of the *Studs Lonigan* trilogy, who wanted to join, but whose nomination (by Novack) Stolberg vetoed, calling Farrell "irresponsible" and compromised for having said publicly that he thought Trotsky innocent.[23] Having said no to Farrell, Stolberg's urgent insistence with Beals can be understood; he really needed Carleton to say yes. In retrospect, Stolberg suffered a bitter irony as his assiduous effort to enlist someone less admiring of Trotsky than Farrell, resulted in Beals's cantankerously critical performance, which was rather more than Stolberg had bargained for.

The intra-left controversy that swirled about the Commission and the Moscow purges that had provoked it was mostly lost on the larger American public, to the extent that they were aware of it at all. But in the community of leftist intellectuals, it was a fiercely-waged polemical contest, played out in a profusion of pamphlets and articles in small journals. The lines were drawn between two broad groups, many of whom—as in the Soviet Union—had been, not long before, on the same side.

The first, which included many American liberals, such as Upton Sinclair and the *Nation*'s editors, while disturbed by Stalin's authoritarian bent and doubtful about the integrity of the Soviet judicial system, nonetheless defined the issue as a choice between an alliance with Stalin to defeat the greater evil of fascism, and a de facto surrender to that latter, greater evil. For others, Communist Party members and sympathizers, sustaining the legitimacy of the Moscow trials was crucial to their own political and moral self-definition.

Against them was a smaller group, many of whom but certainly not all of them Trotskyists, who could not accept the first of two implications eloquently posited by the Trotsky sympathizer Farrell: "if the official version of the Trials were true, then the co-workers of Lenin and leaders of the Bolshevik Revolution must be considered as one of the worst gangs of scoundrels in history; if the Trials were a frame-up then the leaders of Soviet Russia were perpetuating one of the most monstrous frame-ups in all history."[24] For members of this group, Trotsky, the Bolshevik intellectual, theorist, and prolific writer seemed an unlikely co-conspirator with Hitler. At the very least, he deserved the benefit of the doubt, along with a chance to defend himself.

One barometer of the coexisting confusion and polarized debate among American Marxists over Trotsky was the March 1937 issue of Victor Calverton's *Modern Monthly*, devoted to a symposium on the question: "Is Trotsky Guilty?" Its contributors concluded with diverse verdicts—three votes of "guilty," six of "frame-up," and three of bafflement.[25] In the event, Beals decided, without much reflection, to join the Commission.

In addition to Dewey and Stolberg, the Commission—in fact, its subcommittee holding hearings in Mexico—also included Suzanne LaFollette, a journalist and niece of the Progressive Party Wisconsin US Senator Robert LaFollette, and Otto Ruele, an exiled former German Reichstag Social Democratic Party member and biographer of Karl Marx. Lawyer John F. Finerty, who had defended Nicola Sacco and Bartolomeo Vanzetti, was to act as counsel for the Commission, while labor attorney Albert Goldman would be Trotsky's counsel.[26]

\*\*\*

Trotsky had disembarked in the oil port of Tampico on January 9, 1937, accompanied by his wife Natalia. They had come to Mexico as the only passengers aboard the Norwegian oil tanker *Ruth*, with feelings of combined relief and bitter resignation. The first arose because his asylum there ended four months of house arrest in the Norwegian town of Honefoss, a short drive north of Oslo. He had been forced to that after having been denied asylum in France, where the Popular Front government of Prime Minister Léon Blum (1872–1950) was at pains to avoid offending Stalin.

But this relief was embittered because of Mexico's remoteness from Trotsky's Eurasian political theatre of activity. His simple presence in the Aztec capital underlined the fact that, at fifty-seven years old, though still possessed of his formidable political talents, he was unable to exercise them. He had become a footnote, while Stalin, whom he had once considered a plodding camp follower, too insignificant be his adversary, now stood at the head of the Soviet Union, the bulwark against the rising fascist armies of Europe.[27]

Trotsky was welcomed at the Tampico pier by American Trotskyist leader Max Shachtman and Frida Kahlo, then better-known as Frida Rivera for her marriage to the muralist Diego Rivera. The latter could not attend due to a kidney illness, but welcomed the Trotsky couple the following day at the home he shared with Frida in Coyoacán, south of Mexico City. They had been conveyed to the capital aboard a luxury train dispatched by President Cárdenas.[28]

Rivera had embraced Trotskyism with his characteristically voluble enthusiasm. In 1929, he had been expelled from the Mexican Communist Party, apparently after a 1927 visit to Russia, during which he had met Stalin but had failed to show sufficient deference. Other accounts suggest that it was Rivera himself who broke with the Communists, having been disturbed by the expulsions imposed on members of Trotsky's Left Opposition.[29]

In any case, there was a mutual respect and affinity between the two men, who treated one another as friends, at least during the first months of Trotsky's residence in Mexico. Trotsky had an artistic sensibility unusual for a political thinker, and indulged Rivera's self-image as a sophisticated political actor in his own right.

Just two weeks after Trotsky's arrival in Mexico, a second trial got underway in Moscow. In this one, the so-called Trial of the Seventeen, former Trotsky associates such as Karl Radek, Georgy Pyatakov, and Nikolai Muralov, along with former Bolshevik leader Grigory Sokolnikov, and thirteen others sat in the dock to face a string of accusations, all linked to the chief defendant *in absentia*, Trotsky himself. Andrey Vyshinsky, the Stalinist prosecutor, presented charges that Trotsky was conspiring with Hitler and the Emperor of Japan to cede the Soviet Ukraine to them in return for their support against Stalin.[30] Thirteen of the defendants were eventually shot, while the others—including Radek, who implicated Bukharin, setting the stage for a third trial—were sent to labor camps where they perished.

Even if the Moscow trials are now recognized as frame-ups to justify the Great Terror in which millions were killed, imprisoned or exiled, this was not the case in 1937. Joseph E. Davies, whom FDR had named US Ambassador to Moscow after his decision in 1934 to establish diplomatic relations with the Union of Soviet Socialist Republics (USSR), attended some of the trials and reported to Washington that the Kremlin's fears of conspiracy were justified.[31] His credulous account was matched by those of journalists Walter Duranty of the *New York Times*, and Louis Fischer of the *Nation*, and supported in polemical commentaries by writers and intellectuals such as Romain Rolland, Upton Sinclair, and George Bernard Shaw.[32]

Trotsky was therefore seized of an urgent desire to get on with his defense and pressed his US followers Herbert Solow and Shachtman to speed up efforts to convene the Commission of Inquiry.[33]

\*\*\*

Beals and Blanca Rosa left Berkeley by car in early April 1937, timing their departure for Mexico to enable a short border stop at Laredo, Texas. They met Dewey there, along with Stolberg, Novack, LaFollette, and Pearl Kluger, Secretary of the Commission, who were changing trains on their journey from New York and St. Louis aboard the Missouri Pacific's Sunshine Special.[34] The Beals couple, having obtained a cash advance from Stolberg at Laredo to cover their expenses, continued by car to Mexico City, arriving there a couple of days before the Inquiry's opening session on April 10, a clear and sunny Saturday morning.

The Commission's hearings were held in the dining room of the Riveras' so-called Blue House. Given security concerns, the room's French windows facing Londres Street had been barricaded with adobe bricks and sandbags, while policemen stood guard outside.[35]

Trotsky himself was defiant, nattily dressed in suit and tie, exuding vigor and good humor to dispel the tension. Beals sensed pathos in seeing the onetime supremely powerful War Minister of the Soviet Union amid such humble surroundings. He also felt his own distance from the other Commission members almost immediately.

"I found myself in a nest of furibund Trotskyites," he would recall, whose manner was one of "hushed adoration of the master."[36] Suzanne La Follette upbraided him for smoking and chewing gum, both of which, she said, Trotsky could not abide. But, as Beals observed in a caustic account published later, "Frieda Rivera," dressed every day in a different Tarascan *huipil* (traditional embroidered dress) and heavy silver jewelry, sat directly facing Trotsky, and not only chewed gum throughout the hearings, but repeatedly drew it out of her mouth in a long thread, eliciting not the slightest objection from the Old Man. Their infatuation, which would evolve into a full-blown affair shortly after the hearings, was apparently already under way.[37]

Indeed, Farrell, who had traveled to Mexico for the hearings even though he had been passed over for a seat on the Commission, showed some of the awe that Beals so disparaged. "It is . . . a spectacle rare in history. Imagine Robespierre or Cromwell under such circumstances. Well this is more, because neither Cromwell nor Robespierre had the intellectual breadth that Trotsky has."[38]

The first session began with Dewey's reading of an opening statement purportedly on behalf of all the Commissioners. For Beals, this was the beginning of his rocky relationship with the whole undertaking. He had not participated in drafting the statement, mostly because he had not traveled to Mexico with the other commissioners. He took specific issue with its assertion that Trotsky had made "repeated demands" to the Soviet authorities that he be extradited to face the charges laid against him by Stalin's regime. In fact, there was no evidence of such demands having been made. Indeed, had Moscow sought Trotsky's extradition, it would have triggered court proceedings in France or Norway, but significantly, not in Mexico, as diplomatic relations between the two countries remained broken.[39]

At the opening of the third session, on April 12, Beals rose to object to the statement. The Commission damaged its own credibility by making assertions unsupported by evidence, he said. He also insisted that the Commission publish its preliminary findings at the earliest opportunity, and not, as proposed, after unspecified additional investigations had been conducted. This was urgent, he said, because if the Commission's report cast reasonable doubt on Trotsky's guilt, it would similarly cast doubt on charges facing defendants in forthcoming Moscow trials, and "might have some restraining influence which would save their lives."[40] Alternatively, if the Commission failed to raise any reasonable doubt, he said, "this should help to free Soviet justice from unfair imputations and permit it to punish those who are properly guilty, without the disturbance of outside propaganda."[41]

Dewey initially responded by saying that Beals had not been available for consultation on the statement but gave in after Beals challenged him on this point, saying he had been in Mexico City two days before the proceedings began. Dewey then expressed regret for the error regarding extradition. Nonetheless, Beals's stance was seen as hostile by the other commissioners and indeed, by Trotsky himself.

"If Mr. Beals is insisting upon exactitude, I will also," he said. "I am not the 'accused' here; I am a witness." To which Beals responded: "I accept that qualification, Mr. Trotsky, I understand this is an investigation."[42]

Beals remained relatively taciturn throughout the hearings, putting pointed questions only a few times. Nonetheless, his questions were invariably the most searching and provocative put to Trotsky. The other commissioners hewed to simple queries of fact whose answers both they and Trotsky knew beforehand or tossed softball questions that allowed the witness to perorate on revolutionary ideology.

Beals first challenged Trotsky during the second sitting. He started by asking Trotsky if he had brought his complete archives with him to Mexico. Upon his reply that some of his archives had been stolen, by Nazis in Norway and by GPU agents in Paris, Beals pressed him on how he had chosen what to bring with him to Mexico. Trotsky said his selection was adapted to the indictments, to offer proofs "from the political to the philosophical" that they were false.[43]

Beals then showed even more skepticism, by probing Trotsky's willingness during the World War I to surrender Russian territory to Germany under the 1918 Treaties of Brest-Litovsk. Would not Trotsky's attitude be the same now, Beals asked, "if it enhances the return of your group to power to implant the socialism which you believe to be more correct?"[44]

Trotsky dismissed this suggestion, saying that if he were to enter into relations with fascists, he would cease to be a revolutionary, and become "a miserable adventurist." In response to a follow-up question from Suzanne LaFollette, he explained that the Bolshevik government pursued Brest-Litovsk only because the French President Georges Clemenceau (1841–1929) had refused military support for Russia against Germany.[45]

This exchange sowed doubts about Beals among the other, more partisan commissioners, with Otto Rühle, for example, shifting in his chair, muttering "sehr schade" ("what a pity").[46] But it was Beals's second major intervention that provoked the most enduring furor. Late in the afternoon of the eleventh day of hearings, on April 16, he began a line of questions probing the origins of a controversy within the Bolshevik leadership during the early years of the revolution as to whether or not they should seek to foment Communist revolutions in other countries or forswear foreign intrigue to focus instead on building "socialism in one country." Trotsky responded that external fomenting of revolution was "an artificial thing," and that the Bolshevik view in the years immediately following October 1917 was that the Russian Revolution was the first of a series in an inevitable historical process.

Beals suddenly shifted gears, with a sharply specific question: "Do you know Mr. Borodin?"

This was an unexpected tangent that perplexed everyone and caught Trotsky off guard. Mikhail Borodin, whose real name was Mikhail Gruzenberg, was a Communist International, or Comintern, agent Beals had encountered in Mexico City in 1919, back in the days when he was teaching English and drinking at Fat Sing's on Dolores Street. Beals had met him through his friends Manabendra N. Roy and his American wife Evelyn Trent, in whose apartment Borodin was then staying. Roy, a Hindu nationalist, had self-exiled in Mexico, where he was among the founders of the Communist Party of Mexico—the first outside Russia.[47]

Beals remembered his instant dislike for Borodin who, Roy had confided to him, had been sent to Mexico by the Bolsheviks to precipitate Communist agitation and unrest. This conspiracy was intended to provoke US intervention in Mexico, which would distract and dissuade Woodrow Wilson's administration from helping Britain in its putative plan to declare war on Russia.[48] In return for acting on Borodin's direction in founding the Communist Party of Mexico—a breakaway splinter of the Mexican Socialist Party of the day—Roy was named to represent Mexico in the Communist International, and obtained Comintern support for his faction in the liberation struggle in then-British India.

Trotsky, taken aback, replied that he had met Borodin, "one or two times, but I didn't know him as Borodin. I knew him as a political personality."

Beals retorted that Borodin had come "secretly" to Mexico in 1919, had founded the Communist Party and, "at that time made the statement that he was an emissary of yours."[49]

"Of mine?" Trotsky replied, incredulous. "At that time I was in my military train [during the Russian Civil War]. I forgot all the world geography except the geography of the front . . . may I ask the source of this sensational communication? It is published—no?"

"It is not published," Beals replied, to which Trotsky said, "I can only give the advice to the Commissioner to say to his informant that he is a liar."

"Thank you, Mr. Trotsky. Mr. Borodin is the liar."

"Yes; it is very possible," Trotsky concluded.

The exchange so raised tension in the room that Dewey thought it best to adjourn for the day. Finerty approached Beals, telling him angrily that his question was irrelevant. Beals started to explain its context as suggesting evidence that Trotsky had supported cross-border political intrigue in the past. He added that he could prove Borodin's role by producing an article he had published about it, just as Trotsky had taken to citing his own articles as evidence.

Beals then added that he had begun to think that Finerty was "really Trotsky's attorney" rather than counsel to the Commission. "I don't want to speak to you," Finerty replied behind clenched teeth, "except as I must address you at the Commission."[50] At the back of the room, meanwhile, Diego Rivera explained to puzzled Mexican reporters that Beals was hostile to Trotsky because he was "in the pay of the GPU."[51]

The next day, when the twelfth sitting opened at 10 a.m., Beals was nowhere in sight. Trotsky's attorney, Albert Goldman, read a statement by Trotsky denouncing Beals's allegations that Borodin had been sent to Mexico on Trotsky's orders as a "falsehood which he has utilized [for] a definite purpose—to compromise my situation in Mexico."[52] In the statement, he also asked the Commission to investigate the source of Beals's information which, he predicted, would uncover a conspiracy "to prevent me from unmasking the judicial crimes in Moscow."[53]

Dewey replied that this would be difficult because Beals had that very morning submitted a letter of resignation, which he proceeded to read into the record. In it, Beals said that he did not consider the proceedings of the Commission a truly serious investigation of the charges.

Dewey expressed regret at the resignation, claiming that Beals had "prejudged the case" despite having been given full opportunity to ask questions.

He also challenged the assertion in Beals's resignation letter that the sessions had been completed, noting that the hearings were preliminary, and would be complemented by further investigations by "the full Commission."

For journalists covering the Commission, this was a mud fight that boosted the story's prominence. "'Trial' of Trotsky a joke, says Beals," was the headline over a *New York Times* story by correspondent Frank Kluckhohn.[54] In it, Kluckhohn reported Beals's contention that Dewey had distorted the meaning of his resignation, saying that he had not prejudged the case. "I do not know what sort of conclusions the other commissioners will bring in but I do know that to label their efforts as an investigation is to sully a fair word. The hushed adoration of the other members of the commission for Mr. Trotsky throughout the hearings has defeated all spirit of honest investigation."[55]

Kluckhohn was seen as hostile by the other commissioners largely due to his skeptical scene-setting article on the Commission's hearings published in the *New York Times* before they began. The Commission's supporters saw a Stalinist bias in the account, consistent with *Times* man Duranty's uncritical coverage of Stalin's trials in Moscow.[56] They consequently thought suspicious Beals's habit of chatting with Kluckhohn during breaks in the hearings.[57]

The Mexican dailies treated the imbroglio with a flippant derision, as if to punish the Commission for its oversight in not providing Spanish interpretation. The Commission's only concession to the Mexican press consisted—ironically—of a few perfunctory summaries that Beals, its only Spanish speaker, was enjoined to offer on its behalf. These did not include Dewey's appeal to the press at the first hearing, "to safeguard our task by living up to its own highest tradition of scrupulous objectivity."[58]

"Contradiction of ideas, contradictions among men, farce, bloody farce, petulance and narcissism, that is all we see," summarized an editorial in *Excelsior*. "Trotsky doesn't deserve our hospitality. He should have entertained us, and he didn't. Beals did, though, but only for a moment."[59] The same paper's humorist offered a rhyming couplet that doused both sides with sardonic irony:

> Carleton Beals hizo bien su papel.
> Le robó la película al ruso.
> Y ahora todos se fijan en él
> Por aquella renuncia que puso.
> Luego . . . , un libro . . . , dinero y . . . cartel![60]

The controversy did not end there. Just over a month later, before the Dewey Commission had drafted its report and unsurprising not-guilty verdict, Trotsky issued a press release denouncing Beals as a GPU, or Stalinist agent on a deliberate mission to undermine the hearings and the Dewey Commission's credibility, as well as Trotsky's own political asylum in Mexico.[61] Dewey himself had added fodder to the charge by obliquely suggesting that Beals's resignation was of a piece with efforts on behalf of "powerful interests engaged in attempting to disrupt and sabotage [the Commission's] work."[62] In the same breath, Dewey assailed the conduct of "those liberals" trying to discredit the Commission's effort as marking, "an intellectual shirking that is close to intellectual dishonesty . . . more than that, it is treachery to the very cause of liberalism."[63]

These public criticisms of Beals's conduct came just as Trotsky's trenchant critique of Stalin's regime, *The Revolution Betrayed* was published, and coincided with the shocking verdicts in the second Moscow Trial of the Seventeen.[64] Trotsky, persecuted and powerless yet still defiantly denouncing Stalin's tyranny, thus attained a summit of moral stature that, at least for the moment, obscured his own authoritarian instincts. Among those closely following the Commission's deliberations, Beals's only real defender was *New Masses*, whose vitriolic treatment of Trotsky reflected its disciplined Stalinist line. It all cast Beals in a rather bad light.

The furor continued when Beals penned a withering attack on the Dewey Commission's work, published in the *Saturday Evening Post* in June, under the headline, "The Fewer Outsiders the Better." The *Saturday Evening Post*, then under the editorship of conservative anti-New Dealer Garet Garrett, was in other circumstances an unlikely site for Beals's brand of journalism. In this case, his tirade against the Commission ("a chummy club room, a pink tea party") and Trotsky ("an embittered man [of] choleric disposition . . . his mental faculties blurred by a consuming lust of hate for Stalin") may have satisfied broader anti-Communist sentiments embraced by the middle-brow weekly and its three million readers.[65]

Five months later, when Beals's friend Victor F. Calverton invited Trotsky to submit an article on war to his *Modern Monthly*, the Old Man seized on the request to challenge Calverton to remove Beals from the magazine's masthead. He refused to be published in a magazine whose contributors included "a GPU agent" whose presence carried the "contamination" of Stalinism, which Trotsky described as "the syphilis of the workers movement."[66] Trotsky's demand was endorsed by Diego Rivera, also a *Modern Monthly* contributor, who wrote Calverton that he too would sever his association with the magazine's art staff unless Beals was "ejected from the editorial board with an open declaration of the political and moral motives for this action."[67]

Calverton squirmed. He was unwilling to heel to Trotsky's pressure and publicly denounce his friend, but he was also uncomfortable defending Beals's conduct during and after the Commission hearings, which he had thought unjustified.[68] In the end, he resolved the dilemma by removing Beals as a contributing editor, but also writing Trotsky that there was "no shred of evidence" to support the charge that Beals was a GPU agent.[69]

He then shared this correspondence with Beals, noting that he had "spent many hours trying to explain and defend your honesty in the whole Trotsky dispute, even with many of your former and best friends. Knowing you for the years I have, not for one second did I doubt the sincerity of your motivation, however much I disagreed with your conclusions and regretted the unwiseness of certain of your remarks."[70]

Beals was unrepentant and suggested that Calverton had kicked him off the magazine "for believing the same things you do."[71] He added: "It's all cock-eyed to me, all these strange revolutionary egos running around loose. In neither Stalinites nor Trotskyites have I found decency or honor. Stalin for me is a menace to the world. Poor Trotsky reveals all the symptoms of disordered temperament. I repeat: "a plague on both their houses."[72]

In truth, Beals, though obviously not a Trotskyist, was not a Stalinist either. But the timing of his disdainful and public resignation from the Commission was spectacularly unlucky for him, as it cast him as Stalin's apologist, a version that has been recorded in almost all accounts of the episode.[73]

For many American leftist intellectuals, the Moscow Trials were a defining moment. Faced with evidence that the Soviet workers' paradise was now ruled by a tyrant, they found in Trotsky a credible champion whose presence offered at least a glimmer of hope that the Marxist project might be rescued from its usurper. This hope was urgently needed, not only in Russia, they believed, but also in Spain, where the Republican government was locked in struggle against a military uprising to which it would succumb two years later.

But for this hope to endure, Trotsky's stature had to be defended. In the United States, Trotskyism and the Fourth International which sought to carry its message, gained broader support among leftist activists and intellectuals than it did in Europe, where this group was more alarmed by the immediate threat posed by fascist armies than they were by Stalin's tyranny. American writers such as Farrell were joined in their defense of Trotsky by Edmund Wilson and Sidney Hook, as well as Dwight Macdonald and Philip Rahv, these last two editors of *Partisan Review*, which became the center of "literary Trotskyism" in 1937.[74]

It was this stature of Trotsky's that Beals challenged. Although he insisted on objectivity and the rules of evidence when acting as a member of Dewey Commission, Beals unleashed a torrent of invective thereafter. In his *Saturday Evening Post* piece, for example, he went beyond the Commission's procedure to unveil what he saw as Trotsky's conspiratorial proclivities, and to expose his hypocrisy in seeking the help of democrats he elsewhere derided, to serve his purpose of attacking Stalin. Beals had a point, but he was not well-served by his aggressive tone, which seemed more driven by pique and wounded pride than dispassionate analysis.

Still, his position, while it led to his own ostracism from many progressive circles in the United States at the time, holds up comparatively well when considered today. One of Trotsky's more recent biographers, Robert Service, has taken issue with earlier defenders such as Deutscher, citing evidence that Trotsky reacted to the Kronstadt mutiny by Bolshevik sailors in 1921 by dispatching its leaders to labor camps and, on other occasions, voiced no objection to exemplary mass executions.[75] Service also demonstrates that Trotsky even endorsed show trials in the early years of the Bolshevik revolution to eliminate Socialist-Revolutionaries, kulaks and priests, among others.[76]

But in 1937, Trotsky's image as the aggrieved party had more adherents. Also, the feud within the American left provoked by the Stalin-Trotsky split was already long-entrenched, and thoroughly irreconcilable.

Within the small world of intellectuals who focused their energies on leftist committees and journals, the dispute was rooted in the 1928 Comintern order that all Communist Parties denounce non-Communist Party (CP) left groups as "social fascists."[77] In New York's Madison Square Garden, for example, CP members violently disrupted a Socialist Party rally in February 1934. Similarly, in Greenwich Village, Communist activists once confronted Diego Rivera and Frida Kahlo during their visit to the city by shouting them down at a public meeting.[78] Claiming that capitalism was entering imminent crisis, the Stalinist persecution of Trotsky was part of a larger strategy to treat all non-Communist groups, even socialists whose ideology was closest to Marxism, as enemies of the revolution.

First among these were established parties such as Germany's Social Democrats, France's Socialists and Britain's Labour Party. But America's Socialist Party also became a target, along with American leftists sympathetic to Trotsky, part of the so-called Left Opposition. Another of Stalin's targets was Nikolai Bukharin, a onetime Politburo member, editor of *Pravda* and Comintern chairman. He had aroused Stalin's enmity by challenging the latter's collective farms strategy. His position was endorsed by what came to be known as the Right Opposition, led in the United States by labor organizer Jay Lovestone, who mounted an American "Opposition" Communist Party.

Even amid an economic crisis that had put one in four Americans out of work, and millions on breadlines, these revolutionary anti-capitalist groups operated at the margins of US politics. Neither Communists nor Socialists attracted more than a fraction of one percent of the popular vote, and only one of their candidates, the American Labor Party's Vito Marcantonio of East Harlem (to whose campaign Beals made a contribution), was ever elected to US Congress. Still, their intellectual cadre—among whom Beals circulated throughout the 1930s—had a pronounced influence on American journalism and popular culture.[79] Even if, in retrospect, those who advocated Communist revolution in America seem delusional, they were reaffirmed in their convictions by their connection to an international movement, whether led by the Soviet Comintern, or by the Trotskyist Left Opposition, or its successor, the Fourth International.

This helps explain the force with which these left intellectuals waged their ideological battles, breaking friendships and savagely denouncing erstwhile allies over what often seemed, on the surface, to be esoteric points of difference in political strategy. Looking back over the handful of little magazines published in New York, from the Stalinist *New Masses* to the independent Marxist and Trotsky-leaning *Partisan Review*, and to the liberal *Nation* and *New Republic*, whose combined readership did not exceed a hundred thousand, this vitriol seems puzzling, even absurd. But set against the looming struggles in Europe and Asia between communism, socialism, and fascism, and the murderous purges unleashed by Stalin in which millions perished, the bitterness was perhaps not misplaced. For many of them, this ideological clash for supremacy over the international Marxist revolutionary movement was definitive, taking second place to little else in their lives.

In 1934, Stalin, alarmed at the threat posed to the Soviet Union by Hitler's Nazi militarism, decreed an about-face in strategy, calling on Communist Party members, first in France and subsequently everywhere, to join forces with Socialists in a *popular front* against fascism. Trotsky, in exile in France at the time, viewed this as abandoning the Communists' strategic principle. Aside from his personal enmity against Stalin, Trotsky opposed alliances that would divide and distract working class political action into fruitless directions. He also believed it would fail to achieve its stated goal of defusing the Nazi threat to the USSR, as he perceived the French Socialists, elected in 1936—with Communist Party support—under the leadership of Léon Blum, as too weak to challenge Hitler.

Trotsky's followers, loosely organized in a fledgling network across Europe and the United States were not, of course, included in this new putatively large-tent Stalinist approach; indeed, like Trotsky himself, now Stalin's bitter foe, they despised and dismissed it.

Trotsky took issue with Stalin's strategy of "socialism in one country" as it was used to justify alliances with capitalist powers, first to engage in trade and then to fight the common enemy of Nazis bent on world domination. Even more, it concealed a creeping "Bonapartism" in which Tsarist rule had been replaced not by a proletarian dictatorship, but by a *bureaucratic* workers' republic. Trotsky's goal was to free the Marxist-Leninist revolutionary project from its Stalinist prison, and once again anchor it to its first principles, including international solidarity among Marxists against capitalism, whether democratic or fascist.

By 1936, this rather Byzantine intra-Bolshevik intrigue reverberated in America. American Trotskyists—who had pursued a two-year dalliance with followers of Dutch-born socialist pacifist clergyman Abraham Johannes "AJ" Muste in his American Workers Party—now launched their own counter-action to the pro-Stalin Popular Front by adopting a policy called *entrism* into the Socialist Party of America.[80]

American Trotskyist leaders James Cannon and Max Shachtman engineered this new shift as a way of at once challenging the Popular Front and also pushing the Socialist Party away from its farmer-labor populist roots and into a more radical Bolshevik direction. This provoked a struggle for leadership of the American Socialist Party between the Trotskyists who had entered the party and aligned themselves with the so-called "Militants" led by party leader Norman Thomas against "Old Guard" Debsians.

By this time Beals had long ago severed his earlier links to the Socialist Party. Still, he was aware of these new internal fissures, as his mother Elvina, an Old Guard member, filled her always-frequent letters to him around this time with screeds against the militants.

For his part, Beals needed little prodding to take a jaundiced view of Trotsky. He almost instinctively bristled around fifth column types,[81] whether Stalinist or Trotskyist, as he perceived both as manipulators who did not really believe in democracy. Like Beals's associates who followed Muste for a time, independent progressives such as Stuart Chase, Roger Baldwin, and *Nation* editor Freda Kirchwey, he found the Trotskyists were a vaguely disturbing presence. Indeed, Muste himself had once described Trotsky as "quite as much a dictator as Stalin in the Communist Party."[82]

Also, although Beals claimed he bore no special grudge against Trotsky, he did have many contacts and sympathies that suggested the contrary. His good friends and literary agents Max Lieber and Ernestine Evans were both still pro-Soviet at this time, along with Anna Louise Strong, who had guided him during his visit to Moscow.

On the Spanish front where this battle was most intense at the time, Beals once wrote disparagingly of what he called "the Trotskyist revolt behind the lines of the Spanish Loyalist government, the ill-starred uprising of the P.O.U.M."[83]

While Beals's claim to be a member of neither camp was sincere, his habit of holding Stalin and Trotsky to be equally villainous was at least somewhat specious. Evidence of Stalin's purges, and of his role in perpetuating famine in Ukraine was widespread by 1937, while Trotsky had been in exile, running for his life throughout this period. Yet Beals held Trotsky to be of the same ilk. "When in power Trotsky practiced terrorism of the State; Stalin continued the same tactic," he wrote in 1940. "One fell off the horse, the other kept on riding. The man who falls off, blames the successful rider rather than his own incapacity."[84] Beals went out of his way to insist that although Trotsky was no longer an emperor, he was nonetheless without clothes.

How to explain this awkward episode, from which Beals emerged muddied, angry, and alienated from more than a few of his erstwhile friends? It began with his error in judgment in accepting the invitation to join the Dewey Commission in the first place. He showed an almost shocking naivety, to some extent shared by Dewey himself, in failing to appreciate the Commission's central purpose as a platform for Trotsky's political messages. It seems oddly incongruous that his usually sharp instincts honed on close-up exposure to violent political struggle abandoned him at this juncture.

Once he arrived in Coyoacán, though, he realized he had signed on for the choir in a Trotskyist church, and he was horrified. Not a joiner by nature, he developed a quick dislike for the whole enterprise. He felt he had been tricked into signing on, lured by Dewey's stature and—he had been told—the involvement of historian Beard. When he learned that Beard was not of the party, he felt he was being used, and that he would forever be identified as a Trotsky follower if he went along with it.

He gave the exercise the benefit of the doubt for a day or two, but soon concluded that the Commission's origins, purpose and narrow parameters put the lie to its outward pretence of investigation and impartiality. This was a partisan show, not murderous like the Moscow Trials, of course, but not really an inquiry either. He wanted no part of it.

In most of the accounts and analytical literature on the Dewey Commission, the Beals resignation is usually treated as a footnote, in which a self-important, but otherwise irrelevant American writer likely in thrall to Stalinism, perhaps even on its payroll, tried to undermine this challenge to the Moscow Trials' supposed legitimacy.

This is unfair and symptomatic of celebrity culture that defines people, including writers, by their one or few acts that gain the greatest notoriety. More to the point, this interpretation is not plausible, and survives only because Beals's own story is so little-known. Aside from his friendships with intellectuals still in the Soviet camp then led by Stalin, it is quickly forgotten that he had enough closeness with Trotskyists to have been trusted, initially at least, as a Commission member.

As we have seen, Beals simply did not have the temperament of an agent, a spy, or an intriguer. He could not be a soldier in any kind of army. Nor was his participation an opportunistic publicity stunt, as the Mexican journalist's limerick suggested. It was too painful and costly to him for that. Also, Beals was not adept at self-promotion; indeed, he intensely disliked it.

Moving from the imputed motives critics have cited to explain Beals's performance at the hearings to the substance of his questions, one discerns the issue that the Commission avoided. This was not that Trotsky was masterminding a specific conspiracy to violently overthrow Stalin. Rather, it was that Trotsky's writings and personal revolutionary history revealed his endorsement of violence and repression—and conspiracy—as essential tactics in revolutionary strategy. Given Trotsky's position and history, he might well have been expected him to mount an effort to topple Stalin. That he had not done so suggests a lack of support rather than absence of motive.

In his 1919 debates with German social democrat Karl Kautsky, and in his 1920 book, *Terrorism and Communism*, Trotsky left no doubt about his belief that socialism could be achieved only by the violent means of proletarian dictatorship and terrorism.[85] His pursuit of the *end* of an idealized socialist future justified the *means* of generalized terror that would be needed to achieve it.[86] Trotsky did not have the psychopathic or paranoid streak held to explain Stalin's murderous record, but terror was part of the political toolkit he explicitly recommended.

Beals thus found it inconsistent that his fellow Commissioners, who elsewhere defended democratic practice as axiomatic, would be at such pains to defend someone who dismissed it as mere bourgeois affectation. His approach went beyond the boundaries of the Commission's purpose. He sought to unveil Trotsky's conspiratorial history, and thereby expose what he saw as hypocrisy. Perhaps Trotsky was not conspiring as alleged with fascists against Stalin in this particular instance, but the tumultuous events of his life revealed a practiced conspirator.

Not only that, but Beals had seen the effects of Trotsky's strategy in action. His chance encounter with Borodin, whose dispatch to Mexico by the Soviet regime in 1919 is a matter of historical record, betrayed Moscow's conspiratorial inclinations under Lenin and Trotsky. It was an obscure, personal experience of which no one in his audience could have been aware. But it was nonetheless real and relevant to Beals who, by the 1930s, looked back with disgust at an attempt by the Bolsheviks to intrigue and twist Mexico's indigenous revolution to serve their own Marxist-Leninist vision and geopolitical goals.

Still, the reference mystified the mostly partisan assembly, and led many of them to explain it by attributing sinister motives to Beals. They did not know about Mexico's revolutionary history, and they did not know about Beals. In the absence of such knowledge, the explanation was obvious to them. He was a Stalinist infiltrator, a GPU agent. *Reductio ad absurdum*.

Beals's experience aligns closely with that of French-Russian journalist Victor Serge, once Trotsky's acolyte, but whom Trotsky denounced as a "demoralized petty bourgeois" for having called on Marxists to embrace the Declaration of the Rights of Man. Wrote Serge: "Slandered, executed, and murdered, Trotskyism was displaying symptoms of an outlook in symmetry with that of the very Stalinism against which it had taken its stand, and by which it was being ground into powder."[87]

# NOTES

1. Carleton Beals, *The Stones Awake: A Novel of Mexico* (Philadelphia: J. B. Lippincott, 1936); *America South* (Philadelphia: J. B. Lippincott, 1937); *The Coming Struggle for Latin America* (New York: Halcyon House, 1940); and *American Earth: The Biography of a Nation* (Philadelphia: J. B. Lippincott, 1939).

2. David Kinkead to Carleton Beals, October 28, 1935, Carleton Beals Collection (CBC), Howard Gotlieb Archival Research Center, Boston University (hereafter cited CBC).

3. For an overview of the Scottsboro Boys cases, see Daren Salter, "Scottsboro Trials," *Encyclopedia of Alabama*, February 6, 2008; last updated December 6, 2017, http://www.encyclopediaofalabama.org/article/h-1456 (accessed May 25, 2021).

4. Carleton Beals, "Scottsboro Interview," *Nation*, February 12, 1936.

5. Beals, "Scottsboro Interview" (1936).

6. See Robin D. G. Kelley, *Hammer and Hoe – Alabama Communists during the Great Depression* (Chapel Hill: University of North Carolina Press, 1990), 62–63. Also Tom Burke to Margaret Marshall (Associate Editor of the *Nation*), February 20, 1936, CBC.

7. Carleton Beals, "Red Clay in Alabama," *Nation*, April 8 and 16, 1936.

8. Beals, "Red Clay in Alabama," 445.

9. Victor Hugo, *Les Misérables* (Belgium: Lacroix, Verbeckhoven & Cie, 1862).

10. I am grateful to the late Susannah Joel Glusker, daughter of Anita Brenner and author of *Anita Brenner: A Mind of Her Own* (Austin: University of Texas Press, 1998), for pointing this out. In the 1920s, Luz was a life model in several of the open-air art schools in Mexico City, and posed for Diego Rivera, Fernando Leal, Tina Modotti, and especially Jean Charlot, who first sketched and painted her portrait many times over. Beals's rendering in prose is analogous to Charlot's stylized images depicting a quintessential indigenous soul. Luz Jimenez, or Julia "Luciana" Jiménez (1897–1965), was born in the town of Milpa Alta, south of Mexico City—the model for Esperanza's home village of Milpa Verde in Carleton Beals's *The Stones Awake* (Philadelphia: J. B. Lippincott, 1936). Her studies were truncated by the Revolution, and though not a servant (as some recalled), her life was never financially secure. After working as a model, she became a rural schoolteacher in Milpa Alta in the early 1930s and later, a collaborator with linguists studying Nahuatl and visiting anthropologists. She remained in contact with Charlot for decades; he was godfather to her daughter Conchita, and along with Anita Brenner, he long helped support the family.

11. See Carleton Beals, *Brimstone and Chili: A Book of Personal Experiences in the Southwest and in Mexico* (New York: Knopf, 1927), 261–83.

12. Katherine Anne Porter, Review of *The Stones Awake*, by Carleton Beals, *New Republic*, November 18, 1936.

13. Beals, *Stones Awake*, 309–15.

14. Stanley Young, "Mr. Beals's Novel of Revolutionary Mexico; THE STONES AWAKE," *New York Times*, October 18, 1936, B8, https://www.nytimes.com/1936/10/18/archives/mr-bealss-novel-of-revolutionary-mexico-the-stones-awake-by.html (accessed May 23, 2021).

15. Review of *The Stones Awake*, by Carleton Beals, *Saturday Review of Literature*, 15, no. 2, November 7, 1936, 37; S. A. Lavine, Review of *The Stones Awake*, by Carleton Beals, *Boston Transcript*, October 17, 1936.

16. George Novack to Carleton Beals, March 19, 1937, CBC.

17. Glusker, *Anita Brenner*, 161.

18. Benjamin Stolberg to Carleton Beals, March 12, 1937, CBC.

19. Benjamin Stolberg to Carleton Beals, March 25, 1937, CBC.

20. Harold Kirker and Burleigh Taylor Wilkins, "Beard, Becker and the Trotsky Inquiry," *American Quarterly* 13, no. 4 (1961): 519, https://doi.org/10.2307/2710373

21. Corliss Lamont et al., "An Open Letter to American Liberals," *Soviet Russia Today*, March 1937, 14–15.

22. Lamont et al., "Open Letter," 14–15.

23. Alan M. Wald, *James T. Farrell: The Revolutionary Socialist Years* (New York: New York University Press, 1978), 69.

24. James T. Farrell, "Dewey in Mexico," in *John Dewey: Philosopher of Science and Freedom*, ed. Sidney Hook (New York: Daily Press, 1950), 358n.

25. Victor F. Calverton [pseud. George Goetz], "Is Trotsky Guilty?" *Modern Monthly* 10, March 1937, 5–8.

26. Suzanne LaFollette, *The Case of Leon Trotsky, Report of Hearings on the Charges Made Against Him in the Moscow Trials by the Commission of Inquiry* (New York: Merit, 1968; originally published New York: Harper, 1937; 1965).

27. See, for example, Isaac Deutscher, *The Prophet Outcast: Trotsky 1929–1940* (New York: Random House, 1963), 222.

28. Bertrand M. Patenaude, *Trotsky: Downfall of a Revolutionary* (New York: HarperCollins, 2009), 15–18.

29. Deutscher, *Prophet Outcast*, 358.

30. Deutscher, *Prophet Outcast*, 360.

31. Archie Brown, *The Rise and Fall of Communism* (New York: Ecco and HarperCollins, 2011), 75.

32. Deutscher, *Prophet Outcast*, 368.

33. Alan M. Wald, *The New York Intellectuals: The Rise and Decline of the Anti-Stalinist Left from the 1930s to the 1980s* (Chapel Hill: University of North Carolina Press, 1987), 131.

34. Albert Glotzer, *Trotsky: Memoir and Critique* (Buffalo, NY: Prometheus Books, 1989), 255

35. Patenaude, *Trotsky*, 40.

36. Carleton Beals, "Trotsky Rides Again," in Carleton Beals, "Under the Fifth Sun" (unpublished autobiography, c. 1972–1978), in Carleton Beals Collection (CBC), Howard Gotlieb Archival Research Center, Boston University, box 44; and Carleton Beals, "The Fewer Outsiders the Better," *Saturday Evening Post*, June 12, 1937.

37. Beals, "Trotsky Rides Again."

38. Wald, *James T. Farrell*, 70.

39. Dewey, John (Chairman), Commission of Inquiry into the Charges Made Against Leon Trotsky in the Moscow Trials, *The Case of Leon Trotsky: Transcript of Proceedings*. (Merit. New York, 1937; 1968), 66–68 (hereafter cited Dewey, *Case of Leon Trotsky*).

40. Dewey, *Case of Leon Trotsky*, 68.

41. Dewey, *Case of Leon Trotsky*, 68.

42. Dewey, *Case of Leon Trotsky*, 71.

43. Dewey, *Case of Leon Trotsky*, 52.

44. Dewey, *Case of Leon Trotsky*, 54.

45. Dewey, *Case of Leon Trotsky*, 54–55.

46. Beals, "Fewer Outsiders the Better" (1937).

47. Carleton Beals, *Glass Houses: Ten Years of Free-Lancing* (Philadelphia: J. B. Lippincott, 1938), 43–49.

48. Beals, *Glass Houses*, 45.

49. Dewey, *Case of Leon Trotsky*, 412.

50. Marion Hammett and William Smith, "Inside the Trotsky 'Trial,'" *New Masses*, April 27, 1937, 10.

51. Hammett and Smith, "Inside the Trotsky 'Trial,'" 10.

52. Dewey, *Case of Leon Trotsky*, 415.

53. Dewey, *Case of Leon Trotsky*, 416.

54. Frank Kluckhohn, "'Trial' of Trotsky a joke, says Beals," *New York Times*, April 19, 1937.

55. Kluckhohn, "Trial," *New York Times*, April 19, 1937.

56. See Glotzer, *Trotsky*, 266–70. Glotzer, a Trotskyist who was the Commission's verbatim reporter, characterized Kluckhohn's reports as "misleading, antagonistic and pro-Stalinist" and also reports that James T. Farrell wrote him that Beals's friend Harry Block, whom Farrell claimed was a Communist Party member, "was the person who got to Carlton [sic] Beals." The report is corroborated in Beals's own unpublished memoir, although Farrell's and Glotzer's version contains factual errors such as its claim that Block was married to the daughter of (Mexican labor leader Vicente Lombardo) Toledano; in fact, Block's wife was artist Maria

Luisa (Malú) Cabrera, daughter of Carranza's finance minister Luis Cabrera (see Beals, "Under the Fifth Sun" [unpublished autobiography], CBC). Moreover, Toledano, just ten years older than Maria Luisa (how could he be her father?), and in 1937 leader of the Mexican Labor Confederation was, by then, supporting Mexican President Cárdenas (who had granted Trotsky exile), and selected Fidel Velasquez as his successor *against* the candidate backed by the union's CP-linked faction. Finally, Farrell, as we have seen, is hardly an objective observer, especially with respect to Beals's role on the Commission. Nonetheless, Beals wrote in an unpublished manuscript (see Carleton Beals Collection [CBC]) that Block, then the *Nation*'s correspondent in Mexico City, *did* urge him to resign from the Commission.

57. Dewey, *Case of Leon Trotsky*, xxvi.
58. Dewey, *Case of Leon Trotsky*, 3.
59. "Lo del Día – Trotsky nos ha desilusionado," por un Observador, *Excelsior*, April 20, 1937, CBC, box 144.
60. "Epigrama del Día," por Kien, *Excelsior*, April 19, 1937, CBC, box 144. Roughly translated by author:
    Carleton Beals played his role well.
    Stealing the show from the Russian,
    Now all eyes upon him dwell,
    For resigning in high dudgeon,
    He'll write a book that'll sell!
61. Wireless to the *New York Times*, "Trotsky Hints Beals Works for the Soviet," *New York Times*, May 26, 1937, 9, https://timesmachine.nytimes.com/timesmachine/1937/05/26/94379864.html?auth=login-email&pageNumber=9 (accessed May 24, 2021). See also John Dewey, *Not Guilty: Report of the Commission of Inquiry into the Charges Made Against Leon Trotsky in the Moscow Trials* (Brooklyn, NY: Sam Sloan and Ishi Press International, 2008; originally published in 1938).
62. "Meddling Charged in Trotsky Inquiry," *New York Times*, May 10, 1937, 2.
63. "Meddling Charged in Trotsky Inquiry," *New York Times*, May 10, 1937, 2.
64. Leon Trotsky, *The Revolution Betrayed*, trans. Max Eastman (Mineola NY: Dover, 2004), originally published *The Revolution Betrayed: What is the Soviet Union and Where Is It Going?* trans. Max Eastman (Garden City, NY: Doubleday, Doran, 1937).
65. Beals, "Fewer Outsiders" (1937).
66. Leon Trotsky to Victor F. Calverton [pseud. for George Goetz], October 15, 1937, CBC.
67. Diego Rivera to Victor F. Calverton [pseud. for George Goetz], November 3, 1937, CBC.
68. Victor F. Calverton [pseud. for George Goetz] to Carleton Beals, March 30, 1938, CBC.
69. Victor F. Calverton [pseud. for George Goetz] to Leon Trotsky, December 6, 1937, CBC.
70. Victor F. Calverton [pseud. for George Goetz] to Carleton Beals, March 30, 1938, CBC.
71. Carleton Beals to Victor F. Calverton [pseud. for George Goetz], April 11, 1938, CBC.
72. Beals to Calverton (1938), CBC.
73. For example, Deutscher, *Prophet Outcast*; Glotzer, *Trotsky – Memoir and Critique*; Farrell, *Dewey in Mexico*; Patenaude, *Trotsky – Downfall of a Revolutionary*.
74. Deutscher, *Prophet Outcast*, 430.
75. Robert Service, *Trotsky: A Biography* (Cambridge, MA: Harvard University Press, 2009), 223, 243, and 283.
76. Service, *Trotsky: A Biography*, 411.
77. Robert Service, *History of Modern Russia: From Nicholas II to Vladimir Putin*, rev. ed. (Cambridge, MA: Harvard Univeristy Press, 2005), 178.
78. Wald, *New York Intellectuals*, 59; Albert Halper, *Good-Bye Union Square: A Writer's Memoir of the Thirties* (Chicago: Quadrangle Books, 1970), 89–97.
79. See Michael Kazin, *American Dreamers: How the Left Changed a Nation* (New York: Alfred A. Knopf, 2011).
80. Constance Ashton Myers, *The Prophet's Army: Trotskyists in America, 1928–1941* (Westport CT: Greenwood Press, 1977), 112–115.

81. The term "fifth column" originated during the Spanish Civil War, but now refers to any group of conspirators who seek to join a larger group to undermine it from within, usually in favor of an enemy group or nation.

82. Myers, *Prophet's Army*, 120.

83. Beals, *Glass Houses*, 399. The POUM, or Partido Obrero de Unificacion Marxista (Workers' Party of Marxist Unification), was a semi-Trotskyist breakaway group from the Spanish Communist Party, based in Catalonia, and which fought on the Republican side in the Spanish Civil War. Although it endorsed Trotsky's ideas, it was not formally affiliated with the Fourth International.

84. Beals, *The Great Circle: Further Adventures in Free-Lancing* (Philadelphia: J. B. Lippincott, 1940), 155.

85. See Leon Trotsky: *Terrorism and Communism: A Reply to Karl Kautsky* (London: Verso, 2007; originally published 1920).

86. See George L. Kline, "The Defence of Terrorism: Trotsky and His Major Critics," in *The Trotsky Reappraisal*, ed. Terry Brotherstone and Paul Duke, trans. Brian Pearce, Jenny Brine, and Andrew Drummond (Edinburgh: Edinburgh University Press, 1992), 156–65.

87. Victor Serge, *Memoirs of a Revolutionary* (1951), trans. Peter Sedgwick, with George Paizi (New York: New York Review, 2012), 407.

*Chapter Eleven*

# Wartime Visions of America North and South

By the mid-1930s, a collective sense of resignation had taken hold across America that a major war was all but inevitable. Italy had invaded Ethiopia. Japanese troops occupied Manchuria. General Francisco Franco (1892–1975) was leading a military revolt against Spain's Republican government. And most ominous of all, Adolf Hitler had launched a massive rearmament in Germany.

Franklin Delano Roosevelt (FDR) was neither a pacifist nor an isolationist, but his keen political instincts reminded him of America's bedrock popular view: European wars were for Europeans to solve. As he launched his re-election campaign in early 1936, he knew that his prospects depended on reassuring Americans that he would keep America safe, and out of any war.

But a back-door threat put this scenario on thin ice. Roosevelt's ever-feuding foreign policy architects, the earnest, sad-eyed Tennessean US Secretary of State Cordell Hull and the patrician diplomat Sumner Welles, despite their growing differences, agreed that the United States needed to be vigilant lest South America be contaminated by European fascism. Argentina, the continent's largest economy, was the most exposed. A large share of its export trade was with Europe, and its authoritarian, military-backed governing class admired the strong hand of order and discipline they saw in Mussolini, Hitler and soon, Franco.

So it seemed too, with Brazil, where the populist Getúlio Vargas (1882–1954), elected in 1930 as the country's president, showed dictatorial inclinations, and enjoyed, at least for a time, the support of the local fascist brand, the green-shirted *Integralistas* (an extreme-right nationalist movement founded in 1932). Chile, Peru, Bolivia, and Ecuador, all ruled by military men, were likewise exposed.

Hull and Welles feared that growing links between these authoritarian *caudillos* and the emerging Axis belligerents could gel into an alliance in which the Latins would supply vital raw materials—oil, iron, copper, lumber, and foodstuffs—to the fascists bent on global domination. Their alarm mounted as they watched the Latins' trade with Europe rise as that with the Depression-racked United States waned. It could, ultimately, conclude with war in the Western hemisphere.

To stem this prospect, Roosevelt sought to reinforce the Good Neighbor Policy he had undertaken in 1933 with a dramatic gesture that would help build support for the United States among the Latin American countries. In a move that cleverly appealed at once to pacifists and those concerned about security, the President called in January 1936 on leaders of the hemisphere's twenty republics, "to assemble at an early date . . . to determine how the maintenance of peace among the American Republics may best be safeguarded."[1]

This summit conference took place eleven months later in Buenos Aires. Roosevelt, by then just re-elected, sailed down on a triumphant cruise aboard the battleship *USS Indianapolis*, with stops in Rio de Janeiro and Montevideo where, as in Buenos Aires itself, he was met by enthusiastic crowds who lined the streets to cheer as he waved his fedora from an open car.

The summit produced a convention for "the maintenance, preservation and reestablishment of peace."[2] But even if this seemed a historic watershed, the first time since 1889 that the hemisphere's political leaders agreed to take steps against a possible attack from a non-hemispheric aggressor, the convention failed to bridge a divide between the United States and Argentina.

Carlos Saavedra Lamas (1878–1959), Argentina's erudite and stiff-mannered foreign minister, resisted FDR's overture which he perceived as a threat to Argentina's dominance of South America. He rejected the American proposal for compulsory consultation among the American republics whenever a war threat appeared in the hemisphere. He similarly dismissed the US idea of a permanent inter-American committee to conduct such consultation. Most importantly, he rebuffed the United States' push for a declaration of common neutrality by all of the hemisphere's republics.

Saavedra Lamas's opposition to the American position attracted the support of Bolivia, Chile, and Uruguay, and resulted in a watered-down version of the hemispheric commitments that Washington had sought. The republics conceded, almost grudgingly, that while a common neutrality policy was a vague "general objective," the hemisphere's countries who so chose could—and would—continue nonetheless to maintain relations with fascist powers and trade with them.[3]

Carleton Beals followed these events closely, of course. Upon his return from Mexico in early May of 1937, he and Blanca Rosa spent another summer—their third—at Brockett's Point. Their living room was like a shrine for

Beals's typewriter, on which he labored intensely, pouring out analyses of US-Latin American relations in the shadow of the looming world war.

In November 1937, *America South* was published. In this, probably his most enduring book, Beals sought to take in a broader perspective of Latin America as a whole, shifting from his earlier focus on single countries. This allowed him to discern what he considered defining threads in the history of relations between the region and the United States and outline a conceptual framework much aligned with what would later be called the radical, neo-imperialist interpretation, or Wisconsin School.[4]

In its final pages, Beals zeroed in on Roosevelt's trip to Buenos Aires to conclude a wide-ranging discourse on the Monroe Doctrine and Pan-Americanism. In the proposals Hull had tabled in Buenos Aires, Beals saw a dishonest ploy. In effect, Washington was asking Latin America to apply a neutrality policy that would cut off the supply of vital materials to European countries, upon whose purchases the Latins were heavily dependent, which America would be unwilling to have applied against itself.[5]

While conceding that the Latin Americans "like [Roosevelt] very much and so do I," Beals dismissed the final agreement reached in Buenos Aires as "a dishwater soup proposal without efficacy."[6] In his view, the major achievement there, overlooked by the press at the time but cited as significant by historians since then, was the adoption of a protocol against "intervention" by one American republic into the affairs of another.

In a departure from Hull's position at the Montevideo Pan-American conference on the same issue three years earlier, the US delegation did not insist this time on any reservation to its self-imposed embargo on intervention. "This diplomatic victory was entirely Latin America's," Beals wrote, adding that it was, "in the long run more important than any lost neutrality legislation—provided future administrations keep the promise."[7]

In this first detailed critique of pan-Americanism during the Good Neighbor era, Beals struggled with apparently contradictory impulses. His visceral opposition to US intervention in Latin American countries continued, but he was obviously troubled that US failure to intervene had the outcome that the United States acquiesced with murderous despots.

He lamented that FDR's professed embrace in his Buenos Aires speech of "free American republics, the will of the people, the desire for peace, the sacredness of international obligations" was directed at "one of the worst groups of international cutthroat diplomats ever to come together in the Americas, representatives for the most part of governments that have abused their own people, who have no more loyalty to international agreements than Hitler or the Mikado."[8]

He quoted approvingly what he called "more cynical Latin-American critics" who saw in Roosevelt's charm offensive a "New World brand of Holy Alliance" in which the United States embraced reactionary, "semi-

Fascist dictatorships which infest Latin America" as this best served the interests of American companies and banks with economic and financial interests in the region.[9] Beals gave credence to this line of analysis, noting that the Good Neighbor Policy's progenitor, Sumner Welles, had earlier driven US interventions in the Dominican Republic and Cuba.

He added that FDR's fulsome praise for democracy was also compromised by the administration's relative antipathy to Mexico's reformist government led by President Lázaro Cárdenas, arguably more democratic than any other in Latin America. Also, unlike Mexico, the United States pointedly refused to offer even moral support to the elected Spanish Republican government's struggle against Franco's fascist military revolt, then under way.

Beals took issue not with pan-Americanism as an idea, but with what he saw as the US government's self-interested conception of it, and disingenuous purpose in promoting it. Pan-Americanism, as conceived in Washington, Beals argued, was driven not by a desire for multilateral hemispheric comity and cooperation, based on consultation and mutual respect, but rather by an effort to get the Latin American republics to line up behind US policy and priorities.

*America South* was generally well-received by reviewers. The perennial liberal Latin-Americanist Hubert C. Herring, while gently upbraiding Beals for "forever catching someone in a foul plot," nonetheless judged it "a good book . . . the best he has written," an assessment shared by Beals himself.[10] Anthropologist Philip Ainsworth Means, writing in the *New York Times Book Review*, praised it for provoking thought and debate, but mocked what he called Beals's "psychology: evidently he hates the rich, the great and the powerful, and conversely, he loves the tumultuous and the embattled oppressed."[11] Means, perhaps betraying his own pro-establishment bias, took specific issue with what he called a "tirade" in *America South* against the Pan-American Union and its head, American diplomat Leo Stanton Rowe.[12] Beals had charged that Rowe acted as a "correct window-dresser" for the US government at the Pan-American Union, "whitewashing" its Marine interventions, attacking Mexico when it was "non grata to the petroleum companies" and lying about economic progress and school systems in countries which had neither.[13]

As complement to its full-throated critique of pan-Americanism, Beals devotes several chapters of *America South* to outlining a kind of proto-version of what would later come to be known as Dependency Theory.[14] The essence of this is in a chapter, "Why Latin-American Backwardness?" in which Beals summarizes and dismisses a series of then-popular theories seeking to explain Latin America's chronic poverty and underdevelopment. These include racial—or racist—arguments, a tropical climate in many countries that favors lethargy over industry, the absence of coal to develop an industrial base, lack of adherence to moral standards, excessively mystical religiosity, militarism, the absence of a middle class, and poor health.

Beals concludes that rather than any of these, each of which he thought specious, irrelevant or consequences rather than causes, the most plausible argument is rooted in Latin America's feudal legacy. This history, in which Indian and *mestizo* peons or African-descended slaves worked on agricultural estates, was combined in the early twentieth century with the emergence of industrial societies in the United States and Europe, Beals explained, which pushed up demand for raw materials.

"Many of the countries became one-crop countries . . . dependent upon the whims of the world market," he wrote. "Thus their economies have had no stability; hence their politics have had no stability."[15]

Later in the book, he outlines the consequence of "ineluctable demand" for raw materials by US industry as being the expansion of US capital to Latin America, where it demands "settled political conditions . . . and—if not honest governments—at least amenable governments."[16] With new, modern social and economic systems emerging as a result of these investments in mines, oil drilling, and fruit plantations, the feudal order was disturbed, and its evils distorted into new directions.

"The extraction of vast quantities of raw materials has tended to accentuate feudal evils, to accentuate militarism, to forestall democracy, and to prevent the amalgamation of the social groups, the classes, the races and the cultures," Beals wrote.[17]

It was these forces, and the economic crisis that undid even their limited benefits by the early 1930s, that propelled such movements as the Augusto César Sandino Rebellion, the Cuban revolution of 1933, *Aprismo*, and the Lázaro Cárdenas radical revival in Mexico, all of which Beals had witnessed at first hand.

While these trends have been widely acknowledged by historians, Beals's analysis was a radical interpretation in its time, at least within the small community of American scholars and journalists interested in Latin America.[18] There was something preternatural—"awkward" was how *Time* Magazine described Beals—about a widely-published and incontestably well-informed *American* journalist delivering such a hostile reading of America's role in the hemisphere, especially at the apex of the Good Neighbor era.

But if almost heretical at home, in Latin America it constituted, in the early-to-mid-1930s, a compelling challenge to the old order. And by the mid-1940s and later, variations of it would propel leftist or left-leaning populist leaders from Argentina's President Juan Perón (1895–1974) to Cuba's Fidel Castro to power.

Indeed it would become the standard interpretation of political, economic, and social history for Latin America's left. A more elaborately documented and argued version of it would emerge as mainstream among the region's respectable intellectual establishment too. The Argentine economist Raúl Prebisch developed his prescriptive theory of Import-Substituting Industrialization, or ISI, as a way to end the one-crop economy trap, and the negative terms of trade it produced. Prebisch, a United Nations official who founded the Economic Commission for Latin America in 1949, is credited for having developed with Hans Singer, another United Nations economist, what came to be known as the Prebisch-Singer Theory.[19]

In the 1960s and 1970s, this theory would animate neo-Marxist leaders such as Cuba's Castro and Chile's President Salvador Allende (1908–1973), and perhaps find its most eloquent journalistic literary expression in Eduardo Galeano's *Las Venas abiertas de América Latina* (*Open Veins of Latin America*), the book Venezuela's populist left-wing President Hugo Chávez (1954–2013) bestowed on US President Barack Obama (1961–) in 2009.

Coincidentally, Beals reviewed the English-language edition when it first appeared in 1974, calling it "a truly majestic book [that] rips away every defense of imperialism with a determined yet quiet rage. This book surpasses any I have ever read on the theme, and it will endure through all the years to come."[20]

Just as *America South* was being shipped to booksellers in October 1937, a savage massacre of civilians by government troops in the Dominican Republic, and the passive official US response to it, served to underline Beals's *America South* thesis.

Rafael Leonidas Trujillo (1891–1961), the Caribbean country's President since he had seized power in a coup in 1930, ordered his troops to slaughter immigrant Haitian residents living near the border town of Dajabón. He claimed that they were working with his political enemies to destabilize his government.

Trujillo had served two terms as president and had pledged not to contest the upcoming 1938 elections, making a public show of following the US custom of a two-term limit. But he simultaneously maneuvered to place his puppet, Jacinto Peynado (1878–1940), in the presidency while Trujillo would retain control of the army.

The unprovoked brutality and scale of killing was shocking. Over five days, up to twenty thousand civilians were either shot or butchered with machetes, clubs, and knives in what came to be known as the Parsley Massacre.[21]

Beals had received a letter from an American contact in Santo Domingo, who claimed to have seen "truck after truck, dripping with blood and filled with mangled bodies, pass by in the direction of shark-infested seas."[22] The letter's account, borne out by similar reports Beals found in New York's Spanish-language press, formed the basis for a story Beals immediately filed to *Current History*. It was initially turned down by an editor who thought it far-fetched and insufficiently documented, but finally published in the magazine three months later, after coverage in the *New York Times* and *Herald-Tribune* had corroborated Beals's account.[23]

Beals later wrote updated versions for *Readers' Digest* and the *American Weekly*, despite reported efforts by Trujillo's public relations counsel and the State Department to suppress the story.[24]

Just over a year later, in July 1939, FDR and Mrs. Roosevelt hosted Trujillo for tea at the White House.[25] This visit came just two months after Nicaraguan dictator Anastasio Somoza, he who had ordered Sandino's murder in 1934, was an overnight White House guest and honored with an invitation to address both houses of Congress.

These cases sharply illustrated, for those who paid attention, the substance behind *America South*'s depiction of Latin America's economically-dependent, backward states whose dictators—"cut-throats" to use Beals's term—were indulged by US leaders and for whose political survival the Good Neighbor Policy provided a kind of insurance.

\*\*\*

In April 1938, *America South*'s steady sales prompted a reprint, accompanied by the publication that month of *Glass Houses*, a memoir of Beals's freelancing years in Latin America, Spain, and Italy during the 1920s. "The booksellers are already predicting it will be a best seller," Jefferson Jones, the J. B. Lippincott editor, enthusiastically wrote Beals. Indeed, *Glass Houses* was briefly on the *New York Herald-Tribune*'s best-seller list, just behind Isak Dinesen's *Out of Africa*.[26]

*Glass Houses* was more widely reviewed than Beals's previous books, showing his arrival as an established writer. Most of America's big-city dailies included it in their literary pages, as did the major magazines, By and large, reviewers treated it with respect, aside from the now-customary digs at Beals's tendency to lean too far left, or to take himself too seriously. "Mr. Beals strikes you as a man who could always keep himself in hot water—even if he had to boil it himself," jibed Charles Poore in the *New York Times*.[27]

It remains of some historical interest for its eyewitness sketches in which Beals reveals the foibles of some of the era's public figures, along with its *zeitgeist*. We learn, for example, of Diego Rivera's angry outburst upon learning that his [first] wife Lupe is pregnant, fearing that children would "clutter up his studio."[28] Sandino appears here, along with John Dos Passos and Charles Lindbergh, Dwight Morrow, and Benito Mussolini, among many others.

With the success of these books and the passage of time having pushed the bruising Dewey Commission episode into the background, Beals had settled by the summer of 1938 into a lifestyle at once tranquil and productive. He reveled in his country esquire's idyll on the Connecticut shore, absorbing the traditional *latina* attentiveness of Blanca Rosa, always cheerful, chatty, and well-turned out. As her English improved, she helped him by typing manuscripts, in addition to serving up Peruvian specialties such as *papas a la huancaína* (Huancayo-style potatoes).

Not least, Beals, ever the unapologetic admirer of an attractive female form, enjoyed cavorting in Long Island Sound with his slim and petite young wife, and then lounging with her on a towel spread out on nearby Short Beach after their daily dips.

With their more anchored domestic household, and with a growing income from royalties and lectures enabling such luxuries as a Ford Coupe, Beals and Blanca Rosa also welcomed her sister Aurora for a visit of several months in the summer of 1938.

The sisters both liked to entertain and launched what became an agreeable tradition of weekend gatherings that would last several years. It was focused on two couples to whom the Beals's often played host, first at Brockett's Point, and then at the more upscale house they built in 1942 on Uncas Road in Sachem's Head, Guilford. The first was Max Lieber, and his new wife—and business partner—Minna Zelinka, along with Minna's ten-year-old son Ernest. The second was Alberto Rembao, editor of the liberal Christian monthly, *La Nueva Democracia* (New Democracy), published in New York City, and his Spanish-born wife Julia.

Beals had met Rembao through Samuel Guy Inman, head of the Protestant Committee on Cooperation in Latin America, who had been a friendly acquaintance since early Mexico days. Rembao, once a Mexican revolutionary soldier in Pablo Orozco's army who had lost a leg in battle, was possessed of a great gift for friendship. Although Rembao's defining evangelical Christian faith might have been a barrier to intimacy with Beals, who wore his disregard for religious practice on his sleeve, the two men grew close, exchanging several notes a week over many years.

Educated at the Pacific School of Religion in Berkeley, Rembao, his eyes twinkling with merriment, was so full of effervescent warmth and clever ebullience, so open to debate and discussion, that Beals was utterly charmed. The loyalty he inspired in Beals was such that Carleton once interceded forcefully on Rembao's behalf to get him a teaching position at New York's City College over the administration's objections that Rembao did not have his immigration papers in order.

It was in some respects, an unlikely triangle of couples: Beals and Blanca Rosa, still in her late twenties, Lieber, the Jewish Communist Party member and literary agent, and Rembao, the Protestant theologian who sought to apply social gospel ideas to fight injustice and exclusion in Latin America, a kind of precursor to the liberation theology of the 1960s and 1970s.[29] Their debates were animated, with Rembao arguing that the strength of communism came from its tenderness for the downtrodden, which was ultimately rooted in Christian devotion. To which Beals and Lieber would shake their heads in disbelief.

"My disciples are those who deny me," was Rembao's rejoinder, quoting Nietzsche back to his atheistic friends.

A shared sense of irreverent humor combined with literary verbosity sustained this steady light-hearted patter among the three men, punctuated by revolving tournaments at the chessboard.

One evening at Brockett's Point, for example, Max pretended to sulk because Carleton and Alberto were speaking too much Spanish, which Max could not follow. It was decided that Carleton and Alberto would drive from Brockett's Point to New Haven to pick up some wine, while Max would remain with the ladies. Max remonstrated upon their return, complaining that he had been left alone in female company because Alberto's Spanish banter, however hilarious, excluded him.

"You are jealous," said Alberto, "at having to take second-place to a dark-skinned person, an inferior race . . . and resent that we are not speaking in English, the language which the Lord God used when he dictated the Pentateuch to Moses."[30]

To which Max responded, tongue firmly in cheek: "I do not object to your dark skin: that is just surface pigmentation. What I take exception to is your black soul. But you are only a child, so will be permitted to enter the pearly gates."[31]

This happy domestic scene was suddenly interrupted on September 21, when the Great Hurricane of 1938 slammed the Connecticut coast. Its 186-mile-an-hour gusts battered seaside homes and communities there and across six other New England states, killing 682 people.

Brockett's Point was hard hit. A giant wave severed the verandah from the Beals's cottage, while the high winds blew out the windows and dislodged the roof. Comparatively speaking, they were lucky, as many of their neighbors' homes were washed away.

Beals's main concern was rescuing the manuscript for the book on which he was at work, *American Earth*, which came through safely, if a little damp.[32] In the following days, Beals and Blanca Rosa (Aurora, fortuitously, had returned to Peru just days before), rescued their clothing and personal effects from the watery mess, and moved into another cottage offered them by landlord Benjamin Brockett.

***

War fever mounted in 1938, the year of Hitler's Anschluss (union) with Austria, Kristallnacht, his takeover of the Sudetenland, and moves against Czechoslovakia. In America, these developments sustained the wrangling between FDR's White House and Congressional leaders over the continuing embargo on US arms sales to the European powers.

The ban was rooted in the *Neutrality Act of 1935* that the US Congress had passed, driven by the isolationist US Senator from North Dakota, Gerald P. Nye, a populist progressive Republican who reflected widespread feeling in the mid-West even as his countrified bowl haircut triggered snickers in Washington.[33]

FDR, squeezed between Nye-inspired Congressional warnings against US entanglement in Europe and the need to do something to stem what he saw as fascism's rising tide, moved to a renewed embrace of the Good Neighbor Policy in Latin America. It had withered since the President's triumphal December 1936 tour, and reviving it took on new urgency as Roosevelt was stymied in his effort to lean toward Britain in the intensifying conflict in Europe. He would return, as historian Fredrick Pike has observed, to "one of the earliest themes of hemispheric policy as sounded by the 1823 Monroe Doctrine: America for the Americans."[34]

There were grounds for this position, both as a considered response to evidence of a real threat, and also to rising public concern about it across the country. Beals contributed mightily to fueling this wave of concern, in some quarters even alarm, about Nazi penetration in South America. He published a series of articles through the fall of 1938 and winter of 1939 in *Current History*, *Harper's Monthly*, *Foreign Affairs*, and *Readers' Digest* that declaimed against "totalitarian inroads" in the continent.[35]

These articles were expanded, woven together and published around the same time by J. B. Lippincott's Halcyon House, as *The Coming Struggle for Latin America*, whose cover flap cited Hitler's purported boast that once he had subdued Europe, the Latin American continent would drop into his hands "like an over-ripe fruit."[36]

This book's six printings over two years and sales over thirteen thousand—Beals's most popular thus far—fed a strong appetite among the US reading public over this alleged fifth column activity. Beals presented an arresting catalogue of evidence to show how Nazi Germany, Imperial Japan, and Mussolini's Italy were spreading their tentacles to Latin America, through investment, trade, and commercial airlines, as well as propaganda and outright support, including military training, for the continent's panoply of dictators. Beals also documented the depth and range of British ties to the continent, as well as Soviet efforts, albeit less successful.

His brief built on a history in which especially Argentina, but also Brazil, Chile, Uruguay, Peru, and Bolivia maintained friendly ties to Germany, Italy, and Spain. All had sizeable expatriate German, Italian, and in some cases, Japanese communities, with prominent local leaders sympathetic to the fascist or militarist regimes in their countries of origin. These were often politically influential or important players in the local economies, or both.

The close cultural ties were reinforced by trade and investment flows. For example, airline links were maintained by German-owned carriers, with German managers and pilots. A Nazi-controlled German news service, Trans-Ocean, supplied a steady stream of pro-German propaganda to South American newspapers. German military delegations provided training to their South American counterparts.

Another American writer seizing on this issue was John Gunther, whose best-selling *Inside Latin America,* published in 1941, credited Beals as the source for his material on fascist penetration.[37]

Beals berated the FDR administration for what he argued were ineffectual responses to these threats, namely the reciprocity trade deals being pursued by Hull and, once again, an ingenuous reliance on the Good Neighbor Policy. Instead of embracing and arming murderous tyrants such as Somoza, Trujillo, and more importantly, a fascist-sympathizing dictator such as Brazil's Vargas, Beals called on the Roosevelt administration to support the forces of democracy in Latin America.

Latin America's people, Beals argued, wherever given a chance to express themselves freely, "have no sympathy for Fascism, but desire more democracy and more liberty—a process actually obstructed by our own State Department by its false labels and ill-considered support to such tyrannies as those of Brazil, its support of re-armament and its power-politics."[38]

While Beals's description of European fascist inroads to Latin America was disturbing, the policy prescriptions he proposed to undercut them leaned to isolationist withdrawal rather than assertive action, both in Europe and the Western hemisphere. He called on the US government to: (1) get out of the propaganda business in foreign lands; (2) quit helping out in the "dirty" armament business; (3) recall its military missions from Brazil, Peru, Guatemala and Argentina; and (4) get rid of [its] official language and patronizing condescension and superiority."[39]

Almost immediately, Clarence Senior, executive secretary of the Keep America Out of War Congress, an alliance of pacifist, liberal, and socialist groups including the National Council for the Prevention of War, the Women's International League for Peace and Freedom, and the American Friends Service Committee, among others, embraced Beals's argument. The group's campaign took up *Coming Struggle*'s four-point program as the basis for activity of its affiliated groups.[40] Meantime, Senior informed Beals that he had urged the anti-interventionist alliance's local chapters, "to get people to review your book."[41]

Oddly, while left-leaning isolationists embraced Beals's prescriptions, their most prominent opponent on this issue, namely FDR, likewise shared Beals's assessment of the problem, if not its solution. The President, struggling to weaken the isolationists in US Congress who had passed a series of *Neutrality Acts* (of 1935, 1936, 1937, and 1939), made assertions remarkably similar to those found in *Coming Struggle*'s early chapters.

"The vast resources of Latin America constitute the most tempting loot in all the round world," Roosevelt intoned in a December 1940 Fireside Chat. And in May 1941, the President warned that for Hitler, the conquest of Europe was simply "a step towards ultimate goals in all the other continents."[42]

Beals did urge intervention in one place where FDR's administration had shown reluctance and vacillation: Spain. In *Coming Struggle*, he denounced a bill passed by the US Congress in January 1937 at the behest of the US State Department that forbade arms sales to the Spanish Republican government. That bill reversed the previous status quo which permitted the sale of arms to friendly governments suppressing a revolt.

"If weak democratic governments [like Spain's] cannot get arms from the so-called democratic Powers," Beals wrote, "a premium is put on Fascist revolt everywhere, not merely in Europe but in America itself."[43]

He argued that if the United States applied this policy to South American regimes facing challenges from democratic reformers, it would wind up supplying arms to "tyrannical semi-Fascist" governments, thereby snuffing out demands for democracy in those same countries. In the same vein, Beals took issue with America's comparatively frosty stance toward Mexico, then under the left-leaning Lázaro Cárdenas administration and the only country in Latin America, aside from Costa Rica, that supported the Loyalists in Spain. Both countries, Beals noted, were also the only ones in the region "enjoying free speech."[44]

In essence, Beals's argument in *The Coming Struggle for Latin America* was that America's security was most effectively assured by "free peoples" in Latin America, as they would spontaneously resist the intrigue of foreign reactionary powers to control them. It is tidily summed up in the book's final paragraph: "We cannot hope to successfully help defend Latin Americans against the totalitarian powers unless they are thereby enabled to share equally with us the larger freedom that we seek to preserve."[45]

Beals spent most of the winter and fall of 1939 on *The Coming Struggle for Latin America* lecture tours through the Midwestern states and California, speaking at universities and dinner clubs, and traveling by train with Blanca Rosa.

The tours were followed and also encouraged a lively public reaction to the book, with bundles of mail directed to Beals, most of it positive. The critical reception was lively too, with controversy swirling over what should be America's stance in response to the threats of fascism, Soviet communism, and the looming world war.

In its time, Beals's exhortation that America back democracy in the Western hemisphere by ending its support for dictators was seen by many in the foreign policy elite as naïve and wishful thinking that would leave America vulnerable. This kind of *realpolitik* view is one end of a remarkably regular pendulum swing in which US support for democracy is upheld only when it is not trumped by security issues, access to vital resources or other geopolitical considerations. It is worth noting that twenty years after *The Coming Struggle for Latin America*, Presidential candidate John F. Kennedy, speaking in Tampa, Florida two weeks before his election promised that he would, "give constant and unequivocal support to democracy in Latin America. We must end our open and warm backing of dictators."[46]

In the face of evidence of fascist penetration and influence that Beals himself documented, however, his proposed response, essentially withdrawal from the scene, seemed incongruously passive for many Americans. Indeed, his account tended to alarm readers into favoring, if not intervention, at least some kind of assertive US action.

\*\*\*

Beals's productivity was staggering during this period. Just on the heels of *The Coming Struggle of Latin America*, J. B. Lippincott published his *American Earth: The Biography of a Nation*, a kind of documentary companion to John Steinbeck's *The Grapes of Wrath*, which came out at almost exactly the same time. It was "a fighting book, brim-full of the pity and anger that makes the reformer," reviewed Columbia University historian Allan Nevins, "bellicose in a good cause."[47]

*American Earth* gathered together some of Beals's journalism, including the Alabama sharecroppers' stories he had done for the *Nation* in 1936, and combined these pieces with a historical prologue, itself almost book-length, describing the destruction, over three hundred years, of America's lands and forests under the onslaught of Westward expansion. The indictment ranges from the Trail of Tears in which the Cherokee were pushed to Oklahoma, to the onrush of slave barons, cattle companies, extermination of the buffalo and the beaver, land speculation, razing of forests, and spoliation left by mining crews and oil drillers.

The book's driving force, though, is in its second half, which highlights Beals the reporter's firsthand testimony of the impact on rural folk of rising agri-business across the West. This new model of company farms, combined with crushing family farm debt and dust storms, was driving small-hold farmers, like Steinbeck's Joad family, to abandon their own lands to head west, where they became migrant laborers on giant plantations. Beals even visited the same federal labor camp, Weedpatch, south of Bakersfield, California, that inspired Steinbeck's fictional depiction.[48] The real lot of the "Migs" (migrant workers) Beals found there was no less grim than that facing the Joads.

"California really wants the Migs when the crops are ready to harvest," Beals wrote, "and she wishes they were in Timbuktu the rest of the year, for then they can only drift into the cities or into roadside slums, menacing public health, while they starve through to the next crop or through a year until they become eligible for relief. Relief is not so much a subsidy to the Migs as it is to the big growers, but this is not recognized."[49]

After his fall 1939 book tour and a Christmas celebration in New York City with the Rembaos, Beals and Blanca Rosa spent his lecture fees on train fare to Fort Lauderdale, and rental of a bungalow at nearby Dania Beach, where they spent the winter of 1940. There, Beals finished the manuscript of the book that pulled his Latin-US trade argument together and shipped it off to Lieber and Houghton Mifflin. It would come out in November, under the title *Pan America*.

When the couple returned to Connecticut after five months of mostly rainy Florida weather, they had a rude shock. Their Brockett's Point home had been burgled and set alight by a gang of teenage boys. Many of their clothes and personal items were ruined. Once again, Ben Brockett offered up another cottage.[50]

Another surprise awaiting Beals upon his return from Florida was Max Lieber's announcement that he had negotiated a new deal for him with Houghton Mifflin publishers. This would take him away from J. B. Lippincott, the house that had published eight Beals titles over nearly a decade.

Lieber, an inveterate and opinionated booster of his writers whose pushiness grated with some, had long felt that J. B. Lippincott's "casual" promotional efforts on Beals's behalf fell short.[51] Part of Lieber's coolness toward J. B. Lippincott also may have stemmed from Beals's habit of bypassing Lieber to deal directly with J. B. Lippincott editor Jefferson Jones. Beals enjoyed a cordial relationship with Jones that dated back to 1930—before he had hired Lieber as his agent.

Beals decided, with some reluctance, to go along with Lieber's guidance and accept Houghton Mifflin's offer, which included a thousand dollar advance for the *Pan America* manuscript. He also authorized Lieber to press J. B. Lippincott to cancel his outstanding contract for another book with them. It was awkward, as J. B. Lippincott's Jones had just ordered another five thousand–copy printing of *The Coming Struggle in Latin America* and had his staff working on the galleys for Beals's second volume of memoirs, *The Great Circle: Further Adventures in Free-lancing*, which was published in October.[52]

Just weeks after these prickly negotiations, Beals had a start when his new editor at Houghton Mifflin, Paul Brooks, told Lieber he was worried about reports from booksellers that Beals's "reputation has been declining in some quarters and we have a big job before us in starting the upward spiral again."[53]

Lieber sprang to defend Beals, saying that the booksellers were "ignorantly" comparing Beals's fiction books, whose sales were generally desultory, with those of his non-fiction, all of which had topped four thousand, capped

**Figure 11.1.** Carleton Beals in a photo from the jacket flap of *Pan America*, one of three books Beals published in 1940. His expression reflects the satisfaction of an author at the pinnacle of his career. *Photo courtesy of the Beals Family.*

by *The Coming Struggle for Latin America* at more than thirteen thousand.[54] However true, the comment irritated Beals. He had not given up on being a novelist, and Lieber's insensitivity on this point planted a seed of discord that would endure.

*Pan America* came out just a month after *The Great Circle*, putting two new Beals books on the market at once, just as had happened the year before with *The Coming Struggle for Latin America* and *American Earth*. It was an astonishing level of productivity, attesting to Beals's prodigious energy, but the sloppy timing probably hurt sales.

*Pan America*, while it sold enough to satisfy Houghton Mifflin, did not achieve the success of *The Coming Struggle*. Its argument was supported by a persuasive marshalling of facts on Latin America's resources—oil, iron ore, copper, tungsten, rubber, and agricultural commodities—combined with a thorough exposition of trade deals between Germany and Argentina and Brazil. His case extended to Britain too, whose imperial trade system he treats with scorn as "more rigid and coercive than that of the Nazis, [and which] leans far over toward the completely nationalized trade methods of Soviet Russia."[55]

Such was the discursive tone of *Pan America*, in which Beals stepped beyond his earlier descriptive warnings of fascist fifth columns in Latin America and the dictators that gave them succor. He concluded its thorough and well-informed polemic of 517 pages with a proposed program that had much the same purpose as Roosevelt's—or rather, Assistant US Secretary of State for Latin American Affairs Adolf A. Berle's—idea of a hemispheric cartel.

This cartel proposal floated by President Roosevelt in June 1940 called for an arrangement in which the United States and the Latin countries would jointly manage their surpluses, so as to counter the growth of barter trade between South America and the European belligerents. FDR was concerned that Latin America's loss of British trade due to wartime austerity left it exposed to German overtures. To forestall this danger, he suggested that the United States buy up Latin countries' surpluses and resell them on global markets along with US goods.

It was not a workable plan, as the United States exported, in large measure, the same commodities the Latins did, making them competitors rather than complementary partners.[56] The initiative was driven by security concerns rather than economic opportunity; its purpose was to deny the Nazis access to vital resources. As America had imposed a boycott on Germany, so too it sought to ensure that the Latins do likewise. The plan was promptly shelved, however, as it was fiercely opposed by American farm and factory producers who feared Latin competition.

In *Pan America,* Beals dismissed the cartel idea too, but argued that a way could be found—indeed *had* to be found—to get around this problem by negotiating mutually-beneficial managed trade agreements industry by industry, and product by product. The traditional US preference for Open Door trade was a pipedream, Beals wrote, in a world whose trade was mostly within sealed blocs of the fascist regimes and the old British and French Empires.

The book's logic was compelling in 1940. Many Americans believed the Germans would win the war, and Beals made the case that the United States needed to prepare itself for that possibility. *Fortune* magazine published the results of a US opinion survey in which 40 percent of respondents felt certain of an Axis victory, while only 30 percent thought Britain would win. The same poll revealed that 70 percent believed that Germany would try to seize control of South America.[57]

With most of continental Europe under fascist rule or occupation, and a Tripartite Pact between Berlin, Rome, and Tokyo having been concluded in September, Beals's call for a US effort to secure its access to vital commodities by creating some kind of trade arrangement with its hemispheric neighbors was a reasonable idea. It was a variation on the thesis, also published in 1940, by historian Charles A. Beard. Beard's *A Foreign Policy for America*, which Beals quoted in his book, combined an isolationist call to stay out of the European war with a defense of "Continental Americanism" that is, a strategic alliance between the United States and other nations of the Western hemisphere, to protect themselves from European intrusion.[58]

Beals's *Pan America* argument, while stopping short of outright isolationism, struck some as unseemly for the force with which it denounced British trade practices, and sympathized with Germany over the raw deal it had been delivered at Versailles as almost justifying its descent into fascism and warmaking.

"This is a strange volume," wrote Duke University Latin Americanist J. Fred Rippy, who laced into Beals's work with the same regularity as Beals did unto him. "Apparently the author's central thesis is that the United States should permit the British Empire to go down, allow Japan to dominate Asia, and Germany to dominate all Europe and Africa, and center its efforts on the economic solidification of the Western Hemisphere . . . not a new viewpoint, but officially the US had rejected it before the book saw the light."[59]

Peter Drucker, later to become America's premier management guru, reviewed the book too. While he credited Beals's depth of knowledge on trade flows and Latin America, he faulted him for a lack of political realism in thinking that the United States could lead continent-wide economic and trade planning without creating a military and political imperialist apparatus. "His theories are one-third Spengler, one-third Greenwich Village Marxism, and one-third that queer kind of romanticism which passes for realism amongst the young reporters in provincial city-desk rooms," Drucker wrote. "But to say that everything is a racket and everybody is a racketeer is hardly a satisfactory basis for a permanent political program."[60]

These dismissals seem too casual in the light of steps by the Roosevelt administration in 1940 to boost economic collaboration in the hemisphere to achieve essentially the same goals outlined in *Pan America*: keep the Latins onside with the United States as war approached and sustain access to vital resources while denying it to the enemy.

The administration approved a $500 million increase in the ExIm Bank's capital in 1941, thereby raising its lending authority to $700 million, almost all of which was directed south. Technical and financial assistance were added, and US government agencies were asked to favor Latin American products when buying strategic materials abroad. The United States also signed purchase agreements with several Latin American governments to assure access to strategic materials such as rubber, lead, bauxite, copper, tin, and tungsten. By the end of 1941, US trade with the Latin American countries had been restored to its 1929 level, up more than 50 percent from the outbreak of the war in 1939.[61]

By 1940, the US government's stance toward commercial and foreign investment disputes between American companies and Latin American governments had undergone a complete reversal from its earlier knee-jerk defense of US oil, mining, utility, and transport companies. As historian Bryce Wood observed, "the national interest was finally seen by the Department of State as being different from that of the oil companies and as superior to it."[62]

Evidence of this shift was seen in the ultimately conciliatory acceptance, through US Ambassador Josephus Daniels's intervention, of Mexican President Lázaro Cárdenas's decision to expropriate and nationalize Mexico's mostly US-owned oil holdings in 1938. The issue was highly contentious at first but defused over time as Daniels flexed his own personal political muscle to over-rule the more intransigent posture of Hull's State Department.

As the perceived security threat deepened once war had been declared in Europe, subsequent disputes between Bolivia and Standard Oil Company, and between Venezuela's mildly reformist President Eleazar López Contreras (1883–1973) government and US oil companies there, were settled with relative dispatch as US concessions were now more easily offered and accepted.

With this war-driven shift in US policy toward Latin America, Beals found himself in the unusual—for him—position of seeing his views largely having become conventional wisdom in the White House, the US State Department, and even the Pentagon. The fascist threat had, at least temporarily, united those who in other circumstances were ideologically divided.

As if to underline this new status, Beals was approached in early 1941 by Karl Bickel, head of the communications division of the Office for the Coordination of Commercial and Cultural Relations between the American Republics.[63] This Office, headed by Nelson Rockefeller and soon renamed the Office of the Coordinator of Inter-American Affairs, would become what one historian has called "the most fully developed and intensive use of soft power in US history."[64] It recruited some of America's leading creative media artists, from Walt Disney to Orson Welles, as well as writers, painters, journalists, and ad-men to mount lecture tours and film projects, and promote, among others, a Spanish-language version of *Readers' Digest,* and popular American novels. It was all aimed at developing a narrative of hemispheric comity that would serve as cultural glue to ensure that Latin America's wartime alliance would be with the United States, and not its enemies.

Beals, ever skeptical of officialdom, did not wholeheartedly join this initiative, but he did allow his name to be included on a list of speakers specialized in Latin America who might be called upon to participate in public forums organized by the Office or its affiliates.[65] Even as he collaborated in this way with the US government, however, Beals nonetheless remained engaged in the anti-interventionist campaign.

\*\*\*

In the winter of 1941, Beals and Blanca Rosa purchased a three-quarter-acre lot overlooking Long Island Sound in Sachem's Head, outside Guilford, Connecticut, on which they began construction of a new home. Building the house would take almost two years, complicated and interrupted by shortages of money to pay contractors as well as, of course, the national upheaval that followed the Japanese attack on Pearl Harbor, America's entry into World War II, and the rationing of gasoline and other materials that ensued.

During that winter, Beals also cogitated over what eventually would be his fourth and most successful novel, a sprawling futurist tale of an imagined pincer invasion of South America by fascist forces, Germans in Brazil and Japanese in Chile. As he planned this book, however, he grew increasingly frustrated with Houghton Mifflin's refusal even to consider publishing his fiction. "No publisher has ever attempted to rub my nose into it quite so badly," Beals protested to Lieber, "and I want as little to do with them as possible."[66]

The Beals couple continued to live in a Brockett's Point cottage while their new home was being built a short drive away, but this grew uncomfortable with the arrival of colder autumn days and nights. A measure of their financial straits during this period was that Beals failed to travel to Berkeley when his father, Leon Eli Beals, died in October 1941. His mother Elvina remonstrated bitterly with him over this.

Frustrated with Houghton Mifflin's indifference, Beals pressed Lieber to respond instead to an earlier expression of interest in his South American novel idea from Sam Sloan, a partner in Duell, Sloan, and Pearce Publishers, of New York. The timing was right. After the December 6, 1941 Japanese attack on Pearl Harbor, Sloan brought both renewed enthusiasm and razor-sharp focus to the project, giving Beals precise instructions as to plot and desired tone: "Begin the story with the various elements falling into line to fight off the enemy . . . with US engineers and Latin American Bolivars working hand in hand, with white men and brown women loving and suffering together, with wealthy US consuls giving their homes to South American patriots etc. etc. Lay it on thick."[67]

The story line was prompted not only by Pearl Harbor, but also by Roosevelt's Navy Day address in October 1941, in which he claimed to have a secret map which showed Hitler's plan for division of South America into five vassal states.[68] This followed similar allegations the President had made in his Fireside Chats and press conferences.[69] Such fears were underscored in May 1942, when the US ship *Ogontz*, loaded with Chilean nitrates bound for Mobile, Alabama, was sunk by a German U-boat in the Gulf of Mexico, through the connivance of Chilean intelligence with the Nazis.[70] Indeed, throughout 1942, Sumner Welles denounced "back-stabbing by Axis emissaries" enabled by Chile and Argentina, as a threat to freedom and integrity of the hemisphere.[71]

The onward rush of bellicose events was not the only pressure Beals faced to finish the book. Eduardo Leyva, Blanca Rosa's 18-year-old kid brother, had been sent by his parents to New York, where the family hoped that Beals would find medical care to treat the young man for convulsions and chronic headaches. Beals had invested all his liquid savings in the house project and was, for the moment, broke. How would he pay for brain surgery and convalescent care?[72]

He contacted a Dr. Ronald Klemme of St. Louis, a brain surgeon he had met socially in Mexico, and who had attended one of Beals's recent lectures. Klemme acted immediately, sending an associate to New York to examine Eduardo, and following himself shortly thereafter to attend a conference, during which he met Beals and examined Eduardo as well. He then invited Eduardo to move to St. Louis and stay at his home for the weeks the treatment would take, while reassuring Beals that he would charge only for costs, not for his services. Beals had only to pay for transport and the hospital stay.

Beals gratefully praised Klemme's generosity, and set to work on the novel, writing about 500 pages in just two months, which he shipped off without even proofreading the typescript. Duell, Sloan, and Pearce accepted it with alacrity—"it's a grand story," wrote Charles A. Pearce—and quickly paid Beals a thousand-dollar advance.[73]

Beals was able to cover the costs of Eduardo's treatment, which turned out to be limited to extraction of spinal fluid, which, along with medication, had alleviated the convulsions. The teenager returned to New Haven by train from St. Louis, and stayed for several months with Carleton and Blanca Rosa, finding a job in a New York City machine shop. A year later, he returned to Lima, lucky to catch a passenger vessel out of New Orleans before they were suspended due to submarine threats.

Throughout these travails, Beals's novel brought relief and exhilaration. It was selected as book of the month by the Literary Guild of America, which resulted in a sold-out print run of 200,000, the maximum limit allowed during wartime. No other Beals title had sold even half as many copies. Its title, *Dawn Over the Amazon*, "had symbolic meaning for us," Beals reflected. "We were out of the woods financially after many months of near despair."[74]

The story is a remarkable feat of imagination. It may seem an obscure and doubtful pursuit to look backward at a futuristic novel, written hurriedly by a cash-strapped author in 1942, about an imagined post- World War II fascist invasion of Latin America set in 1950 and which, of course, never came to pass. Still, there is something compelling about this tale. Beals was proud of it, not just because it was his only real bestseller, but as his most successfully accomplished fiction. On inventiveness, his self-assessment is deserved. *Dawn*'s imagined pan-Latin American war against Nazi-Japanese invaders fully reveals Beals's depth of knowledge of the region's subterranean political forces, the heroic idealism of some leaders, the perfidy of others, along with his ever-present skepticism of US motives.

Although he disclaimed any relation between his fictional characters and contemporary political figures, the models for his story's puppets are obvious. The central character, a mystical and charismatic political and military genius, Victor de la Hoz Hurtado, "The Reaper," is a stand-in for Beals's friend Victor Raúl Haya de la Torre, the Peruvian populist leader cheated out of power and persecuted for years by the Peruvian military. He is depicted in *Dawn Over the Amazon* as leader of a pro-United States, pro-freedom-and-democracy version of Alianza Popular Revolucionaria Americana (APRA), ready to align with the US in "a continental defense on a truly democratic basis."

This was fully consistent with APRA's real shift, by the early 1940s, from routine denunciations of US imperialism, to a position of strong support for America's war on fascism.[75] Indeed, this was the position of almost all the world's Left at the time, including the Communist parties which, after having preached non-intervention while Stalin and Hitler's nonaggression pact held, immediately called for an all-out effort to defeat fascism after the Nazis invaded the Soviet Union in June of 1941.

Beals built his narrative around a can-do American visionary, Grant Hammond, who wants to transform the Amazon into a vast development of air-cooled cities and modern agribusiness. He seeks support for his plan from the region's political leaders, most of whom are complacent and unmoved—except for the Reaper, with whom he establishes a bond.

When the Nazis invade Brazil while the Japanese attack Valparaiso and occupy much of northern Chile, Hammond's preoccupation shifts from his development project to helping the Reaper gather and deploy a continental army to repel the fascist forces. There is much intrigue among a complex cast of characters, including a corrupt Peruvian president and his sinister British advisor Montague, a Hungarian noble who has become a roué, a heroic Brazilian general and various US diplomats. The fast-paced plot includes a continental army division's march through the Amazon jungle, for which Beals drew from Theodore Roosevelt's 1914 account of his expedition up the Tapajos River to the Amazon, *Through the Brazilian Wilderness.*[76]

*Dawn Over the Amazon* also features pulpy overlapping romances involving Hammond and Szvigurt, the Hungarian baron, with three rather stereotyped Latin women, Marcela, the scheming seductress and erstwhile mistress of the Peruvian president, Gabriela, the Reaper's sister, at once comely and saintly, and Melinda, the backwoods landowner's daughter who becomes a Brazilian *Pasionaria* (modeled on the Spanish Republican fighter and Communist politician Dolores Ibárruri, known as *la Pasionaria*, or passion flower) whose stirring speeches rally her country's people to the Reaper's cause.

However unlikely this seems, it had resonance when it was published in wartime 1943, playing on fears of fifth column activity by fascists in South America, and boosting the Good Neighbor solidarity with Latin America that was reaffirmed in the 1942 Rio Conference Pact, at which all the Latin American countries, save Argentina and Chile, rallied to the US appeal and agreed to defend the hemisphere against attack. It provided, wrote one reviewer, "a graphic picture of what a compromise peace would mean, and what we may have to face in a few years if we merely scratch the snake, not kill it."[77]

## NOTES

1. See Robert Dallek, *Franklin Roosevelt and American Foreign Policy, 1932–1945* (New York: Oxford University Press, 1981), 122.

2. Harold B. Hinton, "America Parley Ends in Peace Act," *New York Times*, December 24, 1936, 1.

3. Dallek, *Franklin Roosevelt*, 132–34.

4. The Wisconsin School is so-named as its chief proponent, historian William Appleman Williams, was on the faculty at the University of Wisconsin in Madison in the 1950s and 1960s. Williams, building on the work of his thesis advisor Fred Harvey Harrington, developed an argument that pursuit by the United States of the Open Door for trade and investment, as originated by US Secretary of State John Hay at the beginning of the twentieth century, had led to a "neo-imperialist" American foreign policy.

5. Carleton Beals, *America South* (Philadelphia: J. B. Lippincott, 1937), 514.

6. Beals, *America South*, 514.

7. Beals, *America South*, 517.

8. Beals, *America South*, 513.

9. Beals, *America South*, 515. This analysis has been backed up by later authors. For example, see Walter LaFeber, *Inevitable Revolutions: The United States in Central America* (New York: W. W. Norton and Company, 1983), 81; and David F. Schmitz, *Thank God They're on Our Side: The United States and Right-Wing Dictatorships, 1921–1965* (Chapel Hill: University of North Carolina Press, 1999).

10. Hubert C. Herring, "A Glowing Canvas of Latin America," *New York Herald-Tribune*, November 28, 1937. Beals's opinion of the book is found in his dedication, "This is one of the better ones, I believe," inscribed in a copy of *America South*, to Carolyn Kennedy, whom he would marry years later. In Christopher Neal (CNC), Private collection, Westmount, Quebec.

11. Philip Ainsworth Means, "Mr. Beals Surveys America South," *New York Times*, January 9, 1938.

12. L. S. Rowe was Director General of the Pan American Union—later the Organization of American States—from 1920 until his death in 1946.

13. Beals, *America South*, 494–95.

14. Dependency Theory emerged in the 1960s, built on the notion that resources flow from a "periphery" of poor and underdeveloped states to a "core" of wealthy states, enriching the latter at the expense of the former. Its various proponents, such as Andre Gunder Frank and Samir Amin, contend that rich and poor states are made so by the global capitalist system. It arose as a reaction to and refutation of Modernization Theory, an earlier stages-of-growth theory of development, which holds that societies progress through similar stages of development, that contemporary low-income countries would also move to wealthier status, a process which can be accelerated by investment, technology transfers, and closer integration into the world market. Dependency Theory argues instead that developing countries are not merely later-blooming versions of developed countries, but have unique features and structures of their own. More importantly, their development has been distorted by the dictates of foreign capital investment, and its capitalist logic of resource extraction and repatriation of profits to the "core" states. This entrenches the unequal relationship, the dependency of the peripheral states, resulting in their systematic impoverishment as weaker members in a global market economy.

15. Beals, *America South*, 354.

16. Beals, *America South*, 473.

17. Beals, *America South*, 355.

18. See for example, Thomas F. O'Brien, *The Revolutionary Mission: American Enterprise in Latin America, 1900–1945* (Cambridge: Cambridge University Press, 1996).

19. The Singer–Prebisch thesis (also Prebisch–Singer thesis, PST, or Prebisch–Singer hypothesis) postulates that terms of trade between primary products and manufactured goods, deteriorate in time. In 1950, the economists Raúl Prebisch and Hans Singer independently developed the thesis that developing countries that were exporting commodities were at a permanent disadvantage, as they were subject to unstable prices for their exports, while facing relatively higher prices for their imported manufactures; Prebisch argued in favor of import-substituting industrialization to solve this problem. While the PST has lost relevance as most developing countries have become emerging industrial market economies, it still influences economists who advise countries that rely heavily on commodity exports to guard against currency overvaluations and Dutch Disease, named after a 1970s economic situation in the Netherlands when rapid development of a sector of the economy (particularly natural resources) precipitates a decline in other sectors.

20. Eduardo Galeano, *Las Venas abiertas de América Latina* (Open Veins of Latin America) (Coyoacán, Mexico: Siglo XXI, 1974), back cover.

21. Richard Lee Turtis, A World Destroyed, A Nation Imposed: The 1937 Haitian Massacre in the Dominican Republic," *Hispanic American Historical Review* 82, no. 3 (2002): 590, https://doi.org/10.1215/00182168-82-3-589. The "parsley" label arose due to likely apocryphal reports that Dominican troops selected those to be killed by holding up a sprig of parsley and asking, "What is this?" Creole-speaking Haitians or Dominicans of Haitian-origin who stumbled in pronouncing the trill in the "r" of the Spanish word *perejil* thereby sealed their fate.

22. Carleton Beals, "Caesar of the Caribbean." *Current History*, 48, no. 1, January 1938, 31.

23. Beals, "Caesar of the Caribbean," 31; and Carleton Beals, "Under the Fifth Sun" (unpublished autobiography, c. 1972–1978), in Carleton Beals Collection (CBC), Howard Gotlieb Archival Research Center, Boston University, box 47 (hereafter cited CBC).

24. Beals, "Under the Fifth Sun" (unpublished autobiography), CBC; and Fausten Winbus to Carleton Beals, April 23, 1938, CBC, box 47.

25. Wood, *The Making of the Good Neighbor Policy* (New York: W. W. Norton, 1961), 155.

26. Best-Seller List, *New York Herald-Tribune*, June 12, 1938.

27. Charles Poore, "Books Notes," *New York Times*, April 15, 1938, 17.

28. Carleton Beals, *Glass Houses: Ten Years of Free-Lancing* (Philadelphia: J. B. Lippincott, 1938), 242.

29. See Ruben Rivera, *Alberto Rembao (1895–1962): Mexican American Protestant for Internationalism and Christian Holism* (Saarbrücken, Germany: VDM Verlag Dr. Müller, 2000).
30. Alberto Rembao to Carleton Beals, July 2, 1942, CBC.
31. Maxim Lieber to Carleton Beals, July 2, 1942, CBC.
32. Brockett's Point Hurricane, *New York World-Telegram*, September 23, 1938, CBC, box 145.
33. US Congress, *Neutrality Act of 1935*, Pub. Res. 74–67, 49 Stat. 1081, 74th Cong., 1st sess., August 31, 1935, https://govtrackus.s3.amazonaws.com/legislink/pdf/stat/49/STATUTE-49-Pg1081.pdf (accessed May 25, 2021). The *Neutrality Acts* refer to a series of *Acts* past in 1935, 1936, 1937, and 1939.
34. Fredrick Pike, *FDR's Good Neighbor Policy – Sixty Years of Generally Gentle Chaos* (Austin, TX: University of Texas Press, 1995), 31.
35. See Carleton Beals, "Totalitarian Inroads in Latin America," *Foreign Affairs,* October 1938, Beals, "Swastika Over the Andes," *Harper's Monthly*, July 1938, 78–89; Beals, "Japan Tiptoes around the Monroe Doctrine," *Current History*, September 1938; Beals, "Black Shirts in Latin America, *Current History*, November 1938; "Red Star South," *Current History*, December 1938; and Beals, "John Bull in Latin America," *Current History*, January 1939.
36. Carleton Beals, *The Coming Struggle for Latin America* (New York: Halcyon House, 1940).
37. John Gunther, *Inside Latin America* (New York: Harper and Brothers, 1941), 480.
38. Beals, *Coming Struggle*, 379.
39. Beals, *Coming Struggle*, 310–11.
40. Clarence Senior to Carleton Beals, December 6, 1938, CBC.
41. Senior to Beals (1938), CBC.
42. Broadcasts of December 29, 1940, and May 27, 1941, in Russell D. Buhite and David W. Levy, eds., *FDR's Fireside Chats* (Norman: University of Oklahoma Press, 1992), 167–68.
43. Beals, *Coming Struggle*, 172.
44. Beals, *Coming Struggle*, 165.
45. Beals, *Coming Struggle*, 472.
46. John F. Kennedy, *Alliance for Progress Speech*, Tampa, Florida, October 18, 1960, DNC Press Release. JFK Library, Boston.
47. Allan Nevins, "How We Ravaged the Riches of a Continent," *New York Herald-Tribune*, April 2, 1939; see also John Steinbeck, *The Grapes of Wrath* (New York: Viking Press, 1939).
48. See Jackson J. Benson,"'To Tom, Who Lived It': John Steinbeck and the Man from Weedpatch," *Journal of Modern Literature* 5, no. 2 (1976): 151–210, https://www.jstor.org/stable/3830940.
49. Carleton Beals, *American Earth: The Biography of a Nation* (Philadelphia: J. B. Lippincott, 1939), 407.
50. Ben Brockett to Carleton Beals, March 5, 1940, CBC; and Note "for release," May 22, 1940, CBC.
51. Max Lieber to Carleton Beals, May 23, 1940, CBC.
52. Jefferson Jones to Carleton Beals, August 13, 1940 and October 2, 1940, CBC; and Carleton Beals, *The Great Circle: Further Adventures in Free-Lancing* (Philadelphia: J. B. Lippincott, 1940).
53. Max Lieber to Carleton Beals, September 19, 1940, CBC.
54. Max Lieber to Carleton Beals, September 24, 1940, CBC.
55. Carleton Beals, *Pan America* (Boston: Houghton Mifflin, 1940), 338–39.
56. Donald Marquand Dozer, *Are We Good Neighbors? Three Decades of Inter-American Relations, 1930–1960* (Gainesville: University of Florida Press, 1959), 49.
57. Pike, *FDR's Good Neighbor Policy*, 231.
58. Charles A. Beard, *A Foreign Policy for America* (New York: Alfred A. Knopf, 1940).
59. J. Fred Rippy, "Review *Pan America: A Program for the Western Hemisphere*, by Carleton Beals," *Hispanic American Historical Review* 21, no. 2 (1941): 300–301, ttps://doi.org/10.2307/2507402.

60. Peter F. Drucker, "A Policy for the Americas," *Saturday Review of Literature*, December 21, 1940, 14.
61. Dozer, *Are We Good Neighbors?*, 76–77.
62. Wood, *Making of the Good Neighbor Policy* (1967), 249.
63. Karl Bickel to Carleton Beals, January 10, 1941, CBC.
64. Darlene J. Sadlier, *Americans All: Good Neighbor Cultural Diplomacy in World War II* (Austin: University of Texas Press, 2012), 2.
65. Francis DeW. Pratt to Carleton Beals, February 14 and 19, 1941, CBC.
66. Carleton Beals to Max Lieber, March 10, 1941, CBC.
67. Sam Sloan to Max Lieber, March 31, 1942, CBC.
68. Dozer, *Are We Good Neighbors?*, 104.
69. Irwin F. Gellman, *Secret Affairs: Franklin Roosevelt, Cordell Hull, and Sumner Welles* (Baltimore: Johns Hopkins University Press, 1995), 259.
70. Bryce Wood, *The Dismantling of the Good Neighbor Policy* (Austin: University of Texas Press, 1985), 12.
71. Wood, *Dismantling of the Good Neighbor Policy*, 8.
72. Beals, "Under the Fifth Sun" (unpublished autobiography), CBC, xi.
73. Beals, "Under the Fifth Sun" (unpublished autobiography), CBC, xi; Max Lieber to Carleton Beals, April 8, 1942; and Charles A. Pearce to Carleton Beals, January 11, 1943, CBC.
74. Beals, "Under the Fifth Sun" (unpublished autobiography), CBC. See also Carleton Beals, *Dawn Over the Amazon* (New York: Duell, Sloan, and Pearce, 1943).
75. John C. Campbell, "Political Extremes in South America," *Foreign Affairs*, April 1942.
76. Theodore Roosevelt, *Through the Brazilian Wilderness* (New York: C. Scribner's Sons, 1914).
77. Victor M. Hamm, "Looking Backward From 1950 in Novel by Carleton Beals," Review *Dawn Over the Amazon*, by Carleton Beals, *Milwaukee Journal*, July 25, 1943, 47.

*Chapter Twelve*

# Hitting a Wall

*Dawn Over the Amazon* was an odd confection: a pot-boiler about a fictional war to entertain readers already absorbed by a real one. Part-thriller, part-romance, part-political-spy novel, it also served as a propaganda piece, a World War II example of the *alternative history* genre that had earlier surfaced to boost patriotic fervor during World War I.

The novel's sales made it the high-water mark of Carleton Beals's literary career. It gave him a financial boost, delivering about $6,000 in royalties in 1943, while also enhancing his public profile. His fictional rendering of Nazi-Fascist threats to the hemisphere also reflected what was the apogee of Franklin Delano Roosevelt (FDR's) Good Neighbor Policy, whose purpose was now concentrated on neutralizing well-substantiated Axis Powers' collaboration with fascist-type groups and dictators in Latin America. In addition to *Dawn Over the Amazon*'s selection by the Literary Guild for distribution to over 120,000 subscribers, *Liberty* Magazine, then America's second-largest circulation general-interest magazine, published a 20,000-word condensed and illustrated version of *Dawn Over the Amazon* in September. The novel was also briefly listed on the *New York Herald-Tribune*'s best-seller list ahead of Ayn Rand's *The Fountainhead*, with which its publication roughly coincided.[1]

*Dawn Over the Amazon*'s curious jungle war, with idealistic guerrillas and air strikes mixed with love affairs, even if clumsily drawn, had—and still has—a certain appeal as suspense with comic touches. "It would be an exaggeration to call this a great novel," wrote author William Barrett, also a frequent correspondent with Beals, in the *Boston Post*, "but this is a thrilling book in more ways than one."[2] And John Selby, while offering a backhanded snipe in his syndicated literary column, nonetheless acknowledged *Dawn Over the Amazon*'s appeal to lower-brow taste: "This is a terrific mélange of sloe-eyed senoritas, rotten barons, flustered planters, bemused diplomats, tangled intrigues and fictional clichés. It left me gasping."[3] "Hot-blooded and swift-paced," said Lewis Gannett, while Nina Brown Baker, writing in the *New York Times*, marked its serious purpose by suggesting that the political and economic views of the protagonists—the Reaper and Hammond—"well merit re-reading," and that Beals's own voice "is that of authority."[4] Beals received plenty of fan mail applauding it, including compliments from other writers and political figures.

As his biggest-selling book, *Dawn Over the Amazon* opened the possibility that Beals's audience might reach beyond his established constituency of Latin Americanists and political radicals who read the *Nation* and similar magazines. Its royalties allowed him and Blanca Rosa to enjoy the comfortable home they now owned, just a stroll from the water's edge along Long Island Sound. They entertained more frequently than ever, with similarly successful, progressive-minded couples, serving up meals with the vegetables they had grown in their wartime victory garden. At weekends, they often welcomed guests with whom they swam and sunbathed on the flat rocks and beach just below their home. In the evenings, there were cocktails, alfresco dinners when the weather allowed, and often dancing.

Among their closest friends during this period were Kyle and May Crichton, he the entertainment editor at *Collier's*, as well as cultural critic—under the pseudonym Robert Forsythe—for the Communist magazine *New Masses*. A big, ebullient mountain of a man capped by a wispy dome, Crichton was every bit as prolific as Beals, while also sharing his leftist political orientation leavened by a chariness of Communist Party apparatchik. Beals admired Crichton's restless intellect and complexity, in which a relaxed, wise-cracking wit was combined with prodigious churning out of pro-bono, left-leaning articles which, he ingenuously hoped, would hasten the collapse of capitalism. Still, Crichton's soul was pluralistic enough that he indulged his Catholic wife May, who sent their four children—one of whom, Robert Crichton, later became a writer as well—to parochial schools. Only there, Beals observed, they might be "immunized from Kyle's darker creeds."[5] Crichton himself recognized the conflicts of interest inherent in his diverging identities, highlighted by his practice of having his alias Forsythe, the Communist, review books by Crichton, the cultural gadfly. To him, it was just an inside joke. "When we win," he would say of the expected Communist revolution, "I'm the first to go. They [Communists] have no humor and they can't stand irreverence."[6]

With Stuart and Marian (Tyler) Chase, who lived in a rambler house in Georgetown Village, Connecticut, the Beals couple often shared Thanksgiving and Christmas dinners, at one or the other's home. Stuart, more earnest in style, was an economist, educator, author, and early consumer advocate, among the founders of *Consumer Reports* magazine. His 1932 book, *A New*

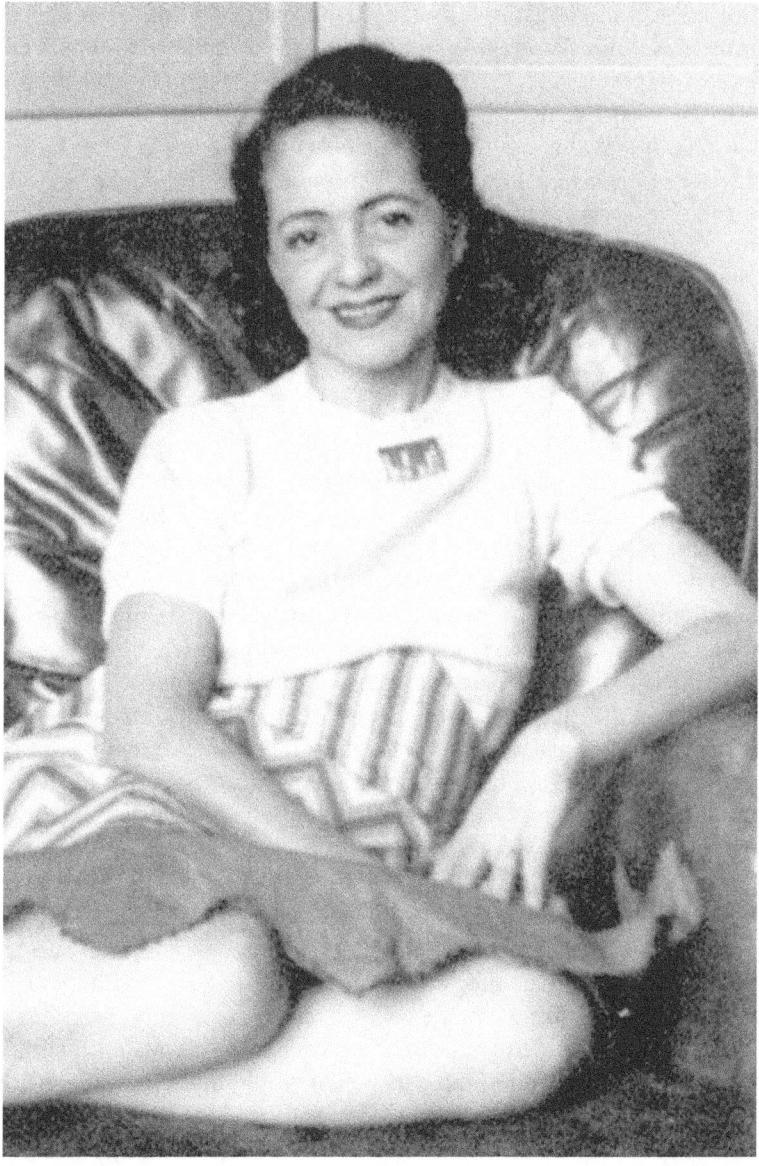

Figure 12.1. Blanca Rosa (Leyva y Arguedas) Beals was for almost twenty years happily married to Beals, whose work she supported and with whom she traveled and enjoyed an active social life. Their marriage collapsed after a furious row at their home in Sachem's Head, Connecticut that coincided with Beals's professional crisis in 1953, not long after this photo was taken. *Photo courtesy of the Carleton Beals Collection, Howard Gotlieb Archival Research Center, Boston University, and Ralph Carleton Beals.*

*Deal for America*, had so influenced FDR that the President adopted not only many of its recommendations, but used its name for his signature policy platform.[7] His wife Marian was an editor at the *Nation*, as well as a concert violinist.

Amid this reassuring comfort and success, Beals had little warning that his triumphal ride was about to derail. The first fissure was a bitter falling-out with his longtime agent and friend Maxim Lieber. While he and Blanca enjoyed the conviviality of their growing Connecticut circle, Beals's frustration with Lieber had smoldered for over a year, ever since Lieber's ill-considered, in retrospect, rupture of Beals's longstanding and largely successful relationship with J. B. Lippincott.

Almost immediately, Beals clashed with Houghton Mifflin editor Paul Brooks, with whom Lieber had promoted a contract. This came to a head in 1942 and early 1943 over the manuscript for *Rio Grande to Cape Horn*, Beals's second title with his new publisher. After the success, albeit modest, of *Pan America*, Houghton Mifflin had agreed to publish this updated overview of Latin America. It was much like *America South* in format, but Brooks demanded major revisions and deletions to passages he deemed too controversial.[8]

In particular, he and his Houghton Mifflin colleagues objected to references which they considered potentially damaging to US State Department efforts to keep Latin American regimes on board with the United States in the Allies' war effort. They singled out Beals's characterization of Latin American rulers such as Getulio Vargas in Brazil, Rafael Leonidas Trujillo in the Dominican Republic, and Nicaragua's Anastasio Somoza, all US allies, as "dictators" and "unsavory." Another contentious point was Beals's allegation that a US official was "strenuously conspiring" to topple Argentine President Ramón Antonio Castillo (1873–1944) and have him replaced by former President Agustín Pedro Justo (1876–1943), who could be expected to abandon Argentina's "neutral" wartime stance, and embrace the Allies.[9] Ultimately, the latter passage was removed as Justo's untimely death in January 1943 made it irrelevant.

Brooks persisted in demanding further revisions. It was not just the content of the changes he sought, most of which would blunt the edge of Beals's broadsides, but also his dismissive tone that rankled. Brooks, who would later encourage Rachel Carson to write *Silent Spring*, took issue with Beals's "tendency to weaken his argument by occasional cracks" and "unnecessarily bitter" comments.[10] Beals, with nineteen published books under his belt, took umbrage at these remonstrations from an editor, not incidentally sixteen years his junior, and whom Lieber had foisted upon him without consultation. He bristled at what he saw as outright censorship of his work.

*Rio Grande to Cape Horn* was nonetheless published in September 1943. Its reviews were mixed. Beals's longtime acquaintance, Latin Americanist historian Hubert Herring, who praised the book in the *American Mercury*, unwittingly discerned Brooks' restraining influence in finding that Beals had grown "mellow."[11] Other critics, even if respectful, still found an unevenness to *Rio Grande to Cape Horn*. The authoritative insights of its chapters on Mexico's complex and protracted transition from Plutarco Elías Calles to Lázaro Cárdenas, along with the country's then-recent rallying to wartime alliance with the United States were found to be in some contrast to Beals's more fanciful assessment that "air-cooled cities" would soon sprout in the Amazon.[12] Indeed, some of the material in the "Future of the Amazon" chapter of *Rio Grande to Cape Horn* seems as if lifted whole from Beals's fictional *Dawn Over the Amazon*, published only three months earlier.

Another chapter of *Rio Grande to Cape Horn* was devoted to Argentina, then South America's largest economic and military power, and whose continuing neutral stance was a source of irritation and suspicion to US leaders. Once again, Beals articulated what was seen by the US foreign policy elite as a provocative contrarian position. He depicted Argentina's effort to sustain trade ties with Axis Powers—as well as with Britain—as being driven by its survival instinct, not an anti-United States or pro-fascist orientation. For the Argentines, he argued, the continuing US "sanitary" ban on Argentine beef imports had grievous consequences, favoring Britain for access to the lucrative US meat market, at Argentina's expense. No surprise, then, that Argentina should seek new markets in neighboring countries that it could dominate, such as Bolivia, and increase collaboration with its similarly isolated mother country, Francisco Franco's Spain, while also expanding trade with Japan. "Covert antagonism" between the United States and Argentina was the inevitable result, he wrote, costly not just in wartime, but also likely to handicap hemispheric solidarity and economic cooperation efforts in the future. Indeed, with the rise of the populist Juan Perón two years later, this antipathy would sharpen, confirming Beals's premonition. But this analysis found few takers in wartime America, where Argentina's stance was seen as too friendly to the enemy. Beals was a "hemisphere isolationist," sniffed Lloyd Mallan in his *New York Times* review.[13]

Despite the rocky navigation of the *Rio Grande to Cape Horn* manuscript into print, and Beals's increasing frustration with his agent, he and Blanca hosted Max and Minna Lieber at their home over the 1944 New Year's holiday. It would be their last amicable get-together. By late spring, their rupture was complete, all of it spilling out in bitter recriminations. Beals complained to Lieber that his relationship with Houghton Mifflin was "the most disastrous and blighting of my whole literary career," and held Lieber fully responsible for it.[14] To which Lieber responded with a bruising comment that revealed problems surfacing in Beals's work, as well as his own hurt feelings. "Years ago you were a pioneer," he wrote, "striking out along new paths and embodying progressive interpretations of political action.

During the past few years, others have caught up with and passed you. Recently your interests have turned inward to such an extent that your books have become chores for you rather than exciting creative challenges."[15]

This conflict over, from Beals's standpoint, his livelihood, was a genuine difference that could not be bridged. Both men were shaken and saddened by it, as it destroyed an irreplaceably warm bond of trusting support and of friendship for over fifteen years that had also included their spouses. Professionally too, it proved a devastating turning point for Beals, as he struggled to find his way with new agents whose success in placing his work, overall, would fall short of Lieber's.

The first of these was Mavis McIntosh, who had started one of New York's first female-led literary agencies in 1927, and whose star client was John Steinbeck. McIntosh immediately set to work placing several Beals manuscripts that had failed to stir Houghton Mifflin editor Brooks's interest. McIntosh, well-connected with book publishers, nonetheless faced an uphill slog. First, she negotiated Beals out of his contract with Houghton Mifflin, which was snarled in a quarrel over the terms of an earlier advance he had received. Then, she tried to stir interest in his work among other publishing houses. The manuscripts ranged from a history of the 1870s populist movement in America's West, to a book on the Panama Canal Zone, and a novel, *Bridge of Royal Delights*.[16]

Sadly for Beals, McIntosh made little headway on these with publishers and, tellingly, she urged Beals to revise the novel before she would promote it further. In the meantime, Beals wrote a piece for *Harper's* on the Soviets' version of soft-power diplomacy in Latin America—now that the USSR's restored wartime alliance with the United States and Mexico allowed it—as well as an analysis of Perón's emergence in Argentina for the *Progressive*. The market for his signature expertise on Latin America was clearly shrinking, though, as public interest had shifted to the war in Europe and the Pacific.

The war's impact also included gasoline rationing that limited Beals's driving, and travel in general. Restrictions on paper and metals encumbered reprints of existing books. Plates for Beals's earlier titles were melted down on government orders for other uses. New projects whose sales prospects were less than best-seller got a thumbs-down. Even Cap Pearce, at Sloan, Pearce, and Duell, Beals's *Dawn Over the Amazon* publisher, once his champion, found his new novel manuscript to be short of the mark. "Maybe the best thing for us is to step aside gracefully," he wrote Beals, "on the theory that some other publisher will have an editor ready . . . to work out a detailed revision with you."[17] The distractions of war hurt magazines too, including such Beals clients as *Common Sense*, driven out of business by lagging demand.[18]

While McIntosh's contacts with book publishers were impeccable, she was not able to match Lieber's connections to magazine editors. Beals took action on his own, seeking out Morris Rubin, editor of the *Progressive* magazine, organ of the Progressive movement, based in Madison, Wisconsin. Rubin, just thirty-four years old, had taken over the reins of the magazine after serving as Wisconsin's Progressive Party Governor Philip La Follette's press secretary until his defeat in 1938. Rubin welcomed Beals as a contributor, who thus joined other *Progressive* collaborators such as his earlier acquaintances Oswald Garrison Villard—who had resigned from the *Nation* in 1940 as he disagreed with its editorial position in favor of rearmament against Hitler—and Roger Baldwin, as well as his friend Stuart Chase. While there was some diversity of opinion among *Progressive* contributors, the magazine's editorial position leaned to pacifist isolationism, and by 1945, focused on finding fault with the war's emerging outcomes.

With travel ruled out, Beals produced a string of opinion pieces for Rubin on the emerging post-war order. He denounced the secrecy that had shrouded the Big-Three Conferences from 1943 to 1945,[19] and its horse-trading which resulted in Poland, the Baltics, and most of Eastern Europe being chained to Stalinist regimes, while allowing Britain to restore its empire, including 300 million disenfranchised Indians.[20] In other columns, he raised doubts about FDR's arms-for-oil deal with Saudi King Ibn Saud (1875–1953), as well as on the post-Yalta Chapultepec Conference in Mexico City, in 1945.

In the latter, Beals quoted the head of Brazil's delegation, who had characterized US Secretary of State Edward R. Stettinius Jr.'s goal at the February-March 1945 meeting as being nothing more than to shore up support for the Yalta agreement among the nineteen Latin governments. They would thus endorse, in effect, an extension of the well-established US hegemony in the Western hemisphere to reach global scale. The same enforced consensus would include approval of US leadership in creating a United Nations Organization at the San Francisco Conference a month later.

While outwardly benign, this consensus was easily achieved only because key players such as Argentina were absent, Beals wrote. Argentina, ruled by reformist military officers among whom Colonel Perón was then the fast-rising star, had sought a Pan-American meeting, but pointedly was not invited to Chapultepec. Canada was similarly absent, as well as the European colonies of the West Indies, and the American one, Puerto Rico. The US economic agenda—a vague endorsement of free trade and the "elimination of government from industry"—was thus endorsed without opposition, as the smaller countries chose not to give voice to their skepticism.[21]

The meeting at Chapultepec, or "grasshopper hill" as Beals translated it, was a defining moment of disillusionment, in which he perceived the first cracks that would rent asunder the Good Neighbor Policy. Beals had repeatedly found flaws in Roosevelt's approach to Latin America, thinking it oversold, often inauthentic and too friendly to dictators. But he also welcomed the Good Neighbor Policy's central plank of non-intervention. It was expedient, of course, but also principled, and an about-turn from the big-footed use of US military force that he had witnessed in the 1920s.

From 1945, however, once the Allies' final victory neared, Beals saw the policy crumbling. He documented its dismantling in a series of articles in the *Progressive* over the next year, culminating in a four-part summation the following year on Argentina's dramatic turn under the populist Perón, who successfully stared down US Ambassador Spruille Braden's meddlesome effort to undermine his presidential campaign.[22]

Braden orchestrated the production of a US State Department report, popularly called the "Blue Book," which catalogued Argentina's putative collaboration with the Nazis during World War II. The report was distributed to Latin American governments on February 24, 1946, just two weeks before the Argentine election. The timing of its release, so obviously aimed at smearing presidential candidate Perón, triggered widespread outrage, of which Perón took full advantage. "Perón SI, Braden NO," screamed headlines and newsboys. Perón was elected with 53.1 percent of ballots cast. Braden, his scheme a fiasco, was promptly summoned back to Washington. Beals related the episode to the *Progressive* readers, reporting Perón's ironic comment to an American official trying to mend diplomatic ties after Braden's exit: "As an Argentinian citizen," Perón said, "I am eternally resentful of Braden's intervention; as Juan Perón, I am eternally grateful."[23]

This piece was part of a year-long stream of articles Beals produced during an ambitious eight-month tour of Latin America that he and Blanca undertook in early 1946. The idea for the trip was born out of his growing frustration at his failure to find outlets for his journalism.

The *Progressive*'s payments of $35 an article were not enough to live on, so Beals decided to invest in a trip to key countries in the region. He would gather enough fresh material for at least one new book, while also sending regular reports to Rubin. He also used the tour to visit old friends and acquaintances who boosted his morale, along with Blanca's, who welcomed a rare opportunity to visit her family in Peru.

In January 1946, the couple took a train to Laredo, Texas, from which they hired a car to Mexico City on the newish Pan-American highway. They later continued south to Nicaragua on the Inter-American Highway, meandering through Guatemala, where Beals stopped to interview the recently-elected reformist President Juan José Arévalo (1904–1990), and then Honduras. From there, they flew to Managua, Nicaragua, and then to Panama, Bogotá, Lima, La Paz, Santiago, and various cities in Argentina, for a trip lasting eight months.

The tour renewed Beals's first-hand familiarity with Latin American trends, politics, and personalities, which had suffered from years of wartime restrictions that kept him in Connecticut. His encounter with Arévalo, the forty-two-year-old "schoolteacher President" in Guatemala City's Presidential Palace stirred his hope for real change in a country emerging from fourteen years of dictatorship under Jorge Ubico (1878–1946). In an interview that was "more like an easy conversation between old acquaintances," Arévalo outlined for Beals his vision for Guatemala, which focused on agrarian reform in a country where 2 percent of the people owned 70 percent of the land. This would include a farming colony in the mostly vacant Petén jungle highlands near the Belize border to end the country's reliance on cereal imports. Arévalo told Beals he wanted to expand education, protect labor rights, and consolidate the fledgling democracy that had brought him to power with 85 percent of the (literate male) vote.

Beals found an "astonishing psychological change" in Guatemala's people. "Not only do [they] seem free and gay, but everybody speaks his mind." He found new newspapers on sale on street corners, and a proliferation of books and magazines, ending the "old hushed whispers in a corner" to which he had grown accustomed on previous visits.[24]

Nicaragua was a contrast, with dictator Somoza at the helm. Nonetheless, at the time of Beals's visit, Somoza had relaxed his repression and backed a labor code passed by the country's Congress that responded to demands of a nascent labor union movement. Somoza's temporary liberality also reflected the influence of the US State Department, then pressuring him to hold elections. In Nicaragua's hot, dusty capital of Managua, Beals—still remembered for his 1928 interview with Sandino—was invited by one of Somoza's adversaries, General Carlos Pasos, to tour his textile factory, Pasos, Arellano y Companía (PAYCO). A founder of the Independent Liberal Party (PLI), Pasos was anxious to one-up Somoza and dampen union activism at his mill by casting himself as the greater friend of labor. This would assuage his pique that Somoza had dispatched his labor minister José Zelaya to settle a strike by PAYCO workers two years before.[25] Pasos found it useful to seize on Beals's visit, publicized in the PLI daily, to associate himself with Sandino's memory, thus giving Somoza, the newly converted union man, a poke in the eye.[26]

For his part, Somoza, then recovering from a bout of malaria at his hacienda, also invited Beals to interview him there. Beals declined, though, not wanting to play this game and chilled as he reminded himself that Somoza, twelve years before, had hosted Sandino for dinner only to have him murdered on the way out. Before their departure for Costa Rica, Beals and Blanca Rosa were the guests of honor at a dinner-dance hosted by Managua's press club and attended by the political elite and US embassy staff. It was an agreeable event, but marred at the end by police who marched half a dozen guests off to jail.[27]

In La Paz, Bolivia, which he reached in August, Beals was the first foreign journalist to tour the battered National Palace after the July 21 uprising, in which a provisional junta of students, workers, court justices and professors had seized power from police and soldiers guarding dictator Major Gualberto Villarroel (1908–1946). Over 500 people had been killed in bloody street clashes, Beals reported, that ended only after Villarroel was fatally shot while hiding in a closet, then hung from a lamp-post in the Plaza Murillo, facing the National Palace. "At first, he did have some popular support," Beals wrote in a minute-by-minute reconstruction, but his rule had degenerated into "totalitarian terrorism" that ultimately led to his regime's collapse.[28]

Despite Beals's demanding travel, research, and writing, and his agent McIntosh's efforts to place his articles, the results from the long trip were meager. Rejections piled up. "I honestly think the books are a better bet for money than the articles, which tend to be slightly off the track so far as the best paying magazines are concerned," McIntosh advised him.[29] This only worsened after his return home. He and McIntosh tried to place more lighthearted, first-person travel pieces on such topics as a tropical bus ride, local manners, and foods. They also recycled short stories and his manuscripts of a couple of novels. None of it worked. Beals's financial reserves were drained. The South American trip had cost him $5,000, but he was not able to capitalize on it. "It has been practically all outgo and nothing coming in," he complained to McIntosh.[30]

The major literary output resulting from Beals's 1946 Latin America tour was *Lands of the Dawning Morrow*, another overview of the region, his third in this genre, and arguably rivalling *America South* a decade earlier as the most illuminating. Bobbs-Merrill publisher John L. B. Williams had paid a $675 advance, hoping for "the best book Carleton Beals has ever written."[31] Beals delivered a meaty manuscript whose meticulous research is evident on every page. Studded with quotes from political leaders and intellectuals from Mexico to Argentina, along with eyewitness descriptions from his exploration of booming cities, hydroelectric dams, mines, and steel mills, it delivered an eerily prescient warning.

Among the signs of progress in the region, Beals highlighted the replacement of military dictators by elected civilians and restored constitutional rule, noting that Chile welcomed delegates from seven Latin American countries at the second international conference of democratic and peoples' parties in 1946.[32] But he also identified the biggest threat to the hoped-for "dawning morrow" in Latin America, namely Washington's foreign policymakers who, in their postwar rush to stamp out Soviet Communism, would only strengthen fascist-style dictatorships. This, he argued, would push the region's long-suffering people to desperation, prompting them to "turn to Communism in earnest."[33] The region's worst dictators—Somoza in Nicaragua, Trujillo in the Dominican Republic, Tiburcio Carías in Honduras, President Eurico Dutra (1883–1974), who had by now replaced Vargas in Brazil, and President Gabriel Gonzalez (1898–1980) in Chile—"have been the first to seize on this [anti-Communist] slogan to buttress up their shaky positions and impose new terror on the people."[34] Many countries, he warned, "especially dictatorial lands, will be hit by serious revolutions before they join the general progress of the continent."[35] Beals's suspicions were spot-on, as later research has shown that Cold War calculations led the late-1940s US State Department to favor cooperation with dictators over promotion of democracy in the region, as their regimes would be more reliably anti-Communist.[36]

This was a particularly striking example of the Cassandra quality of much of Beals's work, accurately identifying signs pointing to the revolutionary blowbacks that came later, led by Fidel Castro, Chile's Salvador Allende, Nicaragua's Sandinistas, and El Salvador's Farabundo Martí National Liberation Front (FMLN).

Beals feared that an exaggerated American use of the Communist bogey would be all the more tragic, given Latin America's recent progress, the growth of its cities, rapid expansion of manufacturing and agro-industry, along with diversified and mechanized agriculture replacing backward feudal estates. Much of this change was propelled by policies that encouraged local control of industry, manufacturing, natural resources, and utilities, introduced by reform-minded governments, more of them elected than ever before.

Most prominent among these in the late 1940s was the Peronist awakening in Argentina, still the focus of barely contained hostility in Washington. An admiring account of Perón's rule is the book's centerpiece, with Perón's effort to repatriate Argentina's hitherto largely foreign-owned vital economic resources highlighted as a model of the "third way" other nations should take to exit the noxious zero-sum choice between US-style capitalism and Soviet Communism.

"Perón is a pretty good guy, in Mr. Beals's estimation," wrote Sam Acheson in the *Dallas News*. "Most of us in the US have gotten the dictator all wrong . . . this is a little hard to take. But coming from a reporter of Mr. Beals' integrity, one who has been cuffed and booted around by more dictators to the South than the law ought to allow, his verdict must give us pause."[37] Beals's friend Samuel Guy Inman, writing in the *Churchman*, noted that Beals had overlooked Perón's flaws, such as his silencing of opposition parties and efforts to control neighboring countries, but acknowledged that Beals had also "told a side of the Perón story which is necessary for the US to understand but which has been carefully hid by most reporters."[38]

Even if *Lands of the Dawning Morrow* earned a raft of admiring reviews, its sales were disappointing, leading Bobbs-Merrill to withdraw its earlier promise to publish another Beals book. It is surprising that such a sharply-observed piece of work by a recognized authority on its subject, should have had such difficulty finding an audience. His publishers, agents and friends seemed mystified. War-weary Americans, it seemed, had grown tired of serious political discussion, of Latin American problems, of overseas strife.

Indeed, by the late 1940s, progressive-minded people who were the bedrock of Beals's readership seemed everywhere divided. The New Deal era had passed. The Henry Wallace campaign had gone down to defeat in 1948. Wisconsin's Progressive US Senator Robert La Follette Jr. had been defeated in 1946 by Joe McCarthy, who would soon begin his Red-baiting. The Left was silenced while anti-Communist hysteria mounted amid the trial of Alger Hiss, the *Smith Act of 1940* (*Alien Registration Act*) trial of labor leader Harry Bridges and convictions of alleged Communists.[39] Overseas, Stalin tightened his grip over Eastern Europe, Mao Zedong's Communist takeover meant the "loss" of China, and President Truman somberly announced in September 1949 that the Soviets had acquired a nuclear bomb.

Carey McWilliams, an editor at the *Nation* who became Beals's principal contact and sponsor there when he rejoined its roster of contributors in the early 1950s, observed a phenomenon accompanying the emerging Cold War. It was a kind of "gray list" to which liberal-minded writers and journalists found themselves consigned. They were not systematically blacklisted and denied work as happened to screenwriters and performers suspected of Communist sympathies after the Hollywood Ten group refused in 1947 to cooperate with the House Committee on Un-American Activities (HUAC). But these "gray-listed" writers and artists fell into an awkward nebulous zone. Questioning the Cold War line, increasingly, invited trouble. And with the HUAC spreading its investigative tentacles ever wider, editors sought to avoid such trouble.

Some erstwhile liberal intellectuals, often those with a Communist past, had become so committed to the new "anti-Communist" ideology that they denounced as un-American and pro-Soviet any criticism of American policy not coupled with a stronger criticism of Russian policy and practice.[40] Some of Beals's friends, such as Bert Wolfe joined this group (Wolfe wrote anti-Stalin scripts for *Voice of America* in the early 1950s), as well as others he despised such as Whittaker Chambers, whose testimony—most prominently against Hiss—unleashed an anti-Communist witch-hunt in the US State Department. Laurence Duggan, head of Latin American Relations at State, was an early victim. Duggan fell to his death from the sixteenth floor of a Manhattan office building after Chambers's allegations about his supposed Communist ties raised enough suspicion at the FBI that they questioned him. Although the evidence was inconclusive, suicide was the most plausible hypothesis. At his funeral, attended by former FDR-era colleagues at State such as Sumner Welles and Adolf Berle, a statement was circulated denouncing HUAC's role in "unjustly profaning" Duggan's memory.[41] This created a chill in the Latin American Relations Division at the US State Department that would become an arctic deep freeze with the arrival of John Foster Dulles as US Secretary of State a few years later.

A forbidding atmosphere for those whose politics leaned left spread through both government and the media, where fewer editors were inclined to buck the shift in attitudes by publishing the provocative perspectives so abundant in Beals's work. Nonetheless, Beals remained unbowed and untroubled, except financially, probably because he had no previous Communist Party membership or espionage activities to conceal. And as a freelancer living modestly without children, he had no established job to protect. His journalistic stance thus remained as uncompromising as his personality. He tried, in vain as it turned out, to stir interest in his *Lands of the Dawning Morrow* by positioning it as a challenge to what he called "foolish" anti-Communist wolf cries in Latin America.

These arose most pointedly in the US response to massive street violence after the assassination in Bogotá, Colombia of populist Liberal leader Jorge Eliécer Gaitán. His killing on April 9, 1948, coincided with the opening day in the same city of an Inter-American Conference at which US Secretary of State George Marshall sought Latin-American support for Washington's emerging policy of containment to check putative Soviet expansionist aims in the Western hemisphere, and elsewhere. The so-called *Bogotazo* violence that ensued was a spontaneous eruption of popular outrage, but some US observers saw a Communist hand in it.

Beals saw little connection between the aspirations of Latin America's poor—those who supported Gaitán, for example—and Soviet designs. "It takes a certain lack of humor, or else great imagination, to see [Soviet foreign minister] Gromyko and some barefoot villager marching under the same flag," he wrote in a letter published in *Newsweek* soon after the *Bogotazo*. "The villager changes his politics according to the corn supply, but only Stalin could change Gromyko."[42] And in an interview with the liberal *PM New York Daily*, Beals dismissed as "poppycock" the suggestion that Communists were behind the *Bogotazo*. "The Communists got 2,000 votes in the last election," Beals said. "There aren't enough of them to stage anything this big ... and why should they want to kill Gaitán?"[43]

However intact his journalistic integrity, Beals was, by 1949, living on a financial shoestring, anxiously counting on small checks for magazine pieces. He could no longer afford the services of a typist, and the quality of his manuscripts suffered as a result. He terminated his relationship with Mavis McIntosh which, though pleasant, had "scarcely been profitable to you or to me," he told her, turning instead to John Schaffner. Outwardly, life at his Sachem's Head home with Blanca was unchanged. Their social life with neighbors and friends continued, seemingly untroubled. "You both have the *don de gentes* (people skills) well developed," complimented historian Lesley Byrd Simpson, a house guest from Berkeley in whose honor they threw a cocktail party.[44]

But Beals's closest friends saw past this surface tranquility and sensed the trouble he was in. Kyle Crichton, whose senior editorial position at *Collier's* provided financial security, sent him a sizeable check in February 1949, with a note saying he should take it as, "a loan, a gift or any damn thing you please."[45] Later Crichton referred millionaire electric and steam car pioneer H. Jay Hayes to Beals to write a short vanity biography. Stuart Chase and Paca Toor also sent him money, the latter several times, both inventing excuses and ruses to do so, to preserve his dignity and ensure that their gifts would be accepted.

As the 1950s began, marked by the rise of McCarthyism and its intolerance, the appetite for Beals's brand of journalism continued to diminish. His new agent, John Schaffner refocused his efforts by securing for him contracts to write popular histories, for example a biography of Texas founder Stephen F. Austin, aimed at young readers, and a history of New Haven, Connecticut, *Our Yankee Heritage*, both published in 1951.[46]

After some initial success in obtaining book contracts, however, Schaffner's promotional initiatives ran aground. Having convinced Beals to produce slice-of-life anecdotal stories from his travels rather than political analysis, he failed to sell these to magazines he targeted such as *Town and Country* and *Family Circle*, or men's adventure magazines such as *Argosy* and *Saga*, none of which were intuitively obvious placements for Beals.[47] Indeed, this genre of dramatized personal experiences was not Beals's forte either. Schaffner also grew frustrated with Beals's slapdash approach to writing, in which everything seemed thrown together in a rush.[48] This had earlier been a fault-line in Beals's work, noticed by other editors and agents. But during this period after the war, it became more pronounced, an added liability when he already faced an uphill struggle to survive as a writer. In late 1952, Beals switched agents again, following up on a referral from *Collier's* editor Joe Alex Morris, whom he had met through Kyle Crichton, to Bertha Klausner, a literary agent whose instinctively shrewd insight and personal warmth immediately inspired the troubled writer's confidence.

Klausner would prove herself a lifesaver for Beals. She was genuinely honored to have been approached to be his agent, and this humility immediately engaged him. Klausner also grasped the root causes of the crisis that had now overwhelmed him. First, his customary freelance markets, the liberal magazines, had all but dried up. Second, his own efforts to retool his brand of journalism were unfocused and hurried, even panicky. She saw that his haste in writing, a tendency itself reinforced by the pitiless stream of rejections he was getting, was tied to a sense of despair that his career was spinning out of control.

Her first step in trying to help him was to learn everything she could about his work. She asked him to hand over all his unpublished manuscripts, some decades old. She pored over them, looking for nuggets or threads of material that could be revived and made marketable, or dreaming up ways to repackage them to suit a changed market. She gave his published work a second look too, managing, for example, to stir a Hollywood producer's interest in the film rights to *Black River*.

Klausner's arrival soon gave Beals a renewed sense of hope that he would publish again. It was a reed of optimism to which he would cling, as it coincided with the deepest personal crisis of his life: the collapse of his marriage. By the spring of 1953, Carleton had grown distant from Blanca, quietly nursing resentments over what he saw as her erratic behavior, and failure to support him through his professional struggle. On her side, she complained that he drank to excess, and that he was unfaithful, suspecting that some of his intellectual friendships with other women might have been sexual as well. The root cause of their discord, however, was Beals's struggle to publish, and the financial abyss into which it pushed them.

Their crisis and Blanca's mental instability seemed locked in a vicious circle. Carleton's brother Ralph had been shocked when, during a visit to the Beals home in Sachem's Head in the early 1950s, Blanca Rosa had tried to seduce him, claiming that she was wildly in love with him.[49] Blanca, who had once "entranced the whole [Beals] family," had become "deeply disturbed," Ralph thought, with "an increasingly pathological obsession with sex."[50]

Things came to a head the afternoon of April 11, 1953, when an angry and agitated Blanca threatened to shoot Carleton. Earlier that day, she had burst into the home of an alarmed neighbor asking to borrow her Colt Automatic pistol. Thinking Blanca had gone mad, the neighbor refused the request, and sent her home. Once there, she was in an unchecked rage and threatened Beals with such force that he rushed out of his home.

The following day, he left her a note that ended the relationship. "Your hate of me and threats of violence are quite terrifying," Beals told her. "I have lost hope of changing you or bringing you back to your senses . . . to realize how false and unworthy your suspicions [are] about me." Adopting a tone more of sorrow than anger, Beals said he would be forever grateful for "the brightness and sweetness and tolerance you once had," but now lamented having to watch "the hate and bitterness [and an] ugly attitude toward so many people, creep into your heart."[51] He concluded by saying he felt "terribly sorry for you," and promised that "everything I have, I am sorry it is so little, you may have."[52]

Over the next months, Beals sank into depression. He wanted to walk away from Blanca altogether, but their straitened finances forced the couple to remain under the same roof for much of 1953. At the same time, Beals faced additional stress caused by a renewed FBI investigation of him. This one was launched after the head of the Connecticut chapter of the Daughters of the American Revolution in Connecticut, Grace Lee Kenyon, wrote FBI Director J. Edgar Hoover asking that the Bureau probe claims that Beals had "Communist sympathies."[53] Kenyon was concerned, as she had hired Beals to write a history of Bristol, Connecticut, and did not want the book's credibility tainted by the author's alleged Communist connections. Beals responded with a furious denial. The FBI investigated nonetheless but found no evidence to support his alleged Communist or Soviet ties.

By early 1954, Beals was exhausted from bickering with Blanca. He found a refuge with his friend, Vlad Janowicz, an abstract expressionist painter who supported himself by renting out chicken coops on nearby New England Road, also in Guilford. Vlad, a blunt, no-bullshit kind of character, had been a Communist activist in Chicago in the 1930s before moving to Guilford to devote himself to art and a simpler rural life. He, too, was going through his own marital separation, and welcomed Beals's company and solidarity.

Amid this upheaval at home, Beals nonetheless kept an eye on political developments in Latin America, and Guatemala in particular, where a democratic revolution faced mounting hostility from the President Dwight D. "Ike" Eisenhower (1890–1969) administration, and its foreign-policy duumvirate of the Dulles brothers, John Foster as US Secretary of State, and Allen as CIA Director. The administration minted its so-called "New Look" policy, outlined in US National Security Council (NSC) Report 162/2, in the summer of 1953, stressing the need for a cheaper, more effective, more mobile approach to waging the Cold War.[54] Significantly, it placed greater emphasis on clandestine covert action as a creative, lower-cost response to reverse what administration officials saw as Communist penetration of peripheral areas like Guatemala.[55]

This crude caricature would become a fixture of the Dulles brothers' drive to intervene to topple left-leaning social reform governments in developing countries. It would get its test run in Guatemala, where the reformist Arévalo—whom Beals had interviewed in 1946—had been succeeded as President in 1950 by his defense minister, Jacobo Árbenz (1913–1971), elected with over 65 percent of the vote.

Árbenz had been among the leaders of the 1944 coup that overthrew the dictator Ubico, and installed Arévalo in power. He was determined to sustain and deepen the social revolution begun under Arévalo, which focused on expanding labor rights and most notably, agrarian reform. The agrarian reform program, launched in June 1952, stirred the ire of the United Fruit Company (UFCO), Guatemala's largest landowner with about 550,000 acres on both coasts.[56] In 1953, the government issued two decrees to expropriate 209,842 acres left idle by the company as insurance against plant diseases that periodically ravaged the bananas.[57] United Fruit took exception to this as a matter of principle, and also more specifically to the terms it was offered, namely compensation based on UFCO's own 1952 land value assessment, which the company had then deliberately underestimated to reduce its land tax bill.[58]

The company's position was difficult to defend on its own in Guatemala. Given its long-dominant position and easy rapport with earlier dictators, UFCO was unaccustomed to negotiating or accepting terms from a government whose politics it despised. The company's executives turned instead to Washington to make their case, and got a sympathetic hearing from John Foster Dulles, who had earlier spent his legal career at Sullivan and Cromwell, the elite New York law firm that represented United Fruit, and whose brief Dulles had handled.

At the same time, UFCO launched an aggressive publicity campaign run by the clever and energetic Edward Bernays, aimed at smearing the Árbenz government as Communist-dominated. Bernays organized tours of Guatemala for reporters with the wire services and major US dailies, in which the newsmen were shepherded around the country for interviews with government critics and UFCO officials. At the same time, he pressured news media executives such as his friend Arthur Hays Sulzberger, publisher of the *New York Times*, to explore the story of Communist penetration in Guatemala, with facilitation by UFCO.[59]

The official decision to move against Árbenz was made in early August 1953, at a meeting of the White House committee on covert operations whose members included Allen Dulles, US Undersecretary of State Bedell Smith, and C. D. Jackson, Eisenhower's psychological warfare adviser.[60] Beals, while not aware of the specifics, smelled out the intrigue. He began to investigate, quickly finding grounds for suspicion, and even some proof that a US-backed conspiracy against Guatemala was under way.

He revealed the intrigue in an article, "Dollar Diplomacy in Guatemala," which he submitted to the *New Republic*. Its editor, Helen Fuller, turned it down, claiming "limited space."[61] Once the June 1954 coup overthrowing Árbenz had happened, and evidence of CIA involvement began to surface, Beals wrote several stories in a burst of outrage, but almost all were rejected, in their turn, by the *Progressive*, *Harper's*, and the *Nation*.[62] At the *Progressive*, editor Rubin had initially signaled that he would run Beals's article on the coup, only to pull it at the last minute. He replaced it with another by Donald Grant, editor of the *St. Louis Post-Dispatch*. Grant closely toed Washington's official line, quoting as justification for the coup a dubious allegation by US Ambassador John Peurifoy that Árbenz, "readily admitted to him that he was a member of the Communist Party."[63] Rubin defended his decision to replace Beals's article, saying a reference in Beals's piece to civil liberties under Árbenz was no longer valid, given the Guatemalan President's decision to suspend such liberties (as a protective measure) in the days leading up to the coup.[64] Beals was unconvinced, and thought Rubin "timid."[65] Rubin's misgivings were likely influenced by former Wisconsin US Senator Robert LaFollette Jr.'s role, shortly before the once-Progressive politician's February 1953 suicide, in lobbying liberal Congressmen and officials to buy the idea that Árbenz was a dangerous radical.[66]

Only the ecumenical *Christian Century* agreed to publish two of Beals's Guatemala investigative analysis pieces. By this time, of course, such accounts no longer had the capacity to forestall what had already happened. In the second of these, published in December 1954, Beals's tone seems self-consciously reined-in by the prevailing anti-Communist hysteria, and almost wistful:

> If our policy [in Guatemala] is to be successful, if communism is to be beaten, the people cannot be denied democratic freedom. They cannot be compelled to accept drastically reduced wages, to be excluded from the land, to suffer forced labor and serfdom ... to improve the people's condition is an obligation we assumed in bringing about the overthrow of the Árbenz government. If we fail we shall have done communism a great service in Guatemala and everywhere else. The stake is not merely Guatemala; it is all Latin America.[67]

Even without Bernays's media smear campaign against Guatemala, and State Department pressure on American media executives, it would have been difficult for Beals to publish his independent perspectives. With the groupthink engendered by this pressure, most editors opted for caution and eschewed a writer whose assessments were so much at odds with the received version from Washington. Beals shared his frustration with his longtime associate, the Protestant missionary and professor Inman, who had visited and written about the Guatemalan revolution in 1950: "I find it almost impossible to get anything published anywhere on Latin America, not even banalities, let alone any attempted analysis of what is going on."[68]

Meantime, Beals's personal turmoil continued. In February 1954, his mother Elvina died after suffering a stroke. His brother Ralph, with whom she had been living in her last years, wrote him a characteristically acerbic note from Santa Monica, asking what he wanted done with Elvina's documents and autobiographical writing, the latter "full of rather artificial sentiments about her children and personal sufferings." He added: "I hope things break better for you soon."[69] Carleton wrote him back immediately, asking if he could advance some money from the estate, to which Ralph responded with a $50 check "to tide you over" until the estate funds became available.[70] It was a sad testimony to the depth of Beals's penury.

It would take three years for the Beals couple's divorce to be granted in March 1956 by a New Haven Superior Court judge, after recriminations aired in court. A Guilford physician testified that Blanca had developed a nervous condition due to her marital unhappiness, exacerbated by financial duress. "In the latter years of her life with Carleton, she didn't know where her next meal was coming from," Dr. Frank McGuire said.[71] Beals agreed to give Blanca their Sachem's Head house, even though he felt betrayed that she had destroyed some of his manuscripts, and refused his request to recover his office furniture, as well as personal mementos and Mexican paintings.

## NOTES

1. Ayn Rand, *The Fountainhead* (Indianapolis, IN: Bobbs Merrill, 1943).
2. William Barrett, Review of *Dawn Over the Amazon*, by Carleton Beals, *Boston Post*, July 25, 1943; Carleton Beals, *Dawn Over the Amazon* (New York: Duell, Sloan, and Pearce, 1943).
3. John Selby, Review of *Dawn Over the Amazon*, by Carleton Beals, *Morning Herald*, Uniontown, PA, June 23, 1943, 13.
4. Lewis Gannett, "Books and Things," Review of *Dawn Over the Amazon*, by Carleton Beals, *New York Herald Tribune*, June 23, 1943, 19A; Nina Brown Baker, "Jungle War, 1950," Review of *Dawn Over the Amazon*, by Carleton Beals, *New York Times*, July 11, 1943, 46, 50.
5. Carleton Beals, "Under the Fifth Sun" (unpublished autobiography, c. 1972–1978), in Carleton Beals Collection (CBC), Howard Gotlieb Archival Research Center, Boston University, 74–75 (hereafter cited CBC).
6. Robert Crichton, "My Father, the Un-American," *New York Magazine*, March 10, 1975, 35.
7. Stuart Chase, *A New Deal for America: The Road to Revolution* (New York: Macmillan, 1932).
8. Carleton Beals, *Rio Grande to Cape Horn* (Boston: Houghton Mifflin, 1943); Beals, *Pan America* (Boston: Houghton Mifflin, 1940); and Beals, *America South* (Philadelphia: J. B. Lippincott, 1937).
9. R. N. Linscott to Maxim Lieber, December 23, 1942, CBC.
10. Paul Brooks to Maxim Lieber, March 19, 1943, CBC. See also Rachel Carson, *Silent Spring* (Boston: Houghton Mifflin, 1962).
11. Hubert Herring, Review of *Rio Grande to Cape Horn*, by Carleton Beals, *American Mercury*, November 1943, 516; Beals, *Rio Grande to Cape Horn*.
12. C.A. Hutchinson, "Circling a Continent," *Saturday Review of Literature*, October 16, 1943, 48.
13. Lloyd Mallan, "Some Notes on Latin America," Review of *Rio Grande to Cape Horn*, by Carleton Beals, *New York Times*, September 26, 1943, BR9.
14. Carleton Beals to Maxim Lieber, May 17, 1944, CBC.
15. Maxim Lieber to Carleton Beals, May 22, 1944, CBC.
16. Carleton Beals, *Bridge of Royal Delights* (unpublished manuscript), Carleton Beals Collection (CBC), Howard Gotlieb Archival Research Center, Boston University.
17. Cap Pearce to Carleton Beals, July 30, 1945, CBC.
18. Varian Fry, Editor of *Common Sense*, to Carleton Beals, December 28, 1945, CBC.
19. The Big Three Conferences, as they were known, were held as follows: Tehran Conference, November 1943; Yalta, February 1945, and the Potsdam Conference, July 1945, the first two attended by Winston Churchill, Franklin D. Roosevelt and Joseph Stalin, and the last by Churchill, Stalin and US President Harry S Truman. There was also a Moscow Conference, October 1944, which Roosevelt did not attend. The Chapultepec Conference was held in Mexico City, February 21 to March 8, 1945, between the United States and nineteen Latin American countries.
20. Carleton Beals, "The Democratic Road to Enduring Peace," *Progressive*, February 12, 1945.

21. Carleton Beals, "Oil Imperialism Imperils the Peace," *Progressive*, May 21, 1945; and Beals, "Meaning of the Meeting on Grasshopper Hill," *Progressive*, March 19, 1945.

22. Carleton Beals, "Prosperous Argentina," *Progressive*, August 26, 1946; Beals, "Argentina on the March," *Progressive*, September 2, 1946; Beals, "Remaking Argentina," *Progressive*, September 23, 1946; and Beals, "Inside Argentina," *Progressive*, September 30, 1946.

23. Beals, "Argentina on the March" (1946).

24. Carleton Beals, "Schoolteacher President," *Asia and the Americas* 46, no. 8, August 1946, 363–67.

25. See Jeffrey L. Gould, "Nicaragua," in *Latin America between the Second World War and the Cold War, 1944–1948*, ed. Leslie Bethell and Ian Roxborough (Cambridge: Cambridge University Press, 1992), 254.

26. *El Liberal Nacionalista* (Managua) (The Nationalist Liberal), April 24, 1946, CBC.

27. Beals, "Under the Fifth Sun" (unpublished autobiography), CBC, box 47, folder 9, 136.

28. Carleton Beals, "Barricades in Bolivia," *Asia and the Americas* 46, no. 11, November 1946, 489–94.

29. Mavis McIntosh to Carleton Beals, June 7, 1946, CBC.

30. Carleton Beals to Mavis McIntosh, January 17, 1946 [*sic*, 1947], CBC.

31. Mavis McIntosh to Carleton Beals, May 16, 1947, CBC.

32. Carleton Beals, *Lands of the Dawning Morrow: The Awakening from Rio Grande to Cape Horn* (New York: Bobbs-Merrill, 1948), 295.

33. Beals, *Lands of the Dawning Morrow*, 280.

34. Beals, *Lands of the Dawning Morrow*, 280.

35. Beals, *Lands of the Dawning Morrow*, 23.

36. Greg Grandin, *Empire's Workshop: Latin America, the United States, and the Rise of the New Imperialism* (New York: Henry Holt, 2006), 40–42.

37. Sam Acheson, "Latter day Humboldt Catches Latin America," *Dallas News*, May 2, 1948.

38. Samuel Guy Inman, Review of *Lands of the Dawning Morrow*, by Carleton Beals, *Churchman*, 162:16 (Hartford, CT), November 1, 1948.

39. US Congress, *Smith Act of 1940* (*Alien Registration Act, 1940*), 54 Stat. 670, Pub. L. 76–670, 76th Cong., 3rd sess., June 28, 1940, https://govtrackus.s3.amazonaws.com/legislink/pdf/stat/54/STATUTE-54-Pg670.pdf (accessed May 26, 2021).

40. Carey McWilliams, *The Education of Carey McWilliams* (New York: Simon & Schuster, 1978), 145.

41. Sam Tanenhaus, *Whittaker Chambers: A Biography* (New York: Random House, 1997), 331.

42. Carleton Beals, Letter to the Editor, *Newsweek*, June 12, 1948.

43. "Latin American Specialist Beals Explains the Riots in Colombia," *PM New York Daily*, April 18, 1948, CBC.

44. Lesley Byrd Simpson to Carleton Beals and Blanca Beals, June 17, 1950, CBC.

45. Kyle Crichton to Carleton Beals, February 4, 1949, CBC.

46. Carleton Beals, *Stephen F. Austin: Father of Texas* (New York: McGraw-Hill, 1951); and Beals, *Our Yankee Heritage: The Making of Greater New Haven* (New Haven CT: Bradley & Scoville, 1951).

47. John Schaffner to Carleton Beals, June 12, 1950, CBC.

48. John Schaffner to Carleton Beals, May 19, 1949, CBC.

49. R. L. Beals, "Memories of My Brother, Carleton Beals" (1982), MBYC.

50. R. L. Beals, "Memories of My Brother, Carleton Beals" (1982), MBYC, 17.

51. Carleton Beals to Blanca Rosa Beals, April 12, 1953, CBC.

52. Carleton Beals to Blanca Rosa Beals (1953), CBC.

53. US Department of Justice, Federal Bureau of Investigation Files on Carleton Beals, Washington, DC, "Memo to Director, FBI, Re: Carleton Beals Security Matter: New Haven Origin," March 5, 1953 (NW#48582, DocId: 32988232), 1–14.

54. US National Security Council, NSC 162/2, A Report to the National Security Council, by the Executive Secretary, James S. Lay, Jr., on Basic Nation Security Policy, October 30,

1953, Washington, DC, https://fas.org/irp/offdocs/nsc-hst/nsc-162-2.pdf (accessed May 26, 2021).

55. Nick Cullather, *Secret History: The CIA's Classified Account of Its Operations in Guatemala, 1952–1954*, 2nd ed. (Stanford, CA: Stanford University Press, 2006), 37.

56. Steven C. Schlesinger and Stephen Kinzer, *Bitter Fruit: The Untold Story of the American Coup in Guatemala*, 2nd ed. (Garden City, NY: Doubleday, 1982), 75.

57. Schlesinger and Kinzer, *Bitter Fruit*, 75.

58. Schlesinger and Kinzer, *Bitter Fruit*, 54.

59. Schlesinger and Kinzer, *Bitter Fruit*, 87–90.

60. Schlesinger and Kinzer, *Bitter Fruit*, 108.

61. Helen Fuller to Carleton Beals, October 22, 1953, CBC.

62. Morris Rubin to Carleton Beals, October 5, 1954; John Fisher to Carleton Beals, October 21, 1954; Victor J. Bernstein to Carleton Beals, October 19, 1954, CBC.

63. Donald Grant, "Last Chance in Guatemala," *Progressive* 18, no. 9, September 1954, 28.

64. Morris Rubin to Carleton Beals, June 22, 1954, CBC.

65. Rubin to Beals (1954), CBC (Beals's marginal note on letter from Rubin).

66. Schlesinger and Kinzer, *Bitter Fruit*, 91–92.

67. Carleton Beals, "Second Thoughts on Guatemala," *Christian Century*, December 8, 1954, 1491.

68. Carleton Beals to Samuel Guy Inman, June 15, 1954, CBC.

69. Ralph L. Beals to Carleton Beals (undated, 1954), CBC.

70. Ralph L. Beals to Carleton Beals, April 4, 1954, CBC.

71. Frank McGuire, "Mrs. Beals Goes Free," *New Haven Sunday Herald*, March 25, 1956, CBC.

*Chapter Thirteen*

# Second Act in Cuba

Carolyn Kennedy lived alone on her hobby farm in Guilford, seven miles north of Carleton Beals's house in Sachem's Head, Connecticut. She was a solitary woman who combined a headstrong attitude with a sensitive soul attuned to the natural world. But even if introverted, she was not anti-social. She had grown up an only child, accustomed to the company of people a generation older than hers. She naturally gravitated toward them at social occasions such as community clambakes and corn roasts. That is how she met Carleton Beals.

Now forty-five years old, she had admired him from a distance for years. She had read all of his books. When each one of them was published, she would stop by Beals's home with her fresh copy to have him sign it. He was flattered by this interest, and charmed by her humor, which was dry but nonetheless conveyed a discreet flirtation.

An aspiring writer herself, she had once asked him to review a manuscript on which she had been working, a story of friendship between two World War I soldiers. He had taken the time to read it and scribble comments in the margins, to which she had responded with fawning gratitude. "I don't think actual publication would give me as much pleasure as your marginal notes," she wrote him.[1]

Carolyn was also friendly with Vlad Janowicz, and with his now-estranged wife Ruth, so she soon learned that Carleton was boarding with Vlad, having left Blanca. It was not long before she invited him to dinner at her home.

"He'd lived such a big life," she recalled years later. "He didn't deserve to be unhappy." It was as though she had decided, on the spot, to become the ideal companion that her instinct told her he needed. He welcomed her attention as a drowning man welcomes rescue.

A brunette of stocky build, Carolyn had dabbled at drama after graduating from Skidmore, a women's college in Saratoga Springs, New York, in the 1930s. But her taciturn reserve made this an unnatural pursuit for her, so she abandoned it for a job as a copywriter in the advertising department at Consolidated Edison. The highlight of her career there had been serving as a guide to the company's dramatic "City of Light" pavilion at the 1939 New York World's Fair.

She was the only child of George P. Kennedy, president of the Lafayette National Bank of Brooklyn, and his wife Ida Burr Kennedy, a schoolteacher.[2] Her father, also a prominent philanthropist, died at 64 years old in 1946, leaving Carolyn a substantial inheritance.

She "worshipped" her father and so was devastated by the loss. Seeking a change from Brooklyn and city life, she moved to Guilford, where she rekindled happy memories of childhood summers that her family had spent there.

**Figure 13.1.   Carolyn Kennedy Beals in the living room of the home she shared with Beals from 1958 until his death in 1979, in Killingworth, Connecticut, c. 1960.** *Photo courtesy of the Carleton Beals Collection, Howard Gotlieb Archival Research Center, Boston University, and Ralph Carleton Beals.*

She liked the town's rural flavor, its relaxed pace, and the opportunity it offered to rediscover her childhood passion for horseback riding.

Carolyn found happiness in horses and other animals, treating them with the solicitous regard one reserves for close friends. Her property soon became known for its horses, goats, and an ever-growing collection of cats, as she adopted all strays. Each animal was known to her as a distinct personality, and each given a name, such as Tiger Pants and Cherry Bounce.

This was a new world for Beals, but he took to it with humor and even delight. The couple was married, quietly, with neither guests nor a reception, almost immediately after Carleton's divorce from Blanca was finalized in March 1956.

At the same time, Beals moved into Carolyn's home on Little Meadow Road, and began re-establishing contact with friends and associates from whom he had withdrawn during his feud with Blanca. Many of them were shocked and saddened to learn of the breakup, as they had seemed a model couple. Few had detected Beals's discomfort at feeling trapped, nor Blanca's creeping sense of desperation, as both had assiduously concealed their troubles. Beals, as always, was measured in word and in gesture, while Blanca had an acutely-honed sense of dignity that kept her poised, giving away nothing when neighbors and friends stopped by or called on the phone.

Now, however, it was all out in the open, and Beals was relieved. "I am free of a terrible nightmare," he wrote an editor who had worked with him on *Our Yankee Heritage*, a series of three textbook histories of New England he had managed to produce during this period of turmoil.[3] To his ever-loyal correspondent Ernestine Evans, he confided that although he was resigned to a "complete loss and crash of everything [in his divorce settlement]," he was now, "in better spirits, more hopeful, and working more—or at least better—than I have for quite some years."[4]

Bertha Klausner's efforts were delivering results too. At fifty-five years old, she was in the prime of her career, able to draw on a vast network of publishing contacts, as well as Hollywood film-makers whom she would pitch on periodic trips to the West Coast. After Beals finished the *Yankee Heritage* series, Klausner lined up contracts for him to do biographies of early Americans such as explorer Robert Gray and missionary pastor John Eliot. She had also encouraged him to rework his script for a musical on a rather unlikely subject, the life of Carry Nation, the axe-wielding prohibitionist of the 1890s from Medicine Lodge, Kansas, Beals's birthplace.

There was renewed interest in Beals's work from the *Nation*, then emerging from its own early-1950s struggle to find funding, finally resolved when George Kirstein used part of his personal fortune to buy the magazine.[5] Kirstein restored the *Nation*'s solvency along with its determination to challenge the continuing assaults from various House Committee on Un-American Activities (HUAC), on both national and state levels.

Its new editor Carey McWilliams, always an admirer of Beals, turned to him for guidance in covering mounting unrest against the Fulgencio Batista regime in Cuba. McWilliams, who had replaced Freda Kirchwey as the magazine's editor in 1955, agreed to publish a series of stories that Beals would produce during a trip to Cuba and Haiti in June and early July of 1957.

Public interest in Cuba had spiked since February, when the *New York Times* published a front-page interview with the rebel leader Fidel Castro, conducted from his Sierra Maestra encampment by veteran reporter and editorial writer Herbert L. Matthews. The story proved that Castro, whom Batista had claimed dead, was not only very much alive, but also in command of a growing and disciplined revolutionary army. Castro later publicly took credit for adroitly staging his encounter with Matthews to convince the American journalist that his rebel force was much larger and better-equipped than it really was. True or not, the incident became a journalistic legend of sorts, and while it served Castro well, it also ultimately destroyed Matthews's credibility and career.[6] For Beals, who naturally compared Matthews's exploit to his own with Augusto César Sandino in 1928, the buzz about Castro opened a new opportunity for his own reports on Cuba.

Beals flew from New York to Havana on June 1, and undertook a whirl of travel to Camagüey, Santiago, and Manzanillo, as well as Havana itself. Although disappointed that he was not able to interview Castro or other 26th of July Movement leaders, he cabled a two-part feature piece to McWilliams, published a week later under the headline, "The New Crime of Cuba." The first part focused on Batista's campaign of terror and the increasingly frequent—almost nightly, during Beals's visit—sabotage attacks by shadowy groups. The second described the sources of resistance to Batista, for the most part students whose future was blighted by Batista's forced closure of Cuba's universities. Calling Cuba "the Hungary on our doorsteps," and citing its secret police, student leaders in prison, kangaroo-court judges, and official corruption, Beals nonetheless dismissed most of the opposition as "terrorists." He seemed dismayed that, despite offering little beyond "a few vague notions about democracy and the constitution," these groups had managed to inspire "a surprisingly strong sympathy in upper social circles."[7]

Beals was no more sanguine about Castro, "this mysterious daredevil of the hills," who had by now gained the support of almost all those opposed to Batista, including both terrorists and those opposed to terrorism. Castro had "become the idol, to the point of fanaticism, of Young Cuba," Beals wrote, even if "what he hopes to bring about nobody seems to know, for he has made no pronouncements of program other than wiping out Batista."[8]

Beals's rather dismal perception of Castro's program was quickly contested after the piece appeared. Mario Llerena (1913–2006), a Cuban intellectual and Castro associate living in Mexico, sent Beals a copy of *Nuestra Razón* (Our Reason), a manifesto setting out the 26th of July Movement's program. Beals, chastened at not previously having been aware of the document, insisted that McWilliams publish his summary of the manifesto's key points in the *Nation*, which he did in September. The manifesto called for labor rights, land reform, nationalization of utilities, public education and health, democratic parties, and honest suffrage.[9] In retrospect, Beals's initial sense that Castro's mercurial character and personality would weigh more heavily in defining Cuba's future than this fairly conventional social democratic program turned out to be closer to the mark. Indeed, Llerena would abandon Castro even before the revolutionary triumph.

From Havana, Beals took a short flight on June 17 to Port-au-Prince, Haiti, also in the throes of violent chaos. Just days before, on June 14, a military coup led by General Antonio Kébreau (1909–1963) had toppled an elected, pro-labor regime led by Daniel Fignolé (1913–1986), after just nineteen days in power. Kébreau's soldiers had killed over 400 pro-Fignolé demonstrators, and seized hundreds more, dumping many of them, without food, on La Gonâve, a sparsely-inhabited island forty miles off shore.[10]

Beals himself felt the repression when three soldiers burst into his hotel room and, finding him undressed, glared at him briefly, looked around the room, and left. Beals alerted the *Nation's* publisher George Kirstein who sent protest cables to US Secretary of State John Foster Dulles and US Ambassador to Haiti Gerald Drew.[11] All this did was provoke the Haitian police to arrest the hotel's owner and threaten him with imprisonment for conspiring with the foreign press against the government.[12]

Beals's poignant descriptions of Haiti's poverty, sadly, are of a character almost identical to those of more recent accounts, showing that little has changed for the average Haitian since his time. He relates, for example, that Kébreau had "turned his soldiers loose on the slum districts . . . the shacks along the harbor front and the boulevard to the airport, one of the filthiest, most sickening conglomerations of misery, disease and horror I have ever seen."[13]

The shaky Kébreau regime would soon relinquish power after "bayonet elections," Beals predicted, to the candidate who "will promise the army the most graft and patronage." This would be, he predicted, François "Papa Doc" Duvalier (1907–1971).[14] Indeed, four months later, Duvalier was elected, and would rule Haiti until his death in 1971, when he was succeeded by his son, Jean-Claude "Baby Doc" Duvalier (1951–2014).

Beals returned to Guilford from this tumultuous Caribbean trip both exhausted and exhilarated. His Cuba and Haiti pieces were featured on the *Nation*'s cover, and the *Christian Century* published his articles on political intrigue within Cuba's Catholic Church and labor union movement.[15] Carolyn, who had written him affectionate letters every day during his tour, had been busy during his absence, preparing for a move both had anticipated for months.

The couple, drawing mostly on Carolyn's inheritance, had purchased a thirty-acre property a few miles east of Guilford, on Fire Tower Road, just north of the village of Killingworth, Connecticut. The stretch of woodland, which they would call Hackamore Farm in a nod to Carolyn's horsey predilection, backed up to a state forest on two sides, and its dwelling was a two-story farmhouse built about 1730. Nearby was a large red barn, and beside it, the original Killingworth schoolhouse.[16]

The schoolhouse was soon transformed into Beals's study. He contracted his neighbor, a carpenter and handyman, to rebuild its roof, install a small furnace and build shelves to accommodate his more than four thousand books. A large desk was set up in the center of the room, and a bed under a window along one side. By mid-winter of 1958, he had "everything in order, the way I want it," he wrote his brother Ralph.[17]

The schoolhouse study became Beals's creative hermitage, in which he soon settled into a daily routine of reading and writing that usually extended late into the night. This stability, combined with Klausner's promotional efforts, focused on juvenile textbooks and popular history markets, soon delivered a steady stream of book contracts. The biography, *John Eliot: The Man Who Loved the Indians,* published in March 1958, was selected as a "choice" by the Literary Guild's division for young readers.[18]

It was followed by Hastings House's publication in May of a light-hearted memoir, *House in Mexico.*[19] Its fifteen chapters of whimsical vignettes, two of them previously published in the *New Yorker*, were drawn from Beals's day-to-day life in Mexico City and Coyoacán in the late 1920s and early 1930s. The book's highlight was a retrospective portrait of Petra, Beals's housekeeper in Coyoacán, whose attitude toward Beals was a winsome hybrid of maidservant and scolding parent. Another tongue-in-cheek essay on manners dealt with the fine art of flirting in the state of Tehuantepec, and a third recalled how Beals got lost, spending a night in the forest, during a hike up Mount Ajusco, south of Mexico City, with Ernest Gruening, who was by now campaigning for Alaska's first-ever US Senate seat. "A delightful book which tourists should read before heading south," wrote Hubert Herring in the *New York Herald-Tribune*, while also noting that Beals was writing about a Mexico of twenty-five years before, now much changed.[20]

Beals had found a new tranquility and balance with Carolyn, his spirit rekindled by her gentle and steadfast affection for him, combined with her rejection of social pretension, much like his own. "He was everything to me," she recalled years later. "A husband, a father, an older brother, a lover, and my best friend."[21]

Carolyn's devotion to her two horses and three goats, to which a cow was soon added, kept her at home most of the time, so the couple's social life was less active than Beals's had been when he lived with Blanca Rosa. They invited neighbors for dinner from time to time, but for the most part, they kept to themselves. Although not quite hermits, they both savored their relative solitude. Beals filled his days at his typewriter, working on manuscripts, as well as letters to friends, editors, writers, admirers, and critics.

He was, of course, caustic in his views of the President Dwight D. Eisenhower administration. One example was a piece he wrote for the *Christian Century* following Vice President Richard Nixon's (1913–1994) disastrous tour of Latin America in May 1958, which ended abruptly in Caracas, where an angry mob attacked his motorcade with such violence that he was lucky to get out alive. US officials were first caught off guard by the anti-Nixon protests there, and those in Uruguay, Argentina, Peru, Bolivia, and Colombia, later blaming them on Communist agitators, immaturity, and envy of the United States.[22] But Beals attributed them to long-standing grievances over US support under Eisenhower for military dictators and trade protection at a time of low commodity prices. In the Venezuelan case, he blamed US backing for the dictator Marcos Pérez Jiménez (1914–2001), overthrown by a provisional junta just four months before Nixon's visit. He urged "a reappraisal of our Latin American policy . . . to recover some of the prestige we gained during our brief good-neighbor policy."[23]

Nixon aide William G. Key challenged "glaring inaccuracies and faulty interpretations," in Beals's critique, describing protests in all cities except Caracas as "minor." He also took issue with Beals's suggestion that US emissaries cultivate the "intellectual elite" to promote democracy in Latin America, arguing that the focus should rather be on students, labor unionists, and the slowly developing middle classes.[24] Beals riposted that these were precisely the groups comprising the intellectual elite to which he had referred, and that Key could not "push me out of this [pro-democracy] church by verbal legerdemain."[25]

Beals was alienated not just by the Eisenhower-Nixon mindset, but also by the self-absorbed consumerism that had America in its embrace. Both, he believed, had provoked the prevailing and troublesome, for his publishing prospects, lack of interest in any journalism like his, that challenged Cold War orthodoxies and explored topics beyond "the dear USA" and its "chromium gadgetry."[26] But even if he was peeved that America's lapse into a complacent repose of conservatism and consumerism had shrunk the audience for his defiantly independent voice, Beals was much too happy at home to be peevish.

\*\*\*

On New Year's Day 1959, when Beals heard the news from Havana that Fidel Castro had seized power, and that Batista had fled, he was as if thunderstruck. He had been following events in Cuba closely, so he sensed that Batista's hold on power was unraveling. All the same, his regime's collapse, and Castro's rapid rise from just a couple of hundred fighters two years earlier, jolted Beals into a suddenly quickened pace. Until then, he had been working on a longer-term work of history, perusing archives for a study of the anti-Catholic Know-Nothings in the United States of the 1850s, to fulfill another book contract Klausner had obtained for him with Hastings House. And he was still limping from the kick to his flank by Carolyn's horse Binkie.

Beals knew instinctively that this was a defining moment. The Cuban Revolution had been launched, and he needed to be there. He called McWilliams, who confirmed that the *Nation* would take stories from him. He packed his things, and two days later, he was on a train from New York to Miami. Once there, he took a ferry to Cuba, reaching Havana on January 5, 1959, where he booked into the colonial-style *Hotel Inglaterra* in the city's old quarter.

Two days later, Castro rode into a jubilant Havana with five thousand of his mostly bearded revolutionary fighters, riding atop armored cars, jeeps, trucks, and Sherman tanks that Batista's regime had bought from the United States for use against them.[27] Beals mingled with the celebrating crowds as they showered the victorious rebels with confetti and waved Cuban flags. He watched as the thirty-two-year-old Castro, dressed in green fatigues and a peaked hat, climbed a rostrum erected on the parade grounds at Camp Columbia where, famously, one of three doves set free by a celebrant chose to land on his shoulder. Picking up the theme of peace, Castro told the forty thousand Cubans who had assembled, that the "military caste has been eliminated." In a two-hour speech, he promised that within days, "we will use our planes to rain shoes, clothing, food and pledges of land reform upon the peasants of Oriente province. Our planes will be symbols of love and not of terror."[28]

Although Castro installed Manuel Urrutia (1901–1981) as President heading a provisional government, Castro alone remained "the arbiter of affairs," Beals reported in the *Nation*. He was also "the hero" not just of his young *guerrilleros*, but of Cuba's youth and students. The country's major professional and civic groups had broken with Batista, and now backed Castro, and he enjoyed the goodwill of a large sector of the Church hierarchy.[29]

The *Nation* published three Beals stories in successive weeks, and the *Christian Century* two others, in which he recounted the Revolution's euphoric first weeks. His mounting admiration for this bold experiment is palpable in these dispatches, as he described life in Havana rapidly resuming its busy routine, a four-day national strike ending peacefully, the garbage and trashed gambling machines carted away.

But he also identified fault-lines. There was the absence of a strong tie between Castro's movement and Cuba's labor unions. Another issue was dealing with the Batista regime's crimes, that is, the need to bring justice to

Batista officials guilty of torture and of murder while also respecting some sort of due process. Beals attended one trial that lasted four hours, in which the prisoner's crimes "were grievous and well-substantiated," and after which the court deliberated for five minutes and pronounced the death sentence. "Two hours later the prisoner was dead," Beals reported. "This was not a show trial. Nearly all the trials that have been held have followed this pattern."[30]

The executions, reaching seventy by mid-January (this number would rise to over five hundred), ignited the first round of tension in revolutionary Cuba's relationship with the United States.[31] This was the most portentous of the emerging fissures, and Beals picked up on it, almost immediately seeking to counter the chorus of criticism already emanating from Washington. Beals warned of the Cubans' hair-trigger sensitivity to the comment January 15 by Illinois Republican US Representative William L. Springer, that nowhere except in Cuba had there been "such a bloodbath" when a dictator took power. Springer's comment was accompanied by a call by US Representative Emanuel Celler, a Democrat from Brooklyn, for a United Nations (UN) investigation of the executions.[32]

"Nothing has done more to solidify the Cuban people behind the revolutionary Government than [these] statements by our Congressmen," Beals wrote.[33] "On every corner, in every bar and restaurant, on every autobus, comes a bitter anti-American reproach," matched and encouraged by Castro who had declared that the United States "will never establish good relations with free Cuba by starting with threats."[34]

In the same piece, Beals criticized the Eisenhower administration's decision to name Philip Bonsal as US Ambassador to Cuba. Bonsal's earlier career had included a stint as an executive with the International Telephone & Telegraph (ITT)–owned Cuban Telephone Company which, Beals reported, had paid a three-million-dollar bribe to have its rates raised by the Batista regime.[35] "Even if Bonsal acts in the most upright manner, he is going to be crucified before long by the Cuban press, and relations between the two countries will be worsened once more."[36]

Beals blamed this myopia among US officialdom and Congressmen on the biases of and curbs imposed on American news media in Cuba under Batista. Honest newsmen, he wrote, could not tell the truth and stay in business on the island. "The failure now," he added, "to present the Cuban picture properly, plus the lack of knowledge of what went on previously, have led to these outbursts in Congress."[37]

While Beals's journalistic coverage of the Cuban Revolution's first months was sympathetic, even effusive, and his criticism of early US reactions sharply pointed, he did harbor some skepticism about Castro. On the eve of the Cuban leader's first visit to the United States in April 1959, Beals wrote his friend, Berkeley historian Lesley Byrd Simpson, that he saw "some good stuff in (Castro), but a lot of phony babble-babble too."[38]

During this early period, official US responses to the Revolution, at least on the surface, remained cordial. Washington recognized Castro's government six days after the revolutionary victory—the second country to do so after Venezuela.[39] In the first six months of 1959, relations were even "rather good" according to one US diplomat.[40] Castro kept himself out of the revolutionary government's first cabinet, headed by Urrutia and which included several middle-of-the-road public figures, but no Communists.[41]

For the US government, the first major irritant arose in March 1959, when the Cuban government "intervened" the Cuban Telephone Company, and the power utility *Compañía Cubana de Electricidad* (Cuban Electricity Company), also US-owned, and reducing rates to where they were before Batista had raised them in 1957.[42] This action came amid a flurry of populist decrees, confiscating properties owned by those associated with Batista's government, reducing by half rents paid by those earning less than $100 a month, and requiring licenses for imports of luxury goods, along with the announcement of a land distribution project in Pinar del Río.[43]

In April, Castro accepted a speaking invitation from the American Society of Newspaper Editors. This visit, concocted by *New York Times* editor Turner Catledge, W. D. Maxwell of the *Chicago Tribune*, and George M. Healy Jr. of the *New Orleans Times-Picayune*, was to have been a one-day dash to Washington, but Castro extended it to three weeks, covering several US states, Canada, Brazil, Argentina, and Uruguay, where he received a generally curious and enthusiastic reception.[44] President Eisenhower, annoyed at the anti-American tenor of Castro's speeches, arranged to be golfing in Georgia during the Cuban leader's visit. Vice-President Nixon spent three hours with him instead, during which he lectured Castro on the dangers of communism, advised him to hold elections, and to welcome foreign capital.[45] After the meeting, Nixon told Eisenhower that Castro had the makings of a strong leader and that, "he is either incredibly naïve about communism or under communist discipline—my guess is the former."[46]

US irritation mounted in May, when an agrarian reform law was promulgated, affecting 40 percent of Cuba's farmland.[47] It prohibited foreigners from owning land, and banned estates over 1,000 acres, or in the case of highly productive sugar and rice plantations, over 3,333 acres. Expropriated owners were offered twenty-year government bonds based on the assessed tax value of the properties—in most cases, grossly undervalued by the owners to evade taxes under Batista—and paying annual interest of 4.5 percent.[48] Many of these were owned by US nationals, who lobbied US Assistant Undersecretary of State Roy R. Rubottom Jr., prompting him to complain to Cuba's ambassador to Washington, demanding more generous compensation to affected landowners.[49] Indeed, American investors' stake in Cuba was significant, with $879 million and $975 million in private US investment in 1958 and 1959 respectively, more than any other Latin American country except oil-rich Venezuela.[50] The Cubans made clear that they had no intention of negotiating.

On Wall Street, Cuban stocks in sugar and the utilities plummeted, and a spate of articles appeared in *Time* and *Newsweek* depicting Castro's Cuba as turning to communism, a contention reinforced by avowed Marxist Ernesto "Che" Guevara's appointment as head of the Agrarian Reform Institute.[51] Castro prodded the resignation of Urrutia as President in July, whom he publicly denounced for raising the issue of communism so as to provoke foreign intervention.[52] Urrutia was replaced by President Osvaldo Dorticós (1919–1983), a lawyer who, as Minister of Revolutionary Laws, had drafted the land reform legislation. Dorticós had been a Communist Party member as a student, but this was unknown to most of the cabinet, who saw him as a moderate; since his student days, he had outwardly adopted the lifestyle of a prominent attorney, serving as head of the Cuban Bar Association.[53]

Beals's keen desire to visit Cuba for a second time in 1959 was stymied by a lack of funds. Still, he was able to draw on notes from his January visit to produce an analysis for the *Nation* that challenged the growing chorus in US media denouncing Castro as a Communist. Published just after Castro's US tour, Beals's article noted that the "hysterical clamor" against Castro was in marked contrast to US media silence when only months earlier, Batista had shuttered newspapers, jailed journalists, destroyed opposition parties, and put the army in charge of labor unions and schools.[54]

Cuba's provisional government had carried out "a tremendous and amazingly competent reconstruction . . . against great odds," Beals wrote, while also defending Castro's contention that "an election now . . . would merely result in automatic victory for himself."[55] Interestingly, the accuracy of this view was confirmed even a year later by an opinion survey conducted in Cuba for the US government, which found 86 percent of Cubans either moderately or fervently supporting Castro.[56]

In late fall, McWilliams offered Beals an advance to return to Cuba to do a "roundup" after Castro's first year in power, but Beals had to delay due to a severe abscess that caused him to lose several teeth and required surgery. In the interim, he vetted—at McWilliams's request—an article for the *Nation* on Cuba, which lauded the Revolution's achievements, by CBS correspondent Robert Taber. Beals judged it "accurate and truthful."[57]

In 1957, just after Herbert Matthews's Castro scoop, Taber had been escorted by Castro associates to interview the rebel leader and spend several days filming his soldiers camped in the Sierra Maestra jungle. He produced another documentary for CBS a year later after traveling with Raúl Castro's column in Oriente.

By late 1959, Taber had grown so dismayed by what he saw as a US media campaign of lies against the Cuban Revolution that he was shifting his posture from journalist to activist. His *Nation* article, which drew on research he had done for a book which Taber would publish in 1961, *M-26: Biography of a Revolution*, emphasized "a virulent press campaign, concocted of ignorance, half-truths, name calling, connotative misdirection and outright fabrication, all tending to erode the first light image of the revolution and to discredit its leadership."[58]

Shortly after Taber's article was published in late January 1960, he invited Beals to a meeting at his Manhattan apartment with him and a New Jersey contractor, Alan Sagner, to discuss setting up a committee to combat "the anti-Cuban . . . counter-revolutionary . . . propaganda with which we are being deluged."[59] Although Beals could not make it, he told Taber that he "heartily backed" what would be called the Fair Play for Cuba Committee (FPCC), offered to help, and authorized that his name be used as an endorsee.[60]

Beals pressed the same theme in a lecture he gave March 9, 1960 on Cuba and Latin America to an audience of seven hundred at New York City's Cooper Union for the Advancement of Science and Art. "We call Castro hysterical," he said. "Who has been more hysterical than our newspaper owners and our Senators and Congressmen?"[61]

Around this time, Castro made moves that further unraveled Cuba's ties with Washington. In February, Soviet Vice-Premier Anastas Mikoyan was lavishly welcomed in Havana, where he signed an agreement under which the USSR would buy one million tons of Cuban sugar annually for five years, more than doubling its largest-ever annual purchase of Cuban sugar to that date and agreed to supply Cuba with Russian crude oil in return.[62]

On March 4, a French munitions ship, *La Coubre*, accidentally exploded in Havana's harbor, killing over seventy-five people and wounding about two hundred.[63] Castro immediately denounced the accident as a US plot against Cuba. Later that month, on March 17, President Eisenhower formally authorized a CIA plan, underway since December 1959, to equip and train Cuban exiles to launch an amphibious assault on Cuba.[64]

Meantime, the FPCC made its first public splash with a full-page ad in the *New York Times* April 6, under the headline, "What is *really* happening in Cuba?" and listing endorsements of twenty-eight writers and intellectuals, including Norman Mailer, James Baldwin, Jean-Paul Sartre, and Simone de Beauvoir. It featured quotes from damning articles about Cuba that had appeared in the Hearst-owned *New York Journal-American*, as well as *US News & World Report*, and *Newsweek*, highlighting, respectively, Cuba's alleged communism, confiscation of property, and chaos. False charges in each case, the ad claimed, citing evidence overlooked by the US reporters. Readers wanting to "know more of the truth about revolutionary Cuba as it is today," were invited to contact the Committee, whose chairman was identified as Waldo Frank, and its co-chairman, Carleton Beals.[65]

Beals, though supportive, had been reluctant to take on the co-chairman role, as he feared it would take too much time away from his writing. "It would have to be on the basis of a certain non-responsibility," he told Taber, adding that he thought Frank made a "fine chairman" and should have direct responsibility.[66] Two weeks later, Beals placed conditions on his support, asking Taber to reassure him that no Communists were part of the FPCC, and that no Cuban government money had been used to publish the ad.[67] With the ad already going to press that same night, Taber had had no time to respond.

Beals's passivity in taking a lead role with FPCC caused a complication when he was contacted by George Sokolsky, the *Journal-American* columnist whose description of Cuba as "a pro-Communist state . . . bargaining with Soviet Russia for the munitions of war" had been denounced as false in the ad. Beals was caught in an awkward bind when Sokolsky demanded to know if Beals could state categorically that no Cuban government money had supported the ad's publication. Beals, not having received the assurance he had sought from Taber, could not offer that guarantee, and so exposed himself to Sokolsky's charge in his syndicated column that the ad's backers "may have let themselves out for hire [by Castro]."[68]

Taber remonstrated with Beals for having "cooperated" with Sokolsky, "by providing him with material which it must have been obvious he would distort for his own slippery purposes."[69] In fact, as would later come to light in testimony before the US Senate Judiciary Committee, the ad had been financed largely by Raúl (Raulito) Roa Jr. of the Cuban Permanent Mission to the United Nations.[70]

Soon after the ad's publication, Beals was invited on an expenses-paid trip to Cuba by none other than Dorticós, the man Castro had installed as President. Beals accepted the invitation, while insisting that his mission include a series of lectures in Havana to justify the Cuban government subsidy for his trip. At the same time, he agreed with McWilliams to file new stories from Cuba for the *Nation*.[71]

A snag delayed his travel plan. Days before his scheduled departure, Beals received a summons to testify before the US Senate Judiciary Committee's Subcommittee on Internal Security, chaired by Democratic US Senator James O. Eastland of Mississippi, now focused on the FPCC as part of a wide-ranging investigation of Communist Party activities in the United States. No stranger to the dangers posed by Red-baiting politicians, Beals was unsettled by the subpoena. As the committee's first witness on FPCC, without an attorney or funds to hire one, he was exceedingly wary. His now-public FPCC connection threatened to draw him into legal trouble he could not afford. At the same time, he was concerned that his planned trip to Cuba was at risk and determined to conceal it. He chose to stifle his defiant instincts, opting instead to be uncharacteristically co-operative with the committee, "abject" in one historian's account. He brushed off the Senators' barbed questions trying to associate him with known Communists, and even offered gratuitous anti-communist remarks.[72]

After the hearing, Beals flew to Havana and spent all of May 1960 in Cuba, traveling to Camagüey, Manzanillo, Yara, Bayamo, Santiago, and the Sierra Maestra. His role with the FPCC now won him interviews with Fidel Castro, as well as his brother Raúl Castro (1931–).[73] Government officials showed up at his Hotel Riviera lobby to escort him on a tour of the new model residential city of six thousand homes under construction just east of Havana, and then to farming cooperatives in Pinar del Rio. He visited a university complex being built that would transform the military barracks at Camp Columbia.

"The famous American writer," as he was often described in Cuban newspapers, was invited to speak to audiences of teachers, workers, and students, often large and enthusiastic, and his comments were reported in the local media. Beals's earlier solidarity with the 1933 Revolution, killed in the egg by US intrigue with Batista, was recalled in newspaper profiles in which this *"amigo de Cuba"* (friend of Cuba) was asked for his views on Cuba's new situation. He was granted a two-hour interview with Education Minister Armando Hart, a Castro intimate, and invited to speak to an audience of academics by Hart's wife Haydee Santamaria, at the *Casa de las Americas*, the new cultural institute she directed.[74] Suddenly, here in revolutionary Cuba, Beals had achieved celebrity status.

He responded in kind to this warm embrace. To the delight of his Cuban hosts, he denounced US policy toward Cuba, as well as America's military-industrial complex, its still-institutionalized racism, and its media whose ownership by a moneyed elite, he charged, undermined its freedom.[75] He even managed a dig at the pro-segregation Senator Eastland, whose committee had questioned him just weeks before, for "keeping 20 million blacks in the US without a vote."[76]

Beals's unusual combination of journalistic chops, fluent Spanish, credibility in progressive circles, and solidarity with the Revolution made a strong impression on Jorge Ricardo Masetti, head of Prensa Latina, the country's fledgling news agency. Masetti was an Argentine journalist who had earlier worked with his fellow Argentine, Che Guevara, to set up a clandestine radio service from the Sierra Maestra during the revolutionary struggle.

After the victory, Masetti was given the task of setting up a news agency that would gather and disseminate both Cuban and international news with a decidedly progressive orientation. Feeling itself increasingly besieged, not just by hostile US policy, but also by negative US media coverage and public opinion against the Revolution, Cuba's leaders looked to Prensa Latina to

Figure 13.2. Carleton Beals and Jorge Ricardo Masetti, head of Cuba's *Prensa Latina* news agency, 1960, are all smiles as they sign a contract for Beals to be a "correspondent-at-large." It would not end happily. *Photo courtesy of the Carleton Beals Collection, Howard Gotlieb Archival Research Center, Boston University, and Ralph Carleton Beals.*

shift perceptions in a more positive direction. It was a knotty challenge: a Gallup poll in the summer of 1960 found that 81 percent of Americans surveyed had "an unfavorable opinion" of Fidel Castro.[77]

More specifically, the new agency's purpose was to counter the influence exerted by Western, and especially US-owned, wire services such as Associated Press (AP) and United Press International (UPI), whose copy dominated United States and global news media. As we have seen, US media coverage of Cuba's revolution had soured by mid-1959 after an initial honeymoon period of friendly curiosity in which Castro was widely depicted as a rebel hero of liberal bent.

Prensa Latina's target audience included not just US media, but newspapers, magazines, radio, and television in Latin America that used US wire service copy. Its campaign of persuasion was an early example of Cuba's soon-to-be-familiar internationalist posture to bolster its own revolution on the global stage by promoting socialist-oriented national liberation movements elsewhere. Prensa Latina sought to challenge, or at least mitigate, the predominance of this US media juggernaut, which the Cuban leaders perceived as locked in a Cold War mindset, implicitly biased against Communism, but also unsympathetic to any socialist or "third way" options that were distinct from the US model of Open Door capitalism.

For the US government, Prensa Latina's own biases and potential reach were seen to pose enough of a threat to warrant close scrutiny. The US Information Agency aggressively monitored the extent to which Prensa Latina dispatches were published in Latin American media, and encouraged US embassy staff to "seek to discredit" Prensa Latina with editors as "unreliable."[78] The Cuban wire service was seen, by US officials, to be implementing the "big-lie technique . . . through (its) false and slanted reporting . . . to create anxiety and tension in other countries of Latin America and to give a slanted picture of the United States."[79] Most US media had the same position on Prensa Latina, either attacking it directly or in UPI's case, sending a circular to newspapers around the world that denounced it as "Communist," and warning them against using its copy.[80]

This propaganda contest in which the United States and Cuba sought to win over public opinion to their competing narratives was a remarkable case study illustrating theories of public discourse at work. Prensa Latina, "Communist" or not, challenged the heretofore dominant US narrative in and about Latin America, and the world, promulgated by US wire services, consistent with the "hegemony" concept posited by Italian Marxist thinker Antonio Gramsci. Cuba's Prensa Latina was also a conscious attack on what French structuralist philosopher and neo-Marxist Louis Althusser would later term the "ideological state apparatus," in this case, of the United States; the news media were a part of this apparatus, he theorized, whose purpose is to sustain elite power in bourgeois societies. This concept was further refined by Michel Foucault, who proposed the idea that power, or the powerful, produce "knowledge and discourses" that discipline the way things are perceived.[81]

Prensa Latina had established bureaus in several Latin American countries and New York City (where its correspondent was a young Gabriel García Márquez), but it lacked a journalist on its roster who could bring real insight to its coverage of US affairs, especially foreign policy. Masetti decided that Beals was uniquely qualified to fill this role, and so approached him during his Havana visit. He proposed that Beals be a correspondent-at-large for Prensa Latina, filing a weekly article on topics of his choosing, in the general field of international affairs, with an emphasis on the United States.[82] Beals, flattered and impressed by the personable thirty-one-year-old Masetti's talent, accepted with alacrity. "It was hard not to like him," Beals wrote, "with his quizzical smile and tousled hair, [and] his generous open spirit."[83] He signed a contract with Masetti in Havana that specified payment of $50 per article.[84]

Another fruitful Havana encounter for Beals was with Lyle Stuart, a freewheeling publisher from New York, also enamored of the Revolution—he was treasurer of the FPCC—and always looking for unorthodox views to promote. Stuart, given to eclectic tastes ranging from radical politics to gambling and erotica, had founded a left-leaning but non-sectarian monthly tabloid, the *Independent*. It was already devoting extensive space to Cuba's unfolding transformation, but Stuart wanted more, so he welcomed Beals as a contributor who combined unusual knowledge with a *sui generis* approach.[85]

For Beals, Stuart's magazine provided another outlet, allowing him to increase his readership and income by adapting some of his Prensa Latina pieces for the *Independent*'s US subscribers, while adding others as well. He also welcomed Stuart's unabashed radicalism and enjoyed his nonconformist Rabelaisian style. Upon their return from Cuba, Stuart and his wife, Mary Louise, invited him to their New York City home to feast on Hawaiian food and abundant libations. Stuart was "a truly nice guy," Beals mused, who "aims to print what no one else will print, or is afraid to print."[86] In addition to writing for Stuart's paper, Beals also gave him referrals to key Cuban contacts. He was also filing at this time to *Política*, a left-wing monthly published in Mexico City.

Beals's dispatches for Prensa Latina, ranging from analysis of Eisenhower's cancelled visit to Japan after Tokyo riots against the Japanese-US security pact, to a story on a pacifists' caravan protesting French nuclear tests in Algeria, gained valuable currency for the upstart agency, as newspapers from Colombia, Japan, and the Soviet Union picked them up.[87]

At the same time—this coinciding almost exactly with John F. Kennedy's (1917–1963) US presidential nomination—Beals's article, "Cuba: Victim or Aggressor?" was published in the *Nation*, accompanied by an editorial, "Go Slow (on Cuba), Goliath," warning against US intervention.[88] "Thrilling stuff," the *Nation*'s China correspondent Anna Louise Strong wrote to editor McWilliams from Peking, which she said she was passing on to the Chinese government, whose leaders "are much impressed with the Cubans."[89]

While Beals found new outlets for his journalism, another previously reliable one, the liberal Protestant *Christian Century* now turned his work down, apparently seeing in it a new, too-far-left tilt.[90] Despite this, along with the "subtle snooping" by federal secret agents triggered by his Cuban activism, Beals rejoiced in his new role with Prensa Latina. "It is about the only time in my life that I've been free to write what I wanted in the way I want," he told Ernestine Evans.[91]

By the fall of 1960, US public attention was increasingly riveted on Cuba, with widespread opprobrium mixed with mounting alarm. Castro delivered a record-long four-and-half-hour speech to the UN General Assembly September 26, denouncing US imperialism and aggressive American moves against Cuba, such as its order in July to cut US sugar purchases. He depicted Cuba's struggle as being in the forefront of a broader one waged by the oppressed poor in all developing countries against the United States and its capitalist and colonialist allies. While singling out the US government and monopoly interests for his sharpest invective, Castro also appealed for solidarity from the American people. He mentioned Beals and Waldo Frank by name, as "distinguished intellectuals" whose example of solidarity with Cuba made it impossible for Cuba to see the US *people* as enemies.[92] Throughout the speech, the *New York Times* reported, Soviet Premier Nikita Khrushchev (1894–1971) directed applause from the socialist bloc delegates, like "the leader of a Russian choir . . . motioning with upward sweeps of his open hands for more enthusiasm."[93]

Castro, more truculent this time than during his first US visit as Cuba's leader the year before, had a major impact on public consciousness thanks, in no small part, to guidance from FPCC activists. On Taber's advice, the Cuban delegation decamped from their upscale Shelburne Hotel in downtown Manhattan, miffed when the hotel's manager demanded a $10,000 advance damage deposit. Taber enlisted the help of Nation of Islam leader Malcolm X (1925–1965) to gain space for Castro and his handlers at Harlem's modest Theresa Hotel, where the Cuban leader held court with Khrushchev and Indian Prime Minister Jawaharlal Nehru (1889–1964), in addition to Malcolm. Castro was also the guest of honor at a reception there organized by the FPCC team and attended by leading New York hip literati and radical activists, black and white. Beals was invited but chose not to attend.

Amid the breakneck pace Beals had set, producing mostly Cuban-oriented journalism through the summer and fall of 1960, his *Brass-Knuckle Crusade*, a popular history of the "Great Know-Nothing Conspiracy, 1820–1860," was published in late June by Hastings House.[94] He also found time to deliver speeches on Cuba at the New School for Social Research, and at the first major FPCC rally in Manhattan, where he shared the stage before 1,500 people with I. F. Stone, and Leo Huberman, of the Marxist *Monthly Review*, who had coauthored a book on Cuba with fellow *Monthly Review* editor Paul Sweezy.[95]

The October 20 rally marked the apogee of consensus among New York intellectuals in support of Cuba's Revolution. These included Marxists such as Huberman and Sweezy, as well as sociologist C. Wright Mills, and erstwhile Communist—and FPCC chairman—Waldo Frank, all of whom published books on Cuba during this period that expressed solidarity with the Cuban revolutionaries, while denouncing official Washington's mounting hostility toward them.[96]

The FPCC rally also came on the same day that presidential candidate Kennedy, whom Castro had derided in his UN speech as an "ignorant, illiterate millionaire," called for aid to Cuban groups seeking to topple Castro, a demand he would repeat the following night in his fourth televised debate with Nixon. It also coincided with the recall to Washington of US ambassador to Cuba, Philip Bonsal, and came a week after Eisenhower imposed a trade embargo on Cuba.[97]

Candidate Kennedy's call for aid to anti-Castro groups sought to show him as an anti-Communist every bit as uncompromising as Nixon. It was also mischievously shrewd, as Kennedy knew, from the secret July 23 briefing he had received from CIA Director Allen Dulles, that Eisenhower had already approved US support for Cuban insurgents who were at that moment being trained at camps in Florida and Guatemala. Nixon could not divulge these activities, of course, so was stuck with haplessly defending a more restrained US strategy toward Cuba that did not, in fact, exist.

In a *Nation* piece, "Cuba's Invasion Jitters," published just after Kennedy's election in November, Beals strongly suggested that a US-backed assault on Cuba was being planned. Citing the US government advisory that American citizens should leave Cuba, and Cuban government claims that army transport planes and other materiel were being assembled in Guatemala and Haiti for use against Cuba, he warned that, "unhappily, the signs are that we intend to proceed on our present path of folly."[98]

More grounds for these fears were added a week later, when McWilliams, in a *Nation* editorial, quoted Ronald Hilton, director of Stanford University's Institute of Hispanic-American Studies, who had learned during a recent visit to Guatemala that the CIA had purchased a million-dollar tract of land there, where it had built a military base with an airstrip. A Guatemalan newspaper, *La Hora*, had reported on October 30 that the base was being used by the CIA to train Cuban counter-revolutionaries, Hilton said. McWilliams's editorial called for public pressure on the Administration "to abandon this dangerous and hair-brained project," and urged US media with reporters in Guatemala to follow up on the story.[99]

The *New York Times* did so, and on January 10, 1961, ran its own front-page story on the base. But the piece, by the paper's Mexico-based correspondent Paul Kennedy, had a strangely restrained, even disingenuous tone. It accepted at face value Guatemalan President Miguel Ramón Ydigoras's (1895–1982) suggestion that the base was to shore up his country's defenses against an eventual Cuban attack *on Guatemala* and failed to challenge the US embassy's "complete silence" on the topic.[100] The Eisenhower administration, now in its final days, declined to comment on it, while a State Department spokesman claimed to know nothing about it.[101]

After President John F. Kennedy's (JFK) inauguration, and his decision to proceed with the Cuban invasion plan, he pressed *New York Times* publisher Arthur Hays Sulzberger to suppress, or at least downplay stories on preparations for it. Similar stories were spiked in early 1961 by the *New Republic* and the *Miami Herald*, after Kennedy aide Arthur Schlesinger Jr. and CIA Director Allen Dulles, respectively, intervened with editors.[102] But stories emerged elsewhere, and the *New York Times* could not ignore them. A frenzy of rumors was sustained, accompanied by an oddly schizoid situation in which the assault was at once denied and expected.

As drumbeats foreshadowing the Bay of Pigs grew louder, Beals's pro-Castro stance also grew more explicit now that he was clearly associated with both Prensa Latina and the FPCC. Among his interventions for Prensa Latina was a fierce denunciation of the Inter-American Press Association, a network of conservative publishers across Latin America and the United States, for having excluded the Cuban news agency from its annual conference in Bogotá. The ban arose, Beals said, from "unproven charges" against Prensa Latina by *Chicago Tribune* correspondent Jules Dubois, whom Beals dismissed as "an ex-secret agent of the US government, Col. Jules Dubois."[103]

On December 23, 1960, Beals flew back to Havana, this time with *Independent* publisher Lyle Stuart, who paid for his trip.[104] Also spending Christmas and New Year's in Cuba were 326 students from campuses across the United States on an FPCC-organized tour to celebrate the Cuban Revolution's second anniversary, as well as over two hundred Americans on a tour organized by New York's *National Guardian*.[105] By this time, the FPCC organization claimed about seven thousand members nationwide, as well as twenty-seven "adult" chapters and forty campus-based "Student Councils."[106] The US State Department had tried to dissuade the FPCC group from going to Cuba, and their flight was delayed at the last minute when the Cuban pilot who had flown the plane to New York to pick them up defected. Another pilot was hastily dispatched to replace him.[107]

The "Christmas tour" was a remarkably successful outreach effort by the FPCC. The young activists visited cooperative farms, housing complexes, and factories, and concluded their tour by attending a major speech by Castro, followed by a reception he hosted. They would return to their campuses to give speeches and write articles for the student press on their Cuban experience. It was altogether too much goodwill for Eisenhower. He imposed a ban on travel to Cuba by Americans on January 3, 1961, while the students were still in Havana.

Beals was still in Cuba too, where he told the Havana daily *El Mundo*'s Waldo Medina, that such decrees made him feel "more like a citizen of Cuba than my own country . . . when the US changes its policy, I will start feeling like a citizen there, but with Cuba still at the center of my heart."[108] Invasion was an ever-present danger, he added, as much under Kennedy's incoming administration as under Eisenhower's, as the US government was "the world's most reactionary," and so dominated the country's media that "even if the government sends young boys to hell, their mothers will not protest."[109] The story was published alongside a UPI story on the no-longer-secret Guatemalan air base.

Castro responded to the travel ban, tit for tat, in early January 1961 by restricting accredited personnel allowed at the US embassy in Havana—"a nest of spies," he said—to just eleven. Eisenhower, in one of his last acts before Kennedy's inauguration, closed the embassy and ended diplomatic relations with Cuba.

Beals returned to Killingworth from Havana in mid-January, having obtained agreement from Masetti to do a three-month tour of Latin America during which he would research and write stories on the region for Prensa Latina, while also giving lectures and media interviews on the Cuban revolutionary process. He delivered lectures in the United States too, which, combined with his FPCC involvement, provoked the FBI to investigate Beals once again, after a hiatus of nearly a decade. One FBI report relied on opinions provided by a Temple University professor, Clement G. Motten, who had participated with Beals in a January 22, 1961, panel discussion on Cuba in Philadelphia. Beals was a "special pleader" for Castro, Motten said, "[who] must be in the pay of the Castro regime."[110]

On March 14, 1961, he began his new journey with a flight to Mexico City, during which he read the *New York Times* front-page story on President Kennedy's White House speech to Latin diplomats the day before, in which he launched the Alliance for Progress, a ten-year development plan for Latin America backed by $500-million in US aid.[111]

A month later, of course, this carrot was complemented by the stick: the infamous Bay of Pigs invasion. Beals was in Guayaquil, Ecuador on April 15, when news broke of the amphibious attack on Cuba. He addressed a gathering of the country's Union of Journalists that evening, telling them that Ecuador—then under the rule of populist President José María Velasco Ibárra (1893–1979)—and all of Latin America, should denounce "this kind of terrorism." They should express their support for Cuba's government and its people, he urged, in remarks reported the next day in a leftist daily, *La Nacion.*[112]

At his next stops in Lima, La Paz, Santiago, and Montevideo, Beals gave more speeches at universities, along with radio and print interviews, usually in left-wing media, in which he repeated his condemnations of the US-backed invasion by anti-Castro Cubans, many of them *batistianos* (Batista loyalists), who had by now been routed by the Cuban army.[113] His audiences had grown in angry protest at the invasion; at San Marcos University in Lima, he addressed a crowd of more than two thousand, which then spilled out into the streets where their demonstration was promptly circled by police.[114]

Everywhere, Beals was respectfully received by media and, often enough, government officials, even Presidents. He was also discreetly tailed by US diplomatic staff who reported on his meetings and public remarks to Washington. Indeed, a review of the US Information Agency's archives on Prensa Latina attests to the tenacity and extent of its effort to counter and disable the upstart Cuban news service and, consequently, its irritation with Beals, described in its reports to Washington as "the Castro apologist" and "the writer of leftist hue."[115] The US Information Agency produced a critical report on Beals's trip and shared it with the FBI's New Haven office, which had already placed Beals's mail, bank transactions and foreign travel under surveillance.[116]

In Bolivia, Beals met with President Victor Paz Estenssorro (1907–2001), visited a resettlement project at Pillapi with Roberto Jordán Pando, Minister of Campesino Affairs, and held a two-hour press conference hosted by Teddy Córdova, editor-in-chief of the pro-government daily *La Nación*, and also Bolivia's Prensa Latina correspondent.[117] At the latter, he dismissed the Alliance for Progress as "an insult," while defending the Castro regime as "fighting the battle for Latin America."[118]

Beals's Latin tour was followed only weeks later by Adlai Stevenson, US Ambassador to the United Nations, whose itinerary was roughly the same, covering ten countries. In Brazil, both men were interviewed by the Sao Paulo newspaper *Jornal do Brasil* on the same day.[119]

Stevenson sought to assuage disgruntled Latin leaders who, while not fervent Castro supporters, were deeply disturbed by what they saw as a violation of international law by the United States. Overall, reaction to the Bay of Pigs in Latin American political and media circles was sharply negative, even among those who had welcomed JFK's Alliance for Progress speech. A typical example was in Uruguay, where *Acción*, the newspaper of the Colorado List 15 Party, edited by its leader Luís Batlle Barres, ran an editorial, "It can't be!" It called the invasion an *atropello* [outrage]" unequalled in North American history for its "impudence and disregard of all international obligations."[120] A survey conducted in May for the US Information Agency in Mexico City, Rio and Lima found at least two-thirds of respondents opposed to unilateral US invasion of Cuba.[121] Stevenson acknowledged this upon his return to Washington, telling reporters after briefing Kennedy on his trip that "US involvement" in the invasion was generally unpopular in Latin America, "where the principle of non-intervention is a religion."[122]

Although Beals, through his "Yankee friend of Cuba" persona, had been among those who fed the swelling disapproval that Stevenson now sought to contain, his informal public diplomacy on behalf of the Cuban regime would soon end. The Bay of Pigs fallout within the Cuban government had engulfed Prensa Latina. Masetti, Beals's sponsor, had been pushed out by Communist hardliners who seized control of the news agency in the wake of the invasion. Beals was suddenly made aware of this change, and its draconian implications, upon his arrival in Montevideo in late May. The local Prensa Latina correspondent told him that he would have to seek advance approval for his public remarks from Prensa Latina's new director, a Spanish *émigré* named Fernando Revueltas.

Beals was furious. He cut short his relationship with Prensa Latina on the spot by firing off an angry missive to Revueltas. "Since you are new in your post, you are apparently unaware that you have no right to instruct any correspondent anywhere to clear what I may say or write with your office before it is released," Beals wrote.[123] "I am an independent writer who has agreed to send you articles for payment . . . what I write and say is therefore none of your business."[124]

His vehement response was partly influenced by pique at Prensa Latina editing heavy-handed enough to so distort some of his copy that its messages wound up being the opposite of what Beals had intended. He appealed for understanding to his closest friend in the Cuban leadership, Haydee Santamaría, who promised to pass on his complaints to President Dorticós.[125] But as Dorticós had ultimately approved Masetti's removal, reportedly upon the demands of the Communist-dominated Cuban newspaper and newsworkers union, he was not now going to intervene on Beals's behalf.[126] Interestingly, Beals was not alone in parting ways with Prensa Latina after Masetti's dismissal; Gabriel García Márquez left, or was fired, at about the same time. Both men had been hired by Masetti.[127]

Beals took the dispute public with a blistering article in the *Independent*, in which he excoriated Prensa Latina's new managers and their intrigue as "a type-example of how a revolution devours its own children."[128] He blamed the debacle on the Communists' "greediness for power in the organization," and dismissed Revueltas, a compromise candidate whom Dorticós had selected as director to end the turmoil, as their pliable servant. The story must have puzzled attentive *Independent* readers as an about-face reversal of Beals's piece in the same paper the previous month. Then, he had reported on coercion *against* the Cuban agency in the United States and elsewhere, by denial of visas—even to pass through Miami, an aviation hub for Caribbean basin travel—harassment, arrest, and deportation.[129]

The only response Beals received was from Prensa Latina's New York bureau chief, Angel Boán, to whom he had written seeking reimbursement for travel expenses. Boán, after having read Beals's second *Independent* article, told him acidly: "Despite your white hair and your old age, which may have played a role in this unfortunate episode, I am duty-bound to call you by your name: old scoundrel (*canalla*)."[130]

Thus ended Beals's association not just with Prensa Latina, but also soon thereafter with the FPCC, itself thrown into an existential crisis by the Bay of

Pigs fiasco. Following his acrimonious break with Prensa Latina, Beals was denied a visa by the Cuban government, and of course, now faced the US-imposed travel ban as well. A few months after his return to Killingworth on June 28, he told Richard Gibson, formerly Taber's colleague at CBS and now heading the FPCC, that he thought it "rather ridiculous" that he should appear on a FPCC platform, "while I remain repudiated by the Cuban government."[131]

In fact, Beals had always been uncomfortably reluctant in fully embracing his public role with FPCC. He joined the committee without much reflection, realizing its personal cost and danger to his livelihood only once he had already been pulled into its controversial vortex. While in Cuba during the FPCC Christmas tour, for example, Beals had been publicly—and wrongly—identified in the *Boston Daily Record* as the FPCC group's leader. Klausner told him this resulted in the loss of potential book contracts, adding to the cold shoulder he had already received from the *Christian Century*.[132]

Cuba placed Beals before a dilemma. He needed to maintain enough detachment to protect his credibility as a journalist. But he also felt a moral obligation to take a public stand against America's Cuba policy—backed by almost all US media—which he despised as the reprise of a familiar theme: US imperialism, or neo-imperialism, now directed in a nuclear age by President Kennedy, whom he perceived as dangerous and unprincipled. The polarized Cold War logic that prevailed while Cuba became America's dominant foreign policy issue in 1960 had made it extremely difficult for a journalist to hew to an independent line. After Bay of Pigs, it became impossible.

The imagined space for "fair play" between Cuba and the United States, always narrow, had vanished now that the two countries were declared enemies. Following the Bay of Pigs, the FPCC became something of a political orphan, as the hardening of positions in Washington and Havana made its call for "fair play" seem naïve at best. Also, in practical terms, the Cuba travel ban deprived FPCC of its most important activity, a key factor leading one of the Committee's key organizers, Berta Green of the Trotskyist Socialist Workers' Party, to take her followers out of it.[133]

In this climate, journalists were forced, willy-nilly, to choose sides, or move on to other issues. Beals remained sympathetic to the Cuban Revolution's ideals, and did not publicly criticize Castro, or his regime, even as it grew explicitly Communist and Soviet-aligned. But he quickly sought a lower profile in the debate, having been burned by his experience with Prensa Latina, and bruised by the FPCC affiliation.

## NOTES

1. Carolyn Kennedy to Carleton Beals, June 20, 1950, Carleton Beals Collection (CBC), Howard Gotlieb Archival Research Center, Boston University (hereafter cited CBC).

2. New York Times, "George P. Kennedy, Banker, Dies at 64," *New York Times*, March 1, 1946, 22.
3. Carleton Beals to David Legerman, July 16, 1955, CBC.
4. Carleton Beals to Ernestine Evans, July 28, 1955, CBC.
5. Victor S. Navasky, *A Matter of Opinion* (New York: Picador, 2005), 174.
6. See Tad Szulc, *Fidel: A Critical Portrait* (New York: Harper Collins, 1986), 445–53; and Anthony DePalma, *The Man Who Invented Fidel: Castro, Cuba, and Herbert L. Matthews of the New York Times* (New York: Public Affairs, 2006).
7. Carleton Beals, "The New Crime of Cuba," *Nation*, June 29, 1957, 566.
8. Beals, "New Crime of Cuba," 567–68.
9. Carleton Beals, Cuban Manifesto, in "Letters," *Nation*, September 27, 1957.
10. Carleton Beals, "Haiti Under the Gun," *Nation* 185, no. 1, July 6, 1957, 3.
11. Telegram George G. Kirstein to Carleton Beals, June 20, 1957, CBC.
12. Beals, "Haiti Under the Gun," 4.
13. Beals, "Haiti Under the Gun," 3.
14. Beals, "Haiti Under the Gun," 8.
15. Carleton Beals, "The Church in Cuba's Civil War," *Christian Century*, July 31, 1957, 915–17; Beals, "Blackjacking Cuban Labor," *Christian Century*, August 21, 1957.
16. Carleton Beals to Ralph L. Beals, June 20, 1958, CBC.
17. C. Beals to R. L. Beals (1958), CBC.
18. Carleton Beals to William Loeb, January 18, 1958, CBC; see also *John Eliot: The Man Who Loved the Indians* (New York: Messner, 1957).
19. Carleton Beals, *House in Mexico* (New York: Hastings House, 1958).
20. Hubert Herring, Review of *House in Mexico*, by Carleton Beals, *New York Herald-Tribune*, July 20, 1958.
21. Carolyn Kennedy Beals, Interview by Christopher Neal, October 10, 2001, Madison, CT.
22. See Max Paul Friedman, *Rethinking Anti-Americanism: The History of an Exceptional Concept in American Foreign Relations* (Cambridge: Cambridge University Press, 2012), 145–46.
23. Carleton Beals, "Viva Nixon!" *Christian Century*, June 18, 1958, 716–18.
24. William G. Key, Administrative Assistant to the Vice President, to Harold E. Fey, Editor, *Christian Century*, June 19, 1958, CBC.
25. Carleton Beals to Harold E. Fey, Editor, *Christian Century*, June 19, 1958, CBC.
26. Carleton Beals to Ralph Beals, June 20, 1958, CBC.
27. R. H. Phillips, "Havana Welcomes Castro at End of Triumphal Trip," *New York Times*, January 8, 1959, 1, 9.
28. Carleton Beals, "Revolution Without Generals," *Nation*, January 17, 1959, 43.
29. Beals, "Revolution Without Generals," 45.
30. Carleton Beals, "Cuba in Revolution," *Christian Century*, February 4, 1959, 131.
31. R. H. Phillips, "Castro Says Cuba Wants Good Ties with Washington," *New York Times*, January 16, 1959, 3.
32. John D. Morris, "US Will Speed Envoy to Havana, *New York Times*, January 16, 1959, 3.
33. Carleton Beals, "As Cuba Sees It," *Nation*, January 31, 1959, 83.
34. Beals, "As Cuba Sees It," 83.
35. Beals, "As Cuba Sees It," 83.
36. Beals, "As Cuba Sees It," 85.
37. Beals, "As Cuba Sees It," 85.
38. Carleton Beals to Lesley Byrd Simpson, April 12, 1959, CBC.
39. Szulc, *Fidel*, 480–81.
40. Wayne S. Smith, *The Closest of Enemies: A Personal and Diplomatic History of the Castro Years* (New York: W. W. Norton, 1988), 43.
41. W. S. Smith, *Closest of Enemies*, 43.

42. Philip W. Bonsal, *Cuba, Castro, and the United States* (Pittsburgh, PA: University of Pittsburgh Press, 1971), 44; Leland L. Johnson, "US Business Interests in Cuba and the Rise of Castro," *World Politics* 17, no. 3 (1965): 444–45, https://doi.org/10.2307/2009288.

43. Hugh Thomas, *Cuba, or The Pursuit of Freedom*, updated ed. (New York: Da Capo Press, 1998), 1201.

44. DePalma, *Man Who Invented Fidel*, 147–48; Bonsal, *Cuba*, 66.

45. Jules R. Benjamin, *The United States and the Origins of the Cuban Revolution: An Empire of Liberty in an Age of National Liberation* (Princeton, NJ: Princeton University Press, 1990), 178.

46. Alan H. Luxenberg, "Did Eisenhower Push Castro into the Arms of the Soviets?" *Journal of Interamerican Studies and World Affairs* 30, no. 1 (1988): 47–48, https://doi.org/10.2307/165789.

47. Thomas, *Cuba, or The Pursuit of Freedom*, 1215–16.

48. Thomas, *Cuba, or The Pursuit of Freedom*, 1216.

49. Benjamin, *United States and the Origins of the Cuban Revolution*, 180.

50. U. S. National Archives and Records Administration (NARA), US Information Agency, Office of Research and Analysis, Research Note 11–61, April 24, 1961, in Fact Book on Latin America, NARA-MD, RG306/A1/1029/1960-62.

51. Robert Smith Thompson, *The Missiles of October: The Declassified Story of John F. Kennedy and the Cuban Missile Crisis* (New York: Simon & Schuster, 1993), 87.

52. Benjamin, *United States and the Origins of the Cuban Revolution*, 184.

53. Szulc, *Fidel*, 466–67.

54. Carleton Beals, "The Squeeze on Castro," *Nation*, May 2, 1959, 402.

55. Beals, "Squeeze on Castro," 402.

56. Lloyd A. Free, *Attitudes of the Cuban People Toward the Castro Regime in the late Spring of 1960* (Princeton, NJ: Institute of International Social Research, 1960); U.S. National Archives and Records Administration (NARA), US Information Agency, Research & Reference Service, NARA IRI. CV.4.

57. Carleton Beals to Carey McWilliams, December 29, 1959, CBC.

58. Robert Taber, "Castro's Cuba," *Nation*, January 27, 1960, 64; see also Robert Taber, *M-26: Biography of a Revolution* (New York: Lyle Stuart, 1961).

59. Robert Taber to Carleton Beals, February 9, 1960, CBC.

60. Carleton Beals to Robert Taber, February 10, 1960, CBC.

61. Carleton Beals, Lecture to Cooper Union for the Advancement of Science and Art, March 9, 1960, New York City, Speech text, CBC, box 149.

62. Bonsal, *Cuba*, 131.

63. Thomas, *Cuba, or The Pursuit of Freedom*, 1269.

64. Stephen G. Rabe, *Eisenhower and Latin America: The Foreign Policy of Anticommunism* (Chapel Hill: University of North Carolina Press, 1988), 129.

65. Fair Play for Cuba Committee, "What is (Really) Happening in Cuba?" (advertisement), *New York Times*, April 6, 1960, 33.

66. Carleton Beals to Robert Taber, March 24, 1960, CBC.

67. Carleton Beals to Robert Taber, April 5, 1960, CBC.

68. George Sokolsky, Syndicated Column, *Middletown Press* (Connecticut), King Features Syndicate, April 21, 1960.

69. Robert Taber to Carleton Beals, April 22, 1960, CBC.

70. Testimony of Dr. Charles A. Santos-Buch, at US Senate, Hearings before the Subcommittee of the Senate Judiciary Committee to Investigate the Administration of the Internal Security Act and Other Internal Security Laws (on the Fair Play for Cuba Committee [FPCC]), 20 days of testimony, 1960–1963, January 10, 1961, 76–81, http://onlinebooks.library.upenn.edu/webbin/book/lookupname?key=United States. Congress. Senate. Committee on the Judiciary. Subcommittee to Investigate the Administration of the Internal Security Act and Other Internal Security Law (accessed May 13, 2021).

71. Carey McWilliams, *The Education of Carey McWilliams* (New York: Simon & Schuster, 1979), 228.

72. See Van Gosse, *Where the Boys Are: Cuba, Cold War America and the Making of a New Left* (London and New York: Verso, 1993), 166n12; and US Senate, Hearings before the Subcommittee of the Senate Judiciary Committee to Investigate the Administration of the Internal Security Act and Other Internal Security Laws (on the Fair Play for Cuba Committee), April 29, 1960, 1–12.

73. Carleton Beals to Lyle Stuart, May 22, 1960, CBC.

74. Carleton Beals to Carolyn Beals, May 27, 1959, CBC.

75. "Movilización obrera contra agresiones a Cuba acuerda el Plenario de la CTC (Cuban Workers Confederation) – Condena el Escritor Carleton Beals las actividades contra Cuba que se están realizando en los círculos imperialistas de EE. UU., *Hoy* (Havana), May 17, 1960; "Haré todo lo posible para que en mi país se conozca la gran fuerza de la Revolución Cubana," *El Mundo* (Havana), June 1, 1960, CBC.

76. *El Mundo*, ibid.

77. Richard E. Welch, Jr., *Response to Revolution: The United States and the Cuban Revolution, 1959–1961* (Chapel Hill: University of North Carolina Press, 1985), 217n.

78. U. S. National Archives and Records Administration (NARA), Lafe Allen, Confidential Joint USIA-State Message to all posts, October 26, 1959, NARA-MD, RG 306/P223/Container 6, USIA Office of Research and Analysis, 1960–61.

79. U. S. National Archives and Records Administration (NARA), US Information Agency, Office of Research and Analysis, Research Note-12–61, May 5, 1961, Recent Trends in Cuban Propaganda, NARA-MD, RG306/A1-1029.

80. Carleton Beals to Lyle Stuart, June 28, 1960, CBC.

81. See Walter L. Hixson, *The Myth of American Diplomacy: National Identity and US Foreign Policy* (New Haven, CT: Yale University Press, 2008). See also Louis Althusser, *Lenin and Philosophy, and Other Essays*, trans. Ben Brewster (New York: Monthly Review Press, 1971; Michel Foucault, *Power/Knowledge: Selected Interviews and Other Writings, 1972–1977*, ed. Colin Gordon (New York: Pantheon, 1980).

82. Carleton Beals to Prensa Latina, June 5, 1960, CBC.

83. Carleton Beals, "Shakeup at Latin-American News Agency Threatens Its Integrity and Future Impact," *Independent* (New York), July 1961.

84. About $437 in 2021.

85. Lyle Stuart to Carleton Beals, May 31, 1960, CBC.

86. Carleton Beals to Bob Taber, June 26, 1960, CBC.

87. Jorge Ricardo Masetti to Carleton Beals, July 21, 1960, CBC.

88. Carleton Beals, "Cuba: Victim or Agressor [*sic*]? Report from Havana (1)," *Nation*, July 23, 1960.

89. Anna Louise Strong to Carey McWilliams, September 5, 1960, CBC.

90. Carleton Beals to Robert Taber, June 26, 1960, CBC.

91. Carleton Beals to Ernestine Evans, August 12, 1960, CBC.

92. David Deutschmann and Deborah Schnookal, eds., *Fidel Castro Reader* (North Melbourne: Ocean Press, 2008), 185.

93. Sam Pope Brewer, "Castro Gets His Applause Mainly from Soviet bloc, Led by Khrushchev—Latins Show Little Interest," *New York Times*, September 27, 1960, 20.

94. Carleton Beals, *Brass-Knuckle Crusade: The Great Know-Nothing Conspiracy, 1820–1860* (New York: Hastings House, 1960).

95. Fair Play for Cuba Community (FPCC) newsletter; Leo Huberman and Paul M. Sweezy, *Cuba: Anatomy of a Revolution* (New York: Monthly Review Press, 1960).

96. See Rafael Rojas, *Fighting Over Fidel: The New York Intellectuals and the Cuban Revolution*, trans. Carl Good (Princeton, NJ: Princeton University Press, 2016). Rojas reviews the fertile 1960s debate among left-leaning American intellectuals, including writers, Beats, and Black activists on Cuba's revolution, defining nuanced differences among them based on ideology, the changing geopolitical stakes, and the Cuban leadership's shifting ideological positions based on Cold War calculations. See also C. Wright Mills, *Listen Yankee: The Revolution in Cuba* (New York: Ballantine Books, 1960); and Waldo Frank, *Cuba: Prophetic Island* (New York: Marzani & Munsell, 1961).

97. E. W. Kenworthy, "US Recalls Ambassador In Cuba for Extended Stay, *New York Times*, October 21, 1960, 1, 4; Thompson, *Missiles of October*, 101.

98. Carleton Beals, "Cuba's Invasion Jitters," *Nation* 191, no. 16, November 12, 1960, 360–62.

99. Carey McWilliams, "Are We Training Cuban Guerrillas?" *Nation* 191, no. 17, November 19, 1960, 378.

100. Paul P. Kennedy, "US Helps Train An Anti-Castro Force At Secret Guatemalan Air-Ground Base," *New York Times*, January 10, 1961.

101. See Gosse, *Where the Boys Are*, 211; McWilliams, *Education*, 228–30; and Peter Kornbluh, "Cuba Libre," *Nation* (150th Anniversary ed.), April 2015, 60–63.

102. D. D. Guttenplan, *American Radical: The Life and Times of I. F. Stone* (New York: Farrar, Straus, and Giroux, 2009), 353–54.

103. Carleton Beals's statement to the President of the Sociedad Interamericana de Prensa (SIP) (Inter-American Press Association) in Bogotá, October 1960, CBC.

104. Carleton Beals to Angel Boán, December 12, 1960, CBC.

105. Gosse, *Where the Boys Are*, 161.

106. Peter Kihss, "Pro-Castro Body Reports US Gain," *New York Times*, November 20, 1960; and Gosse, *Where the Boys Are*, 207.

107. Skye Stephenson, "International Education Flows between the United States and Cuba (1959–2005): Policy Winds and Exchange Flows," in *Cuban Studies 37*, ed. Louis A. Pérez Jr. (Pittsburgh, PA: University of Pittsburgh Press, 2006), 129.

108. Waldo Medina, "Entrevista al Escritor Carleton Beals - Cuba Despertó a los Pueblos Sonolientos," *El Mundo* (Havana), January 11, 1961, CBC.

109. Medina, "Entrevista al Escritor Carleton Beals" (1961), CBC.

110. US Department of Justice, Federal Bureau of Investigation Files on Carleton Beals, Washington, DC, New Haven, Special Agent John J. Ward, *Carleton Beals: Internal Security: Cuba Registration Act* (NH 100-14584, Bureau File 100-333614, August 10, 1961; NW#48582 DocId: 32988232), 8–9.

111. W. H. Lawrence, "President Gives 10-year Aid Plan to Latin America," *New York Times*, March 14, 1961.

112. *La Nación* (Guayaquil), April 16, 1961, CBC; U. S. National Archives and Records Administration (NARA), College Park, Maryland, Foreign Service Despatch, American Consulate General Guayaquil, April 24, 1961, NARA-MD, RG 84, NND 959107.

113. Teddy Córdova-Claure, "Ni La Libre Empresa Ni El Comunismo Han Encontrado El Camino' Dijo Beals" (Neither Free Enterprise Nor Communism has Found the Way, says Beals), *La Nacion* (La Paz), April 26, 1961; "El Personaje de la Semana Carleton Beals" (Personality of the Week, Carleton Beals), *El Pueblo* (La Paz), April 24, 1961; "John Kennedy, 'Un Hombre Frustrado, Bastante Poco Sensato y Muy Peligroso' Dijo Carleton Beals, Famoso Escritor Norteamericano" (John Kennedy 'a frustrated, very unwise and dangerous man' says Beals, Famous American Writer), *El Siglo* (Santiago), May 5, 1961; "Yanqui Defiende a Cuba: Presentamos a Carleton Beals, El Amigo de los Latinoamericanos" (Yankee Defends Cuba: Introducing Carleton Beals, Friend of Latin Americans), *Clarín* (Santiago), May 8, 1961, CBC.

114. Carleton Beals to Haydee Santamaría, June 15, 1961, CBC.

115. U.S. National Archives and Records Administration (NARA), College Park, Maryland, Foreign Service Despatch, Howard I. Blutstein, Second Secretary, La Paz, to Department of State, "Activities of Carleton Beals." May 26, 1961, NARA-MD, RG59/920.6211/5-2661/NND949612; Foreign Service Despatch, Ward P. Allen, Guayaquil, April 24, 1961, NARA-MD, RG59/NND959107.

116. US Department of Justice, Federal Bureau of Investigation Files on Carleton Beals, Washington, DC, New Haven, Special Agent John J. Ward, *Carleton Beals: Internal Security – Cuba Registration Act* (NH 100-14584, Bureau File 100-333614, February 2, 1961; May 26, 1961 & August 10, 1961; NW# 48582 DocId 32988232).

117. Howard I. Blutstein, US Department of Justice, Federal Bureau of Investigation Files on Carleton Beals, Washington, DC, New Haven, Special Agent John J. Ward, *Carleton Beals*.

118. Howard I. Blutstein, US Department of Justice, Federal Bureau of Investigation Files on Carleton Beals, Washington, DC, New Haven, Special Agent John J. Ward, *Carleton Beals*.

119. Carleton Beals to Richard Gibson, July 6, 1961, CBC.
120. U.S. National Archives and Records Administration (NARA), College Park, Maryland, Amembassy Montevideo, Colorado List 15 Reaction to Invasion of Cuba. Foreign Service Despatch, June 1, 1961, NARA-MD, RG 84/NND 948831/350/1961.
121. U.S. National Archives and Records Administration (NARA), College Park, Maryland, Cuban Landings Survey, May 1961, NARA-MD, RG 306, 230/46/35/02, ZP6102.
122. United Press International (UPI), "Reds Gain in Latin America through Feeding on Poverty," *St. Petersburg Times*, June 24, 1961.
123. Carleton Beals to Fernando Revueltas, undated but probably June 15, 1961, CBC.
124. Carleton Beals to Fernando Revueltas (c. 1961), CBC.
125. Haydee Santamaria to Carleton Beals, July 7, 1961, CBC.
126. Carleton Beals to Sam Shapiro, June 29, 1961, CBC.
127. "El trabajo de Gabo en Prensa Latina fue destruida bajo sospecha ideologica – Rogelio García Lupo" (Gabo (Gabriel García Marquez's work for Prensa Latina destroyed due to ideological suspicions – says Rogelio García Lupo), *Clarín* (Buenos Aires), December 4, 2014, http://www.clarin.com/sociedad/Gabo-Prensa-Latina-destruido-ideologica_0_1124287593.html (accessed May 27, 2021); Joe Stephen, "Love in the Time of Surveillance: FBI Agents Tracked Gabriel García Márquez," *Washington Post*, September 4, 2015.
128. Carleton Beals, "Shakeup at Latin-America News Agency Threatens Its Integrity and Future Impact," *The Independent* (New York), July 1961.
129. Carleton Beals, "The Deadly Drive to Silence the Press in Latin America," *Independent* (New York), June 1961.
130. Angel Boán to Carleton Beals, July 14, 1961, CBC.
131. Carleton Beals to Richard Gibson, January 21, 1962, CBC.
132. Carleton Beals to the Editor, *Boston Daily Record*, December 28, 1960, CBC.
133. Gosse, *Where the Boys Are*, 253n122.

*Chapter Fourteen*

# Radical in Winter

Even if Prensa Latina had produced only a modest income for Beals, he needed to replace it. His rupture with Prensa Latina left him without a steady outlet for his journalism, on which he had relied to bridge the income gaps between book advances and royalties. A man of unusually frugal tastes, Carleton Beals neither sought nor ever enjoyed real wealth, even at the best of times. But, in 1961, as he neared his sixty-eighth birthday, his options had narrowed. His physical stamina had diminished, even if his health remained remarkably good, especially for such a heavy smoker. His recent Cuban involvement, for all its adrenaline excitement, had distracted him from book projects. In the Cold War groupthink of the early 1960s, it had also underlined the left-wing, and at times, false pro-Communist label with which he had to contend. *Brass-Knuckle Crusade* had not sold well, despite some good reviews[1]. Bertha Klausner was tenacious, though, unstinting in her faith in Beals's talent. But even she needed to draw on reserves of optimism in the face of rejections from publishers which, however politely delivered, were numerous enough to have discouraged many agents.

As Beals had not been an employee anywhere since his early twenties, he had no pension beyond a paltry social security payment of less than $50 a month. He and Carolyn owned their home outright, having purchased it with her inherited wealth, by now nearly depleted. They kept their costs low, driving a used Studebaker, eating simply and at home, and never traveling except for Beals's work trips, which were always solo, and would now end altogether. Carolyn had not worked since her thirties, so there was no nest egg, and no pension on her side either. Beals would work until the end of his life, and even then, his discipline would not always spare him from financial distress.

Happily, this time, his Prensa Latina turn was soon supplanted by another with the *National Guardian*, an independent socialist-oriented weekly newspaper out of New York, founded in 1948 as part of the Henry Wallace Presidential campaign, under the banner of the Progressive Party. Its editor, former *New York Times* reporter James Aronson, had followed Beals's work for years, and now asked him to file analytical pieces on Latin America.[2]

He and co-editor Cedric Belfrage had launched the *National Guardian*, with business manager John McManus, soon after their return to America from Germany, where they met while guiding the post-Nazi rehabilitation of the country's newspapers. Both, like Beals, had since suffered Red-baiting from US Senator James O. Eastland's Internal Security Subcommittee, and US Senator Joe McCarthy's House Committee on Un-American Activities (HUAC), which launched a push, achieved in 1955, to deport the British-born Belfrage.[3] Belfrage shared with Beals a passionate interest in Latin America; he had lived Cuba between 1960 and 1961, where he was international affairs editor for the pro-Castro daily *El Mundo,* and was now preparing to move, with his fifth wife, Mary Bernick, to Cuernavaca, Mexico.

Beals's first files for the paper covered the overthrow of Ecuador's durable populist President Velasco Ibarra, President Joaquin Balaguer's (1906–2002) takeover in the Dominican Republic after dictator Rafael Leonidas Trujillo's assassination in 1961, and the shifting of Venezuelan President Romulo Betancourt (1908–1981) from a pro-Castro to a pro-US position, driven, Beals surmised, by his need for financing and its availability through the new Alliance for Progress.

Beals reworked, expanded, and added to these *National Guardian* pieces, to produce another Latin America overview book. He worked on it through 1962, and it was published by Abelard-Schuman, after some delay, in October 1963, as *Latin America: World in Revolution.* In it, Beals presented the Mexican and Cuban revolutions as bookends in a half-century history of revolutionary ferment in the region driven, in large measure, by the habitual interference of the United States, economic, political, and military. Each chapter is devoted to a specific country's experience, each a breezy and opinionated review of coups, economic crises, revolutions and intrigue. Many chapters are enriched by firsthand detail drawn from Beals's 1961 tour of South America on behalf of Prensa Latina. Presidents, army chiefs, and prelates are curtly dismissed with *ad hominem* epithets, and accused of various perfidies. Arching over the whole is an indictment of US meddling, with emphasis on the 1950s and early 1960s.

In the Argentina chapter, for example, Beals covers President Juan Perón's rise, decline and overthrow in 1955 by General Pedro Arámburu. He then relates the "sad career of treacherous [Arturo] Frondizi," the Radical Intransigent Party leader elected with Peronist support in 1957. Frondizi immediately faced an acute balance of payments crisis, to which he responded by approving an austerity plan to appease foreign creditors. The plan succeeded in releasing new credits from the International Monetary Fund (IMF), US Export-Import Bank and private banks. Although the investments they financed in oil and steel boosted economic growth, the benefits were not well distributed. Real wages dropped as inflation rose in 1959 and 1960, and a wave of crippling strikes ensued. President Eisenhower's administration had considered Perón's earlier removal "a great boon," Beals claimed, and welcomed the military's restoration of democracy, along with Frondizi's austerity plan. But when Frondizi was no longer able to defend his economic policy against the labor unrest and protest from the Peronists who felt he had betrayed them, the military removed him.

Beals wrote that the US embassy did not oppose the military action, but insisted only that the regime have "an appearance of legality" to ensure the country's continued access to credit.[4] This was achieved by the Argentine Army installing the head of the Congress, José María Guido (1910–1975), as provisional President, upon which, "this miserable creature . . . dissolved the national Congress, dispersed Congressmen by bayonets and tear-gas, and set up an all-military council so the newly-elected deputies could not be seated."[5] The military-appointed finance minister, Álvaro Alsogaray, obtained a new US loan of $200 million on condition that the economic plan be sustained, and as Beals writes "in spite of our [America's] sudden repugnance for military dictatorship."[6]

Such is the tone throughout the book, revealing an almost jaded weariness with the region's history, so inexorably saddled with America's big-footed dominance. Beals seemed weighed down by the familiarity of the story, by what he saw as its tragic predictability.

Although the book was translated into Spanish by an Argentine publisher and enjoyed a reportedly good sale there, it was the first of Beals's Latin America books to be ignored by *New York Times*, and most US media. This was partly due to its infelicitous publication around the time of Kennedy's assassination on November 22, 1963. Beals held nothing back in the book's final chapter, a long, withering polemic denouncing the Alliance for Progress. For most readers, the young President's recent and tragic death ennobled him, making such splenetic criticism of one of his legacy projects seem tasteless.

For others, the book's style was crude at any time. Harold Davis of American University found it full of "flippant, purple phraseology, careless of facts." He also judged that Beals's "ingrained habits of vitriolic vituperation . . . [and] intellectual demagoguery," led him to "make whipping boys of the Church, landowners, the military and "United States imperialism," and stood in the way of "objective historical analysis."[7]

From greater distance, however, Beals's critique of what he calls the "Holy Alliance," for all its strident tone, draws early conclusions about the

Alliance for Progress that were confirmed by later critics. Indeed, the Alliance was orphaned by JFK's assassination, and suffered from neglect as President Lyndon B. Johnson (LBJ) (1908–1973) evinced less interest in Latin America. Under LBJ, the earlier insistence that Alliance funds be limited to democracies was abandoned, as anti-Communism became the new litmus test for US aid, and authoritarian dictatorships—such as Brazil's military regime—passed it. In 1967, the US Congress refused Johnson's request for additional funds for the Alliance and, by 1970, even the late President's brother, US Senator Edward M. Kennedy, lamented that the Alliance, "has been a major economic disappointment . . . a social failure . . . a political failure."[8]

Despite the book's unfortunate timing, it sold better than the two Beals books immediately preceding it, *Nomads and Empire Builders: Native Peoples and Cultures of South America*, and *Cyclone Carry: The Story of Carry Nation*, both published by the Chilton Company in 1961 and 1962 respectively.[9] Beals's lifelong interest in Carry Nation, the temperance zealot who smashed saloons with her hatchet, was rooted in the happenstance that she was from Medicine Lodge, where Beals was born. She was also known to his parents, and intensely disliked by his mother Elvina who recalled how she relentlessly hectored her husband Leon Beals, then the county's attorney, into prosecuting bootleggers even where evidence was lacking. The book's meager sale, below three thousand copies, was undoubtedly due to its subject's lack of appeal. Though "well-written and well-documented," wrote one reviewer, "Carry Nation is such a repulsive personality that after 347 pages of smashing, you are tempted to hit her with her own biography."[10]

A more compelling project that Beals undertook in 1963 was the translation to English of a book by Guatemala's reformist former President Juan José Arévalo, *Anti-Kommunism in Latin America*, published by Lyle Stuart. The translation, which Beals completed over a few weeks between March and April, was prompted by his shared outrage with Stuart over the Kennedy administration's continuing hostility to Cuba's Revolution, and by its use of the Organization of American States (OAS) to whip up anti-Communist hysteria.

It soon became timely. Arévalo returned to Guatemala on March 29, 1963, after seven years in exile, to prepare his candidacy for Presidential elections scheduled for November of that year. But the elections were scrapped just two days later, on March 31, when Colonel Enrique Peralta (1908–1997) overthrew his predecessor, Miguel Ramón Ydígoras, the military ruler who had presided over the Bay of Pigs training base.

Peralta, who had been defense minister in Ydígoras's cabinet, seized power amid concerns among Guatemala's economic and military elite that Arévalo, whom they saw as a dangerous socialist who would tolerate Communists in any government he led, would easily win the planned election.

That possibility, suddenly made real by Arévalo's arrival in the country, was the spark that led Peralta to launch the coup.

Although Beals did not know it at the time, he anticipated what scholars later discovered: the Kennedy administration, on the advice of U.S Ambassador John O. Bell, had endorsed the coup beforehand, giving Peralta the green light.[11] It was a textbook example of the very phenomenon denounced by Arévalo in his book, prophetic in this case, as he was its direct victim. Peralta, whose regime the United States recognized seventeen days after the coup, was, Beals wrote, "a creature well trained in the United States for such monkeyshines (i.e. how to administer the local police state), and has been provided by our own authorities with an over-kill supply of weapons and planes."[12]

This context was overlooked in a dismissive review in the *New York Times* by veteran Latin America reporter Tad Szulc, who found it "a demonological study of a situation that has long ago ceased to exist," and "utterly out of touch with the realities of the hemisphere."[13]

Beals, however, found Arévalo's analysis relevant. The book's title derided Washington's regular invention of shadow enemies in Latin America, namely "Kommunists" with a "k," a flourish then popular on Madison Avenue, to distinguish the bogus enemy—land reformists, socialists, and social democrats—from real Communists. The 1963 coup in Guatemala, like the infamous one concocted by the CIA in 1954, Beals claimed, was driven by "a *reductio ad absurdum* of the McCarthy mind." Its goal was to keep a reformist like Arévalo, who might threaten the interests of the United Fruit Company, out of power.

Arévalo, whom Beals had interviewed in Guatemala's National Palace during his presidency in 1946, was among the Latin American political philosopher-leaders Beals most admired. Arévalo's book outlines a schema in which the phony crusade by Latin American governments, mostly military regimes, against "Kommunism" is a Washington-induced mimicry of the US Cold War against Soviet Russia. He argues that it was also supported—each for their own reasons—by the Catholic Church, and the "Geese of the Capitol," that is, the US media, advertising, and public relations industries. *Anti-Kommunism* followed an earlier Arévalo book on a similar theme, *The Shark and the Sardines*, which denounced a predatory combination of US corporate investment, oil, mining and cash-crop operations, political influence and military intervention in the region.[14] Both were best-sellers in Latin America, and both described a vision of the US role in shaping Latin America's history to produce an early-1960s outcome of dictatorship, widespread poverty, social inequality, and economic dependence. It was a vision that Beals considered "powerful, fearless . . . enlightened," and that he wholly shared.[15]

\*\*\*

Beals had turned seventy years old just days before John F. Kennedy was shot in Dallas in 1963. He was shocked at the assassination, of course, but had never shared the enthusiasm around the New Frontier presidency, and was not transfixed by the "fallen hero" moment as were most Americans. A disturbing footnote for him was the almost immediate discovery that JFK's assassin, Lee Harvey Oswald, had rented an office in New Orleans on behalf of the Fair Play for Cuba Committee (FPCC). This ensured that Beals's record as FPCC's co-chairman, however fleeting and tentative, would forever be tarnished by an association with the "pro-Castro Red" who killed the President.

He was not particularly bothered. His life continued quietly and happily through the 1960s, as he produced columns from his schoolhouse study. He continued to write on Latin America, denouncing the 1964 military coup in which Brazil's elected President João Goulart (1918–1976) was overthrown, as well as the "police action" in which LBJ sent US troops to the Dominican Republic in 1965. Increasingly, he also turned his attention to US policy in Southeast Asia. These articles, freighted with polemics as predictable as the outrages he felt the need to decry, were published in the *National Guardian*, Lyle Stuart's *Independent*, and *Política* in Mexico as before, and also in *Liberation*, a radical pacifist monthly out of New York founded by A. J. Muste, Dave Dellinger, Bayard Rustin, and Sidney Lens. He also wrote for *Revolution*, another monthly published in French and English in Paris by his ex-FPCC contacts Robert Taber and Richard Gibson. *Revolution* had evolved from *Révolution africaine*, the organ of the Algerian *Front de Libération Nationale*, and was leftist in orientation, "even Marxist," Taber told him, but non-sectarian.[16]

These columns were complemented by a steady stream of books that he churned out with his usual industry. A group biography of Simon Bolívar and other heroes of South American independence, *Eagles Over the Andes*, was published along with the Arévalo translation in the fall of 1963.[17] The following year, Beals was pleasantly surprised to win a Grammy Award for Best Album Notes, which he had drafted for a Columbia Records long-play of traditional Mexican music.[18]

This was followed in 1965 by *War Within a War: The Confederacy Against Itself*, about dissenters within the rebel South during the Civil War, and in 1966 by an easy-to-read illustrated history of the Mayas.[19]

He rarely ventured from Killingworth now, where Carolyn doted on him, interrupting his work only to insist he walk the fifty yards from his schoolhouse to the kitchen of the main house to share lunch and dinner. One exception was a lecture tour in November 1966, which took him to university campuses in New York, Baltimore, Chicago, Milwaukee, and North Dakota.

By this time, about 400,000 US troops were fighting Ho Chi Minh's (1890–1969) nationalist forces in Vietnam, backed up by large-scale US bombing of North Vietnamese villages. American involvement in Vietnam had provoked widespread protest among students, with the first teach-ins having been held the year before at the University of Michigan and University of California Berkeley. Beals, always opposed to imperialist wars, had embraced the anti-nuclear peace movement that had arisen in the late 1950s. Now, he was among those who demanded an end to the US war to shore up the puppet military regimes of South Vietnam, and made this the focus for his campus tour stump speech. While pleased by the "thoughtful and marvelous" reception he was given at most places, he found the travel exhausting, and did not repeat the experience.

Coinciding with America's descent into the Vietnam quagmire was the rise of the New Left, led by the Students for a Democratic Society, founded in 1962. This movement gave Beals some hope as a radical renewal. He admired its theoretical progenitor Herbert Marcuse, a Weimar-era German Marxist who had immigrated to the United States with several other fellow members of the Frankfurt School, as well as the work of sociologist C. Wright Mills, who had coined the term *New Left*. Its postures in opposition to the war and militarism in general, its challenges to consumerism, middle-class conformity, institutionalized racism ("so far-reaching and deeply permeating [yet] scarcely recognized even by those who disclaim such prejudices," Beals wrote) and gender roles, as well as its libertarian flavor, all appealed to Beals. But the New Left lacked "a studied program," he thought, and this prevented it from posing a serious threat to the established parties.[20]

Its leaders had turned away from a focus on ending the Vietnam War but had not succeeded in rallying mass public opinion against poverty or what Beals saw as America's crumbling society.[21] Instead of this, he lamented that too many of the New Left's proponents devoted themselves to stirring up self-defeating sectarian disputes within the ranks of progressive-minded Americans.

This tension reached his Killingworth study when a mutiny by ostensibly New Left staffers at the *National Guardian* forced the resignation, in March 1967, of its editors James Aronson and Cedric Belfrage. Among the proposals by the rebellious staff members was to dispense with contributors they deemed "irrelevant to the needs of the new radicalism." Among these were Anna Louise Strong (in China), Julio Álvarez del Vayo, the Spanish Republic's exiled foreign minister who was the *National Guardian*'s international affairs commentator, and Beals.[22]

When Aronson resigned, Beals supported him for having "hewed to the great principles . . . above the ugly bickering of the dogmatic zealots who pressured him constantly from within and without the paper." Not knowing who was to replace Aronson, and not wanting "to buy a pig a poke," Beals asked the paper's new editors to remove his name from the list of contributors.[23]

With Vietnam, Beals's dismay at having witnessed, by now, six decades of US militarism hardened into disgust. It is a caricature that old men become curmudgeonly, but it applies to Beals who, earlier given to occasional choleric outbursts, now gave them freer rein. By the late 1960s, he was spending most of his time alone. Even now, in his mid-seventies, he worked most days from 9 a.m. to 2 a.m., but his frustration mounted as his work was more often rejected than published. His income shrank while high blood-pressure complicated his well-being. His daily regimen included maintaining a steady correspondence with friends, fans, and critics, alternating between his often-gracious responses to requests for assistance and referrals to journalists, historians, and students, and irascibility, cantankerous sarcasm, and thin-skinned impatience with critics.

In early 1968, for example, he wrote his friend Vlad Janowicz about the US presidential race, then in the primaries.

> The most honest contender, and for how long one cannot know is Eugene McCarthy... Robert Kennedy has proved himself already to be a thoroughgoing louse with a Harvard accent and slap-me-on-the-wrist-Percy, sweet-cookie type of speaking. Nixon is a new Nixon calling for "new" leadership. He's so new, with so much spit and polish, with a new nauseating floor-walker smile, anybody but the typical USA dupe would know him to be a faker from way back... Mush-head [George] Romney has gone back to attending the Mormon Church, a racist outfit that owns the beet-sugar industry and exploits Mexicans and Puerto Ricans shamelessly.[24]

While Beals's life was largely secluded, prompting writer George Black to describe him as a "cranky political version of J. D. Salinger," he was fully awake to the *zeitgeist*: a tumultuous period of African-American civil rights and anti-war protest, youth counterculture and radicalism, the assassinations of Malcolm X, Martin Luther King Jr., and Robert F. Kennedy, and violent demonstrations at the 1968 Democratic and Republican conventions.[25] Despite his steady slide at once to old age and obscurity, Beals kept provoking his critics publicly too, to the extent that publishers enabled him. Two books on which he worked in tandem during this period, *Great Guerrilla Warriors* and *The Nature of Revolution*, were published in 1970, respectively by Prentice-Hall and Thomas Y. Crowell Company.[26] In both, he developed a historical thread tracing the origins of what had come to be known as Third World revolution, and which he found in American and French revolutions. *The Nature of Revolution* was dismissed by one reviewer as the work of a "poor man's Brinton," referring to Harvard University historian Crane Brinton, whose 1938 *The Anatomy of Revolution* remains a reference of choice on the topic. Certainly, Beals's work does not meet Brinton's standard of analytical depth. Nonetheless, Beals makes sound observations in it about the restive politics of late-1960s America, considered in the context of earlier revolutions, both historical and those he had witnessed firsthand. He concludes it with a lament that is remarkably timely, even timeless:

> Perhaps we can figure out how our system, seemingly so efficient, has become so close to being unworkable, our future so uncertain, our way of life so menaced—and in so short a number of years. The reasons are not far to seek: five wars in my lifetime—imperialism, neocolonialism; trying to run the world; millions of underprivileged people in the wealthiest land on earth; social injustice; the desecration of our habitat and the reckless destruction of animal and plant life—the fouling of our own nest so to speak; the too rapid exhaustion of our natural resources; our top-heavy military and police establishment; the narrowing by government of the duties and rights of citizens; the improper exploitation of the Third World.[27]

In *Great Guerrilla Warriors*, Beals drew on his experience with Augusto César Sandino over forty years before, as an early example of a phenomenon in which a charismatic individual inculcates the revolutionary impulse, captures a public following, and creates a movement. He placed this story alongside other biographical essays starting with Aguinaldo in the Philippines, Pancho Villa and Emiliano Zapata in Mexico, Abdel Krim of Morocco, Yugoslavia's Marshal Tito, Mao Zedong, and Fidel Castro.

*Warriors* also included a sympathetic portrait of Ho Chi Minh, a timely but controversial choice, as the book's publication came after more than fifty thousand American troops had been killed fighting Ho's forces in Vietnam.

It was too much for some. One Vietnam veteran wrote to accuse Beals of "glorifying Communists" in *Warriors*, provoking a bristling denunciation: "I have never before written to a confessed, smug self-righteous murderer.... Such brave fighters you were! Fighters for what? Not for a free America or a free South Viet Nam, that's for sure. For an honorable peace? Bosh! There ain't no such animal... never has America so misused its power and nobility so disgustingly as in Viet Nam. Cuddle up to your bravery, my little man."[28]

Just before the book was published, Beals reunited with his old friend and erstwhile *Nation* editor Ernest Gruening, now a Democratic Party US Senator from Alaska. The two met for dinner in mid-April 1970 at Gruening's home in Washington, where Beals had stopped on his way home from a trip to New Orleans. This renewed a friendship that had been frayed and neglected, as Gruening's political career and role in guiding Alaska to statehood took him a long way from Beals's continuing iconoclastic journalism focused on Latin America. Nonetheless, Beals had applauded Gruening's vote—one of just two in the US Senate—against the 1964 Gulf of Tonkin Resolution, which marked the beginning of the escalation of US involvement in the Vietnam War.[29]

Gruening and Beals both had the cold satisfaction of having been proven right when the United States was forced to withdraw in defeat from Vietnam in 1975. This ended the waging of the Cold War with such ferocity, at least during Jimmy Carter's (1924–) one-term presidency.

But even if the Vietnam War had transfixed America with bitter debate and angry division throughout this period, Beals's effort to address it through the lens of his experience in *Great Guerrilla Warriors* and *The Nature of Revolution* ultimately met with failure. Both books were panned when they were noticed at all. The later disregard that comes with advancing age was upon him. His work was characterized by his familiar polemical tone, but now shorn of the immediacy of witness, it came across as more of a rant than the documented accounts he had produced in earlier years.

In late 1972, Beals was approached by John Britton, a young historian from South Carolina who had discovered Beals's work in the course of his own research on Mexican-American relations during the Mexican Revolution. Britton sought Beals's collaboration for a biography he wanted to do on him. Flattered by the attention, Beals invited Britton to visit him in Killingworth, to look over his manuscripts, correspondence, and other papers. When Britton saw the binders filling twenty-five feet of shelf space in Beals's study during his first visit in January 1973, he quickly grasped the scale of work ahead of him, and the time it would take. "It's too bad that you are not closer at hand," Beals told him, almost apologetic.

Britton was undeterred, however, and that summer rented a cottage in Killingworth with his wife Kathy for six weeks, spending most days with Beals, whose loyal, large gray cat Smokey watched like a lazy sentry in the schoolhouse study. He tape-recorded Beals's meandering responses to his questions and borrowed materials to read overnight. A friendly rapport grew between them that included Carolyn and Kathy to whom, Britton noticed, Beals paid special attention. "Even in his eighties, he was still a lady's man," he recalled. In all, Britton visited Beals six times between 1973 and 1978. His biography would be published after Beals's death.[30]

Another young man, Melvin Yoken, a French teacher at the University of Massachusetts in nearby New Bedford, showed spontaneous interest in Beals in his twilight years. Yoken had developed a hobby of befriending writers such as André Gide, Jules Romains, and Lewis Mumford, among others, by initiating a correspondence with them. He wrote Beals a flattering letter in 1974, thus beginning a friendship with the old writer. It culminated with Beals's visit to New Bedford in March 1975, where he gave a lecture at the university, was interviewed on a local radio station and celebrated with a dinner in his honor attended by Yoken and his faculty friends.

Even as biographer Britton continued his research and interviews, Beals worked in parallel on his own autobiography. Tentatively titled *Under the Fifth Sun* in a nod to Aztec mythology, it was a sprawling piece of work, covering hundreds of pages, parts of which Klausner sent off as enticements to potential publishers. The project, as well as two novels and a biography on

**Figure 14.1. Carleton Beals, aged eighty-two, at a dinner held in his honor before delivering a lecture at the University of Massachusetts (Dartmouth), near New Bedford, in March 1975.** *Photo courtesy of the Carleton Beals Collection, Howard Gotlieb Archival Research Center, Boston University, and Ralph Carleton Beals.*

the ill-fated nineteenth-century Hapsburg rulers of Mexico, Maximilian I (1932–1867) and his wife Carlota, which Klausner had retrieved from Beals's stack of unpublished manuscripts, failed to elicit interest. This spiral of rejection demoralized him, deepening stress caused by his straitened finances.[31]

In 1976, Beals's health faltered severely, as his high blood pressure was compounded by an intestinal ailment that required surgery and a hospital stay. The couple's money woes lapsed into penury; Beals had almost no income that year other than his and Carolyn's social security payments which together totaled only $211 a month. Their Killingworth property was paid for, but they had to seek relief as they could not cover the taxes on it.[32]

Beals's final years coincided with a revival of the memory of Augusto César Sandino in the form of a new generation of Sandinistas fighting to topple Nicaraguan dictator Anastasio "Tachito" Somoza Debayle (1925–1980), second son of the *Guardia Nacional* general who had ordered

Sandino's murder in 1934. With post-Vietnam America having elected Jimmy Carter as President, there would be no US military intervention to defend this last of the Somozas. But Carter administration diplomats nonetheless prevaricated, trying to find a middle ground between the Sandinistas, whose collective leadership was dominated by Marxists in thrall to Fidel Castro, and the increasingly desperate Somoza dictatorship.

In December 1978, the *Nation* published a front-page story on the advancing Sandinistas, comparing the situation in Nicaragua to the one Beals described there fifty years before. Its author, Marc Lindenberg, inserted boxed quotes from Beals's Sandino interview, to complement his own report on the new Sandinistas—then just six months away from their revolutionary triumph in July 1979—in which he criticized the Carter administration for its confused policy. Although that policy had removed some support for Somoza in a futile effort to pressure him to resign, it had also failed to recognize the Sandinistas as a legitimate political force. The *Nation*'s editorial in the same issue called for a full US withdrawal of support for Somoza and his National Guard.

The situation was not so far removed from what Beals had seen, in which US-supervised elections were held that pointedly excluded the Sandinistas of his time. The *Nation*'s then-assistant editor, Kai Bird, wrote Beals asking if he wanted to contribute a short commentary.[33] Beals was in hospital, once again for intestinal surgery, and did not respond. Bird nonetheless cited Beals's journalistic legacy in his editorial: "A final American withdrawal is long overdue. But perhaps it is too much to expect this administration to break the cycle of foreign-inspired violence so vividly reported a half century ago by Carleton Beals on the trail of Sandino."[34]

By now, Beals was frail and weakened after his hospital stay. He spent most days resting in bed in his schoolhouse, while Carolyn brought him his meals from the house. Seven months later, on June 26, 1979, less than a month before the victorious Sandinistas rode into Managua, Beals died. There was no funeral.

Carolyn, now widowed, donated his voluminous papers to Boston University, but preserved his schoolhouse study and desk as he had left it. Every year until her death in 2002, on his birthday, she placed a card on his desk. Its inscription: "Please come back!"

## NOTES

1. Carleton Beals, *Brass-Knuckle Crusade: The Great Know-Nothing Conspiracy, 1820–1860* (New York: Hastings House, 1960).
2. James Aronson to Carleton Beals, November 21, 1961, Carleton Beals Collection (CBC), Howard Gotlieb Archival Research Center, Boston University (hereafter cited CBC).

3. See Cedric Belfrage and James Aronson, *Something to Guard: The Stormy Life of the National Guardian, 1948–1967* (New York: Columbia University Press, 1978), 178–209, for Belfrage's first-person account of his testimony, detention at Ellis Island, and deportation.

4. Carleton Beals, *Latin America: World in Revolution* (New York: Abelard-Schuman, 1963), 206.

5. Beals, *Latin America*, 206.

6. Beals, *Latin America*, 206.

7. Harold Eugene Davis, Review of *Latin America: World in Revolution*, by Carleton Beals, *Americas* 21, no. 2 (1964): 212–13, https://doi.org/10.2307/979063.

8. Joseph Smith, *The United States and Latin America: A History of American Diplomacy, 1776–2000* (New York: Routledge, 2005), 126.

9. Carleton Beals, *Nomads and Empire Builders: Native Peoples and Cultures of South America* (Philadelphia: Chilton Books, 1961); and *Cyclone Carry: The Story of Carry Nation* (New York: Chilton Books, 1962).

10. *Cyclone Carry: The Story of Carry Nation*, by Carleton Beals, "A Vulgar Woman and Demon Rum," *Toronto Telegram*, February 16, 1963.

11. Max Paul Friedman, *Rethinking Anti-Americanism: The History of an Exceptional Concept in American Foreign Relations* (Cambridge; Cambridge University Press, 2012), 151–55.

12. Carleton Beals, trans., "Introduction," in *Anti-Kommunism in Latin America An X-Ray of the Process Leading to a New Colonialism*, by Juan José Arévalo (New York: Lyle Stuart, 1963), 9.

13. Tad Szulc, "Who's Conspiring Where?" Review of Anti-Kommunism in Latin America by Juan José Arévalo, *New York Times Book Review*, March 29, 1964, BR12.

14. Juan José Arévalo, *The Shark and the Sardines*, trans. June Cobb and Raul Osegueda (New York: Lyle Stuart, 1961).

15. Beals, "Introduction," in *Anti-Kommunism*, 13.

16. Robert Taber to Carleton Beals, August 7, 1963, CBC.

17. Carleton Beals, *Eagles of the Andes: South American Struggles for Independence* (Philadelphia: Chilton Books, 1963).

18. *Mexico: A Columbia Records Legacy Album*, Mexican Orchestra conducted by Carlos Chavez, 1964, Carleton Beals and Stanton Catlin, album notes writers, Winner Best Album Notes, 7th Grammy Awards, 1964. https://www.grammy.com/grammys/awards/winners-nominees/132 (accessed May 31, 2021).

19. Carleton Beals, *War Within a War: The Confederacy Against Itself* (New York: Chilton Books, 1965); and Beals, *Land of the Mayas: Yesterday and Today* (New York: Abelard-Schuman, 1966).

20. Carleton Beals, *The Nature of Revolution* (New York: Thomas W. Crowell, 1970), 267.

21. See Andrew E. Hunt, *David Dellinger: The Life and Times of a Nonviolent Revolutionary* (New York: New York University Press, 2006), 142; Beals, *Nature of Revolution*, 266.

22. Cedric Belfrage and James Aronson, *Something to Guard*, 326.

23. Carleton Beals to the staff of the *National Guardian*, April 22, 1967, CBC.

24. Carleton Beals to Vlad Janowicz, March 11, 1968, CBC.

25. George Black, "Our Man in Managua," *Nation*, December 19, 1987, 761.

26. Carleton Beals, *Great Guerrilla Warriors* (Englewood Cliffs, NJ: Prentice-Hall, 1970); and Beals, *The Nature of Revolution*.

27. Beals, *Nature of Revolution*, 273–74.

28. Carleton Beals to Bob Martin, January 27, 1973, CBC.

29. US Congress, Gulf of Tonkin Resolution (Southeast Asia Resolution), 78 Stat. 384, Pub. L. 88–408, 88th Cong., 2nd sess., August 10, 1964, https://www.govinfo.gov/content/pkg/STATUTE-78/pdf/STATUTE-78-Pg384.pdf (accessed May 27, 2021).

30. John A. Britton, *Carleton Beals: A Radical Journalist in Latin America* (Albuquerque, University of New Mexico Press, 1987).

31. Carleton Beals, "Under the Fifth Sun" (unpublished autobiography, c. 1972–1978), in Carleton Beals Collection (CBC), Howard Gotlieb Archival Research Center, Boston University.

32. Carleton Beals to US Department of Health, Education, and Welfare, August 3, 1976, CBC.
33. Kai Bird to Carleton Beals, November 15, 1978, CBC.
34. Kai Bird, editorial, *Nation*, December 9, 1978, 628.

*Chapter Fifteen*

# A Stranded Ghost's Journalistic Legacy

In 1938, *Time* magazine described Carleton Beals as "the best informed and *most awkward* living writer on Latin America." The original meaning of "awkeward" in Middle English was "in the wrong direction," derived from "awke," meaning "turned the wrong way."[1] This description of Beals is apt, perhaps, but it is fair to insist that the source be cited along with the epithet. In 1938, and for many years thereafter *Time* was the media preserve of Henry Luce, as stout a defender of America's version of capitalism and its overseas extension as could be found anywhere. He was fiercely anti-Communist, and suspicious of any drift in the Left direction. He did not brook deviations from these positions in his flagship newsmagazine. For that reason, probably, *Time* never published anything by Beals.

Carleton Beals was, by the late 1940s, increasingly marginalized, not by accident, but because of his views on US foreign policy in Latin America, and because his analyses of political events in the region and in the world diverged too much from the reigning consensus in the mass media and among political elites. He was a journalist outcast during the deepest freeze of the Cold War, when the Dulles brothers, US Secretary of State John Foster and CIA Director Allen, crafted a foreign policy driven by an obsession with what they saw as expansionist Soviet Communism. Everything was seen through that lens then, and for many years thereafter. Beals's awkwardness lay in his refusal to adapt to it.

By then, Beals was in his sixties, a stage when many journalists are winding down their careers. But even with Beals's then-shrinking audience, US Vice President Richard Nixon found reason enough to ask the FBI to investigate him. It had not been the first time that Beals's commitment to an independent path brought him trouble. It had earlier triggered his arrest by

Mexican police, and US diplomats and information service officials tracked him overseas, on and off, throughout his life.

But his independence and determination not to be a joiner also kept him out of the Communist Party. It was a decision driven by his headstrong character, democratic socialist orientation, and commitment to disinterested journalism, but had the convenient result of keeping him free of the ideological baggage that put many of his left-minded contemporaries on blacklists that destroyed their careers in the 1940s and 1950s. In the event, he was nonetheless considered suspicious and "un-American" enough to see his livelihood grievously damaged too.

Most awkward about Beals was his analysis of US foreign policy, specifically his critique of "US imperialism" in Latin America, as articulated in what he saw as a distorted twentieth-century interpretation of the Monroe Doctrine, and as practiced in US military interventions in countries to protect US property and financial interests.

In his denunciations of "dollar and gunboat diplomacy," Beals challenged elite capture of foreign policymaking which, he argued, served elite—as opposed to public—interests. He claimed that this led the United States to support and arm dictatorships in Latin America, which undermined the Jeffersonian ideal of encouraging, by example rather than force, the expansion of democratic freedom in other countries.

As a lifelong freelancer whose work appeared mostly in liberal and, in his later years, radical magazines, Beals was at the margins of a media industry largely owned by members of America's corporate elite. He was a precursor of many other dissident investigative journalists who blew, and still blow, whistles on what they see as US neo-imperialist hubris, overreach, or excess, such as the late David Halberstam on Vietnam, Seymour Hersh, Mark Danner, Raymond Bonner, and, more recently, Glenn Greenwald, who broke the Edward Snowden story.

Such journalists matter. They are often pushed aside or limited to publication in smaller magazines and alternative media.[2] But they and these media, though often dismissed as catering to small and dissident audiences, perform a canary in the mine function. They are often the first to dig out uncomfortable—awkward—truths, forcing those who wield power in government and in business, including the mass-audience mainstream media, to cover stories that had earlier escaped their notice.

Beals himself was deeply cynical about the mainstream news media. "There's only one difference between a newspaper and a whorehouse," he once wrote. "The newspaper doesn't have a piano in the parlor." More seriously, he denounced the US media of his time in a two-part series filed in 1960 (awkwardly) through the Cuban agency, Prensa Latina. Despite their apparent freedom, they are not imbued with the "spirit of freedom," Beals wrote. This spirit, essential to an honest discussion of public affairs, had been eaten away, he thought, by the closeness between big business, including media owners and Washington officialdom. As a result, media reports were often "inadequate, biased and in support of the status quo, bitterly opposed on every occasion to the new forces of liberation in the world."[3]

Beals was disturbed by the commercialism and conformity he found in US media, as these had the dangerous result that the American people, in his judgment, were poorly informed, especially about the world outside the United States, and therefore unable to properly understand the meaning of international events. They were thus easy prey for the media power elite, in Beals's time, the Luce, Hearst, and Newhouse empires, their advertisers, and the political status quo they helped mightily to shape, and consequently served and defended.

In foreign affairs, most media followed "the official State Department line," Beals charged. He certainly did not, and suffered harassment as a result. Journalists seen as friendlier to the US State Department got cooperation from US embassy staff, while Beals got surveillance. Beals's experience taught him that federal agents quietly pressured media managers, dropping in to "talk over" articles they had not liked. As we have seen, this practice resurfaced throughout the Cold War, coexisting then and later with more subtle forms of pressure. In Beals's case, US officials found a great deal that they did not like.

Beals's journalism placed him firmly in the "radical" tradition of American foreign policy experts. He was more reporter than academic analyst, but he did develop a consistent and coherent analytical framework sound enough to command respect, even from the historians and international affairs theorists whom he sometimes disparaged. Informed by an unusual breadth of experience, Beals was an autodidact of vast, informal, and eclectic scholarship who never lost his popular touch.

He did not consider himself an intellectual in the formal sense and was more inclined to tell stories and unveil hidden facts than to invent theories. But his journalism routinely included insights that revealed the elite economic and political forces behind events, and these contained the germ of, or illustrated, theories that later became fully-fledged schools of thought. Usually, these were simply his observations of specific situations, such as his view of elite dominance of media in America. In this case, one discerns a similar perception in the neo-Marxist French structuralist thinker Louis Althusser's delineation of the media and of other cultural industries as part of an "ideological state apparatus" that reinforces the power structure in capitalist societies.[4] Similarly, Beals's interpretation of US imperialism shares common ground with Antonio Gramsci's idea of hegemony, as well as Michel Foucault's reflections on "knowledge" and "discourses" produced by the powerful that discipline the way things are perceived. Foucault, for example, argued that specific discourses have shaped and created meaning systems that have gained the status and currency of "truth." These meaning systems dominate how individuals define and organize themselves and their social world, whilst alternative discourses are deliberately marginalized. These last, nonetheless, potentially offer a public space—or a public sphere, to use Jürgen Habermas's[5] term—where hegemonic practices can be contested, challenged and even resisted.[6]

Beals argued that most US media presented a distorted picture that led Americans to perceive the US role in the world as promoting freedom and democracy, disguising its true neo-imperialist goals. He would have recognized the ideas of these thinkers, as well as the "Orientalism" of Edward W. Said, as being roughly parallel to his own views, differing only in their form of expression in the esoteric language of philosophy and critical theory.[7] Said cites Richard Barnet's observation that, "a United States military intervention in the Third World had occurred every year between 1945 and 1967 [when he stopped counting]," and that such interventions have "all the elements of a powerful imperial creed . . . a sense of mission, historical necessity, and evangelical fervor."[8] To Said, "the amazing thing about this is not that it is attempted, but that it is done with so much consensus and near unanimity in a public sphere constructed as a kind of cultural space expressly to represent and explain it."[9]

Later in his life, Beals explicitly shared the analysis of Herbert Marcuse, the most activist of the Frankfurt School émigrés to the United States, that consumerism and mass media culture had lulled America into passive distraction under elite domination.[10] Marcuse's and the Frankfurt School's critical analysis has found renewed relevance amid the twenty-first-century crisis facing the United States and all liberal democracies, as inequality has risen amid globalized capitalism.

On a related front, dependency theory, a framework to describe unequal economic relations between developed and so-called Third World countries, was tentatively sketched out by Beals in *America South*, even before the postwar era of decolonization. His description of one-crop dependent economies in Latin America was a *sui generis* observation, but fully consistent with more elaborate—and much later—formulations by Raúl Prebisch and Andre Gunder Frank, couched in the vernacular of economics and political science.[11] Dependency theory has been overtaken, or rather modified, by globalization and anti-globalization theory in recent decades, but elements of it endure today.

Perhaps most important, however, is Beals's status as a forerunner of revisionist historian William Appleman Williams, and late twentieth-century US foreign policy critics such as Noam Chomsky, Chalmers Johnson, Andrew Bacevich, Greg Grandin, and Chris Hedges whose analyses of American foreign policy Beals also anticipated.

Beals's first prominent foreign policy analysis surfaced in his 1923 book, *Mexico: An Interpretation*, an account of the Mexican Revolution and US policy responses to it. In it, as well as articles in the *Nation* and the *New Republic*, he denounced US oil companies in Mexico for trying to goad Presidents Wilson and Harding administrations into military intervention to stifle Mexico's claim to own sub-soil minerals—including oil—on its territory.[12] Wilson balked on intervention, but Harding withheld recognition of Mexican President Álvaro Obregón's government for almost four years until oil claims negotiations concluded in 1923. Hostility resumed under President Coolidge, until the latter dispatched Dwight Morrow as ambassador to patch the persisting rift.

"The tragedy of the whole business," Beals wrote, "resides in the fact that we were stirred so close to war-pitch over petroleum technicalities that we jeopardized our entire peace and good-will with Latin America, and to some extent with the world, in futile conflict in which, little by little, we have had to yield to the Mexican position and to respect the sovereign right of Mexico to enact its own legislation."[13]

With smaller countries, such as Nicaragua, there were fewer restraints to "war-pitch," as military intervention became the policy of choice to snuff out Sandino's rebellion in the 1920s. The US Marines also organized, supervised and certified political parties for Nicaragua's presidential election; it was nation-building, 1928-style, and Beals was unsparing in his criticism of it. His series, "With Sandino in Nicaragua," in the *Nation* and the *New York Herald-Tribune*, as we have seen, coincided with an effort by Peace Progressives in the US Congress, led by Idaho US Senator William Borah, chairman of the US Senate Foreign Relations Committee, to try to end the US Marine presence in Nicaragua. Beals's six-part series, cited by several Senators, came at the end of two months during which the US troop presence in Nicaragua had been doubled to 2,570, along with the dispatch of fifteen fighter aircraft, making this the Western Hemisphere's first air war.[14]

While the US State Department justified the intervention with the claim that Sandino was a "bandit" who threatened Americans' lives and property, Beals's *Nation* series depicted Sandino as a revolutionary patriot battling US forces of occupation whom, Beals presumed derisively, were "fighting for the Monroe Doctrine."[15] The US Marine occupation of Nicaragua was already controversial, with the *New York Times*, *New York World*, and *Baltimore Sun* suspecting "imperialistic motives," so Beals's firsthand account of his interaction with Sandino reinforced existing skepticism.

Beals's criticism of the 1926–1934 US intervention in Nicaragua was an example of what David C. Hendrickson has described as "the antipodal tendencies" generated by the "regularly recurring historical pattern of American imperialism."[16] It is a dissident rather than a mainstream tendency. Though pervasive and recurring, it is often derided as unpatriotic. Given the popular currency of liberty, democracy, and free markets as characteristics defining America's identity, and widely held to shape US foreign policy, Beals's repeated attacks on the Monroe Doctrine, and especially its Roosevelt Corollary, earned him the enmity of the foreign policy elite of his day. Like conservative historian Mark Falcoff, who has described Beals's legacy as "doleful," they saw him "siding with our enemies," or impugning US policymakers' motives.[17]

Beals's status as a dissident journalist limited his access to mass media, and his critical stance, frequently at odds with the dominant consensus, often prevented him from getting published. His work appeared in liberal magazines such as the *Nation* and the *New Republic*, but he was in the *New York Times* only occasionally, and with less frequency as he grew older.

Sociologist Jürgen Habermas's concept of "the public sphere" in which public policy is discussed and in which consensus forms, offers a useful tool to explain the marginalization to which Beals—and many other critical journalists—have been subjected. The US public sphere is one in which few dissident voices, or even distinct perspectives, are heard. This has led to groupthink in many crises, prompting errors in public and foreign policy due to blind spots in critical areas. These blind spots arise as a relative uniformity of views heard in the media results, systematically, in significantly overlooked and under-covered aspects of public policy issues, including foreign policy.

On Latin America, for example, Americans were not aware of Mexican opinion that led to the Revolution, or of the short-sightedness of backing Fulgencio Batista in 1934, or of the seeds of later conflict sown by unseating Jacobo Arbenz in Guatemala in 1954. These were pre- and early Cold War "victories" that were cancelled out by later reversals: Fidel Castro's takeover in 1959, the Farabundo Martí National Liberation Front (FMLN) challenge in El Salvador in the 1980s, the 1979–1990 Sandinista Revolution, and later, the leftist challenges posed by Hugo Chávez and Nicolás Maduro in Venezuela, and Evo Morales in Bolivia. These challengers to US power arose from animosity sowed by earlier US policies, promulgated without sufficient challenge inside the United States, because US foreign policy is discussed and developed by a small elite in a handful of universities—Johns Hopkins, Harvard, Georgetown, and think-tanks such as the American Enterprise Institute, the Heritage Foundation, and Brookings, the State Department and the Pentagon. So the groupthink is not only unchallenged, but reinforced by the smallness of the circle, or public sphere to use Habermas's term, in which it develops. This puts American leaders at risk of missing cues that would steer them in a better direction in dealing with other countries.

By 1931, for example, Henry L. Stimson admitted he had made a mistake in investing his confidence in Nicaragua's Moncada at El Espino in 1927.[18] He saw that he had been used by Moncada, who wanted a deal that would put him in the President's chair. Again and again, US leaders have made deals with military dictators, first in Central America and the Caribbean, Mexico, Brazil, and others. Later, this was carried to Pakistan (General Zia and Nawaz Musharraf), Egypt (Hosni Mubarak), Indonesia (Suharto), Iran (House of Pahlavi), and many others. It has proven short-sighted, costly, and a failure even in terms of achieving the ends of the Open Door Policy that the strategy purported to serve.

But if Beals was an anti-imperialist in the radical tradition, he also drew from the well of a Jeffersonian philosophy, as defined by another historian, Walter Russell Mead. Beals shared Jefferson's suspicion of the nexus of mutual support between large corporations and big government, in both foreign and domestic policy.[19] In his reporting on Mexico, Nicaragua, Cuba, and other countries in the Caribbean and South America, Beals decried what he saw as the spilling of US blood and the spending of its treasure on behalf of American bondholders, bankers, railway concession holders, oilmen, and owners of utilities, mining, sugar, and fruit companies.

In this, his position was similar to that of his contemporaries, historians Charles A. Beard and Mary Ritter Beard, both Jeffersonians whom Beals admired. Observing US bankers testifying at the US Senate Finance Committee in 1931 to 1932 on the sale of Latin American bonds in the United States, the Beards concluded that "their testimony demonstrated . . . that the promotion, flotation, and outcomes of foreign loans in the United States had a direct bearing upon the foreign policies and relations of the Federal Government." The US State Department and the US Navy, they added, "lost some of their glamour" as a result.[20]

Like Beals, Charles Beard agreed that US military intervention would not solve internal national struggles in other countries. "Social issues are not settled by bayonets, for we cannot sit on them or live by them," Beard wrote about Mexico during its Revolution. "If a process is inevitable, it is better to let it alone or to aid in its culmination."[21]

Beals's argument against the brief for American business carried by US foreign policymakers in Latin America, and their willingness to support them by undermining even mildly reformist governments while shoring up dictators, was that this approach contradicted the democratic ideals of the American republic.

By the 1930s, under the Good Neighbor Policy, Franklin Delano Roosevelt's (FDR) US Secretary of State Cordell Hull pursued reciprocity agreements with Latin American countries, cultivating friendly relations with over a dozen dictators. While this policy consciously rejected the earlier military interventions, it still violated American values, Beals argued. "In Latin America, we are not supporting democracy and freedom any more than we are in Spain," Beals wrote in the late 1930s. "We are actively supporting

Fascist trends, under the noble cloak of brave words about freedom, democracy and international justice."[22]

In this regard, just a couple of years earlier, in his book *America South*, Beals had noted with approval Jefferson's preference in 1823 for accepting British Foreign Secretary George Canning's offer of a joint stance by Britain and America against any effort by France, or any other power, to take control of former Spanish colonies in the Western Hemisphere. "Had we co-operated in 1823," Beals wrote, "we would early have promoted the founding of principles of international control which our Monroe Doctrine wounded and continues to wound."[23] Instead, Beals argued, the Monroe Doctrine, in its "self-satisfied paternalism," gave the US unilateral license to intervene as it saw fit in the hemisphere.

In his two books, *Coming Struggle for Latin America* and *Pan-America*, that had multiple printings just before US entry into World War II, Beals fed mounting alarm about fascist German, Italian, Spanish, and Japanese tentacles extending to dictatorships in Latin America, with expanding trade ties.[24]

The legacy of America's hitherto highly-unequal, neo-colonial exploitation of Latin America's mineral, oil and agricultural resources was now biting back, Beals claimed. In 1938, for example, Mexico's President Lázaro Cárdenas nationalized his country's petroleum sector, most of it US-owned. Beals argued that had US investors respected Latin countries' sovereignty, and forsworn the bully tactic of calling out the US government to defend their interests, America would not now be facing competition from its fascist enemies for access to strategic resources in Latin America.

This analysis anticipated the critique of William Appleman Williams, and it either reflected or influenced (or both) the *zeitgeist*, as FDR promised in 1940 to undertake "a new approach . . . to these South American things. Give them a share."[25] More broadly, Beals anticipated Williams's analysis that the Open Door guiding principle behind US foreign policy, conceived in the "Open Door Notes" by John Hay, US Secretary of State in 1899 and 1900, helped explain the evolution of the Cold War. Rigid adherence to the Open Door trumped any effort at accommodation with Communist, or even socialist-leaning regimes.[26] United States policymakers systematically opposed such regimes, attacking, or covertly sabotaging them where feasible, and engaging with the Soviet Union only in the exceptional circumstance of the war against Nazi Germany and Imperial Japan.

One might have thought Beals would welcome FDR's Good Neighbor Policy as a break with the troubled past of intervention. While he did acknowledge it as a necessary wartime expedient by 1941, he had earlier decried it as a "Goodwill Racket" that enabled dictatorships to take hold, stifling democratic aspirations across the Western Hemisphere. As US policy in Latin America shifted after World War II, from non-intervention to Cold War-driven containment of Communism, Beals wrote critical assessments of covert US military action in Guatemala (1954) and Cuba (1961), and of JFK's Alliance for Progress, all of which he saw as US imperialism at work.

Beals's exceedingly skeptical, even cynical, perspective on US intervention explains his dismissal of so-called US liberal internationalism in the Wilsonian tradition, as reeking of hypocrisy. By the 1960s, the Bay of Pigs delivered a kind of *coup de grâce*, confirming for Beals that, from a Latin American standpoint, US policy toward revolutions had come full circle, returning to the kind of unabashed violation of international law in practice against Sandino in Nicaragua.

Indeed, for Latin America, the constraints imposed by US hegemony in the hemisphere had not changed. But the postwar growth of the United States to superpower status, and the Cold War, anti-Soviet, anti-Communist framework used by American foreign policymakers raised the stakes. Through the CIA-backed coups against Mohammed Mossadegh in Iran in 1953, Arbenz in Guatemala in 1954, the Bay of Pigs fiasco, and the protracted war in Vietnam, US policy, Beals argued, visited suffering and death upon millions. At the same time, the policy failed to achieve its own purported goals of promoting democracy, freedom, and open-door markets, while it also—particularly in the case of Vietnam—imposed large costs on Americans.

Not least, this disconnect between America's claim to defend democracy and freedom, and its practice of labelling as Communist and treating with hostility almost all political movements seeking economic and social justice in developing countries, eroded America's credibility in Latin America, as elsewhere in what are now called developing and emerging-market countries. This was underlined in Cuba, Beals maintained, where, just four years after Castro's takeover, more had been accomplished "in matters basic for the peoples' welfare and for economic expansion . . . than was accomplished in nearly sixty years of US rule."[27]

This invidious comparison, typical of Beals's journalism and judged heretical by many Americans, marked him as an "engaged journalist," as much advocate as observer. But Beals, for all his opinionated and often bilious invective, was also exceedingly prescient. Looking back at his journalism and his judgments, one is struck by the extent to which his so-called radical assessments are now mainstream. The US opening to Cuba is perhaps the most striking example. In August 2015, US Secretary of State John Kerry declared, upon re-opening the US embassy in Havana that, "U.S policy is not the anvil on which Cuba's future will be forged . . . Cuba's future is for Cubans to shape."[28] It was remarkably similar to Beals's prediction in 1963, "that Latin America's future would be defined not "between the narrow prison walls of the Cold War," as defined by Washington or Moscow, but that "their destiny is their own, not ours, to dictate."[29]

In a similar vein, Kerry told ambassadors at the Organization of American States in 2013, that "the era of the Monroe Doctrine is over." He said the

United States would not propose "a declaration about how and when it will intervene in the affairs of other American states," but sought instead a partnership among equals with its Latin American neighbors.[30]

This position was reinforced by Antony Blinken, President Joe Biden's US Secretary of State who promised, in his first major foreign policy speech in March 2021, that "we will not promote democracy through costly military interventions or by attempting to overthrow authoritarian regimes by force. We have tried these tactics in the past. However well intentioned, they have not worked. They've given democracy promotion a bad name, and they've lost the confidence of the American people. We will do things differently."[31]

In Beals's time, the kind of restraint he wished the United States to practice in the Americas, and the world, was called, usually derisively, an "isolationist" position. But while suspicious of military interventions, except when America was directly attacked, Beals leaned to a discreet—rather than crusading liberal internationalist—support for democracy in other countries.

"Does 'global responsibility' have to remain aggressive and require armed intervention everywhere the smoke of freedom rises?" he wrote in one of his last books, published in 1970. "Must decency in international relations be equated with isolationism?"[32] He offered no specific answer, but was inclined toward what the conservative economist Martin Feldstein has called an "inward-first approach" to *economic* policy reform, that is, toward a focus on setting an example at home for the reform you want your neighbors to emulate.[33] Beals implicitly argued for a similar approach in promoting democracy; "there is," he wrote, "a growing awareness that for every social injustice, crime and international misdeed committed by others abroad, the United States has committed the same abuses at home."[34]

He also favored, when wartime prompted him to be concerned about securing America's access to important natural resources, an emphasis on international commerce as a force for promoting stability.

Consistent with his socialist progressive roots, however, he insisted in 1939 that America needed to break down the cabal joining Washington's political elite and Wall Street, and its excessive influence over foreign policy, to build an authentic free trade area with Latin America. This would create a "special sphere of interest and protection" he argued, replacing, "our attempt to exercise merely political and military influence, without a proper economic basis, [which] now exposes us increasingly to future defeat and to the constant charge of imperialism."[35] Again, this is an idea that has become common currency; the United States now has free trade agreements with eleven Latin American countries.[36]

Beals saw America's support for dictators in Latin America as a liability in the fight against fascist enemies in World War II. "We cannot hope to successfully defend Latin America against the totalitarian powers," Beals wrote, "unless they are thereby enabled to share equally with us the larger freedom that we seek to preserve."[37] On the economic front, he believed, like President Abraham Lincoln's US Secretary of State William Seward, for example, that America's political influence in favor of democracy would come through the power of *mutually beneficial* trade.[38] Finally, like President Thomas Jefferson, he believed that America's "duty" toward Latin America was, "to wish them independence and self-government, because they wish it themselves; and they have the right, and we none, to choose for themselves."[39]

Beals continued to apply the same principle in his critique of US foreign policy as the Cold War containment doctrine shaped it from the Truman administration until the collapse of the Soviet empire, which came a decade after Beals's death. He was one of only a few voices denouncing the CIA-orchestrated Guatemala coup in 1954 when it happened, even anticipating it. In the forbidding climate of blacklists and Red-baiting, however, he could not get his stories on it published at the time.

By the early 1960s, he found more company in denouncing US hostility to the Cuban Revolution, and the Bay of Pigs invasion, which led directly to the 1962 Cuban missile crisis. The timing of Beals's 1963 translation of Juan José Arévalo's *Anti-Kommunism in Latin America*, was appropriate as the US paranoia about Communism had reached its apogee just as the Communist presence in Latin America had declined to its lowest point, save for Cuba.[40] Indeed, Castro's turn to the Soviet Union was, as many scholars have shown, largely a reaction to US policy. Jorge Dominguez, for example, has observed that, "the international system permitted this move; (Castro's) own political circumstances required it."[41] Elsewhere in Latin America, Communism was a "perceived rather than a visible threat to US interests," with Communist parties in decline throughout the region.[42]

This protest against the Cold War foreign policy deepened as the Vietnam war death toll mounted to the point that public disgust with it made a Bealsian kind of dissident position almost mainstream. By then, of course, Beals was an old man, a hermit in the winter of his life, forgotten by all but the left progressives who read his occasional pieces in the *National Guardian*. Even so, he was vindicated in seeing his longstanding, heretofore lonely and somewhat old-fashioned radicalism suddenly joined. With tens of thousands of Americans having been killed in Vietnam by the late 1960s, the anti-war movement was surging and with it, the New Left, Ban-the-Bomb, Black Power, civil rights, feminist and peace movements, demonstrations at the 1968 Democratic and Republican conventions, and the hippie counterculture. For Beals, it was as if the cavalry had arrived.

This underlined Beals's status as a curmudgeonly, but clear-eyed Cassandra, who identified political trends early, and warned of their dangers. He smelled the menace of fascism during Benito Mussolini's March on Rome in 1922. He lamented the double-standard US officials applied to Mexico's legitimate claim to subsoil petroleum rights. He correctly denounced, in the 1920s, the US dollar and gunboat diplomacy in Central America and the Caribbean as short-sighted and doomed to fail. He saw the self-defeating myopia in US support for authoritarian military rulers from Latin America to Vietnam. He anticipated the bloc called the Third World even before it acquired that moniker and championed the "third way" between US capitalism and Soviet Communism that so many of its then-emerging leaders sought. He decried the US failure to understand the thirst for economic independence in developing countries in favor of an insistence on a rigid and misplaced Cold War lens for interpreting their fledgling societies' effort to find their own destiny. He also calculated, in advance, the cost to American prestige and credibility of its neo-imperialist adventures from Nicaragua in the 1920s to Cuba and Vietnam in the 1960s.

Beals's refusal to yield in demanding strict adherence to the highest principles of the American Republic in crafting and carrying out its foreign policy, and his refusal to accept *realpolitik* arguments to justify parsing those principles, even at the cost of watching his successful but always precarious career disintegrate, is an example that deserves attention. Was he a foolish idealist, a stubborn malcontent, or a model of intellectual honesty on a trashed landscape?

In reviewing his life's work, I have concluded that he was the latter. As a journalist, Beals unconsciously applied, *avant la lettre*, philosopher John Rawls's maximin principle of testing the legitimacy of one's actions by asking whether they maximize liberty and minimize inequality, and importantly, asking how they affect the worst-off. He found America often wanting on this score.[43] Beals made enemies easily with his take-no-prisoners denunciations of US diplomats as "stuffed shirts" and "apologists" of businessmen as "kissers of the feet of aristocrats," and so on. His prose sometimes lacked polish, and his invective had a back-street crudeness, too rarely tempered by whimsy or politesse. Mostly, he regarded the representatives of US interests, whether business or government, as unprincipled, or ignorant yokels, or both. Unable himself to rein in his passions and adapt to the constraints of working in an institution, he was unforgiving of conformists who, though not personally venal, were willing to carry out the policy, whatever it was.

Then as now, it is usually socially unacceptable for journalists to adopt this position. It is perceived as unseemly, discourteous, or jejune to openly challenge the morality of US motives in foreign interventions, or the character of those who direct them. Such defiance has currency among so-called radicals marching in the streets or on Washington's Mall, or with crusaders such as Ralph Nader or US Senator Bernie Sanders, but too often, it is frowned upon as undignified in the genteel circles of mainstream journalism.

Beals did not live to witness President Ronald Reagan's military interventions and covert operations in Nicaragua, El Salvador, Grenada, and Panama, or the Persian Gulf, Iraq and Afghanistan Wars launched respectively by the two Presidents Bush, George H. W. (1924–2018) and later his son George W. (1946–). He certainly would have opposed them all and been dismayed but unsurprised by the role played by prominent media in shaping, or at least acquiescing to, an elite Washington consensus supporting them. While President Donald J. Trump's (1946–) unprecedented public mendacity may have scrambled some of the rules in reporting on the Presidency, Beals would have denounced the active support he has enjoyed from some media, and the casual accommodation made by many others.

Journalists' own fear of being confused with megaphone ideologues or ingenuous naïfs or, perhaps, of being ejected from the elite circles to which they have been admitted, has cowed many of them. This climate has softened their bile and, along with it, sadly, much of their fire and skepticism. That journalistic maxim, "comfort the afflicted and afflict the comfortable," is only selectively observed. Shorn of universal application, it has lost its power as an organizing principle for the practice, craft, and industry of journalism, and generated cynicism among thinking audiences.

Beals's posthumous marooning as a stranded ghost in the annals of American journalism history is due, in large measure, to intolerance of journalists who make a habit of challenging the ethics behind the actions of America's leaders. This intolerance has stifled all but a few of our journalists from developing the capacity to conceive of an alternative vision of the world's possibilities outside the parameters of US foreign policy interests, as defined by the US government. It is hard to exaggerate the disservice to America's attentive public of this repeated failure to think outside the box.

A few contemporary journalists do not fit this mold and are, in some sense, in the Beals tradition. David Halberstam's reporting on Vietnam was legendary not just for its exhaustive research, but also for its willingness to challenge received orthodoxies from the powerful. Raymond Bonner reported with fearless clarity on the US-backed Savadorean army's atrocities in the 1980s. More recently, Glenn Greenwald, the journalist who broke the Edward Snowden revelations on US National Security Agency (NSA) surveillance practices with filmmaker Laurie Poitras, regularly denounces groupthink among journalists, their excessive closeness to government sources, and willingness to channel points of view that please both those sources and the media for which they work. Others include the late Christopher Hitchens, whose campaign to have US Secretary of State Henry Kissinger tried as a war criminal is reminiscent of Beals's public attack on US Ambassador to Mexico Henry Lane Wilson for his alleged role in Mexican President Francisco Madero's overthrow and murder. Finally, Noam Chomsky, like Hitchens more public intellectual than reporter, has delivered a withering critique of US foreign policy as imperialism for decades and, like Beals, has been largely denied access to mass-audience media.

The work of these journalists and public intellectuals, like that of Beals, is salutary, necessary to the republic and to the world around it. In their work, and in that of Beals, we find a bracingly distinct version of often familiar events, whose veracity compels even as its difference from the mainstream induces some doubt. Even if the contemporary media landscape is utterly transformed since Beals's time, a new generation of freelancers is emerging to rescue coverage of "global" stories from larger media that have shuttered their overseas bureaus.[44]

Journalists from this tradition will, one hopes, wrest control of our public conversation from the hysterical blowhards on cable television and radio talk shows, most of whom, despite hardnosed personas, are thinly-disguised proxies for the powerful, reinforcing a status-quo discourse. Unlike them, Beals and those following in his journalistic tradition stand out. Some have emerged with the media's transformation to online platforms, enabling backpack and citizen journalists to build audiences. These reporters believe what they say, and have the facts to prove their stories, however unpopular or unorthodox. These rare journalists include men and women whose lives are fraught by risk and sacrifice in devotion to their craft. They are exciting because they are unafraid to call it as they found it and bear the consequences. They are "awkward." And necessary.

## NOTES

1. Time editors. "Books: Stone-Thrower," Review of *Glass Houses*, by Carleton Beals, *Time* 31, no. 18, April 25, 1938, http://content.time.com/time/subscriber/article/0,33009,931058,00.html (accessed May 27, 2021); *Merriam-Webster Dictionary*, s.v. "awkward," http://www.merriam-webster.com/dictionary/awkward.

2. See Silvio Waisbord, "Advocacy Journalism in a Global Context," in *The Handbook of Journalism Studies*, ed. Karin Wahl-Jorgensen and Thomas Hanitzsch (New York: Routledge, 2009), 371–85. Waisbord juxtaposes what he calls "advocacy journalists" motivated by a desire to redress power imbalances and guided by a reformist impulse to promote perspectives that are typically under- or misrepresented in the media, against the "gate-keeper" model (371), the notion of professional journalism guided by the ideals of objectivity and public service. Beals would qualify as an advocacy journalist under Waisbord's definition; like many others in this category, his work was mostly found in alternative publications, described by Waisbord as "flag-carriers for advocacy journalism, such as the publications of anti-war, feminist, gay, environmental, and ethnic rights movements" (373).

3. Carleton Beals, "Press Freedom in the United States," November 11 & 18, 1960, *El Sol* (Montevideo), Carleton Beals Collection (CBC), Howard Gotlieb Archival Research Center, Boston University (hereafter cited CBC).

4. See Louis Althusser, "Ideology and Ideological State Apparatuses," in *Lenin and Philosophy, and Other Essays*, trans. Ben Brewster (New York: Monthly Review Press, 1971), 127–86.

5. See Jürgen Habermas, *The Structural Transformation of the Public Sphere – An Inquiry into a Category of Bourgeois Society*, trans. by Thomas Burger (Cambridge: MIT Press, 1991; original German: *Strukturwandel der Öffentlichkeit*, 1962). Habermas defines the public sphere as a neutral space between civil society and the state that arose as democracy developed in the 18th and 19th centuries. He attributes its creation to the emergent bourgeoisie which sought to challenge and curtail the power of the absolutist state by enabling informed and critical dis-

course in a public sphere. This public sphere enables political journalism, among other forms of expression. Habermas argues that the public sphere's effectiveness as a restraint on state power has been compromised by advertising, public relations, and other directed strategies to shape public opinion. These have transformed this sphere from a platform that allows open discussion in which people's private opinions can become public, to one that favors powerful players' efforts to manage consensus and promote consumer culture.

6. Antonio Gramsci, *Antonio Gramsci: Selections from the Prison Notebooks*, ed. and trans. Quintin Hoare and Geoffrey Nowell Smith (New York: International, 1971), 12, 259, 260–63; Michel Foucault, *Power/Knowledge: Selected Interviews and Other Writings, 1972–1977*, ed. Colin Gordon (New York: Pantheon, 1980), 93–95.

7. See Walter L. Hixson, *The Myth of American Diplomacy: National Identity and US Foreign Policy* (New Haven, CT: Yale University Press, 2008). Hixson subjects the history of US foreign policy to a postmodern analysis that integrates the ideas of these and other critical theorists to conclude that American foreign policy has been driven by a "myth to power" hegemony that has produced a "pathological aggression against enemy-others," and whose stubbornly unilateral approach prevents the US from participating in, or leading, the construction of a genuinely cooperative global community. He cites Beals's reporting of Augusto César Sandino as an example of a foreign actor challenging America's "imperial anxiety."

8. Edward W. Said, *Culture and Imperialism* (New York: Random House, 1994), 285–86. See also Richard J. Barnet, *Roots of War* (New York: Atheneum, 1972).

9. Said, *Culture and Imperialism*, 285–86.

10. Beals, *The Nature of Revolution*, 257–274; Herbert Marcuse, *One-Dimensional Man* (Boston: Beacon Press, 1964).

11. James William Park, *Latin American Underdevelopment: A History of Perspectives in the United States, 1870–1965* (Baton Rouge: Louisiana State University Press, 1995), 149.

12. Carleton Beals, *Mexico: An Interpretation* (New York: B. W. Huebsch, 1923).

13. Carleton Beals, "Dwight Morrow Agrees with Mexico," *Nation*, January 25, 1928, 91–93.

14. US Senate. Hearings before the Committee on Foreign Relations. *Use of the United States Navy in Nicaragua*. 70th Congress, 1st Session, Pursuant to S. Res. 137, Use of the United States Navy in Nicaragua. February 11 and 18, 1928, at February 11, 1928, 1.

15. Carleton Beals, "With Sandino in Nicaragua," *Nation*, February 22 & 29, 1928; and March 7, 15, 21, & 28, 1928.

16. David C. Hendrickson, *Union, Nation, or Empire: The American Debate over International Relations, 1789–1941* (Lawrence: University Press of Kansas, 2009), 14.

17. Mark Falcoff, *A Culture of Its Own: Taking Latin America Seriously* (New Brunswick, NJ: Transaction, 1998), 131–39.

18. "Our Intervention Limited by Hoover," *New York Times*, April 16, 1931, 9; See also Godfrey Hodgson, *The Colonel: The Life and Wars of Henry Stimson, 1867–1950* (New York: Knopf, 1990), 90–91.

19. Walter Russell Mead, *Special Providence: American Foreign Policy and How It Changed the World* (New York: Alfred A. Knopf, 2001), 179.

20. Charles A. Beard and Mary Ritter Beard, *America in Midpassage. Volume 3. The Rise of American Civilization* (New York: Macmillan, 1939), vol. 3, 400.

21. Charles A. Beard, "The Key to the Mexican Problem," *New Review*, 1914, 324.

22. Carleton Beals, *The Coming Struggle for Latin America* (New York: Halcyon House, 1940), 315.

23. Carleton Beals, *America South* (Philadelphia: J. B. Lippincott Company, 1937), 464.

24. Beals, *Coming Struggle*; and Carleton Beals, *Pan-America* (Boston: Houghton Mifflin, 1940).

25. William Appleman Williams, *The Tragedy of American Diplomacy* (New York: W. W. Norton, 1959), 183.

26. Williams, *Tragedy*, 49–51.

27. Carleton Beals, *Latin America: World in Revolution* (New York: Abelard-Schuman, 1963), 135.

28. US Department of State, US Secretary of State John Kerry, Remarks at Raising of the US Flag at US Embassy, Havana, Cuba, August 14, 2015, Diplomacy in Action, https://2009-2017.state.gov/secretary/remarks/2015/08/246121.htm (accessed May 27, 2021).

29. Beals, *Latin America*, 331.

30. US Department of State, US Secretary of State John Kerry, Remarks on US Policy in the Western Hemisphere, Organization of American States, Washington, DC, November 18, 2013, Diplomacy in Action, https://2009-2017.state.gov/secretary/remarks/2013/11/217680.htm (accessed May 27, 2021).

31. US Department of State, US Secretary of State Antony J. Blinken, Speech: "A Foreign Policy for the American People," Washington, DC, March 3, 2021, https://www.state.gov/a-foreign-policy-for-the-american-people/ (accessed May 27, 2021).

32. Carleton Beals, *The Nature of Revolution* (New York: Thomas Y. Crowell, 1970), 273.

33. Martin Feldstein, quoted in Henry R. Nau, *At Home Abroad: Identity and Power in American Foreign Policy* (Ithaca, NY: Cornell University Press, 2002), 117.

34. Beals, *Nature of Revolution*, 267.

35. Beals, *Pan-America*, 516.

36. US Office of the President, Office of the United States Trade Representative, Free Trade Agreements, https://ustr.gov/trade-agreements/free-trade-agreements (accessed May 27, 2021).

37. Beals, *Coming Struggle*, 472.

38. See Robert Kagan, *Dangerous Nation: America and the World 1600–1898* (New York: Alfred A. Knopf, 2006), 250–51.

39. See Robert W. Tucker and David R. Hendrickson, "Thomas Jefferson and American Foreign Policy," *Foreign Affairs* 69, no. 2 (1990): 153, https://doi.org/10.2307/20044308.

40. See Carleton Beals, trans., "Introduction," in *Anti-Kommunism in Latin America an X-Ray of the Process Leading to a New Colonialism*, by Juan José Arévalo (New York: Lyle Stuart, 1963).

41. Jorge I. Domínguez, *To Make a World Safe for Revolution: Cuba's Foreign Policy* (Cambridge, MA: Harvard University Press, 1989), 21.

42. Lester D. Langley, *America and the Americas: The United States in the Western Hemisphere*, 2nd ed. (Athens: University of Georgia Press, 2010), 189.

43. See John Rawls, *A Theory of Justice*, revised ed. (Cambridge: Harvard University Press, 1999).

44. See Lars Willnat and Jason Martin, "Foreign Correspondents: An Endangered Species?" in *The Global Journalist in the 21st Century*, ed. David H. Weaver and Lars Willnat (New York: Routledge, 2012), 495–510.

# Bibliography

## ARCHIVES AND COLLECTIONS

Carleton Beals, Special Collections Division, Joseph Mark Lauinger Library, Georgetown University Library, Washington, DC.
Carleton Beals Collection (CBC), Howard Gotlieb Archival Research Center, Boston University.
Christopher Neal (CNC), Private collection, Westmount, Quebec.
Francis White Papers (FWP), Milton Eisenhower Library, Johns Hopkins University, Baltimore.
George Washington University Library, Washington, DC.
Katherine Anne Porter Room, University of Maryland, College Park.
*Liberation,* Special Collections, Howard University Library, Washington, DC.
Melvin B. Yoken Collection (MBYC), John Hay Library, Brown University, Providence, Rhode Island.
*The New Masses,* Special Collections, George Mason University Library, Fairfax, Virginia.
U.S. Department of Justice, Federal Bureau of Investigation Files on Carleton Beals, Washington, DC.
U.S. Department of State, Records of U.S. Department of State Relating to Latin American & Caribbean States 1930–1934. LM 157.
U.S. Library of Congress (LOC), Washington, DC.
U.S. National Archives and Records Administration (NARA), College Park, Maryland.
U.S. National Archives and Records Administration (NARA), Washington, DC.
Victor Calverton Papers, New York Public Library, New York City.

## PRIMARY SOURCES

Beals, Carleton. *Adventure of the Western Sea.* New York: Henry Holt, 1956.
———. *American Earth: The Biography of a Nation.* Philadelphia: J. B. Lippincott, 1939.
———. *America South.* Philadelphia: J. B. Lippincott, 1937.
———. *Banana Gold.* Philadelphia: J. B. Lippincott, 1932.
———. *Black River.* Philadelphia: J. B. Lippincott, 1934.
———. *Brass-Knuckle Crusade: The Great Know-Nothing Conspiracy, 1820–1860.* New York: Hastings House, 1960.

———. *Bridge of Royal Delights* (unpublished manuscript), Carleton Beals Collection (CBC), Howard Gotlieb Archival Research Center, Boston University.
———. *Brimstone and Chili: A Book of Personal Experiences in the Southwest and in Mexico*. New York: Knopf, 1927.
———. *Colonial Rhode Island*. Camden, NJ: Thomas Nelson, 1970.
———. *The Coming Struggle for Latin America*. New York: Halcyon House, 1940.
———. *The Crime of Cuba*. Philadelphia: J. B. Lippincott, 1933.
———. *Cyclone Carry: The Story of Carry Nation*. New York: Chilton Books, 1962.
———. *Dawn Over the Amazon*. New York: Duell, Sloan, and Pearce, 1943.
———. *Destroying Victor*. New York: Macaulay, 1929.
———. *Eagles of the Andes: South American Struggles for Independence*. Philadelphia: Chilton Books, 1963.
———. *Fire on the Andes*. Philadelphia: J. B. Lippincott, 1934.
———. *Glass Houses: Ten Years of Free-Lancing*. Philadelphia: J. B. Lippincott, 1938.
———. *The Great Circle: Further Adventures in Free-Lancing*. Philadelphia: J. B. Lippincott, 1940.
———. *Great Guerrilla Warriors*. Englewood Cliffs, NJ: Prentice-Hall, 1970.
———. *The Great Revolt and Its Leaders: The History of Popular American Uprisings in the 1890s*. New York: Abelard-Schuman, 1968.
———. *House in Mexico*. New York: Hastings House, 1958.
———. *The Incredible Incas: Yesterday and Today*. New York: Abelard-Schuman, 1973.
———, trans. "Introduction." In *Anti-Kommunism in Latin America An X-Ray of the Process Leading to a New Colonialism*, by Juan José Arévalo, 9–16. New York: Lyle Stuart, 1963.
———. *John Eliot: The Man Who Loved the Indians*. New York: Messner, 1957.
———. *Land of the Mayas: Yesterday and Today*. New York: Abelard-Schuman, 1966.
———. *Lands of the Dawning Morrow: The Awakening from Rio Grande to Cape Horn*. New York: Bobbs-Merrill, 1948.
———. *Latin America: World in Revolution*. New York: Abelard-Schuman, 1963.
———. *The Making of Bristol*. Bristol, CT: Bristol Public Library Association, 1954.
———. *Mexican Maze*. Philadelphia: J. B. Lippincott, 1931.
———. *Mexico: An Interpretation*. New York: B. W. Huebsch, 1923.
———. *The Nature of Revolution*. New York: Thomas W. Crowell, 1970.
———. *Nomads and Empire Builders: Native Peoples and Cultures of South America*. Philadelphia: Chilton Books, 1961.
———. *Our Yankee Heritage: The Making of Greater New Haven*. New Haven, CT: Bradley & Scoville, 1951.
———. *Pan America*. Boston: Houghton Mifflin, 1940.
———. *Porfirio Díaz: Dictator of Mexico*. Philadelphia: J. B. Lippincott, 1932.
———. *Rio Grande to Cape Horn*. Boston: Houghton Mifflin, 1943.
———. *Rome or Death: The Story of Fascism*. New York: Century, 1923.
———. *Stephen F. Austin: Father of Texas*. New York: McGraw-Hill, 1951.
———. *The Stones Awake: A Novel of Mexico*. Philadelphia: J. B. Lippincott, 1936.
———. *The Story of Huey P. Long*. Philadelphia: J. B. Lippincott, 1935.
———. *Taste of Glory: A Novel*. New York: Crown, 1956.
———. "Under the Fifth Sun." Unpublished autobiography. c. 1972–1978. In Carleton Beals Collection (CBC), Howard Gotlieb Archival Research Center, Boston University. Box 45. [One title among several given to unfinished and unpublished autobiography.]
———. *War Within a War: The Confederacy Against Itself*. New York: Chilton Books, 1965.
Beals, Carleton, and Stanton Catlin, *Mexico: A Columbia Records Legacy Album*. Mexican Orchestra conducted by Carlos Chavez, 1964. Winner Best Album Notes, 7th Grammy Awards, 1964. https://www.grammy.com/grammys/awards/winners-nominees/132 (accessed May 31, 2021).
Beals, Carleton, and Clifford Odets. *Rifle Rule in Cuba*. American Commission to Investigate Labor and Social Conditions in Cuba. New York: Provisional Committee for Cuba, 1935.
Beals, Carleton, and Ross, Edward Alsworth. *The Church Problem in Mexico*. New York: Academy Press, 1926.

# SECONDARY SOURCES

Aaron, Daniel. *Writers on the Left: Episodes in American Literary Communism*. New York: Harcourt, Brace, and World, 1961.
Agee, James, and Walker Evans. *Let Us Now Praise Famous Men*. Boston: Houghton Mifflin, 1941.
Aguilar, Luis E. *Cuba 1933: Prologue to Revolution*. New York: W. W. Norton, 1974.
Alpern, Sara. *Freda Kirchwey: A Woman of "The Nation."* Cambridge, MA: Harvard University Press, 1987.
Althusser, Louis. "Ideology and Ideological State Apparatuses," in *Lenin and Philosophy and Other Essays*, translated by Ben Brewster, 127–86. New York: Monthly Review Press, 1971.
Arévalo, Juan José. *Anti-Kommunism in Latin America: An X-Ray of the Process Leading to a New Colonialism*. Translated by Carleton Beals. New York: Lyle Stuart, 1963.
———. *The Shark and the Sardines*, trans. June Cobb and Raul Osegueda. New York: Lyle Stuart, 1961.
Bacevich, Andrew J. *Diplomat in Khaki: Major General Frank Ross McCoy and American Foreign Policy, 1898–1949*. Lawrence: University Press of Kansas, 1989.
Barnet, Richard J. *Roots of War*. New York: Atheneum, 1972.
Basadre, Jorge. *Historia de la República del Perú, 1822–1933*. 6th ed. 17 vols. Lima, Perú: Editorial Universitaria, 1963.
Beals, Ralph L. "Memories of My Brother, Carleton Beals." 1982. Prepared for Melvin B. Yoken. Melvin B. Yoken Collection (MBYC), John Hay Library, Brown University, Providence, Rhode Island.
———. "Prospective Diary of Trip to Mexico in 1918–1919." Unpublished manuscript. c. 1932. Courtesy of Alan R. Beals. In Christopher Neal, Private collection (CNC), Westmount, Quebec.
Beard, Charles A. *A Foreign Policy for America*. New York: Alfred A. Knopf, 1940.
Beard, Charles A., and Mary Ritter Beard. *America in Midpassage. Volume 3. The Rise of American Civilization*. vol. 3 of 4. New York: Macmillan, 1939.
Belfrage, Cedric, and James Aronson. *Something to Guard: The Stormy Life of the National Guardian, 1948–1967*. New York: Columbia University Press, 1978.
Benjamin, Jules R. *The United States and the Origins of the Cuban Revolution: An Empire of Liberty in an Age of National Liberation*. Princeton, NJ: Princeton University Press, 1990.
Benson, Jackson J. "'To Tom, Who Lived It': John Steinbeck and the Man from Weedpatch." *Journal of Modern Literature* 5, no. 2 (1976): 151–210. https://www.jstor.org/stable/3830940
Bethell, Leslie, and Ian Roxborough, eds. *Latin America between the Second World War and the Cold War, 1944–1948*. Cambridge: Cambridge University Press, 1992.
Black, George. *The Good Neighbor: How the United States Wrote the History of Central America and the Caribbean*. New York: Pantheon, 1988.
Bondil, Nathalie, ed. *Cuba: Art and History from 1868 to Today*. Produced by Montreal Museum of Fine Arts; Museo Nacional de Bellas Artes and the Fototeca de Cuba in Havana. Westminster, MD: Prestel USA, 2008.
Bonsal, Philip W. *Cuba, Castro, and the United States*. Pittsburgh, PA: University of Pittsburgh Press, 1971.
Brenner, Anita. *Idols Behind Altars*. New York: Payson & Clarke, 1929.
———. (Unpublished journal, November 21, 1925). Courtesy of Susannah Joel Glusker, Mexico City.
Brenner, Anita, and George R. Leighton. *The Wind that Swept Mexico: The History of the Mexican Revolution of 1910–1942*. New ed. Austin: University of Texas Press, 1971. First published in 1943.
Brinkley, Alan. *Voices of Protest: Huey Long, Father Coughlin, and the Great Depression*. New York: Alfred A. Knopf, 1982.
Britton, John A. *Carleton Beals: A Radical Journalist in Latin America*. Albuquerque: University of New Mexico Press, 1987.

———. *Revolution and Ideology: Images of the Mexican Revolution in the United States.* Lexington: University Press of Kentucky, 1995.
Brotherstone, Terry, and Paul Dukes, eds. *The Trotsky Reappraisal.* Translated by Brian Pearce, Jenny Brine, and Andrew Drummond. Edinburgh: Edinburgh University Press, 1992.
Brown, Archie. *The Rise and Fall of Communism.* New York: Ecco and HarperCollins, 2011.
Buhite, Russell D., and David W. Levy, eds. *FDR's Fireside Chats.* Norman: University of Oklahoma Press, 1992.
Calverton, Victor F. *The Liberation of American Literature.* New York: Charles Scribner, 1932.
Campbell, John C. "Political Extremes in South America." *Foreign Affairs* 20, no. 3 (1942): 517–34. https://doi.org/10.2307/20029172.
Carson, Rachel. *Silent Spring.* Boston: Houghton Mifflin, 1962.
Catholic Church. National Conference of Catholic Bishops. *Pastoral Letter of the Catholic Episcopate of the United States on the Religious Situation in Mexico.* Committee of the American Episcopate. New Haven, CT: Committee of the American Episcopate, 1926. https://catalog.princeton.edu/catalog/2336775 (accessed May 19, 2021).
Chase, Stuart. *A New Deal.* New York: Macmillan, 1932.
Charlip, Julie A. "At Their Own Risk: Coffee Farmers and Debt in Nicaragua, 1870–1930." In *Identity and Struggle at the Margins of the Nation-State*, edited by Aviva Chomsky and Aldo Lauria-Santiago, 94–121. Durham, NC: Duke University Press, 1998.
Chomsky, Aviva, and Aldo Lauria-Santiago, eds. *Identity and Struggle at the Margins of the Nation-State: The Laboring Peoples of Central America and the Hispanic Caribbean.* Durham, NC: Duke University Press, 1998.
Chomsky, Noam, and Edward Herman. *Manufacturing Consent: The Political Economy of the Mass Media.* New York: Pantheon, 1988.
Cosío Villegas, Daniel, ed. *Historia general de México.* 4th ed. 2 vols. México City: El Colegio de México, 1998.
Cowie, Jefferson R. *The Emergence of Alternative Views of Latin America: The Thought of Three U.S. Intellectuals, 1920–1935.* Working Paper 3. Durham, NC: Duke-University of North Carolina Program in Latin American Studies, September 1992.
Croly, Herbert. *The Promise of American Life* (1909). Princeton, NJ: Princeton University Press, 2014.
Cullather, Nick. *Secret History: The CIA's Classified Account of Its Operations in Guatemala, 1952–1954.* 2nd ed. Stanford, CA: Stanford University Press, 2006.
Currie, Harold W. *Eugene V. Debs.* Boston: Twayne, 1976.
Dallek, Robert. *Franklin D. Roosevelt and American Foreign Policy, 1932–1945.* New York: Oxford University Press, 1979.
Davis, Harold Eugene. Review of *Latin America: World in Revolution*, by Carleton Beals. *Americas* 21, no. 2 (1964): 212–13. https://doi.org/10.2307/979063.
Deas, Malcolm. "John A. Britton, Carleton Beals. A Radical Journalist in Latin America." *Journal of Latin American Studies* 21, nos. 1–2 (1989): 187–88. https://doi.org/10.1017/S0022216X00014723.
Delpar, Helen. *The Enormous Vogue of Things Mexican: Cultural Relations between the United States and Mexico, 1920–1935.* Tuscaloosa: University of Alabama Press, 1992.
Dennis, Lawrence. "Revolution, Recognition and Intervention." *Foreign Affairs* 9, no. 2 (1931): 204–21. https://doi.org/10.2307/20030344.
Denny, Harold Norman. *Dollars for Bullets: The Story of American Rule in Nicaragua.* New York: L. MacVeagh, Dial Press, 1929.
DePalma, Anthony. *The Man Who Invented Fidel: Castro, Cuba, and Herbert L. Matthews of the New York Times.* New York: Public Affairs, 2006.
Deutscher, Isaac. *The Prophet Outcast: Trotsky 1929–1940.* New York: Random House, 1963.
Deutschmann, David, and Deborah Schnookal, eds. *Fidel Castro Reader.* North Melbourne: Ocean Press, 2008.

Dewey, John (Chairman). Commission of Inquiry into the Charges Made Against Leon Trotsky in the Moscow Trials. *The Case of Leon Trotsky: Transcript of Proceedings*. New York. Merit, 1968. Originally published 1937.

———. *Not Guilty: Report of the Commission of Inquiry into the Charges Made Against Leon Trotsky in the Moscow Trials*. Brooklyn, NY: Sam Sloan and Ishi Press International, 2008. Originally published in 1938.

Domínguez, Jorge I. *To Make a World Safe for Revolution: Cuba's Foreign Policy*. Cambridge, MA: Harvard University Press, 1989.

Dozer, Donald Marquand. *Are We Good Neighbors? Three Decades of Inter-American Relations, 1930–1960*. Gainesville: University of Florida Press, 1959.

Dur, Philip, and Christopher Gilcrease. "US Diplomacy and the Downfall of a Cuban Dictator: Machado in 1933." *Journal of Latin American Studies* 34, no. 2 (2002): 255–82. https://doi.org/10.1017/S0022216X02006417.

Falcoff, Mark. *A Culture of Its Own: Taking Latin America Seriously*. New York: Routledge, 1998.

Farrell, James T. "Dewey in Mexico." In *John Dewey: Philosopher of Science and Freedom*, edited by Sidney Hook, 351–77. New York: Daily Press, 1950.

Fergusson, Erna. *Mexico Revisited*. New York: Alfred A. Knopf, 1955.

Foucault, Michel. *Power/Knowledge: Selected Interviews and Other Writings, 1972–1977*. Edited by Colin Gordon. New York: Pantheon, 1980.

Frank, Waldo. *Cuba: Prophetic Island*. New York: Marzani & Munsell, 1961.

Free, Lloyd A. *Attitudes of the Cuban People Toward the Castro Regime in the late Spring of 1960*. Princeton, NJ: Institute of International Social Research, 1960.

Friedman, Max Paul. *Rethinking Anti-Americanism: The History of an Exceptional Concept in American Foreign Relations*. Cambridge: Cambridge University Press, 2012.

Galeano, Eduardo. *Las Venas abiertas de América Latina*. Coyoacán, Mexico: Siglo XXI, 1974.

Garner, Paul. *Porfirio Díaz del héroe al dictador: Una biografía politica*. Mexico: Planeta, 2003.

Gellman, Irwin F. *Secret Affairs: Franklin Roosevelt, Cordell Hull, and Sumner Welles*. Baltimore: Johns Hopkins University Press, 1995.

Gibson-Brenman, Margaret. *Clifford Odets: American Playwright, The Years 1906–1940*. New York: Applause Theatre and Cinema Books, 2002.

Gilderhus, Mark T. *Diplomacy and Revolution: U.S.-Mexican Relations under Wilson and Carranza*. Tucson: University of Arizona Press, 1977.

Glad, Betty. *Charles Evans Hughes and the Illusions of Innocence: A Study in American Diplomacy*. Urbana: University of Illinois Press, 1966.

Glotzer, Albert. *Trotsky: Memoir and Critique*. Buffalo, NY: Prometheus Books, 1989.

Glusker, Susannah Joel. *Anita Brenner: A Mind of Her Own*. Austin: University of Texas Press, 1998.

Goldstein, Robert Justin. *Political Repression in Modern America: From 1870 to 1976*. Chicago: University of Illinois Press, 2001.

Gosse, Van. *Where the Boys Are: Cuba, Cold War America and the Making of a New Left*. New York: Verso, 1993.

Gould, Jeffrey L. "Nicaragua." In *Latin America between the Second World War and the Cold War, 1944–1948*, edited by Leslie Bethell and Ian Roxborough, 243–79. Cambridge: Cambridge University Press, 1992.

———. "Vana Ilusión!": The Highlands Indians and the Myth of Nicaraguan Mestiza, 1880–1925." In *Identity and Struggle at the Margins of the Nation-State*, edited by Aviva Chomsky and Aldo Lauria-Santiago, 52–93. Durham, NC: Duke University Press, 1998.

Gramsci, Antonio. *Antonio Gramsci: Selections from the Prison Notebooks*. Edited and translated [from the Italian] by Quintin Hoare and Geoffrey Nowell Smith. New York: International, 1971.

Grandin, Greg. *Empire's Workshop: Latin America, the United States, and the Rise of the New Imperialism*. New York: Henry Holt, 2006.

Gronbeck-Tedesco, John A. *Cuba, the United States and Cultures of the Transnational Left, 1930–1975*. New York: Cambridge University Press, 2015.
Gruening, Ernest. *Many Battles: The Autobiography of Ernest Gruening*. New York: Liveright, 1973.
———. *Mexico and Its Heritage*. New York: Century, 1928.
Guggenheim, Harry Frank. *The United States and Cuba: A Study in International Relations*. New York: Macmillan, 1934.
Gunther, John. *Inside Latin America*. New York: Harper and Brothers, 1941.
Guttenplan, D. D. *American Radical: The Life and Times of I. F. Stone*. New York: Farrar, Strauss, and Giroux, 2009.
Halper, Albert. *Good-Bye Union Square: A Writer's Memoir of the Thirties*. Chicago: Quadrangle Books, 1970.
Hendrickson, David C. *Union, Nation, or Empire: The American Debate Over International Relations, 1789–1941*. Lawrence: University Press of Kansas, 2009.
Herman, Edward S., and Noam Chomsky. *Manufacturing Consent: The Political Economy of the Mass Media*. New York: Pantheon Books, 1988.
Hixson, Walter L. *The Myth of American Diplomacy: National Identity and U.S. Foreign Policy*. New Haven, CT: Yale University Press, 2008.
Hook, Sidney, ed. *John Dewey: Philosopher of Science and Freedom*. New York: Dial Press, 1950.
Hooks, Margaret. *Tina Modotti: Radical Photographer*. New York: Da Capo Press, 1993.
Huberman, Leo, and Paul M. Sweezy. *Cuba: Anatomy of a Revolution*. New York: Monthly Review Press, 1960.
Hugo, Victor. *Les Misérables*. Belgium: Lacroix, Verbeckhoven & Cie, 1862.
Hunt, Andrew E. *David Dellinger: The Life and Times of a Nonviolent Revolutionary*. New York: New York University Press, 2006.
Inman, Samuel Guy. *Intervention in Mexico*. New York: Association Press, 1919.
Instituto de Estudio del Sandinismo. *Ahora sé que Sandino Manda*. Managua, Nicaragua: Editorial Nueva Nicaragua, 1986.
———. *General Augusto C. Sandino*. Managua: Instituto de Estudio del Sandinismo/Editorial Nueva Nicaragua, 1986.
———. *General Augusto C. Sandino: Padre de la revolución popular y antimperialista, 1895–1934*. Managua, Nicaragua: Editorial Nueva Nicaragua, 1986. http://books.google.com/books?id=kFFqAAAAMAAJ.
Jacobs, Dan N. *Borodin: Stalin's Man in China*. Cambridge, MA: Harvard University Press, 1981.
Johnson, Leland L. "U.S. Business Interests in Cuba and the Rise of Castro." *World Politics* 17, no. 3 (1965): 440–59. https://doi.org/10.2307/2009288.
Johnson, Robert David. *The Peace Progressives and American Foreign Relations*. Cambridge, MA: Harvard University Press, 1995.
Kagan, Robert. *Dangerous Nation: America and the World 1600–1898*. New York: Alfred A. Knopf, 2006.
Trotsky, Leon. *Terrorism and Communism: A Reply to Karl Kautsky*, London: Verso, 2007; originally published 1920.
Kazin, Michael. *American Dreamers: How the Left Changed a Nation*. New York: Alfred A. Knopf, 2011.
Kelley, Robin D. G. "The Share Croppers Union." In *Encyclopedia of the American Left*, edited by Paul Buhle, Mari Jo Buhle, and Dan Georgakas. New York: Garland Publishers, 1990.
Kennedy, John F. *John F. Kennedy, Alliance for Progress Speech*, Tampa, Florida, October 18, 1960, DNC Press Release. JFK Library, Boston.
Kirker, Harold, and Burleigh Taylor Wilkins. "Beard, Becker and the Trotsky Inquiry." *American Quarterly* 13, no. 4 (1961): 519–25. https://doi.org/10.2307/2710373.
Klarén, Peter F. *Modernization, Dislocation, and Aprismo: Origins of the Peruvian Aprista Party, 1870–1932*. Austin: University of Texas Press, 1973.
———. *Peru: Society and Nationhood in the Andes*. New York: Oxford University Press, 2000.

Kline, George L. "The Defence of Terrorism: Trotsky and His Major Critics." In *The Trotsky Reappraisal*, edited by Terry Brotherstone and Paul Duke, translated by Brian Pearce, Jenny Brine, and Andrew Drummond, 156–65. Edinburgh: Edinburgh University Press, 1992.

Krauze, Enrique. *Mexico: Biography of Power: A History of Modern Mexico, 1810–1996*. Translated by Hank Heifetz. New York: HarperCollins, 1998.

La Botz, Dan. "American 'Slackers' in the Mexican Revolution: International Proletarian Politics in the Midst of a National Revolution." *Americas* 62, no. 4 (2006): 563–90. https://www.jstor.org/stable/4491137.

———. "The Mexican Communist Party." *Medium*. December 18, 2019. https://danlabotz.medium.com/the-mexican-communist-party-83a3f5ffbca1 (accessed May 13, 2021).

LaFeber, Walter. *Inevitable Revolutions: The United States in Central America*. New York: W. W. Norton, 1983.

Langley, Lester D. *America and the Americas: The United States and the Western Hemisphere*. 2nd ed. Athens: University of Georgia Press, 2010.

———. *The Banana Wars: An Inner History of American Empire, 1900–1934*. Lexington: University Press of Kentucky, 1983.

———. *The Banana Wars: United States Intervention in the Caribbean, 1898–1934*. Wilmington, DE: Scholarly Resources, 2002.

Lewis, Sinclair. *Main Street*. New York: Harcourt, Brace and Howe, 1920.

López Torres, Alejandra. "La biografía 'historica' de Carleton Beals a través de sus lectores." *Tzintzun. Revista de Estudios Historicos* 40 (2004): 107–34. http://www.tzintzun.umich.mx/index.php/TZN/article/view/316.

Luxenberg, Alan H. "Did Eisenhower Push Castro into the Arms of the Soviets?" *Journal of Interamerican Studies and World Affairs* 30, no. 1 (1988): 37–71, https://doi.org/10.2307/165789.

Lyons, Eugene. *Assignment in Utopia*. New York: Harcourt, Brace, 1937.

Macaulay, Neill. *The Sandino Affair*. Chicago: Quadrangle Books, 1971.

MacMillan, Margaret. *Paris 1919: Six Months That Changed the World*. New York: Random House, 2001.

Marcuse, Herbert. *One-Dimensional Man*. Boston: Beacon Press, 1964.

Mariátegui, José Carlos. *Seven Interpretive Essays on Peruvian Reality*. Translated by Marjory Urquidi. Austin: University of Texas Press, 1971.

Marnham, Patrick. *Dreaming With His Eyes Open: A Life of Diego Rivera*. Berkeley: University of California Press, 2000.

Masterson, Daniel M. *Militarism and Politics in Latin America: Peru from Sánchez Cerro to Sendero Luminoso*. Westport, CT: Greenwood Press, 1991.

McWilliams, Carey. *The Education of Carey McWilliams*. New York: Simon & Schuster, 1979.

Mead, Walter Russell. *Special Providence: American Foreign Policy and How It Changed the World*. New York: Alfred A. Knopf, 2001.

Mencken, H. L. *Prejudices: First Series*. New York: Alfred A. Knopf, 1919.

———. *Prejudices: Second Series*. London: Jonathan Cape, 1921.

———. *Prejudices: Third Series*. New York: Alfred A. Knopf, 1922.

*Merriam-Webster Dictionary*, http://www.merriam-webster.com/dictionary/.

Meyer, Lorenzo. "El primer tramo del camino." In *Historia General de México*, 4th ed., edited by Daniel Cosío Villegas, vol. 2, 1183–1272. México City: El Colegio de México, 1994.

Mills, C. Wright. *Listen Yankee: The Revolution in Cuba*. New York: Ballantine Books, 1960.

Munro, Dana Gardner. *The United States and the Caribbean Republics, 1921–1933*. Princeton NJ: Princeton University Press, 1974.

Myers, Constance Ashton. *The Prophet's Army: Trotskyists in America, 1928–1941*. Westport CT: Greenwood Press, 1977.

Nau, Henry R. *At Home Abroad: Identity and Power in American Foreign Policy*. Ithaca, NY: Cornell University Press, 2002.

Navasky, Victor. "Oswald Garrison Villard." *School of Cooperative Individualism*. 1990. https://www.cooperative-individualism.org/navasky-victor_oswald-garrison-villard-1990.htm (accessed May 20, 2021).

Navasky, Victor S. *A Matter of Opinion*. New York: Picador, 2005.

Needler, Martin C. Book Review of "Britton, *Carleton Beals: A Radical Journalist in Latin America* (Albuquerque: University of New Mexico Press, 1987)." *Hispanic American Historical Review* 68, no. 2 (1988): 374–75. https://doi.org/10.1215/00182168-68.2.374.

O'Brien, Thomas F. *The Revolutionary Mission: American Enterprise in Latin America, 1900–1945*. Cambridge: Cambridge University Press, 1996.

Orwell, George. *Nineteen Eighty-Four: A Novel*. London: Secker & Warburg, 1949.

Othón, Manuel José. *La Casita* (lyrics). Music by Felipe Llera. Recorded 1923. https://www.loc.gov/item/jukebox-67326/ (Library of Congress (LOC) audio-recording, accessed May 31, 2021).

Park, James William. *Latin American Underdevelopment: A History of Perspectives in the United States, 1870–1965*. Baton Rouge: Louisiana State University Press, 1995.

Patenaude, Bertrand M. *Trotsky: Downfall of a Revolutionary*. New York: HarperCollins, 2009.

Paxton, Robert O. *The Anatomy of Fascism*. New York: Alfred A. Knopf, 2004.

Pérez, Louis A., Jr., ed. *Cuban Studies 37*. Pittsburgh, PA: University of Pittsburgh Press, 2006.

———. *Cuba Under the Platt Amendment, 1902–1934*. Pittsburgh, PA: University of Pittsburgh Press, 1986.

———. "In Defense of Hegemony: Sumner Welles and the Cuban Revolution of 1933." In *Ambassadors in Foreign Policy: The Influence of Individuals on U.S.-Latin American Policy*, edited by C. Neale Ronning and Albert P. Vannucci, 28–48. New York: Praeger, 1987.

Phillips, R. Hart. *Cuban Sideshow*. Havana: Cuban Press, 1935.

Pike, Fredrick B. *FDR's Good Neighbor Policy: Sixty Years of Generally Gentle Chaos*. Austin: University of Texas Press, 1995.

Porter, Katherine Anne. *The Collected Stories of Katherine Anne Porter*. New York: Harcourt Brace, 1965.

Raat, W. Dirk. *Mexico and the United States: Ambivalent Vistas*. Athens: University of Georgia Press, 1992.

Rabe, Stephen G. *Eisenhower and Latin America: The Foreign Policy of Anticommunism*. Chapel Hill: University of North Carolina Press, 1988.

Rand, Ayn. *The Fountainhead*. Indianapolis, IN: Bobbs Merrill, 1943.

Rathbone, Belinda. *Walker Evans: A Biography*. New York: Houghton Mifflin, 1995.

Reed, John. *Ten Days that Shook the World*. New York: Boni & Liveright, 1919.

Rippy, J. Fred. "Review *Pan America: A Program for the Western Hemisphere*, by Carleton Beals." *Hispanic American Historical Review* 21, no. 2 (1941): 300–301. ttps://doi.org/10.2307/2507402.

Rivera, Ruben. *Alberto Rembao (1895–1962): Mexican American Protestant for Internationalism and Christian Holism*. Saarbrücken, Germany: VDM Verlag Dr. Müller, 2008.

Robinson, Ione. *A Wall to Paint On*. New York: E. P. Dutton, 1946.

Rojas, Rafael. *Fighting Over Fidel: The New York Intellectuals and the Cuban Revolution*. Translated by Carl Good. Princeton, NJ: Princeton University Press, 2016.

Ronning, C. Neale, and Albert P. Vannucci, eds. *Ambassadors in Foreign Policy: The Influence of Individuals on U.S.-Latin American Policy*. New York: Praeger, 1987.

Roosevelt, Theodore. *Through the Brazilian Wilderness*. New York: C. Scribner's Sons, 1914.

Rosenberg, Emily S. *Financial Missionaries to the World: The Politics and Culture of Dollar Diplomacy, 1900–1930*. Cambridge, MA: Harvard University Press, 1999.

Rushdie, Salman. *The Jaguar Smile: A Nicaraguan Journey*. London: Pan Books, 1987.

Sadlier, Darlene J. *Americans All: Good Neighbor Cultural Diplomacy in World War II*. Austin: University of Texas Press, 2012.

Said, Edward W. *Culture and Imperialism*. New York: Random House, 1994.

Salter, Daren. "Scottsboro Trials." *Encyclopedia of Alabama*. February 6, 2008. Last updated December 6, 2017. http://www.encyclopediaofalabama.org/article/h-1456 (accessed May 25, 2021).

Sánchez, Luis Alberto. *Haya de la Torre y el APRA*. 2nd ed. Lima, Perú: Editorial Universo, 1980.

Schlesinger, Stephen C., and Stephen Kinzer. *Bitter Fruit: The Untold Story of the American Coup in Guatemala.* 2nd ed. Garden City, NY: Doubleday, 1982.

Schmitz, David F. *Thank God They're on Our Side: The United States and Right-Wing Dictatorships, 1921–1965.* Chapel Hill: University of North Carolina Press, 1999.

Schoultz, Lars. *Beneath the United States: A History of U.S. Policy Toward Latin America.* Cambridge, MA: Harvard University Press, 1998.

Schroeder, Michael J. "Bandits and Blanket Thieves, Communists and Terrorists: The Politics of Naming Sandinistas in Nicaragua, 1927–36 and 1979–90." *Third World Quarterly* 26, no. 1 (2005): 67–86. https://www.jstor.org/stable/3993764.

———. "Horse Thieves to Rebels to Dogs: Political Gang Violence and the State in the Western Segovias, Nicaragua, in the Time of Sandino, 1926–1934," *Journal of Latin American Studies* 28, no. 2 (1996): 383–434. https://doi.org/10.1017/S0022216X00013055.

Serge, Victor. *Memoirs of a Revolutionary* (1951). Translated by Peter Sedgwick, with George Paizi. New York: New York Review, 2012.

Service, Robert. *History of Modern Russia: From Nicholas II to Vladimir Putin.* Revised ed. Cambridge, MA: Harvard Univeristy Press, 2005.

———. *Trotsky: A Biography.* Cambridge, MA: Harvard University Press, 2009.

Smith, Joseph. *The United States and Latin America: A History of American Diplomacy, 1776–2000.* New York: Routledge, 2005.

Smith, Wayne S. *The Closest of Enemies: A Personal and Diplomatic History of the Castro Years.* New York: W. W. Norton, 1988.

Spenser, Daniela. *Stumbling Its Way Through Mexico: The Early Years of the Communist International.* Translated by Peter Gellert. Tuscaloosa: University of Alabama Press, 2011.

Steinbeck, John. *The Grapes of Wrath.* New York: Viking Press, 1939.

Stephenson, Skye. "International Education Flows between the United States and Cuba (1959–2005): Policy Winds and Exchange Flows." In *Cuban Studies 37,* ed. Louis A. Pérez Jr., 122–57. Pittsburgh, PA: University of Pittsburgh Press, 2006.

Stimson, Henry L. *American Policy in Nicaragua: The Lasting Legacy.* New York: Markus Wiener, 1991.

Suchlicki, Jaime. *Cuba: From Columbus to Castro and Beyond.* 5th ed. Dulles, VA: Brassey's, 2002.

Szulc, Tad. *Fidel: A Critical Portrait.* New York: Harper Collins, 1986.

Taber, Robert. *M-26: Biography of a Revolution.* New York: Lyle Stuart, 1961.

Tanenhaus, Sam. *Whittaker Chambers: A Biography.* New York: Random House, 1997.

Tannenbaum, Frank. *Peace by Revolution: Mexico after 1910.* New York: Columbia University Press, 1933.

———. *Whither Latin America? An Introduction to Its Economic and Social Problems.* New York: Thomas Y. Cowell, 1934.

Thomas, Hugh. *Cuba, or The Pursuit of Freedom.* Updated ed. New York: Da Capo Press, 1998.

Thompson, Robert Smith. *The Missiles of October: The Declassified Story of John F. Kennedy and the Cuban Missile Crisis.* New York: Simon & Schuster, 1993.

Torres-Rioseco, A., and Carleton Beals. "Correspondence: On Peruvian Literature and an Article by Carleton Beals." *Books Abroad* 9, no. 2 (1935): 147–49. https://doi.org/10.2307/40076208.

Trotsky, Leon. *The Revolution Betrayed.* Translated by Max Eastman. Mineola NY: Dover, 2004. Originally published *The Revolution Betrayed: What Is the Soviet Union and Where Is It Going?* Translated by Max Eastman. Garden City, NY: Doubleday, Doran, 1937.

Tucker, Robert W., and David C. Hendrickson. "Thomas Jefferson and American Foreign Policy." *Foreign Affairs* 69, no. 2 (1990): 135–56. https://doi.org/10.2307/20044308.

Turtis, Richard Lee. "A World Destroyed, A Nation Imposed: The 1937 Haitian Massacre in the Dominican Republic." *Hispanic American Historical Review* 82, no. 3 (2002): 589–635. https://doi.org/10.1215/00182168-82-3-589.

Ulloa, Berta. "La lucha armada (1911–1920)." In *Historia General de México,* 4th ed., edited by Daniel Cosío Villegas, vol. 2, 1171–80. México City: El Colegio de México, 1998.

U.S. Congress. *Congressional Record*. 70th Congress, 2nd Session. Volume 70, Part 6 (December 3, 1928, to March 4, 1929), 9–236. https://www.govinfo.gov/app/details/GPO-CRECB-1929-pt6-v70/GPO-CRECB-1929-pt6-v70-1 (accessed May 13, 2021).

———. *Espionage Act of 1917*. Pub L. 65-24, 40 Stat. 217. 65th Cong., 1st sess. June 15, 1917.

———. Gulf of Tonkin Resolution (Southeast Asia Resolution), 78 Stat. 384, Pub. L. 88-408, 88th Cong., 2nd sess., August 10, 1964, https://www.govinfo.gov/content/pkg/STATUTE-78/pdf/STATUTE-78-Pg384.pdf (accessed May 27, 2021).

———. *Neutrality Act of 1935*. Pub. Res. 74-67, 49 Stat. 1081. 74th Cong., 1st sess. August 31, 1935, https://govtrackus.s3.amazonaws.com/legislink/pdf/stat/49/STATUTE-49-Pg1081.pdf (accessed May 25, 2021)

———. Platt Amendment. 1901 U.S. Army Appropriations Bill. 31 Stat. 895, Pub. L. 56-803. 56th Cong., 2nd sess. March 2, 1901.

———. Smith Act of 1940 (*Alien Registration Act, 1940*). 54 Stat. 670, Pub. L. 76-670. 76th Cong., 3rd sess. June 28, 1940. https://govtrackus.s3.amazonaws.com/legislink/pdf/stat/54/STATUTE-54-Pg670.pdf (accessed May 26, 2021).

———. *Tariff Act of 1930*, 19 U.S.C. ch. 4, Pub. L. 71-361, 71st Cong., 2nd sess. March 13, 1930.

U.S. Department of State. *Foreign Relations of the United States: Diplomatic Papers*. 1932. Vol. 5. Latin America. Washington, DC: United States Government Printing Office.

———. U.S. Secretary of State Antony J. Blinken. Speech: "A Foreign Policy for the American People." Washington, DC. March 3, 2021. https://www.state.gov/a-foreign-policy-for-the-american-people/ (accessed May 27, 2021).

———. U.S. Secretary of State John Kerry. Remarks at Raising of the U.S. Flag at U.S. Embassy. Havana, Cuba. August 14, 2015. Diplomacy in Action. https://2009-2017.state.gov/secretary/remarks/2015/08/246121.htm (accessed May 27, 2021).

———. U.S. Secretary of State John Kerry. Remarks on U.S. Policy in the Western Hemisphere, Organization of American States. Washington, DC. November 18, 2013. Diplomacy in Action. https://2009-2017.state.gov/secretary/remarks/2013/11/217680.htm (accessed May 27, 2021).

U.S. National Security Council. NSC 162/2. A Report to the National Security Council, by the Executive Secretary, James S. Lay, Jr., on Basic Nation Security Policy. October 30, 1953. Washington, DC. https://fas.org/irp/offdocs/nsc-hst/nsc-162-2.pdf (accessed May 26, 2021).

U.S. Office of the President. Office of the United States Trade Representative. Free Trade Agreements. https://ustr.gov/trade-agreements/free-trade-agreements (accessed May 27, 2021).

U.S. Senate. Hearings before the Committee on Foreign Relations. *Use of the United States Navy in Nicaragua*. 70th Congress, 1st Session, Pursuant to S. Res. 137, Use of the United States Navy in Nicaragua. February 11 and 18, 1928.

———. Hearings before the Subcommittee of the Senate Judiciary Committee to Investigate the Administration of the Internal Security Act and Other Internal Security Laws (on the Fair Play for Cuba Committee), 20 days of testimony, 1960–1963. http://onlinebooks.library.upenn.edu/webbin/book/lookupname?key=United States. Congress. Senate. Committee on the Judiciary. Subcommittee to Investigate the Administration of the Internal Security Act and Other Internal Security Law (accessed May 13, 2021).

Valcárcel, Luis E. *Tempestad en los Andes*, Lima, Perú: Populibros Peruanos, 1964.

Wahl-Jorgensen, Karin, and Thomas Hanitzsch, eds. *The Handbook of Journalism Studies*. 2nd ed. New York: Routledge, 2009.

Waisbord, Silvio. "Advocacy Journalism in a Global Context." In *The Handbook of Journalism Studies*, edited by Karin Wahl-Jorgensen and Thomas Hanitzsch, 371–85. New York: Routledge, 2009.

Wald, Alan M. *Exiles from a Future Time: The Forging of the Mid-Twentieth-Century Literary Left*. Chapel Hill: University of North Carolina Press, 2002.

———. *James T. Farrell: The Revolutionary Socialist Years*. New York: New York University Press, 1978.

———. *The New York Intellectuals: The Rise and Decline of the Anti-Stalinist Left from the 1930s to the 1980s*. Chapel Hill: University of North Carolina Press, 1987.

Walsh, Thomas F. *Katherine Anne Porter and Mexico: The Illusion of Eden*. Austin: University of Texas Press, 1992.
Weaver, David H., and Lars Willnat, eds. *The Global Journalist in the 21st Century*. New York: Routledge, 2012.
Welch, Richard E., Jr. *Response to Revolution: The United States and the Cuban Revolution, 1959–1961*. Chapel Hill: University of North Carolina Press, 1985.
Welles, Benjamin. *Sumner Welles: FDR's Global Strategist*. New York: St. Martin's Press, 1997.
Whitney, Robert. *State and Revolution in Cuba: Mass Mobilization and Political Change, 1920–1940*. Chapel Hill: University of North Carolina Press, 2001.
Williams, William Appleman. *The Tragedy of American Diplomacy*. New York: W. W. Norton, 1959.
Willnat, Lars, and Jason Martin. "Foreign Correspondents: An Endangered Species?" In *The Global Journalist in the 21st Century*, edited by David H. Weaver and Lars Willnat, 459–510. New York: Routledge, 2012.
Wolfe, Bertram D. *The Fabulous Life of Diego Rivera*. New York: Stein and Day, 1963.
Wood, Bryce. *The Dismantling of the Good Neighbor Policy*. Austin: University of Texas Press, 1985.
———. *The Making of the Good Neighbor Policy*. New York: W. W. Norton, 1961; 1967.
Woods, Kenneth F. "Samuel Guy Inman and Intervention in Mexico." *Southern California Quarterly* 46, no. 4 (1964): 351–70. https://doi.org/10.2307/41171358.

# Additional Sources

This list includes selected newspaper and magazine articles by Carleton Beals, as well as those interviewed by Christopher Neal and the names of newspapers and magazines consulted for this book.

*Selected Articles* by Carleton Beals, listed by date. Articles coauthored with Beals are included at the end of this list.

Beals, Carleton. "Fascismo—The Reaction in Italy." *Nation* 112, no. 2913, May 4, 1921, 656-57.
———. "Where Italy Stands." *Nation*, May 24, 1922.
———. "The Fate of Trieste: Redenta." *Nation*, July 12, 1922.
———. "The Fascist Labor Movement in Italy." *Nation*, October 4, 1922.
———. "The Black-Shirt Revolution." *Nation*, December 13, 1922.
———. "The Dictatorship of the Middle Class." *Nation*, January 17, 1923.
———. "The Italian Labor Line-Up." *Nation*, February 14, 1923.
———. "The Dictatorship of Benito Mussolini." *Current History* 18, no. 2, May 1923.
———. "What Calles Faces." *Survey Graphic*, December 1924.
———. "What Spain Faces." *Nation*, January 14, 1925.
———. "Tasks Awaiting President Calles." *Current History*, February 1925.
———. "Italian Fascism Developing a New Phase." *Current History*, May 1925.
———. "The Mexican Church Goes on Strike." *Nation*, August 18, 1926.
———. "Calles is Gaining in Mexico." *Nation*, October 6, 1926.
———. "Baron Banana in Puerto Barrios." *Nation*, September 15, 1926.
———. "Mexico Seeking Central American Leadership," *Current History* 24, September 6, 1926.
———. "The Religious Problem in Mexico." *Nation*, December 8, 1926.
———. "The Nicaraguan Farce." *Nation*, December 15, 1926.
———. "Mexico's Bloodless Victory," *Nation*, January 26, 1927.
———. "Whose Property is Kellogg Protecting?" *New Republic*, February 23, 1927.
———. "Who Wants War with Mexico?" *New Republic*, April 27, 1927.
———. "Civil War in Mexico – How It Strikes an Observer." *New Republic*, July 6, 1927.
———. "Mexico's Coming Election." *New Republic*, August 17, 1927.
———. "The Revolution in Mexico." *New Republic*, October 26, 1927.
———. "Whither Mexico?" *New Republic*, December 21, 1927.

———. "Dwight Morrow Agrees with Mexico," *Nation*, January 25, 1928.
———. "With Sandino in Nicaragua." *Nation*, February 22 & 29, 1928; March 7, 15, 21 & 28, 1928.
———. "The McCoy Election Law." *Nation*, April 4, 1928.
———. "Chamorro, the Strong Man of Nicaragua." *Nation*, April 11, 1928.
———. "This is War, Gentlemen!" *Nation*, April 11, 1928.
———. "Obregon: Bold Master of Mexico." *New York Times Magazine*, July 22, 1928.
———. "Digging Graves in Mexico." *Nation*, August 1, 1928.
———. "Calles: A Record of Statesmanship." *Current History*, January 1929.
———. "Mexico's Labor Crisis." *Nation*, March 13, 1929.
———. "Mexico Rises Out of Chaos." *Nation*, April 3, 1929.
———. "Mexican Military Adventurers in Revolt." *Current History*, May 1929.
———. "Spain: The Wreck of an Empire (1)." *Nation*, June 26, 1929.
———. "Spain: How Strong is the Dictatorship? (2)" *Nation*, July 3, 1929.
———. "Modern Spain: Censorship (3)." *Nation*, July 10, 1929.
———. "Modern Spai: Official Corruption (4)." *Nation*, July 17, 1929.
———. "Mexico and the Communists." *New Republic*, February 19, 1930.
———. "Latin-American Social and Political Progress." *Current History*, August 1930.
———. "Poet of Mexico." *Saturday Review of Literature*, August 16, 1930, 57.
———. "Valle Inclan in the Café." *Bookman* 72, November 1930.
———. "Mexico Turns to Fascist Tactics." *Nation*, January 28, 1931.
———. "Color in Our Foreign News," *Outlook and Independent*, February 25, 1931.
———. "Is America a Menace?" *Scribner's Magazine*, March 1931.
———. "Has Mexico Betrayed Her Revolution?" *New Republic*, July 22, 1931.
———. "Sandino Keeps His Word." *Nation*, February 22, 1933.
———. "The Crime of Cuba." *Reader's Digest,* April 1933.
———. "Young Cuba Rises." *Scribner's Magazine.* November, 1933.
———. "A New Code for Latin America." *Scribner's Magazine*. January 1934.
———. "American Diplomacy in Cuba." *Nation* 138, no. 3576, January 17, 1934.
———. "Burning Saints in Mexico." *Nation*, December 26, 1934.
———. "Aprismo: The Rise of Haya de la Torre." *Foreign Affairs* 13, no. 2, January, 1935.
———. "Latin America Grows Up." *Current History.* February 1935.
———. "Socialism on a Platter." *Nation*, April 10, 1935.
———. "Cuba's John Brown." *Common Sense*, July 1935.
———. "Revolt in Panama*."* *Nation*, July 24, 1935.
———. "The New Machado in Cuba." *Nation* 141, no. 3657, August 7, 1935, 153.
———. "The Scottsboro Puppet Show." *Nation*, February 5, 1936.
———. "Scottsboro Interview." *Nation*, February 12, 1936.
———. "Red Clay in Alabama." *Nation*, April 8, 15, 1936.
———. "Yankee in Havana." *Nation,* May 20, 1936.
———. "Serenade in Mexico." *Virginia Quarterly Review*, Autumn 1936.
———. "The Fewer Outsiders the Better." *Saturday Evening Post*, June 12, 1937.
———. "Pan-Americanism 1937-Style." *Political Quarterly* 8, no. 4, October 1937.
———. "Caesar of the Caribbean." *Current History* 48, no. 1, January 1938.
———. "The Mexican Challenge." *Current History* 48, no. 4, April 1938.
———. "Swastika Over the Andes." *Harper's Monthly*, July 1938.
———. "Japan Tiptoes Around the Monroe Doctrine," *Current History* 49, no. 1, September 1938.
———. "Totalitarian Inroads in Latin America." *Foreign Affairs*, October 1938.
———. "Black Shirts in Latin America," *Current History* 49, no. 3, November 1938.
———. "Red Star South," *Current History* 49, no. 4, December 1938.
———. "John Bull in Latin America." *Current History*, January 1939.
———. "South America: A Map Story," *Current History*, February 1939.
———. "Colombia: Again the Good Neighbor," *Current History* 50, no. 1, March 1939.
———. "Argentina versus the United States." *Current History*, July 1939.
———. "Defense of the Americas." *Common Sense*, December 1940.

———. "How to Flirt in Tehuantepec." *New Yorker*, July 14, 1942.
———. "A Modern Don Quixote." *Virginia Quarterly Review*, Spring 1943.
———. "Inside the Good Neighbor Policy (Bolivian Tin)." *Harpers*, August 1943.
———. "Our Crumbling Good Neighbor Policy." *Progressive*, January 15, 1945.
———. "The Democratic Road to Enduring Peace." *Progressive*, February 12, 1945.
———. "The Meaning of the Meeting on Grasshopper Hill." *Progressive*, March 19, 1945.
———. "Oil Imperialism Imperils Peace." *Progressive*, May 21, 1945.
———. "Poland and Argentina." *Progressive*, June 4, 1945.
———. "New Empires for Old." *Progressive*, September 3, 1945.
———. "Good Neighbors Don't Wear Brass Knuckles." *Progressive*, September 24, 1945.
———. "London: Peace versus Loot." *Progressive*, October 8, 1945.
———. "Where Do We Stand in Latin America?" *Progressive*, November 19, 1945.
———. "Golden Spike." *Asia and the Americas*, December 1945.
———. "One Man's Prison." *Progressive*, January 7, 1946.
———. "This is Mexico Today" *Progressive*, April 1, 1946.
———. "Crisis in Mexico." *Progressive*, April 8, 1946.
———. "Guatemala Turns to Liberty." *Progressive*, May 6, 1946.
———. "Getting the Truth about Latin America." *Progressive*, July 15, 1946.
———. "Crisis in Chile." *Progressive*, July 29, 1946.
———. "Schoolteacher President." *Asia and the Americas* 46, no. 8, August 1946, 363-67.
———. "Prosperous Argentina." *Progressive,* August 26, 1946.
———. "Argentina on the March." *Progressive,* September 2, 1946.
———. "Remaking Argentina." *Progressive*, September 23, 1946.
———. "Inside Argentina." *Progressive*, September 30, 1946.
———. "Revolution in Bolivia." *Progressive*, November 4, 1946.
———. "Barricades in Bolivia." *Asia and the Americas* 46, no. 11, November 1946, 489-94.
———. "Oil and Blood." *Progressive*, May 19, 1947.
———. "End of the World Strikes Oil." *Collier's*, August 2, 1947.
———. "It's Later than We Think." *Progressive*, August 18, 1947.
———. "Bayonet Labor Rule." *Current History*, January 1948.
———. "Dollar Diplomacy Sneaks Back." *Progressive*, June 1948.
———. "Why South America Growls." *Christian Century*, September 26, 1948.
———. "Buttering our Bread on the Wrong Side." *Saturday Review of Literature*, March 26, 1949.
———. "Neighborly No More." *Progressive*, August 1949.
———. "Explosion in Puerto Rico." *Progressive*, December 1950.
———. "Copper, Chile and Communism." *Nation*, October 13, 1951.
———. "Explosion in Bolivia." *Progressive*, June 11, 1952.
———. "The Vargas Story: Nation in Transition," *Nation*, September 4, 1954.
———. "Tragic Guatemala." *Progressive*, May 1955.
———. "Arms Come Home to Roost." *Christian Century*, June 1, 1955.
———. "Everywhere South." *Nation*, September 17, 1955.
———. "Who Won in Argentina?" *Nation*, October 1, 1955.
———. "Fountain of Light – A Dictator Disports." *Nation*, January 14, 1956.
———. "Rifle Rule in Cuba." *Christian Century*, November 21, 1956.
———. "Where Does Charity Begin?" *Christian Century*, January 30, 1957.
———. "The New Crime of Cuba." *Nation*, June 29, 1957, 566-68.
———. "Haiti under the Gun." *Nation*, 185, no. 1, July 6, 1957, 3-8.
———. "The Church in Cuba's Civil War." *Christian Century*, July 31, 1957, 915-17.
———. "Blackjacking Cuban Labor." *Christian Century*, August 21, 1957.
———. Cuban Manifesto, in "Letters," *Nation*, September 27, 1957.
———. "Gentleman as Diplomat." *Nation*, March 22, 1958.
———. "Wild Ducks for Cuba." *Christian Century*, April 2, 1958.
———. "Viva Nixon!" *Christian Century*, June 18, 1958, 716-18.
———. "Such a Little Country." *Nation*, August 2, 1958.
———. "Revolution without Generals." *Nation*, January 17, 1959, 43-45.

———. "Terror in Cuba?" *Nation*, January 24, 1959.
———. "As Cuba Sees It." *Nation,* January 31, 1959, 83-85.
———. "Cuba in Revolution." *Christian Century*, February 4, 1959, 131.
———. "The Squeeze on Castro." *Nation*, May 2, 1959, 402.
———. "Invasion by Rowboat." *Nation*, July 18, 1959.
———. "Cuba: Victim or Agressor [*sic*]? Report from Havana (1)." *Nation*, July 23, 1960.
———. "Cuba's Invasion Jitters," *Nation* 191, no. 16, November 12, 1960, 360-62.
———. "The Deadly Drive to Silence the Press in Latin America." *Independent* (New York), June 1961.
———. "Shakeup at Latin-American News Agency Threatens Its Integrity and Future Impact." *Independent* (New York), July 1961.
———. "Outhouse Economy." *Liberation*, September 1961.
———. "Castro and the OAS." *Nation*, January 13, 1962.
Beals, Carleton, and Abel Plenn. "Louisiana's Black Utopia." *Nation*, October 30, 1935.
———. "Louisiana Skin Game." *Nation*, December 25, 1935.

## MAGAZINES, NEWSPAPERS, AND NEWS AGENCIES

*Christian Century*
*Collier's*
*Common Sense*
*Current History*
*Diario de la Marina* (Cuba)
*Excelsior* (Mexico)
*Foreign Affairs*
*Harper's*
*Havana American-News*
*Havana Post*
*New York Herald-Tribune*
*Liberation*
*Mexican Folkways*
*Mexican Life*
*Modern Monthly*
*El Mundo* (Havana)
*La Nación* (Buenos Aires)
*Nation*
*National Guardian*
*New Masses*
*New Republic*
*News* (Mexico City)
*New Yorker*
*New York Post*
*New York Times*
*New York Times Magazine*
*La Prensa* (Managua)
*Prensa Latina*

*Progressive*
*Readers' Digest*
*Saturday Evening Post*
*Saturday Review of Literature*
*Scribner's Magazine*
*Time* (magazine)
*El Universal* (Mexico)
*Washington Post*

## INTERVIEWS

John A. Britton
Alan R. Beals
Carolyn Kennedy Beals
Ralph Carleton Beals
Lenny Cavallero
Melvin Yoken

# Index

ABC militants, 160, 161, 169–170, 173, 174, 179n6
ACLU. *See* American Civil Liberties Union
AFP. *See* American and Foreign Power Corporation
agrarian reform. *See* land reform
*agrarista* (Mexico), 22
Alfred Knopf Publishers, 17, 78, 147
Algonquin Hotel, 68
Alianza Popular Revolucionaria Americana (APRA) (American Popular Revolutionary Alliance): Beals, C., on, 184–185, 190, 253; Haya and, 184, 185, 186, 187, 253; persecution of, 184–185, 187
Allende, Salvador (Chile president), 238, 269
Alliance for Progress (US), 301, 302, 312, 313, 314, 333
Álvarez del Vayo, Julio, 138, 155n13, 317
American and Foreign Power Corporation (AFP), 176, 179n19
American Civil Liberties Union (ACLU), 14, 73, 92
*American Earth* (Beals, C.), 207, 241, 245–246, 247
American Federation of Labor, 100
American High School (Mexico): dismissal from, 38; teaching at, 30
American Popular Revolutionary Alliance. *See* Alianza Popular Revolucionaria Americana
American Protective League (APL), 15
American Republic peace summit, 234
American Socialist Party, 11, 12; Beals, E., in, 13, 14, 225
*America South* (Beals, C.), 177, 207, 262, 268, 332; Dependency Theory in, 234, 236–237, 255n14, 328; on Latin America and US, 235, 236, 238, 239; reviews of, 236, 239
d'Annunzio, Gabriele, 42–43
*Anti-Kommunism in Latin America* (Arévalo), 314, 315, 335
APL. *See* American Protective League
APRA. *See* Alianza Popular Revolucionaria Americana
Árbenz, Jacobo, 274–276, 333
Arévalo, Juan José (Guatemala president), 266–267, 274, 314–315, 335
Argentina: Beals, C., on, 263, 264, 265, 266, 312; FDR and, 234; military dictators in, 312–313. *See also* Perón, Juan
Association for the Protection of American Rights in Mexico, 58
Association of Oil Producers in Mexico, 58
Avellaneda, Juan de Dios, 27
awkwardness: Beals, C., with journalistic, 1, 5, 6–7, 237, 325, 326; in journalism,

359

196, 226, 270, 293, 326, 338

Baldwin, Dorothy, 74, 196
Baldwin, Roger, 14, 73–74, 198, 199, 225
*Banana Gold* (Beals, C.), 78, 103
Batista, Fulgencio (Cuba dictator), 3; Beals, C., on, 199–200, 284; Castro, F., and, 176, 284, 287, 288–289, 290; as coup leader, 171; Cuba repression by, 197, 330; government control by, 176; on Grau, 176, 183; Mendieta and, 176, 197, 198, 199; unrest on, 284; Welles and, 173
Bay of Pigs: Beals, C., on, 299, 301, 333; Cuban missile crisis and, 335; Latin America on, 302; as US fiasco, 3, 178n1, 300, 301, 302, 303, 314, 333, 335
Beals, Carleton: autobiography, 10, 23n2, 178n1, 320; beginnings of, 4; health and death of, 321, 322. *See also specific subjects*
Beals, Carolyn Kennedy (wife), 9–10, 254n10; with Beals, C., 281, 282, 283, 285–286; early life of, 282–283
Beals, Elvina (mother): on Beals, C., incarceration, 14; death of, 276; relationship with, 10, 21, 44, 47, 56, 67, 178, 251, 314; in US Socialist Party, 13, 14, 225
Beals, Leon Elverson (father), 13
Beals, Ralph Carleton (nephew), 50
Beals, Ralph Leon (brother), 10, 24n38; Mexico trek with, 16, 17, 18, 19, 20–21, 74
Beard, Charles A., 212, 213, 226, 249, 331
Becker, Maurice, 74, 196
Benavides, Óscar R. (Peru president), 184
Betty. *See* Daniel, Elizabeth
Bickel, Karl, 126n6, 250
Biden, Joe (US president), 334
*Black River* (Beals, C.), 183, 193–194, 195–196, 273
Blackshirts, 42, 43, 44, 45, 73
Blair, Albert, 38
Blanca. *See* Leyva y Arguedas, Blanca Rosa
Block, Harry, 78, 147–148, 149, 229n56
Boas, Franz, 10

Bolívar, Simón, 92, 100, 251, 316
Bolivia, 263, 330; Beals, C., and, 268, 287, 302; oil and, 250
Bonsal, Philip, 289, 299
Borodin, Mikhail (Gruzenberg, Michael), 31–32, 40n25; Beals, C., on, 31, 218–219, 227; Trotsky and, 32, 39n24, 218–219, 227; Wilson, W., and, 218
Braden, Spruille, 266
*Brass-Knuckle Crusade* (Beals, C.), 298, 311
Brazil, 290, 314, 330; Beals, C., and, 242, 265, 302, 316; fascism and, 248, 251, 253–254; Vargas of, 233, 243, 262, 269
Brenner, Anita, 55–56, 75, 77, 78
*Bridge of Royal Delights* (Beals, C.), 264
*Brimstone and Chili* (Beals, C.), 17, 24n38, 36, 74, 75, 78
Britton, John A., 320
Brooks, Paul, 246, 251, 262, 264
Broun, Heywood, 68, 91
Bucareli Treaty, 60
Bush, George H. W. (US president), 337
Bush, George W. (US president), 337

Caffery, Jefferson: Cuba and, 174, 197, 198–199; in El Salvador, 104, 174, 197, 198–199
Calles, Plutarco Elías (Mexico president), 2, 19, 49–50, 69; Beals, C., on, 71–72; on Beals, C., 62; on Communist Party, 135; Cristero Rebellion and, 79, 85, 86, 131, 133, 134; on Mexico revolution and military, 133–134; Morones and, 72; in New York City, 70; Obregón supporting, 63, 64, 64n1, 131; opposition to, 78–79
Calverton, Victor F. (George Goetz), 4, 196, 207, 221–222; *The Liberation of American Literature* by, 191
Carranza, Venustiano (Mexico president), 2, 19; Beals, C., and English teaching for, 25, 34; Beals, C., on, 35; Huitrón on, 22–23; influence loss by, 35, 36–37; oil and, 58, 59
Carrillo Puerto, Felipe, 49, 63–64, 66n48
Carter, Jimmy (US president), 320, 321–322

Castro, Fidel (Cuba dictator), 178n1; Batista and, 176, 284, 287, 288–289, 290; Beals, C., on, 284, 288, 289, 291, 292, 294, 300; Eisenhower on, 290, 292, 299, 300; *fidelistas* and, 3; JFK and, 299, 314; Revolution and, 284, 288, 289–290, 292, 294, 300, 330; Sandinistas and, 321; Soviet Union and, 292; to United Nations, 297; in US, 290, 297–298; on US, 292, 301; US on, 289, 290–291, 294–295, 299
Castro, Raúl, 291, 294
Catholicism, 138; Beals, C., on, 79; on Obregón, 131, 132, 133; on Sandino, 1; Toral and, 132, 133, 135, 137. *See also* Cristero Rebellion
Catt, Carrie Chapman, 80–81
de Céspedes, Carlos Manuel (Cuba president), 170, 171–172, 174
Chamorro, Emiliano (Nicaragua president): coup by, 96–97, 98, 101, 102; interview of, 113, 114; presidency of, 95–96, 115; Solórzano ousted by, 95–96
Chapultepec Conference (Mexico), 265–266, 277n19
Chase, Stuart, 88n24, 225, 260–262, 265, 272
Chávez, Hugo (Venezuela president), 238, 330
Chile, 269; Allende of, 238, 269
Cholita. *See* Gonzalez, Soledad
Cleveland, Grover (US president), 13
CO. *See* conscientious objector
Cobb, Frank I., 68
Colombia, 162, 188, 271, 297
*The Coming Struggle for Latin America* (Beals, C.), 207, 242–243, 244–245, 246–247, 332
Communism: Beals, C., and, 73–74, 325; Beals, C., and Mexico, 146–147; Beals, C., on, 88n24, 141, 155n25, 326, 335; FPCC and, 293; in Latin America, 271; liberal intellectuals as against, 270; Mexico on Party of, 135, 136, 144, 146; Modotti, T., and, 75–76; Mussolini on, 43; *New York Times* on, 275; Palmer on, 51; Portes Gíl, on, 134, 135, 144; Siqueiros, D., and, 54, 135; Stalin on,

224; Stalin on Mexico and, 144; Wolfe, B., and Wolfe, E., on, 52–53
Communist Party, 135
Confederación Regional Obrera Mexicana (CROM) (Regional Confederation of Mexican Workers), 63, 72
Connecticut: Beals, C., home in, 9, 207, 209, 234, 239, 240, 241, 246, 251, 262, 267; neighbors on Beals, C., 9
conscientious objector (CO), 12
Coolidge, Calvin (US president), 3, 52, 63; Honduras and, 104; Mexico and, 71, 77, 85, 97, 99, 195, 329; Nicaragua and, 93, 97, 99, 115; Pan-American Congress and, 107, 111, 118, 125; Sandino and, 92, 125; Welles and, 169, 170
Crichton, Kyle (Robert Forsythe), 208, 260, 272
*The Crime of Cuba* (Beals, C.), 190, 193; on Cuba and US, 159, 162, 163, 164, 165, 166, 167, 168, 170, 198; promotion of, 173, 177; reviews of, 170
Cristero Rebellion, 83–84, 85; Calles and, 79, 85, 86, 131, 133, 134; Obregón and, 131, 133, 134; Portes Gíl and, 135
Croly, Herbert, 3, 29, 81–82; *New Republic* magazine of, 68, 81, 82, 83
CROM. *See* Confederación Regional Obrera Mexicana
Cuba: ABC militants of, 160, 161, 169–170, 173, 174, 179n6; Bay of Pigs fiasco in, 3, 178n1, 300, 301, 302, 303, 314, 333, 335; Beals, C., on, 6, 160, 161, 197, 198, 284, 288, 289, 292, 293, 294, 333; Caffery and, 174, 197, 198–199; de Céspedes of, 170, 171–172, 174; *The Crime of Cuba* on US and, 159, 162, 163, 164, 165, 166, 167, 168, 170, 198; democracy and, 176–177, 284; Dorticós of, 291, 303; Evans, W., photos of, 165, 168, 170, 180n40; Ferrara and, 161; FPCC on, 292–294, 297, 298–299, 300, 301, 303–304, 316; Grau San Martín of, 174, 176, 177, 183; Great Depression on, 159, 168, 180n40; Guggenheim, H., and, 163–167, 168, 170, 171, 179n22; *New York Times* and, 170, 199, 284, 290, 292, 297, 299; people of, 160, 162,

164–166; Platt Amendment and, 162–163, 167, 168, 174, 177, 198; sugar economy of, 159–160, 162, 163, 167, 172, 176, 197, 290, 292, 297; trip to, 173; UFCO and, 160; on US, 289; US and enemy, 304; US on, 159–160, 176–177, 297; US populace on, 294. *See also* Batista, Fulgencio; Castro, Fidel; Machado, Gerardo; student-army government
Cuban missile crisis, 335
Cuban Revolution (1933), 177, 294
Cuban Revolution (Castro, F.): Beals, C., on, 304; Castro, F., and, 284, 288, 289–290, 292, 294, 300, 330; Stuart on, 297, 300, 314, 316; US leftist intellectuals on, 298, 307n96
culture war, 51
*Cyclone Carry* (Beals, C.), 314

Daniel, Elizabeth (Betty) (wife), 150, 151, 159, 168; marriage trouble with, 177–178
Davis, Richard Harding, 4
*Dawn Over the Amazon* (Beals, C.), 251–252, 253–254, 263; reception of, 253, 259–260, 264
Deas, Malcolm, 5
Debs, Eugene V., 12–13, 44, 74, 225
Delpar, Helen, 65n7
democracy, 338n5; Beals, C., on, 190, 227, 243, 334; Cuba and, 176–177, 284; dictators as not, 333, 334; FDR and, 236; Guatemala and, 267; JFK on, 245; Latin America and, 47, 287; Machado and Cuba, 159, 160, 169–170; Mexico and, 80, 146; Mussolini transforming, 42, 46, 48n12; US betraying, 2, 97, 120, 198, 203, 236, 237, 244, 245, 268–269, 314, 315, 326, 328, 331, 332, 333
Dennis, Lawrence, 97, 98
Denny, Harold Norman, 93, 127n26, 170
Dependency Theory: in *America South*, 234, 236–237, 255n14, 328; Latin American leaders and, 237–238
depression, 47, 48, 67, 69, 137, 273
*Destroying Victor* (Beals, C.), 142–143
DEU. *See* Directorio Estudiantil Universitario

Dewey, John: Commission of, 220, 221, 222, 226, 239; Mexico "Preliminary Commission of Inquiry" and, 217, 219; as philosopher, 2, 164, 212, 214, 216, 217, 219–220
*Diario de la Marina* (Navy Daily Journal), 160
Díaz, Adolfo (Nicaragua president), 92, 95; US supporting, 98, 99
Díaz, Porfirio (Mexico dictator), 4, 19, 22, 152; Angel of Independence statue and, 26; Beals, C., on, 73, 150, 151–152, 159
dictators: Argentina with military, 312–313; Batista as Cuba, 3; Beals, C., on, 268–269, 313, 334; Castro, F. (Cuba dictator), 178n1; Chamorro as Nicaragua, 95–96, 115; Chávez as Venezuela, 238, 330; as not democracy, 333, 334; Díaz, P., as Mexico, 4, 19, 22, 152; Duvalier, Papa Doc as, 285; Hitler as Germany, 265; Jiménez, M., as Venezuela, 287; Mao as, 40n25; Ortega as Nicaragua, 1, 3; Somoza, A. D., as Nicaragua, 1, 7n2, 267, 268, 321; Stalin as Soviet Union, 225; Trujillo as Dominican Republic, 262, 269, 312; US for, 331, 332, 334; Vargas as Brazil, 233, 243, 262, 269; Velasco Ibárra as Ecuador, 301, 312. *See also* Chamorro, Emiliano; Díaz, Porfirio; Somoza, Anastasio García
Directorio Estudiantil Universitario (DEU) (University Students' Directory), 169, 171, 172, 173
Doheny, Edward L.: Beals, C., and, 83, 204n51; on book publishing, 60, 193; Kellogg for, 83, 195; on Mexican law and oil reserves, 58, 59, 60, 85, 93; as oil tycoon, 58, 80, 83, 85, 100, 193, 195, 204n51; Teapot Dome scandal and, 4, 60, 83, 86, 193, 204n51
"Dollar Diplomacy in Guatemala" (Beals, C.), 275
Dominican Republic, 169, 236, 238–239, 316; Trujillo as dictator of, 262, 269, 312. *See also* Trujillo, Rafael Leonidas
Dorticós, Osvaldo (Cuba president), 291, 303

downtrodden masses, 21
draft resisters: APL against, 15; CO and, 12; *Oakland Tribune* and, 14; to World War I, 14–15
Durant, Kenneth (Rosta/TASS), 72–73, 74, 142
Duvalier, François (Papa Doc) (Haiti dictator), 285

*Eagles of the Andes* (Beals), 9, 316
Eberhardt, Charles, 96, 118; Beals, C., and, 104, 114–115
Ecuador, 233, 301, 312
Eisenhower, Dwight D. (US president), 274, 275; Beals, C., on, 287, 289, 297; on Castro, F., 290, 292, 299, 300; on Perón, 313
El Salvador: Beals, C., and, 103, 104, 114, 115; Caffery and, 104, 174, 197, 198–199; FMLN in, 269, 330
English Institute, 28, 30
Europe: imperialism and, 13, 14; lecturing in, 138
Evans, Ernestine, 73, 225, 283, 297
Evans, Walker, 165, 168, 170, 180n40
exile: in Mexico City, 15, 16, 28–30, 52; over World War I, 15, 16–17; Weisner in, 20–21, 24n38
expatriate community, 51, 52

Fair Play for Cuba Committee (FPCC), 6; Beals, C., and, 292, 293; Beals, C., leaving, 303–304; Christmas tour by, 300; on Cuba, 292–294, 297, 298–299, 300, 301, 303–304, 316; Oswald and, 316; US on Communism and, 293
fake news, 6
Falcoff, Mark, 4
Fall, Albert B., 59; Teapot Dome scandal and, 4, 60, 83, 86, 193, 204n51
Farabundo Martí National Liberation Front (FMLN), 269, 330
Farrell, James T., 195, 213, 214, 216, 222, 229n56
fascism: American Republic peace summit on, 234; Beals, C., on, 46, 245, 248, 332, 334; Beals, C., on Nazis and, 242–243; Brazil and, 248, 251, 253–254; Hull and Welles on South America and, 233, 234, 331; industrialization and, 47, 48n12; Latin America and, 46–47, 242; Stalin on, 224
*fascisti* (fascists), 43–44, 45–46
FBI. *See* Federal Bureau of Investigation
FDR. *See* Roosevelt, Franklin D.
Federal Bureau of Investigation (FBI), 6, 274, 301, 325
Fernandez de Castro, José Antonio, 160
Ferrara, Orestes, 161
*fidelistas* (Fidelists), 3
Fidelists. *See fidelistas*
finances, 56, 271–272, 273, 276; *Prensa Latina* on, 311; problems with, 11, 42, 47, 48, 277, 320–321, 326; success with, 253
*Fire on the Andes* (Beals, C.): on Peru, 184, 186, 187, 189, 191, 196, 197; response to, 190, 191, 192
flu. *See* influenza epidemic
FMLN. *See* Farabundo Martí National Liberation Front
Fonseca, Carlos, 1, 121
Forsythe, Robert. *See* Crichton, Kyle
FPCC. *See* Fair Play for Cuba Committee
Franco, Francisco, 233
Freeman, Joseph, 88n24, 141–142
Frente Sandinista de Liberación Nacional (FSLN) (Sandinista National Liberation Front): by Amador, 1; by Fonseca, 121; repressive remnant of, 1; on Somoza, A. G., regime, 7n2
Fuentes, Carlos, 4

Gale, Linn A. E., 27, 31
Gale, Magdalena, 27
Galeano, Eduardo, 238
*Gale's International Monthly* (Gale, L.), 27
García Márquez, Gabriel, 296, 303
Giolitti, Giovanni (Italy prime minister), 43
*Glass Houses* (Beals, C.), 39n24, 41, 239
Goetz, George. *See* Calverton, Victor F.
gold, map for, 16, 18, 19
Gold, Michael, 31, 69, 74
González, Manuel (Mexico president), 152–153

Gonzalez, Soledad (Cholita), 49–50, 75
Good Neighbor Policy (US): Chapultepec Conference on, 265–266, 277n19; FDR and, 2, 169, 175, 177, 190, 199, 234, 236, 331, 332; Hull and, 233, 234, 235, 243; purpose of, 259
GPU. *See* Russian state security police
Grau San Martín, Ramón (Cuba president): Batista on, 176, 183; of Cuba, 174, 176, 177, 183; student-army government and, 171, 172, 173, 174, 175, 176, 177, 183; on Welles, 174, 176, 177, 183
Great Depression, 197, 208, 234; on Beals, C., 150, 192, 200; on Cuba, 159, 168, 180n40
*Great Guerrilla Warriors* (Beals, C.), 318, 319–320
Greenwald, Glenn, 5, 326, 337
groupthink, 6, 311, 330, 337
Gruening, Ernest: as editor, 147, 164, 167; as *Nation* magazine editor, 30, 36, 55, 56, 58, 60, 63, 82, 91; politics and, 69, 71, 192, 286, 319
Gruzenberg, Michael. *See* Borodin, Mikhail
Guatemala: Árbenz of, 274–276, 333; Arévalo of, 266–267, 274, 314–315, 316, 335; Beals, C., on, 275–276, 315; democracy and, 267; *New York Times* on, 299; UFCO and, 274–275, 315; US airbase in, 299, 314; US coup in, 3, 274, 275, 335; Ydígoras and, 299, 314
Guggenheim, Harry Frank: Beals, C., and, 163–167, 168, 170, 171, 179n22; FDR and, 166; Machado and, 163, 166, 170, 179n22; *New York Times* and, 166
Guggenheim Foundation, 73, 142, 150
Guzmán, Martin Luis, 138

Haberman, Robert, 49
Haiti, 238, 255n21, 284; Beals, C., on, 285, 299; Duvalier, Papa Doc of, 285; Welles and, 169
Harding, Warren (US president), 52; Hughes, C., and, 97; on oil, 59, 60
Haya de la Torre, Victor Raúl (Peru), 3; APRA and, 184, 185, 186, 187, 253; Beals, C., and, 184, 186; on Indigenous population, 186, 189

Hearst, William Randolph, 68
Hemingway, Ernest, 168
hemispheric cartel, 248; FDR and, 249–251
Herring, Hubert, 5, 81, 166–167, 171
Hitchens, Christopher, 5
Hitler, Adolf (Germany dictator), 265; Latin America and, 242, 244, 252; Trotsky and, 212, 214, 215, 224; war maneuvers by, 233, 235, 241, 253
Hollander, Paul, 65n7
Honduras, 118; Beals, C., and, 78, 94, 103, 104, 122; Coolidge and, 104; Sandino and, 100, 104, 117, 118
Houghton Mifflin: Beals, C., on, 251, 262, 263; Lieber and, 240, 246, 251, 262, 263–264
House Committee on Un-American Activities (HUAC), 270–271, 283, 312, 326
*House in Mexico* (Beals, C.), 286
HUAC. *See* House Committee on Un-American Activities
Huebsch, Ben, 30, 47, 60
De la Huerta, Victoriano (Mexico president), 37, 58, 59, 63
Hughes, Charles Evans, 58, 97, 117, 177
Hughes, Langston, 69, 208
Huitrón, Evangelina, 22–23
Hull, Cordell, 199; Good Neighbor Policy and, 233, 234, 235, 243; on Latin America and fascism, 233, 234, 331; Welles and, 166, 168, 172, 174–175, 234

imperialism: Beals, C., on, 4, 46, 77, 80, 115; Europe and, 13, 14; Latin America and, 52, 55, 91, 92, 94, 104; Sandino against, 1, 3, 92, 93, 108, 119; by US, 1, 58, 97, 98, 108, 111, 115, 117–118, 119, 120, 121, 336
Import-Substituting Industrialization (ISI), 238
Indigenous population: Beals, C., on, 189; Beals, R., on, 21; fascism and, 46–47; Haya on, 186, 189; Jiménez, J., and, 228n10; land reform and, 61–62; Peru and, 189, 191; *The Stones Awake* on, 210; Trotsky and, 227; Vasconcelos on,

55
Industrial Workers of the World (IWW) unions, 100
influenza epidemic (1918), 19, 22
Inman, Samuel Guy, 59, 60, 240, 269, 276
Institutional Revolutionary Party. *See* Partido Revolucionario Institucional
*Intervention in Mexico* (Inman), 59
intervention protocol, 235
ISI. *See* Import-Substituting Industrialization
Italy: Beals, C., finances in, 42, 47; Blackshirts of, 42, 43, 44, 45, 73; Giolitti of, 43; moving to, 41; politics of, 43. *See also* Mussolini, Benito
IWW. *See* Industrial Workers of the World unions

*The Jaguar Smile* (Rushdie), 1
J. B. Lippincott & Company: Jones of, 73, 183, 197, 239, 246; Lieber on, 246
Jefferson, Thomas (US president), 2, 331, 332, 335
JFK. *See* Kennedy, John F.
Jiménez, Julia (Luciana, Luz), 209, 228n10
*John Eliot* (Beals, C.), 9, 286
Johnson, Lyndon B. (LBJ) (US president), 314, 316
Jones, Jefferson, 73, 183, 197, 239, 246
journalism: as advocacy, 62, 326, 337–338, 338n2; awkwardness in, 196, 226, 270, 293, 326, 330, 338; Beals, C., and TASS, 72–74, 145; Beals, C., technique of, 29, 44–45, 126, 164, 326, 327, 328–329, 333, 336, 337; Beals, C., writing in, 29, 44, 82–83, 327; of Beals, C., 29, 44; Bickel on US State Department and, 126n6, 250; "gray list" on liberal, 270–271; lecture circuit and, 137–138; in Mexico City, 28, 29; on Monroe Doctrine, 92; in New York City, 68; in retirement, 9–10; success in, 4, 116, 125, 132, 196, 211, 272, 283, 294; on Trotsky Mexico trial, 220; US leftist intellectuals on, 223–224
Juárez, Benito, 145, 150

Kahlo, Frida, 2, 53, 55, 210; Trotsky and, 212, 215, 223

Kellogg, Frank B., 92, 100, 104, 117, 118; for Doheny, 83, 195; Nicaragua peace initiative by, 97
Kennedy, Edward M., 314
Kennedy, John F. (JFK) (US president), 297, 300–301, 304, 315; Alliance for Progress by, 301, 302, 312, 313, 314, 333; assassination of, 313, 316; Castro, F., and, 299, 314; on democracy, 245. *See also* Bay of Pigs
Kennedy, Robert, 318
Kerry, John, 333
Khrushchev, Nikita (Soviet Union premier), 297–298
King, Martin Luther, Jr., 318
Kirchwey, Freda, 88n24, 133, 155n13, 225, 284; on Sandino story, 103, 116, 118
Kissinger, Henry, 5
Klausner, Bertha, 272–273, 283, 286, 287, 304, 311

labor activism, 100. *See also* Confederación Regional Obrera Mexicana; Industrial Workers of the World unions
La Follette, Philip, 265
La Follette, Robert, 69; US Progressive Party/movement and, 214, 265, 275
La Follette, Robert, Jr., 270, 275
LaFollette, Suzanne, 214, 216, 218
land reform: Indigenous population and, 61–62; for Mexico, 61–62; *Mexico* on, 61; Obregón on, 61
*Lands of the Dawning Morrow* (Beals, C.), 268, 269, 271
Lane Wilson, Henry, 5, 80, 81, 82, 176, 337
Larsen (Lieutenant), 114
Latin America: American Republic peace summit on, 234; *America South* on, 235, 236, 238, 239; on Bay of Pigs, 302; Beals, C., on, 1–2, 6, 274; on Beals, C., 5; Communism in, 271; democracy and, 47, 287; Dependency Theory and, 237–238; Hitler and, 242, 244, 252; Hull and Welles on fascism and, 233, 234, 331; imperialism and, 52, 55, 91, 92, 94, 104; intervention

protocol in, 235; ISI on one-crop economies and, 238; Nazi fascism and, 46–47, 242; return to, 266–268
*Latin America* (Beals, C.), 312, 313–314
LBJ. *See* Johnson, Lyndon B.
lecturing: Beals, C., on, 137; in Europe, 138; in US, 137, 138
leftist intellectuals (US): Beals, C., on, 225; on Beals, C., 227; on Castro, F., Cuban Revolution, 298, 307n96; on journalism, 223–224; on Moscow Trial of the Seventeen, 222; on Stalin, 225; Stalin on, 223; on Trotsky, 222, 223
León, Carlos, 94
Lewis, Sinclair, 52, 65n6, 69, 195
Leyva y Arguedas, Blanca Rosa (Blanca) (wife): attraction to, 183–184; marriage trouble with, 273–274, 276, 283; marriage with, 196, 239–240, 261, 271; from Peru, 240, 241
liberal intellectuals, 270
*The Liberation of American Literature* (Calverton), 191
Lieber, Maxim: as agent, 192, 196, 207, 225, 265; Houghton Mifflin and, 240, 246, 251, 262, 263–264; on J. B. Lippincott, 246
Lindbergh, Charles, 86–87, 239
literary marketplace: Beal, C., pursuing, 16; efforts in, 28, 29, 70, 268; Evans, E., and, 73; opinions on, 69, 75; rejection in, 44, 47
Lliteras, Juan Andrés, 179n6
Long, Huey P., 4, 197, 200–203
Luciana. *See* Jiménez, Julia
Luz. *See* Jiménez, Julia
Lyons, Eugene, 140–141

Machado, Gerardo (Cuba president), 3; Beals, C., on, 159, 162, 163, 178n1; FDR on, 170; Ferrara on, 161; Guggenheim, H., and, 163, 166, 170, 179n22; Mella and, 125, 136–137, 159; resignation of, 170; unrest on, 159, 160; violence and responses by, 160, 162, 164, 167
Madero, Francisco (Mexico president), 58, 80, 177
Madre Conchita, 133, 135, 137

*Main Street* (Lewis), 52, 65n6, 68, 195
Makar, Alexandr, 145
Malcolm X, 298, 318
Manchester, Dorothy, 21
Mao Zedong (China dictator), 40n25
Mariátegui, José Carlos, 3, 6, 186, 188–189, 191
Marines (US): McCoy and, 117; Mexico and, 122; Nicaragua and, 1, 3, 93, 95, 96, 98, 99, 103, 119, 122, 123–124, 125; on Sandino, 105–107, 109, 110, 114, 115, 329; on Somoza, A. G., 120
marriage. *See* Beals, Carolyn Kennedy; Daniel, Elizabeth; Leyva y Arguedas, Blanca Rosa; Rhein, Lillian
Marx, Karl, 1, 2, 231n83
Masetti, Jorge Ricardo, 294, 295
McCarthy, Joe, 6, 270, 272, 312, 315, 318
McCoy, Frank R.: on Nicaragua election, 111, 115–116; on Sandino, 115–116; US Marines and, 117
McIntosh, Mavis, 264, 265, 268, 271
Mella, Julio Antonio, 125, 136, 159; Modotti, T., and, 136–137, 178n1
Mendieta, Carlos (Cuba provisional president), 160, 170, 173, 174; Batista and, 176, 197, 198, 199
*Mexican Maze* (Beals, C.), 77, 148–149, 150
Mexico: *agrarista* of, 22; anti-Communist by, 136; Beals, C., and American expatriates in, 25, 27; Beals, C., and political activists in, 31–32; Beals, C., and US expatriates in, 25; Beals, C., at American High School, 30, 38; Beals, C., at Miguel Lerdo de Tejada High School, 49, 50, 52; Beals, C., on, 26–27, 57, 71, 144; Beals, C., on art and, 55, 56; Beals, C., on revolution and, 3; Beals, C., promiscuity in, 32–33, 56–57; Beals, C., trek in, 18–23, 25; Beals, R., and Beals, C., trekking, 16, 17, 18, 19, 20–21, 74; Bucareli Treaty of US and, 60; Chapultepec Conference of, 265–266, 277n19; on Communist Party, 135, 144, 146; Coolidge and, 71, 77, 85, 97, 99, 195, 329; Cristero Rebellion of, 79, 83–84, 85, 86, 131, 133, 134, 135; debts of, 85;

Index 367

democracy and, 80, 146; Doheny on oil and, 58, 59, 60, 85, 93; exile in, 15, 16, 28–30, 52; expatriate community in, 51, 52; gold search in, 16, 18, 19; González of, 152–153; De la Huerta of, 37, 58, 59, 63; journalism in, 28, 29; land reform of, 61–62; leaving of, 38; Madero of, 58, 80, 177; Mexico City of, 25–26, 28, 29, 52; Obregón on land redistribution and, 61; oil reserves of, 58, 194, 195, 329, 332, 336; Ortiz Rubio of, 144, 146; Portes Gíl of, 134, 135, 145; return to, 47, 49, 75, 121–124, 144, 150, 216; revolutionary war in, 18, 26, 330; on Soviet Union, 145; Stalin and Communist Party in, 144; teaching in, 25; trek to, 17–18; Trotsky to, 214–215; US Marines and, 122; Yaqui Indians of, 16, 18, 19, 20, 35, 37. *See also* Calles, Plutarco Elías; Carranza, Venustiano; Díaz, Porfirio; Obregón, Álvaro; Rivera, Diego

Mexico (Beals, C.): Huebsch editing, 30, 47, 60; land reform in, 61

Mexico "Preliminary Commission of Inquiry" on Trotsky, 226; Beals, C., on, 216, 217, 220, 221, 226, 227; on Beals, C., 212–213; Dewey and, 220, 221, 222, 226, 239; journalists on, 220; for Trotsky, 211, 213, 216, 226–227; Trotsky on, 216; US populace on, 213–214. *See also* Dewey, John

Miguel Lerdo de Tejada High School, 49, 50, 52

Modotti, Mercedes, 75, 76–78

Modotti, Tina, 2, 210, 228n10; Communism and, 75–76; Mella and, 136–137, 137, 178n1; Rivera and, 76–77; Robinson and, 155n25; Stalinism and, 53

Moncada, José María (Nicaragua president): Beals, C., interviewing, 113, 114–115, 125; as Nicaragua Liberal, 96, 102, 116, 120; Stimson and, 93, 99–100, 102; US on, 119, 330

Monroe Doctrine (US): Beals, C., on, 80, 125, 235, 326, 329–330, 332; FDR and, 242; as greed, 118; journalists on, 92; as over, 333–334

Moore, Michael, 166

Morocco, 138, 139, 319

Morones, Luis, 57–58, 63, 100, 135, 145; Calles and, 72; CROM by, 63, 72

Morrow, Dwight W., 77, 131, 132, 134, 239, 329; on oil claims, 85–86

Moscow Trial of the Seventeen: *New York Times* on, 216; on Trotsky and associates, 211, 215–216, 221; US leftist intellectuals on, 222; US populace on, 213–214

Mussolini, Benito, 42; Beals, C., on, 42, 45, 335; Blackshirts of, 42, 43, 44, 45, 73; on Communism, 43; on democracy, 42, 46, 48n12; *fascisti* violence for, 43–44, 45–46

NAACP. *See* National Association for the Advancement of Colored People

*Nation* (magazine), 2, 3, 10; Álvarez del Vayo and, 138, 155n13, 317; Gruening editing, 30, 36, 55, 56, 58, 60, 63, 82, 91; Kirchwey editing, 88n24, 103, 116, 118, 133, 155n13, 225, 284; McWilliams editing 164, 180n26, 213, 270, 284, 288, 291, 293, 297, 299; as Progressive Party/movement (US), 91; Spain series in, 138–139; Villard of, 68, 74, 91, 120, 199

National Association for the Advancement of Colored People (NAACP), 91

National Committee for the Defense of Political Prisoners (NCDPP), 208

*National Guardian* (newspaper), 312, 316, 317, 335

National Revolutionary Party. *See* Partido Nacional Revolucionario

*The Nature of Revolution* (Beals, C.), 318–319, 320

Navy Daily Journal. *See Diario de la Marina*

NCDPP. *See* National Committee for the Defense of Political Prisoners

Needler, Martin, 5

Nehru, Jawaharlal (India prime minister), 297–298

"The New Crime of Cuba" (Beals, C.), 284

New Left, 317

"New Look" policy, 274

*New Republic* (magazine), 2, 68, 81, 82; Doheny and, 83
New York City: Beals, C., in, 10, 70–71; Calles in, 70; journalism in, 68; return to, 67–68, 150, 159
*New York Times* (newspaper), 68, 301, 312; Beals, C., in, 2, 4, 29, 125, 132–133, 134, 150, 197, 330; on Beals, C., 80, 82, 152, 170, 175, 192, 193, 211, 220, 236, 239, 260, 263, 313, 315, 329; on Communism, 275; Cuba and, 170, 199, 284, 290, 292, 297, 299; on Guatemala, 299; Guggenheim and, 166; Lindbergh and, 87; on Moscow trials, 216; Reed, A., of, 64; on Sandino, 92, 93, 117
Nicaragua: Beals, C., and, 95, 97, 98–99, 103–109; Coolidge and, 93, 97, 99, 115; Díaz, A., of, 92, 95, 98, 99; Kellogg and peace for, 97; McCoy on election and, 111, 115–116; Ortega of, 1, 3; politics of, 95–97; revolution and, 1; Stimson agreements on, 93, 99, 102, 119, 120, 330; UFCO in, 98, 100, 121; US Marines occupying, 1, 3, 93, 95, 96, 98, 99, 103, 119, 122, 123–124, 125; violence and rural elite of, 101. *See also* Chamorro, Emiliano; Moncada, José María; Sacasa, Juan Bautista; Sandino, Augusto César; Somoza, Anastasio García
Nixon, Richard (US vice president and president), 5, 287, 290, 299, 318, 325
*Nomads and Empire Builders* (Beals, C.), 314

*Oakland Tribune* (newspaper), 15
Obama, Barack (US president), 3, 238
Obregón, Álvaro (Mexico president), 2, 19, 27; assassination of, 131, 132; Beals, C., on, 62, 71, 132; on Beals, C., 62; Calles supported by, 63, 64, 64n1, 131; Catholicism on, 131, 132, 133; Cristero Rebellion and, 131, 133, 134; on land reform, 61; as president, 51, 54, 59, 64, 64n1, 131; presidential bid by, 35; takeover by, 36, 37
OGPU. *See* Russian state security police

oil reserves: Bolivia and, 250; Bucareli Treaty and, 60; Carranza and, 58, 59; Doheny and, 58, 59, 60, 80, 83, 85, 93, 100, 193, 195, 204n51; Harding on, 59, 60; Kellogg and US, 83, 195; of Mexico, 58, 194, 195, 329, 332, 336; Morrow on, 85–86; Teapot Dome scandal on, 4, 60, 83, 86, 193, 204n51; US on, 59; Wilson, W., on Mexico, 58, 59, 194–195, 329
Olmedo, Dolores, 54
Open Door policy (US), 141, 248, 254n4, 295, 330, 332
*Open Veins of Latin America. See Las Venas abiertas de América Latina*
Orlando, Vittorio (Italy prime minister), 42
Orozco, José Clemente, 54
Ortega, Daniel (Nicaragua dictator), 1, 3
Ortiz, Fernando, 167, 173
Ortiz Rubio, Pascual (Mexico president), 144, 146
O'Shaughnessy, Mike, 16, 19
Oswald, Lee Harvey, 316

Paca. *See* Toor, Frances
Palmer, A. Mitchell, 51
Palmerín, Ricardo, 64, 66n48
*Pan America* (Beals, C.), 247–249, 332
Pan-American Congress, 107, 111, 118, 125
Pancho Villa. *See* Villa, Francisco
Papa Doc. *See* Duvalier, François
Parsley Massacre, 238–239, 255n21
Partido Nacional Revolucionario (PNR) (National Revolutionary Party), 72, 144
Partido Obrero de Unificacion Marxista (POUM) (Workers' Party of Marxist Unification), 231n83
Partido Revolucionario Institucional (PRI) (Institutional Revolutionary Party), 72
"La Peregrina" (De la Vega and Palmerín), 64, 66n48
Pérez Jiménez, Marcos (Venezuela dictator), 287
Perón, Juan (Argentina president): Beals, C., on, 269, 312; Eisenhower on, 313; as leftist, 237, 263; US and, 264, 265, 266, 313

Peru: army possibilities in, 188; Benavides of, 184; Blanca from, 240, 241; *Fire on the Andes* on, 184, 186, 187, 189, 190–191, 196, 197; Indigenous population and, 189, 191; 1931 election of, 204n18; Sánchez Cerro of, 185–186, 187, 188; sugar economy of, 185, 186, 187, 190. *See also* Haya de la Torre, Victor Raúl
Pestkovsky, Stanislav, 53, 75, 145
Phillips, Charles, 31
Phillips, Howard, 54, 75, 94, 148, 150
Platt Amendment (US), 162–163, 167, 168, 174, 177, 198
PNR. *See* Partido Nacional Revolucionario
Poltiol, George, 28, 30
Porfiriato, 58
*Porfirio Díaz* (Beals, C.), 152, 153, 154
Porter, Katherine Anne, 57
Portes Gíl, Emilio (Mexico interim president), 134, 135, 145
Positivism (religion), 12, 14
POUM. *See* Partido Obrero de Unificacion Marxista
Prebisch–Singer (PST) thesis, 237, 255n19, 328; United Nations and, 238
*Prensa Latina* (Cuba news service): Beals, C., for, 6, 10, 294, 295–296, 297; Beals, C., on change and, 302–303; finances and, 311
PRI. *See* Partido Revolucionario Institucional
Primo de Rivera, Miguel, 138, 139
*Progressive* (magazine), 264, 265, 266, 275
Progressive Party/movement (US): Beals, C., and, 39n24, 260, 263, 270, 294, 317, 334, 335; Beard and, 212, 213, 226, 249, 331; Dewey and, 212; La Follette, R., as part of, 214, 265, 275; publications of, 69, 91, 264, 265, 266, 275; on Trotsky, 212, 225; in US government, 93, 116, 117, 173, 242; Wallace as part of, 270, 312; Wilson, W., and, 51, 333
*The Promise of American Life* (Croly), 81
propaganda model, 120
PST. *See* Prebisch–Singer thesis
public sphere, 327–328, 330, 338n5

Pulitzer, Joseph, 68

Quevedo y Zubieta, Salvador, 152, 153–154

Reagan, Ronald (US president), 3, 336
Reed, Alma, 64
Reed, John, 73
Regional Confederation of Mexican Workers. *See* Confederación Regional Obrera Mexicana
Rembao, Alberto, 240–241, 246
Rhein, Lillian (wife): marriage collapse with, 47, 56, 57, 67; marriage with, 11, 32, 33–34, 38–39, 41, 42, 139, 143
*Rio Grande to Cape Horn* (Beals, C.), 262–263
Rivas (messenger), 103–104, 122
Rivas, Alfredo, 96
Rivas, Antonieta, 38
Rivera, Diego, 2, 53, 54; Beals, C., on, 77; on Beals, C., 219, 221; Modotti, T., and, 76–77; Robinson and, 155n25; on Stalin, 215; on Trotsky, 215
Robeson, Paul, 69
Robinson, Ione, 142, 155n25
Rockefeller, John D., 55
*Rome or Death* (Beals, C.), 42, 45, 46
Roosevelt, Franklin D. (FDR) (US president): Argentina and, 234; Beals, C., on dictators and, 177; Chase and, 88n24, 225, 260–262, 265, 272; Cuba and Welles by, 5, 168–169, 170–172, 174–175; Cuban Revolution of 1933, 177; democracy and, 236; Good Neighbor Policy by, 2, 169, 175, 177, 190, 199, 234, 236, 331, 332; Guggenheim, H., and, 166; hemispheric cartel and, 249–251; Latin America intervention protocol and, 235; on Machado, 170; Monroe Doctrine and, 242; on Trujillo, 239; Trujillo and, 239; on US and World War II, 233, 243–244
Roosevelt, Theodore (US president), 68, 81, 98, 254
Rosta/TASS. *See* TASS
Roy, Manabendra N., 31, 218
Rubin, Morris, 265, 266, 275
Rushdie, Salman, 1

Russian state security police (OGPU): Beals, C., in Soviet Union and, 217, 219, 220, 221, 227; secret police as, 140, 155n20

Sacasa, Juan Bautista (Nicaragua vice president), 94; as Nicaragua Liberal candidate, 95; as Nicaragua vice president, 95, 96, 97, 98, 99, 100, 101, 102; Sandino and, 120; against US, 97
Said, Edward W., 328
Sánchez Cerro, Luís (Peru president), 185–186, 187, 188
Sandinista National Liberation Front. *See* Frente Sandinista de Liberación Nacional
Sandinistas: Castro, F., and, 321; triumph of, 322, 330
Sandino, 105–107, 109, 110, 114, 115, 329
Sandino, Augusto César (Nicaragua), 1; Beals, C., interviewing, 1, 3, 5, 93, 94, 103, 109–112, 113, 114–115, 119, 120, 125, 329; on Beals, C., 107; Coolidge and, 92, 125; Honduras and, 100, 104, 117, 118; against imperialism, 1, 3, 92, 93, 108, 119; Kirchwey on, 103, 116, 118; McCoy on, 115–116; *New York Times* on, 92, 93, 117; as Nicaragua Liberal, 100–102; Sacasa and, 120; sombrero image of, 1; Somoza, A. G., murdering, 7n2, 119, 120; Stimson on, 118; support for, 92–93, 102–103, 109, 111, 112, 119, 121; US Marines on, 105–107, 109, 110, 114, 115; US on, 93, 104, 117, 118, 119; US State Department on, 329; Villard on, 92–93, 94
Schaffner, John, 271, 272
Scottsboro trial, 6, 208–209
Sellers, David F., 111, 117, 119
Sheffield, James R., 63, 83
Sinclair, Harry F., 60; Teapot Dome scandal and, 4, 60, 83, 86, 193, 204n51
Sinclair, Upton, 68, 82
Siqueiros, David Alfaro, 54, 135
Siqueiros, Santos, 105, 108, 110–111
Sokolsky, George, 293
Solórzano, José (Nicaragua president), 95–96

sombrero image, 1
Somoza, Anastasio García (Nicaragua dictator): dictatorship by, 1, 7n2, 267, 268; FSLN on, 7n2; on Sandino, 120, 239, 243, 262, 267, 268; Sandino murdered by, 7n2, 119, 120; US confidence in, 120; US Marines on, 120
Somoza, Anastasio "Tachito" Debayle (Nicaragua dictator), 1, 321–322; on Sandino, 119, 121
Soviet, definition of, 58
Soviet Union: Beals, C., in, 139–141; Beals, C., on, 145; Borodin and, 31–32, 39n24–40n25, 218–219, 227; Castro, F., and, 292; Mexico on, 145; Moscow Trial of the Seventeen and, 211, 213–214, 215, 220, 221, 222; Reagan on, 3. *See also* Stalin, Joseph; Trotsky, Leon
Spain: Beals, C., on, 138–139; moving to, 38–39, 41; Primo de Rivera and, 138, 139; Stalin and Republicans of, 138
Stalin, Joseph (Soviet Union dictator), 225; Beals, C., on, 139–140, 222; on Communism, 224; on fascism, 224; Lyons on, 140–141; on Mao Zedong, 40n25; on Mexico Communist Party, 144; Moscow trials by, 211, 213–214, 215, 220, 221, 222; Rivera, D., on, 215; Spanish Republicans and, 138; targets of, 223; on Trotsky, 39n24, 211–212, 214–215; Trotsky on, 221, 224; on US leftist intellectuals, 223; US leftist intellectuals on, 225
Stalinism: Beals, C., on, 141, 144, 196, 211; Modotti, T., and, 53; Trotsky and, 211–212, 213, 217, 220, 222, 223
State Department (US): on Beals, C., 6, 329; on Sandino, 329
Steinbeck, John, 264
Stevenson, Adlai, 302
Stimson, Henry L., 163; Moncada and, 93, 99–100, 102; Nicaragua agreements by, 93, 99, 102, 119, 120, 330; on Sandino, 118; on Somoza, A. G., 120
*The Stones Awake* (Beals, C.), 143, 207, 209–211, 228n10; on Indigenous population, 210
Stuart, Lyle, 297, 300, 314, 316

student-army government (Cuba): on de Céspedes, 170, 171–172, 174; of Cuba, 171, 172; Grau and, 171, 172, 173, 174, 175, 176, 177, 183; US on, 171
sugar: Cuba economy and, 159–160, 162, 163, 167, 172, 176, 197, 290, 292, 297; Peru economy and, 185, 186, 187, 190

Taber, Robert, 291–292, 293, 298, 303, 316
Taft, William Howard (US president), 80, 81, 98, 99
Tannenbaum, Frank, 58, 63, 71
TASS (Soviet news agency) (Rosta/TASS), 4, 53, 57, 116, 139; Beals, C., with, 72–74, 145; Durant and, 72–73, 74, 142; Freeman for, 88n24, 141–142
teaching: at American High School, 30; at English Institute, 28, 30
Teapot Dome scandal, 4, 60, 83, 86, 193, 204n51
Téllez, Manuel C., 70
*Ten Days that Shook the World* (Reed, J.), 73
Third World: Beals, C., on, 2, 318–319, 336; US on, 328
Thompson, Hunter S., 5, 166
*Time* (magazine), 1, 291, 325
Toor, Frances (Paca), 53, 55–56, 69, 75
Toral, José de León, 132, 133, 135, 137
Trotsky, Leon (Soviet Union), 2; Beals, C., on, 217–218, 222–223, 225, 227; Beals, C., on Borodin and, 218; on Beals, C., 217, 220, 221; Borodin and, 32, 39n24, 218–219, 227; Hitler and, 212, 214, 215, 224; Kahlo and, 212, 215, 223; to Mexico, 214–215; on Mexico "Preliminary Commission of Inquiry," 216; Mexico "Preliminary Commission of Inquiry" for, 211, 213, 216, 226–227; Moscow trials on, 211, 215–216, 221; POUM for, 231n83; Rivera on, 215; on Stalin, 221, 223, 224; Stalinism and, 211–212, 213, 217, 220, 222, 223; Stalin on, 39n24, 211–212, 214–215; US leftist intellectuals on, 222, 223. *See also* Borodin, Mikhail

Trujillo, Rafael Leonidas (Dominican Republic dictator), 262, 269, 312; FDR and, 239; Parsley Massacre and, 238–239, 255n21
Truman, Harry S. (US president), 270, 277n19, 335
Trump, Donald (US president), 3, 337
Turcios, Froylán, 94, 104–105

UFCO. *See* United Fruit Company
*Under the Fifth Sun* (Beals, C.), 10, 23n2, 178n1, 320
"Under the Fifth Sun," 126n12, 156n64
United Fruit Company (UFCO), 98, 100, 121, 160, 274–275, 315
United Nations, 265, 289; Castro, F., to, 297; PST thesis and, 237; Stevenson and, 302
United States (US): *America South* on, 235, 236, 238, 239; on Árbenz, 274–276, 333; Bay of Pigs and, 3, 178n1, 300, 301, 302, 303, 314, 333, 335; Beals, C., followed by, 122–124; Beals, C., on, 28, 328; Beals, C., on foreign policy and, 2, 5, 6, 58, 62, 79–80, 162–163, 171, 243, 250, 268–269, 294, 304, 325, 326, 327–328, 331, 335; Beals, C., on pan-Americanism and, 236; Beals, C., on politics and, 318; on Beals, C., 5, 63, 125, 302; Bickel on journalism and State Department of, 126n6, 250; Biden of, 334; Bucareli Treaty of Mexico and, 60; Carter of, 320, 321–322; Castro, F., in, 290, 297–298; Castro, F., on, 292, 301; on Castro, F., 290–291, 294–295, 299; for de Céspedes, 170, 171–172, 174; Cleveland of, 13; Connecticut home in, 9, 207, 209, 234, 239, 240, 241, 246, 251, 262, 267; *The Crime of Cuba* on Cuba and, 159, 162, 163, 164, 165, 166, 167, 168, 170, 198; on Cuba, 159–160, 176–177, 297; Cuba and enemy, 304; Cuba on, 289; on Cuba student-army government, 171; culture war in, 51; democracy betrayed by, 2, 97, 120, 198, 203, 236, 237, 244, 245, 268–269, 314, 315, 326, 328, 331, 332, 333; Díaz, A., supported by, 98, 99; for

dictators, 331, 332, 334; FDR on World War II and, 233, 243–244; as foreign invader, 61, 339n7; groupthink of, 6, 311, 330, 337; with Guatemala airbase, 299, 314; Guatemala coup by, 3, 274, 275, 335; Harding of, 52, 59, 60, 97; HUAC of, 270–271, 283, 312, 326; imperialism by, 1, 58, 97, 98, 108, 111, 115, 117–118, 119, 120, 121, 336; Jefferson, T., of, 2, 331, 332, 335; LBJ of, 314, 316; on Machado, 170; on Moncada, 119, 330; "New Look" policy of, 274; on Nicaragua dictator, 97; Nicaragua occupation and Marines of, 1, 3, 93, 95, 96, 98, 99, 103, 119, 122, 123–124, 125; Nixon of, 5, 287, 290, 299, 318, 325; Obama of, 3, 238; on oil reserves, 59; for Open Door policy, 141, 248, 254n4, 295, 330, 332; Perón and, 264, 265, 266, 313; Platt Amendment of, 162–163, 167, 168, 174, 177, 198; populace on Cuba, 294; populace on Dewey Commission and Moscow purges, 213–214; propaganda model in, 120; Reagan of, 3, 336; revolt money from, 127n26; Roosevelt, T., of, 68, 81, 98; on Sacasa, 97; on Sandino, 93, 104, 117, 118, 119; on Somoza, A. G., 120; Taft of, 80, 81, 98, 99; Teapot Dome scandal in, 4, 60, 83, 86, 193, 204n51; on Third World, 328; Truman of, 270, 277n19, 335; Trump of, 3, 336; UFCO helped by, 98, 100, 121, 160, 274–275, 315; US leftist intellectuals on, 223–224; in Vietnam, 316, 333; on World War I, 11–12; on World War II, 233, 241–242. *See also* Coolidge, Calvin; Eisenhower, Dwight D.; Kennedy, John F.; Monroe Doctrine; Progressive Party/movement; Roosevelt, Franklin D.; Wilson, Woodrow

University Students' Directory. *See* Directorio Estudiantil Universitario

Vargas, Getúlio (Brazil dictator), 233, 243, 262, 269
Vasconcelos, José, 54–55, 144, 146
de la Vega, Luis Rosado, 64, 66n48

Velasco Ibárra, José María (Ecuador dictator), 301, 312
*Las Venas abiertas de América Latina* (Galeano) (*Open Veins of Latin America*), 238
Venezuela: Bolívar of, 92, 100, 251, 316; Chávez and, 238, 330
Vietnam: Beals, C., on, 318, 319–320, 335; US in, 316, 333
Villa, Francisco (Villa, Pancho), 19, 183
Villard, Oswald Garrison, 3, 4, 212, 265; as *Nation* editor, 68, 74, 91, 120, 199; on Sandino, 92–93, 94

Wallace, Henry, 270, 312
*War Within a War* (Beals, C.), 316
Weinberger, J. L., 53, 55
Weisner, Ernesto, 20–21, 24n38
Welles, Sumner, 181n86; AFP and, 176; Batista and, 173; Beals, C., on, 176; Coolidge and, 169, 170; Cuba and, 5, 168–169, 170–172, 174–175; on fascism and South America, 233, 234, 331; on Grau, 174, 176, 177, 183; Haiti and, 169; Hull and, 166, 168, 172, 174–175, 234. *See also* Good Neighbor Policy
Weston, Edward, 2, 53, 75, 76, 77
Williams, George, 105
Wilson, Edmund, 222
Wilson, Henry Lane. *See* Lane Wilson, Henry
Wilson, Woodrow (US president): Borodin and, 218; Durant and, 72; on Mexico oil reserves, 58, 59, 194–195, 329; Progressive era and, 51, 333; World War I and, 11–12, 13, 15, 73, 81
*The Wind That Swept Mexico* (Brenner), 55–56
Wisconsin School, 254n4
Wolfe, Bertram, 52–53
Wolfe, Ella Goldberg, 52–53, 69, 72
Workers' Party of Marxist Unification. *See* Partido Obrero de Unificacion Marxista
World War I, 2; Beals, C., on, 10, 11, 12; draft resister to, 14–15; exile over, 15, 16–17; military discharge for, 15; *Oakland Tribune* and draft resister account in, 14; US on, 11–12; Wilson,

W., and, 11–12, 13, 15, 73, 81
World War II: FDR on US and, 233, 243–244; on publishing, 264; US on, 233, 241–242
writing. *See* journalism; literary marketplace

Yalta agreement, 265, 277n19
Yaqui Indians (Mexico), 16, 18, 19, 20, 35, 37

Ydígoras, Miguel Ramón (Guatemala president), 299, 314
Yoken, Melvin, 320

Zamora, José de Jesús, 103
Zapata, Emiliano, 26, 37, 61, 80, 183, 319
Zepeda, Pedro José, 94–95
Zimmerman, Arthur, 12

# About the Author

**Christopher Neal** is a journalist and communications professional. He was a freelance correspondent in Central and South America in the 1980s and also worked as a reporter for the *Montreal Gazette* and *Ottawa Citizen*. He managed media relations for the World Bank's Latin America and Caribbean department, and earned a Masters of International Policy and Practice (MIPP) from George Washington University. A dual citizen of the United States and Canada, Neal lives in Montreal.

www.ingramcontent.com/pod-product-compliance
Lightning Source LLC
Chambersburg PA
CBHW052043220426
43663CB00012B/2421